INFORMATION SYSTEMS
A MANAGEMENT APPROACH
THIRD EDITION

STEVEN R. GORDON

Babson College

JUDITH R. GORDON

Boston College

WILEY

CREDITS

Acquisitions Editor *Beth Lang Golub*
Marketing Manager *Gitti Lindner*
Production Manager *Lari Bishop*
Assistant Editor *Lorraina Raccuia*
Developmental Editor *Camille McMorrow*
Designer *Kris Pauls*
Illustration Editor *Benjamin Reece*
Copy Editor *Ann Whetstone*
Indexer *Sandy Schroeder*
Cover Design *Jennifer Fisher*
Cover Images *Top left: ©PhotoDisc, Inc, Bottom left: © Corbis Digital Stock, Top right: Prada New York Epicenter store courtesy of Prada,*
        Bottom right: © Corbis Digital Stock, Middle: © Corbis Digital Stock

This book was set in Minion and printed and bound by Von Hoffmann. The cover was printed by Von Hoffmann.

This book is printed on acid free paper.∞

ISBN 0-471-27318-X

Printed in the United States of America

10 9 8 7 6 5 4 3 2 1

DEDICATION

WE DEDICATE THIS BOOK TO
MICHAEL, LAURIE, STEVE, BRIAN, AND LOGAN,
WITH MUCH LOVE.

BRIEF CONTENTS

CONTENTS

CHAPTER 2

THE ORGANIZATION AND INFORMATION MANAGEMENT   34

PART II
EVALUATING INFORMATION TECHNOLOGIES   63

CHAPTER 3

COMPUTER HARDWARE AND SOFTWARE   64

CHAPTER 5

TELECOMMUNICATION AND NETWORKS   156

PART III
DESIGNING SYSTEMS FOR BUSINESS   197

CHAPTER 6

INTRODUCTION TO E-COMMERCE AND E-BUSINESS   198

CHAPTER 8

■ **MANAGEMENT SUPPORT AND COORDINATION SYSTEMS 276**

PART IV
MANAGING THE INFORMATION RESOURCES 311

CHAPTER 9

SYSTEMS PLANNING, DEVELOPMENT, AND IMPLEMENTATION 312

CHAPTER 10

MANAGING THE DELIVERY OF INFORMATION SERVICES   358

PREFACE

All people use information in their personal and professional lives, but most fail to appreciate that they must *manage* information to maximize its usefulness. Although you may be bombarded with information from an array of media, you probably have little difficulty filtering it and retaining the information that is most important to you. You may use a relatively simple non-computerized information system, such as a date book, checkbook, or address book, or a simple computer-based system, such as an electronic calendar or personal financial manager, to assist you in dealing with this information. At the organizational level, however, and sometimes even at the personal level, the volume or complexity of information being processed, its importance to the organization or individual, and the difficulty of sorting and interpreting the information require careful control, systematic processing, and refined analyses. Increasing the rigor of information management normally involves the development of more complex formal, typically computerized systems that collect, organize, retrieve, and communicate information.

The third edition of *Information Systems: A Management Approach* focuses on the manager's use of information technology to support the management of information. Specifically, it addresses the use of computer-based systems for the following: (1) determining the type of information that is needed for the effective performance of organizational activities; (2) collecting, accessing, and organizing this information; (3) retrieving, handling, and processing the information once it is available; and (4) interpreting and communicating information to diverse constituencies both inside and outside the organization. Although the book presents information and information management concepts primarily from a manager's perspective, it also considers the perspectives of knowledge workers and other job holders in diverse functions, such as marketing, manufacturing, human resources management, engineering, and finance, in organizations of all sizes.

This book is intended for use in a management information systems course in either undergraduate or graduate programs of business or management. Its goal is to prepare future managers to use information systems to meet their information needs. It includes extensive examples of real-world situations in which managers successfully and unsuccessfully use information systems and technologies.

THE MANAGEMENT APPROACH

Information Systems: A Management Approach, Third Edition, presents a framework for thinking about and improving the management of information by using high-quality information systems and technology. It offers a unique four-step approach (see figure on next page) to the process of managing information. This approach is integrated throughout the text; and minicases and activities are structured around it as well.

First, managers begin with a diagnosis of information needs. This diagnosis requires a description of the existing problem, the context in which it occurs, the type of information available, the type of information required to solve it, and the possible ways of securing the needed information. Next, managers evaluate the options to meet these needs.

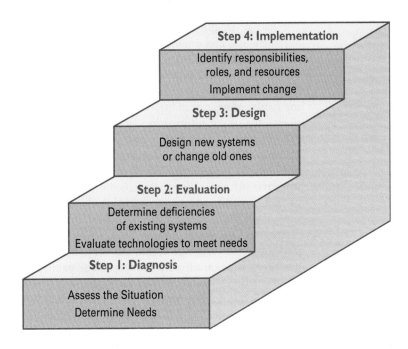

Managers assess the hardware, software, database, and telecommunication networks to meet their information needs. Then, if needs are unmet, they move to the design or selection of appropriate systems. Design involves correcting deficiencies in existing systems and integrating state-of-the-art practices and technology into them. Finally the managers implement these changes. They must identify each party's responsibility for implementation, including the roles individual managers, information systems staff, or specialists from outside the organization will play, as well as the implementation budget and timetable.

ORGANIZATION OF THIS TEXT

The text is organized into four parts, corresponding roughly to the four-step approach described above. Each part follows the four-step approach throughout, however the parts differ in their emphasis (see table below).

	Part I Diagnosing Information Needs for Management	Part II Evaluating Information Technologies	Part III Designing Systems for Business	Part IV Managing the Information Resource
Step 1 Diagnosis	✓✓✓	✓✓	✓✓	✓
Step 2 Evaluation	✓✓	✓✓✓	✓✓	✓
Step 3 Design	✓	✓✓	✓✓✓	✓✓
Step 4 Implementation	✓	✓	✓	✓✓✓

Key: ✓✓✓ (Strong emphasis); ✓✓ (Moderate emphasis); ✓ (Light emphasis)

Part I, "Diagnosing Information Needs for Management," focuses on the way managers, groups, and organizations use information. Chapter 1 sets the stage by describing the nature of information management, the context of information management in the modern world, the role of the manager, and the four-step management approach. Chapter 2 looks at the organizational context of information management, focusing on the changing nature of organizations, new organizational structures and their information requirements, the use of information technology to support team-based management, and the role of information in setting and implementing organizational strategy.

Part II, "Evaluating Information Technologies," illustrates how managers evaluate technologies available to meet their information needs. Chapter 3 discusses hardware and software, and how they are packaged into complete computer systems. Chapter 4 investigates database management systems, including their use and functionality, their development through data design, their technical underpinnings, and their management. Chapter 5 discusses telecommunications and networks, including their types and uses, the infrastructure of the communication industry, the hardware and software components of networking technology, Internet concepts, and principles of network management.

Part III, "Designing Systems for Business," presents how organizations use information systems and technology to solve problems and improve business processes. Chapter 6 introduces e-commerce and e-business principles and concepts, including the objectives of doing business electronically, electronic business models, and difficulties of doing business electronically. Chapter 7 drills down into the design of information systems for specific business functions, cross-discipline enterprise systems, and systems designed to support processes across company boundaries. It addresses information systems that help manage customer and channel relationships, manufacturing and production, supplier relationships, warehousing, transportation, human resource management, and accounting. Chapter 8 investigates management support and coordination systems, including management reporting systems, decision support systems, groupware, and executive information systems.

Part IV, "Managing the Information Resource," investigates issues associated with developing information systems and managing the information they process. Chapter 9 looks at the elements of systems development, including assessing requirements; analyzing alternatives; designing, developing, and implementing new systems; and maintaining and reviewing systems. It also addresses the unique problems of developing and managing Web sites. Chapter 10 looks at ways of structuring and managing the parts of the organization that deliver information services.

FEATURES OF THIS TEXT

The third edition of *Information Systems: A Management Approach* provides an integrated presentation of each topic using text, cases, exercises, and Web activities. The text is designed to be versatile in its use, offering flexibility in the sequencing of chapter coverage and the selection of instructional materials. Additional major features include the following:

- *Current, real-world examples* integrated throughout the text illustrate key concepts in action.

- Extensive integration of *Web-based references and material* ensures that the third edition remains current.

- *The four-step management approach* helps develop critical thinking skills. Students learn to analyze a situation, evaluate existing systems for managing information, design the features of new systems, and consider the issues associated with implementing them.

- *Emphasis on e-business* in the selection of cases and examples in all chapters.

- *A new chapter on e-commerce and e-business* (Chapter 6) discusses the ways that modern businesses are using the Internet, mobile communication, and other information technologies to support existing business processes and to implement new business models.

- *A new chapter on functional and enterprise systems* (Chapter 7) provides extensive in-depth examples of how functional departments use information systems and technology to automate and improve their processes, and how organizations integrate these systems with one another and with the systems of customers, suppliers, and other business partners.

- Issues associated with the *globalization of business* are highlighted throughout the text. Students consider the implications of managing information in transnational organizations with diverse cultures, skills, languages, and legal systems.

- *A strong ethical focus* permeates each chapter, with an activity in each chapter encouraging students to consider the ethical implications of various managerial choices.

- *Strong focus on current and future technologies* ensures that students know about an array of technological possibilities. Updates on the book's Web site ensure that the discussion of technologies remains current.

- *A short case* introduces each chapter. Key concepts throughout the chapter are applied-to the opening case where appropriate.

- An *integrated and comprehensive* pedagogy supports student learning. The pedagogical elements include a chapter outline, learning objectives, chapter summary, key terms, review questions, minicases, activities, notes, and recommended readings.

- *Minicases* allow students to experience real-life situations without leaving the classroom.

- *Activities* at the end of each chapter provide students the opportunity to understand information needs, assess the effectiveness of information management strategies, and apply course concepts to developing aspects of information systems.

- *IS on the Web Exercises.* These exercises at the end of each chapter make use of the Internet as a tool for further exploring chapter concepts.

SUPPLEMENTARY MATERIALS

The following supplementary material is provided for adopting instructors on the text's companion Web site:

- PowerPoint slides: A Microsoft PowerPoint presentation by Jeff Caldwell and Tyler Caldwell is available for each chapter of the text. Instructors are authorized to provide electronic copies of these presentations to their students.

- Instructor's manual: An instructor's manual by Paula Ruby provides, for each chapter, a lecture outline; teaching suggestions; answers to review questions, discussion questions, and case questions; and Web resources.

- Image library: The image library contains almost every figure and table contained in the text. Instructors are authorized to reuse this material for classroom presentations created in PowerPoint or other presentation software.

- Test bank: The test bank, created by Paula Ruby, contains questions of various types (true/false, multiple choice, short answer, and essay) at various levels of difficulty keyed to the learning objectives.

The text's companion Web site (located at www.wiley.com/college/gordon and available to both students and instructors) provides access to additional activities not found in the text. Also, this site provides new material to keep the text current in the face of a rapidly changing environment and technology, links to companies mentioned in the text, and links to supplementary readings and related material.

ACKNOWLEDGMENTS

The development of this book has been influenced by the contributions of many people. We would like first to thank the reviewers of this book, who made important contributions that significantly influenced its development and quality. We thank:

Bay Arinze
Drexel University

Gary Armstrong
Shippensberg University

Nancy W. Davidson
Auburn University at Montgomery

Barbara Denison
Wright State University

Jack Van Deventer
Washington State University

Bryan Foltz
East Carolina University

William H. Friedman
University of Central Arkansas

Tim Goles
University of Texas at San Antonio

Veronica Hinton-Hudson
University of Louisville

Brian Kovar
Kansas State University

Brett Landry
University of New Orleans

David W. Letcher
The College of New Jersey

Jane Mackay
Texas Christian University

John Melrose
University of Wisconsin at Eau Claire

Enrique Mu
University of Pittsburgh

Bruce A. Reinig
San Diego State

Paula Ruby
Arkansas State University

Linda Salchenberger
Loyola University of Chicago

Charles Small
Abilene Christian University

Carlos Urcuyo
University of Toledo

Vince Yen
Wright State University

Dale Young
Miami University

In particular, we thank Paula Ruby of Arkansas State University for her outstanding work on the instructor's manual and test bank.

We greatly appreciate the editorial and technical support provided by the professionals at Leyh Publishing. In particular, we thank Jennifer Fisher, Lari Bishop, and Camille McMorrow for their attention to design, layout, copy editing, and pursuit of permissions. Rick Leyh deserves special thanks for his guidance and inspiration from the conception of this project through its implementation.

Our greatest thanks go to our extended families, whose enthusiasm has always been the deepest source of our strength. Finally, to Michael, our sole remaining at-home child, we give extra thanks for sacrificing his time with us so that this project might succeed.

ABOUT THE AUTHORS

Steven R. Gordon is an Associate Professor of Information Systems and Technology at Babson College. He is a co-author of *Information Systems: A Management Approach* and *Essentials of Accounting Information Systems*. Dr. Gordon's research and consulting interests focus on two areas: governance and structure of the information technology function in organizations and e-commerce in the financial service industry. His research appears in the *Communications of the ACM, Information & Management, Information Systems Management,* the *International Journal of Service Industry Management,* and other academic journals. He is a Global Associate Editor of the *Journal of Information Technology Cases and Applications* and serves on the Editorial Review Board for the *Journal of End User Computing.*

Before arriving at Babson College, Dr. Gordon founded and served as president of Beta Principles, Inc., which developed and marketed accounting software and resold computer hardware. Dr. Gordon also consulted to the airline industry at Simat, Helliesen & Eichner, Inc. He holds a Ph.D. in Transportation Systems from the Massachusetts Institute of Technology.

Judith R. Gordon is an Associate Professor of Management in the Carroll School of Management at Boston College and has twice served as chairperson of the department. Dr. Gordon's research and publication interests focus on the career development of women, work–family issues in the workplace, organizational change, information systems delivery, and managerial effectiveness. She has regularly presented papers at the Academy of Management meetings and has published articles in such journals as the *Academy of Management Executive, Women in Management Review, Human Resource Planning, Information Systems Management, Information & Management, Sloan Management Review, and Academy of Management Review.* She is the author of *Organizational Behavior: A Diagnostic Approach, Information Systems: A Management Approach* and *Human Resources Management: A Practical Approach.*

Dr. Gordon was the first woman to receive a doctorate from the Sloan School of Management at the Massachusetts Institute of Technology. She is currently a member of the Commission on Institutions of Higher Education of the New England Association of Schools and Colleges.

Part I

Diagnosing Information Needs for Management

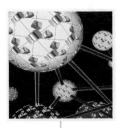

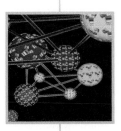

Managers today face the challenge of managing information effectively. Information technology can support information management and help organizations compete successfully in a global environment. This part introduces the management of information at the managerial, team, and organizational levels. Chapter 1 presents the basic issues related to information and its management. It defines information and information management and discusses information's role in managerial jobs. The chapter concludes with the four-step management approach used throughout the remainder of this text. Chapter 2 continues the introduction to information management by examining how organizations use information to address the information requirements of new organizational structures, the role of information management in supporting team-based management, and the relationship between information and organizational strategy. ∎

1

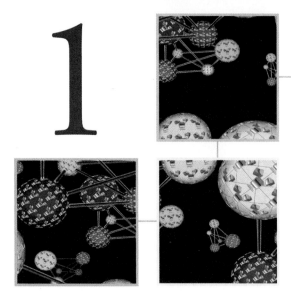

Information Management in a Global Economy

LEARNING OBJECTIVES

After completing Chapter 1, you will be able to:

- Define information and discuss its role in organizations.
- Identify the role of information technology in organizations.
- Classify information systems according to their purpose and scope.
- Identify five key issues in managing information in today's organizations.
- Describe managers' use of information in their jobs.
- Identify the information requirements for effective management.
- Offer an approach to addressing ethical issues in information management.
- Identify the four steps in the effective management of information.

Managing Information at Marriott International

Marriott International Inc., known worldwide for its Marriott hotels, manages 21 distinct brands, including the Ritz-Carlton and Ramada chains, with over 2,200 units in 60 countries and territories.[1] Managing its information is the key to managing its diverse and far-flung properties.

The Ritz-Carlton was one of the first hotel chains to provide its employees with the information that they needed to make their clients feel special. Clients at Ritz-Carlton hotels expect top-notch, personal service. The more information employees have about the guests, the more they can ensure that visits at the Ritz meet or exceed their guests' expectations. Does a guest want her bed turned down at 9 p.m.? Does a guest want a city or garden view? Does a guest want a chocolate on his pillow in the evening? Hotel employees collect anecdotal information about guest preferences and record them on cards that the clerical staff keys into an international guest preferences database. Employees use this information to provide a more personal level of service.[2]

This type of customer knowledge creation and use is now standard not only at the Ritz but also at all other Marriott hotels. Still, managers such as Tony Reid, vice president of sales information and planning systems, know that customer knowledge, no matter how good, is poorly used if restricted to an individual hotel. Marriott also needs to coordinate the use of information among its hotels and even among its chains. As most people stay frequently at several different hotels, sharing information about them can help improve service and lead to better customer satisfaction. Reid remembers one example, when salespeople from two different Marriott hotels were competing for the same customer and the same event—a company meeting. One hotel's salesperson had already interviewed the meeting planner and had collected information about the event. As a result, the customer didn't have to waste time repeating the information for the second hotel's salesperson. The two salespeople prepared a joint proposal and won the contract.[3]

How do managers at Marriott and other companies ensure that their employees have the information they need? How do they share critical information among business units around the world? Once they get the required information, how do managers guarantee that their employees can use it to do their jobs well? How do managers and their employees handle the daily challenge of managing information effectively and ethically?

In this chapter we first explore the role and management of information in organizations. Then we investigate the issues involved in the management of information in today's organizations. We next examine how managers use and manage information in their jobs. We conclude by examining the four-step management approach to information management used throughout this book.

WHAT IS INFORMATION MANAGEMENT?

Managers deal with information in all aspects of their work. Managers at Marriott need information about their customers to provide the best service they can. They use information about their employees to train them properly and to create appropriate incentives for them to act in the best interest of the company. They use information to determine where to build new hotels, to set or change prices for their rooms and facilities, and to create reward programs that provide incentives for frequent travelers to stay at Marriott hotels.

What Is Information?

We define **data** as fundamental facts, figures, observations, and measurement, without context or organization. A weather station, for example, might report the following data: 2597, 1400, 35, 30.2R, 10NW, 28. We define **information** as processed data—data that have been organized and interpreted, and possibly formatted, filtered, analyzed, and summarized. The weather station data might provide the following *information,* for example. Weather station 2597 reported at 14:00 (2:00 p.m.), a temperature of 35 degrees Fahrenheit, a rising barometric pressure of 30.2, a wind velocity of 10 mph from the northwest, and a humidity of 28 percent. A map, summarizing the data from many stations, provides information about the location and movement of fronts and storms. We present and use information today in many media, including sound, graphics, and video.

Managers can use information to obtain knowledge. **Knowledge** is an understanding, or model, about people, objects, or events, derived from information about them, as illustrated in Figure 1-1. Knowledge provides a structure for interpreting information, usually by assimilating and explaining variations over time or space. For example, managers at Marriott obtain knowledge about customers' preferences from the information obtained as a result of accumulating data about specific customer requests. **Wisdom** is the ability to use knowledge for a purpose. Computer systems collect data, produce and present information, and help create knowledge. We trust people to apply their wisdom to make information systems effective.

The Role of Information in Organizations

Organizations use information as a resource, an asset, or a product, as Figure 1-2 illustrates.

- *Information as a Resource.* Like money, people, raw materials, machinery, or time, information can serve as a **resource,** an input into the production of goods and services. Marriott International, for example, uses information as a resource to provide better service for its customers. Managers can use information to replace capital and labor, often reducing costs at the same time. For example, managers at Scottish Courage Brewing (SCB), the leading brewer in the United Kingdom and one of the largest in Europe, use information about demand, production rules, inventory, and supplies to make better use of their

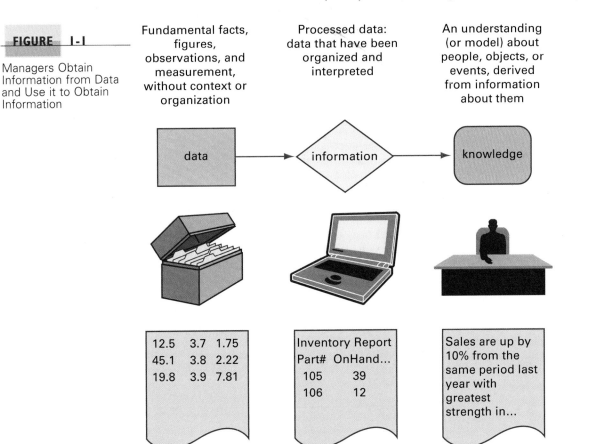

FIGURE 1-1

Managers Obtain Information from Data and Use it to Obtain Information

brewing tanks. As a result, they have been able to reduce SCB's need for more production capacity and can better meet urgent customer orders.[4]

- *Information as an Asset.* Information can serve as an asset, the property of a person or an organization that contributes to a company's output. In this way, information resembles plant, equipment, goodwill, and other corporate assets. Managers may view information as an investment that they can use strategically to give their company an advantage over its competitors. Although generally accepted accounting rules typically prevent companies from listing information as an asset on their public balance sheets, many companies, such as truckline Roadway Express, internally assign a value to their information to calculate a return on investment for proposed information systems.[5]

- *Information as a Product.* Companies can also sell information, the output of its production, as a product or service or as an embedded component of a product. In our service-oriented economy, an increasing number of companies view information in this way. Publishers of directories, television guides, and airline guides make a profit from selling information. The American Medical Association plans to create a subsidiary called "Preference Solutions" to sell information about physicians and other health-care workers in the United States to drug companies and other interested parties.[6] Often the sale of information in this manner raises ethical issues (see Activity 1.4). Information is an embedded component of LG Electronics' high-end microwave oven. LG Electronics, a $54 billion Korean firm formerly known as Goldstar, makes a microwave oven that stores up to 20 frequently used settings and can download recipes and cooking information over the Internet.[7]

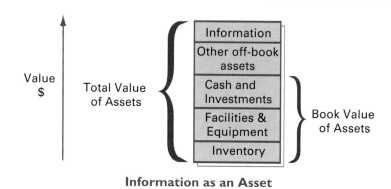

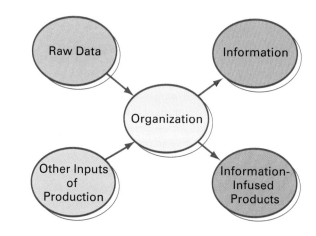

FIGURE   1-2

Managers Use
Information as a
Resource, Asset, or
Product

Information as a Resource

Information as an Asset

Information as a Product

The Role of Information Technology

Information technology has allowed individuals, groups, and organizations to manage information effectively and efficiently. Think about the information available through the Internet and on internal company networks. Information technologies ease communication among people within and between organizations. Consider the ability of a company to track thousands of products in its warehouses and sales of the products in hundreds of retail outlets. Significant advances in information technology have made it possible to acquire, manage, and use such large quantities of information at a relatively low cost.

The widespread availability of affordable computer technology has dramatically changed the way people acquire, process, store, retrieve, transmit, communicate, and use information. Ellis Don, a Toronto-based construction company, for example, plans to use information technology to track thousands of paper documents and images. On any given project, the company may deal with 50 or more subcontractors, and, without computerized systems, the contracts and engineering drawings become voluminous and hard to control.[8] Boston's Beth Israel Deaconess Medical Center links hospitalized premature infants with their parents through videoconferencing, a high-speed Internet connection, and database software. The Baby CareLink system, as it's called, allows parents to monitor their babies at all times, improves the quality and amount of information that doctors have at their disposal when making life-saving decisions, and even reduces the amount of time that babies spend in the Neonatal Intensive Care Unit.[9] In this book, we will explore how information technology affects how we work.

Information technology (**IT**) includes computer hardware, software, database management systems, and data communication technologies.

Computer hardware refers to the equipment used in electronic information processing. Today affordable desktop and portable computers can outperform the room-sized, million-dollar computers of ten years ago.

- Input hardware captures raw data and information from interactive uses.
- Processing hardware converts or transforms data.
- Storage hardware includes removable and fixed media that allow rapid access to information.
- Output hardware provides copies of data on paper, microform, and video screens.

Computer software provides the instructions, in the form of computer code and its accompanying documentation, for processing data electronically.

- Systems software directs the functioning of the hardware.
- Applications software assists in the acquisition, processing, storage, retrieval, and communication of information.
- Software development tools facilitate building and modifying software to respond better to an organization's information needs.

Database management systems offer vehicles for storing and supporting the processing of large quantities of business information, such as data on employees, products, customers, and suppliers. This technology allows managers to easily access, sort, and analyze databases of information along a variety of dimensions. For example, Larry Durrett, president of Southern Multifoods Inc., the owner of 100 Taco Bell franchises, uses sophisticated database management systems to organize and analyze the huge amount of raw sales data collected by their computer systems on a daily basis.[10] Managers at Intermountain Health Care have used its database on medical services provided to about 500,000 residents of Utah and Idaho to improve customer service, control costs, and make better decisions. For example, by analyzing data on the company's use of supplies, managers were able to improve the company's purchasing contracts and obtain volume discounts. They were also able to integrate clinical, claims, and financial data to better understand tradeoffs between clinical outcomes and cost. They found, for example, that frequent cholesterol tests and regular eye examinations increased the effectiveness of treatments provided to diabetics.[11]

Data communication technologies, specifically company networks and the **Internet,** a worldwide network of networks, have dramatically improved the communication of information across small and large distances. Managers and other employees can easily send data from one plant location to another or access data located halfway around the world using dial-in options, computer networks, videoconferencing, and other electronic media. Advances in communication technology occur frequently, reducing the cost and increasing the accuracy and speed of data transmission. Companies use the Internet for communication and for electronic commerce.

Employees at Krispy Kreme Doughnuts can access information stored at company headquarters from any store using a simple Web browser over a secure Internet hookup called a VPN (see Chapter 5). They can take company surveys, examine productivity statistics, order new supplies, and even train new employees. They can also submit financial information rather than faxing it, saving time and increasing accuracy.[12]

Managing Information with Information Systems

An **information system** combines information technology with data, procedures for processing data, and people who collect and use the data, as shown in Figure 1-3. A human resources department might have an information system that tracks all current and potential employees' work and salary history, training experiences, and performance evaluations and regularly provides reports to their managers summarizing the data. Microsoft, for example, uses a human resources information system to store information about each employee, such as Social Security number, manager, hire date, and employment status, as well as to manage processes, such as benefits enrollment, vacation and sick time reporting, payroll, and stock purchase programs.[13] In addition to using technology, such as computers and database management systems, this system includes data about the employees, procedures, such as when and how to implement performance reviews, and people, such as the human resources professionals who collect, analyze, and disseminate the information.

Organizations and their employees use a variety of computerized systems to help manage information. Managers may use computerized systems to maintain information about employee performance, customer preferences, and industry trends, as well as to motivate and develop employees, communicate with other managers, make decisions, negotiate agreements, and manage resources. As managers become more sophisticated in performing their tasks, they require increasingly sophisticated systems to help them meet their information needs.

Organizations that lack quality information systems may experience problems in accessing the data they need for executive decision making. They may lose important data during a relocation or power failure. They may also perform the wrong activities in dealing with customers or suppliers or fail to respond quickly to changes in the marketplace or industry.

Types of Information Systems

Although you can classify information systems in many ways, in this book we use two dimensions: their purpose and their scope. On the purpose dimension, we distinguish

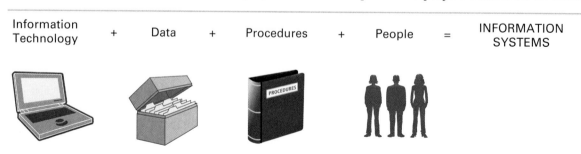

| Information Technology | + | Data | + | Procedures | + | People | = | INFORMATION SYSTEMS |

Information systems include information technology, data, data processing procedures, and people who use the data.

among automation systems, transaction processing systems, and management support systems. On the scope dimension, we distinguish among individual, departmental/functional, enterprise, and inter-organizational systems.

The Purpose of Information Systems

In this section, we differentiate among information systems according to the intent of their use. We briefly describe three distinct categories of purpose: automation, transaction processing, and management support.

Automation systems use information technology to perform tasks or to make them easier or less labor intensive. Although automation systems may use or collect information, that is not their primary purpose. The electronic key systems used by Marriott International are excellent examples of automation systems. Electronic keys are created at check-in time for every customer. Their function is to open doors, and they simply replace physical keys that perform the same function. Another example of an automation system would be the robotic systems that major automobile manufacturers use to assemble cars. These systems replace physical laborers with machines that perform the same functions. The computer systems in advanced thermostats, which provide temperature control by time of day, are also automation systems. The following examples illustrate the broad range of automation systems applications:

- Office automation systems speed the processing of information and aid in time management, communication, document preparation, and filing.

- Workflow systems coordinate the movement of documents and other data among various groups in the organization. AAA Missouri uses workflow to automate the handling of insurance policy applications, which previously required four instances in which the policy forms needed to be reopened, sorted, and date-stamped.[14]

- The automation of manufacturing and design through computer-aided design and computer-aided manufacturing systems often improves product quality, worker efficiency, and organizational performance.

- Automation of education and training through the use of computer-aided instruction can make large amounts of diverse information available to students inexpensively and easily.

- Expert systems automate functions that require highly specialized knowledge, such as product design, medical diagnosis, or equipment repair.

Transaction Processing Systems (TPSs) process and record an organization's transactions. A **transaction** is a unit of business activity, such as purchasing a product, making a banking deposit, or reserving an airline seat. Transaction processing includes activities such as recording, filing, and retrieving records or filling out order forms and checks. Transaction processing systems support low-level employees in performing routine business functions by providing data to answer questions, such as those shown in Figure 1-4. At Marriott International hotels, reservation agents use transaction processing systems to reserve rooms for customers. Housekeeping managers might use transaction processing systems to keep track of which rooms need to be cleaned. Desk clerks use transaction processing systems to check in customers and assign them a cleaned room.

Transaction processing systems have transformed the work done by clerical and other low-level employees. Now, for example, they input hotel or airline reservation data directly into online electronic forms. The West Florida Medical Center Clinic in Pensacola, Florida, reduced its claims denial rate by 70 percent, affecting the collection of $1 million per month, simply by computerizing the entry of its claim codes so that they could be

FIGURE   1-4

Transaction processing systems help managers answer numerous questions that keep their businesses running smoothly and profitably.

- From whom do we buy our copier paper?
- How many envelopes did we purchase in the last order?
- Which sweaters were delivered last week?
- Where has the inventory of lug nuts been stored?
- How much does the company owe its chemicals supplier?
- How much of the money owed to company X has been paid?
- How many hours have employees worked?
- How much is the total payroll this week?
- How much should be deducted from each paycheck for taxes and benefits?
- What is the customer's account balance?
- Has the shipment arrived at the customer's site or is it in route?
- Has the customer paid yet?

entered by the physician or nurse who was making the decision about the type of treatment their patients received.[15]

Management Support Systems (MSSs), the subject of Chapter 8, supply information that managers need to make decisions and coordinate their activities. Many people use the term "management information system (MIS)" to mean MSS, but others consider an MIS to be any type of information system, whether or not it provides information for management. In this text, we consider MSS and MIS to be synonymous. A human resources manager at Marriott International might use a management support system to evaluate the performance of an employee before deciding whether or not to give him a raise. A marketing manager might use a management support system to assess the effectiveness of a recent advertising campaign or to estimate the impact of alternative future campaigns. Management support systems might alert a financial executive that the profitability of one hotel property is significantly below that of others in the chain.

Management support systems include management reporting systems, decision support systems, groupware, and executive information systems. **Management reporting systems** provide information that low-level managers need to make routine decisions. They organize and summarize key data collected by transaction processing systems. Reports might be prepared periodically, at the request of the manager, or when appropriate conditions arise.

Decision support systems assist managers in making nonroutine decisions. Typically, decision support systems include models that managers can use to evaluate the impact of alternative choices and to help them decide which choice is best. South African Petroleum Refineries Ltd., a joint venture of Royal Dutch/Shell and British Petroleum, saved $1.5 million in one year with a decision support system that helped managers adjust the blending and cooling operations in their refineries.[16]

Groupware supports the group activities of managers and other workers. Groupware helps them exchange information, coordinate activities, and manage the flow of work. Wunderman, an international marketing company with 80 offices in 40 countries, uses groupware to coordinate multicountry projects, develop proposals, share documents, and coordinate schedules. Wunderman also allows clients to participate in groupware activities associated with their projects and has found that their participation reduced the need for redoing parts of projects and increased clients' happiness with the results.[17]

Executive information systems provide the information that top executives need to quickly identify problems, scan data for trends, communicate with employees, and set strategic objectives. Manila Electric Company is designing an executive information system to manage its corporate planning and decision-making processes using a performance measurement tool known as the Balanced Score Card. The system will help executives weigh and balance the company's performance across perspectives, such as financial health, customer satisfaction, the efficiency of internal business processes, and corporate learning and growth.[18] Executive information systems are often built to satisfy the needs of a particular executive.

The Scope of Information Systems

Information systems can be distinguished by how broadly they are used. **Individual information systems** target a single person in the organization. Often, someone with a unique information need creates an individual information system for his or her own use. For example, a sales manager at a Marriott hotel might create a spreadsheet that helps her forecast the demand for conference room space based on the historical trends and patterns at her hotel. The bookmarks, or favorites list, that you've created for your Web browser could be considered a type of individual information system. Although individual information systems might use information that others in the organization collect or create and might feed information into systems with a wider scope, they are intended to be used by an individual in the performance of his or her job.

Functional information systems or **departmental information systems** address the needs of individual functions or departments. Examples of such systems include accounting systems, sales management systems, order entry systems, and warehouse management systems. Chapter 7 provides many examples of such systems and examines their features. Functional systems may stand alone or be part of a more comprehensive enterprise information system.

The word *enterprise* means a partnership, corporation, association, union, or any group of individuals working together as an organization.[19] **Enterprise information systems** fully integrate the functions of a company or enterprise and provide a single, comprehensive repository for its information. On the transaction processing side, for example, when a customer orders a product, an enterprise information system might arrange for the product to be pulled from inventory, shipped, and invoiced to the customer. If necessary, it might arrange for replacements to be manufactured, which could also require the ordering of supplies. Accounting entries would also be made where appropriate. Because an activity in any one part of a company typically affects other parts, companies use enterprise information systems to coordinate all processes and update all affected data. On the management support side, enterprise information systems include tools to analyze corporate-wide data and to evaluate the overall effect of changes in one part of the company. For example, managers can analyze alternative manufacturing plans to determine their impact on staffing, cost, quality, availability of supplies, and ability to meet demand.

Inter-organizational information systems are those that provide a common point of interaction and common repository of information for a company, its suppliers, distributors, customers, and/or shippers. Sometimes even competitors are included to a limited extent. Humana, a health-care organization based in Louisville, Kentucky, boasts approximately 6.5 million members in 18 states and Puerto Rico. Humana is testing an inter-organizational information system that allows doctors, patients, and administrators to share data, such as claims status and prescription history, and to automate certain functions, such as plan authorization. Humana expects the system to save money, improve execution, and attract both customers and providers.[20]

INFORMATION MANAGEMENT IN TODAY'S WORLD

Diagnosing needs for information, evaluating information technology to meet these needs, and designing responsive information systems form the backbone of effective performance in today's environment. Even well-managed companies can fail as a result of unexpected events or a few bad decisions. Good managers can increase the likelihood of their companies' success by using information to make good decisions, motivate employees, and initiate necessary changes.

Succeeding in a Global Environment

Managers function in a global marketplace, in which organizations deal within and across national boundaries. Understanding this global context and sharing information worldwide have become challenges that face managers. Differences of time, culture, and language create barriers to effective communication that information systems can reduce. Managers at different Marriott hotels, for example, want to share information about guests so they can meet their needs at any location. Information systems can support such sharing, making information about a specific customer available instantly at any location in the world.

Profiting from an Electronic Economy

Businesses operate in an increasingly electronic economy. Managers can take advantage of this trend to improve profitability. Electronic business transactions drive down cost, increase speed, and create flexibility for customers. Businesses can take orders electronically to reduce sales costs and eliminate errors. They can distribute coupons electronically. They can purchase goods electronically, reducing paperwork, and automatically search for and secure the best price from qualified providers. Managers can communicate by e-mail and videoconferencing, reducing postage, telephone, and travel expenses.

Focusing on Performance

To survive in a competitive environment, businesses need to focus on performance. Customers may be won over by promises of lower prices, better service, higher quality, and devoted attention. However, they will not return unless the company can deliver on its promises. Managers are responsible for assuring that their companies deliver what they promise. Information systems help them to monitor performance and to take steps to improve it.

Increased competition from abroad has required U.S. companies to reexamine the quality of their goods and services. Large numbers of defects, complaints from customers about outdated products, and declining productivity caused U.S. manufacturers to introduce **total quality management (TQM)** as a solution to these problems. Companies such as Xerox, Motorola, Teradyne, Texas Instruments, and others introduced broad-based, system-wide programs to address these concerns. TQM programs emphasize responding to customers' needs as a top priority. They give workers more responsibility for making decisions and change the way they perform work. TQM programs foster continuous improvement in both an organization's product and the processes for creating it. Statistical control techniques use extensive information collected about the organization's functioning to improve its product and processes. Managers also collect information about other companies' best practices as a way of establishing a standard of high-level performance for their company.

Supporting a Mobile Workforce

Information and communication technologies help workers to be as effective as possible no matter where they are. Sales people can use laptop computers equipped with the latest product information and with software that allows them to customize solutions to meet the needs of their most demanding customers. They can obtain the assistance of specialists in their organization over Web or chat links. They can analyze the status of their prospects, keep track of sales, notify headquarters of any changes in the field, and receive directions from their superiors. Mobile phones keep them in voice and e-mail contact at all times.

Advances in telecommunications allow managers around the world to conference and even to assemble documents as if they were in the same room. The ability to do business without having to wait for faxes or overnight mail delivery improves productivity dramatically.

Information and communication technologies also support telecommuting. **Telecommuters** are mobile employees who rarely, if ever, visit their employers' offices. They may work at home or on the road, satisfying their individual or family needs, while at the same time reducing the demand for and cost of office space.

Building Individual Capabilities and Productivity

High-performing organizations emphasize the employment of **knowledge workers**— employees, such as engineers, accountants, lawyers, and technical specialists, who have specialized skills and knowledge that allow them to function effectively in today's organizations. These knowledge workers rely on information to help them perform well. British Petroleum (BP) believes that its knowledge workers, while being part of a business unit, also have a role in supporting the welfare of the entire company through their participation in a program called "Sharing Know-how." They are encouraged to use the "Connect" system, which includes Web-based personal profiles of more than 18,000 engineers, scientists, and technicians as well as commercial and administrative support personnel. *Connect* organizes these professionals into networks, such as the Refinery Operations Managers Network, that provide databases to assist them in solving problems and connecting with knowledge workers who have needed expertise.[21]

Through extensive training and development, companies build individual capabilities and productivity. Information systems contribute directly by helping people process the large quantities of information available. British Telecom (BT) uses Intellact to provide 90,000 of BT's 137,000 employees with Web-based access to data, news, and research about practically every topic of importance to the company. Approximately 7,000 users log in each day for an average of seven to eight minutes.[22]

THE MANAGER AND INFORMATION MANAGEMENT

Management refers to the process of achieving organizational goals by planning, organizing, leading, and controlling organizational resources. Managers face an array of challenges in performing their work in a global environment. They must deal with increasing competition, decreasing resources, and rapidly changing technology. They must understand and respond to dramatic cultural differences, imposing legal constraints, and dynamic customer requirements.

The Manager's Job

Managers at all levels cope with less than perfect information in an uncontrollable environment. They perform a great quantity of work at an unrelenting pace.[23] This level of activity requires managers to continually seek and then quickly process large amounts of information, generally without time for leisurely reflection. Managers also participate in a variety of brief activities that result in significant fragmentation of their time. They become accustomed to the rapid exchange of information with others and hence must have the needed information readily available. Think of the function manager at a Marriott hotel faced with the possibility of booking a large conference. She needs to agree with the customer on which conference and function rooms will be used at what times, how many rooms to reserve for conference participants, and what meals to plan. She needs to know that her staff can deliver what she promised in a timely, cost-effective fashion and without conflicting with commitments made to other customers. She needs to quote a reasonable price and then present a signed contract almost instantly. Because time is precious and managers tend to deal with issues that are current and specific, they seek ways to secure information as efficiently as possible.

Managers also spend extensive amounts of time communicating with other managers, both inside and outside the organization. As more information becomes available to them, managers seem to want and need even more information to perform effectively. Increasingly managers will spend more time interpreting historical data, anticipating future trends, setting accurate goals, measuring performance against goals, identifying variances quickly, allocating resources dynamically, and adapting to unanticipated events.

Managers at different hierarchical levels in the organization have special concerns, as shown in Figure 1-5.

The Strategic Focus of Top Management Teams

Top-level managers establish the overall, long-term direction of an organization by setting its strategy and policies. They develop programs and activities in line with stated profit or service objectives. Top executives typically have both an internal and an external orientation. They must ensure that work gets done within their particular subsidiary or division while they interact with executives in other organizations and the general public. Increasingly, such interactions span regional and national boundaries, requiring executives to have large repositories of information about an array of global issues. Richard Parsons, CEO of AOL Time Warner, for example, oversees AOL, the world's largest Internet service, cable channels CNN and HBO, Warner Brothers movie studios, 64 magazine imprints, including *Time, People,* and *Sports Illustrated,* six record labels, and the Atlanta Braves baseball team. [24] He needs strong management skills and quality information to succeed.

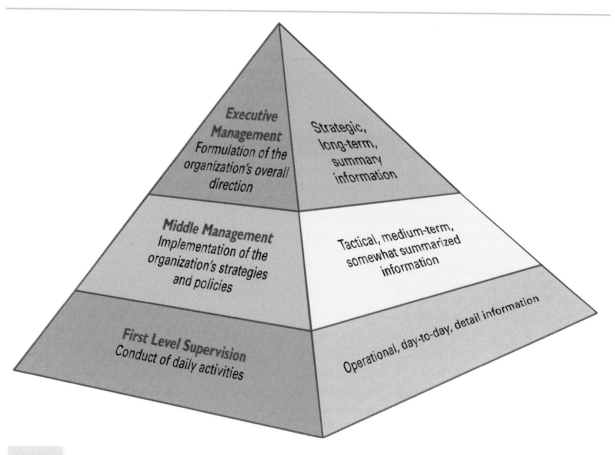

FIGURE   1-5   Managers at different levels in the organizations have different information needs.

Top executives often need performance-related information about the results of various divisions or product groups. They may require summary data about sales, production levels, or costs to assess the organization's performance. Top executives also use information about new technology, customers, suppliers, and others in the industry to gain a competitive advantage over other firms. They may want detailed information about particular aspects of their organization, such as the total number of employees or sales at any particular time. They may also want general information that focuses on a division's profitability, market share, return on investment, or trouble spots. As you can see, the information needs of top executives vary considerably.

Consider the job of a senior marketing manager in a hair-care products division of a large company. She must determine the best mix of products for the company, authorize advertising and marketing research expenditures, and supervise a staff of managers responsible for accomplishing the department's goals. What types of information might she require? Now compare her information needs to those of a senior financial manager or even to those of a senior marketing manager in a computer software firm. Clearly these managers have some needs in common, but they also have needs unique to their jobs, organizations, and industries. Diagnosing the particular information needs of a senior executive requires tracking organizational and job goals and then assessing the information that helps accomplish them.

Planning and Implementation Needs of Middle Managers

Middle managers focus primarily on implementing the policies and strategies set by top management. They translate the long-term direction set by top management into medium-term decisions and activities that affect the way the organization does business. Plant managers, regional sales managers, directors of staffing, and other middle managers almost always deal with internal organizational issues, such as finding ways to increase productivity, profitability, and service. Middle managers must meet production schedules and budgetary constraints while still acting independently. They participate actively in an array of personnel decisions, including the hiring, transfer, promoting, or firing of employees. Middle managers pass top management's directives to lower levels of the organization and communicate problems or exceptional circumstances up the hierarchy. They may work in the United States or abroad, directly managing one or more work teams, coordinating interdependent groups, or supervising support personnel. Middle managers might also serve as links between their own work groups and others in the organization.

Middle managers require more detailed information than executives about the functioning of the groups or workers they supervise; generally, however, they don't require as detailed information as first-level supervisors. Often middle managers need detailed budget data, extensive information about workers' performance, schedules, and skills, and data about their group's products or services to perform their jobs well and to ensure their work group focuses on organizational goals. Often they cannot obtain perfect information and must use the best information they can secure.

Middle managers who act as **project managers** might have responsibility for one or more unique projects, such as the development of new spreadsheet software or a new computer chip, or ongoing projects, such as the provision of accounting services to a small business. A Project manager typically supervises a team of workers who together must accomplish a specific goal. The project manager must ensure that the project team works together effectively toward its common goal. She must have information about the project's goal, task, timetable, and team members.

Operational Needs of First-Line Supervisors

First-level managers have the most direct responsibility for ensuring the effective conduct of the daily activities in the organization. The supervisor of long-distance telephone operators handles any problems that arise in servicing customers. The customer services manager in an insurance company oversees the interactions between customer service representatives and policyholders. Such supervisors might plan work schedules, modify subordinates' job duties, train new workers, or generally handle problems employees encounter. They ensure that their subordinates accomplish their daily, weekly, and monthly goals and regularly provide workers with feedback about their performance. They screen problems and may pass particularly significant, unusual, or difficult problems on to middle managers.

First-line supervisors also spend large amounts of time in disturbance handling roles, such as replacing absent workers, handling customer complaints, or securing repairs for equipment. They, too, may experience imperfections in the information they receive; they must recognize these deficiencies and respond accordingly. Diagnosis of information needs must be ongoing and responsive to the particular situations these managers face.

The Roles of the Manager

Managers assume a variety of roles on the job, as shown in Table 1-1.[25] Plant managers have different information needs from corporate controllers. The vice president of human resources has different information needs than the chief financial officer. Managers perform roles such as the following, each with their own information needs:

- *Gathering Information and Monitoring the Environment.* Managers gather information from the environment inside or outside the organization. They review written information about the company and its industry, attend meetings that present information about the organization, or participate in task forces or committees that provide additional information about organizational functioning. They look for a variety of information from worldwide sources to assist them in their duties. Information systems can assist with both the collecting and the processing of this information.

- *Sharing Information.* Having collected information about the organization's functioning, managers then share it with subordinates, peers, supervisors, or people outside the organization. Managers share information about the environment in which the organization functions, including industry trends, technological developments, and market requirements. Managers also share their knowledge of the organization—its structure, goals, resources, and culture. They share information in face-to-face meetings, at meetings, or using electronic systems.

- *Leading, Motivating, and Coaching Employees.* Managers establish a formal reporting structure and a system of accountability among workers. Managers attempt to build effective work teams by encouraging cooperation and handling conflicts that arise. They direct and motivate employees to accomplish personal and organizational goals. They train, coach, and evaluate their employees and help them develop the skills, knowledge, materials, equipment, and time to perform their jobs.

- *Making Decisions and Plans.* All managers act as decision makers. Top managers determine their company's goals and the strategy for accomplishing them. Lower-level managers decide the number and type of employees necessary to accomplish the organization's goals. Managers require information about individuals, groups, and organizations involved in or affected by the problem situation. They need information about the alternatives available and the costs and benefits associated with each. Managers often incorporate their decisions into long-term and short-term plans for the organization. They should diagnose each decision situation to identify its unique information needs.

Role	Examples of Information
TABLE 1-1 Managers perform numerous roles as part of their job. The use of information gathering technology can make performing these roles easier.	
Gathering information and monitoring the environment	Company and industry information Minutes of task force and committee meetings Competitor information
Sharing information	Industry trends Technological developments Market requirements Organizational information
Leading, motivating, and coaching employees	Performance management Training opportunities Job descriptions
Making decisions and plans	Problem situations Operational and strategic plans Company goals
Distributing and negotiating about resources	Employee assignments and scheduling Budget Available equipment
Resolving problems and developing strategic responses	Problems and possible solutions Attitudes toward change Local political and economic conditions
Providing control	Performance standards Corporate goals Performance measurements

- *Distributing and Negotiating about Resources.* Managers determine the assignment of people to tasks, the allocation of money and materials to individuals, departments, and other work groups, and the scheduling of various employees' time. To allocate resources effectively, managers need information about enterprise goals and resource availability and employees' existing work assignments, capabilities, and vacation schedules. They also should know the costs of various projects or products. They need to understand the tradeoffs between various scheduling or budgeting alternatives. Managers frequently negotiate with their subordinates or other managers about how to best allocate resources to accomplish various group or organizational goals. Information systems can provide managers the information they need to improve this allocation.

- *Resolving Problems and Developing Strategic Responses.* In conjunction with resource allocation and negotiation, managers define problems in a situation, analyze them, and then propose solutions. Managers can act as change agents in dealing with problems. As change agents, they need data about workers' and management's attitudes toward change, the resources available for the change, and the consequences of similar changes in other situations. Developing strategic responses in organizations that function globally may pose special challenges. Managers may need to account for significant currency fluctuations, unpredictable local political conditions, or an unknown labor pool. They may need to consider variations in national customs, worker expectations, and product acceptance.

- *Providing Control.* Control means ensuring that performance meets established standards, workers' activities occur as planned, and the organization proceeds toward its established goals. In the control process, as shown in Figure 1-6, managers establish standards and methods for measuring performance, assess performance, and then compare performance to the standards. They require information about the organization's functioning to help them anticipate and handle organizational problems and challenges. For example, when a sales report shows that one

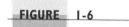 **I-6**   Managers implement the control process to ensure that actual performance meets expected standards.

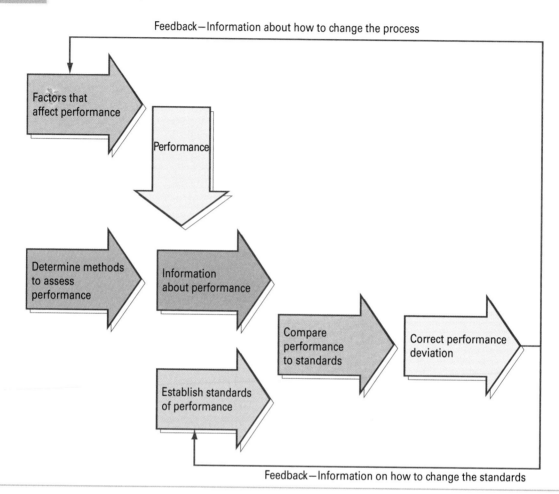

salesperson has fallen significantly behind forecast, the sales manager can act to identify and rectify the problem. When a budget variance analysis shows that an account is approaching its budget too early in the year, financial managers can analyze past and projected spending to determine the cause and correct the problem.

The Challenges for Effective Information Management

Managers need to collect, process, and disseminate information quickly and accurately to help their organizations compete effectively in today's global marketplace.

Using Technology Appropriately to Meet Information Needs

Although computers can make large quantities of information available, such information may not address managers' or employees' needs. Managers need to continually reassess whether they have the information they need for performing their various roles.

Using information technology effectively means ensuring that the technology chosen best meets these information needs. Companies must frequently make tradeoffs between securing the best technology and making cost-effective choices. The rapid pace of new technology introductions challenges managers to continuously assess how well existing technologies meet information needs.

Using technology effectively also requires a continuous updating of technical skills. Although many companies provide training to their employees, others do not. Ensuring that employees have the appropriate skills has both financial and time cost implications. As a result, employees may find their mobility and productivity limited by the extent to which they can learn new technical skills independently of their employers.

Dealing with Too Little, Too Much, or Conflicting Information

The gap between the amount of information an organization can collect and the ability of its employees to make sense of the information has widened rather than narrowed. Often employees face an **information glut,** an overload of information. For example, Universal Product Code scanners provide 100 to 1,000 times as much information about product sales as was available before their use. The size of Wal-Mart's corporate database, which includes data about sales, shipments, inventory, customers, and suppliers, among other facts, now exceeds 101 terabytes, the equivalent of more than 25 billion pages of text.[26] As managers move higher in the organization and assume more responsibilities, information overload becomes a more significant challenge.

To avoid such overload, people must carefully assess their information needs and then find effective ways of managing the information. Because computers process input from diverse sources, users may also obtain conflicting information if one source updates information more frequently than another does. Bob Evans' Farms, the $1 billion owner and operator of more than 450 family restaurants in 22 states, uses business intelligence software to tackle its glut of information. This software allows its marketing managers to organize and summarize information in a meaningful way, to focus their attention on out-of-the-ordinary events and statistics, and to put the right information into the hands of those who need it at the right time.[27]

Responding in a Timely Fashion

Manual filing systems satisfy many personal needs for organizing and retrieving information, but they make it difficult for managers to easily retrieve large quantities of information. They also make it impossible to collect information from different sites worldwide. Computerized systems not only ease access to material in a single location, but also allow managers to retrieve information from multiple locations, often instantly. They can also support quick, repeated searches of data. For example, people who require patent information for engineering inventions can use software to perform sophisticated and rapid patent searches.[28]

A variety of information industries, such as the newspaper, magazine, radio, television, and advertising industries, assist people in acquiring timely information for use at work. The Web, in particular, makes information readily available through the Internet. For example, not only can moviegoers obtain film schedules on the Web, they can also view movie previews, read reviews, and purchase their tickets so that they can be certain of a seat when they arrive at the cinema.

Ensuring Cost Effectiveness

Although information can be valuable, it is costly to use. Acquiring, processing, storing, retrieving, transmitting, communicating, and using information all have costs. Generally, acquiring information through informal sources, such as conversations with customers or suppliers, costs less than through formal ones, such as electronic forms or monitoring equipment, but the information acquired may be harder to organize and use effectively. Experts estimate that electronic forms for capturing data cost at least 70 percent less to design, purchase, use, carry, and revise than the equivalent paper forms.[29] Electronic processing, such as electronic scanning, can significantly reduce the costs of handling information. The Lourdes Hospital in Paducah, Kentucky, a 389-bed facility, saved $120,000 in paper and supplies and freed a 400-square-foot forms storage room by replacing pre-printed and stock forms with electronic forms. The forms are printable on demand and easily input into its medical records system. The electronic forms also increased the hospital's accuracy in tracking patients, their treatments, and lab needs. Based on the success at Lourdes, Catholic Health Partners, of which Lourdes is a member, intends to implement a similar system with estimated savings of $10 million.[30]

The primary cost of storing information is the cost of the storage medium and space. The cost of media, physical facilities, and staff for backup systems also contribute to the storage costs. Storing large amounts of data calls for simultaneously developing and storing an index or map that assists in locating the data. Electronic systems provide rapid and inexpensive retrieval of electronically stored information. Transmitting information long distance or exchanging large volumes of data can occur more effectively by electronic communication.

Ensuring Security

Users of computer systems must pay special attention to the security of their information. With the widespread use of the Internet, security issues have become more common. Computer files are highly susceptible to theft and sabotage, particularly because these security breaches are not easily noticeable. The threat to computer files has increased as many people have unprecedented access to them through the Internet. Levels of security can be placed on information systems so that only specified information can be shared with others.

Ethical Principles for Information Management

Because the power of information is so great, people who manage information and those who design information systems are right to be concerned about its potential misuse. Unfortunately, information systems, like most other tools, can be used for good or bad.

Philosophers distinguish between the concepts of **morality** and **ethics.** Morality refers to what is good or bad, right or wrong. Philosophers differ as to whether or not morality is relative or absolute. The relative theory holds that different people may have different standards for what is right or wrong depending on their culture, upbringing, religion, or even their financial circumstance. The absolute theory maintains that the standards of what is right or wrong are absolute and apply to all people in all situations.

No matter which philosophy you accept on morality, you will occasionally be faced with situations where applying your moral standards is difficult. For example, consider a person whose moral standard states that all lives have equal value. He holds one dose of an antidote for a poison that has affected both a criminal and an outstanding citizen who has done good deeds throughout his life. The outstanding citizen has a 10 percent chance of surviving if given the antidote while the criminal has a 90 percent chance of surviving if given the antidote. Both will die if the antidote is not administered. What should the person do? This example presents a moral dilemma because his desire to save the person whose moral standards are most like his own conflicts with his moral standard to maximize the likelihood of saving a life. Ethics is the study of how to apply your moral standards to particular situations, such as this one. It makes no assumptions about what is right or what is wrong. Rather, it examines how to be consistent in the application of your moral principles.

Ethical issues in information systems relate to security, privacy, use of company resources, computer viruses, and unprofessional behavior, among others. They can involve any type of information technology and any type of information system. The ethical use of information systems has become a major concern for managers and IS professionals.

Controls over access to information, particularly on the Web, have raised ethical concerns related to censorship. Most of the limitations have focused on preventing children from reading pornographic material. However, businesses also routinely limit or monitor their employees' use of the Web to protect themselves from lawsuits for sexual harassment and to counter the loss of productivity associated with Web surfing. More than half of all companies now monitor their employees' e-mail or Web surfing.[31]

Protecting personal privacy has also become a key issue as computer information systems can maintain large amounts of data about individuals without their knowledge. Privacy advocates call for policies and procedures to protect individuals' privacy, such as ensuring the legal collection of correct and up-to-date data relevant to the organization's goals.[32]

People often face options regarding the use of information that they cannot label clearly as right or wrong, moral or immoral. For example, what should you do if, after promising your employees that their data are private, you learn that one employee has stolen company information? What if you learn that one employee has plans to harm another? Should you examine their data files? People can apply a variety of ethical principles to determine what is or is not ethical in cases such as these.[33]

- *The principle of harm minimization.* Make the decision that minimizes harm. To apply this principle, you must look at how the decision affects all parties, not only you and your company. You will probably have to weigh the harm done to one person against the harm done to another.

- *The principle of consistency.* Assume that everyone who faces a similar decision makes the same choice as you. Would you approve of the consequences? For example, if you believe that copying software rather than purchasing it is ethical, examine the implication of everyone copying software.

- *The principle of respect.* Make the decision that treats people with the greatest respect. This implies that you act towards them in the same way that you hope they would act towards you.

If these principles conflict, are too difficult to apply, or provide no clear solution, you can also use a variety of practical approaches for making ethical decisions.[34]

- *Use the law to guide your ethical choice.* For example, apply existing copyright protection laws to determine whether permission or payment is necessary to use a software product for a specific application.

- *Apply the formal guidelines of your company or an appropriate professional organization.* These guidelines might help you decide among legal choices. For example, the Code of Ethics and Professional Conduct of the Association for Computing Machinery includes provisions, which you could legally ignore, for respecting the privacy of others and honoring confidentiality.

- *Use one of the following informal guidelines.* What would your mother (or father) say if you acted in that way? How would you feel if you saw your situation described in the newspaper? Does the situation "smell bad?" How would you feel if the roles were reversed, and the act was done to you? Would you use your behavior as a marketing tool?

- *Avoid decisions that answer the following questions with "no":* Does the action cause unnecessary social harm or fail to serve the public interest? Does the action violate any basic human rights? Does the action abridge any commonly accepted duties?

Texas Instruments offers the quick ethics test shown in Figure 1-7.

THE FOUR-STEP MANAGEMENT APPROACH

How can managers meet the challenges of managing information efficiently and effectively? We propose that a systematic approach to diagnosing needs, evaluating information technology, designing information systems, and then implementing them will improve information management. This model involves four steps, as shown in Figure 1-8: diagnosis, evaluation, design, and implementation. While this model has some of the same characteristics as the Systems Development Life Cycle (see Chapter 9), the four-step management approach helps managers and other employees, rather than information systems professionals, improve their information management.

Diagnosing Information Needs

Managers, employees, and other individuals must first assess their needs for information within a particular situation they face. Diagnosis requires a description of the existing problem, the context in which it occurs, the type of information available, the type of information required to solve it, and the possible ways of securing the needed information. Executives at Marriott International, for example, must determine the types of information they need to make such organizational decisions as setting strategic direction, general marketing policies, and human resources practices. Each manager has different information needs. How can each effectively get and process the information most important to his decision making?

FIGURE 1-7

Managers and employees can use this quick test to determine whether an action is ethical.

- Is the action legal?
- Does it comply with company values?
- If you do it, will you feel bad?
- How will it look in the newspaper?
- If you know it is wrong, don't do it!
- If you are not sure, ask.
- Keep asking until you get an answer.

SOURCE: Texas Instruments Inc. Reprinted in Diane Trommer, "Lead Us Not into Temptation—Supply Chain Model Poses New Ethical Challenge," *Electronic Buyers' News*, 4 August 1997, www.tecvhweb.com/se /directlink.cgi?EBN19970904S0005. Used with permission.

FIGURE 1-8

Managers should use the four-step approach to managing information.

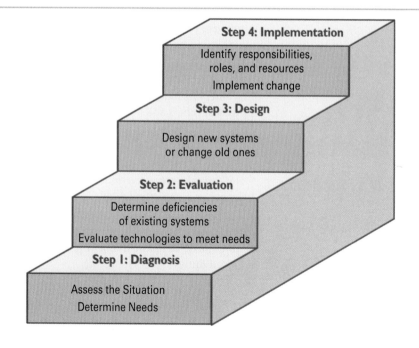

Diagnosis of information needs can occur at the individual, managerial, organizational, or societal level. Employees must assess the information they need to do their jobs effectively. Managers often have needs for transaction processing, financial control, project management, and communication, among others. Organizations use information to increase their competitive advantage or implement their strategy, such as by improving customer service, cost control, or quality monitoring.

Society, too, uses information for communication, economic development, and generally improving the quality of life. Like business managers, public decision makers need to diagnose their information needs so that they can properly execute their roles. The city of Fairfax, Virginia, equipped its busses with Global Positioning Systems and installed a wireless system to gather the information that they needed to improve the bus schedules and services. The system also allows waiting passengers to get precise information about the location and likely arrival times of approaching busses.[35]

Evaluating Information Technology and Systems

Evaluation of the hardware, software, database, and data communication used to handle information follows the diagnosis of needs. Evaluation has several steps, as shown in Figure 1-9:

1. *Assess the current technology and systems for handling information.* A manager, for example, might first describe the components of the information technology and systems used to acquire, process, store, retrieve, or communicate information.

2. *Compare these components to available systems* and ask the following: How well does the current technology and systems respond to the information needs? Are technologies and systems available that would significantly improve the handling of information? Are they likely to be cost-effective? What consequences will result from changing the handing of information?

3. *Determine what information needs are not or cannot be handled.*

Figure 1-10 offers a list of questions the manager might ask as part of the evaluation step.

FIGURE 1-9

Evaluating information technology and systems involves comparing existing systems to state-of-the-art systems that meet information needs.

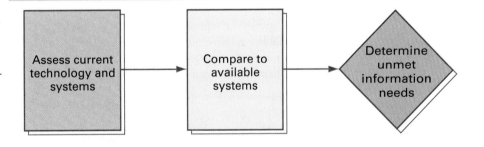

FIGURE 1-10

Answer these questions to evaluate your company's information systems and technology.

- What are the current systems for handling information?
- Are they manual or computerized?
- What are the components of the information systems and technology?
- How do these components compare to available state-of-the-art systems?
- How well does the current system respond to the information needs?
- Would other systems respond better to the information needs?
- Would state-of-the-art systems significantly improve the handling of information?
- What consequences will result from a change in the way information is handled?
- What information needs are not handled and cannot be handled, regardless of the information technology or information systems used?

Designing Responsive Systems

If an evaluation determines that existing technology and systems do not adequately meet information needs, managers, staff specialists, and information users, together with information systems professionals, then need to design coherent systems for information management. Design involves correcting deficiencies in existing systems and integrating state-of-the-art practices and technology into them.

The design phase involves making decisions about specific information technology and their integration into information systems. It involves a cost-benefit analysis to ensure that the new design provides a sufficient return for the additional costs incurred. System users and skilled professionals often collaborate to ensure the best design.

Implementing Information Systems

The final step focuses on issues associated with implementing the new or altered systems. Who will be responsible for overseeing the implementation? How will it occur? What additional resources will be required for implementation? What types of follow-up will occur? How will the change affect other aspects of an individual's or organization's functioning? Identifying the parties' responsibility for implementation involves determining the roles individual managers, information systems staff, or specialists from outside the organization will play. Specifying the timetable for implementation typically follows.

Top management must ensure that sufficient resources are available for the implementation and for dealing with changes that occur as a result of the implementation. They must also assess whether the information systems professionals function effectively throughout the four phases. Recognizing that the new system and technology likely will have unanticipated consequences should be a key aspect of planning; monitoring such effects and providing solutions for problems that arise should be part of the implementation. Implementation also includes ensuring that the new systems perform as expected and result in the predicted costs and savings.

ORGANIZATION OF THIS BOOK

This book applies the four-step approach to examining the management of information, as shown in Table 1-2. Part One, composed of Chapters 1 and 2, diagnoses information needs by focusing on the way managers, groups, and organizations use information. Part Two, which includes Chapters 3 through 5, evaluates the information technologies available to meet these

TABLE 1-2

This book follows the four-step approach of information management.

	Part I Diagnosing Information Needs for Management	Part II Evaluating Information Technologies	Part III Designing Systems for Business	Part IV Managing the Information Resource
Step 1 Diagnosis	•••	••	••	•
Step 2 Evaluation	••	•••	••	•
Step 3 Design	•	••	•••	••
Step 4 Implementation	•	•	•	•••

KEY: ••• (Strong emphasis); •• (moderate emphasis); • (Light emphasis)

needs. Part Three, Chapters 6 through 8, examines how organizations use information systems and technology to solve problems and improve business processes. Part Four, Chapters 9 and 10, investigates implementation issues and managing the information resource.

SUMMARY

This book investigates the management of information. We define information as processed data. Information can be used as a resource, asset, or product. Information technology, in the form of computer hardware, software, database management systems, and data communication technology, helps meet the information needs of managers and employees. We can create information systems for purposes of automation, transaction processing, or management support and with personal, departmental, enterprise, or inter-organizational scope.

Information management poses unique challenges to managers. They must succeed in a global environment. Companies focus on performance in an increasingly electronic and mobile economy. They build individual capabilities and productivity by creating a knowledge-based work force.

Managers in the global marketplace face a dynamic and unpredictable environment. They perform a great quantity of work at an unrelenting pace. Differences exist in the types of information needed by managers at different levels. All managers perform a variety of roles that require different types of information. They also face a variety of challenges in managing information. Sometimes, they need to apply ethical principles to decide how information should be used.

Managers can use a four-step analytical model to improve their management of information. They first assess their situation and assess their information needs. Next they evaluate the quality of their existing information systems for meeting their information needs. Third, if needs are not adequately met, they propose modifications in the systems to better meet their needs. Fourth and finally, they deal with issues of implementation and follow-up.

KEY TERMS

automation systems	functional information system	management
computer hardware	groupware	management reporting system
computer software	individual information system	management support system (MSS)
data	information	morality
data communication technology	information glut	project manager
database management system	information system	resource
decision support system	information technology	telecommuter
departmental information system	inter-organizational information system	Total Quality Management (TQM)
enterprise information system	Internet	transaction
ethics	knowledge	transaction processing system (TPS)
executive information system	knowledge worker	wisdom

REVIEW QUESTIONS

1. What is information management?
2. What is information?
3. How do data, information, and knowledge differ?
4. In what three ways do organizations use information?
5. What is information technology?

6. What are four major types of information technology?

7. For what three purposes do people use information systems?

8. What is a transaction?

9. What types of management support systems exist?

10. How might the scope of an information system be described?

11. What major issues do managers face in managing information today?

12. What aspects of the manager's job influence his management of information?

13. How does the global marketplace affect information management?

14. What roles does a manager perform?

15. How do managers use information to improve the quality of their products and services?

16. How does a manager use information and information systems in performing each of her roles?

17. What challenges do managers face in ensuring effective information management?

18. What ethical issues do managers face?

19. What steps comprise the four-step management approach?

20. Why should managers diagnose their information needs?

21. What steps should they take in evaluating information technology and systems?

22. What issues should they consider in designing responsive systems?

23. What issues must they resolve as part of implementation?

MINICASE

HOSPITALITY COMPANY GETS THE MESSAGE AROUND THE WORLD

When Carlson Hospitality—which franchises, owns, and manages hotels such as Country Inns & Suites, Radisson, and Regent—considered getting rid of its binder-size monthly status reports and replacing them with sleek handhelds that would deliver real-time information about occupancy, VIP visits, and overbooking, the company knew the project wouldn't be a walk in the park. Any system that the company built would eventually have to work at 750 hotels in 55 countries and accommodate more than 2,000 users. For many global corporations, the very thought of offering so many far-flung people access to so much information would place the project on the chopping block, ready to be scaled down, but Carlson scaled up.

During the last three years, the Minneapolis-based company spent $21 million re-architecting its core systems and integrating data from at least six databases. And while that restructuring was not done with a vast wireless project in mind, the resulting order made it possible for the technology team to push the hospitality company's key indicators out over a wireless local area network (LAN), as well as a wired network. The integration was vital to the wireless project because it organized the data (occupancy rates, pricing information, and so on) from all the company's different databases in ways that will someday make worldwide distribution feasible.

"That new architecture was a prerequisite to having the data available to work with," says CIO Scott Heintzeman. But it tied managers to their desks because that information could only be accessed from PCs. Carlson wanted to "[get] managers out from behind their desks and talking to the customers," Heintzeman said. "We're not just pushing out static information, [but] information in a graphical format that makes it easy [for managers] to spot trends." For example, a room-booking screen lets managers view day-by-day or year-by-year occupancy rates.

To achieve this goal Heintzeman and his team had to build an application that would make sense of the information as it was presented on handheld computers. And, of course, Carlson had to set up wireless LANs in each hotel where the wireless system would be used. Heintzeman and his team chose to implement the new system on Pocket PCs from Compaq Computer Corp. rather than on the Palm Pilot or similar handheld computers because it was easier to develop software on PocketPC's Microsoft operating system than on the Palm Pilot's operating system.

In March 2001, the company began a trial of the new system in a Minneapolis hotel and quickly expanded the test to four other locations. Managers in those hotels use their desktop computers to select the pieces of data, such as occupancy rates, and set up alerts for the key indicators, such as a sudden increase in demand. They then download the data to their handhelds so that they can access it from almost anywhere on their hotels' property.

Today, Carlson managers are pushing data to the handhelds in one of three ways. Most managers use a cradle to connect their handheld to a computer, some sync the data over a wireless LAN, and a few use AT&T's digital wide area network.

In all, Heintzeman says, Carlson has put about 200 people on handhelds at a cost of about $100,000. He reports that things are working well and plans to expand the program to deploy about 6,000 Compaq iPaq Pocket PCs, equipping corporate executives as well as general managers and frontline personnel at more than 600 hotels.

SOURCE: Adapted from Danielle Dunne, "Wireless That Works," CIO 15 February 2002, 60; and Bob Brewin, "Hotel Chain Moves to Wireless Data Access," Computerworld, 4 December 2000, 6. Reprinted through the courtesy of CIO. ©2002, CXO Media Inc. All rights reserved.

Case Questions

Diagnosis

    1. What information needs did Carlson's managers and operations personnel have?

Evaluation

    2. What types of information systems did the company have?

    3. How well did these systems meet their needs?

Design

    4. What changes in information systems did the company make?

    5. Did these changes better meet their needs?

Implementation

    6. What implementation issues did Carlson face?

    7. How will Carlson know whether or not the new systems are effective?

1-1 MANAGERIAL ACTIVITIES ANALYSIS

ACTIVITY

Step 1: Review the excerpt of the daily work diary shown in Figure 1-11 of Joseph Michaelson's morning. Michaelson is the plant manager for one of five plants of a large manufacturer that produces and sells components for computers. The plant operates twenty-four hours a day, seven days a week.

Step 2: For each activity performed, record the information the manager used during that activity as follows:

    Activity   **Information Used**

Step 3: Now select a manager to interview. Ask him or her to describe in detail two or three activities he or she performed during the previous workday. Then ask the manager to tell you

Joseph Michaelson holds numerous meetings and performs a variety of activities as part of his job.

8:00	Joseph meets the night supervisor for their daily meeting. They discuss the production runs during the previous night, problems with staffing, and plans for tonight's runs.
8:30	Joseph runs into the plant's human resource representative at the coffee machine. They discuss some new federal regulations that affect their plans for hiring temporary workers.
8:40	Joseph receives a telephone call from the corporate accounting department. He has been meeting regularly with a representative from accounting to discuss new ways of accounting for unused inventory. They chat for twenty minutes about the project as well as exchange some corporate gossip.
9:00	Joseph meets with the five people who report directly to him to review their plans for the week. They spend much of the meeting discussing their plans for increasing the number of self-managing work teams on the plant floor. They also spend some time talking about problems they are having with machining several key parts.
10:00	Joseph participates in a conference call with the four other plant managers to discuss the installation of some new assembly-line technology on the plant floor.
10:30	Joseph completes the paperwork for the performance evaluations of his subordinates that he performed over the past two weeks.
11:00	Joseph meets with two newly hired team leaders to welcome them to the plant.
11:15	Joseph speaks at length with a vendor who has been providing problem parts for use in one of the computer components. Together they discuss ways of solving the problem and schedule another telephone conversation for the next day.
11:30	Joseph takes his daily walk about the plant, speaking with about thirty workers on the floor.

what information was required to perform these activities. Ask the manager what additional information he or she needed to perform the activities more effectively.

Step 4: Answer the following questions, in small groups or with the entire class:

1. Which activities did the managers perform?
2. What information did the managers use during those activities?
3. How did the managers secure the needed information?
4. What additional information did the managers require to perform the activities more effectively?

I-2 FINE LEATHER STORES

ACTIVITY

Step 1: Read the following scenario.

The owner of a chain of five leather goods stores has decided to install a computerized information system to support the accounting, sales, operations, and human resource functions for the stores. Located in small suburban shopping centers, these stores carry an assortment of luggage, briefcases, wallets, and other leather products as well as travel accessories and small electronic products. So far, each store in the chain has operated independently, with a single personal computer to support store functions at the manager's discretion. Some stores use it to record transactions; others maintain inventory records on it; still others use it for primitive payroll systems.

Step 2: Individually or in small groups, diagnose the situation. List the types of information each store manager requires.

Step 3: In small groups or with the entire class, share the lists you have developed. Then prepare a comprehensive list of information after answering the following questions:

  1. What elements do these lists have in common?
  2. What information has been omitted from the lists?
  3. Which information can be part of a computerized information system?

I-3 WHAT INFORMATION IS NEEDED?

ACTIVITY

Step 1: Read each managerial problem below. For each situation, decide what information the manager needs to solve the problem.

Problem 1: The manager of benefits in a moderate-size manufacturing company has just received four complaints from employees who state that their retirement accounts have not been properly credited for the third quarter in a row. What information does the manager need to ensure the correct assignment of money?

Problem 2: The owner of a chain of five ice cream stores has just spoken with one of his managers about an ongoing supply problem. The manager noted that a large number of comments in his customer suggestion box were complaints that the store was out of stock of the flavor of ice cream the customer wanted to purchase. Although such complaints do not seem to have affected sales yet, the manager is afraid that he will soon lose valuable customers to a competing chain. What information do the manager and the owner need to ensure the correct supply of ice cream to each store?

Problem 3: As the project manager of a major audit, you are responsible for allocating the work to the various associates working on the project. You have heard one of the associates complaining that you play favorites in assigning tasks. She complained that the male associates get the more visible tasks that require fewer hours to complete. You do not believe that you discriminate in this way. What information do you need to refute this charge?

Step 2: For each situation, describe two ways the manager could secure the information he or she requires.

Step 3: Individually, in small groups, or with the entire class, answer the following questions:

  1. What types of information needs do managers have?
  2. How can they secure the information they require?
  3. What role can information systems play in providing the needed information?

I-4 ETHICAL ISSUES IN THE SALE OF PERSONAL INFORMATION

ACTIVITY

Step 1: Read the following paragraphs about the AMA and its database plans.

The American Medical Association (AMA) was founded in 1847 "to act as the unified voice of physicians working together to improve health care across the country."[36] Membership in the AMA is open only to doctors, and most doctors are members. The AMA provides many services to physicians, including publication of several journals, lobbying activities, and education.

The AMA is planning to launch a new for-profit subsidiary called "Preference Solutions" to assemble and sell information about health-care professionals. The AMA already receives an income of about $23 million from the sale of information from its current database, which includes data only about doctors. The subsidiary, a joint venture between the AMA and marketing firm Acxiom Corp., will supplement the AMA's database with additional data about the doctors as well as data about other health-care professionals, such as nurses and optometrists. The new database will include demographic information, contact information, and career information, including medical degrees, specialties, certifications, and practice history. The database is expected to be particularly useful to drug, insurance, and advertising companies to help them target audiences most likely to buy their products.[37]

Step 2: Assume that you are a doctor. Individually or in small groups, identify the controls you would want to impose on the use of this database to protect your privacy and prevent its possible misuse. Decide whether or not you would object to the sale of information from this database with and without the controls you have identified.

Step 3: Your instructor will ask you to share the controls you have identified with the class. A list of these controls will be placed on the board or otherwise be made available for Step 4.

Step 4: Assume that you are the president of the AMA. You understand that you can make the most money and incur the smallest cost by avoiding any controls on the database that you plan to assemble. Nevertheless, you might have some moral objections to the uncontrolled sale of this information. Individually or in small groups, answer the following questions:

1. What moral objections, if any, do you have to the uncontrolled sale of information from the database?

2. Which controls, if any, address your objections?

3. How will you decide how to act given the conflicting objectives of maximizing profit from the sale of data and addressing your moral objections?

1-5 PLANNING FOR "GOING GLOBAL"

ACTIVITY

Step 1: You have recently assumed the position of chief information officer of a medium-size company that manufactures and sells professional sports-related products in the United States. The company's market research shows that a demand exists for similar products in Europe, and the executive team has decided to open outlets in three major European cities. If these outlets are successful, top management plans to open ten more within a year, move at least one manufacturing plant to Europe, and continue this rate of expansion over the next three to five years.

You have the assignment of preparing recommendations for updating the company's information systems to meet the needs of a global company. As a first step in this planning, you have decided that you need to develop a comprehensive checklist of the issues you and your staff need to consider about the move to a global company. You know that at a minimum you must consider tax implications of purchasing hardware and the availability of telecommunications services into each location. What else will influence your plan?

Step 2: Individually or in small groups, develop a checklist of issues that you should consider when making your recommendations about information systems in this company.

Step 3: Share the checklist with the rest of the class, and together develop a comprehensive checklist of issues for global companies. For each issue included on the checklist, answer the following two questions:

1. What implications does this issue have for the company's information systems?
2. What would happen if you ignore this issue?

IS ON THE WEB

IS ON
THE WEB

Exercise 1: Visit the Web sites of three companies that provide products or services to help companies do business internationally. Examples of such companies are those providing telecommunication services, logistics services, translation services, accounting software, or sales management software. Explain how these products and services help companies to collect and process data and use the resulting information to improve the efficiency of their global operations.

Exercise 2: Visit one of the sites on the Web page for Chapter 1 in the section called "Cyberethics." Summarize the ethical issues involved in writing laws to control the electronic dissemination of documents, software, and other intellectual property.

RECOMMENDED READINGS

Anthony, Robert. *Planning and Control Systems: A Framework for Analysis.* Boston: Harvard University Press, 1965.

Brynjolfsson, Erik, and Brian Kahin (Eds.). *Understanding the Digital Economy.* Cambridge, MA: MIT Press, 2000.

Lipnack, Jessica, and Jeffrey Stamps. *Virtual Teams: People Working across Boundaries with Technology.* New York: John Wiley & Sons, 2000.

Mintzberg, Henry. *The Nature of Managerial Work.* New Jersey: Harper Row, 1973.

Santos, Jose, Peter Williamson, and Yves L. Doz. *From Global to Metanational: How Companies Win in the Knowledge Economy.* Boston, MA: Harvard Business School, 2001.

Spinello, Richard A. *CyberEthics: Morality and Law in Cyberspace.* Sudbury, MA: Jones & Bartlett Publishing, 2001.

Wheaton, Kristan J. *The Warning Solution: Intelligent Analysis in the Age of Information Overload.* Fairfax, VA: AFCEA International Press, 2001

NOTES

1. Marriott International, *2000 Annual Report.*
2. James Cash, "Gaining Customer Loyalty," *Informationweek,* 10 April 1995, 88. Laura Struebing, "Measuring for Excellence," *Quality Progress* 29 (1996): 25–28.
3. Elana Varon, "Suite Returns," *CIO* 13 (15 August 2000): 114–122.
4. David Spacey, "Roll Out the Barrels," *Supply Management* 6 (9 August 2001): 32–33.
5. Bob Brewin, "Short-Haul Trucker to Roll Out Location-Tracking System," *Computerworld,* 5 February 2001, 7.
6. Michael Romano, "Broadening the Base," *Modern Healthcare* 31 (29 October 2001): 20–21.
7. Tatyana Sinioukov, "LG Electronics: Ready to Roll into the U.S. Market," *Dealerscope,* July 2001, 26.
8. Michael MacMillan, "Fighting Paper with Paper," *Computing Canada* 26 (13 October 2000): 35.
9. John Halamka, "Inside a Virtual Nursery," *Health Management Technology,* June 2001, 37–38.
10. Lori Doss, "Taco Bell Franchisees Try 'Above-Store' Systems to Lift Efficiency," *Nation's Restaurant News,* 22 October 2001, 55.

11. Rick Whiting, "Data Analysis to Health Care's Rescue," *Informationweek,* 24 September 2001, 68.
12. Jennifer Disabatino, "New Krispy Kreme Intranet a Recipe for Success," *Computerworld.com,* 26 July 2001, http://www.computerworld.com/databasetopics/data/story/0,10801,62556,00.html, accessed on 2 September, 2002.
13. Kimberly Mecham, "How Microsoft Built a Cost-Effective HR Portal," *HR Focus* 78 (August 2001): 4–5.
14. Julie Gallagher, "AAA Missouri Takes Direct Route," *Insurance & Technology,* November 2001, 16.
15. Ronald E Keener, "Clean Claims, More Money," *Health Management Technology,* May 2001, 20–21.
16. Avi Breiner and Rafi Maman, "Refinery Reaps the Benefits of New Decision Support Tool," *Oil & Gas Journal,* 8 January 2001, 46–48.
17. Larry Stevens, Groupware Out of the Box— Some Companies Find That No-Frills Web Collaboration Software Is a Welcome Alternative to a Pricey Notes or Exchange

Rollout, *Internetweek,* 1 October 2001, PG33–PG34.
18. "Meralco Info System," *Businessworld,* 20 March 2001, 1.
19. Paraphrased and adapted from the 'Lectric Law Library's Lexicon at http://www.lectlaw.com/def/e022.htm, accessed on 1 January 2002.
20. David Lewis, "Managed-Care Firm Takes Lead with Diverse Extranet," *Internetweek,* 21 May 2001, 50.
21. David C Barrow, "Sharing Know-How at BP Amoco," *Research Technology Management,* May/June 2001, 18–25.
22. Jason Compton, "Dial K for Knowledge," *CIO,* 15 June 2001, 136–138.
23. H. Mintzberg, *The Nature of Managerial Work,* 2d ed. (Englewood Cliffs, NJ: Prentice-Hall, 1979).
24. Peter J. Howe, "The Point Man Richard Parsons, 'Consummate Diplomat' and Longtime Insider, Faces a Tough Job Steering AOL Time Warner through Turbulent Times in the Net-Media Industry," *Boston Globe,* 16 December 2001, E1. Betsy Streisand and Joellen Perry, "You've Got a

New CEO: AOL Time Warner Picks a Diplomat to Bring Unity to Its Many Parts," *U.S. News & World Report,* 17 December 2001, 32–33.

25. The roles presented here are drawn in large part from Henry Mintzberg, *The Nature of Managerial Work,* 2nd ed. (Englewood Cliffs, NJ: Prentice-Hall, 1979).

26. Paul Sheldon Foote and Malini Krishnamurthi, "Forecasting Using Data Warehousing Model: Wal-Mart's Experience," *The Journal of Business Forecasting Methods & Systems,* fall 2001, 3–17.

27. C. Dickinson Waters, "Bob Evans' Tech Chief Attacks Information Overload," *Nation's Restaurant News,* 16 April 2001, 58. James Peters, "Bob Evans Growth Plan Falls Flat As Unit Expansion Falters," *Nation's Restaurant News,* 3 December 2001, 4–6. www.bobevans .com, accessed on 29 August, 2002.

28. "Patent Searches and More," *Manufacturing Engineering,* March 2001, 32.

29. M. Bragen, "Form Fitting," *Computerworld,* 14 September 1992, 105–107.

30. "Documented Savings," *Health Management Technology,* October 2001, 56–57.

31. Sandra Swanson, "Beware: Employee Monitoring Is on the Rise," *Informationweek,* 20 August 2001, 57–58.

32. Michael H. Agranoff, "Protecting Personal Privacy Exposed in Corporate Data Bases," *Information Strategy: The Executive's Journal* 7 (summer 1991): 27–32.

33. This discussion is based on Ernest A. Kallman and John P. Grillo, *Ethical Decision Making and Information Technology: An Introduction with Cases* (New York: McGraw-Hill, 1993).

34. Kallman and Grillo, *Ethical Decision Making.*

35. Alan Radding and Julia King, "Leading the Way," *ComputerworldROI,* September/October 2001, 14–22.

36. http://www.ama-assn.org/ama/pub/category /1915.html, accessed on 15 January 2002.

37. Romano, "Broadening the Base," 20–21.

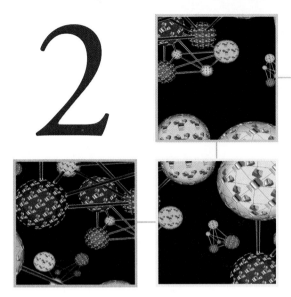

2

The Organization and Information Management

LEARNING OBJECTIVES

After completing Chapter 2, you will be able to:

- Describe the business context in which today's organizations operate.
- Discuss the five information requirements of today's organizations.
- Describe the new organizational forms that have arisen and their information requirements.
- Identify the information needs of team-based management.
- Illustrate the types of information required to make and implement strategic decisions in an organization.
- Comment about the relationship of information to the design and implementation of organizational structures.
- Offer ways of using information for achieving a competitive advantage.

Kodak Faces Challenges

When Daniel Carp, chairman, president, and CEO of Eastman Kodak Company, examined the sales data for the 2000 Christmas season, he must have felt that they signaled both good news and bad. The good news was that digital cameras were among the hottest items of the holiday season and that Kodak's cameras beat the competition handily, achieving a 50 percent share, according to one market survey. The bad news was that film, film paper, and film processing had been Kodak's primary source of income and profit since the company was founded in 1892. Kodak was clearly at a crossroads, with many possible paths to follow.

Carp had to answer some important questions. Was film a technology of the past, doomed by the digital revolution, or would film and film processing continue to be prosperous areas of business even as digital photography grew? To compete in the digital world, should Kodak focus on cameras, picture printing, or picture paper? Kodak was already a player in all of these markets. Its Easy Share camera was a best seller. Its PalmPix camera turns a handheld organizer into a digital camera. Its Ofoto.com subsidiary provides a Web site for customers to share digital photos with friends and relatives, edit photos, and have them printed or made into cards and delivered to their door. Kodak's photo-quality inkjet paper was popular. One market in which Kodak did not compete was that for photo-quality digital printers.[1]

The threat posed by digital technology to Kodak is clear. What other threats does Kodak face? What are its strengths and weaknesses, and how might these affect its response? What opportunities exist for revenue and profit growth, and how should Carp prioritize these opportunities? Which divisions should be downsized or eliminated? What companies might Kodak want to acquire to strengthen its competitive position? What information does Carp need to make these decisions? How can Kodak's information systems help?

Once Carp sets a strategic direction for Kodak, how can he communicate his vision so that the entire company pulls effectively toward the same goals? How can information systems translate his vision into action?

Managers in all companies face similar questions. In this chapter we answer them by first looking at the nature of organizations and their information requirements. Next we examine a number of new organizational structures and consider the information required to support them. We then investigate the trend toward using teams in the workplace and review the information that team-based management requires. Finally, we explore the use of information in determining and implementing an organization's strategy, as well as achieving a competitive advantage.

THE CHANGING ORGANIZATION

Organizations function in a dynamic, global marketplace, with numerous challenges and opportunities. They must bring high-quality products to market quickly and at a competitive price, while meeting customer needs. Kodak faces these challenges in the imaging industry.

The Business Context

The following characteristics provide the backdrop for organizational functioning:

- *The globalization of business* calls for managers with strong leadership skills in cross-cultural situations. They must respond to continuous and unpredictable economic changes and dramatic political upheavals. They need to think creatively about the best locations for operations to take advantage of low labor costs around the world. They also need to think about how to market and sell common products in different countries to take advantage of economies of scale and scope. DaimlerChrysler AG, for example, a German company, is bringing together engineers, marketing managers, and executives from Europe, North America, and Asia to develop a "world engine" that could power cars from Chrysler, Mitsubishi, and Hyundai.[2]

- *Rapid technological change* constantly threatens established products and services. The rate of technological change has been increasing. As a result, companies have to upgrade their technology more frequently than they have in the past just to remain competitive. For example, in 1970, the productivity of the average factory was just 15 percent below that of the best factories. By 2000, that figure had jumped to 40 percent.[3] The average factory just cannot keep up with the pace of technological change. Today's organizations must provide a learning environment, where employees can constantly upgrade their skills as technology changes. In addition, managers need to be vigilant and adept at evaluating the threat and potential of new technologies.

- *Organizational flexibility, adaptability, and collaboration* characterize the changing organization. Companies need the capability to reorganize quickly to respond to changing market conditions. They need to put resources where they achieve the greatest payback. They need to reengineer their business processes to become more effective and efficient. Today's organizations often create partnerships with other companies, even competitors, to meet customer demands and create new product niches. Extensive, rapid communication has become a key to effective organizational functioning. Companies have introduced flexible organizational structures to ease communication within and between organizations. Nortel Networks, a $30 billion network and communications leader, has recently moved from a vertically integrated firm to one that now outsources nearly all of its manufacturing. This change in structure allows Nortel to use only the most current manufacturing sources for the components it needs, and it also allows Nortel to adjust quickly to geographical changes in demand and manufacturing needs.[4]

- *Work teams and empowered workers* accompany the need for greater flexibility, adaptability, and collaboration. Companies use cross-functional teams to bring products to market more rapidly and cheaply. They give workers new responsibilities in decision making so that employees with the best knowledge can quickly respond to changing conditions. Bell Atlantic, now Verizon, tested the concept of work teams by organizing half of its customer call centers to operate in teams. It found that the team-based centers produced greater service quality, greater employee satisfaction, greater productivity, and increased sales.[5]

- *The changing workforce* has caused companies to consider the value that women and minorities bring to organizations with their special perspectives and knowledge. Combined with the traditional white male workers, the more diverse workforce creates a powerful mechanism for understanding the marketplace and improving organizational performance. Companies also grapple with the benefits and challenges created by the growing contingent labor market, where workers move among companies on a contract basis. The temporary work market in the United States, which varies according to the state of the economy, is valued at approximately $70 billion, with upwards of two million placements daily.[6] One estimate holds that one in four working Americans are "free agents," working for themselves or on temporary projects or jobs.[7]

- *Knowledge management* has emerged as a new discipline in organizations.[8] We define **knowledge management** as the identification, capture, systemization, and dissemination of knowledge so that it can be used it improve the operation and efficiency of the organization. You may recall that we defined knowledge as an understanding derived from information. Because understanding is an intensely personal experience, knowledge is also personal. The challenge of knowledge management is to translate such personal knowledge into organizational knowledge. **Knowledge workers,** those who understand the information maintained by the organization and can use it wisely, are particularly valuable to an organization's success. Imagine, for example, the additional value that a reception desk worker at a hotel can offer when trained as a knowledge worker rather than as a simple clerk.

Information Requirements for Organizations

Today's organizations have special and increased requirements for information to support their new ways of doing business. They must ensure the accessibility, reliability, accuracy, privacy, and security of information at a reasonable cost.

- *Making Information Accessible.* Companies need to make the appropriate information available to users at the right time, the right place, and in the right format. Increasingly, organizations use computerized systems to increase information accessibility. Kodak is spending more than $200 million to integrate its information systems and make its data available for use in all processes and throughout the enterprise. It anticipates having as much as 500 terabytes (equivalent to 500 trillion characters) of data accessible to its employees.[9] Although information systems, such as Kodak's, can satisfy the need to make information accessible, they can also make data inaccessible when they break down or when managers design them to withhold information from employees.

- *Ensuring the Reliability and Accuracy of Information.* The proper design and use of information systems ensure the availability of accurate and reliable data. Managers need consistent and correct information to make good decisions. Corrupted or unavailable data can significantly and negatively affect organizational performance. PSS Medical, a medical supplies company based in Jacksonville, Florida, estimated that as many as 2,000 employees left the firm each year within weeks of being hired because they were denied insurance or paid late due to bad or misplaced data. A new information system that allows employees to enter information directly into Web-based forms significantly simplified the paperwork, reduced the errors, eased the workload of the human resources department, and stabilized the workforce. The value of the increased accuracy and reliability of information far exceeds the $17,000 per month that the company spends to support the system.[10]

- *Respecting Privacy.* Companies collect a great deal of information about their customers and visitors to their Web sites. They have a responsibility to use this information in a way that is consistent with the desires of the people who have provided it. A person who fills a prescription, for example, at an online drugstore, probably does not expect the drugstore to share information about his illness with others. A person who registers her new set of golf clubs online may or may not want the manufacturer to share her sports interests with others. Companies need to determine the expectations of their information sources and provide appropriate measures to ensure that information given in confidence is not used inappropriately.

- *Creating Secure Information.* Security means protection against theft, manipulation, and loss of data. Companies protect their information to preserve their competitive advantages and to guarantee the integrity of their operations. Without security, competitors or disgruntled employees could steal or modify key information, including proprietary technology, production methodologies, product data, and research and development breakthroughs. Financial companies and companies in the health-care industry have taken leading roles in securing data. Cardinal Health, for example, a Fortune 100 health-care manufacturer and distribution company, employs a team of 15 security specialists to investigate corporate practices for collecting and securing data. The team is charged with developing and promulgating security policies and responding to any attempts to breach security.[11] Although the need for security may seem obvious, research shows that most often companies fail to improve their security practices until confronted with a major breach of security.[12]

- *Making Information Available at an Appropriate Cost.* Because the cost of acquiring, manipulating, and maintaining information can be high, reducing these costs by a small percentage can greatly increase profitability. Information systems specialists need to focus on the costs of collecting and maintaining information as well as on the value of the outputs of information systems when justifying their costs. A company's financial managers need to compare the return on any investments in information systems with other possible uses of the company's financial resources. MetLife, for example, wanted to build a database that would consolidate customer information from more than 30 different business systems. Although the price estimate for the database was more than $50 million, the net benefit to the company was high enough that CEO Robert Benmosche felt comfortable approving the project.[13]

Cemex, a $6 billion international cement company headquartered in Mexico, created an advantage over its competitors by using information systems to enable it to react quickly to its customers' needs. Cemex employees and customers require information that is accessible, reliable, and secure at a cost that keeps Cemex competitive in a commodity business. Cemex's cement plants and a central database are linked together over the Internet and a satellite network to coordinate production activities, track demand, exchange financial information, and automate record keeping. Its trucks are equipped with satellite geographic positioning systems, transmitters, and phones, so that they can be monitored and rerouted if customers' needs should change. The reliability and accessibility of its information allow Cemex to provide customers with a 20-minute delivery window, as opposed to the three-hour window that had been customary in the industry. Customers can also access delivery and billing information over the Internet, increasing their satisfaction and driving up Cemex's sales.[14]

NEW ORGANIZATIONAL STRUCTURES AND INFORMATION REQUIREMENTS

Organizational structure refers to the division of labor, coordination of positions, and formal reporting relationships within an organization. This structure may promote specific information needs for an organization.

The traditional hierarchical structure of organizations supports a control and command mode of operation. Information filters from low levels of the hierarchy up to decision-making managers. Managerial decisions filter down to lower levels where they are executed. The more important the decision, the higher up and down the hierarchy the information flows, taking time in the process and increasing the likelihood that information and decisions are misinterpreted.

Today's changing organizations have two important characteristics. First, managers give more responsibility for decision making to employees rather than retaining as much control as possible. Systems that make information readily available to workers at all levels in the organization can replace managers, service staffs (e.g., legal, public relations), and central management. As Figure 2-1 illustrates, this flatter structure increases each manager's span of control and reduces the need to move information up the corporate hierarchy for decision making. The company can respond faster to changes in the marketplace because decision makers are closer to the source of information.

Second, organizations more often have an organic structure. This structure emphasizes lateral communication and involves more flexible interactions among parts of the organization. A bank manager might serve on a task force to develop new products for the bank at the beginning of the year and several months later participate in a reorganization of the sales functions in the bank. Organizations might institute project and product management structures that group workers according to the project or product on which they work. The matrix form and other integrated structures simultaneously group employees on multiple dimensions, such as functional area, project, client, and geographical location, as illustrated in Figure 2-2. These structures create intense information needs for workers throughout the organization to ensure the coordination of activities.

Alliances and Joint Ventures

Organizations do not always need to acquire and develop their own resources to compete. Sometimes it is faster and cheaper to form a mutually beneficial **alliance,** an official working partnership, with another organization. Companies may license technologies to other com-

FIGURE 2-1

FIGURE 2-1

Flattening the organizational structure increases managers' span of control and moves decision making closer to the source of information.

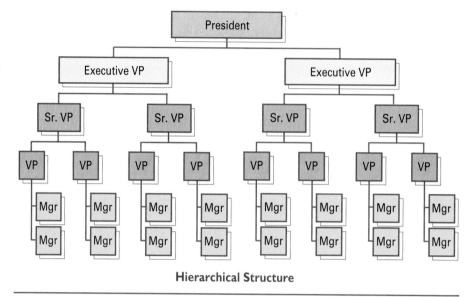

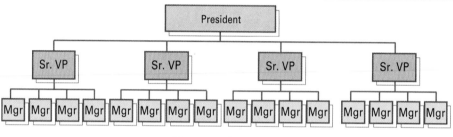

FIGURE 2-2

A matrix organizational structure such as the one shown here and other organic structures create intense information needs to coordinate activities and planning.

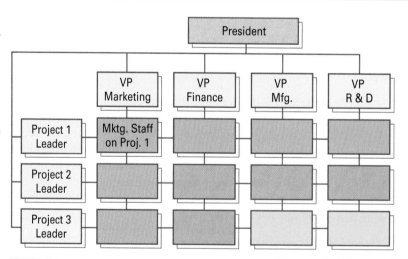

panies. They may form **joint ventures,** where together they develop or market specific products or services with partners here and abroad. Such alliances help organizations compete successfully because they bring additional resources to solving organizational problems. Drugstore.com, an online pharmacy, and General Nutrition Centers (GNC), a distributor of vitamins and health foods, with more than 5,000 stores worldwide, formed a partnership that gave Drugstore.com the exclusive rights to sell GNC-branded products and created a GNC LiveWell store within the Drugstore.com Web site. This partnership extended GNC's reach to customers far from a GNC store and allowed the company to sell 24 hours a day, 7 days a week, with no investment in Web technology, equipment, and labor. The partnership gave Drugstore.com increased name recognition and helped it overcome a potential lack of customer trust.[15] These companies must now find ways to share information effectively.

The health-care industry has experienced widespread consolidation through the formation of joint ventures, umbrella organizations, and alliances. Intermountain Health Care (IHC), the medical provider for the 2002 Olympics, includes health insurance plans, physicians, 21 hospitals, and 80 clinics. IHC uses information technology to integrate and coordinate its services, lower costs, and improve clinical outcomes.[16]

Managers in these situations need to blend different cultures and management styles, reconcile variations in job design, and develop compatible human resources systems. Information systems support these and other tasks. They require compatible information systems to ease the sharing of relevant information on a timely basis.

Interorganizational information systems can meet information needs by serving as information links that enable the creation and efficient functioning of alliances, joint ventures, and partnerships.[17] These pathways for communication between two organizations meet the need for coordination between an organization and its customers and suppliers. Information links enable or improve the collection and communication of information regarding inventory, sales, and other areas in which the two organizations interface.

Modular Structures

Modular structures break organizations into key processes and let individual subcontractors perform these key processes, as shown in Figure 2-3.[18] A small corporate staff develops the company's strategy, subcontracts the work to others, and then monitors the interface with the various subcontractors.[19] The core firm may *sell* appliances, but subcontractors handle their design, manufacturing, sales, and distribution. Modular organizations add or subtract parts as needed to meet changing market conditions. Brokers assemble these business subgroups by subcontracting with independent organizations for required services, creating linkages among partners, or locating such functions as design, supply, production, and distribution. They use market mechanisms, such as contracts or payment for results, rather than plans, controls, or supervision to hold the functions together.[20]

Full-disclosure information systems link the various network components. They require a clear understanding of the information requirements of all members of the network as well as the strategy and goals of the modular corporation. Such systems must have reliable data that all members can readily access.

Dell Computer could be considered a modular organization. Dell assembles computers, but it sources the design and manufacture of most of its components and software to other companies. Dell relies on its network of partners and suppliers to produce a broader range of goods than it could produce on its own, and its flexible alliances allow it to respond rapidly to the changes in the market due to technological advances or unexpected customer demands.[21]

The **virtual organization** is a modular structure tied together by computer technology, as shown in Figure 2-4.[22] Information technology links the components of the network and allows them to share skills, costs, and access to markets. Each participating organization contributes only its core competencies. The ability to easily regroup companies into virtual corporations creates the flexibility required to seize new opportunities and remain competitive.

Virtual companies have five major characteristics:[23]

- *Absence of Borders.* The virtual corporation lacks the traditional corporate borders because the extent of cooperation among competitors, suppliers, and customers spans normal borders.

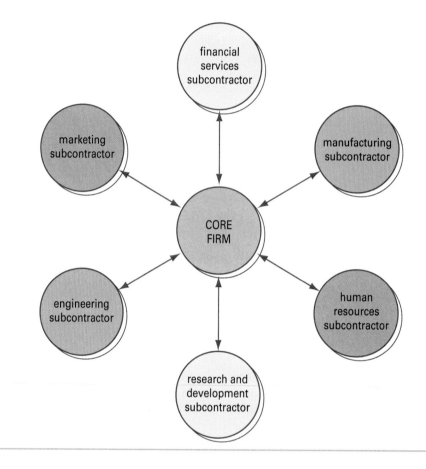

FIGURE   2-3

Modular organizations are networks of subcontractors, who each perform a specific function. Dell Computer has a modular structure.

- *Technology.* Computer networks link distant companies, and they use electronic contracts to form partnerships.
- *Excellence.* Each partner brings its core competencies to the corporation, allowing the creation of a "best-of-everything" company.
- *Opportunism.* Partnerships are relatively impermanent, informal, and more opportunistic because companies join to meet a specific market opportunity and then disband after meeting it.
- *Trust.* The relationships in a virtual corporation require mutual trust because of their great interdependency.

A virtual company has intensive information needs because it exists essentially as a function of shared information. Computer systems must link the various members of the network, providing current, complete, and compatible information. Agile Web Inc. is a virtual company composed of 21 small, Pennsylvania-based manufacturing companies with complementary expertise and capabilities. Through sophisticated software, they are able to combine their resources to bid on contracts that no individual member could win on its own. For example, Agile Web won a contract to produce a forklift handle that required one of its members to provide the plastic parts, another member to shape and mold the metal parts, and a third member to solder the handle together and test its circuits and switches. Currently, Agile Web generates about $4 million in annual sales for its members.[24]

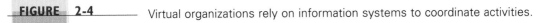

FIGURE   2-4 Virtual organizations rely on information systems to coordinate activities.

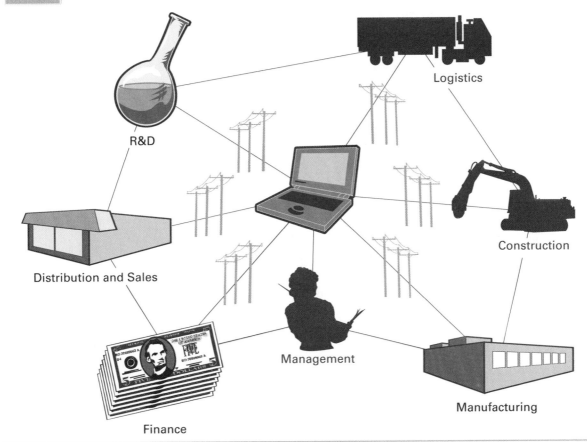

SUPPORTING TEAM-BASED MANAGEMENT

Companies in the United States and abroad have altered their cultures to encourage team-work and collaboration. Pillsbury's Green Giant frozen vegetable plant in Belvidere, Illinois has been using work teams since 1987. The success of the team concept at the plant has led to its increased use to achieve efficiency in operations and to solve problems. The plant now has 48 business teams in addition to several temporary process-improvement teams. One such team, called L.I.F.E., for Living in an Injury Free Environment, reduced accidents by 38 percent in its first year and another 52 percent in its second year. Team members have a great deal of authority to solve problems, creating a culture in which team members have a passion for their work.[25]

Teams in the Workplace

Teams can vary in their leadership, longevity, and composition, as illustrated in Figure 2-5.

- *Traditionally-managed Versus Self-managed.* **Traditionally-managed teams** have a designated individual who serves as the official leader or manager. This person oversees the daily activities of the team, sets its direction, evaluates its employees, and ensures the accomplishment of its goals. **Self-managed teams** have members who share responsibility for managing the work group without an officially

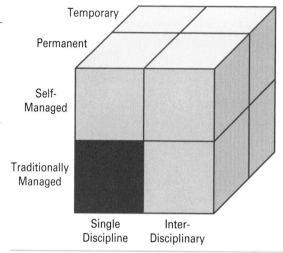

FIGURE 2-5

Team types differ along three dimensions. The box in the lower left-hand corner represents the common traditional-ly-managed, permanent, single-discipline team.

appointed leader. Such teams have full responsibility for completing a well-defined part of the work, generally the finished product or service or a significant component of it. They normally have discretion over decisions relating to how they achieve their goals. Managers do not oversee the daily activities of a self-managed team, but they may coach it, develop an overall strategy for the teams in their area, champion innovation, and provide resources for the team. The managers may also serve as liaisons to other parts of the organization, suppliers, and customers. Harley-Davidson, the motorcycle manufacturer, began implementing self-directed teams in 1995. Union and salaried employees now work in teams in which decisions are made by those most knowledgeable or informed about the alternatives and in which consensus must be reached. Harley-Davidson attributes many positive outcomes to the cooperation, trust, and teamwork provided by this structure, including an 88 percent increase in manufacturing productivity, a 50 percent drop in dealer preparation work, significant reductions in scrap and damage, a 200 percent increase in customer satisfaction, and dramatically improved employee satisfaction.[26] The success of self-managed teams, however, depends in part on various cultural factors and attitudes toward jobs, such as individualism and desire for authority, which may differ among countries.[27]

- *Permanent Versus Temporary.* **Permanent teams** work together for long periods of time, generally at least one year, on a repetitive set of tasks. **Temporary teams** form for short, pre-specified amounts of time to complete a unique set of tasks or projects. Conseco, an Indianapolis-based insurance company with 13 million customers, uses temporary project teams to improve customer service and internal operations. Teams are expected to complete their work in six months or less, and to generate savings for the company of approximately $150,000 per project.[28]

- *Single Discipline Versus Multiple Disciplines.* Companies can form teams that include workers from a single functional area, such as research and development, manufacturing, or marketing. Increasingly, companies form interdisciplinary or **cross-functional teams** that include employees from several functional areas. Often the people with the required expertise are not situated at the same location. In such cases sharing information effectively is more difficult. Hewlett-Packard created cross-functional teams that they called "virtual" because their members were often in different locations and operating at different times of the day. These teams developed and launched a commercially successful medical care system in half the time normally needed.[29]

Information Needs of Teams

Empowered workers need access to diverse types of information from throughout the organization. Because teams often assume managerial functions, they have information needs similar to those of managers, as discussed in Chapter 1. They require information for:

- Monitoring the environment
- Updating employees and managers about team activities
- Leading, motivating, and coaching team members
- Planning
- Making decisions
- Allocating resources
- Resolving problems
- Monitoring quality and performance

Team members need to communicate information quickly as a way of coordinating their actions. Because teams often function at dispersed locations, even at sites in different time zones, they need access to current information and should have the ability to update it in real time. For example, teams need to schedule, track, and ensure the timely completion of team activities. They need information about individual performance and task accomplishment to coordinate the team's attainment of its goals.

Using Information Systems for Team Activities

Computerized systems can more easily provide teams with the types of information they require. Teams use automation systems to improve workflow, design, and manufacturing. They use transaction processing systems to track orders, shipments, and accounts payable and receivable. They use management support systems for forecasting and analyses.

Groupware, computer software that particularly supports the coordination of team activities, has seen explosive growth. Groupware, which is described in more depth in Chapter 8, supports electronic messaging, schedules meetings, facilitates conferencing, and performs other functions, as shown in Table 2-1. Although groupware supports team operations, it can be used for additional functions that include, but are not restricted to, team operation, as shown in Table 2-2. For example, project team members around the world can update specifications of a new product in real time, so that the team continues to progress in its product development.

TABLE 2-1

Groupware Can Be Classified According to the Application's Functionality.

- electronic mail and messaging
- group calendaring and scheduling
- electronic meeting systems
- desktop video and real-time data conferencing
- non-real-time data conferencing
- workflow management
- group document handling
- workgroup utilities and development tools
- groupware services
- groupware applications
- collaborative Internet-based applications and products

SOURCE: Based on David Coleman, "Groupware for Collaboration," *Virtual Workgroups*, July/August 1996, 28–32. Table from McGraw Hill. Reproduced with permission.

Rank	Most Important Applications
	TABLE 2-2
1	Office productivity
2	Business process redesign
3	Group project management
4	Publications coordinating/routing
5	Customer service
6	Electronic meeting facilitation
7	Integrate compound documents and multimedia
8	Change management
9	Distribute/restructure organization
10	Sales force automation
11	Downsizing support
12	Move from mainframe to local area networks

TABLE 2-2

A survey of the most popular business applications for groupware showed that the top three were office automation and productivity, business process redesign, and group project management.

SOURCE: Adapted from Table 1 in David Coleman, "Groupware for Collaboration," 28–32. Table from McGraw Hill. Reproduced with permission.

These systems allow teams to process information more quickly and accurately. They can obtain the information they need to help their organization sustain its competitive advantage. Norsk Hydro, a diversified Norwegian company with operations in 75 countries around the world, uses an IBM groupware product called Lotus Notes to coordinate projects, share expertise, and collaborate on software development. The culture at Norsk had been one in which business units around the globe operated with a great deal of autonomy. As part of its modernization strategy, Norsk sought to establish global operations with standardized processes, shared information, and more central control. Senior company managers felt, correctly, that the use of groupware would help achieve these goals. Although it met with some resistance at first, groupware is now being used in over 1,500 applications within the company.[30]

INFORMATION AND ORGANIZATIONAL STRATEGY

Regardless of its structure, each organization must develop a **strategy**—a long-term direction or intended set of activities for attaining its goals. Strategic-level decisions include plans for accomplishing long-term goals of market share, profitability, return on investment, service, and performance. Managers who make strategic decisions need to determine their organization's distinctive competence by answering questions such as those shown in Figure 2-6. Answering these questions calls for obtaining information from both outside and inside the organization.

What strategy should Kodak pursue to remain competitive in the digital age? How will Daniel Carp and other Kodak executives decide what information Kodak's top managers need to determine its strategy? Clearly, they will need to track technological developments

FIGURE   2-6

Managers can assess the distinctive competencies of their organization by answering these questions.

- What kind of business should we be in?
- What should be the organization/s markets?
- What market niches exist in which the organization can compete?
- What products or services should the organization offer?
- What technological investment is required?
- What human resources are available and required?
- What financial, time, material, or other resources are available and required?

in digital imaging. They will also need business intelligence about what products and features consumers are buying. They will need to review the expertise of their engineers and developers to assess their strengths and weaknesses in preparation for new hiring or the acquisition of companies that possess the skills and knowledge Kodak is missing.

Levels of Strategy

Companies can develop strategy at three levels, as shown in Figure 2-7. **Corporate-level strategy** addresses which lines of business a company should pursue. It views an organization as a portfolio, agglomeration, federation, or amalgam of businesses or subunits. Strategic management at the corporate level focuses on decisions about acquiring new businesses, divesting old businesses, establishing joint ventures, and creating alliances with other organizations.

To determine its corporate-level strategy, top management needs to obtain information about the speed of industry growth and the portion of the industry market captured by the business unit, among other information. Information on industry growth and market share is often public, at least in the United States, due to the disclosures required of companies issuing stocks and bonds. Industry lobbyists, stock market researchers, trade magazine journalists, and other researchers also act as sources of this information. Information systems can regularly provide organizations with such information by tapping into commercially sold databases or Web-based information resources that offer extensive economic, technological, demographic, and even legal information. This ongoing availability of information allows organizations to determine their strategic position, as well as the appropriate actions to maintain or change this position.

Information systems can provide the information for making resource allocation and other investment decisions. Information about market share, profit margins, ownership of patents, technical capability, customer requirements, and competitive strengths and weaknesses helps management determine its investment strategy.

Business-level strategy matches the strengths and weaknesses of each business unit or product line to the external environment to determine how each unit can best compete for customers. Strategic decisions include what products or services the company should offer, what customers it should service, and how it will deploy resources of advertising, research and development, customer service, equipment, and staffing. The Home Depot, a 1300-store company selling home improvement goods, pursued an aggressive growth strategy throughout the 1990s, becoming the third largest retailer in the United States. However, in response to a softening economy in the year 2000 and a sense that the market was becoming saturated, the company switched its strategy, focusing instead on increasing productivity, expanding services, and fine-tuning its product line.[31]

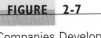

FIGURE 2-7

Companies Develop Strategies at the Corporate, Business, and Functional Levels.

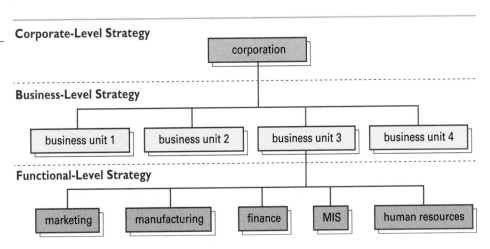

Strategic management also addresses how functions such as finance, marketing, research and development, operations, and human resource management can best support the organization's strategies. **Functional strategies** direct the way individual departments perform their tasks to accomplish organizational objectives.[32] Marketing strategies focus on product development, promotion, sales, and pricing. Finance strategies focus on the acquisition, allocation, and management of capital. Operations strategies include decisions about plant size, plant location, equipment, inventory, and wages. Research and development strategies emphasize basic, applied, or developmental research. Human resource strategies revolve around the deployment of employees and the relations between labor and management. Managers need information about state-of-the-art practice and competitors' activities in each functional area to help develop their companies' strategies.

Determining the Organization's Strategy

Many forces constrain and help shape an organization's strategy. Figure 2-8 illustrates this concept in a model called the **five forces model,** popularized by Michael Porter.[33] The bargaining power of suppliers and buyers, the threat of new entrants, the possibility of product or service substitutes, and the rivalry of competitors, all affect the success of an organization's strategy. Consider Kodak. In its traditional market of film and film processing, its market dominance assured that it had good bargaining power relative to its suppliers and buyers. New entrants faced high barriers to overcome its entrenched brand and reputation for quality. Although competitors existed for both film and processing, Kodak had established its place among its competitors. However, digital imaging, once only a limited

FIGURE 2-8

According to Porter's five forces model, the bargaining power of suppliers and buyers, the threat of new entrants and product or service substitutes, and the rivalry of competitors constrain and help shape an organization's strategy.

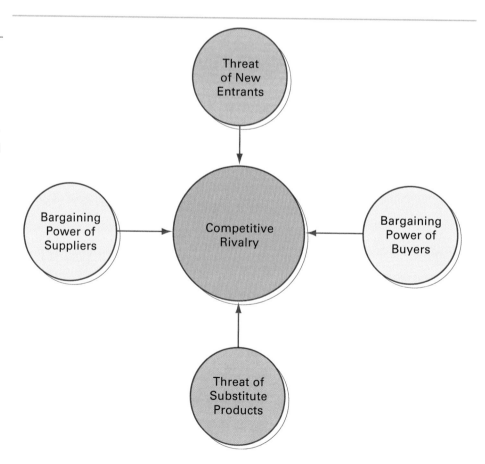

threat, has become a substitute product that Kodak can no longer ignore. It will either need to establish its position in this market or lose market share.

In the digital world, Kodak needs to assess its competitive position. It needs to examine, for example, whether it can build sufficient bargaining power with suppliers of flash memory and other digital camera and imaging components to succeed in digital photography. It will need to assess its strength relative to its competitors and will need to determine the extent to which new entrants are likely to upset the competitive balance. Only then can it decide whether to compete on cameras, printing, Web-based photo storage, or combinations of these markets.

Managers often use a **situational analysis**—the process of collecting and analyzing information about a company's strengths, weaknesses, opportunities, and threats—to help determine its strategy. The acronym *SWOT* is often used for these four components of situational analysis. **Strengths** and **weaknesses** are internal characteristics of the organization that enhance and impede its ability to compete. A reputation for quality exemplifies strength while having costs above the industry average typifies weakness. **Opportunities** and **threats** are external or environmental factors that might help or hinder an organization from meeting its strategic goals. Weak competitors illustrate an opportunity while adverse regulatory rulings represent a threat. Table 2-3 displays some major issues to consider in situational analysis.

TABLE 2-3

Managers can use a SWOT analysis to determine strengths, weaknesses, opportunities, and threats in developing a strategy.

Potential Internal Strengths	Potential Internal Weaknesses
A distinctive competence	No clear strategic direction
Adequate financial resources	Obsolete facilities
Good competitive skill	Lack of managerial depth and talent
Well thought of by buyers	Missing key skills or competence
An acknowledged market leader	Poor track record in implementing strategy
Well-conceived functional area strategies	Plagued with internal operating problems
Access to economies of scale	Falling behind in R&D
Insulated from strong competitive pressures	Too narrow a product line
Proprietary technology	Weak market image
Cost advantages	Weaker distribution network
Better advertising campaigns	Below-average marketing skills
Product innovation skills	Unable to finance needed changes in strategy
Proven management	Higher overall unit costs relative to key competitors
Ahead on experience curve	
Better manufacturing capability	
Superior technological skills	

Potential External Opportunities	Potential External Threats
Serve additional customer groups	Entry of lower-cost foreign competitors
Enter new markets	Rising sales of substitute products
Expand product line to meet broader range of customer needs	Slower market growth
Diversity into related products	Adverse shifts in foreign exchange rates and trade policies of foreign governments
Vertical integration	Costly regulatory requirements
Falling trade barriers in attractive foreign markets	Vulnerability to recession and business cycle
Complacency among rival firms	Growing bargaining power of customers or suppliers
Faster market growth	Changing buyer needs and tastes
	Adverse demographic changes

SOURCE: Adapted from Arthur A. Thompson, Jr., and A. J. Strickland III, *Strategic Management: Concepts and Cases*, 5th ed. (Homewood, IL: BPI/Irwin, 1990), 91. Table from McGraw Hill. Reproduced with permission.

Situational analysis requires extensive internal and external data. To evaluate internal strengths and weaknesses, such as reputation for quality or above average costs, a company must compare data on its internal condition with industry and competitor averages. Quality information systems can assist organizations in securing comprehensive information for the SWOT analysis. Organizations can use them to maintain, update, or access environmental and organizational data, such as demographic trends, potential customer lists, financial data, or staffing patterns. Strategic management involves matching the strengths and weaknesses of each business unit or product line to the external environment to determine how the business unit can best compete for customers.

Types of Strategies

Firms can adopt five strategies, as shown in Figure 2-9, to reap a competitive advantage: differentiation, cost leadership, focus, linkage, and information leadership.[34] Information systems can provide the information required to support these strategies.

- **Differentiation** seeks to distinguish the products and services of a business unit from those of its competitors through unique design, features, quality, or other factors. Companies pursuing a differentiation strategy need current and accurate information about the market, including detailed information about competitors' products, customers' requirements, and changing environmental conditions. CIGNA Insurance manages its knowledge about customers to identify profitable market niches. It developed a performance model for underwriters

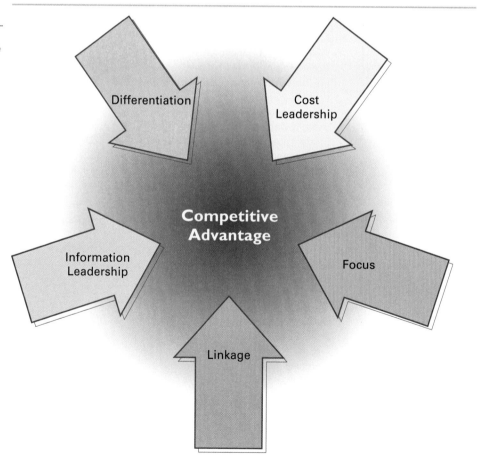

FIGURE 2-9

Companies can use five strategies to develop and sustain a competitive advantage.

that systematized the key steps in reviewing an application for insurance and linked each step to the relevant database of information. In this way it improved the quality of information available to underwriters, which in turn increased the company's profitability.[35]

- **Cost leadership** achieves a competitive advantage by carefully controlling costs, which allows the business unit to make more profit than its competitors on products sold at the same price. Complete information about costs lets companies better control costs and gives them a competitive advantage. A company uses internal corporate information to reduce costs by achieving efficiencies in production, distribution, and sales.

- **Focus** achieves competitive advantage by concentrating on a single market segment. A company following the focus strategy concentrates its resources to become a big player in a small market rather than a small player in a larger market. Tiffany, for example, focuses on the high-end jewelry market. Whole Foods, an Austin, Texas retailer with 129 stores in the United States, focuses on the market for natural and organically grown foods. These companies require information about the nature of available markets and the characteristics of the players in them.

- **Linkage** obtains a competitive advantage by establishing special, exclusive relationships with customers, suppliers, and even competitors. These organizations require detailed information about customers' needs, special arrangements with suppliers, and potential synergies with competitors. Aerospace manufacturer Boeing links directly to some of its key suppliers with an information system called iCollaboration. This system models Boeing's manufacturing process to let suppliers know exactly when it will need parts. The system reduces Boeing's supply costs, cuts manufacturing delays due to out-of-stock parts, and allows Boeing's suppliers to better plan their own production.[36]

- **Information leadership** increases the value of a product or service by infusing it with expertise, information, and information processing capability. Managers can supplement products with summary and activity reports for an account or customer, product and market information relevant to the customer, or information about related products and services. Federal Express and UPS, for example, consider package tracking and Web-based pickup requests to be integral parts of their delivery services. Luxury cars are now equipped with information processing capabilities. Motorola is testing new technology that will allow manufacturers to embed considerable intelligence into your car. The product is expected to provide information verbally to drivers about impending traffic congestion and the best route around it, weather conditions, directions to a service station when fuel is low, and perhaps even advice about whether or not there is a parking spot at the traveler's destination.[37]

Using Information to Achieve a Competitive Advantage

In many organizations, information management is a back-room operation intended to support the other functions of the business. Information systems can also be used proactively and strategically as a competitive weapon, as shown in Table 2-4.

Reacting to Market Conditions

A firm that can respond quickly to market conditions has an advantage over its slower competitors in a number of ways. It can keep its costs lower by reducing excess inventory, eliminating mistakes in purchasing, and cutting production on slow-selling products. It

TABLE 2-4	Company Gains a Competitive Advantage by	Information Systems Assist by Helping Organization to
Managers can use information systems to help their company achieve a competitive advantage.	Reacting to market conditions	Reduce excess inventory Tailor prices to the market React quickly to lagging sales Leverage cash Introduce new products Set prices
	Improving customer service	Maintain appropriate inventory Respond to customers' needs Monitor customer service
	Controlling costs	Classify expenditure Monitor spending Control budgets
	Improving quality	Provide feedback Give production workers immediate access to analyses
	Expanding globally	Ease communication Support coordination

can tailor its prices more accurately to what the market will bear. It can react more quickly to lagging sales by adjusting advertising and price promotions. It can leverage its cash better, taking long or short positions and moving money quickly to where the opportunity for profit is the greatest. It can more quickly introduce products that the consumer wants. Being first in the market gives a company the opportunity to be a market share leader, with resulting scale efficiencies in manufacturing and marketing.

Companies can also use competitive pricing to give them a strategic advantage.[38] Information from computer systems can assist the process. Restaurants can assess the impact of various pricing and promotion strategies on their profit margins. A resort hotel can evaluate the success of special promotional packages by tracking an individual guest's expenditures by revenue center (e.g., golf course, restaurant, and health club) and can then adjust the promotions offered to increase their effectiveness.

The ability to react rapidly to the market depends on a firm's ability to monitor external conditions. The government, news providers, and many private enterprises collect leading indicators of economic and market trends that organizations can use to monitor external conditions. To collect business intelligence, executives at Kodak probably also read magazines such as *Popular Photography, Photo District News, Photo Trade News, Photographic Processing,* and *Digital Photography and Imaging International,* and visit online sources, such as Photo.net.

Most companies also collect information about external conditions in the normal course of business. For example, the record of customers' purchases can also become a weather vane of consumer opinion and product evaluation. Companies need to view such data not only from the context of operations management but also from the context of planning for competitive advantage. Information systems help companies organize and use such data. Organizations with information systems that facilitate the collection and processing of such data have a competitive advantage over those that do not.

Improving Customer Service

Good service has become a requirement of business in most industries. Management theory now advises companies to become customer-centric, obsessed with knowing what the customer wants or needs and providing it.[39] Information systems are critical to implementing a customer-centric philosophy. They allow companies to collect data about how their customers use their product and services, enable immediate responses to customer problems, and, often through the Web, allow customized responses to consumer demands or preferences. Information systems that target Customer Relationship Management (CRM) have become very popular, as discussed in Chapter 7.

General Motors knows that its customers want cars that are safe and reliable. That's why it equips its luxury vehicles with OnStar, a technology and service that can run diagnostics on your engine while you drive, locate your vehicle and dispatch emergency assistance if the vehicle breaks down or if your airbag inflates, and provide many other services 24 hours a day, 365 days a year. The system has been installed in more than two million cars since 1997. Recently, OnStar has added a concierge service to help GM car owners purchase tickets or plan events from their car when they travel.[40]

When many dot-com companies went bust in 2001 and the economy turned down after the terrorist attacks on the World Trade Center and the Pentagon, online auction company eBay bucked the trend with continued success. eBay attributed much of this success to the attention it pays to its customers.[41] eBay makes a practice of watching what its customers buy and listening to what they want.[42]

Controlling Costs

An organization can create a competitive advantage by becoming a low-cost producer. But how does a firm keep costs below its industry's average? It can do so by achieving economies of scale in production, distribution, and sales. However, as volume increases, keeping track of and rationalizing business activities becomes more complex. The ability to handle, process, and summarize large amounts of information is, therefore, a prerequisite to achieving cost reduction through volume growth. Information systems can easily serve this function.

Systems to classify, monitor, and limit spending also ease cost control. To set budgets, managers need information about previous spending and about new plans and objectives. Budgetary information, in turn, permits managers to optimize their resources within prescribed limits.

Companies can also cut costs by using the Web to streamline processes. Proctor & Gamble, for example, uses the Web to get feedback from its focus groups about new products. Moving the focus groups online lowered costs by ten to twenty percent. Honeywell uses the Web to monitor its networks, saving more than $150 million annually by doing preventative, rather than corrective, maintenance. General Motors lowered its cost by purchasing supplies over the Web.[43]

Improving Quality

Having a reputation for quality offers a strategic advantage for any organization. Consumers will usually pay more for a product or service that they know always meets their expectations than one whose quality varies or is known to be poor. Improving quality also decreases costs by reducing waste, eliminating rework, and permitting more orderly processing.

Achieving quality requires production workers to have constant feedback about the production process so that they can spot problems immediately and correct them. In the past systems were built so that production workers collected and entered data about production but did not have immediate access to analyses performed on the data that they had collected. Management support systems provided summary and exception reports to the managers who then intervened in the process. Generally, managers would know about production problems before the production workers did. Companies operating in this fashion shipped inferior goods and provided inferior services. Now, information systems can immediately process, analyze, and report information to production workers who can intervene quickly to improve the process and improve quality.

Expanding Globally

Although language differences, regulation of information flows, and lack of a communication infrastructure remain barriers to the exchange of information, in general companies of all sizes now have the resources and information systems to allow them to operate globally. Information systems meet the need for coordination of diverse enterprises in distant locations.

Going global remains one of the easiest ways for a company to expand its market. A company pursuing the strategy of rapid growth and high market share increases its opportunities for success by considering the entire world as its market. After the terrorist attacks on the World Trade Center and the Pentagon, when it seemed logical for U.S.-based companies to follow a more inward-looking strategy, a PriceWaterhouseCoopers survey found instead that 27 percent of companies planned to increase their global expansion, compared to only 19 percent before the attack.[44] A likely explanation is that companies were looking to expand in new areas to compensate for falling domestic sales.

Going global is also a strategy for reducing costs. Companies with global manufacturing and production abilities can match their production plans to where raw goods and labor are the cheapest. Applica Inc., for example, a Florida-based manufacturer of small kitchen and garment care appliances, including some sold by Black & Decker and others sold under the Windmere brand, keeps costs down by manufacturing in the People's Republic of China and in Mexico.[45]

Information technology helps multinational companies compete internationally by supporting foreign subsidiaries, better integrating worldwide operations, allowing greater flexibility in responding to local market needs, and serving clients more innovatively.[46] Creating a mature technological environment abroad helps meet customer needs for new products and management's needs for consistency and control in worldwide locations.

SUMMARY

Today's organizations need information to help them function effectively in the changing marketplace. They have experienced a globalization of business and accompanying need for flexibility, adaptability, and collaboration. Their managers create teams and empower workers to make better decisions more quickly. They employ a changing workforce that views diversity as an advantage. These organizations require accessible, reliable, private, and secure information at an appropriate cost.

Managers create a variety of teams in the workplace: traditional and self-managing, permanent and temporary, single discipline and multiple discipline. These teams have information needs that focus on the managerial, communication, and task functions the teams perform.

The new forms of today's organizations also have special information requirements. Alliances and joint ventures use information systems to ease the sharing of relevant information on a timely basis. Modular structures require full-disclosure information systems to link the various components of the network. Virtual organizations could not exist without information systems, which link their various parts.

Information also plays a key role in determining and implementing an organization's strategy. Organizations need information to make strategic decisions and can use it to develop a competitive advantage. They require information, such as about business growth rate and market share, to make decisions about acquiring new businesses, divesting old businesses, establishing joint ventures, and creating alliances with other organizations. They also obtain information to help match the strengths and weaknesses of each business unit with its external environment. Firms can adopt the following strategies to obtain a competitive advantage: differentiation, cost leadership, focus, linkage, and information leadership. Information can help organizations attain a strategic advantage by reacting to market conditions, improving customer service, controlling costs, improving quality, and expanding globally.

KEY TERMS

alliance	information leadership	situational analysis
business-level strategy	joint venture	strategy
corporate-level strategy	knowledge management	strength
cost leadership	knowledge worker	temporary team
cross-functional team	linkage	threat
differentiation	modular structure	traditionally-managed team
five forces model	opportunity	virtual organization
focus	organizational structure	weakness
functional strategy	permanent team	
groupware	self-managed team	

REVIEW QUESTIONS

1. What characteristics describe the business context that organizations function within?
2. Why do organizations need to ensure the accessibility, reliability, accuracy, privacy, security, and cost-effectiveness of their information?
3. How do information systems help companies operate in the global marketplace?
4. How do information systems allow organizations to adopt more flexible structures?
5. What new organizational structures exist in organizations?
6. How do alliances and joint ventures use information?
7. What characteristics should information systems have to support alliances and joint ventures?
8. How do modular structures use information and information systems?
9. What role do information systems play in virtual organizations?
10. What types of teams are found in the workplace?
11. How do the information needs of self-managing teams differ from those of other teams?
12. Do permanent and temporary teams have the same information needs?
13. How can companies use information systems to support team activities?
14. How can groupware support team activities?
15. What is a strategy?
16. What five forces affect an organization's strategy according to Porter?
17. How does a SWOT analysis help determine an organization's strategy?
18. What information does a SWOT analysis require?
19. What five strategies can companies use to attain a competitive advantage?
20. How do companies use information to sustain a competitive advantage?

KNOWLEDGE MANAGEMENT AT MARCONI

When Marconi went on a shopping spree and acquired ten telecommunications companies over a three-year period, it faced a serious challenge: How could the $3 billion manufacturer of telecommunications equipment ensure that its technical support agents knew enough about newly acquired technology to provide quick and accurate answers to customers on the phone? And how could Marconi bring new agents up to speed on all the company's products?

Marconi's technical support agents—500 engineers scattered in 14 call centers around the globe—field approximately 10,000 questions every month about the company's products. Before the acquisitions, agents had relied on Tactics Online, a private company Web site where they and customers could search for frequently asked questions and text documents. As new agents and products joined the company's ranks, Marconi wanted to supplement the Web site with a more comprehensive knowledge management system. As engineers from the newly acquired companies came on board, however, they were hesitant to share their knowledge about the products they had been supporting. "They felt that their knowledge was a security blanket that helped guarantee their jobs," says Dave Breit, director of technology and R&D for managed services in Warrendale, Pennsylvania. "With all of the acquisitions, it was essential that we all avoid hoarding knowledge and share it instead."

At the same time, Marconi wanted to streamline its customer service organization by making more of its product and systems information available directly to customers and shortening the length of customer calls. "We wanted to leverage the Web for customer self-service versus increasing the number of agents," Breit says. "We also wanted to provide our frontline engineers [who interact directly with customers] with more information more quickly so that they could resolve more calls faster."

Building on a Knowledge Management Foundation

The concept of sharing knowledge among agents was nothing new to Marconi. In 1997, Marconi had started basing a percentage of agents' quarterly bonuses on the amount of knowledge they submitted to Tactics Online as well as their involvement with mentoring and training other agents. "Each agent was expected to teach two training classes and write 10 FAQs to earn their full bonus," says Breit. "When we brought new companies online, the new agents received the same bonus plan. This approach allowed us to build a very open knowledge-sharing environment."

To augment Tactics Online, Marconi chose software from ServiceWare Technologies. Breit's division spent six months implementing the new system and training agents. The system—dubbed KnowledgeBase—is linked to the company's Customer Relationship Management system and is powered by a database management system. The integrated view of Marconi's customers and products provides agents with a comprehensive history of interactions. Technical support agents can, for example, put markers in the database and immediately pick up at the point where the customer last spoke with another agent.

On the Front Line

Tactics Online complements the new system. "The data stored in KnowledgeBase are specific troubleshooting tips and hints on our various product lines," says Zehra Demiral, manager of knowledge management systems. "Tactics Online, on the other hand, is more of a doorway for customers to come into our customer support organization. From there, customers can access KnowledgeBase or their service requests or our online training manuals."

Technical support agents now rely on KnowledgeBase for the latest solutions to customers' product and systems problems. Level 1 agents answer all incoming calls, solve customers' problems when possible, record the calls in the company's CRM system, and transfer the more difficult calls up the line to Level 2 agents. Level 2 agents, meanwhile, are the heart of the organization, composing about 70 percent of the technical support organization. They handle the more difficult calls and troubleshoot and diagnose equipment and network problems. "They're the majority of our knowledge users and contributors," says Breit. "They write up a synopsis of the call and feed it into KnowledgeBase [on an ongoing basis] so that other agents can refer to the solution later."

After Level 2 agents submit their knowledge "raw" to a holding queue, Level 3 agents confirm the accuracy of the information, make any necessary changes, and then submit the document to Demiral. (Level 3 agents also act as consultants, helping Level 2 agents solve problems and serving as intermediaries between the agents and the company's engineering departments.) The entire process of updating the KnowledgeBase system with a new solution typically takes between three days and two weeks.

Changing Roles

As Breit anticipated, implementing KnowledgeBase has changed the agents' roles. Level 1 agents, for example, now do more in-depth troubleshooting because they have more information available at their fingertips. In fact, they solve twice as many calls themselves (50 percent instead of 25 percent) in a shorter time (10 minutes versus 30 minutes). Since Level 1 agents can handle more calls, this group has doubled in size during the last two years.

The transition wasn't quite as painless, however, for the Level 2 and Level 3 agents. "Rather than simply submitting HTML pages to Tactics Online, they were now asked to analyze the problems in a very procedural way and create diagnostic 'trees,'" says Breit. "That's a more analytical way to think through a problem. Most of these guys had thought in terms of 'what is the fastest way to solve a problem' rather than 'what is the most efficient way to solve a problem.'"

With hundreds of people submitting solutions, Marconi tended to get a lot of wheel reinvention. "There can be five or six ways to solve the [same] problem, but there's one way that's most efficient," Breit says. To unearth and disseminate the most efficient solutions, agents were required to flowchart each of their solutions for the first three months following KnowledgeBase's launch. "It's amazing how many [agents] were unconscious of their own methodologies," says Breit. "It was somewhat painful, but they eventually felt they benefited because they understood how they solve problems."

As a result, agents now create technical solutions for customers in the most efficient—and logical—way possible instead of simply offering a "quick and dirty" solution. Think of the difference between simply being told what keys to strike on your PC and being taught how your software works and the logic behind executing a certain sequence of keystrokes. Once you actually understand how the product works, you can use the software more effectively and resolve more problems yourself.

Making It Work

Demiral spent a lot of time working with the Level 3 agents to make their solutions less complex and streamline the review process. "We had to go through two iterations of how to organize and present the content," Demiral says. "Customers tend to think in terms of the product and then the problem. But engineers often think about the problem first and then the product."

The result: Customers often wouldn't fully understand the solution. At the same time, Marconi had to work at easing Level 3 agents' concerns that making them responsible for reviewing solution content would suddenly turn them into technical writers.

Marconi confronted cultural issues as well. "Business needs are different in different parts of the world," says Demiral. "What may be normal business practice for Americans may not be common elsewhere." In Europe, for example, the value of the KnowledgeBase system was not readily accepted. But once employees there saw that customers could use the system to solve some of their own problems, they got on board. Such an experience has been incorporated into how Marconi approaches knowledge management. "We sometimes have to introduce the idea of knowledge management over time, validate it, and then move forward," Demiral says.

SOURCE: Adapted with permission from Louise Fickel, "Know-It-Alls," *CIO*, 1 November 2001, 90–95. Reprinted through the courtesy of CIO. ©2002, CXO Media Inc. All rights reserved.

Case Questions

Diagnosis

1. What information needs did Marconi's technical support and customer service agents have?

2. How has Marconi's acquisitions affected these needs?

Evaluation

3. What types of information systems did Marconi use before the acquisitions?

4. How well did these systems meet Marconi's needs?

Design

5. What changes in information systems would most greatly benefit Marconi's agents and customers?

6. How would such changes better meet their needs?

7. How might KnowledgeBase increase Marconi's competitive advantage?

Implementation

8. What implementation issues does Marconi face in maximizing the value of KnowledgeBase to its agents and customers?

9. How has Marconi addressed these issues?

2-1 RECRUITING AT COMMUNITY UNIVERSITY

ACTIVITY

Step 1: Read the following scenario.

The graduate business school at Community University recently experienced significant declines in the number of inquiries and applicants for both its full-time and part-time M.B.A. programs. The recently hired director of admissions, Susan Sellers, believed that the decline resulted in part from the decreasing interest in management education. Sellers also believed that the decline could be attributed to a lack of a clear strategy for selling the program. She intended to change the recruiting focus from students with business undergraduate degrees to recent graduates with a liberal arts background and significant work experience.

Sellers planned to use a large part of her budget to improve the information systems in the admissions office. Her initial step was to identify the particular information needs of the new strategic direction of the admissions process.

Step 2: Individually or in small groups, develop a list of information Susan Sellers needs to support the new recruiting strategy.

Step 3: In small groups or with the entire class, share the list you have developed. Then answer the following questions:

1. What are the information needs of the new recruiting strategy?

2. How can the organization satisfy these needs?

2-2 SAVING JOBS AT MANSFIELD UNIVERSITY

ACTIVITY

Step 1: Mansfield University has decided to redesign all of its business processes over the next three years, automating as many as possible by using advanced technologies. The university's goals in the redesign, known as Project Millennium, include improving service to students and their families and reducing costs.

You are the vice president for human resources at Mansfield. You have just returned from a meeting at which you have been asked to lead an effort to reduce the number of employees by 20 percent as part of Project Millennium. While you know that the redesign will improve the university and help guarantee its success over the next decades, you feel that cutting jobs in this way is not ethical. What should you do?

Step 2: Individually or in small groups, analyze the situation using the basic ethical criteria.

Step 3: Based on your analysis, develop an action plan. Share the action plan with the rest of the class.

2-3 INCREASING THE COMPETITIVE ADVANTAGE

ACTIVITY

Step 1: Read the descriptions of the situations below. For each situation, offer two strategies for increasing the organization's competitive advantage over others in its industry. Then list three types of information required to implement each strategy.

Problem 1: Stable pricing is difficult for restaurants like Red Lobster that specialize in such foods as crabmeat or shrimp, where costs are volatile. Customers react unfavorably to frequent changes in menu prices; therefore, the restaurant must protect itself against overpricing and losing customers or underpricing and losing margins. How can Red Lobster use information to maintain a competitive advantage?

Problem 2: The owner of a small company manufacturing digital scales has recently exhibited her product at a trade show in Germany. She has also begun to speak with representatives of the Chamber of Commerce in several small towns in Ireland about the issues associated with opening a manufacturing plant in the town. How can the company use information to increase its competitive advantage?

Problem 3: A small real estate office that had specialized in residential properties recently began to list a small number of commercial properties. It also began a trial membership in a national network of real estate offices. The consortium provides national advertising and referrals and also assists in human resource functions, such as payroll, training, and recruiting. How can the small real estate office use information to further develop a competitive advantage over other real estate offices?

Step 2: In small groups, compile the strategies that organizations can use to attain a competitive advantage. Then list the types of information required to implement these strategies.

Step 3: Individually, in small groups, or with the entire class, answer the following questions:

1. In what ways can an organization increase its competitive advantage?
2. What types of information are required to do this?
3. How can the organizations secure this information?
4. What role can information systems play in providing the needed information?

2-4 ASSESSING THE QUALITY OF INFORMATION

Step 1: Individually or in small groups, design a questionnaire to assess how well an organization's information meets the criteria of low cost, accessibility, reliability, privacy, and security.

Step 2: Select a department in your college or university or in an organization of your choice, and administer the questionnaire to two or three members of that organization.

Step 3: Tabulate the results.

Step 4: Individually, in small groups, or with the entire class, share your results. Next, list the conclusions you can draw from the data. Then, answer the following questions:

1. How well does organizational information meet the criteria of low cost, accessibility, reliability, and security?

2. What two recommendations would you offer for improving the quality of the organization's information?

2-5 SWOT ANALYSIS AND INFORMATION

Step 1: Individually, in twos, or in threes, choose a local business to analyze.

Step 2: Locate four sources of information about the company.

Step 3: Using the information, list three of each of the following:

- Strengths:
- Weaknesses:
- Threats:
- Opportunities:

Step 4: In small groups, list the types and sources of data you used to perform the SWOT analysis.

Step 5: With the entire class, formulate a comprehensive list of the sources and types of data used to perform a SWOT analysis. Then answer the following questions:

1. Which sources provided the most useful data? The least useful data?

2. What other information would be helpful in doing the SWOT analysis?

3. How could computerized information systems assist with the SWOT analysis?

IS ON THE WEB

Exercise 1: The Web page for Chapter 2 will direct you to several stories providing examples of corporate business strategy. Select one of the stories, and supplement the material in the story by your own research about this company and others in its industry. Then, using the principles of this chapter, evaluate the company's strategy. In particular, analyze how information systems and information technology can support the strategic direction that the company has taken.

Exercise 2: Visit two of the sites on the Web page for Chapter 2 in the section called "Examples of Virtual Companies." In what ways are these companies similar? In what ways do they differ? How does information technology enable them to operate as virtual organizations?

RECOMMENDED READINGS

Aaker, David A. *Developing Business Strategies,* 6th ed. New York: John Wiley, 2001.

Daft, Richard L. *Organization Theory and Design,* 7th ed. Cincinnati, OH: South-Western College Publishing, 2001.

Duarte, Deborah L. and Nancy Tennant Synder. *Mastering Virtual Teams: Strategies, Tools, and Techniques That Succeed,* 2nd ed. San Francisco: Jossey-Bass, 2001.

Porter, Michael E. *Competitive Strategy: Techniques for Analyzing Industries and Competitors.* New York: Free Press, 1980.

Spekman, Robert E., Lynn A. Isabella, and Thomas C. MacAvoy. *Alliance Competence: Maximizing the Value of Your Partnerships.* New York: John Wiley & Sons, 2000.

NOTES

1. Geoffrey Smith and Faith Keenan, "Kodak Is the Picture of Digital Success," *Business Week,* 14 January 2002, 39. Michael Slater, "Soon Digital Photography Will Rule," *Fortune,* Supplement: *Tech Review* (winter 2002): 43. Michael Slater, "Kodak Advances in Market Share of Digital Cameras," *Wall Street Journal,* 21 December 2001, B2(E). Kodak, *Annual Report* (December 2000). Also, http://www.ofoto.com, accessed at 10 January 2002.

2. Jeffrey Ball, Todd Zaun, and Norihiko Shirouzu, "DaimlerChrysler Ponders 'World Engine' in Bid to Transform Scope into Savings," *Wall Street Journal,* 8 January 2002, A3(E).

3. Steve Liesman, "Productivity Growth May Be Here to Stay," *Wall Street Journal,* 7 January 2002, A1(E).

4. Thomas C Lawton and Kevin P Michaels, "Advancing to the Virtual Value Chain: Learning from the Dell Model," *Irish Journal of Management* 22:1 (2001): 91–112. Frances Cairncross. "Survey: E-management—The shape of the New E-Company," *The Economist,* 11 November 2000, S37–S38.

5. Priscilla S Wisner and Hollace A Feist, "Does Teaming Pay Off?," *Strategic Finance,* 82 (February 2001): 58–64.

6. Tom McGhee, "Temp Jobs Fall, Though Demand for Work Rises: Downturn Catches Up with Industry," *Denver Post,* 16 December 2001, I01.

7. David Burcham, "Tech Outlook," *Compensation & Benefits Management* 18 (winter 2002): 59.

8. Yogesh Malhotra, "Knowledge Management for E-Business Performance: Advancing Information Strategy to 'Internet Time' Information Strategy," *The Executive's Journal* 16 (summer 2000): 5–16.

9. Lucas Mearian, "Sun Inks Five-Year, $200 Million Contract with Kodak," *Computerworld,* 21 May 2001. Accessed on 17 January 2002, from http://www.computerworld.com/storyba/0,4125,NAV47_STO60752,00.html.

10. Leslie Jaye Goff, "At Their Fingertips," *Computerworld,* 10 December 2001, 19–21.

11. Tracy Mayor, "Someone to Watch over You," *CIO,* 1 March 2001, 82–88.

12. Jaikumar Vijayan, "Survey: Breaches Drive Security Upgrades," *Computerworld,* 5 March 2001, 43.

13. Lucas Mearian, "MetLife Building Giant Customer Relational DB," *Computerworld,* 1 January 2002, 10.

14. Simone Kaplan, "Concrete ideas," *CIO,* 15 August 2001, 78. Dean Ilott, "Success Story—Cemex: The Cement Giant Has Managed Concrete Earnings in a Mixed Year," *Business Mexico* 11 (January 2002): 34–35.

15. Drugstore.com Corporate Profile, http://www.drugstore.com, accessed on 17 January 2002. Simone Kaplan, "The Right Fit," *CIO,* 1 December 2001, 72–76.

16. Susanna Moon, "Improving Care through Integration," *Modern Healthcare,* 7 January 2002, 32–33. Rick Whiting, "Data Analysis to Health Care's Rescue," *Informationweek,* 24 September 2001, 68. Also, http://www.ihc.com, accessed on 23 January 2002.

17. Ram L. Kumar and Connie W. Crook, "A Multi-Disciplinary Framework of the Management of Interorganizational Systems," *Database for Advances in Information Systems* 30 (winter 1999): 22–37.

18. S. Tully, "The Modular Corporation," *Fortune,* 8 February 1993, 106–115.

19. G. Morgan, *Creative Organization Theory: A Resourcebook* (Newbury Park, CA: Sage, 1989).

20. R. E. Miles and C. C. Snow, "Organizations: New Concepts for New Forms," *California Management Review* 28 (spring 1986): 62–73.

21. Melissa A. Schilling and H. Kevin Steensma, "The Use of Modular Organizational Forms: An Industry-Level Analysis," *Academy of Management Journal,* December 2001, 1149–1168.

22. William M. Fitzpatrick and Donald R. Burke, "Form, Functions, and Financial Performance Realities for the Virtual Organization," *S.A.M. Advanced Management Journal* 65 (summer 2000): 13–20. J. A. Byrne, "The Virtual Corporation," *Business Week,* 8 February 1993, 98–99.

23. Byrne, "The Virtual Corporation."

24. Alorie Gilbert, "Virtual Company Wins New Business," *Informationweek,* 2 April 2, 2001, 79–82.

25. John Gregerson, "A League of Their Own," *Food Engineering,* November 2001, 36–40.

26. Joe Singer and Steve Duvall, "High-Performance Partnering By Self-Managed Teams In Manufacturing," *Engineering Management Journal* 12 (December 2000): 9–15.

27. Bradley L. Kirkman and Debra L. Shapiro, "The Impact of Cultural Values on Job Satisfaction and Organizational Commitment in Self-Managing Work Teams: The Mediating Role of Employee Resistance," *Academy of Management Journal* 44 (June 2001): 557–569.

28. Ron Panko, "Stealth Solution," *Best's Review,* November 2001, 53–57. Also, http://www.conseco.com, accessed on October 2, 2002..

29. Thomas L. Legare, "How Hewlett-Packard Used Virtual Cross-Functional Teams to Deliver Healthcare Industry Solutions," *Journal of Organizational Excellence* 20 (autumn 2001): 29–38.

30. Ole Hanseth, Claudio U. Ciborra, and Kristin Braa, "The Control Devolution: ERP and the Side Effects of Globalization," *Database for Advances in Information Systems* 32 (fall 2001): 34–46.

31. Debbie Howell, "The Super Growth Leaders—The Home Depot: Diversification Builds Bridge to the Future," *DSN Retailing Today,* 10 December 2001, 17–18.

32. J. F. Stoner and R. E. Freeman, *Management,* 5th ed. (Englewood Cliffs, NJ: Prentice-Hall, 1992).

33. Michael E. Porter, *Competitive Strategy: Techniques for Analyzing Industries and Competitors* (New York: Free Press, 1980). Michael E. Porter, "How Competitive Forces Shape Strategy," *Harvard Business Review,* March/April 1979, 137–145.

34. Michael Porter, *Competitive Strategy: Techniques for Analyzing Industries and Competitors* (New York: Free Press, 1980). Michael E. Porter, "From Competitive Advantage to Corporate Strategy," *Harvard Business Review,* May/June 1987): 43–59. S. Barrett and B. Konsynski, "Inter-Organizational Information Sharing Systems," *MIS Quarterly,* Special Issue (December 1982): 92–105. H. R. Johnson and M. E. Vitale, "Creating Competitive Advantage with Interorganizational Systems," *MIS Quarterly* (June 1988): 153–165. J. F. Rockart and J. E. Short, "IT in the 1990s: Managing Organizational Interdependence," *Sloan Management Review,* winter, 1989. Stan Davis and Bill Davidson, *2020 Vision* (New York: Simon & Schuster, 1991).

35. Harry M. Lasker and David P. Norton, "The New CIO/CEO Partnership," *Computerworld Leadership Series,* 22 January 1996, 1–7.

36. James Cope, "App Helps Boeing Link Factory Floor to Suppliers," *Computerworld,* 19 March 2001, 12.

37. "Motorola Developing Smart Car Technology," *BusinessWorld,* 10 August 2001, 1.

38. Cynthia M. Breath and Blake Ives, "Competitive Information Systems in Support of Pricing," *MIS Quarterly,* March 1986, 85–96.

39. Laura Mazur, "Keep Improving Service Levels or Lose Out to Rivals," *Marketing,* 15 November 2001, 18.

40. Gail Kachadourian, "OnStar Adds Services," *Automotive News,* 24 December 2001, 2. Lillie Guyer, "OnStar Pushes Safety in Technology," *Automotive News,* 3 December 2001, 6TN. Also, http://www.onstar.com accessed on October 2, 2002.

41. Andy Kessler, "No More New Economy Schadenfreude," *Wall Street Journal,* 25 January 2002, A18. Anonymous, Margaret C. Whitman, *Business Week,* 14 January 2002, 69.

42. Joseph T. Sinclair, *eBay The Smart Way: Selling, Buying, and Profiting on the Web's #1 Auction Site,* 2nd ed. (New York: AMACOM, 2001).

43. Mark Veverka, "The Real Dot.coms," *Barron's,* 24 December 2001, 19–21.

44. Jon E. Hilsenrath, "Globalization Persists in Precarious New Age," *Wall Street Journal,* 31 December 2001, A1.

45. Ibid. Also, http://www.applicainc.com/about .htm, accessed on 29 January 2002.

46. B. S. Neo, "Information Technology and Global Competition: A Framework for Analysis," *Information & Management* 20 (March, 1991): 151–160.

Part II

Evaluating Information Technologies

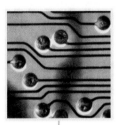

Managers use information technology—computer hardware, software, and telecommunications networks—to meet their information needs. Although managers can no longer expect to have the technical expertise required to design, select, or install information technology, they should have enough knowledge to ask specialists key questions and provide relevant information for selecting the best information technology to meet their information needs. Part II provides such an overview of information technology. Chapter 3 examines computer hardware—the physical equipment used for data input, processing, storing, and output—and computer software—the instructions that command a computer to perform a desired task. Chapter 4 considers database management systems. Specifically it looks at the functions, applications, and technological underpinnings of database management systems, and the design, development, and management of databases. Chapter 5 explores telecommunications and networks. It addresses telecommunication principles, applications, infrastructure, technology, and security along with topics on the Internet and network management.

3

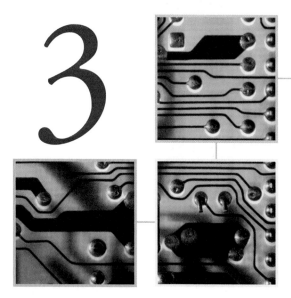

Computer Hardware and Software

LEARNING OBJECTIVES

After completing Chapter 3, you will be able to:

- Describe how data flows among a computer's devices.
- Contrast active and passive data entry.
- Identify six basic types of input devices and cite examples of each.
- Describe how a processor performs its work.
- Describe Moore's Law and discuss its implications.
- Compare and contrast the uses and characteristics of primary and secondary storage devices.
- Discuss ways of measuring the quality of graphics output.
- Describe three softcopy and two hardcopy devices.
- Describe how manufacturers package hardware by size and function.
- Describe the difference between hardware and software and explain how they work together.

- Compare and contrast the functions of application software, systems software, and systems-development software.
- Compare and contrast vertical and horizontal software.
- Cite the relative advantages of packaged, customized, and custom vertical applications software.
- Explain the role of the operating system kernel.
- Describe how people use utility software to manage the resources of their personal computers.
- Describe four ways in which computer languages differ from one another.
- Describe the difference between the two-tiered, three-tiered, and multi-tiered client/server models.
- Discuss the meaning of artificial intelligence and describe the implications of artificial intelligence for the future of computing.

Designing Prada's Epicenter Store

The opening of Prada's Epicenter Manhattan boutique in the spring of 2002 rocked the New York retail establishment. The excitement was driven partly by the store's avant-garde design, the vision of Dutch architect Rem Koolhaas. Its glass walls, its stadium-style bleachers designed to display the Milan fashion house's shoes, and its 30-foot floor/stage shaped like a wave portrayed a flair befitting the Prada name. But even more interesting was the design of the systems to support Prada's customers and salespeople inside the store.

Miuccia Prada, co-CEO of the $1.5 billion Prada empire, envisioned a simple but highly rewarding customer experience. To achieve this goal, each salesperson carries a handheld computer shaped like a flashlight. If a shopper expresses an interest in a particular item, the salesperson can quickly scan it and receive a host of relevant information—what colors and fabrics it comes in, which of these are in stock, what accessories look good with it, and how it is priced. Then, at computer terminals throughout the store, the salesperson can display photos of other garments in the collection, videos of the garment being worn at fashion shows, and even the original designer sketches. If the customer uses a customer card, the salesperson has additional access to the customer's preferences, tastes, and previous purchases, making it easier for the salesperson to provide knowledgeable service. When the customer takes garments to a dressing room, sensors in the room identify the garments. A touch-screen display allows the customer to examine how an accessory, such as a scarf or belt, or even the shoes she bought last month might look with the selected items. The customer can also activate a "magic mirror," that captures and plays back a video of the customer wearing the item. A customer can use the magic mirror, for example, to twirl and see the back of a dress, which would be difficult in a traditional mirror.[1]

How did Prada translate the objectives of superior customer service into the reality of the Epicenter store? What did its managers and their consultants need to know about computer technology even to envision the final result?

Managers usually don't need to understand exactly how a computer works to do their jobs, any more than drivers need to understand how an automobile works in order to drive. But, just as drivers becomes better at driving and purchasing cars, the more they understand about automobile mechanics, so too does a computer user become a better user, purchaser, and director of computer use in her organization, the more she understands about how computers work. This chapter provides an overview of what every intelligent consumer of computer technology needs to know. Depending on your involvement with computer technology, you may need to acquire additional knowledge in one or more of the topics covered in this chapter.

In recent years, the essence of computing has moved away from the computer and toward networks of intelligent devices. The computer, in this evolving model of computing, is simply one of many devices connected to perform a business function. At Prada, for example, a salesperson's handheld device would be useless without access to the knowledge stored in a computer elsewhere in the company. Although we allude to networks at times in this chapter, we have deferred coverage of network concepts to Chapter 5. Also central to computing is the technology that enables organizations, such as Prada, to retain and access the tremendous amount of information they need about customers, suppliers, and processes. Chapter 4 addresses the heart of this technology, database management systems.

In this chapter, we focus on the computer itself. A computer needs hardware and software to work. *Hardware* is the physical equipment used to process information. It includes all the components inside the box that we call a computer. It also includes *peripheral devices,* those devices attached to a computer, such as keyboards, video screens, printers, and scanners, that collect, display, communicate, and store data. *Software* refers to the instructions that, with the help of people, command the hardware to perform desired tasks. Sometimes we use the terms *program, package,* and *application* to refer to software products, although each has a slightly different connotation. Although this chapter addresses hardware and software in separate sections, you will see how the two work together as you read through the chapter. We conclude the chapter with a peek at some exciting advances at the cutting edge of computing technology.

Because of its length, this chapter is divided into two learning modules. Module A covers computer hardware. Module B covers software and a peek into the future.

MODULE A—COMPUTER HARDWARE

COMPUTER HARDWARE

Figure 3-1 provides a conceptual illustration of a computer and its peripheral devices. Managers often make choices about purchasing or upgrading each of these components after diagnosing their needs and evaluating available computer hardware. Prada, with its focus on the customer, was particularly concerned about its input and output devices.

- *Processing hardware* controls the peripheral devices, as directed by computer software.

- The **data bus** is the electrical connection between various parts of the computer, managing the flow of data between the processing hardware and the rest of the computer. The processing hardware puts data in the form of electrical signals on

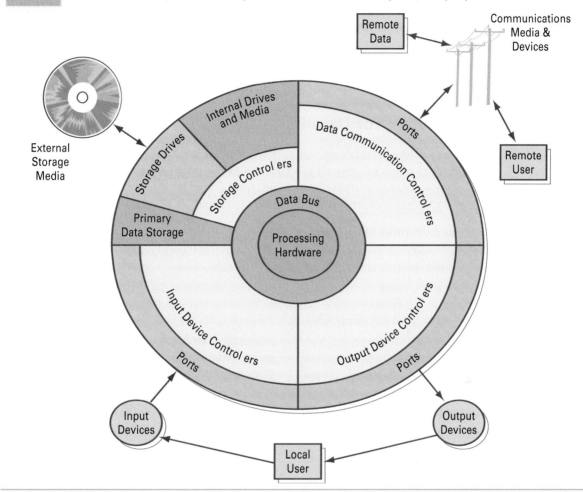

FIGURE **3-1** This conceptual illustration of computer hardware shows processing hardware at the core, surrounded by the data bus, controllers, ports, and peripheral devices.

the bus to direct the other devices. It accepts data from the bus to determine the state of these devices and acquire data that they may provide. Some computers have additional specialized buses for faster connections to certain devices.

- *Controllers,* or **adaptors,** reside inside the computer and convert commands and data from the data bus into signals that peripheral devices can use.

- A **port** is a connection between the computer box and a device outside the computer. Usually, it consists of a receptacle protruding through the computer box that attaches to a controller inside the computer and to a cable connector outside the computer. An infrared port also protrudes through the computer box but connects an external device to the computer by an infrared signal rather than a cable. Some devices, such as computer screens on laptop computers, connect directly to their controllers without a port or cable.

- Input, output, and communications devices transfer data between a computer and its users or other computers.

- Storage devices save data for later processing.

Not all computer hardware actually processes data. For example, a *power supply* regulates the voltage and amperage supplied to other components within the computer. A box called a cabinet holds the computer devices. In this chapter, however, we focus only on hardware that is directly related to processing data. We first focus on the input devices that acquire data. Then, we address how that data is processed. Next, we examine storage devices, which are closely integrated with processing. The last set of devices we examine are output devices, those that present the results of processing to the user. Finally, we explore the different ways that hardware is packaged and marketed.

Hardware for Data Input

Input hardware consists of devices that send signals to a computer. These devices allow people to communicate with computers and allow computers to sense their environment. In this section, we examine the uses and types of input devices that managers might choose as they design computer systems to meet their needs.

Uses of Input Hardware

Input hardware gets information into the computer. We use input hardware for three types of tasks: control, active data entry, and passive data entry.

- *Control.* A person uses an input device to control the tasks or actions of the computer. For example, you might use an input device for control when you select a word processing program from a menu of choices or from a screen full of icons.

- *Active data entry.* A person uses an input device to enter data into a computer. Most business transactions are entered this way.

- *Passive data entry.* The computer obtains information without the active participation of a user. For example, as a car passes through a tollbooth, a device could read the identification of a transponder on its windshield and record the car's passage electronically.

Types of Input Hardware

Input hardware devices use the following technologies to recognize data: keyboards, pointing devices, formatted text readers, image capture devices, instrumentation, and sensors. As shown in Table 3-1, different types of devices are best suited for different purposes. Table 3-2 lists examples of each type of input device.

Keyboards

A *keyboard* consists of a plastic or metal housing containing keys that, when pressed, send a signal to the computer. Every key sends a different signal. Figure 3-2 illustrates two common types of keyboards—data processing keyboards and point-of-sale keyboards.

TABLE 3-1

Different types of devices are best suited for different purposes.

Type of Input Device	Use of Input Device		
	Control	Active Data Entry	Passive Data Entry
Keyboard	•	•	
Pointing Device	•	•	
Formatted Text Reader			•
Image Capture Device		•	•
Instrumentation	•	•	
Sensor			•

	Device Type	Device Examples
TABLE 3-2 Examples of input devices of various types.	Keyboard	Data Processing Point of Sale
	Pointing Device	Mouse Trackball Joystick Light Pen Touch Screen Trackpoint
	Formatted Text Reader	Bar Code Reader MICR Reader Mark Sense Reader
	Image Capture Device	Scanner Digital Still Camera Digital Camcorder
	Instrumentation	MIDI (Musical Instruments) Robotic Controller
	Sensor	Microphone Electromagnetic Receiver (e.g., Radio) Pressure Sensor Chemical Detector Thermometer

FIGURE 3-2

People use data processing keyboards for most computer work.

Sales people use point-of-sale terminals for registering customer sales.

General-purpose computing requires data processing keyboards. You'll find this type on most personal computers. Computers dedicated to sales order processing and certain other applications might use point-of-sale keyboards. These keyboards usually have two areas, one for numeric data entry and one for registering sales of different products. At Burger King or McDonalds, for example, one key may represent the sale of a chicken sandwich while another represents the sale of a fish sandwich.

Pointing Devices

Pointing devices (see Figure 3-3) allow the user to control the movement of a *cursor,* or pointer, on the screen. They are among the most varied and versatile of the input devices.

- *Mouse.* A user operates a mouse, the most popular pointing device for desktop computers, by placing his hand on it and rolling it across a tabletop or other surface. As the mouse moves, it sends a signal about its direction and amount of movement to the computer. The computer processes this signal and moves an arrow or similar symbol in parallel on the screen. A mouse also has two or three buttons that a user can *click* to send additional signals to the computer.

FIGURE 3-3

Pointing devices are among the most varied and versatile of the input devices.

- *Trackball.* A trackball, popular for mobile computing, differs from a mouse in that the user rotates rather than moves it. A user can operate a trackball with a single finger, making it possible to use without lifting the hand from the computer.

- *Joystick.* A joystick acts as a steering device. The user pushes the stick in the direction of the desired movement and releases the stick to stop movement. The speed of movement may depend on the pressure placed on the stick. Joysticks are popular for computer games.

- *Light Pen.* A light pen consists of a stylus that transmits a narrow light beam to a transparent sensor overlaying the surface of a computer screen. Compared to a mouse, trackball, and joystick, a light pen has the advantage of directly identifying a point on the screen without having to move and stop a cursor.

- *Touch Screen.* A touch screen is a transparent surface overlaying a computer screen. When touched with a finger or stylus, it signals the computer indicating the point of contact. Finger-based systems work well for public-access systems because they have no moving parts and novice users can easily operate them. Stylus-based systems work better where more accuracy is desired, such as for handwriting and drawing on a PDA.

- *Touch Pad.* A touch pad, popular for mobile computers, is a pressure sensitive input device. The user controls a cursor on the screen by moving his thumb along the touch pad. A touch pad is small, has no moving parts, and allows the user to control the position of the cursor without lifting fingers from the keyboard.

- *Trackpoint.* A trackpoint is a tiny joystick placed between the G and H keys of a keyboard and operated with the thumb of either hand. Like the touchpad, it allows the user to control the cursor without lifting a hand from the keyboard.

Formatted Text Readers

Formatted text readers, as the name implies, read text formatted specifically for the device in use. Most formatted text readers support passive input and can acquire a large amount of data rapidly. Figure 3-4 illustrates three types of formatted text—bar codes, mark sense forms, and MICR text. *Bar codes* have the broadest market acceptance of all formatted text. Figure 3-4 shows two types of bar codes—a UPC (Universal Product Code) bar code, a

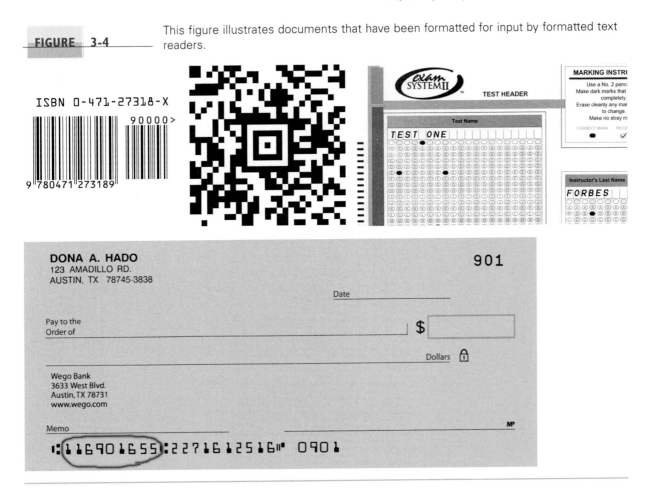

FIGURE   3-4   This figure illustrates documents that have been formatted for input by formatted text readers.

standard adopted by retailers worldwide, and a 2-dimensional matrix bar code, which can contain much more data per unit of space. Many bar code formats and standards exist, including standards for 3-dimensional codes that use raised bars on surfaces subject to abrasion or on surfaces that do not easily accept print. Bar code readers capture data quickly, cheaply, easily, and relatively accurately.

Pratt & Whitney Canada (P&WC), which makes engines and engine parts for aircraft and industrial power generators, uses 2-dimensional bar codes to track the 5,000 components in its typical engine. For tracking purposes, each part is tagged with a combination of serial, factory, and manufacturing numbers. P&WC's bar codes, which can hold as many as 2,000 characters, have reduced the number of data entry errors by 95 to 98 percent, reduced the number of lost parts, improved inventory control, improved employees' ability to select properly among look-alike parts, and dramatically reduced the amount of labor associated with data entry.[2]

A *mark sense form* has boxes or bubble shapes that appear in specific locations on the page. A user enters data by checking a box or filling in a bubble. Mark sense forms are commonly used as test answer forms, voting ballots, and survey instruments. A device that senses the existence or absence of marks in expected locations reads the form and sends its data to a computer.

An **MICR** (Magnetic Ink Character Recognition) reader senses the shape of characters written with magnetic ink. MICR characters have a very stylized form. MICR is used almost exclusively on bank checks.

Image Capture Devices

Image capture devices include scanners, digital still cameras, and digital camcorders. *Scanners* input pictures and other graphics into a computer after first converting them into a binary format, called a bitmap, which the computer can process. Scanners differ in their ability to capture detail, the number of colors they support, and the number of pages they can scan in a minute. High-end scanners have a sheet feeder, read at least six pages per minute, provide a resolution of more than 1,200 dots per inch, and distinguish differences among more than 16 million colors. Flatbed scanners scan books, magazines, and other media that cannot be fed through a sheet feeder. Scanners can also capture images from slides or photo negatives.

To use scanners as an input device for text and numbers, software called **optical character recognition (OCR)** software must convert the images received into data that word processing and spreadsheet programs can process. Low-priced OCR software now typically achieves greater than 99 percent accuracy on clear typed or printed material input through a quality scanner. Delta Dental Plan of Michigan found that the use of scanners with OCR technology allowed it to increase claims capture efficiency by more than 325 percent and to pay 85 percent of submitted paper claims automatically, greatly reducing its backlog and improving customer service.[3]

Digital still cameras produce a digital representation of a picture that a computer can store and process. Outwardly, these cameras appear similar to film-based cameras. Digital cameras use a digital storage device, typically flash memory (see "storage devices" later in this chapter), rather than film to save their images. *Digital camcorders* capture moving pictures electronically. They also look like their non-digital counterparts. They typically use magnetic tape for image storage. The technology and understanding necessary to extract meaningful information from still or moving pictures remains immature. As a result, companies use video technology primarily to capture images for storage and output rather than processing. Nevertheless, Prada could use this technology, along with some simple processing, to improve the function of its magic mirrors. Although data gathered by camera devices can be compressed, digital images, and particularly digital moving images, require much more storage than text documents.

Instrumentation

Computers can receive input through other devices that produce electrical output. For example, a piano keyboard or an electric guitar can be equipped to send signals to a computer as the musical instrument is played. The computer can process the signals to record the notes that were played. Similarly, a computer can capture the output produced by a machine operator who presses buttons or turns a wheel to control a robot or mechanical piece of equipment.

Sensors

Humans sense light, sound, smell, taste, and touch. Computers can also sense characteristics of their environment. Input **sensors** for computers are devices, such as microphones, electromagnetic receivers, pressure sensors, chemical sensors, and temperature sensors, that respond to the environment with a signal that a computer can interpret.

Potential applications of microphones (sound sensors) include monitoring mechanical equipment, such as turbines, processing SONAR data, saving and replaying voice messages or recorded concerts, and recognizing and responding to data or commands spoken by a human. Colorado-based Corporate Express, a provider of office products, found that a voice-based warehouse management system installed in its Detroit warehouse increased worker productivity by 40 percent and reduced errors by 73 percent. Warehouse workers use a headset with a microphone that gives them hands-free ability to communicate with a central computer about what stock to pick.[4]

Manufacturers and warehouses often use electromagnetic sensors to read radio frequency ID tags, which are more durable and reliable than bar codes. Prada uses RFID tags rather than bar codes for its clothing so sensors in the changing room can detect which clothes are hanging in the rooms' interactive closets without the customer having to scan them.

Applications of pressure sensors include touch-screen devices, pen-based input devices, intelligent scales, and control systems for aircraft and missiles. Sensors that measure moisture, temperature, chemical composition, and almost any form of sensory data can convert their readings into digital signals that can then pass to a computer. Manufacturing industries use sensor technologies extensively to collect data about and to automate manufacturing processes. Sensors can even detect brain wave patterns and intensity. Computers can use such sensors to respond to people's thoughts.[5] Table 3-3 provides examples of other applications of sensor technologies.

Hardware for Processing Data

Processing hardware implements the instructions encoded into software. A special hardware device called an *instruction register* or *instruction counter* contains the address of a location in the computer's memory that holds the instruction a computer needs to start its operation. Turning on the computer activates this instruction. Thereafter, the processor executes instructions sequentially in the order they exist in memory unless it encounters an instruction that resets the instruction counter to a different memory address.

Figure 3-5 illustrates the steps needed for a computer processor to perform its work. First, the processor retrieves or fetches the instruction stored at the location indicated by the instruction register. Next, it decodes the instruction, that is, determines what the instruction tells it to do. Finally, it executes the instruction. The processor repeats the three steps of fetch, decode, and execute until someone or a computer instruction turns off the power.

Measuring Processing Power

A manager who purchases a computer needs to understand how computer professionals talk about computer processing power so that he can evaluate and trade off price against performance. Among similar processors and within a single processor family, clock speed is the most common measure of processor power. An electronic circuit called a *clock* emits a regular electronic beat or pulse that synchronizes the operation of the processor. With each pulse, the processor performs one operation, such as fetching or decoding. Some operations, particularly the execution of complex instructions, may take several pulses. We

---

TABLE 3-3

Sensors can be used to detect almost any type of input. The table above illustrates some of their applications.

Check the freshness of food—When you buy food at a grocery store, you may smell it to see if it is fresh. Microsensors can "smell" it for you and alert clerks to pull spoiled food from the shelves.

Monitor vital signs—Microsensors can read a patient's blood pressure, blood oxygen content, pulse rate, etc. and input them continuously to a monitoring computer.

Detect gas leaks—Microsensors can "smell" gas leaks in mining or industrial settings or the leaks of other chemicals to monitor the safety of the work environment.

Detect need for auto maintenance—Sensors can detect engine oil viscosity, heat, if water is mixed with oil, and other problems that demand automobile service.

Intelligent smoke detectors—Sensors can identify the chemical components of airborne particles, determining if particles are related to smoke from fire, mist from a shower, or dust from other sources.

Humidity detectors—Microsensors that monitor humidity can save water by shutting off automatic sprinkler systems after they have delivered the right amount of moisture and keeping them from operating after rain storms.

SOURCE: Virginia Dudek, "Microsensors: Devices that Feel," *MIS Week,* 11 September 1989. Used with permission.

FIGURE   3-5

A processor follows the execution cycle - fetch, decode, and execute - to perform its work.

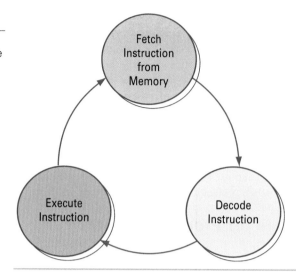

use the term "hertz" to refer to the number of pulses a clock produces per second. The prefixes shown in Table 3-4 modify hertz to express greater speeds. For example, a gigahertz is a billion pulses per second.

Managers and computer professionals can't compare different types of processors on clock speed alone. Table 3-5 describes several other aspects of a processor that affect its power. The input, storage, and output devices that surround a processor will also influence its power. Slow access to memory, for example, will make a fast processor run slowly. You can best evaluate a computer by using it for a sample of tasks similar to those that it will perform.

Choosing Parallel Processing

Managers who work with employees who solve complex problems may choose hardware with parallel processing. **Parallel processing** uses two or more processors in a single computer. These processors either share a common bus and devices or operate more independently. A parallel processing computer overcomes limits in the speed of any one processor by dividing the work among its processors.

Symmetric Multi-Processing (SMP) systems combine multiple processors in a computer with a common bus and common input, output, and storage devices. In *massively parallel processor (MPP)* computers, which connect tens or hundreds of processors, each processor or SMP-processor group has its own bus, memory, and copy of the operating system software.

Although MPP manufacturers originally targeted scientists, many business applications can take advantage of the MPP's parallel construction. For example, ShopKo Stores, a regional mass retailer based in Green Bay, Wisconsin, uses an MPP system to analyze data in its data warehouse and to improve customer response.[6] United Air Lines' reservation systems use an MPP computer to determine how many seats to set aside for last-minute business travelers, how many seats to overbook, and how to manage reservations for flight connections. The company believes that these reservation management functions can add as much as $100 million to its annual profits.[7]

Specialized Processors

Specialized processors respond to a limited set of commands to perform highly specialized tasks. They lack a general capacity to manipulate data and change the order of their

TABLE 3-4

Prefixes use to modify measures of processor speed and quantity of storage.

Prefix	Meaning
Kilo	One thousand
Mega	One million
Giga	One billion
Tera	One trillion
Peta	One quadrillion

Word Length and Bus Width

The word length, or the number of bits a computer can process at one time, is usually at least 32 for personal computers and 64 for organizational computers. The bus width refers to the number of bits a computer can move at one time from one area of memory to another and is generally less than word length.

Doubling the word length will more than double the speed of certain arithmetic operations, such as multiplying large numbers. It will also increase the amount of memory that the processor can address directly. Doubling the bus width will double the speed of moving characters from one area of memory to another.

Speed of Arithmetic

The flop (number of floating point operations per second) measures arithmetic prowess. Modern computers operate in the gigaflop to teraflop range.

Computers use more than a single clock cycle to perform an arithmetic operation. Floating point arithmetic—calculations with numbers having a decimal point and stored in exponential format—consume the most time.

Instruction Speed

MIPS (millions of instructions per second) measures instruction speed for a given processor type.

Instruction speed usually varies directly with the clock speed. A 2 gigahertz Pentium 4 will have twice the MIPS of a 1 gigahertz Pentium 4.

So, you can use MIPS and clock speed interchangeably when comparing similar processors. Because one type of processor may average one instruction every 1.5 cycles while another averages one instruction every 2 cycles, you should use MIPS rather than clock speed to compare different processors.

Instruction Set

The number of different instructions a processor can decode and execute.

Generally, the more instructions a processor can decode and execute, the greater its power. Complex instructions, however, require many more cycles to perform than simple instructions, so they reduce a computer's effective speed relative to its clock speed.

Reduced Instruction Set Computing (RISC) processors understand only a few instructions but execute them faster than traditional Complex Instruction Set Computing (CISC) processors. For example, a 200 MIPS RISC processor may perform tasks no faster than a 150 MIPS CISC processor.

Pipelining

A processor's ability to overlap the fetching, decoding, and executing of different instructions.

A processor with pipelining will operate faster than one without. While a pipelined processor decodes one instruction, it simultaneously fetches a second instruction. Then, while it executes the first instruction, it decodes the second and fetches a third.

---

instruction execution. Because their instructions have been "hard wired" into their chips and their chips have been optimized for their designed tasks, they can perform these tasks more quickly than general-purpose processors.

- *Video accelerators*, also called graphics accelerators, rapidly manipulate images—rotate them, zoom in and out, present appropriate views of three-dimensional objects, color regions, and detect and draw edges.

- *Voice processors* can translate sound-wave inputs into sound-groups called phonemes and then into written words. They can increase the intelligibility and amplification of voice communications. They can also digitize and reproduce audio stored in computer files.

- *Cryptographic coprocessors* offload time-consuming cryptographic computations from the main processor to add security by encoding or encrypting data without affecting the performance of the main processor.

- *Digital signal processors* convert an electronic wave signal, such as one arising from sound or other sensory inputs, to a stream of digital bits and vice versa. **Digital signal processor** (**DSP**) applications include digitally encoding cellular telephone transmissions to prevent eavesdropping and increase clarity, modifying recorded music to sound as if it were recorded in a specific concert hall, and suppressing noise from vehicles and appliances by generating sounds that will cancel the offending sounds.[8]

A computer's processor can off-load work onto a specialized processor, such as a video accelerator, to increase its own efficiency. Some specialized processors, such as those that handle input or output, can achieve further efficiencies by performing their tasks while the main processor independently acts on the next set of instructions. Modern processors now perform many of the tasks previously relegated to specialized processors. For example, since 1999, Intel's newest processors provide functions that had previously required special floating-point (decimal arithmetic) and graphics coprocessors.

Processing Trends

Computer processing power for newly introduced processors has increased at a rate of about 20 to 25 percent a year. At this rate, processing power doubles every three or four years and increases by a factor of ten every ten to twelve years with no increase in cost. This exponential increase in processing power reflects **Moore's Law,** a 1965 prediction by Gordon Moore, a co-founder of Intel, that the amount of information storable in a square inch of silicon would double about every 18 months, as illustrated in Figure 3-6. That prediction has held eerily true for more than 35 years. Some would argue that Moore's Law, fits the growth in computing (as opposed to computer) power since about 1900.[9] However, Moore's Law is not a law of physics. Moore himself predicts that by 2017, his law will end because it will be impossible to cram more logic circuits into a computer chip because each would need to be smaller than an atom.[10]

Scientists see at least two ways to extend Moore's Law beyond 2017. One is to pack transistors vertically onto three-dimensional chips.[11] This technology is already feasible, and such 3D chips are beginning to be shipped.[12] Another solution is quantum computing. Quantum computing improves computing power by dramatically increasing the number of computations that can occur simultaneously, not by decreasing the size of the

---

FIGURE   3-6

This log-linear graph shows how the number of transistors in a typical processor chip have increased exponentially in accordance with Moore's Law.

SOURCE: http://www.intel.com /research/silicon/mooreslaw .htm. Used with permission.

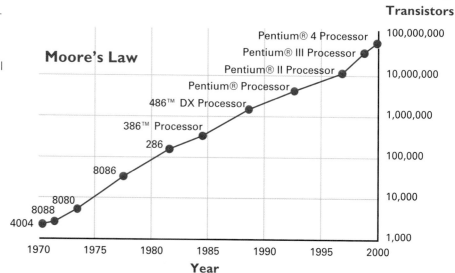

physical components. Although scientists are making progress in demonstrating that quantum computing may one day be possible,[13] the practical applications of the technology remain decades away.

Hardware for Storing Data

Managers and other computer users rarely discard data immediately after collecting, processing, and printing them. In this section we first address the question they ask most often: "How much storage do I need?" Then we investigate the types of storage and alternative devices of each type.

Measuring Storage

Sequences of **bits,** whose value can be zero or one, can represent all information. For example, newspapers and magazines print a black and white picture as a series of inked dots separated by white space. If you lay a 1,000 by 1,000 line grid over a picture, you can observe the color, black or white, at each of the million points lying at the grid intersections. You can then represent the picture by one million bits set to one for black or zero for white. If you require a finer resolution, you can increase the number of lines in the grid and the number of bits used to represent the picture. To represent different colors, you can increase the number of bits dedicated to each point and use different sequences to represent different colors.

Bits can represent letters, numbers, and other characters in this fashion. But a coding scheme, such as the Morse code with bits set to one for a dot and zero for a dash, can represent a character with many fewer bits. Codes that use only seven bits, for example, can represent as many as 128 different characters. Two coding schemes that use eight bits have become industry standards. Most personal computers use a code called *ASCII* to represent characters. IBM uses a code called *EBCDIC* for its largest computers, as do some other manufacturers. Because of the historical widespread use of these eight-bit coding schemes, we now measure storage capacity in **bytes,** where one byte equals eight bits. The same prefaces that we used to modify the word "hertz" (see Table 3-4) can also be attached to the word "byte" to indicate orders of magnitude. With the recent growth in international computing, the *Unicode* standard, which provides up to 49,194 distinct characters in one to four bytes, has gained widespread acceptance.

Companies are finding that as the price of storage declines, the relative benefit of saving corporate data for future analysis increases. A recent survey found that companies have been increasing or plan to increase their data storage by more than 33 percent every year. It also found that more than 22 percent of the respondents' 2001 information technology budget was allocated to storage.[14] Harry Roberts, CIO of Boscov's Department Stores, headquartered in Reading, Pennsylvania, estimates that his company's storage needs are growing at 50 percent per year.[15] Wal-Mart's data warehouse holds 7.5 terabytes of the company's inventory, forecast, customer, competitor, and market basket information.[16] At the high growth rates and huge volumes that companies such as these experience, the importance of wisely managing corporate storage becomes obvious. Managers need to consider carefully the impact on storage when considering plans for new information systems.

Types of Storage

Storage can be primary or secondary and volatile or non-volatile. **Primary storage** is electrical, resides on the bus, and is directly accessible to the processor. **Secondary storage** is storage that the processor cannot access directly. When the processor needs data, it commands the controller to obtain the data from the secondary storage device and place it on the bus. The processor then uses the data immediately or keeps it in primary storage.

Volatile storage requires electrical power to retain its data. **Non-volatile storage** retains its data even in the absence of electrical power. As Table 3-6 shows, primary storage

TABLE 3-6

Types and examples of data storage devices

	Primary	Secondary
Volatile	RAM Cache	
Non-Volatile	ROM	Disk Tape CD DVD Flash

may be volatile or non-volatile, but secondary storage is almost always non-volatile.

A computer needs only enough primary storage to support the tasks its user plans to perform simultaneously. The computer should have enough secondary storage to maintain all data and programs its user will collect. Access to data in secondary storage occurs at speeds several thousands to a million times slower than access to data in primary storage. Still, secondary storage offers three advantages over primary storage. First, it is much less expensive. Second, it retains data without electrical power. Third, it can often be removed from its computer, allowing the transfer of data between computers or the shipping of data as products.

Primary Storage Devices   Because processors access primary storage directly, a computer equipped with primary storage that runs slower than its processor will operate more slowly than it should. Remember that a processor in a single machine cycle will want to retrieve its next instruction from memory. As processors operate at billions of cycles per second, primary access devices must be able to retrieve and store whatever data the processor wants within a few billionths of a second. This requirement precludes the use of mechanical devices for primary storage and suggests the use of chips that store electrical signals. Today's primary storage devices pack millions of transistors, each able to represent a single bit of data, into a chip (see Figure 3-7). Tomorrow's primary storage devices may be opto-electrical, operating at or near the speed of light.

Cache memory describes a small amount of primary storage that is faster than the rest of the primary storage in a computer. In recent years, as computer processor speeds increased, memory speeds failed to keep pace, at least not inexpensively. To compensate for this problem and to keep processors from having to wait while retrieving data and instructions from memory, computer designers equip computers with a small amount of fast, expensive cache memory. When the processor requests data or instructions from an address not in cache memory, the computer moves that data along with a block of nearby addresses into the high speed cache. Then, if the computer requests the instruction or data from nearby addresses, as it usually does, it can find it rapidly in cache memory.

Most memory chips cannot store data without power. This volatile storage, known as **RAM** (**random access memory**), loses whatever data it has if someone turns off the computer. Without any data or programs in its memory, the computer could not do anything when turned on. Some portion of the computer's memory must retain instructions that the computer needs to start functioning and to copy or load the operating system software from secondary storage into primary storage. Computer designers use a type of electron-

FIGURE   3-7

The circuit board holds 256 megabits of data on four chips.

ic storage device known as **read-only memory** (**ROM**) that retains its state in the absence of electrical power to hold the computer's initial instructions. The (non-volatile) ROM devices do not change their state in response to an electronic signal; data must be burned into ROM memory using special equipment. Because of the expense of ROM and because data on ROM cannot be changed, computers contain only kilobytes of ROM compared to megabytes of RAM.

Secondary Storage Devices   Computer users employ secondary storage devices, such as hard disks, diskettes, tapes, CDs, and DVDs, to retain data temporarily and permanently. These devices save data on non-electrical media, such as magnetic or optical films covering tapes or disks. Although these media are non-volatile, they require mechanical devices to position the recording device to save or retrieve data. This mechanical positioning process makes retrieval of data from secondary storage much slower than retrieval of data from primary storage.

Secondary storage devices can use fixed or removable media. Fixed media devices tend to be faster than removable media.

Fixed Media Secondary Storage   A fixed media storage device cannot be removed from its computer. The most common type, a **hard disk,** consists of magnetic-coated metal platters arranged on a spindle, encased in a vacuum chamber, and packaged with a motor, electronics, and magnetic sensors. A hard disk stores a single bit of data by orientating the magnetic field at a disk location in one direction to indicate a zero and in another direction to indicate a one. Because it rotates rapidly, a hard disk provides quick access to any randomly selected bit of information.

The small size and low power needs of hard disks allow vendors to package them inside the cabinet housing of personal computers. People unfamiliar with computer technology often confuse hard disk storage with RAM primary storage because both are internal to the computer and both have capacities specified in bytes.

A technology called **RAID** (**redundant arrays of inexpensive disks**) uses a large number of relatively small hard disks to create what appears to be a single storage device. RAID reduces the time required to read or write data because the computer can simultaneously read or write to each of the disks in the RAID array. RAID storage also takes significantly less room than conventional large disks. Most types of RAID also include redundant storage and circuitry to automatically detect storage errors. If any of the disks in the RAID array malfunctions, it can be replaced without loss of data and without shutting down the computer or the RAID system.

Removable Media Secondary Storage   Removable storage media include diskettes, cartridge disks, magnetic tape, optical media, and flash memory (see Figure 3-8).

- *A diskette* is a random access magnetic medium consisting of a circle of Mylar or similar material coated with a magnetic film and protected with a cardboard or hard plastic cover. Standard 3.5" diskettes hold small amounts of data, typically 1.44 MB, although some types, such as Iomega's Zip disk and Imation's laser-servo diskettes, which require special drives, hold up to 240 MB. The development of low-cost optical drives and media (see below) has reduced the market for diskettes from 42 million units in 2000 to only 30 million in 2001.[17] Forecasts are for this downward trend to continue.

- *Cartridge disks* are similar to removable hard disks. The disk is sealed in a cartridge reducing the possibility of contamination due to dust and allowing the read/write head to approach the disk surface more closely. Disk cartridge capacities are similar to those of hard disk drives.

- *Magnetic tape* storage devices use a thin Mylar tape covered with a magnetic coating. Cartridge tapes resemble those used to record music, and reel tapes

FIGURE 3-8

This figure illustrates many types of removable media.

look like reels of movie film. Tape offers a low cost per unit of storage capacity. A tape capable of archiving 20 gigabytes can be purchased for under $50. Tape lacks random access, so it may take several seconds or even minutes to retrieve a desired item of data. Therefore, tape offers an ideal medium for archiving files.

- *Optical media* store data by changing their reflective properties or their form when struck by a laser. Light from a lower-powered laser determines the state of the medium to retrieve information. The most common optical media include *CD-ROM,* with storage capacities ranging from 580 to 777 MB, depending on format, and *DVD,* with capacities of about 4.7 GB. Both media now come in formats that are read-only, writable, and rewritable.

- *Flash memory* is an electro-magnetic storage device that stores data onto computer chips in a non-volatile fashion. Although expensive, flash memory requires no moving parts, low power, and is more rugged than a diskette. For this reason, it is popular as a storage medium for handheld computers and digital cameras.

Devices exist to automate the insertion and removal of removable media into a computer. For example, Sony's PetaSite 8400 automated mass-storage library stores up to 11 petabytes of data on up to 56,000 tape cartridges simultaneously available through as many as 828 tape drives.[18] Such libraries are ideal for archiving a company's data. *Jukeboxes* automate the switching of optical disks into and out of a single drive in 10 seconds or less. Pioneer's DRM 7000 library stores up to 720 CDs or DVDs, placing them automatically on any of up to 16 drives.[19]

Distributed Storage   A **storage area network** (**SAN**) is a virtual storage device created by connecting different types of storage devices, such as tape libraries, RAID disks, and optical jukeboxes, over a high-speed network. Rather than organizing the storage so that each device is accessed through its own server, a SAN centralizes storage so that any server connected to the SAN has access to its entire storage capacity (see Figure 3-9). A SAN operates on its own optical fiber cabling connecting storage devices as far apart as 10 kilometers and moving data as fast as 4 gigabits/second. A SAN appears to users as a single storage device that can accommodate any or all of a company's data. A SAN not only simplifies the maintenance, backup, and recovery of files for systems administrators, but it also removes the flow of backup data from a company's primary network.

FIGURE 3-9 A storage area network centralizes access to data storage devices.

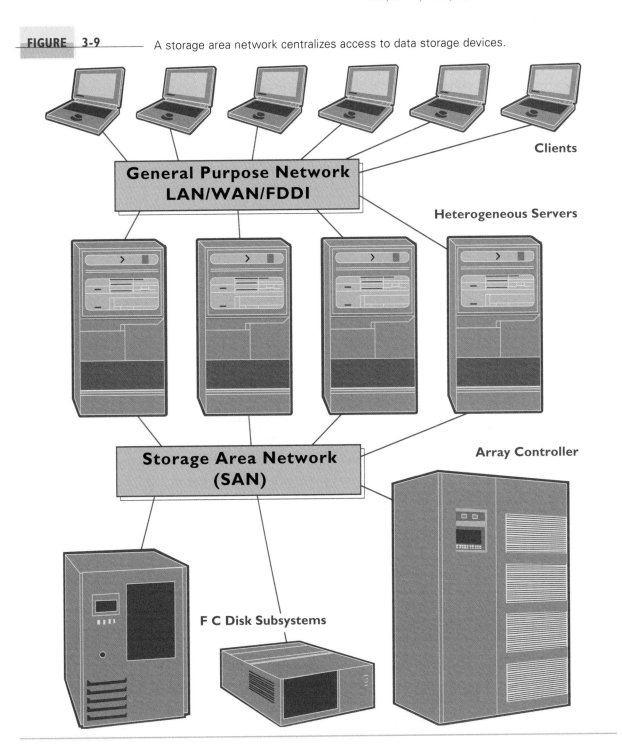

Clients

General Purpose Network LAN/WAN/FDDI

Heterogeneous Servers

Storage Area Network (SAN)

Array Controller

F C Disk Subsystems

When YellowBrix, a Web content provider headquartered in Alexandria, Virginia began to grow at 200 percent per year, its data storage was growing even faster. Periodically, the company had to upgrade its storage in a process that took four days and required recabling the old storage devices as well as the new ones. To make smoother transitions and ease the burden of managing its vast data resources, YellowBrix switched to a SAN. It now takes only a few hours to add additional storage, and no recabling is required. Also, the switch increased service availability and reduced backup time from ten to four hours.[20]

Volumetric Storage Technologies   The amount of data that a DVD or CD-sized disk can store is limited by its surface area and the density at which data can be effectively packed. As data are packed more densely, it becomes more and more difficult and costly to separate individual bits of data for reading and writing. One solution to this dilemma is to store data not only on the surface of the storage medium, but throughout the volume of the medium.

Holographic technologies store data as a 3D image throughout the thickness of the recording material. In addition, millions of bits of data can be written and read in parallel with a single flash of light, making access to the data much faster than with conventional technologies. Industry research and development laboratories have been studying holographic storage since about 1980.[21] The first commercial versions of such storage, however, have only recently been announced. Initially, holographic devices will hold about 100 gigabytes of data on a DVD-sized disk and will transfer data at a rate about 15 times that of the standard DVD technology, but the storage medium will not be rewritable.[22]

Multi-layered fluorescent disk (MFD) technology also promises substantial increases in disk capacity. This technology is similar to current DVD technologies except that the disk is formed in layers of transparent fluorescent material. Researchers have demonstrated the effectiveness of media with up to 100 layers. Since multiple layers can be read at the same time, this technology also promises increases in reading and writing speed.[23]

Hardware for Data Output

Computer systems use output devices to transfer information from computer storage into a form that individuals can see, hear, or feel. Managers need to decide what type of output they need: **softcopy, hardcopy,** or **robotic.**

- *Softcopy*—output on an unmovable medium, such as a computer screen.
- *Hardcopy*—output on a medium, such as paper, that can be removed from the computer.
- *Robotic*—output into devices that physically move in response to signals from a computer.

Most hardcopy and softcopy output devices produce output by placing dots of ink on a page or dots of light on a screen. **Density** refers to the number of dots a device produces per inch horizontally and vertically. The use of a single dot-per-inch (dpi) statistic in its specifications means that the vertical and horizontal directions have the same density (e.g., 300 dpi or 1,000 dpi). When horizontal and vertical dpi differ, manufacturers usually quote both numbers. For text, 300 dpi produces very good quality, although professional typesetters usually operate at 1,200 dpi. Computer screen manufacturers often specify density by the total number of dots in each direction, such as 640 x 480. Alternatively, they might specify the space between adjacent dots, known as the *dot pitch.* Experts recommend dot pitch of not more than .35 millimeters to minimize eyestrain. **Resolution** may be used to refer to density or dot pitch.

Softcopy Devices

The most commonly used softcopy output devices are display units, projectors, and speakers. Each of these devices consists of electronics that reside on a circuit board inside the computer and a physical device, such as a cathode ray tube or a speaker, that produces the output.

A display unit, generally called a *display* or *screen* on laptop and handheld computers and a *monitor* on desktop computers, provides graphical visual output. Each dot, or **pixel,** on the display corresponds to a location in the computer's primary memory or in the memory on the *video adaptor*—a circuit board inside the computer that supports the display.

The most common display technologies are cathode ray tube, liquid crystal, and plasma. A *cathode ray tube (CRT)* is built and operates like a television. It is inexpensive to produce, creates a bright, high-resolution picture, but is heavy and bulky. A *liquid crystal display (LCD)* is a bit more expensive than a CRT to produce at the same size and resolution, is not as bright, but can be made quite thin and light. Thin panel displays using LCD technologies, are increasingly popular as their cost has declined to approach that of CRT display units. *Plasma displays* are also thin. Although they produce a bright image of even higher quality than that produced by a CRT, they are much more expensive. Increasingly, they are becoming competitive for large displays, such as those that might be hung on a wall.

Stereoscopic and volumetric technologies provide 3D display images. *Stereoscopic displays* provide a three-dimensional image as seen from a single point in space using a flat screen. Stereoscopic 3D works on the principle that each eye sees a different image. Most require special polarized or colored glasses, but newer technologies using LCD crystals can point the images so that some pixels can be seen by only one eye while others can be seen by the other eye.[24] **Volumetric displays** produce an actual three-dimensional image that the viewer can walk around. Drug companies have found that volumetric displays, such as the one illustrated in Figure 3-10, are tremendously useful in enabling them to visualize the genetic and physical structure of viruses and other pathogens and to design molecules to disable them.[25]

Projectors allow computer images to be displayed to an entire room. They are more expensive than most display units. Projectors can be compared on the basis of their brightness, contrast, resolution, and sharpness. Of the two most common technologies, digital light processing (DLP) projectors produce images with the best contrast, while LCD projectors produce the sharpest images.

A sound controller, also called a *sound card,* produces an electrical signal that drives one or more speakers. This signal can produce music, special effects, such as the sound of a passing train, or the sound of a voice.

Recent advances in DSP processors (see section on specialized processors) have made voice output relatively inexpensive to produce. As a result, a number of products take advantage of this technology. Consider voice mail. When a person leaves a message on a

FIGURE 3-10

A volumetric display manufactured by Actuality Systems shows the structure of the HIV

Source: http://computerworld .com/hardwaretopics/hardware /story/0,10801,69675,00.html

voice mail system, a DSP digitizes the message and sends it to a computer. The computer saves the data on a hard disk. When the message recipient signals the computer to play the message, the computer outputs the message to a device containing a DSP that reverses the digitizing process, converting the data back into a signal that sounds just like the person who left the message.

Commercial software development tools now exist to help programmers create software to translate text into speech output that sounds very much like that of a human voice. The applications of speech synthesis range from improving the interface of electronic commerce encounters to providing books in electronic form, which blind people can play and listen to on their computers. Office Depot has used speech synthesis, in combination with speech recognition, to power a telephone-based order entry system. The company reports that orders taken by this system cost 88 percent less to process and have more items per order on average than orders placed through a human operator.[26]

Hardcopy Devices

Hardcopy devices produce output on media that can be removed from a computer and hence can be retained for a long time. The most common hardcopy medium for computer output is paper, and the most common output devices are printers and plotters. In selecting a hardcopy device, the user must consider the density and resolution of output desired.

Printers, used by most individuals and businesses for the bulk of their output, produce text and graphics on paper without using a pen. Printers include laser, ink jet, matrix, and character impact, as described in Table 3-7.

Plotters operate by moving a pen or pens over paper, much the way a person writes (see Figure 3-11). Architectural and engineering firms often use plotters rather than printers to produce drawings. The plotters produce high-resolution graphical output. They work on oversized paper and on long rolls of paper.

Devices also exist to produce output directly onto transparencies, microfilm, microfiche, CD-ROM, and slides. These devices generally cost more than devices that produce output of similar quality on paper. For example, most laser and ink jet printers can print

TABLE 3-7   Although companies can choose among four types of printers, most use ink jet and laser printers.

Type of Printer	Quality	Speed	Cost	Process
Laser	Produces high quality text and graphics; 300 to 1,200 dpi	15 pages per minute for personal versions; high-end systems can print up to 464 pages per minute	$300 to $500 for personal systems; more for high-end systems	Uses an internal laser to place dots of selective charge on a heated cylinder, called a drum or platen. The charges attract particles of a dark powder called a toner. As paper rolls over the drum, the drum transfer the toner to the paper and the heat fuses the toner permanently, fixing the image.
Ink Jet	Similar to laser printer quality; copies can smudge when wet	Three to five pages per minute	Less than $200	Sprays streams of ink, which produce dots, at the paper
Matrix Printer	Poorer resolution than ink jet or laser printers; relatively noisy; useful for printing multi-part forms	Some print 700 characters per second; 1,400 lines per minute	Less than $200	Uses a print head that contains pins that can individually be fired at a print ribbon. Each pin hits the ribbon and leaves a dot on the paper.
Character Impact	Used in corporate data centers, and called band printers or chain printers	Can print at 2,200 lines per minute	More costly than ink jet and laser printers	Presses a metal or hard plastic image of a character into a ribbon, which leaves an ink impression on paper. Cannot print graphics

FIGURE   3-11

FIGURE   3-11

Architects and designers often use plotters rather than printers to draw output. A plotter uses a pen or group of pens to create line drawings. A flat-bed plotter can produce large blueprints.

overhead transparencies. Special equipment, not necessarily found in every office, is needed to produce output onto microfilm, microfiche, and CD-ROM. Increasingly, people create slides in their computer program and show them directly from the computer.

Robotic Devices

Robotic output devices physically move in response to signals from a computer. Usually, a robotic device interprets a digital code output by the computer as a signal to turn on, turn off, speed up, or slow down a motor. In more complicated devices, the output signal also addresses one of several motors. Advances in robotics depend less on the sophistication of such output devices than on the software needed to direct the output and processors that can rapidly run software to interpret input video and pressure signals. Only recently have scientists programmed computers to control a robot so that it avoids bumping into objects as it proceeds toward its goal. Such software must first synthesize the two two-dimensional signals produced by the robot's two eyes, into a three-dimensional representation of its world. Then, the software must logically plan and execute a route that safely negotiates this three-dimensional world.

Packaging Computer Hardware

Many different markets exist for computers. The needs of a student, a salesperson, a marketing manager, and a scientist all differ. The computer needs of an organization for tasks such as transaction processing differ further from the needs of an individual computer user. Manufacturers package the components of computers in different ways to meet these various needs.

One way to characterize computer hardware is by its size. The terms "handheld," "laptop," and "desktop" refer to computer hardware intended for personal use. The terms themselves clearly indicate the size objective for these computers. Handheld computers generally do not have a keyboard. Data entry for most handheld computers is through a touch screen and a stylus, often with a special set of easily recognized hand-drawn characters. The screens of handheld computers are integrated into the products and are one of their weakest features, being limited by the size of the unit. Some products integrate handheld computers with cellular telephones.

Laptop computers are meant to be carried and are powered by battery. Their weight and battery life are their primary competitive characteristics, although the quality and size of their display are also factors. Most laptop units are designed to easily connect to a **docking station,** a desktop device with a full screen, keyboard, power source, and network connections, so that the laptop can be used as a desktop unit when docking stations are available. Desktop units, despite their name, are often designed to be placed under rather than on top of the desk. Desktop units designed to connect to a network may not have any secondary storage devices. The display units of desktop computers are almost always separate devices connected to the computer through a port.

Computers to address the needs of an organizational enterprise are classified typically by their power and function. **Mainframe** computers are the most powerful, typically running many application packages simultaneously and serving hundreds of users. *Midrange computers* are less powerful, typically serving a department. **Servers,** no matter what their power, run a single application, such as a database or a Web connection. They may directly serve end users, but are just as likely to serve other computers running more general applications. Mainframes, midrange computers, and even personal computers can be operated as servers. A *blade server* is a computer constructed on a single circuit board that can be mounted on a specially constructed rack of similar servers rather than in a computer box. Because of their low energy and space requirements, companies use blade servers extensively in their data centers, where a single rack may accommodate 200 or more such servers.

SUMMARY

Computers require hardware and software to run. Managers need to understand enough about how computers operate to be intelligent consumers of computer equipment and to make reasoned decisions about the hardware and software necessary to meet their information needs.

Computer hardware is the physical equipment used to process information. It includes processing hardware, the data bus, controllers, ports, and devices for input, output, and data storage.

Input hardware captures raw data in an active or passive mode and can be used to control the computer. Types of input devices are keyboards, pointing devices, formatted text readers, image capture devices, instrumentation devices, and sensors.

Processing hardware implements the instructions encoded into software. Parallel processing and specialized processors can augment a computer's power. Moore's Law describes the rate at which the amount of processing power that can be purchased at a given cost has increased over time.

Bits and bytes measure the quantity of storage. Storage devices may be volatile or nonvolatile and primary or secondary. The processor has direct access to primary storage devices and indirect access to secondary devices, which tend to be slower and less expensive than primary storage.

Output devices transfer information from computer storage into softcopy, hardcopy, or robots. Hardware can be packaged in different sizes and for different purposes. Handheld, laptop, and desktop systems serve personal needs, while midrange and mainframe systems, as well as servers, address organizational needs.

KEY TERMS

adaptor

bit

byte

cache memory

data bus

density

digital signal processor (DSP)

docking station

hard disk

hardcopy

mainframe

MICR (Magnetic Ink
   Character Recognition)

Moore's Law

optical character recognition (OCR)

parallel processing

pixel

plotter

port

primary storage

RAID (redundant arrays of
   inexpensive disks)

random access memory (RAM)

read-only memory (ROM)

resolution

robotic

secondary storage

sensor

server

softcopy

storage area network (SAN)

volatile/non-volatile storage

volumetric display

REVIEW QUESTIONS

1. Define hardware.
2. Describe how processing hardware communicates with peripheral devices.
3. Define active data entry and give an example. How does it differ from passive data entry and control?
4. How do point-of-sale keyboards differ from general-purpose data processing keyboards?
5. Describe three types of pointing devices used for data input.
6. What is the advantage of using 2D bar codes as opposed to UPC bar codes?
7. Describe two types of image capture devices.
8. Identify the steps that a computer processor goes through to perform its work.
9. What factors other than clock speed affect a computer's processing power?
10. Describe four types of specialized processors.
11. What is Moore's Law, and what does it imply for the growth of processing power?
12. Explain why computers typically have more secondary than primary storage.
13. What is cache memory? Why do computers use it?
14. What is ROM? Why do computers need ROM?
15. What is RAID? Why is it popular?
16. Identify three types of removable storage.
17. What is the difference between hardcopy and softcopy output?
18. What is the difference between stereoscopic and volumetric displays? For what applications are these devices most useful?
19. Describe the difference between a printer and a plotter.
20. How do mainframes, midrange computers, and servers differ in their power and function?

MODULE B—COMPUTER SOFTWARE AND A PEEK INTO THE FUTURE

COMPUTER SOFTWARE

Hardware would be of no use without software to tell the computer what to do. It makes sense, then, to classify computer software according to who uses it and what tasks it performs, as shown in Figure 3-12. *Application software* helps perform business tasks, such as word processing, taking an order, billing a customer, or analyzing the causes of weak product sales. We divide application software into vertical and horizontal software, according to whether it addresses tasks common to a specific industry (vertical) or generic tasks that apply to any industry (horizontal), as illustrated in Figure 3-13. *Systems software* is used to control computer devices, interface with network devices, and manage the scheduling and allocation of computer resources for other software. *Systems-development software* is used to create new software.

Understanding all types of computer software helps managers make sense of how computers work and how different software products relate to one another. We start with vertical application software because this class of software affects managers' jobs the most. Also, managers are most likely to have choices about the vertical application software they use, so it is important that they understand their options. We then address horizontal application software, systems software, and systems-development software. Finally, we show how the functions of software can be layered to improve its design and flexibility and to make better use of hardware resources.

Vertical software

Vertical software performs tasks common to a specific industry, such as real estate development, or a function within an industry, such as government contracting for defense contractors and accounting for advertising agencies. Information needs are often very specific to an industry or even a branch of an industry. For example, managers of continuous manufacturing processes, such as chemical production or oil refining, have different infor-

Types	Application software		Systems-development software		Systems software		
Task	Meet business needs		Develop software		Manage computer environment		
Sub-Types	Vertical software	Horizontal software	Computer languages	CASE tools	Systems utilities	Network & systems management	Operating system kernel
Users	Business people		Computer professionals		Business people	Computer professionals	

FIGURE 3-12 — Application software, systems development software, and systems software perform different tasks for different types of users.

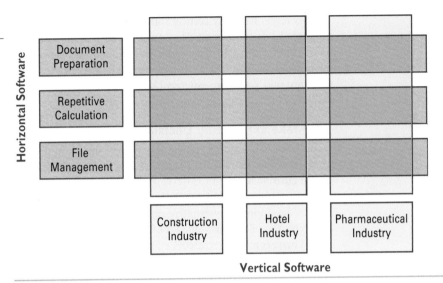

FIGURE 3-13

Horizontal software crosses industry types to perform functions common in all or most industries. Vertical software meets application needs within a single industry or industry group.

mation needs and so require different software than managers of discrete manufacturing processes, such as the assembly of automobiles or consumer goods. A generic manufacturing package will very likely not satisfy either group. Airline and railroad managers, although both in the transportation industry, have unique information needs and require different software for tracking baggage or ticketing passengers. Prada's software is clearly vertical software, as it would be useless in a non-retail environment.

Vertical software cannot capture a mass market because it addresses specialty needs. Its manufacturers generally distribute it through non-retail channels, such as consulting firms, **integrators,** and **value added resellers.**

- *Consulting firms* with expertise in application areas such as architectural planning or government contracting. Accenture's Global Chemical Industry group, for example, has worked with companies such as Dow, DuPont, Elemica, PolyOne, and Ticona to help them select and implement their vertical software.[27]

- *Integrators,* companies that package hardware and software to meet a customer's specification. SchlumbergerSema, for example, tied together hardware and software for the computer systems used at the 2002 Winter Olympic Games.[28]

- *Value added resellers (VARs),* companies that represent the manufacturer and have personnel trained by the manufacturer and authorized to customize the software. For example, Information Technology Inc., headquartered in Lincoln, Nebraska, is a VAR for NCR Corporation's payment and check-processing systems.[29]

Vertical software costs more than mass-marketed software because vertical software developers need to recover their investment over many fewer sales and because the vendors have higher selling costs.

In evaluating vertical software, managers should focus on whether the software supports the way their company conducts its business. Companies that lack resources to purchase or develop customized software sometimes change their business practices to fit with available software. Others, particularly those, such as Prada, who have the resources and whose business practices blaze new trails to create a competitive advantage, need to obtain or create software that supports they way that they do business.

Managers who buy vertical software must also consider the quality and availability of support and customization. They must believe that the software vendor can respond to their unique needs and that the vendor has enough installations to guarantee its existence for many years. Because businesses rely on vertical software in their daily operations, vendors must respond rapidly to emergencies and to requests for changes in the software's design. Failure of the software or of its vendors can have disastrous consequences for businesses.

The Make versus Buy Decision

A company can acquire vertical software in three ways: (1) purchase packaged software from a software manufacturer and use it without modification; (2) purchase software that can be customized; and (3) develop the software from scratch, creating custom software. Business managers and information technology specialists need to decide which acquisition or development alternative makes the most sense for each application. Figure 3-14 illustrates the relative advantages of packaged, customized, and custom vertical software.

Managers and other users can purchase a large variety of uncustomized vertical software products for all types of computers through retail outlets or directly from software developers. Known as packaged or **commercial off-the-shelf (COTS) software,** these uncustomized software packages exist for a wide range of applications and industries. For example, ChemSW Inc. of Fairfield, California develops and sells COTS software called CISPro Desktop that tracks and manages a company's inventory and use of chemicals.[30] Champaign Associates of Manchester, New Hampshire develops and sells GiftMaker Pro, a donor management system for organizations that do fundraising.[31]

Packaged software offers three major advantages: low price, extensive features, and high reliability. These advantages arise from the software's use by multiple companies. In general, the more popular the software is, the greater these advantages become. Packaged

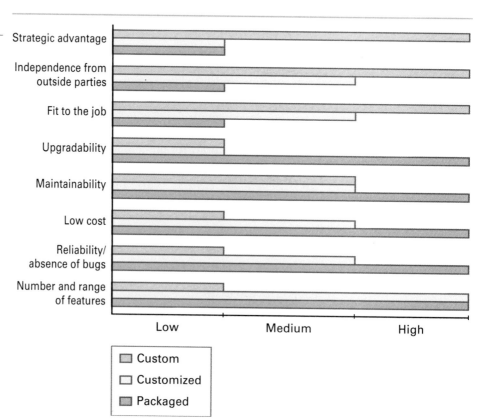

FIGURE   3-14

Custom, customized, and packaged software differ in their strategic advantage, independence from outside parties, likelihood of satisfying business needs, upgradability, maintainability, cost, reliability, and opportunity to provide features.

software often benefits from the large number of users who have tested the software in a variety of environments. This widespread use decreases the likelihood that the software will have major defects and will omit desired features.

On the negative side, packaged software can create a dependency on the software manufacturer. Once a company installs one vendor's vertical software, it will incur heavy costs in licensing, training, and work redesign if it changes to another vendor. As a result, the vendor can charge high prices for upgrades and support. In addition, whenever business managers want a new feature, they can only ask and wait for a future software release. Finally, a company that purchases packaged software does not own it. It just has a license to use it. That license may come with many restrictions, such limitations on the number of people who can use it at once, how many copies can be made, and whether or not the software can be customized.

Most vertical software requires some degree of customization. Packaged software usually provides options during installation and may offer an "options" menu from which authorized users can change set-up features. But, many users require more options than can possibly be set in this fashion. *Customized software* modifies packaged software with computer programs specifically designed to a customer's specifications.

Two questions managers should ask about customized software are (1) who performs the customization and (2) how is the software customized? The software's original developer, a VAR, or the buyer of the software can perform the customization. Software developers know best how their software works and would be likely candidates to perform the customization. However, in most cases, the original developers of the software do not want to divert their product focus by performing individual customizations. Frequently, they partner with a VAR who not only represents their software but has also been authorized to customize it. A company that chooses to customize software on its own probably does so because it believes that it would be harder for a VAR to learn about its specific needs than it would be for the company to understand the software well enough to customize it.

Two alternatives exist for customizing software. One alternative is to change the code that was written by the original software developer. This technique is rarely used because most software developers consider their code to be proprietary and will not release it to their customers or VARs. Also, as discussed above, few developers will customize their own code. A more common approach is to use **application programming interfaces (APIs)** that are provided with the original software. An API allows one program to communicate with another. A typical communication might be, "don't do this task because I (the custom program) need to do it," "do this task using the following data," or "do this task using a specific alternative method rather than the way it's usually done." Developers who want to provide users with an option to customize their software typically provide a rich set of APIs to allow their software to be customized easily and flexibly.

Customized vertical software may suffer from a disproportionate number of software *bugs*, situations where the software doesn't work as expected or desired. While developers of packaged software spend a great deal of time and effort designing and testing their software, custom software developers can't test their product as much because only one company uses it. Customized software also can't readily accommodate new releases without being totally customized again. As a result, companies using customized software do not benefit from the software manufacturer's continuing development efforts. A company may spend a lot to add a feature that the manufacturer might include in its next release for a minimal upgrade fee.

Organizations develop their own software, known as *custom software,* from scratch rather than use or customize packaged software for three reasons. First, no packaged software meets the required specifications, and modifying existing software is too difficult. Second, the company plans to resell the custom software at a profit. Third, custom software may provide the company with a competitive advantage by providing services for customers, increasing management's knowledge and ability to make good decisions, reducing costs, improving quality, and providing other benefits. Only custom software can provide such a competitive advantage since the competition can easily buy packaged and customized software.

Custom software is expensive to produce, costly to maintain, subject to bugs, and usually takes many years to develop. Not only does this development time delay the benefit, but it also reduces the value of the software, as company needs and the competitive environment change constantly. Finally, if software developers can mimic the key features of the software's design and resell it to a company's competitors, they may quickly dilute any competitive advantage the company has gained. As a result, the development and use of custom software has fallen out of favor, and most companies seek packaged or customized software whenever possible.

Integrating Vertical Software

One of the greatest challenges that companies face in using vertical software is integrating the applications of different software vendors. Companies can avoid this integration problem by purchasing software that is already integrated and that performs all or most of the functions that the company needs from a single vendor. Such software, called **enterprise resource planning (ERP) software,** provides seamless support for the operational and administrative processes of a company. It integrates diverse activities internal and external to the company, supports many languages and many currencies, and helps companies integrate their operations at multiple sites and business units.

Most ERP applications are customized products. The major vendors begin with an application template that is pre-customized by industry. Then, the vendors, consultants, or the company purchasing the software further customize it to meet individual company needs. Although the ERP vendors build their software to minimize the amount of customization and to simplify the customization process, most large companies will spend anywhere from 100 percent to 500 percent of the cost of the software for its customization. Chapter 7 addresses ERP software in more depth.

An alternative approach to vertical software integration is to use a middleware product. **Middleware** is software that coordinates application software by processing the output of one product so that it can be fed automatically into another product as input. We address middleware in the context of functional and enterprise systems in Chapter 7.

Horizontal software

Horizontal software addresses tasks that are common to users in all or almost all industries. Managers should understand the options for horizontal software and help find software that best meets their needs. Typically, information systems professionals and corporate purchasing agents rather than business managers assume responsibility for selecting and buying horizontal application packages. They may purchase these packages in volume or purchase a single-site license for the entire organization. They often value a low price and good terms over the particular features offered by competing packages. Horizontal software appeals to a mass market. Its developers and manufacturers can sell it at a relatively low price and still recover their costs. They can distribute it at low cost through retail outlets and mail order houses.

In this section we discuss two generic types of horizontal software: office automation software and business function application software. We then address the steps companies should take in purchasing horizontal software.

Office Automation

Managers, clerks, and other office workers use office automation software to perform routine office tasks. Office automation products include software for word processing, presentation graphics, spreadsheets, database management, electronic mail, scheduling, and workflow, as described in Table 3-8.

Many vendors sell several types of office automation application software in a single package called an *office suite*, such as Microsoft's *Office* or Sun's *Starsuite*. Most office suites

TABLE 3-8

Functions of common office automation software.

Word Processing

Word processing software, such as Microsoft's Word and Corel's Wordperfect, assists users in creating, modifying, and printing text-based documents. These documents may include graphics and other non-textual elements, although presentation graphics software and desktop publishing software work better for creating documents that are more visual than textual.

Presentation Graphics

Presentation graphics software, such as Microsoft's Powerpoint and Lotus's Freelance, helps people without graphics training produce professional-looking slides, overheads, or prints to support their presentations.

Spreadsheet Software

Spreadsheet software, such as Microsoft's Excel, calculates tabular information containing interdependent values and helps automate the process of performing repeated calculations. Managers can use spreadsheets to track budgeted amounts, calculate pay increments, or support other analytical activities.

Electronic Mail

Electronic mail software allows users sends messages to other users and to attach documents and other data to their messages. It organizes messages received into folders, supports the creation and use of personal and organizational telephone directories, and provides various mail handling options, such as setting priority and acknowledgement of receipt.

Database Management Software

Database management software, such as IBM's DB2 and Microsoft's Access, allows users to store, organize, and retrieve data of any type. Database management software generates screens for data entry, cross references data of different types (for example, which employee is the sales representative for a given customer), and retrieves data meeting a selected set of criteria and in a specified sorted order. We explore database management software in more detail in Chapter 4.

Scheduling Software

Scheduling software helps automate the maintenance of appointment calendars and to-do lists. This software reminds users of appointments and activities they have entered with a visual and audio prompt. Users can schedule periodic appointments with a single entry. Scheduling software also helps people share calendars and can automatically suggest appointment dates and times for a set of networked users. It can organize to-do lists by date due, project, and other characteristics.

Workflow Software

Workflow software controls the flow of electronic documents and activities between workers or groups of workers. Workflow software can generate documents or mail in response to certain conditions, route documents, request that users add their digital signature, notify managers of tasks done late or improperly, and select free workers from among a pool to perform certain processes. It can also help managers document and redesign their processes. In this respect, workflow software has many applications beyond office automation.

include word processing, spreadsheet, database management, and presentation graphics software. Some may also include scheduling and electronic mail software. Vendors sell their suite products at a significant discount relative to the prices of the components they include. The components present a common look and feel to the user and can easily exchange information with one another. For example, someone working on a document in the word processor can include tables and charts created with the spreadsheet and presentation graphics software.

Office automation software is also sold as *integrated office software.* Integrated office software compresses several office automation packages into a single program. *Microsoft Works,* for example, consists of software for word processing, spreadsheet, database management, and scheduling. Integrated software doesn't make the user switch between programs to use its different functions as a suite does. Integrated software also costs less than a suite and can be so inexpensive that computer manufacturers package it for free with their hardware. However, integrated office software offers less functionality than similar software in a suite.

Business Function Applications

Vendors sell horizontal software to address many types of functional activities common to most industries. These activities include sales force management, human resources management, inventory management, bookkeeping, customer support, project management, and the production of marketing materials. For example, HRM Software, headquartered in London, has sold its ExecuTRACK software to such varied companies as printer manufacturer Lexmark International, food company H. J. Heinz, and media company Cox Enterprises. ExecuTRACK is horizontal software for leadership development, succession planning, and employee competency management.[32]

Many small companies and some mid-size firms buy packaged generic software to support their business functions. As they grow, these companies' information needs tend to become more specialized and less suited to horizontal software. When this happens, they can replace their horizontal software with vertical software that crosses functions and addresses many of their information needs in a more integrated and industry-specific fashion.

Purchasing Horizontal Software

In evaluating a horizontal software package, buyers consider not only the quality of the software, but also the quality of the vendor or manufacturer, the quality of its documentation, and the availability of ancillary materials, such as textbooks and training courses. The stability and market position of a software manufacturer affect the likelihood of continued development and support of its products and the continued availability of third-party auxiliary software and publications. The quality and responsiveness of a manufacturer's technical support staff are important, even for organizations that have excellent internal support staffs. Often only the software manufacturer can diagnose the causes of problems, find ways to work around the difficulties, and, if necessary, fix them. Buyers can use trade magazines and the World Wide Web as primary sources of information about a vendor's market share and support quality.

Buyers of horizontal applications software also assess a manufacturer's policies and pricing for support and upgrades. Vendors differ in the length of time for which they provide free technical support, as well as in the price of technical support after this period. Some vendors offer a money-back guarantee to unhappy users of their products. Most vendors provide free access to an electronic bulletin board for sharing information about known flaws or bugs, ways of working around problems, and upgrade release notices. Other vendors provide bulletin boards that users can use to talk with other users about their experiences with the product. Buyers should consider the hours of the vendor's technical support, particular if the vendor is located in a distant time zone.

Buyers in an organization that uses several different types of computer systems (for example, IBM mainframe, IBM-PC, and Macintosh) or several different types of systems software should assess whether the horizontal software can run on all systems. The organization benefits from the lack of retraining needed to use horizontal software on different computers. In addition, the computers' hardware and systems software can be changed without affecting the users' ability to perform their work.

Horizontal software commands a higher selling price when used on multi-user computers and servers, although the price per user, often called the price per seat, will be lower than that of similar software sold for individual use. Software vendors may offer *site licenses*. These allow an organization the right to use a specified number of copies of the licensed software or to give a certain number of users access to a single copy of the software at a discount relative to the price of an individual license. Sometimes, in exchange for this discount, the vendor requires all contact to pass through a single representative at the organization's site and provides only a single copy of software documentation.

Systems Software

Systems software performs tasks to manage the devices and resources of a computer and its network. Systems software includes the following types:

- *The operating system kernel* consists of computer programs that perform the most basic housekeeping, resource allocation, and resource monitoring functions for a computer. The kernel operates with a minimum of user input or control. No computer can operate without it.

- **Systems utilities** allow computer owners and users to perform basic maintenance and resource control functions. A computer can operate without systems utilities, although users would find it extremely cumbersome.

- *Network and systems management software* allows computer professionals to monitor and control computer and network resources.

The Operating System Kernel

The **kernel** includes programs that start the computer when the user turns the power switch on, that find and initiate application programs the user wants to run, and that transfer input to the application program and data from the program to output, storage, and network devices. The **operating system** refers to software packaged with the operating system kernel. Traditionally, it includes many utilities, some network and system management software, and even some horizontal software. Exactly where the kernel ends and the system and network management utilities begin is often unclear.

When multiple users or multiple tasks share a computer, the operating system must keep the data and commands of each task and user separate while it provides an opportunity for sharing information among them. A sales manager, for example, can run a monthly sales report at the same time that a warehouse manager checks the inventory of a particular product. The operating system allows systems administrators to establish the rules and priorities for sharing computer resources. A customer credit request, for example, might temporarily delay completion of a sales report because the credit request, with the customer waiting, has a higher priority.

Application software calls on the operating system kernel to request computer resources such as memory, storage, the network, or the display unit. These **system calls** vary among operating systems, making changes and upgrades difficult. Microsoft wrote the kernel for later versions of its Windows operating system to honor system calls for earlier versions, so software written for earlier versions continued to operate as Windows was upgraded. Newer versions of Windows, however, had new system calls. As a result, programs written to run under Windows XP, for example, may not run on earlier versions of Windows.

The operating system kernel must be written for a specific type of computer hardware because it handles the most basic functions of a computer. However, users want operating systems that will work on a range of computers. System calls that perform the same way on different computers ease developers' abilities to create software that runs on different systems. A common user interface reduces users' training needs because the same knowledge then applies to an array of computers.

UNIX was designed as such a common operating system. When first introduced, UNIX was the proprietary software of AT&T, although it ran on several different types of computers. AT&T provided licenses at relatively little cost to vendors who wanted to modify it for other computers. In spite of UNIX's portability, users found that the versions of UNIX provided by their hardware manufacturers often lacked consistency with AT&T's standard and with one another. As a result, it remained difficult to develop application software that ran on different types of computers.

A variant of UNIX called Linux became popular in the late 1990s. A Finnish graduate student named Linus Torvalds developed the software and purposely disclaimed any rights to it, leaving it in the public domain, with the condition that its code and all future versions developed from it remain open to view and change. Several companies, most notably Red Hat and Caldera, modified the software and then created versions having the same system calls and user interface to operate on many different types of computers. As a result, developers can easily create software that will run on many different types of computers under Linux.

Systems Utilities

Systems utilities operate primarily under user control and provide basic resource management functions, such as the ability to copy or back up files, change file names, or sort data, as shown in Table 3-9. Most vendors of operating systems include many systems utilities as an integral part of their operating system software.

A variety of systems utilities are available to purchase or for free to augment or improve the systems utilities included with an operating system. For example, Adobe and RealNetworks provide free software to read files produced in their proprietary formats.[33]

Network and Systems Management

Network management software monitors the state of a company's network and the devices connected to it. This software can provide real-time displays of the traffic on various parts of the network relative to the network capacity, as well as reports that show patterns of usage over time. These reports allow network service management to anticipate capacity shortages and to plan for hardware upgrades in a rational manner. Network management software can also query the status of devices connected to the network, including workstations, printers, routers, switches, hubs, scanners, and any other shared equipment. The software can automatically adjust network parameters so as to avoid malfunctioning devices. For example, the software can route jobs for an out-of-service printer to a printer designated as its standby.

Systems management software monitors the state of a particular computer. Technical specialists generally run this software on key system servers such as file servers, network servers, or Internet servers. Systems management software can identify what programs are running, how much of the computer's resources they use, and why certain performance problems have arisen. It can alert management to impending problems and can provide periodic reports to document usage and performance. It can prioritize and schedule the running of programs that are not time-critical. Systems management software can identify and remove temporary files that abnormally terminated programs have left.

	Utility	Description
TABLE 3-9	Archiving	Allows users to remove data to a permanent storage medium, such as a floppy or optical disk; may compress and/or encrypt the data for improved storage capacity and security. May maintain an archive history and do incremental as well as complete archiving.
Computer operating systems include a variety of systems utilities.	Diagnostics	Allows the user to diagnose problems with various parts of the computer, including files created and used by the operating system.
	Font extenders	Provides type fonts to change the shape of characters. Some font extenders allow the user to edit, rotate, shade, and manipulate fonts in many ways.
	Keyboard modifiers	Allow keys on a keyboard to be reassigned and specified keystrokes to act as shortcuts to words or phrases.
	Miscellaneous	Programs to capture and recall screen displays; programs to recover data that has been erased; programs to allow you to use a mouse in place of arrow keys for programs that do not support a mouse.
	Screen savers	Displays moving designs on your screen if the computer has not been used for a period of time. May prevent others from using the computer without knowing a password.
	Security	Keeps unauthorized users from using your computer or from accessing your data; encrypts data so that they cannot be read or profitably stolen; checks the integrity of your data and/or programs to make sure that they have not been altered.
	Viewers	Read documents created by a variety of software packages and saved in special formats.
	Virus checkers	Identify and eliminate computer viruses.

SOURCE: University Knowledge Database

Packaging the Operating System

Operating system vendors bundle a variety of software with the kernel of the operating system. In most cases, the software packaged as an operating system includes a large number systems utilities and some horizontal software. For example, Microsoft Windows XP includes screen savers, diagnostic software, a Web browser, photo editor, music player, and even a movie maker and player. One reason for putting as much functionality as possible into the operating system is that it improves the product. Skeptics have claimed that another reason is for competitive, or perhaps anti-competitive, purposes.

An operating systems vendor that sells database management software can package the database management software with the operating system so that users have no reason to purchase a competing product. Microsoft recognized the wisdom of this strategy by packaging its Explorer Web browser with its Windows 95 and subsequent operating systems. It quickly captured a market share that it could not otherwise have achieved had it tried to sell Explorer against the Netscape browser. The legality of such packaging, especially if its practitioner has monopoly power and its purpose is to drive a competitor out of business, has been questioned in the courts in the case of the *United States vs. Microsoft*. Although the court ruled that Microsoft had behaved as a predatory monopolist and cited Microsoft's practice of bundling its Web browser with its operating software as part of that evidence, other evidence of Microsoft's monopolistic practices was also cited.[34] The ruling, therefore, makes it difficult to determine if bundling application software with Microsoft's operating system would have been sufficient to judge against it.

Systems-Development Software

Although most managers rely on IS professionals to create or change software, they should know that each type of computer recognizes and responds to a different set of instructions. Computer programs organize and sequence these instructions. Programmers use computer languages, such as C, COBOL, Java, or Visual Basic, to create a single computer program that performs the same task on different computers. Programs written in such languages can be translated into the language of the target computer before being run. Languages also increase the efficiency of software development because programmers can use simple, understandable commands rather than instructions written in a format required by the target computer.

Computer languages differ in the way they are translated, their level of abstraction, whether they are procedural or non-procedural, and whether they are command/data oriented or object oriented. Table 3-10 describes some common computer languages according to these parameters.

Language Translation Method

A *language translator* translates software from the language used by software developers into a computer's language (known as **machine language**) and so lets developers use a common language for software destined for many different types of computers. Each computer translates the same software into instructions that it alone can use.

Two types of language translators exist: compilers and interpreters. A **compiler,** such as one used for C, COBOL, and FORTRAN, translates a program, called **source code,** written in the developer's language into computer code called an **object module.** A linker combines object modules that perform related tasks with already-compiled object code from a library of commonly used functions to create a program called an **executable module,** or a **load module** (see Figure 3-15). A user can load the executable into a computer and run it. The computer running the executable doesn't need a copy of the compiler because the

	TABLE 3-I0

Common computer languages differ on at least four dimensions.

Language	Primary Translation Method	Level of Abstraction	Procedural	Object-Oriented
BASIC	Interpreted or compiled	Moderate	Yes	No
C	Compiled	Low-Moderate	Yes	No
C++	Compiled	Low-Moderate	Yes	Somewhat
C#	Compiled	Low-Moderate	Yes	Yes
COBOL	Compiled	Moderate	Yes	Somewhat*
FORTRAN	Compiled	Moderate	Yes	No
Java	Intermediate code	Moderate	Yes	Yes
Javascript	Interpreted	Moderate	Yes	No
LISP	Interpreted or compiled	Moderate	Yes	No
Pascal	Interpreted or intermediate code	Moderate	Yes	No
Perl	Interpreted or intermediate code	Moderate-High	Yes	No
Prolog	Interpreted	Moderate-High	No	No
Smalltalk	Interpreted	Moderate-High	Yes	Yes
SQL	Interpreted or compiled	High	No	No
Visual Basic	Interpreted or compiled	High	Yes	Yes

*Object-oriented COBOL

program has already been translated. Many languages allow a program to link or unlink an object module as the program runs, a feature called dynamic linking.

An **interpreter,** such as one used for BASIC and Pascal, translates language commands into computer code one instruction at a time and then executes each instruction before translating the next instruction. The user simply loads the interpreter into the computer and runs it. The interpreter treats the source code as data, reading, translating, and obeying its commands.

Interpreters have two major advantages relative to compilers. First, the developer can distribute his source code to anyone who has an interpreter. The same source code will run on any computer and in any operating system. This makes interpreted languages, such as Javascript and HTML, ideal for programming Web pages. In contrast, a developer using a compiled language must create executable modules for each combination of computer type and operating system. Second, an interpreter offers a friendly environment for the software developer. The developer can interrogate the interpreter about the state of the program, reset data values, and continue or restart the program. In contrast, every time a developer makes a change in a compiled-language program, she must recompile the program and relink it before testing and using it.

Interpretive languages also have several disadvantages. An interpreted program runs slower than a similar compiled program because it must be translated while it runs. A user running an interpreted program must have a copy of the interpreter on her computer while a user running a compiled program does not need a copy of the compiler. Users of interpreted programs must have access to the source code to run the programs; thus, protecting interpreted software from piracy is much harder than protecting compiled software.

Some languages, such as BASIC and LISP, exist in both interpretive and compiled forms. Developers can develop their software using the interpretive form of the language and distribute their software in the compiled form, but the compiled programs can't run on any computer. Other languages, such as Java, compile source code into an intermediate code that preserves much of the source language in a highly compact, incomprehensible form, yet still requires an interpreter. This solution allows the program to remain propri-

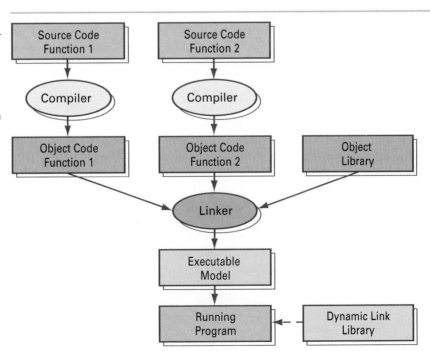

FIGURE   3-15

A compiler translates source code into object modules. A linker combines these object modules with others from an object library to create an executable module.

etary yet run on any computer. It also speeds program execution, although not to the extent of a compiled language.

Level of Abstraction

Although IS professionals rather than managers choose the language to use for a given application, managers should know that they can probably understand and use some high-level interpretive languages, such as SQL, sufficiently well to meet some of their information needs. Computer languages differ in the number of steps the translator has to go through to get from the user's command to computer-executable commands and, so, in the amount of instruction a single command provides.

- *Second generation languages* are relatively low-level and require many steps. A single command provides very limited instruction.

- *Third generation languages* are moderately abstract and require fewer steps. A single command includes a medium amount of instruction.

- *Fourth generation languages (4GLs)* are relatively high-level and require the smallest number of steps. A single command includes an extensive amount of instruction.

Consider the following analogy. How do you give a robot instructions to brush its teeth? If you have a sufficiently intelligent and trained robot, you might simply say, "Brush your teeth." If it has not performed this task before, you might say, "Take the toothbrush from its holder. Open the tube of toothpaste. Squeeze enough toothpaste onto the brush to cover the bristles. Turn on the cold water. Wet the toothpaste and toothbrush bristles. Brush the toothpaste onto your teeth. Rinse your mouth." If the robot has less intelligence or training, you might have to give it even more detailed instructions. It might need to know how to take the toothbrush from its holder, or how to squeeze the tube.

The earlier general-use programming languages, known as assembly languages or second generation languages, required programmers to specify in painstaking detail every step they wanted the computer to perform. Later languages, such as COBOL, FORTRAN, and Pascal, included much more powerful commands. A single command in such a third generation language might substitute for ten to fifty second generation commands. Later languages, such as SQL, operate in conjunction with database management software to convey even more meaning with each instruction. A single instruction in such a fourth generation language often equals hundreds or even thousands of instructions written in a second generation language. Since developers can convey a great deal of meaning with a few instructions, they can reduce development time by about 25 percent relative to that required using languages such as COBOL.[35]

Low-level languages, such as 8086 Assembler and C, have two advantages over higher level languages. First, they can provide more flexibility and speed in performing a job. Using the robot analogy, a robot instructed at the highest level to brush its teeth will likely have a fixed way of doing it, perhaps brushing the top teeth before the bottom. If you wanted the robot to brush its bottom teeth before the top ones, you might have to resort to a lower level language. Low-level languages allow more control over how the computer handles its data and instructions for some programming tasks. Higher-level languages generally do more checking and allow for more contingencies than the same code written in a lower level language.

Programmers can use both high- and low-level languages to develop a single software application. Where possible, they use the highest level language available to maximize their productivity and reduce development time. If parts of the program run too slowly or if the higher-level language is too inflexible to accomplish some tasks, the programmers can write some code in a lower level language. The programmer would compile each part of the program using its own language translator and link the compiled parts into one complete program with a software development tool called a **link-loader.**

Procedural versus Non-Procedural

Procedural languages, such as C, COBOL, or FORTRAN, force a software developer to give step-by-step instructions to the computer. Procedural languages allow the computer to vary its steps depending on the data supplied. Extending the robot analogy, one instruction might read, "If the tube of toothpaste is empty, get a fresh tube from the closet." The steps performed by the robot following this command depend on the state of the toothpaste tube. Software written in a procedural language also allows the computer to determine its directions based on the data it finds.

Non-procedural languages were developed after the first fourth generation languages. The first type, such as SQL, requires the software developer to state an outcome he desires. The language processor rather than the programmer determines the instructions to give the computer to achieve this outcome. For example, a command in such a language might read, "Produce a report showing the name, address, and telephone numbers of all customers in the Northeast region owing over $3,000." The language translator, not the software developer, decides how to achieve this output.

A second type of non-procedural language, such as Prolog, states facts and rules. Products called **expert systems shells** use an **inference engine** to process the language statements and data supplied by users to reach conclusions, answer questions, and give advice. The developer of expert systems software does not know and generally can't specify the order or steps that the inference engine will use to reach its conclusions.

Following is a simple example of a short program (two facts and one rule) that might be expressed in the language of an expert systems shell (see Figure 3-16). Fact 1: Jane is Alan's mother. Fact 2: Mary is Jane's sister. Rule 1: An aunt is the sister of one's mother or the sister of one's father. An inference engine would use this program to determine whether or not Mary is Alan's aunt. The order in which the facts and rules are processed in reaching this answer cannot be determined from the program. Expert systems and their applications are described in fuller detail in Chapter 8.

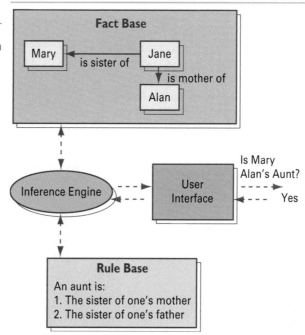

FIGURE   3-16

In an expert system, an inference engine uses a rule base and a fact base to respond to user queries.

Command/Data Oriented versus Object Oriented

Command/data oriented programming languages, such as FORTRAN, COBOL, and Pascal, separate data storage from procedural parts of a program. The procedural parts of a program operate on the data received.

Object oriented languages, such as C#, Java, and Smalltalk, merge procedures and data into a structure called an object. A programmer uses an object-oriented language to build objects. She then builds a program by linking such objects to one another and to objects in a prewritten object class library.

The software developer who uses an object orientation specifies the relationships among objects in two ways. First, the developer establishes a hierarchical relationship in which occurrences (called instances) of similar objects create an object class, and one object class may belong to other classes. For example, Helen and Paul may be objects of the object class "employee." The object class employee may be a member of the class "person," from which it inherits many of its characteristics (see Figure 3-17). Second, the software developer specifies how objects communicate with one another through messages. For example, any person object should respond in an appropriate way to the message "what is your name?" Figure 3-18 illustrates a more complex example of message communication among objects.

In an object-oriented environment, a software developer models the objects and processes in an organization that are necessary to manage its information. Using such objects, the programmer can easily and relatively quickly create a limited prototype of a program to perform almost any information processing function required by the organization. Once developers create software objects that represent the real objects in their business environment, they can use these software objects repeatedly, saving development time and cost. Norfolk Southern Railway, for example, estimated that its switch from COBOL to object-oriented development saved it between $20 and $30 million per year.[36] Companies can save additional time by buying ready-made software object classes from vendors to include in their own software. PepsiCo believes that the use of such classes

FIGURE   3-17

Objects and their classes form a hierarchy, illustrating the principle of inheritance. An employee, for example, inherits the attributes of a person. In this example, Paul and Helen are objects of the object class employee.

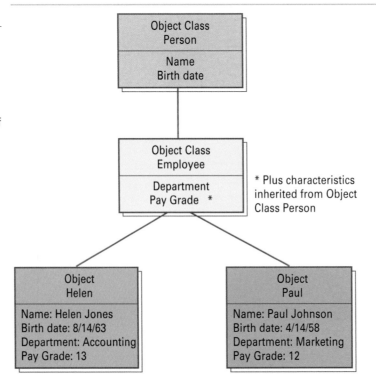

FIGURE   3-18

The customer object responds to the message "Can we offer you credit?" by sending messages to the customer receivable object(s) associated with the customer. It processes the receivable objects' replies and responds with an appropriate return message.

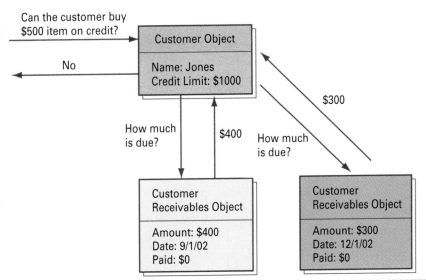

increases the speed with which it can develop new software, increasing its flexibility, adaptability, and market agility.[37]

CASE Tools

Software developers, like the designers of physical products, think of software as a product to engineer. Computer-assisted software engineering (CASE) tools are software products that apply engineering principles to the design, development, and maintenance of software products. They can form the basis for modeling, measurement, and management of systems development and maintenance. Chapter 9 addresses CASE tools in greater depth.

A Layered View of Software

As Figure 3-19 illustrates, at least two layers of software usually exist between the computer and the user—the operating system and application software.

When application software needs computer or network resources to perform its work, it calls upon the operating system kernel to provide them. This division of labor lets application software developers create software that runs on different types of computer systems. An application can run on computers with different designs and configurations because the operating system kernel handles the interface between the application and the hardware.

Client/Server and Multi-Tier Models

The **client/server model** divides a software application into at least two separate but interdependent parts called the *client* and the *server*. Sometimes software is divided into more parts, resulting in a multi-tiered structure. This section discusses how and why application software is designed in this way.

The client/server model in its most basic, two-tier form, assigns the responsibility to the client software for handling the interface with the user. The server software is responsible for data storage and management. Either the client or the server can perform any other processing that may be needed. Consider, for example, software that an insurance agency might use to process its accounts. To add a new insurance policy, client software presents the data entry screen, processes the data entered by the user, and, perhaps, calculates a rate class and a premium amount. The server software stores the policy data in a central database, retrieves rate tables so that the client software can calculate premiums, and, perhaps, even retrieves information, such as customer address, from other policies

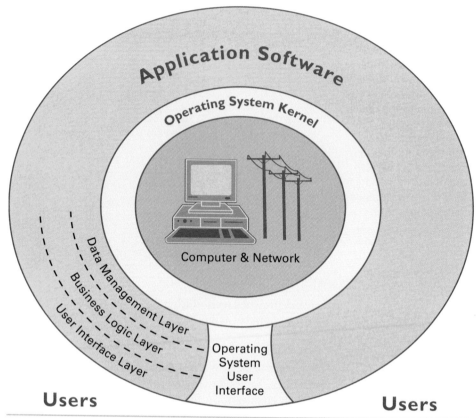

FIGURE   3-19

A layered model of software shows how the operating system mediates between the application and the computer and how both the application and the operating system interface with the user. The application layer can also be divided into data management, business logic, and user interface layers.

held by the same customer to simplify data entry. The server might also perform other functions, such as generating letters to lien-holders.

The client/server division provides three major benefits. First, it allows different parts of the software to be built and modified independently. If a company wants to change the user interface, for example, it must change only the client software. The server software would remain unaffected. Second, it allows server software to be built to serve multiple applications. For example, if the insurance company creates other programs to access the same data, it can use the existing server software and simply build new client applications. Finally, it allows the different parts of the software to run on different computers. This separation of functions reduces the processing load on the data storage computer. The server software can handle requests from copies of the client software running simultaneously on different computers. For example, a single server can store new policy information and process requests from ten insurance agents, each with his or her own computer running a copy of the client software.

The *three-tier client/server* model divides an application into user interface, business logic, and data-handling components (see Figure 3-19). It produces two pairs of client/servers, as shown in Figure 3-20. The user interface is the primary client, obtaining data from the user and issuing a request to the business logic server to process these data. The business logic server becomes a client to the data manager, issuing requests as needed for its own processing. When done, the business logic server sends its results to the user interface client, which in turn presents them to the user.

The three-tier model reduces the resources required at the desktop and at the data interface. Business programs tend to be large and complex, requiring a great deal of stor-

FIGURE   3-20

A three-tier client/server model includes a user interface, business logic, and data management layers. The business logic layer serves the user interface and acts as a client to the data management

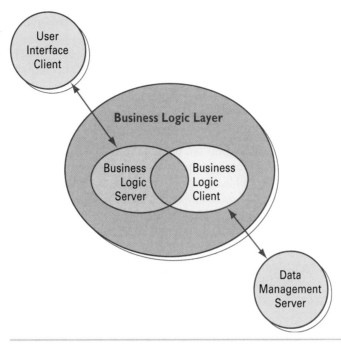

age even when not in use and demanding significant amounts of computer memory when in use. Separating the business logic from the user and data interfaces allows the business logic software to run on a centralized computer, reducing the demands on the desktop computer and the data storage/retrieval computer. The impact is most significant at the desktop. Employees can use less powerful and less costly computers, known as *thin clients*, which include little software, often just a Web browser, with or without secondary storage. For companies that support thousands of desktop computers, using thin clients can result in major cost savings. Two-tier models, in contrast, result in clients with a lot of software and storage, called *fat clients*. Matrix Rehabilitation, a firm that provides outpatient physical therapy in more than 200 clinics in 13 states, switched its computing to a three-tier model with thin clients in mid-1998 rather than upgrade the computers of its 1,000 users. The company found that it saved $2 million in the first two years, improved performance and response time by 150–200 percent, and was better able to manage its software on its 30 application servers rather than 1,000 desktop computers.[38]

The three-tier model also eases the task of upgrading software. When business rules change, computer professionals can modify the middle tier without upgrading the software on each desktop computer and without upgrading the data interface. For this reason, the three-tier model is particularly popular in organizations that use mobile computers because mobile computers are often off-site and unavailable for upgrade.

The *multi-tier client/server* model or *n-tier client/server* model divides application software into multiple components, each of which can call on the others to perform services for it. Consider for example order-entry software. This software might pass a variety of related tasks to inventory management, sales-scheduling, and accounting systems. These systems might run on the same or a different computer as the order-entry system. Splitting the application allows these systems to change without affecting the order-entry system. This approach also splits the processing load among different computers, but increases processing and network overhead by sending messages and requests back and forth among the interrelated systems.

A PEEK INTO THE FUTURE

The technology of computing is evolving rapidly. Although we have some faith that Moore's Law will predict how rapidly computer power will grow, it is futile to attempt to forecast which technologies will fuel that growth. All we know is that computers will be getting smaller and smarter. In this section, we explore the limits of size and intelligence.

Nanobots and Nanotechnology

The prefix "nano" means one billionth. **Nanotechnology** refers to building structures on a scale of one-billionth of a meter, about five times the diameter of a carbon atom. Imagine if you could assemble molecules, or perhaps even atoms, into any sequence and shape you wanted. You could build any drug or, perhaps, even repair or replace body parts that had been injured. You wouldn't need to grow food—you could make it!

IBM first demonstrated the ability to move single atoms more than a decade ago (see Figure 3-21). Scientists have since made great strides in nanotechnology. They have produced a single-molecule machine that converts light energy to work.[39] They have developed feasible designs for nanometer scale motors that are powered by lasers.[40] They have also created wires that are no thicker than a few atoms. When organized into a grid, these wires can produce transistors at their junctions, leading to the promise of computers composed of only a few atoms.[41]

Nanotechnology holds a lot of promise. But, perhaps the greatest promise of all is that of building nanobots, nanometer-sized robots. These robots would be able to perform nano-assembly under the direction of a computer. Conceivably, they would be able to build copies of themselves, and each nanobot built would increase the amount of work that could be done. The concept of self-reproducing computers might be scary, but it's no longer beyond the realm of possibility.

Artificial Intelligence—(When) Will Computers Be Smarter Than You?

What is intelligence? How is it measured? What does it mean to say that you are smarter than a computer?

Intelligence is actually a very complicated concept. Psychologists and educators have argued among themselves for years as to how to measure how smart a person is. And yet, there is no agreement. We might say, for example, that a person is "book smart" but has no "street smarts" or "common sense." Some people can perform amazing feats of arithmetic in their head and yet cannot write a cohesive paragraph. Others can learn to speak many languages, but have little ability to conceptualize or to follow a mathematical proof. In 1983, Gardner proposed a controversial theory of multiple intelligences.[42] He argued that at least eight dif-

FIGURE   3-21

Xenon atoms on a nickel surface

SOURCE: accessed at http://www.rpi.edu /dept/materials/COURSES /NANO/shaw/IBM.gif. Courtesy of International Business Machines. Used with permission.

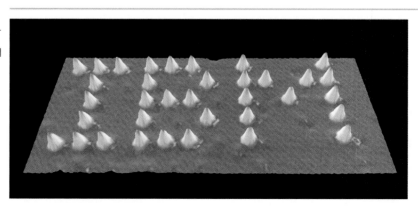

ferent measures of intelligence are needed to describe how smart a person is (see Table 3-11). If Gardner's theory is true, then one person might be smarter than another in one way yet not as smart in another. Nevertheless, you can probably agree that most people are smarter than dogs and that dogs are smarter than computers on most measures of intelligence.

Computer scientists have been trying, unsuccessfully, for years to make computers smart. The key technologies in this field of **artificial intelligence (AI)** have been rule-based systems, neural networks, and evolutionary algorithms. A **rule-based system** is one in which the computer makes decisions based on logical rules. We addressed rule-based systems briefly earlier in this chapter in the descriptions of expert systems shells and inference engines (see Figure 3-16). Rule-based systems have shown some success in limited domains, such as playing chess and making medical diagnoses, where the decisions to be made are limited in scope, the knowledge needed to make those decisions is well defined, and the data bearing upon the decisions are readily available.

Computer scientists have learned to apply **fuzzy logic,** logic based on probabilities, when rules are less clear. Computers use fuzzy logic to make sense of language. For example, when a computer hears the word "understand," it can be reasonably sure that the speaker did not mean "under stand," as those words are unlikely to appear right next to one another. By examining probabilities in this way, a computer can derive probabilities of meaning for phrases, sentences, and then paragraphs.

Other advances in rule-based systems rely on increasing the amount of knowledge that a computer has available in applying the rules. To become smart, a computer needs to be taught knowledge that people take for granted, such as, "One should always carry a box of cookies with the open end up." The Cyc Project is an attempt to codify common sense into basic rules. Doug Lenat, head of Cycorp Inc., believes that the typical person knows about 100 million things about the world. He believes that mapping this knowledge, like mapping the human genome, is doable and will be completed soon.[43]

The **neural network** approach to artificial intelligence operates by mimicking the human brain. Rather than using built-in or programmed rules and an inference engine, a neural network identifies and recognizes patterns. A neural network simulates connections between the nerves in the human brain called neurons that are thought to be responsible for sensation and reasoning. As in the brain, each simulated neuron connects to many other neurons and may simultaneously receive signals from them. The networks "learn" by strengthening or weakening these interconnections.

The *evolutionary algorithm* approach to artificial intelligence operates by observing the success or failure of millions of different sets of rules and approaches to solving a problem. Initially, those rules are randomly generated, but as the computer learns what works and what doesn't, the successful rules are kept and the less successful ones dropped. Then, additional random changes are added, so that the computer's intelligence evolves, as with biological species, through mutation and survival of the fittest.

Despite advances in AI techniques, the consensus among scientists and the general populace is that computers are not very smart. Yet, there is little doubt that they have been

TABLE 3-11

Gardner's eight dimensions of intelligence.

- Linguistic intelligence—"word smart"
- Logical-mathematical intelligence—"number/reasoning smart"
- Spatial intelligence—"picture smart"
- Bodily-Kinesthetic intelligence—"body smart"
- Musical intelligence—"music smart"
- Interpersonal intelligence—"people smart"
- Intrapersonal intelligence—"self smart"
- Naturalist intelligence—"nature smart"

gaining intelligence. Until today, these gains have been almost imperceptible. But, argues Ray Kurzweil, one of the early leaders in AI research, it is usually hard to see progress in the early stages of exponential growth. When progress passes a certain threshold, however, the impact of exponential growth can be astounding. Kurzweil calculates that today's personal computers have barely the power to simulate an insect's brain. However, if Moore's Law continues to hold, as it has for 30 years or more, he calculates that a $1000 computer (in today's dollars) will be able to simulate a mouse's brain by the year 2010 and a human brain sometime around the year 2020. Doubling its power every few years, it would have the capacity to simulate all human brains on earth by the year 2060.[44]

When will computers be smarter than you? It may be sooner than you think!

SUMMARY

Software refers to commands that direct a computer to process information or data. Managers should understand the role of systems software and systems-development software, but they are most affected by business application software, both vertical and horizontal.

Vertical software performs tasks common to a specific industry. It includes packaged software, customized software, and custom software, which differ in the amount of customization the software allows. Horizontal software performs generic tasks common to many types of problems and applications within and across industries. It includes office automation software and some business function applications.

Systems software includes utilities, network and systems management software, and the operating system kernel. Systems utilities operate primarily under user control and provide basic resource management functions. Network and systems management software allows computer professionals to monitor and control computer and network resources. The operating system kernel performs the most basic housekeeping, resource allocation, and resource monitoring functions for a computer.

Systems-development software includes computer languages and computer-aided software engineering (CASE) tools. Computer languages differ in their language translation method, their level of abstraction, whether they are procedural or non-procedural, and whether they are command/data oriented or object oriented. CASE tools help automate the software development process.

In the future, computers will be smaller and smarter. Nanobots will likely assemble structures, perhaps even copies of themselves, out of atoms and molecules. Artificial intelligence software, such as rule-based systems, neural networks, and evolutionary algorithms, combined with increasing computer power, has been predicted to simulate human intelligence by the year 2020.

KEY TERMS

application programming
   interface (API)
artificial intelligence (AI)
client/server model
command/data oriented
   programming languages
commercial off-the-shelf
   (COTS) software
compiler
enterprise resource planning
   (ERP) software
executable module

expert systems shell
fuzzy logic
horizontal software
inference engine
integrator
interpreter
kernel (operating system kernel)
link-loader
load module
machine language
middleware
nanotechnology

neural network
object module
object oriented language
operating system
procedural/non-procedural language
rule-based system
source code
system call
systems utility
value-added reseller (VAR)
vertical software

REVIEW QUESTIONS

1. Define software.
2. Compare and contrast horizontal software and vertical software.
3. What factors should managers consider in evaluating and purchasing vertical software?
4. What are the relative advantages and disadvantages of packaged, customized, and custom software?
5. Why might a company purchase software through a value added reseller (VAR) rather than the software's original manufacturer.
6. Why do software vendors often supply application programming interfaces (APIs) to their products?
7. What options exist for ensuring that an organization's vertical software applications are sufficiently integrated with one another?
8. List two types of horizontal software.
9. What factors should managers consider in evaluating and purchasing horizontal software?
10. Explain how application software uses the operating system kernel.
11. What types of software are typically packaged with the kernel in an operating system?
12. How does a language interpreter differ from a compiler?
13. Why is software development generally quicker and easier in a high-level rather than a low-level language?
14. What is meant by a non-procedural computer language?
15. What does an inference engine do?
16. What is the difference between an object and an object class?
17. Compare and contrast the two-tier client/server model with the three-tier client/server model.
18. Define nanotechnology.
19. List and describe three key technologies in the field of artificial intelligence.
20. Describe Gardner's theory of multiple intelligences.

PAVING OVER PAPERWORK

MINICASE

Construction technician Bill Young remembers when he had to load his truck each day with paper forms before he drove around central Michigan inspecting road construction sites for the Michigan Department of Transportation (MDOT). He had so many boxes "there was no room to even move," recalls Young, sporting a plaid flannel shirt and the deep tan he's acquired working in the field for the last 12 years. Today, the only evidence of paperwork in his truck is a notebook computer mounted on the dash. "Now I'm like a one-man band," Young says. "It's just my laptop and me."

Young is one of hundreds of technicians and inspectors from 37 MDOT offices, 120 local transportation agencies, and 71 private companies in Michigan using FieldManager, a suite of road construction management software developed and co-owned by MDOT and Info Tech, a Gainesville, Florida-based software company. It's a groundbreaking system for a government agency and an industry that has changed little since 1909, when MDOT laid the first mile of concrete highway in the country.

"FieldManager is consistent with my goal of putting more of our state's transportation dollars into preserving our roads and less into administrative overhead," says MDOT Director Greg Rosine. Now, others are following MDOT's lead. FieldManager has been licensed to seven states, two Indian tribes, and 223 private companies.

In the past, a field technician used to go to every work site with a printout of his required Inspector's Daily Report. He would fill it out by hand, tracking thousands of work items and materials for each project—everything from earth excavators to grout. At the end of the day he would hand the report in to the office. Assuming the handwriting was legible, the information on materials used, work completed, and payments required would be copied and hand tallied by as many as five people before the contractor got paid. MDOT needed an army of office workers to verify contractors' work, and inspectors often could handle only one project per season. Larger projects required as many as 20 inspectors onsite each day. Today, MDOT rarely sends more than one field technician to a site. He enters data into a laptop and uploads it to FieldManager, either from the road or back at the office. Office technicians use the information to automatically generate payment estimates. Meanwhile, inspectors and office workers can get up-to-date reports on their projects to settle contractor disputes, amend contracts, check the status of budgets, and make other routine administrative queries.

FieldManager's origins go back to a 1989 program called the Construction Project Record Keeping System (CPRKS—pronounced ka-perks). CPRKS eliminated some transcribing, but it was not integrated with the other major construction management system MDOT used. MDOT's CIO, C. Douglass Couto, hired Info Tech, which had created a PC-based system called Field Book that MDOT thought could be upgraded to replace CPRKS. A financial partnership between a state government department and a software company was unprecedented. Contract negotiations between the Michigan attorney general's office and Info Tech's lawyers dragged on for nearly two years as they searched for a politically acceptable solution. "We had to focus on MDOT's business, which is building roads, not marketing and distributing software to local agencies and consultants," explains Couto.

MDOT and Info Tech stuck through the negotiations because they saw the value of FieldManager to others in the construction business, says Couto. The final agreement allowed MDOT and Info Tech to co-own the source code. Info Tech got the right to sell the software, but had to dedicate licensing fees paid by other states for the further development of FieldManager. The contract also granted Michigan's state and local transportation agencies a perpetual license to the software, mandated that MDOT approve any future changes to it, and paid MDOT royalties from sales to private users. It was a far cry from the standard contract that gave the vendor all control over the software and all the financial benefit from its sales. "If we had done it the usual way, we would have had to pay to make any changes," says Couto.

Couto and Kevin Fox, systems administrator for FieldManager, also had to convince MDOT's legions of end users to embrace the product. "One person took the laptop and said, 'The only thing I'm going to do with this is put it behind my truck and back over it,'" recalls Fox. MDOT overcame the opposition by including users at every stage of development and letting FieldManager sell itself. Today, some of the early resistors are FieldManager evangelists. "If you went to some of those people who had been the most reluctant and tried to take the software away from them now, you'd get hurt," says Daniel Rutenberg, senior systems analyst for the construction and technology division.

SOURCE: Adapted from Stephanie Overby, "Paving over paperwork," *CIO*, 1 February 2002, 82–86. Reprinted through the courtesy of CIO. ©2002, CXO Media Inc. All rights reserved.

Case Questions

Diagnosis

1. What are the information needs at MDOT?

Evaluation

 2. What alternatives does MDOT have to meet these needs?

Design

 3. What are the advantages of FieldManager in meeting these needs?

 4. Why did Couto feel that MDOT needed custom or customized software?

 5. What risks did the MDOT incur in co-developing and co-owning the software?

 6. What benefits, if any, does MDOT derive from co-owning the software?

 7. What hardware is needed for FieldManager to work properly?

 8. Given the construction environment, would you make any changes to the hardware selected?

Implementation

 9. Why did MDOT hire Info Tech to help develop the system?

 10. How did MDOT get its employees to use FieldManager?

 11. What benefits does MDOT derive from using FieldManager?

3-1 CHILDLIFE CENTERS INC.'S PURCHASING PROBLEM

ACTIVITY

Step 1: Read the following scenario.

You have just been hired as the first business manager for Childlife Centers, a chain of ten day care centers for infants, toddlers, and preschool-age children. Jane Stewart began the company ten years ago when she expanded a small preschool in her home into Childlife's first full-service center. Since that time Ms. Stewart has added nine additional centers to the company. During the next five years she expects to double the size of the company by opening ten additional centers. Each center services approximately 60 children and has 12–15 staff members. Until recently Jane used a combination of part-time clerical employees and outside services to meet the administrative needs of the company. Jane's secretary has the only computer owned by the company; she uses it solely for preparing correspondence.

You have been given a budget of $50,000 during this fiscal year to begin computerizing the company's administration. You and your small staff will eventually be responsible for handling personnel data, student information, accounts payable, accounts receivable, payroll, and purchasing. You have hired a consultant to assist you in making the final decisions about appropriate computer hardware and software, but you want to use her time as effectively as possible. Therefore, you want to list the general types of hardware you expect to purchase.

Step 2: Prepare the case for class discussion.

Step 3: Answer each of the following questions, individually or in small groups, as directed by your instructor:

Diagnosis

 1. What are the information needs at Childlife Centers Inc. in the areas for which you are responsible?

Evaluation

 2. What problems are likely to exist with the manual systems that are currently in place?

3. Which of these problems are most critical to the survival of the company?

Design

4. Describe in broad terms your solution to the company's information needs.

5. Describe as specifically as possible the input and output devices that you would recommend.

6. What type of processing and storage would you recommend?

7. Describe as specifically as possible what software you would recommend.

Implementation

8. How should you plan to use the consultant you have hired?

9. What issues should you expect to address when implementing the new system?

Step 4: In small groups, with the entire class, or in written form, share your answers to the questions above. Then answer the following questions:

1. What are the information needs at Childlife Centers Inc.?

2. What are the similarities and differences among the hardware and software options proposed?

3. What types of hardware and software would most effectively meet the company's needs?

3-2 SELECT THE INPUT TECHNOLOGY

ACTIVITY

Step 1: Read the following scenarios. Each describes the data needs of one area of operations in a company or professional organization.

Problem 1: In a law office, lawyers need to keep track of how much time they spend on each activity for every case in which they are involved. They also need to identify and access any documents relevant to the case as quickly as possible when clients call. Some of these documents may be kept electronically, while others need to be kept in paper form. (The office may keep electronic copies.) Some cases are assigned to a single lawyer in the firm, while others may be assigned to several lawyers.

Problem 2: In a hospital while visiting a patient, doctors need to access the patient's chart. This chart contains records of the patient's critical signs, the results of tests performed, and medications administered. The doctor also needs to be able to give orders to the nurses attending the patient and to prescribe medications. Nurses need to access the doctor's orders, to enter critical signs, and to update the record of medication. The pharmacy needs access to the prescriptions the doctor has ordered. The lab needs access to the patient's records in order to update the results of tests performed. Some of the tests, such as cardiograms and x-rays, produce graphical results.

Problem 3: In a warehouse, receivers unload materials from a truck or train car and compare them to the order placed with the supplier. They will note all discrepancies. Stockers move the material to the shelves or bins where they should be stored. At that point, they update the inventory count so that it is available to sales people, assemblers, and others who need to access inventory amounts. Pickers remove inventory from the shelves and place them in a bin for shipment. They respond to a pick list that is generated in response to orders from customers, stores, or assemblers. Picked items should be removed from the inventory count.

Step 2: For each scenario identify what data are required, who requires the data, and who generates and inputs the data.

Step 3: Individually, or in small groups, as directed by your instructor, identify the best two input technologies for each scenario and each type of data. Consider keyboard, voice, bar-coding, scanning, and other technologies covered in this chapter. Identify the pros and cons of each technology and select the one that you think is best.

Step 4: In small groups, with the entire class, or in written form, share your answers to the questions above.

3-3 WRITING SOFTWARE TO DRINK A CAN OF SPRITE

ACTIVITY

Step 1: Imagine this. An alien from outer space who looks quite human and understands your language is a guest of yours for the weekend. However, the alien is not used to your culture. On finding an unopened can of Sprite, he or she asks what to do with it. Naturally, you would like to demonstrate how to open and drink it (right from the can, of course). But since you have just read this chapter on software, you have decided to give the alien verbal instructions instead. If people can instruct computers how to do useful work, surely you can instruct an alien how to drink a can of Sprite.

Step 2: Using between eight and twelve commands, instruct the alien how to open and drink the can of Sprite he or she has found. Number each instruction. You may use instructions of the form, "Repeat instructions 8 through 10 until the can is empty." That, of course would count as one of your instructions. You may also use instructions of the form, "If the tab is on the bottom of the can, continue with instruction 6."

Step 3: Switch your set of instructions with a classmate. Evaluate your classmate's instructions. Try to find bugs in his or her commands. Remember that a bug is a flaw in software. For example, your classmate might have instructed the alien to lift the tab. However, if you lift the tab on a can without holding the can down with the other hand, the can will simply rise, not open. Exchange your evaluation with your classmate.

Step 4: Rewrite the instructions using between 24 and 36 commands and considering your classmate's input.

Step 5: Exchange your set of instructions with a different classmate. Evaluate your classmate's instructions. Try to find bugs in his or her commands. Exchange your evaluation with your classmate.

Step 6: Answer the following questions on your own. Then, as directed by your instructor, share your views with the class.

1. Does increasing the level of detail make it easier or harder to write good instructions?
2. Why is it hard to write bug-free code?

3-4 SOFTWARE FOR PARTY PLANNERS PLUS

ACTIVITY

Step 1: Read the following scenario.

Party Planners Plus is a six-person organization that provides party planning services. Jessica Tanner began the company in 1985 in the basement of her home. She offered planning services for a variety of social events, including weddings, anniversary parties, Bar and Bat Mitzvah celebrations, graduation parties, and major birthday parties. She advised her clients about the party's menu, decorations, and entertainment; ordered invitations, flowers, catering services, rental tables and chairs, party favors, tents, and tablecloths and napkins; set up the party location; and provided necessary staff, such as serving personnel, valets, coatroom attendants, and entertainers. As her business increased, Jessica added part-time and then full-time employees. She moved from merely ordering some supplies, such as unusual centerpieces, to actually hiring a craftsperson to make them onsite. When the company was seven years old, Jessica moved Party Planners Plus into a small storefront office.

In the early days of her business Jessica managed the flow of paperwork manually. Basically it involved making lists of orders, recording payments to vendors of the supplies, and tracking payments by her clients. Two years ago she bought an Apple Macintosh computer to assist with the paperwork. She purchased a good word processing package, which she used to replace much of the manual information recording. Still, the paperwork took a great deal of time and provided her with very little information about her costs and profits and minimal assistance in setting appropriate prices. She knows, however, that she should be able to use the computer for much more support in meeting her information needs.

Step 2: Prepare the case for class discussion.

Step 3: Answer each of the following questions, individually or in small groups, as directed by your instructor.

Diagnosis

1. What do you think are Jessica Tanner's information needs?
2. How are these information needs currently being met?

Evaluation

3. What problems exist with the current methods?

Design

4. What software should Tanner purchase to meet these information needs?

Implementation

5. Should Tanner hire a consultant to help her select and install software to meet her information needs?
6. What purchases should receive the highest priority?
7. Which purchases can be delayed if money is tight?

Step 4: In small groups, with the entire class, or in written form, share your answers to the questions above. Then answer the following questions:

8. What issues did you consider in identifying the information needs of Party Planners Plus?
9. What types of software should receive the highest priority?
10. What other issues should Tanner consider in purchasing software for her company?

3-5 DEALING WITH SUSPECTED SOFTWARE PIRACY

ACTIVITY

Step 1: Read the following scenario.

You work in a company of about 600 employees. One day, while working on a project, you conclude that you need to use a small database management system. After doing some research, you conclude that Microsoft Access is the product you would like to use. You call your rep at the Technical Services Department.

"John," you say, "Will you please order me a copy of Microsoft Access?"

"No problem," he replies. "We have a copy of the distribution CD on the network. Let me mail you instructions on how to install it on your computer."

"Thanks, John. I didn't realize that we had a site license."

"Well, we don't exactly. But we do have quite a few licenses, and I'm sure that not everyone is using their copy."

"In that case," you say, "I'd prefer you order me a licensed copy."

"I'm afraid we're out of budget. Really, don't worry about it. We do this all the time. I've had some misgivings about it myself, but the boss says it's OK."

Step 2: Identify your alternatives. Be sure to consider such actions as going directly to the president of the company and calling the Microsoft software piracy hotline anonymously.

Step 3: Answer each of the following questions, individually or in small groups, as directed by your instructor.

1. For each alternative, who benefits and who is harmed?

2. From the ethical principles of least harm, rights and duties, professional responsibilities, self-interest and utilitarianism, consistency, and respect, how would you evaluate each alternative?

3. What course of action would you take? Why?

IS ON THE WEB

Exercise 1: The Web page for Chapter 3 will direct you to several articles that relate to hardware or software. Select one of the articles and describe the technology it addresses. Then summarize the article's opinion or present your opinion about how this technology affects a particular business, business in general, or society as a whole.

Exercise 2: You have a friend who recently started a small interior design business. Your friend has told you that she wishes to purchase a personal computer to help keep track of her accounts payable, accounts receivable, orders, and customers. Your friend knows that you are taking a course in information systems and wants your advice about which computer and what software she should buy. Use the Web to learn more about the software and hardware she will need and then to compare products. Compare and contrast three computers on their relative speed, features and options, price, and any other relevant factors. Compare and contrast the features of three software packages that might meet her needs. Then write a brief review of your findings for your friend so that she can understand the pros and cons of each option.

RECOMMENDED READINGS

Hennessy, John L., and David A Patterson. *Computer Architecture: A Quantitative Approach.* 3rd ed. San Francisco: Morgan Kaufmann Publishers, 2002.

Meyers, B. Craig, and Patricia Oberndorf. *Managing Software Acquisition: Open Systems and COTS.* Boston: Addison Wesley Longman, 2001.

Negnevitsky, Michael. *Artificial Intelligence: A Guide to Intelligent Systems.* Boston: Addison Wesley Longman, 2001.

Norton, Peter, and H. A. Clark. *Peter Norton's New Inside the PC.* Indianapolis, IN: Sams Publishing, 2001.

Sebesta, Robert W. *Concepts of Programming Languages.* 5th ed. Boston: Addison Wesley Longman, 2001.

Vacca, John R. *The Essential Guide to Storage Area Networks.* Upper Saddle River, NJ: Prentice Hall PTR, 2001.

The following publications provide regular features about computer hardware and software:

Computerworld, Information Week, Software Magazine.

NOTES

1. Jeanette Brown, "Prada Gets Personal," *Business Week,* 18 March 2002, EB8. "Prada Personalizing Customer Experience at New York Epicenter Store Using Texas Instruments RFID Smart Labels," *Business Wire,* 23 April 2002, 2315. IconMedialab, "Texas Instruments & IconMedialab Bring Experience to RFID Retail Solutions," http://www.iconmedialab.com/our_offer /industries/ICON-TIRFID.pdf, accessed on May 31, 2002. Ideo, "Staff Devices & Dressing Rooms for Prada: Information Architecture of High-Fashion Store," http://www.ideo.com/portfolio /re.asp?x=50120, accessed at May 31, 2002.

2. Ken Kirzner, "2D Bar Codes Make Their Mark, for Life," *Frontline Solutions,* May 2001, 18–19.

3. "Major Restoration for Dental Claims," *Health Management Technology,* September 2000, 60.

4. Ken Krizner, "Talking Efficiency," *Frontline Solutions,* April 2002, 16–21.

5. Jerry Zeidenberg, "Multimedia Computing: A Virtual Reality by 2001," *Computing Canada,* 9 November 1992, 17.

6. Renee M. Kruger, "ShopKo's Information Edge," *Discount Merchandiser,* January 1999, 74–75.

7. Stewart Deck, "United Taps Massively Parallel Application," *Computerworld,* 28 June 1999, 66.

8. Ibid. Alicia Hills Moore, "A U.S. Comeback in Electronics," *Fortune,* 20 April 1992, 77–86. Stephan Ohr, "Hot DSP Market Tantalizes Analog and Digital IC Makers," *Electronic Business,* July 1992, 106–109.

9. Ray Kurzweil, *The Age of Spiritual Machines* (New York: Viking/Penguin Putnam, 1999): 25.

10. Michael Kanellos, Moore says Moore's Law to Hit Wall, *CNET News.com,* 30 September 1997, accessed at http://news.com.com/2100-1001-203750.html?legacy=cnet on 3 June 2002.

11. Thomas H. Lee, A Vertical Leap for Microchips, *Scientific American,* January 2002, 52–59.

12. James Detar, A New Dimension to Matrix Chips, *Investor's Business Daily,* 10 May 2002, accessed at http://www.matrixsemi.com/files /10219291820.pdf on 3 June 2002.

13. See, for example, "Computers Take Quantum Leap," *Signal,* February 2002, 6. "EM Noise Cuts Herald Quantum Computing," EE Times, 25

February 2002, 14. "Crystal Traps Light," *Dr. Dobb's Journal,* April 2002, 16.

14. Lorraine Cosgrove Ware, "Managing Storage: Keeping Up with Data," *CIO Research Report,* 7 March 2002, accessed at www.cio.com on 30 May 2002.

15. Carol Hildebrand, "What Elephant?," *CIO,* 15 May 2002, 102-108.

16. Paul Sheldon Foote, and Malini Krishnamurthi, "Forecasting Using Data Warehousing Model: Wal-Mart's Experience," *The Journal of Business Forecasting Methods & Systems,* fall 2001, 13–17.

17. Kim Hyun-chul, "The Passing of a Pint-Sized Friend," *Joins.com,* 25 January 2002. The data are attributed to the Korean-based polyester film manufacturer, SKC Limited.

18. Cybernetics, http://www.cybernetics.com /tape_backup/dtf/petasite.html, accessed on 3 June 2002.

19. Todd Enterprises, http://www.toddent.com /drm-7000.htm, accessed on 3 June 2002.

20. Andrew Conry-Murray, Content Provider Spins Gold from a Storage Area Network, *Network Magazine,* March 2001, 64–69.

21. For a history and explanation of the technology, see Sergei S. Orlov, "Volume Holographic Data Storage," *Communications of the ACM,* November 2000, 47–54.

22. Andy Vuong, "Longmont, Colo.-Based Firm to Unveil New Holographic Storage Technology," *Knight Ridder Tribune Business News,* 8 April 2002, 1.

23. http://www.c-3d.net/tech_frameset.html, accessed on June 3, 2002.

24. Russel Kay, "True 3-D without Glasses," *Computerworld,* 30 April 2001, 53.

25. Russel Kay, "3-D Vision Speaks Volumes," *Computerworld,* 1 April 2002, 44.

26. Amy Helen Johnson, "Helping Web Sites Take Phone Calls," *Computerworld,* 5 February 2001, 65.

27. http://www.accenture.com, accessed on 2 June 2002.

28. Julia King, "Q&A: Bob Cottam, IT Chief for the Olympics, Wants a Perfect 10," *Computerworld,* 11 February 2002, 8.

29. "ITI to Be Value Added Reseller for NCR's Payment Solutions and Check Imaging Business," *Item Processing Report,* 23 May 2002, 1.

30. http://www.chemicalinventory.com/, accessed on 11 September 2002.

31. http://www.campagne.com/gmpro.html, accessed on 11 September 2002.

32. http://www.hrmsoftware.com, accessed on 2 June 2002.

33. http://www.adobe.com/products/acrobat/read-step.html and http://www.real.com accessed on 3 June 2002.

34. *United States vs. Microsoft,* 87 F. Supp. 2d 30 (D.D.C. 2000).

35. Robert Klepper, "Third and Fourth Generation Language Productivity Differences," *Communications of the ACM,* 38 (September 1995): 69–79.

36. Elizabeth Heichler, "Railway Switches Tracks to Objects," *Computerworld,* 26 June 1995, 71.

37. Doug Bartholomew, "Objects Take Off," *Information Week,* 26 February 1996, 14–16.

38. Justine Brown, "PCs Go on a Diet," *CIO,* 1 May 2001, 154-160. "Citrix Case Studies: Matrix Rehabilitation," http://www.citrix.com/press /news/profiles/matrix.htm, accessed on 30 May 2002.

39. Elizabeth Wilson, "Molecular Machine," *Chemical & Engineering News,* 13 May 2002, 6.

40. Mike Martin, "Lasers Power Nanomotors," *Insight on the News,* 27 May 2002, 29.

41. David P. Hamilton, "Technology (A Special Report)—The Nanotechnician: How Small Can Computer Chips Get? According to Charles Lieber, a Few Atoms Are All You Need," *Wall Street Journal,* 13 May 2002, R17.

42. Howard Gardner, *Frames of Mind: The Theory of Multiple Intelligences* (New York: Basic, 1983).

43. Gary H. Anthes, "Computerizing Common Sense," *Computerworld,* 8 April 2002, 49. Michael Hiltzik, "A.I. Reboots," Technology Review, March 2002, 46–55.

44. Ray Kurzweil, *The Age of Spiritual Machines* (New York: Viking/The Penguin Group, 1999): 102–105.

4

Database Management Systems

LEARNING OBJECTIVES

After completing Chapter 4, you will be able to:

- Define database and database management system.
- Describe eight functions that database management systems should provide.
- Define and describe how organizations use metadata.
- Explain why information systems seek to preserve transaction atomicity.
- Explain why managers use data warehouses and data marts.
- Explain how database management systems help make Web pages dynamic.
- Use the entity-relationship model to present the relationship among data items in a pictorial fashion.
- Describe four distribution architectures and the advantages and disadvantages of each for managers.
- Describe the five database models and the advantages and disadvantages of each for managers.
- List the responsibilities of a database administrator and data administrator.

118

Sherwin-Williams Builds a Data Warehouse

Sherwin-Williams has been manufacturing and selling paint and painting supplies since its formation in 1866. It achieved annual sales of more than $5 billion by selling its products at more than 2,500 company-operated stores in North and Central America and about 15,000 third-party retailers worldwide, including Wal-Mart, Target, and The Home Depot.

Keeping track of the information needed to make intelligent business decisions was challenging. Consider that Sherwin-Williams carries 300 different brands and more than 130,000 different products. Because the company grew partly through the acquisition of smaller companies, many of its transaction and control systems were also acquired and not well integrated. For example, at one point it had seven order entry systems running on different types of computers and located in different states and countries. Managers somehow needed to consolidate and organize the data so that they could ask questions such as, "What are our margins by brand and by customer?" and "How do we stack up against the competition by brand within region?" Without adequate business intelligence, Sherwin-Williams' managers couldn't hope to price their products correctly, nor could they effectively plan production or order supplies.

Sherwin-Williams' solution was to build a data warehouse, a database that would hold and organize all the information that the company collected.[1]

Organizing and centralizing a company's data might seem like a good idea, but it is not as easy as it might appear. First, the company's management needs to decide what data it needs to collect and how those data should be used. Then standards must be put into place to ensure the consistency in meaning of data coming from different sources. You might be surprised at the results of a recent survey that showed, for example, that only 20 percent of companies use the same customer code to identify a given customer among all their product lines and functions.[2] Finally, the data must be stored in such a way that the company's managers and operational employees can easily retrieve and manipulate the data. Database management systems can help satisfy these needs.

In this chapter we first answer the questions, "What is a database management system," "What are its functions," and "How is it used?" Next, we address how to organize data for storage in a database. Then, we examine and compare alternative technologies underlying different types of database management systems. Finally, we look at the management infrastructure necessary to support the effective use of the data and database resources.

WHAT IS A DATABASE MANAGEMENT SYSTEM (DBMS)?

A **database** is an organized collection of related data. The key terms here are "organized" and "related." A collection of data is not *per se* a database. Organized means that you can easily find the data you want. For example, a file cabinet, with folders sorted alphabetically, is a database; a bunch of papers stuffed into a drawer is not. A collection of data about the books you own and your friends' telephone numbers is not a database because these data do not relate to one another. Instead, they form two separate collections, or two databases. Many organizations consider all of their organized data part of a database because of their potential interrelationship.

What databases does Sherwin-Williams have? It has data about its customers and products. It also has data about prior orders, which clearly relate to both its customer and product data. It probably also has great deal of data about its suppliers. Whether these data form a database or databases depends on the extent to which they are organized in a meaningful and systematic way and the degree to which they are related.

Managers and employees often use computerized databases, those stored on computer-readable media, such as disks, diskettes, tapes, or CD-ROMs. Computerization of data doesn't ensure that they form a database. For example, many companies use word processors to computerize their correspondence; however, they organize these documents in a haphazard fashion and should not consider them to be a database. Many companies keep both computerized and non-computerized, or manual, databases. For example, Sherwin-Williams maintains a computerized customer database, but it might keep a manual database of employee training materials.

A **database management system (DBMS)** comprises programs to store, retrieve, and otherwise manage a computerized database and to provide interfaces to application programs and to non-programming users. Today, every company developing serious application software should use one or more DBMSs for its data management functions. DBMSs are a key component of almost all vertical application software.

FUNCTIONS OF A DATABASE MANAGEMENT SYSTEM

Managers find DBMSs valuable because they perform the following functions:

- Storing and retrieving data
- Managing metadata
- Limiting and controlling redundant data in multiple systems

- Supporting simultaneous data sharing
- Providing transaction atomicity
- Providing backup and recovery services
- Providing authorization and security services
- Enforcing business rules

How can managers at Sherwin-Williams use DBMSs? The following sections examine their use for each of these functions.

Storing and Retrieving Data

A database management system makes it easier for managers and employees to store and retrieve data. People using a DBMS can permanently store and retrieve data without running any other programs or doing any computer programming. Users can create data-entry forms, such as the one in Figure 4-1, that automatically check the validity of entered data. Managers and other users can retrieve data sorted in a pre-specified way or according to criteria that they specify at the time of retrieval. Jody Schucart, president of the Hawaiian retail store The Pocketbook Man, uses a database to track customers by age, sex, and nationality and purchases by dress size, color, and style.[3]

A store manager at Sherwin-Williams using the company's DBMS can secure any information she wants about a customer. For example, she can make a simple query to the database to identify what a particular customer last purchased. She might also request a sales history, showing subtotals by product category. If the company has a sale on a particular product, the store manager can identify all customers in her region that purchased that product within the past year.

Managers might require programmers to quickly modify programs that use data. Before DBMSs existed, each program stored its data in data files. Programmers typically compressed different types of data, such as dollar amounts, customer codes, or invoice numbers, in different ways to minimize the amount of file storage and maximize speed of retrieval. Other programmers writing code to access the same files had to know their compression format. The result was many errors, especially in large, complex systems. An efficient file format for one application might not be efficient for others. If programmers needed to change the file format

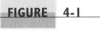

FIGURE 4-1

DBMSs can generate data-entry screens, such as this contact management data entry screen generated by Microsoft Access.

Contacts	
First Name	Contact ID 1
Last Name	Title
Company	Work Phone
Dear	Work Extension
Address	Mobile Phone
	Fax Number
City	
State/Province	
Postal Code	
Country	

Calls...   Dial...   Page: 1 2

Record: 1 of 1

for some data, they would have to change all programs addressing that data, often rewriting programs if the nature of the data changed. For example, if the space required for the customer zip code increased from five to nine digits, programmers probably would have had to modify any programs that accessed the customer files, whether or not they used the zip code.

Now, using a DBMS, the programmer specifies only what data to store or retrieve. The DBMS decides the data's physical organization and representation on the storage medium. The database sees the **physical view** of the data but presents a **logical view** to the user and programmer. The physical view includes how the data are compressed and formatted, which data are stored near each other, and which indexes are created to simplify and speed finding data on the storage medium. The logical view organizes and presents data elements in ways that managers and other users find helpful. As a result, if an organization changes the form of its data, it usually doesn't have to rewrite its programs.

In the late 1990s, companies had to modify many programs, written long before the year 2000, because these old programs allocated only two digits for all date fields, assuming that the first two digits were 19. Programs written around a DBMS, however, were much easier to fix, as data administrators simply increased the space for data fields to four digits and added 1900 to all existing two-digit dates in the database.

Managing Metadata

Metadata are data about data. For example, the fact that a company's invoice numbers are six digits long, with the first digit being either a 1 or 3, is metadata. Metadata about zip codes might indicate that these codes have nine digits, the last four of which are optional, that leading zeros in the code must always be displayed, and that when nine digits are displayed, a dash must be shown between the fifth and sixth digit. Also, metadata might indicate that zip codes in a report should be titled "Zip" and centered, but that zip codes in a data entry screen should be titled "Zip Code:" and shown right justified.

Metadata also have a management purpose. They provide a context for understanding how the data were collected, what they mean, and how they are used. For example, a manufacturer might have a database entry for quarterly sales of a particular product. A manager using such data might need to know, for example, whether the sales represent units or dollars, and, if in dollars, whether foreign sales are converted at the time of sale or at the end of the quarter. The manager might also want to know whether or not returns are subtracted from the sales or kept as a separate entry. If subtracted from the sales, were they subtracted in the quarter when the return was made or in the quarter when the sale was made?

Metadata also include the logical views of data called schemas and subschemas. A **schema** represents an integrated, enterprise-wide view of how data relate to one another. For example, a schema might indicate that customers have shipping and billing addresses, and that they are billed with invoices that have invoice numbers, discount rates, and invoice lines with part numbers and extended prices.

Managers can focus employees on the elements of data that are most relevant to their work, can hide sensitive data, or can present unusual relationships among data in views called **subschemas.** For example, they might create views that eliminate the sensitive discount rate code for employees who shouldn't see it. Workers in shipping might not see a billing address, only a shipping address for customers. Warehouse workers might see invoice lines as a pick list, with shelf locations rather than part numbers.

The **data dictionary** refers to the part of a database that holds its metadata and acts as a CASE tool for automating programming (see Chapters 3 and 9). Figure 4-2 illustrates the contents of a hypothetical data dictionary entry. Many data dictionaries contain information about what programs, reports, and data entry screens use or refer to each data element. This information makes it relatively easy to analyze the impact of changing the characteristics of data. Data dictionaries are also available as stand-alone products that can connect to a number of different databases. Top-level managers use such data dictionaries along with their DBMS's data dictionaries to maintain a consolidated view of data across all their databases.

Why are metadata important? Metadata allow a program to know enough about an item of data that it accesses, such as an invoice number or zip code, to store and display it properly. Metadata allow a DBMS to check for data entry errors. Data managers can request metadata reports to identify changes in the database structure or to compare user needs against existing data. They can query the data dictionary to determine the creation or update date of a particular data item, find what system it came from, and what tools have accessed it. If a manager would like to change an element of data or access an element of data, he can see who controls access or approves changes to it.

Limiting and Controlling Redundant Data in Multiple Systems

Companies often collect and store the same data in two or more different information systems. For example, a company that manufactures and sells office equipment might maintain information about its customers in three places: a service system that tracks customer service requests and mails service bulletins; an accounts receivable system that tracks the amount that customers owe the company; and a sales system that assists its sales agents in identifying customers who might need additional equipment. This duplication of computer storage not only wastes storage capacity, but also wastes time and might cause inconsistencies in data entry. For example, if a customer moves to a new location, employees must reenter the customer's address in all three systems. If the customer told a sales agent about the address change, the agent might forget to inform the people in charge of the service or

FIGURE   4-2
 	
A data dictionary holds metadata. This hypothetical entry shows metadata for the data item Customer Payment Amount.
	Attribute of: CUSTOMER-PAYMENT
	
	Data input screen:
	    Prompt: Amount of Payment:
	    Edit(s): >0
	                <100,000
	    Type: Currency
	    Display: $99,999.99
	
	Report heading:
	    Payment
	    Amount

Aliases: CUST-PAYMENT, CHECK-AMOUNT, CPAMT

Appears in the following views: ACCTS-PAYBLE, CUST-RECRD, PAYMNT-RCRD

Appears in the following programs: ARP-84X, ARP-85Z, CUS-RECPT-PROC, 154X3T22, 123X4T23, P94.XX.2;2

Security level (without view): 12

Owner(s): John Marshall

Help prompt: Enter payment amount without dollar signs or commas.

Integrity:
        On creation of CUSTOMER-PAYMENT:
                Update TOTAL-PAYMENTS = TOTAL-PAYMENTS + CUSTOMER-PAYMENT-
                        AMOUNT
        On update:
                Update TOTAL-PAYMENTS = TOTAL-PAYMENTS + change

accounts receivable systems. The company might then have two or more inaccurate addresses for the customer.

A DBMS reduces the need to store redundant data because it easily joins together information about different business components. As illustrated in Figure 4-3, Sherwin-Williams needs to store only a customer number in the data it retains about an order. If a manager requests a list of orders sorted by customer name, a DBMS would look up the customer number in the customer contact list to retrieve the detailed customer data, such as the company name, contact name, and phone number, associated with each order. In the example shown, use of a customer number saves repeating the customer name, its telephone number, and, conceivably, other information, such as its address, in the records for Orders 567891 and 567892. Similarly, a DBMS makes it easy to combine this general customer information with information unique to other systems. For example, it could combine the customer address with her unpaid invoices for accounts receivable, her previous orders for the sales agent, and her calling record for the service agent. The DBMS stores the customer information only once, reducing redundancy and eliminating the possibility of inconsistent records.

Supporting Simultaneous Data Sharing

Without sophisticated control procedures, errors arise when two people or programs attempt to access and update the same data at the same time. Consider the following example. John and Mary call the same national mail order company to order two sweaters in style #1037. The clerk handling John's order determines that there is an inventory of three such sweaters. Simultaneously, the clerk handling Mary's order obtains the same information. John and Mary, both believing that the two sweaters they want are in stock, request immediate shipment. As John's clerk registers the sale, the computer completes the transaction by changing the available stock to one. At the same time, Mary's clerk registers the sale, also changing the available stock to one. Although the available stock can't fill both orders, such processing allows the clerks and customers to think that the orders had been fulfilled.

Concurrency control describes the proper management of simultaneous attempts to update a database by multiple users or multiple software programs. DBMSs employ a variety of techniques to ensure concurrency control.[4] In critical applications, such as disbursing cash or reserving inventory, a DBMS will allow only one user to update the spe-

---

FIGURE 4-3

A DBMS allows information from different tables to be joined. This example shows how customers and their orders combine to provide the customer telephone number and the order date in the same row.

Order Information

Order #	Customer #	Order Date	Order Status	Ship Date
567891	397	02/07/02	1	02/08/02
567892	221	02/07/02	2	
etc.	...	...	...	...

Customer Information

Customer #	Company Name	Contact	Phone
221	Al Smith Painting	Alan Smith	312-555-2189
397	Arlington Builders	Joe Hudson	617-555-3838
etc.	...	...	...

Combined Information Sorted by Company

Order #	Order Date	Company Name	Phone
567892	02/07/02	Al Smith Painting	312-555-2189
567891	02/07/02	Arlington Builders	617-555-3838
etc.	...	...	...

cific data at a given time. For example, it would show both John's and Mary's clerks the inventory of three sweaters. However, when both clerks decide to reserve two of the sweaters, the computer would only allow one update to proceed. Then, before processing the second update, it would again read the inventory data and would find that the request for two sweaters exceeded the inventory of one and inform the clerk.

Providing Transaction Atomicity

Most business transactions change a database in several ways. Consider what happens, for example, when a banking customer transfers $100 from a savings to a checking account. The bank must reduce the customer's checking account balance, increase her savings account balance, and record the transaction. If the DBMS reduces the checking balance or increases the savings balance and the computer crashes before it changes the other balance, then the balances will be inconsistent, resulting in an unwarranted and undesired loss for the bank or the customer.

Atomicity is the concept that a transaction cannot be split into smaller parts. The term originated at a time when people thought that a physical atom was indivisible. In practice, a DBMS must split a transaction into its parts, as it cannot simultaneously perform multiple updates to the data. However, it must treat these parts as if they are components of a unified whole. If any part of the transaction fails, it must appear as if the transaction never occurred. This may require the DBMS to undo some previous updates.

Most DBMSs provide tools to identify and correct incomplete transactions before they can cause damage.[5] For example, the DBMS can create a temporary record, known as a *log*, at the start of each transaction. It adds to the log upon each successful update and closes this record when the transaction is complete. After a system failure, the DBMS uses the log to trace the transaction process and undo all partially completed transactions. Incorporating such security into every program that processes multiple-update transactions, rather than using a DBMS, is exceedingly complex and difficult.

Software developers can use a product called a **transaction processing monitor (TP monitor)** to enforce transaction atomicity. Table 4-1 lists some basic functions of a TP monitor. Developers typically use TP monitors instead of the TP features of a DBMS when writing software that simultaneously updates several uncoordinated DBMSs.

Providing Backup and Recovery Services

Many databases are much too large to be backed up as normal files. Multi-terabyte databases are not uncommon and some companies are anticipating petabyte-sized databases. These databases would take hours to copy to backup disks or tapes. Companies cannot afford to operate without their databases for so long. They need to be able to back up these databases while they are being used and changed. Database management systems typically provide several options for dealing with this problem:

- Some DBMS products offer the ability to operate in parallel on two storage devices. Periodically, the database administrator detaches one of the storage devices from the database application to create a back-up copy. Afterwards, the DBMS updates this storage device using the database log from the storage device that remained attached.

- Some DBMS products create a small, temporary, update database during the backup process. The main database remains unchanged during the backup. The DBMS uses both the main database and the temporary database to answer queries so that the user always "sees" current versions of the data. After the backup finishes, the temporary database brings the main database up-to-date.

	Function	Benefits Provided
TABLE 4-1 TP monitors provide a range of functions that simplify and coordinate transaction processing on distributed systems.	Enforce data integrity and atomic updates.	When transactions affect data on multiple computers a TP monitor maintains data integrity if some computers involved in the transaction fail or the network fails.
	Log transaction errors	Error logs provide data for reports that managers use to diagnose unreliable processes and technicians use to identify network hardware or software problems.
	Provide queue services that allow business applications to accept transactions faster than the database can handle them for short periods.	This feature is particularly important for web-based transactions whose volumes can't be reliably predicted (as opposed to local transactions limited by the number of terminals).
	Provide a common language for transactions that affect different databases.	They provide a common interface that databases from different vendors use to pass data among themselves.
	Prioritize requests for database services.	They ensure reliable response times for critical applications.
	Provide centralized management of distributed applications.	They ensure coordination among the applications.

Providing Authorization and Security Services

Organizations must control who sees the data they collect. For example, managers often treat salary data, personnel evaluations, and financial information as confidential. In addition, managers must protect accounting information from tampering and fraud.

Most DBMSs can limit who has access to specific data. A DBMS makes a prescribed subschema, or logical view of a portion of the database, available for certain classes of users or applications. For example, most users may see a view of employee data that contains job title, length of service, and name of health care insurance, but does not contain salary information. Managers can also create views for metadata. Such views, for example, might prevent certain users from knowing whether the database contains salary information.

In addition to views that hide data, most DBMSs allow views of aggregated data or joined data. For example, a manager might authorize a user to view average salary by department but not individual salary data. Managers must exercise care in allowing statistical views of data.[6] Sophisticated users can often infer detailed data by asking dividing and overlapping queries. Joined views can combine data that users often view together. For example, a manager might use a view that combines customer name with data relating to the customer's sales representative; the manager will see the name, telephone, and address of each customer's sales representative as if the DBMS stored them with the customer. Non-DBMS systems generally can't hide data from all users because users have access to the entire record of data. DBMSs make it easier to control access to systems with hundreds of programs written by different programmers. They centralize the access control function, dramatically simplifying software development and providing additional power to a data administrator.

Enforcing Business Rules

A DBMS enforces rules that ensure related data are logically consistent. For example, assigning a sales representative to every customer expresses a relationship between two types of data: customer and sales representative. Without a DBMS, each program that modifies information about either sales representatives or customers would have to check that the assignment of sales representative to customer occurred. For example, a program deleting a sales representative would have to check that all of his customers had first been reassigned. Deleting a sales representative and thus leaving some customers without a representative breaks the assignment rule. When a DBMS modifies data, it can enforce such rules, simplifying the programs and ensuring that a programmer or program designer cannot violate business rules due to ignorance.

DATABASE APPLICATIONS

Because a DBMS performs so many different critical functions, it is central to many different types of business applications. In this section, we examine three typical uses of database management systems: supporting application software, warehousing data, and serving dynamic Web pages.

Supporting Application Software

In today's world, a database management system is at the heart of almost every business software application. The reasons are simple:

- A database provides a common, consistent repository for organizational information; and
- A DBMS reduces programming time and effort by performing many of the functions that application programs would otherwise have to perform.

Common Repository

Without a consistent and organized repository of data, every application program would be responsible for coordinating with every other application that needs to access the data it collects or uses. When a customer places an order, for example, the order-taking software performs the primary task of recording the order and communicating with the customer. However, the information associated with the order is also used by the billing program, the program that schedules production of the product ordered, the program that orders supplies necessary to produce the product, the program that arrange for shipping, and many others. Building such programs in the absence of a coordinated data repository is nearly impossible because there are too many interactions among the programs.

DBMS Functions

Because a DBMS provides many of the functions that programmers would otherwise have to develop on their own, a DBMS increases programmer productivity tremendously. For example, programmers do not have to worry about indexing data for rapid retrieval. They don't have to perform validity checks on data added to the database—the rules built into the database will perform the necessary checks and return an error code if the data are invalid. Programmers do not have to build code to recover data if the system crashes in the middle of a transaction. Every one of the eight functions addressed in the section on database functions eliminates a concern for application programmers.

Because a DBMS allows users to retrieve data easily from a database without any programming, business applications don't have to anticipate every conceivable use of the data they collect. Programmers build the most common and useful reports directly into the application's user interface, but managers can analyze the data in many other ways using the DBMS directly. As a result, application programs are smaller and more manageable.

The DBMS/Application Interface

The **ODBC (Open Database Connectivity)** standard allows application programs to access databases through a DBMS in a uniform way. The ODBC standard specifies a protocol for "connecting" a program to the DBMS and then issuing commands or messages to store or retrieve data. The ODBC standard makes it relatively easy to write programs that will work equally well with the DBMS products of different vendors.

Warehousing Data

A **data warehouse** is an enterprise-wide database designed to support business intelligence and management decision making rather than operational needs. While a data warehouse might contain copies of some current transaction data, it mostly contains historic and summary data aggregated at various levels and along various dimensions. For example, it might contain daily, weekly, and monthly sales by store, state/province, country, and region. It might also aggregate sales by product, product group, and business unit. It might aggregate sales by type of customer as well.

The China Merchants Bank, headquartered in Shenzhen, uses a data warehouse to analyze the profile and preferences of its customers and the performance of its departments.[7] Interfoods of America, the franchisee of 166 Popeyes Chicken & Biscuit restaurants, uses a data warehouse to compare the performance of individual franchises and groups of franchises by region. Interfoods also uses the data warehouse to compare inventory, costs, and other transactions across the company and credits the warehouse for enabling the company to reduce food costs by more than 2 percent in some areas.[8]

Why would an organization create a separate database for business intelligence and analysis when most of the information it desires can be obtained directly from its operational databases? It would seem that a data warehouse would add to a company's storage needs and could lead to inconsistencies among the data being analyzed and the data being used for day-to-day operations. One reason for building a data warehouse is to allow the operational database to run more smoothly. No company wants to keep its customers waiting because its DBMS is busy retrieving large volumes of data for a complicated analysis started by some manager in the marketing department. Also, companies like to keep their operational database slim by removing transactions that are no longer necessary for business operations. However, these transactions have historical value for management analysis and, therefore, should be kept within the data warehouse. Companies that have multiple operational databases find that a data warehouse is useful for consolidating data. Finally, data warehouses make it simpler to do management analyses because data are summarized and aggregated as they are entered into the data warehouse.

Data extraction is a primary concern of data warehouse managers. How often should they move data from production systems to the data warehouse? Extracting the data places an extra-heavy processing burden on the production systems. Warehouse managers must implement systems that identify inconsistencies in data extracted from different locations. Extraction of data from non-DBMS systems complicates loading the data warehouse. Often the data must be cleaned and transformed before being loaded into the data warehouse. Software products called *ETL* (extract/transform/load) *products* simplify such extraction. The Automobile Association of the United Kingdom (AA) used Evoke Software's ETL product (Evoke) to analyze and extract 5,000 data attributes from more than 20 data sources and load them into its data warehouse. For example, Evoke determined that AA spelled beige twelve different ways in its different systems. Without an ETL product such as Evoke, the company would not be able identify the different spellings and automatically transform them into a common spelling before loading them into its data warehouse. Therefore, its market researchers would not have been able to analyze vehicle makes, models, and colors accurately.[9] Guinness Limited, the British brewer, found it easier and quicker to use ActaWorks, an ETL product from Acta Technology, to extract its data from its ERP systems and load them into its data warehouse than to use the software provided by the ERP vendor, SAP.[10]

Many tools, including data mining and online analytic processing tools, exist to help managers use the data collected in a data warehouse effectively. *Data mining* describes the process of identifying patterns in large masses of data. Bharti Televentures, a $306 million (Rs 1,500 crore) telecom service provider based in Delhi, India, uses data mining to identify reasons why its mobile customers switch to other providers and, then, rectify the problems. For example, when a data mining analysis discovered that many complaints in one busy region came from users operating out of basement offices, the company set up extra powerful transmitters in that region. When it revealed that a large number of pre-paid subscribers in Delhi were business visitors who subscribed to Bharti's services back in their hometowns, the company launched a regional roaming service program for these customers.[11] *Online analytical processing (OLAP)* tools aggregate, display, and analyze data to draw inferences and make decisions. Marcus Corporation, which owns, manages, or franchises 186 Baymont Inns & Suites and 7 Woodfield Suites, uses OLAP tools to slice and dice data about sales, occupancies, average room rates, revenue per available room, and future bookings by property, location, type of room, manager, type of guest, etc. Such analysis allows it to set rates, serve its guests better, and evaluate its managers.[12] We discuss data mining and OLAP tools and their applications more thoroughly in Chapter 8.

A **data mart** is similar to a data warehouse, but it provides summary and historical data for business intelligence and decision making for a single department or division rather than an entire organization. Data marts cost less to develop and operate than data warehouses and can be built more quickly. Designers can more easily meet the needs of managers who want them without imposing on the limited time of managers who will not use them.

Managers sometimes create data marts by extracting data from an existing data warehouse. In this way, they can, perhaps, provide a longer history or more levels of aggregation than the warehouse might provide. Managers also develop data marts when their company hasn't implemented a data warehouse. For example, Borders Group, the book and music retailer, created a data mart for its marketing department, as Borders had no data warehouse. The data mart helped Borders consolidate customer information from its Web store, borders.com, and its physical stores. Also, together with its customer relationship management software, the data mart helped Borders create services that could be customized for specific customers, perform cross-channel analyses, and target its marketing campaigns better.[13]

Many companies, including Sherwin-Williams, create a data mart as a stepping-stone to the creation of a data warehouse. Sherwin-Williams built four data marts—for sales analysis, category management, contribution analysis, and raw materials—before attempting to integrate them into a data warehouse. To avoid creating independent islands of information, it followed a "start small, think big" approach, selecting a common and scalable set of software products with which to implement the data marts. Its objective was eventually to integrate the data marts into an enterprise-wide data warehouse. It took only about two years after the first data mart was rolled out for an integrated data warehouse with 1.1 terabytes of data and supporting 200 users to be operating.[14]

Serving Dynamic Web Pages

Have you ever noticed how the home Web page of a news provider, such as CNN.com, differs every day you return to its site? The Web pages of auction and sales catalog sites also change rapidly to reflect changes in their products. When you log into a Web site that you've previously registered with, it's likely that the site reflects preferences that you've explicitly entered or preferences inferred from your previous visits to the site. Web sites such as these generate Web pages automatically by pulling the data from a database into a Web page template.

Content management software is designed to ease the development of dynamic Web pages. Web designers use content management software to develop templates with spaces, or fields, designed to display certain types of information. Then, the content management tool pulls selected information into the Web template, just as a mail-merge program pulls names and addresses into a letter template. The content management software feeds the Web page to a Web server, which in turn presents it to the reader. Using content management software, employees with no Web training can easily update Web pages simply by filling in a database form.

Recently, Ford used Microsoft's Content Management Server product to rebuild totally its Ford.com Web site in only 13 weeks. Because users are now able to update much of the Web data simply by entering new information into Ford's databases and because much of the information is drawn automatically from its databases, Ford found that it was able to reduce the staff devoted to maintaining the Web site from five to two. Ford believes that it has approximately 280 additional customer-facing Web sites that could benefit from content management that have not yet been converted.[15]

DEVELOPING DATABASES THROUGH DATA DESIGN

Data design is the process of identifying and formalizing the relationships among the elements of data that will form an organization's database. Managers often work with computer specialists to determine the design that best meets their business's needs. For example, must a customer have a sales representative? If so, how should the database store a customer, if at all, before the company assigns her a sales representative? How many customers can a sales representative represent? What happens to a sales representative's customers when the sales representative leaves the company? Should the database contain the same information for walk-in customers as for repetitive customers? If the customer's shipping and billing address are the same should the address be stored twice?

Decisions such as these are not simple and tend to evolve over the life of a database application. DBMSs, however, make it possible to consider an organization's data design independently of its application programs. As a result, it is often possible to change the design without a massive reprogramming effort. Nevertheless, software developers, database managers, and functional managers must understand the interrelationships that business processes require for an organization's data elements to properly reflect them in the database.

Data Elements

From a logical perspective, we can consider a database to be a combination of data elements. Figure 4-4 shows how these elements form a hierarchy. At the highest level is the database itself. You might think of this as a file cabinet. Continuing the analogy, think of the database as composed of **files,** groups of data about similar things, just like the files in your file cabinet. A customer file, for example, holds all data about a company's customers.

A file contains **records.** Each record generally holds data about a person, place, or thing, concrete or abstract. For example, data about a particular customer might be a record in the customer file. Data about a particular invoice might be a record in an invoice file. Each record contains **fields,** also known as **attributes,** data about one of the characteristics of a record. For example, a phone number might be a field in a customer record. An invoice number or invoice amount might be a field in an invoice record. A field, the lowest element of data that has meaning, contains words, bytes, and bits of data (see Chapter 3).

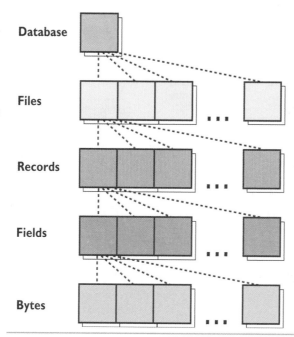

FIGURE 4-4

In the hierarchy of data elements, a database contains files, files contain records, records contain fields, and fields contain bytes of data.

Database

Files

Records

Fields

Bytes

As we will see shortly, this hierarchical model of data is too simplistic. It ignores the relationships between elements at the same level in the hierarchy. For example, Sherwin-Williams' customer file relates to its order file: each customer has one or more orders. This model also ignores actions as opposed to attributes of data elements. For example, this model can't indicate that a customer may do such things as order paint or pay bills when due.

The Entity-Relationship Model

Although a number of models express the relationship among an organization's data elements, the Entity-Relationship (E/R) Model is among the most widely used. The E/R model offers a pictorial way of showing the interrelationships among various types of data.[16]

Figure 4-5 illustrates a portion of an E/R model for a hypothetical wholesaler. Rectangles identify entities about which the organization collects data, corresponding to files, as shown for customers and orders. Diamonds enclose and name relationships between entities. In the figure, the *places* relationship indicates the fact that customers place orders. The lines connecting entities to the diamond represent the relationships among them and show whether the relationship is exclusive. In this example, each customer places zero to many (M) orders, but every order is placed by one (1) customer. This relationship is called one to many. Relationships can also be one to one, as when each employee has a company car and each car is assigned to one employee, or many to many, as when each order may be an order of many products and each product may appear on many orders. Ovals indicate attributes of entities and relationships. For example, in Figure 4-5, tel# is an attribute of customer and Total Quantity is an attribute of the relationship "order_of."

TECHNOLOGICAL UNDERPINNINGS

Managers who understand the fundamental ways databases can differ can generally work more effectively with computer specialists to choose the DBMS that best meets their

FIGURE   4-5 ——————— An Entity-Relationship Diagram illustrates how entities relate to one another and describes the attributes of all entities and relationships.

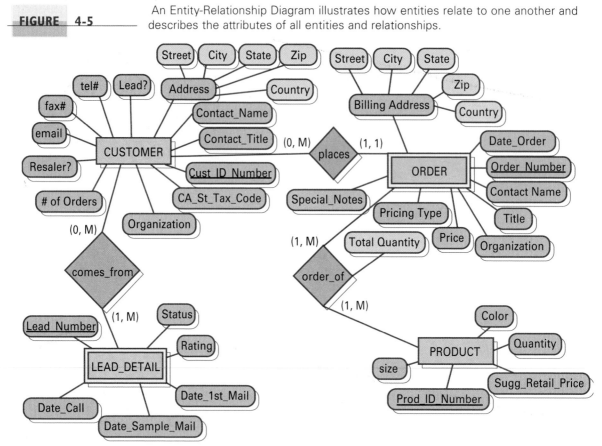

SOURCE: accessed at http://www.ieor.berkeley.edu/~hans/er2.html. Adapted from a diagram created by Handy Halim, Trevor Oelschig, and Amie Wang for Back-a-Line, a company that makes athletic belts for back support.

information needs. In this section we look at two fundamental properties: the distribution architecture and the database model.

Distribution Architectures

Distribution architecture refers to how the organization distributes data and database processing physically among the computers in a network. Distribution architecture has important consequences for database performance and database use. Computer networks allow a DBMS running on one computer to access data stored on another computer. We will study computer networks in Chapter 5 and learn how data flow through a network. Obtaining data through a network is likely to be slower than obtaining it directly from the storage devices of the computer running the DBMS. Moving data across a network consumes network resources and capacity needed for other tasks.

Managers and computer specialists can choose DBMSs with one of four data architectures: decentralized, centralized, client/server, and distributed. Table 4-2 identifies differences among these architectures and shows their advantages and disadvantages.

Decentralized Architecture

A *decentralized architecture* involves no data sharing; it has "islands of information." Generally, this architecture arises from users developing databases as required by individual applications, without central planning and without central control.

TABLE 4-2 The four data architectures differ in their basic characteristics, as well as their performance and use.

		Decentralized	Centralized	Client/Server	Distributed
Defining Characteristics	**Shared Data**	No	Yes	Yes	Yes
	Data Location	Distributed	Centralized	Centralized	Distributed
	Processing Location	Distributed	Centralized	Shared	Distributed
Performance and Usage Characteristics	**Performance**	Excellent	Network Constrained	Network Constrained	Mixed
	Ease of Management	Simple	Easy	Moderate	Difficult
	Redundancy	High	Low	Low	Moderate
	Consistency	Low	High	High	High
	Scalability	High	Low	Moderate	High

The absence of central planning in the decentralized architecture gives users freedom to develop applications that meet their needs and maintain control over the applications they develop. But this architecture generally prevents users from easily combining or comparing data in various databases. It also encourages data duplication, requiring dual entry and dual storage, possibly leading to inconsistencies. Decentralized architectures often arise in companies having a decentralized management approach and in companies built through acquisition.

Centralized Architecture

A *centralized architecture* has a single DBMS running on a single computer and maintaining data centrally. This architecture provides a consistent set of data to authorized users with limited redundancy. It is relatively easy to control and manage, at least for small databases. Having a centralized storage capability also makes it easy to consolidate corporate-wide data and determine whether a data item currently exists within the database.

With centralized processing, a single program accepts the input of many users and sends output to them accordingly. Therefore, a centralized architecture needs more concentrated processing power than a decentralized architecture. Usually, PCs are insufficient to addressing these processing needs, resulting in the use of more sophisticated equipment and a staff dedicated to computer operations.

As database size and usage grow, more powerful equipment must often replace the existing hardware to respond to greater processing and data storage needs. Hardware upgrades of mainframe systems are expensive and sometimes require software changes to support them. The integration of new with existing applications becomes more complex and time consuming as the centralized database grows.

Client/Server Architecture

A **client/server architecture** (see Chapter 3) divides the functions of a DBMS among connected computers on a network, while centralizing permanent storage for all data on a computer called the **database server.** The computers connected to the server are called its *clients.* The clients run the parts of the DBMS that process user requests and display results. The server runs the parts of the DBMS that store and retrieve data. A variety of models exist to divide the functions of the DBMS between the client and the server. In three-tiered client/server systems, applications that access the database might run on servers separate from the database server and separate from the user clients.

To illustrate the application and benefits of the client/server architecture, consider an accounts receivable program running on one client and a customer service application running on another client (see Figure 4-6). At the accounts-receivable station, the data entry clerk processes a customer's check, first entering the customer-ID. The accounts-receivable program sends a request to the client DBMS to determine whether the customer-ID is a valid one. The client DBMS passes this request to the server DBMS, which accesses the database to determine whether the ID is valid. The server responds to the client DBMS, and the client DBMS responds to the application program, which then proceeds to accept data about the check. When the user finishes entering the payment data, the client DBMS processes and compresses the data and forwards them to the server DBMS for storage. At the customer service station, the clerk also accesses client data, such as a list of payments outstanding, through a program running on his or her computer. If the server receives two requests to update the same data at the same time, it mediates the conflict. The server may also keep a log to recover from system crashes.

The primary advantage of the client/server architecture is that it off-loads the application programs and many of the functions of the DBMS from the server. In the example above, the accounts-receivable station operates almost autonomously, barely affected by the number of other programs running on the network. With a centralized architecture, the accounts receivable and customer service applications run on the same computer.

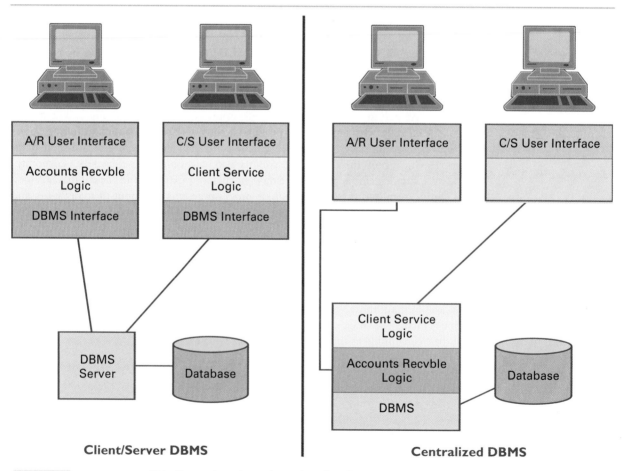

Client/Server DBMS   **Centralized DBMS**

FIGURE 4-6   This illustration shows how the client/server architecture reduces the load on the computer running the DBMS. In this example, the accounts receivable and customer service programs are off-loaded to the client station

When the company adds new applications, accounts receivable processing will slow down unless the company upgrades the computer to provide more processing power.

The client/server architecture encourages the movement of a large amount of data over the network. Because processing occurs at many client locations, and the client and server interact frequently and extensively, data must flow rapidly between server and clients for adequate DBMS performance. The client/server DBMS thereby places a heavy load on the network capacity.

Another disadvantage of the client/server architecture is difficulty controlling data. Employees with access to diskettes on client computers can remove data that the organization means to keep confidential. As a result, some organizations insist that no client computers be equipped with removable media. This, however, limits the usefulness of such computers for other functions.

Distributed Architecture

A *distributed DBMS architecture* distributes both data and processing.[17] It differs from the client/server architecture in that the distributed architecture does not necessarily have centralized data storage; all data may reside at decentralized locations. It differs from the decentralized architecture by treating data as a single database, giving every database client and every server access to all the data in the database no matter where it resides. If the DBMS can obtain requested data locally, it executes the request locally. If the data are not local, then the DBMS determines the location of the data, issues a request to obtain the data from the appropriate computer, and processes the data upon receiving them.

A distributed architecture reduces network traffic by keeping data close to where they are needed (see Figure 4-7). For example, the West Coast sales office of a national company can keep information about its customers on the West Coast computer while the East Coast office keeps similar data on the East Coast computer. Both computers can retrieve data from and store data at either site, but most processing is local. If an East Coast firm calls the Western sales office, the DBMS will try to find the customer's data locally; failing to do that, it will send a message to the remote (East Coast) computer to retrieve the data. The West Coast computer user won't need to know where the data are stored. In addition to reducing network traffic, the distributed architecture allows most transactions to occur rapidly since the local computer maintains the data affecting these transactions.

To improve performance and reduce network traffic, a distributed DBMS will often store the same data in two or more locations. This feature of distributed DBMS is called **replication.** The DBMS manages the consistency of replicated data, ensuring that they be entered only once. If a user or application changes the replicated data at one location, the

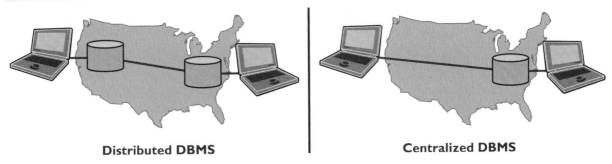

Distributed DBMS　　　　　　　　**Centralized DBMS**

FIGURE　4-7　　The distributed DBMS keeps local data locally and rarely has to move data from one coast to another. The centralized DBMS in this example has to move all West Coast data to the East Coast for storage and back again for usage.

DBMS changes the data at all locations. Various strategies exist for synchronizing the data depending on how important it is that the replicated data always be consistent.

A distributed, replicated database is most applicable when employees use handheld or laptop computers at customer sites. The replication allows employees to access the company's database without having to connect to the home office. Employees can, for example, determine product specifications, pricing, and even product availability, allowing them to respond rapidly and accurately to customer questions. They can also place their orders directly into the local database and be assured that the order will be accounted for when the distributed databases are synchronized, either from a hotel room or when the employee returns to the office.

Distributed DBMSs are more complex than single-computer DBMSs for several reasons. First, the distributed DBMS must be able to determine the location of specific data. Second, it must be more sophisticated in determining the optimal way to request data. The order in which the DBMS processes a request can make a significant difference in the amount of data transmitted over the network. Finally, anticipating computer failures and prioritizing requests for data are extremely complex. Sometimes it is difficult to determine whether a computer has completed an update before it or the network fails. In addition, when two requests to access the same data occur at about the same time, it is not easy to determine which request came first or what other requests are part of the same transaction if one of the requests must be blocked.

Besides the technical difficulties, organizational issues sometimes impede the acceptance of distributed DBMS.[18] Traditionally, a single administrator or administrative office designs and controls the corporate database. DBMSs exist to reduce redundancy in data entry and processing by centralizing such control. Distributing authority and control over the data resource negates this reason for using a DBMS. Many managers believe that isolated and potentially conflicting islands of data will arise as local managers add their favorite modifications to the enterprise data model. Of course, an organization can use a distributed architecture purely for its technical advantages, such as reducing network flow and increasing response time, while refusing to relinquish control to local managers. Still, many managers view distributed architecture as the first step towards distributed control and potential loss of personal information and power.

Mixed Architectures

In practice, mixed architectures arise frequently. Companies with multiple sites may use a distributed architecture with redundant data to maximize performance. The company might use a centralized architecture at one site to consolidate processing; it might use a client/server architecture at another site to distribute processing. Even at companies that centralize their data planning, some managers will create unshared databases for their own personal use. For example, they may keep an electronic Rolodex or a list of customer contacts in a personal database. While the company might prefer that managers share such data, in practice they may find sharing impractical or too invasive of privacy. As a result, some elements of a decentralized architecture arise.

Database Models

Different DBMSs treat the relationships among the elements of data differently. Their approaches fall into a few broad categories, known as **database models.** A DBMS's database model can have profound implications for its performance and might also affect database design.

In this section, we begin with the relational model, as it is the most widely accepted. We then cover two models that have recently achieved a degree of market acceptance, the object and XML models. Finally, we cover the network and the hierarchical models solely because of their historical significance. The less technical reader can skip these two sections without loss of continuity.

Table 4-3 compares these data models. They differ in whether or not standards exist, the speed with which they save and retrieve complex data and associated transactions, the ease with which inexperienced users can search their data, their support for software development, the types of applications they aim to support, and the ease with which their data can be distributed. Generally, technical specialists rather than managers decide on the database model when selecting a DBMS for a particular application.

Relational Model

The **relational model,** first proposed as a theoretical model in 1970 but not widely adopted until the late 1980s, acts as the basis for most DBMS products.

In the relational model, a **table** represents a file with rows called **tuples** and columns called **attributes.** For example, the data in Figure 4-8 represents the customer file with rows, or tuples, identifying each customer's number, name, address, and credit limit. Each column presents a specific attribute for all customers: the left-most column shows all customer numbers, the right-most column all credit limits.

How does this model link two tables, for example customer and invoices? The relational model connects tables by including identifying data from one table in another table. For example, it might include in the invoice table a column that identifies the customer responsible for the invoice, as shown in Figure 4-8. The DBMS can then link the customer table to the invoice table to obtain more detailed information about the customer for a particular invoice. The DBMS would answer any questions about an invoice's customer by first looking in the invoice table, then finding the row for that invoice and identifying the responsible customer from the customer column. Next, the DBMS finds the row of information about the specific customer in the customer table. The DBMS can also identify all invoices of a particular customer by scanning the invoice table and selecting only those who have the specified customer identifier (customer number, for example) in the appropriate column. Most relational DBMSs internally organize the data to make such retrievals quick and efficient.

Because the relational model specifies all relationships among data through data elements, a user can retrieve the data he wants simply by identifying those data in prescribed ways. The standard for specifying such retrieval is an easy-to-use language called **SQL.**[19]

	Relational	Object	XML	Network	Hierarchical
Standards	SQL	ODMG JDOQL	None	CODASYL	None
Speed	Low	Moderate	Moderate	Moderate	High
Ease of query	High	Moderate	Moderate	Low	Low
Ease of software development	Moderate	High	High	Low	Low
Primary target	Decision support	GUI	Document	Transaction	Transaction
Ease of data distribution	Moderate	Moderate	Moderate	Low	Low
Representative products	Access DB2 Oracle Sybase	ObjectStore Objectivity Versant	Xindice Cerisent Coherity	IMS	IDS IDMS

TABLE 4-3

Database model differ in standards, speed, ease of use, and target

In this relational example, the customer number links the Invoice Table to the Customer Table.

Customer Table

Cust #	Customer Name	Address	Credit Limit
16340	Arlington Software	341 Woodward Rd.	5,000
37126	Hanson Widgets	21 Park Dr.	10,000
21371	Marion Assoc.	19 Avalon Ave.	5,000
31319	Generic Products	113-51 71st St.	25,000
87615	Electric Co.	1 Electric Plaza	25,000

Invoice Table

Inv #	Inv Date	Cust #	Inv Amount
100231	11/08/02	37126	301.37
100232	11/08/02	37126	500.23
100233	11/08/02	87615	128.00
100234	11/15/02	16340	200.00
100235	11/15/02	37126	921.00

Unlike most other programming languages, SQL is non-procedural; the user specifies only the characteristics of the data desired, not the steps the DBMS must take to retrieve the data. For example, to find all customers with a credit-limit of over $5,000, the command might be:

```
SELECT CUSTOMER_NAME FROM CUSTOMER_TABLE WHERE
CREDIT_LIMIT > 5000.
```

Joining data from two or more tables is only slightly more complex. For example, to list the invoice numbers and amounts of all customers having a credit limit of less than $5,000, the SQL command would be

```
SELECT INV_NUMB, INV_AMT FROM INVOICES, CUSTOMER_TABLE
WHERE INVOICES.CUST_NUMB = CUSTOMER_TABLE.CUST_NUMB
AND CUSTOMER.CREDIT_LIMIT < 5000.
```

One of the basic principles of relational database management is that no two rows of a table should be identical. The **primary key** of a table is the attribute or attributes that uniquely identify a row in that table. In the example of Figure 4-8, the customer number is a good candidate to be the primary key of the customer table. Customer name is also a potential primary key, as is address, but the credit limit cannot be a primary key, as two different customers might have the same credit limit.

Although the relational model of data is conceptually the simplest to use, poor design of the data tables would negate its benefit. Relational designers use **normalization** to group data elements into tables to simplify retrieval, reduce data entry and storage, and minimize the likelihood of data inconsistencies.

One principle of normalization is that every attribute in a table should depend on the primary key and only the primary key. Look at Figure 4-9 to see the logic behind this principle. In the top table, the phone and region of the sales representative depend directly on the sales representative and only indirectly on the primary key, the customer number, violating the normalization principle. As a result, the phone and region information for Harris (and Jones) appears twice because Harris represents two customers. Several problems arise from this situation. First, if Harris represents hundreds of customers, the database wastes storage by saving Harris's information so many times. Second, if Harris's telephone number were to change, it would have to be changed in hundreds of rows. Third, as shown in the example, this design does not prohibit inconsistency in the data for Harris among the rows of the table, leading to confusion. Finally, if all of Harris's customers were to be deleted, the database would lose all information about Harris. The bottom of Figure 4-9 normalizes the data by breaking it into two tables, one for customers and one for the sales representatives. Note how this solution satisfies normalization principles and solves the problems identified above.

Normalization of relational tables includes several additional principles, which are beyond the scope of this text. How to normalize a relational database is a major component of most courses in database management and is considered an art among database practitioners.

Object Model

The **object model** derives from object-oriented programming (see Chapter 3).[20] Recall that this type of programming views an object as an encapsulation of attributes (or data) and programs (called methods), tightly bundled and closed from the view of users and other programs. For example, a customer might be an object with attributes, such as name, sales-rep, credit-limit, and invoices, along with methods, such as change-credit-limit and pay-invoice. Some attributes, such as invoice, may themselves be other objects. Messages, which give directions to the object, provide the only interface between the user and an object or between objects. A customer object might send its name in response to the message "tell me your name." It might change its representation of the customer's credit limit and reply with the message "done" in response to the message "change credit limit to 3000."

Object-oriented DBMSs store objects and object-class metadata. Objects may belong to an object type, normally called an object class. Figure 4-10 shows a company object class with attributes of name, phone-numbers, and contact, and the method add-phone-numbers, which accepts and processes messages about additional phone numbers. All subtypes of an object, such as a customer company, retain the characteristics of their object (e.g. company name, phone number, contacts, and add-phone), and could have other attributes and methods, such as orders and take-order.

Unnormalized Table with Conflicting Phone Numbers for Rep Harris

Cust #	Customer Name	Customer Address	Sales Rep	Rep Phone	Rep Region
16340	Arlington Software	341 Woodward Rd.	Jones	351-4567	North
37126	Hanson Widgets	21 Park Dr.	Harris	259-8558	South
21371	Marion Assoc.	19 Avalon Ave.	Arnold	346-9666	West
31319	Generic Products	113-51 71st St.	Harris	741-2559	South
87615	Electric Co.	1 Electric Plaza	Jones	351-4567	North

Customer Table

Customer #	Customer Name	Customer Address	Sales Rep
16340	Arlington Software	341 Woodward Rd.	Jones
37126	Hanson Widgets	21 Park Dr.	Harris
21371	Marion Assoc.	19 Avalon Ave.	Arnold
31319	Generic Products	113-51 71st St.	Harris
87615	Electric Co.	1 Electric Plaza	Jones

Sales Rep Table

Sales Rep	Rep Phone	Rep Region
Jones	351-4567	North
Harris	259-8558	South
Arnold	346-9666	West

FIGURE 4-10

A hierarchy of object classes. Customer and supplier are two sub-types of the company class and inherit their attributes and methods. In this example, customers automatically have a name, phone number, and contacts, and an add-phone-number method.

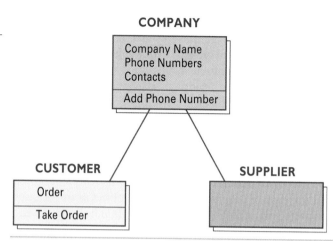

The object model easily integrates with object-oriented programs and readily represents complex data types such as images, sound, and objects embedded within other objects. For example, object-oriented models can easily represent organization charts and engineering drawings, which are hard to represent using the traditional data models. As multimedia becomes more predominant in computing, so too does the use of objects. Object-oriented DBMSs provide a facility to capture such objects in a database.

Current implementations of object DBMSs have evolved in two ways. First, proponents of object-oriented languages have created object DBMSs to provide permanence for objects represented in the languages that they use. [21] Second, relational DBMS vendors have added object features to their products. [22] This second approach has produced hybrid object-relational DBMSs, commonly known as **universal servers.**

Most universal servers store objects such as pictures, signatures, or sound recordings simply as a series of bytes. Because the model doesn't represent object properties, users can't find all photographs of birds in the database unless the records with those photos include captions containing the word "bird." The current standard for queries on object databases is a programming interface standard, but most object-oriented DBMSs support SQL to the extent it is applicable in the context of the database objects.

The existence of standards for representing object data independent of any computer language, operating system, or hardware has increased the popularity of object DBMSs. Most software vendors have adopted the *CORBA (Common Object Request Broker Architecture)* standard; Microsoft has instead adopted *DCOM (Distributed Component Object Model)*. Most object DBMSs support both standards, simplifying their interface to object-oriented programming languages.

XML Model

XML is a language used to mark and identify components of Web-based transaction documents, such as the date or amount of a purchase order or invoice, as well as components of other Web-based documents. XML identifies not only the meanings of these components in the context of the document, but also the layout of the document for printing or display. Native XML database management systems are designed to simplify storing information about layout, which can be highly unstructured and is generally unsuited to storage in a relational format. Layout information is important for many applications, such as users manuals, marketing brochures, and information that designers would like to present as a newspaper or magazine page. Pages that do not change rapidly can easily be stored and retrieved in their word-processing or desktop publishing formats. However, when components and layouts change rapidly, XML databases allow users to store and retrieve documents easily.

The **XML model** is fairly young, and has yet to be standardized. To be considered as a native XML database, a database should conform to a model in which an XML document is the fundamental entity, just as the row is the fundamental entity in the relational model. The model must include elements, attributes, data, and layout information. An XML database can be used to store articles, chapters, and glossary entries, as well as document metadata, such as authors, revision dates, version information, readers, signatories, and workflow path.

Many relational DBMSs, even though they cannot be considered native DBMSs, have been *XML-enabled*. This means that they can accept data in XML format. To enable a database for XML input, the database administrator or an authorized user must identify which XML tags are associated with which database items. Then, for example, if the DBMS is sent an invoice document, the DBMS will recognize it as an invoice document and will recognize the parts of the document, such as the customer ID, the billing address, the invoice amount, and the invoice date, by their XML tags. The DBMS can then extract the data from the document and store it properly in the database.

Network Model

The **network model** builds a tighter linkage (called a **set**) between elements of data, such as between customers and sales representatives. A customer/sales-rep set implements the rule that each customer must have a sales representative. Each entry in the set includes data about a single sales-rep and all of his customers. The network model doesn't store the sales-rep identifier with the customer's data, as would the relational model. It stores the customer's data as part of the set belonging to its representative. One data element may belong to several sets. In Figure 4-11, for example, each order line is part of an order/order-line set and a product/order-line set. An item may be a member of one kind of a set and an owner of another. For example, in Figure 4-11 an order is a member of a customer/order set and an owner of an order/order-line set.

Using sets retrieves related information faster and more efficiently than with the relational model. The database administrator may specify that the DBMS store members of a set near one another so that a single access to the storage medium retrieves them all. For example, one disk access might retrieve a customer and all of its orders.

From the user perspective, sets complicate rather than simplify data access. The user can't access data simply by its title or characteristics. Instead, she must prescribe procedures to get the data by navigating through the network of related items. How would a

FIGURE   4-11

In this example of a network DBMS, Order 3 is a member of the customer/order set of Customer #1 and the owner of an order/order-line set that includes two order lines. The second order line is also a member of the product/order set of Product #1.

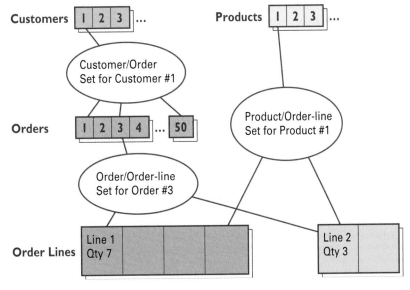

customer services manager determine which customers to contact about delays in processing their order due to a product recall? First, the manager would use the order-line/product set to identify all order lines in which the defective product appeared. The order-line/order set for each line would identify the affected orders. The order/customer set would identify the affected customers. The manager or a technical support person uses a procedural language such as COBOL to search through the related items for the answer. A manager using the relational model, in contrast, would simply specify the relationships among the data requested without doing any programming. Loosely speaking, the user would ask the DBMS to obtain the names of all customers whose ID matched a customer id in the order table and which order contained an order-line matching the defective part. Modern network DBMSs generally include an SQL user interface that translates SQL requests into programs that navigate the databases to extract the desired data.

Several factors explain the popularity of the relational model over the network model:

- The decreasing cost of faster computer processing makes using the relational model more cost effective, while the programming costs required to use the network model remain high.

- The increasing availability of personal computers has caused users who aren't computer professionals to insist on the ability to access data without programming.

- The relational model is more flexible than the network model. Simply adding and deleting columns changes the relationships among data; programs rarely must be changed as with the network model.

Hierarchical Model

We can view the **hierarchical model,** a precursor to the network model, as a network model with additional restrictions. The hierarchical model, also called **hierarchial,** views data as organized in a logical hierarchy. An entity may be a member of no more than one type of set: for example, customers can belong only to sales-rep, not to discount-class or any other data set.

The hierarchical restriction makes it extremely difficult to represent many interrelationships among data. Consider, for example, the order-line in Figure 4-12. Although order line logically deserves to be part of the order set and the product set, the hierarchical model prohibits this dual membership because it violates the hierarchical view of data. Instead, the model requires two hierarchies to represent the data, forcing the DBMS to store the order lines twice.

Most implementations of the hierarchical model have technical ways to loosen the hierarchical restriction somewhat, eliminating data duplication. Nevertheless, it remains cumbersome for data modelers. Although access is intrinsically faster for the hierarchical model than for the network model, current computer technology has removed this advantage.

Despite its drawbacks, the hierarchical model remains one of the most widely used models because of the large installed base of a product called IMS. Developed by IBM in 1968, millions of applications have used IMS. In many cases, and particularly for transaction-based systems, the cost of reprogramming these applications outweighs the benefits of converting them to a network or relational form.

MANAGING THE DATA RESOURCE

A manager's effectiveness in using data depends greatly on how her organization sets up, administers, and manages its databases. In this section, we explore issues and options in organizing and managing the data resource for most effective use.

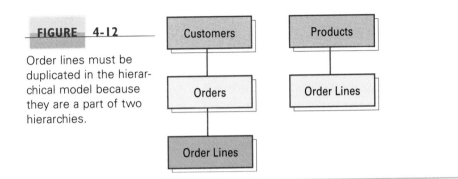

Order lines must be duplicated in the hierarchical model because they are a part of two hierarchies.

Managing the data resource is both a business and a technical problem. Business managers must define their data needs and data sources. Information professionals must make data easily and rapidly accessible to managers, ensure the consistency and accuracy of information collected and stored, and set standards and procedures for reacting to changes in the business information needs. Data administration describes the business role while database administration describes the technical role. These two roles often overlap and fall to a single person in the organization. More frequently, however, a company will have one data administrator and multiple database administrators, one or more for each DBMS used.

Data Administration

A **data administrator** ensures the integrity of the data resource. The data administrator must know what data the organization collects, where it stores the data, and how it names data items.

The data administrator:

- Tries to minimize the redundancy of data by keeping centralized documentation of all data elements. She may impose naming standards on the data throughout the organization and use a data dictionary to keep track of data names and uses.

- Establishes the security of data and sets up appropriate access controls. She works closely with business people to set up appropriate logical views.

- Ensures that data loaded into corporate databases are clean.

- Helps the business establish rules regarding data formats and relationships. For example, rules establishing credit limits for customers may differ not only by type of customer but also by business units within a company, even for the same type of customer.

A data administrator should have a background in database design. Most importantly, a good data administrator needs a broad understanding of the business. Business managers ultimately determine business rules, establish data quality standards, set authorization policy, and decide other matters relating to data integrity. The data administrator needs to work well with business managers, asking them probing questions that result in proper decisions about design and process.

Database Administration

A **database administrator (DBA)** oversees the overall performance and integrity of a DBMS on one or more databases. The DBA regularly backs up the databases and recovers them after a system crash. The DBA supervises and monitors the development of software that uses or affects the databases. He creates separate development databases for testing new software and approves the transfer of such software to a production database after completing testing. The DBA monitors and installs bug fixes and new releases from the DBMS vendor.

Most DBMS vendors include tools to monitor database performance. The DBA can address performance problems in a number of ways:

- The DBA can make procedural changes that improve performance to satisfactory levels. For example, he can restrict certain types of database activities to off-peak periods or reduce their priority so that they don't impair performance.

- The DBA can build indexes into the database to speed frequently performed queries.

- The DBA may be able to change the amount of cache storage and working memory available to the database.

- The DBA can modify the data design through denormalization. When users rejoin records after breaking them apart to reduce duplicate storage and eliminate possible inconsistencies, the database must correctly respond to their requests. Denormalization puts the records back together permanently, reducing the load on the database.

The DBA should have strong technical skills, extensive experience with the DBMS in use, and excellent communication skills. Companies that operate several types of DBMSs usually employ at least one database administrator for each type of DBMS.

SUMMARY

A database is an organized collection of related data. Database management systems perform numerous functions in organizations, including storing and retrieving data and metadata, limiting and controlling redundancy, supporting simultaneous data sharing, ensuring transaction atomicity, providing backup and recovery services, providing authorization and security services, and enforcing business rules.

Databases support business application software by providing a common repository for information and by performing functions that otherwise would have to be performed by application software. Databases, in the form of data warehouses and data marts, are used for business intelligence and to support management decision making. A data warehouse addresses an entire enterprise, while a data mart focuses on an application or department. Databases, along with content management software, support the creation of dynamic Web pages.

Data design describes the process of identifying and formalizing the relationships among the elements of data in a database. The entity-relationship model shows these relationships pictorially.

Distribution architecture refers to the physical distribution of data and database processing among the computers in an organization. A decentralized architecture provides no data sharing. Individual application designers create databases on an ad hoc basis, without central planning or control. A centralized architecture refers to running a DBMS on a single computer. A client/server architecture divides DBMS processing among networked computers while centralizing permanent storage on a database server. The distributed architecture distributes processing and allows data to reside anywhere on the network of computers. Replication of data in this architecture improves performance.

Database models reflect the logical relationships among data in a DBMS. The relational model describes a data object by a table of rows and columns. Normalization of data ensures the effective grouping of the data elements of a database. The object model portrays an object as a combination of attributes and methods. Universal servers provide support of objects within a relational framework. The XML model has a document rather than a record as the fundamental element. The network model builds a tight linkage, called a set, between elements of data. The hierarchical model resembles a network model but also views data as organized logically into a hierarchy.

A data administrator ensures the enterprise-wide integrity of the data resource. A database administrator focuses on the overall performance and integrity of a single DBMS on one or more databases. Both jobs require good technical and business skills.

KEY TERMS

atomicity	database server	relational model
attribute	distribution architecture	replication
client/server architecture	field	schema
concurrency control	file	set
content management software	hierarchical (or hierarchial) model	SQL
data administrator	logical view	subschema
data design	metadata	table
data dictionary	network model	transaction processing monitor
data mart	normalization	(TP monitor)
data warehouse	object model	tuple
database	ODBC (Open Database Connectivity)	universal server
database administrator (DBA)	physical view	XML model
database management system (DBMS)	primary key	
database model	record	

DISCUSSION AND REVIEW QUESTIONS

1. Do data have to be computerized to form a database?
2. What are six reasons that a manager might want to use a database management system?
3. Why do DBMSs store metadata?
4. Why is reducing data redundancy advantageous?
5. Why is concurrency control necessary?
6. Provide an example to show why transaction atomicity should not be violated.
7. Why do database management systems usually have their own backup and recovery capability?
8. How do views enhance data security?
9. Why is it better to enforce business rules in a database rather than through the programs that access the database?
10. How do database management systems increase programmer productivity?
11. How does a data warehouse differ from a data mart?
12. How does a database management system help make Web pages dynamic?
13. Compare and contrast four distribution architectures.
14. What are the advantages and disadvantages of a distributed architecture relative to a centralized architecture?
15. What are key characteristics of the five database models?
16. How does the relational database model represent relationships between tables?
17. What problems might arise from using a data model that has not been normalized?

18. What are the advantages of the object model relative to the relational model?

19. What advantages and disadvantages do sets give the network model relative to the relational model?

20. What is the role of a data administrator?

21. What is the role of a database administrator?

22. What options does a database administrator have to improve database performance?

MINICASE

DATA WAREHOUSING AT NORTH JERSEY MEDIA GROUP

Headquartered in Hackensack, New Jersey, North Jersey Media Group Inc. (NJMGI) publishes two daily and 27 weekly newspapers, most in affluent suburbs just west of New York, as well as four specialty publications. It also operates an Internet portal and owns a substantial commercial printing business.

Its growing data warehouse will allow managers to more easily use content from a variety of databases fed from both internal systems and external sources. At the same time, the company's production-tracking system keeps tabs on the work flow—from plate-ready page files to the printed products—for a wide range of company and contract publications printed (on several different presses) in two of the company's three principal locations.

Not surprisingly, production tracking and the data warehouse are linked. The purpose of both is to allow managers, ultimately from all departments, to explore possibilities and make better decisions about products and services, production, and distribution based on a better knowledge of customers and operating capabilities within the organization.

Company executives say that when fully implemented and integrated, the data warehouse and production tracking should provide a comprehensive view of all company operations and any available information pertinent to those operations.

The Vision

In describing the data warehouse project, strategic development director Richard Webber cites one simple example: getting a better grasp of carrier routes for the company's daily and weekly publications. This information has resided in two different databases, making it "cumbersome" to bring it together through several intermediate programs for analysis. The data warehouse should make accessing and using the information easier.

Maybe more than anything else, the company looks to the data warehouse for help in improving or creating entirely new revenue-generating opportunities. Industry wide, an obvious objective is targeted delivery—locating specific advertisers' likeliest customers among readers and nonreaders, figuring out what new or existing products will best reach those prospects, and determining how to deliver them cost-effectively. Advertisers, says Webber, "want to use their dollars a lot better than they are ... now." The data warehouse, he adds, will enable his company to find the right person and deliver an appropriate message.

For some accounts, the undertaking may initially appear to be pulling back because some ads will reach fewer people. That it costs less is, of course, only half the reason to do it in cases where the value isn't in the volume. The other, more important half, is that those who do see the printed or inserted ads (or receive certain publications) are the ones most likely to respond. Not only is the resulting advertising of higher value but so, too, may be the services provided.

New Opportunities

Tools used with the data warehouse permit the viewing of consumers and advertisers in concert. It is a capability Webber describes as layering, or visually assembling, categories of information, one upon another, allowing them to be understood within various contexts. By importing an advertiser's information and helping with analysis for decision making (say, examining customer traffic patterns), Webber says, "I can use the data warehouse for new-business development"—part of providing advertisers with "better consultation on where they can spend their dollars." Webber pointed out that because the warehouse is Web-accessible, a sales rep can extract and work with information on a laptop while calling on an advertiser.

Moreover, targeting that matches market demography (e.g., interests, incomes, tastes, ages) with geography (edition zone, local publication, single-copy sales locations, carrier routes) or with a particular product or service (daily, weekly, total market coverage, specialty pub, audiotex, Web site, broadcast outlet) can be extended into direct marketing opportunities that exploit local brand recognition, says Webber. It's an area of serious interest and initial involvement for NJMGI. About 12 percent of New Jersey advertising expenditures goes to direct marketing, according to NJMGI president Jonathan H. Markey. "Right now," he says, "none of that goes through our door."

Whether it's where an advertiser wants her ad displayed or where a reader wants his paper dropped, "the data warehouse will allow us to have a relationship with our customers that we've never had before," says Webber. That may include "pay[ing] more attention to our loyal subscribers," for whom "we do nothing" as an industry, he says.

NJMGI has other ideas for the data warehouse. "We think this is the time to go after incremental revenue," says vice president and CIO William E. Toner. Among other things, the company will look for new markets for specialty publications, and it sees commercial potential in two North Jersey counties other than its Bergen County home, as more people move to the outer suburbs.

Development and Implementation

In all, the project encompasses six phases over a period of about a year. Phases one and two, specialty publications and circulation, are already complete. Phase three will cover campaign analysis and retention; phase four will deal with home delivery and single-copy sales; and phases five and six will focus on advertising and marketing, respectively.

NJMGI called on Dublin, California-based Sybase to provide the database and data warehouse software. The company then selected Sybase-partner Business Objects for software to simplify access to the data through a user-friendly front end. Other partners include Silicon Graphics Inc. for its visualization tools for data mining and analysis of trends and patterns, MicroStrategy Inc. for its development tools and application templates, and Cognos Inc. for its decision support software (reporting, analytical, and financial applications, graphical and simultaneous presentation of multiple business metrics, and automatic alerts to defined events).

Implementation of the data warehouse has been undertaken by six IT and business staffers. Three or four will remain to manage the system. Webber estimates that when the system is complete, there will be licenses for 50–75 named concurrent users, most likely managers, with secured levels of access for all but a global-level group. "This spans everything from editorial to production, with emphasis on circulation, advertising, and marketing," he reports. An ETL process—a function that must be written for each existing data-holding system—"acts as a conduit between [that] system and the [new] database," says Webber. The legacy systems remain in place and are used as before. The ETL function is periodic, rather than a constant flow. Now manually activated, it will become automatic, says Webber, once "all the kinks are worked out."

The Payoff

Having used multiple business systems, the specialty publications (for police, parents, health care, and Hispanic readers) used to pull information "into home-grown [Microsoft] Excel spreadsheets. Now that arm of the company gets its information directly from the data warehouse," says Webber.

The weekly division will be able to draw on the system in helping advertisers determine when to advertise what and in which papers. Local marketing data will be consulted on matters of circulation, editorial content, and a possible redesign at the *Herald News,* a 43,604-weekday-circulation paper in West Paterson, New Jersey, which focuses on Passaic County and available in parts of three other counties.

Webber explained that until now, requests to run special reports were passed to an information technology manager, who wasn't always able to fulfill the often time-sensitive requests while the information was still useful. With drop-down menus and the quick visualization possible with Business Objects, "it's not a hard system to learn," says Webber, adding that super-users will be available for help, special projects, and any customized setups. He finds it a "challenge to convince people that they have the information they never had before"—that they no longer must ask and wait. "You've got an idea? Turn on your computer," he says.

SOURCE: Adapted from Jim Rosenberg, "They Went Data Way," *Editor & Publisher,* 14 January 2002, T6-T12. Reprinted through the courtesy of CIO. © 2002, CXO Media Inc. All rights reserved.

Case Questions

Diagnosis

   1. What are the information needs of NJGMI's business managers?

Evaluation

   2. What problems did business managers at NJGMI face in obtaining information prior to the development of NJGMI's data warehouse?

Design

   3. What benefits does NJGMI hope to achieve with a data warehouse?

   4. How are NJGMI's production-tracking system and its data warehouse linked?

   5. What tools augment the power of the data warehouse?

   6. Where does the data come from to populate NJGMI's data warehouse? What is the role of ETL software in populating the data warehouse?

Implementation

   7. Why do you think NJGMI used a phased approach to the implementation of the data warehouse?

   8. What benefits has NJGMI already achieved?

   9. What challenges lie ahead for the developers and potential users of the data warehouse?

ACTIVITY

4-1 DIRTY DATA AT THE MONTANA STATE DEPARTMENT OF CORRECTIONS

Step 1: Read the following scenario.

For years, the Montana Department of Corrections was a prisoner of data quality problems. Aging IT systems perpetrated countless data entry offenses in reports that the prison system was required to submit to state and federal authorities. And while the department's IS group put in hours of manual labor to try to maintain some level of reporting integrity, overall confidence in the quality of data was nonexistent and morale in the IS group was low. The situation came to a head when the department nearly lost a coveted $1 million federal grant. The culprit: information systems that, lacking business rules and a data dictionary, failed to accurately forecast how many of a particular type of offender would be incarcerated. "We had an egregious data quality problem. Not to the point where we were losing offenders—but we weren't able to accurately portray how many we thought we'd have over the next two to five years," says Dan Chelini, the department's bureau chief for information services

With the go-ahead from the state prison's board of directors, Chelini's department mounted an aggressive campaign to turn around data quality as part of an overhaul of the prison system. The first step was to bring in a team from Information Impact International, a consultancy specializing in data quality, to evaluate organizational processes, acquaint the department with the concept of data stewardship, and set up a methodology for data entry. Although some employees were leery at first of the new demands, they bought into the new standards once trained in basic data modeling and data cleansing techniques. A data validity officer was also appointed to rally support for the program and enforce the new rules.

The department now claims to see some real results. Instead of a handful of programmers holding all of the responsibility for prisoners' information, 30 data stewards from all walks of prison life—from probation officers and attorneys to the guy who showers prisoners when they first enter a facility—now function as data quality gatekeepers. They are accountable for accurately entering information on prisoners, such as names, last known addresses, and identifying scars and disfigurements. The Montana Department of Corrections' data quality problem has been detained. "For the first time in years, we're meeting deliverables" such as reports to federal overseers, says Data Validity Officer Lou Walters. "People are involved and excited about pushing data quality."

SOURCE: Extracted and modified with permission from Beth Stackhouse, "Wash Me," *CIO*, 15 February 2001, 100-114,

Step 2: Prepare the case for class discussion.

Step 3: Answer each of the following questions, individually or in small groups, as directed by your instructor:

Diagnosis

1   What are the information needs of Montana's Department of Corrections?

Evaluation

2.   What problems existed when programmers were responsible for data quality?

Design

4.   What was the objective of appointing data stewards and a data validity officer in this situation?

5.   Do you think that the department would have been equally successful had it appointed a data administrator to be in charge of data quality and a database

administrator to build data quality rules and other business rules into the database? Why or why not?

Implementation

6. How should the department proceed to ensure that data quality doesn't deteriorate once the novelty and excitement of pushing data quality wears off?

Step 4: In small groups or with the entire class, share your answers to the questions above. Then answer the following questions:

1. How important is data quality to the Montana Department of Corrections?

2. How well does the stewardship approach address the data quality problems that the department experienced?

3. What are the strengths and weaknesses of the stewardship plan as compared to a plan based on a data administrator and business rules built into the database?

4. What should the department do to ensure the continued success of the stewardship plan?

4-2 USING A MICRO DBMS

ACTIVITY

Step 1: Your instructor will give you instructions for accessing a DBMS on your computer system. Then follow the directions presented below.

Step 2: Create the structure for the STUDENTS table with seven fields of the lengths shown: SID (3), LAST (20), FIRST (20), MIDDLE (1), SEX (1), MAJOR (3), GPA (3 with one decimal place). Specify SID as the primary key.

Step 3: Add the data for the 10 student records shown below.

SID	LAST	FIRST	MIDDLE	SEX	MAJOR	GPA
987	Peters	Steve	K	M	Mgt	3.2
763	Parker	Charles		M		2.7
218	Pichard	Sally		F	Fin	3.6
359	Pelnick	Alan	R	M	Fin	2.4
862	Fagin	Emma		F	Mgt	2.2
748	Meglin	Susan	B	F	MIS	3.8
506	Lee	Bill		M	Fin	2.7
581	Cambrell	Ted		M	Mkt	2.8
372	Quigley	Sarah		F		3.5
126	Anderson	Robert	F	M	Acc	3.7

Step 4: Sort the records to appear in descending GPA.

Step 5 Modify the structure of the table to reflect the possibility of a student last name of 25 characters.

Step 6: Create a data entry form that forces the user, when inputting data, to limit GPA values to between 0.0 and 4.0.

Step 7: Create a query that finds all female students who have a GPA greater than 2.5.

Step 8: Create a printed report of the information about each student that allows the dean of students to identify only those who qualify for Latin honors (top 5 percent of their class).

4-3 PROBLEMS IN DATABASE ADMINISTRATION

Step 1: Read the following problems with administering a centralized database system. For each problem, decide what you would do, and then offer a way of preventing the situation from occurring again.

Problem 1: Since its installation, the centralized database at Watson Manufacturing has had duplicate records. When customer service converted to its new system, it did not want any duplicate records transferred from the centralized database to the new system. Therefore, the department personnel carefully reviewed all records, identified duplicates, and purged them from the system. Several months after this cleansing occurred, the director of market research attempted to analyze the potential customer base for a new product the company was considering. The director was distressed to find that some customers were labeled "duplicate record" and that no further information about them existed. The director was further outraged that information about customers could be erased from the database.

Problem 2: Human resources (HR) is responsible for capturing and maintaining personnel data. HR quit the centralized system because of concerns over system security. However, certain personnel data, which had been maintained by HR, were also used by a number of other offices. When HR abandoned the system, it informed administrative systems that it would not pass new or changed information to other offices. Maintaining employee addresses, locating employees in emergencies, generating mailing labels, verifying employment, and countless other functions now had to be routed through HR because data on the central system became unreliable. Management reports or analyses requiring the merging of HR data with other system data (e.g., employee workload analysis) became impossible. Multiple, alternative, and disparate personnel files began to be maintained by various offices, each for its own office's use. The advantages of a common database were lost, and people could not understand why administrative systems, which maintained the database, couldn't just "fix" this.[*]

Problem 3: Jennifer Smith recently joined the Hartley Engine Company as its first database administrator. Hartley Engine had a sophisticated distributed database management system that encompassed all basic business functions. The system had grown from a multitude of individually designed applications into a coherent system that an external consultant had designed and implemented. Managers at Hartley were used to making their own decisions about what data would be included in the database, who would have access to the data, and what applications should be included. Making changes in the system had been as easy as writing a request for the IS department to make the adjustment. After her first month on the job, Jennifer discovered that the system was not working as efficiently as it should be.

Managers often had to use convoluted ways to access data held in remote locations. The security for data access was ineffective, and anyone could read confidential information. No rationale existed for placing data on the corporate database as opposed to retaining it on local microcomputers. The system was overloaded, processing was slow, and it was costing the company at least three times the money that was reasonable for a firm the size of Hartley.

SOURCE: Reprinted from P. T. Farago, J. Whitmore-First, and E. A. Kallman, "Managing Data Standards and Policies in an Integrated Environment," *Journal of Systems Management*, March 1992, 33. Used with permission.

Step 2: In groups of four to six students, reach a consensus about how to handle each situation.

Step 3: In small groups, with the entire class, or in written form, as directed by your instructor, offer a set of five guidelines for developing an effective way of administering a centralized database system. How would these guidelines change if the database system were distributed?

ACTIVITY

4-4 EXPERIAN AUTOMOTIVE HISTORY

Step 1: Read the following scenario.

Experian Automotive has built what is reported to be the largest relational database in the world. The database contains more than 16 billion records on more than 384 million vehicles. Experian uses an ETL tool called ETI*Extract from Austin, Texas-based Evolutionary Technologies International to extract data about United States vehicles within 48 hours after the data is entered into any department of motor vehicles computer in the country. It then transforms the data from one of 175 different formats into a form suitable for loading into its own, consolidated database. The company then sells the data, charging just $10.99 for a complete history of any car bought or sold in the United States.

Here's what bothers some privacy advocates: Experian is also a credit bureau, which maintains credit information on some 205 million U.S. consumers and 14 million U.S. businesses. To increase its revenues and to provide better service to its automotive customers, Experian has merged its automobile data with its credit data and with data from other sources, including address-change information from the United States Postal Service, vehicle accident and emission reports, and vehicle auctions.

Recently, Ford Motor Credit informed 13,000 consumers that hackers broke into an Experian database containing their Social Security numbers, addresses, account numbers, and payment histories.

SOURCE: Pimm Fox, "Extracting Dollars from Data," *Computerworld*, 15 April 2002, 42. http://www.befree.com/company/pressroom/releases/2002/041002.htm, accessed on 17 June 2002. http://www.automotive.experian.com/, accessed on 17 June 2002. Jay Lyman, "Hackers Expose Consumer Info from Ford, Experian," *osOpinion.com*, accessed at http://www.osopinion.com/perl/story/17826.html on 17 June 2002.

Step 2: Prepare the case for class discussion. Assume that you have been appointed by Experian's president to review the company's policy about merging its data from different sources.

Step 3: Answer each of the following questions, individually or in small groups, as directed by your instructor.

1. What alternatives do you have?

2. For each alternative, who benefits and who is harmed?

3. From the ethical principles of least harm, rights and duties, professional responsibilities, self-interest and utilitarianism, consistency, and respect, how would you evaluate each alternative?

4. What course of action would you recommend? Why?

ACTIVITY

4-5 SIEMENS TRANSPORTATION SYSTEMS TRACKS INSPECTION REPORTS

Step 1: Read the following case.

Sacramento-based Siemens Transportation Systems (STS) is the largest provider of light rail vehicles in North America. The company, a subsidiary of Siemens AG, a global leader in electronics and engineering, has more than 500 light rail systems operating in ten cities in the United States. In addition to manufacturing and assembling rail vehicles, the company develops and installs signaling, communications, and network control systems. It also partners with its customers in providing maintenance for infrastructure and rolling stock to maximize system availability and to ensure efficiency and safety.

The maintenance task involves frequent inspection of track and rolling equipment. Inspectors cannot be expected to carry computers with them. Until recently, they carried a clipboard and would simply jot down their observations on a paper form. Their reports, including requirements for repair and parts, would be placed in a three-ring binder left with the vehicle and copied to the production or parts managers. When the car was repaired, the repair would be noted in the car's binder and the car would be released to the field. The problem was that this manual process was inefficient and sometimes ineffective. Specifically, inspectors spent up to 40 percent of their time shuffling paper rather than inspecting vehicles, and sometimes the papers would get lost.

The solution, designed jointly by the inspectors and systems integrator Bear River, required inspectors to record their observations into a database maintained on handheld Palm computers. At the end of each day, the inspectors' handheld computer databases were synchronized with a central database. Production and parts managers were able to access the central database to better plan and manage their functions.

SOURCE: Kristen Kenedy, "Next Stop: Information Age," *CRN*, 29 April 2002, 39. http://www.sts.siemens.com, accessed on 17 June 2002.

Step 2: Prepare the case for class discussion.

Step 3: Answer each of the following questions, individually or in small groups, as directed by your instructor:

Diagnosis

1. What information do STS's vehicle inspectors need?

2. What information do STS's production and parts managers need?

Evaluation

3. What were the drawbacks of STS's paper-based systems?

Design

4. Why do you think STS chose a database-based solution?

5. What problems do you think might have arisen in trying to fit inspectors' repair notes into the rigid structure of a database?

6. Why was a distributed database the right approach for STS in this situation? Would any other distribution architecture have been feasible?

Implementation

7. How did STS help assure its inspectors' acceptance of the ultimate design?

Step 4: In small groups, with the entire class, answer the following questions:

1. Why did STS choose to replace its paper-based inspection reporting system?

2. How did a database management system simplify development of a computerized system for inspection and repair?

3. Why was a distributed database the right approach for STS in this situation?

IS ON
THE WEB

IS ON THE WEB

Exercise 1: The Web page for Chapter 4 will direct you to an article about the use of database management systems for business or government purposes. Read the article and then answer any one of the following questions:

a) What features of a DBMS are most critical to the success of the database application described in the article?

b) What are the difficulties of administering the database described in the article?

c) What privacy and security issues are associated with the database described in the article, and how are these issues being addressed?

Exercise 2: Visit the Web sites of the object-oriented and XML database vendors listed on the Web page for Chapter 4. Read their FAQs and white papers. Then, compare the strengths and weaknesses of object and XML models to the relational DBMS model.

RECOMMENDED READINGS

Date, C. J., and Hugh Darwen. *Foundation for Future Database Systems: The Third Manifesto*. Boston: Addison Wesley Longman, 2000.

Hoffer, Jeffrey A., Mary B. Prescott, and Fred R. McFadden. *Modern Database Management*, 6th ed. Upper Saddle River, NJ: Prentice Hall PTR, 2001.

Ponniah, Paulraj. *Data Warehousing Fundamentals*, vol. 1. New York: John Wiley & Sons, 2001.

Silverston, Len. *The Data Model Resource Book: A Library of Universal Data Models for All Enterprises*, vol. 1. New York: John Wiley & Sons, 2001.

Tannenbaum, Adrienne. *Metadata Solutions: Using Metamodels, Repositories, XML, and Enterprise Portals to Generate Information on Demand*. Boston: Addison Wesley Longman, 2001.

Thuraisingham, Bhavani M. *XML Databases and the Semantic Web*. Boca Raton, FL: CRC Press, 2002.

The following publications provide regular features about database management systems:

Database Trends and Applications (http://www.databasetrends.com).

DB2 Magazine (http://www.db2mag.com).

DMReview (http://www.dmreview.com).

Journal of Conceptual Modeling (http://www.inconcept.com/JCM/index.html).

Journal of Database Management (http://www.idea-group.com).

NOTES

1. Stacy Collett, "Incoming! External Business Intelligence Can Be a Powerful Addition to Your Data Warehouse, But Beware of Data Overload," *Computerworld,* 15 April 2002, 34. Hugh J. Watson, Barbara H. Wixom, Jonathan D. Buonamici, and James R. Revak, "Sherwin-Williams' Data Mart Strategy: Creating Intelligence across the Supply Chain," *Communications of the AIS,* 5 May 2001. Jim Revak, "Sherwin-Williams' Data Warehouse: The Intelligence in the Supply Chain," *Journal of Innovative Management,* Winter 2001–2002. The Sherwin-Williams Company, *2001 Annual Report.*

2. Paul R.Hagen, with David M.Cooperstein, Christopher Renyi, and Jennifer Schaeffer, *The Forrester Report: Implementing Customer Heuristics,* Cambridge, MA: Forrester Research, 2001, 3. Percentage is based on interviews of 35 executives of department stores, catalog stores, and travel service companies.

3. Erika Engle, "Software Takes Customer Service beyond First Sale," *Pacific Business News,* 9 July 1999, 15.

4. See Gerhard Weikum and Gottfried Vossen, *Transactional Information Systems: Theory, Algorithms, and the Practice of Concurrency Control,* Morgan Kaufmann Publishers, 2001; Quazi N. Ahmed and Susan V. Vrbsky, "Maintaining Security and Timeliness in Real-Time Database System," *The Journal of Systems and Software,* 1 March 2002, 15–29.

5. See Philip M. Lewis, Michael Kifer, and Arthur J. Bernstein, *Database and Transaction Processing,* Boston: Addison Wesley, 2001.

6. See, for example, George T. Duncan, and Sumitra Mukherjee, "Optimal Disclosure Limitation Strategy in Statistical Databases: Deterring Tracker Attacks Through Additive Noise," *Journal of the American Statistical Association,* September 2000, 720–729.

7. Queenie Ng, "Chinese Bank Deploys BI for Faster Sales Analysis," *Asia Computer Weekly,* 10 June 2002, 1.

8. Alan J. Liddle, "Popeyes Franchisee Relies on 'Intelligence' to Convert POS Data into Actionable Information for Improved Performance," *Nation's Restaurant News;* 27 May 2002, 44–46.

9. http://www.evokesoft.com/pdf/uk.pdf, accessed on 16 June 2002.

10. http://www.acta.com/customers/guinness.htm, accessed on 16 June 2002.

11. Roshni Jayakar, "Bharti Televentures Calming the Churn," Business Today, 15 September 2002, 84. Himalee Bahl, "Bharti Televentures' Results: False Rings?," Yahoo News, accessed at http://in.biz.yahoo.com/020513/110/1nxk6 .html on 8 September 2002.

12. "Marcus Corporation Enhancing Business Performance with MicroStrategy Software," *PR Newswire,* 4 September 2002.

13. Marion Agnew, "CRM Plus Lots of Data Equals More Sales for Borders," *Informationweek,* 7 May 7, 2001, 114–118.

14. Hugh J. Watson et al, "Sherwin-Williams' Data Mart Strategy."

15. Carol Sliwa, "Ford Settles on Microsoft Content Management Server," Computerworld.com, 5 April 2002, http://www.computerworld. com/softwaretopics/software/story/0,10801,699 04,00.html, accessed on 18 June 2002.

16. P. Chen, "The Entity-Relationship Model— Toward a Unified View of Data," *ACM Transactions on Database Systems* 1 (1976); Robert W. Blanning, "An Entity-Relationship Framework for Information Resource Management," *Information & Management* 15 (September, 1988): 113–119.

17. For more details, see M. Tamer Ozsu and Patrick Valduriez, *Principles of Distributed Database Systems,* 2nd ed., Upper Saddle River, NJ: Prentice Hall, 1999.

18. S. R. Gordon and J. R. Gordon, "Organizational Hurdles to Distributed Database Management Systems (DDBMS) Adoption," *Information & Management* 22 (1992): 333–345.

19. American National Standards Institute, Database Language SQL, ANSI X3.168-1992, 1992. (See International Organization for Standardization, *Database Language SQL, ISO DIS 9075:1991,* 1991.)

20. W. Kim, "Object-Oriented Databases: Definition And Research Directions," *IEEE Transactions of Knowledge and Data Engineering,* 2 September 1990, 327–341. N. Leavitt, "Whatever happened to object-oriented databases?" *Computer,* August 2000, 16–19.

21. See, for example, Mickey Jordan, Malcolm P. Atkinson, and Ron Morrison, Eds., *Advances in Persistent Object Systems: Proceedings of the Eight International Workshop on Persistent Object Systems (POS-8) and the Third International Workshop on Persistence and Java,* Morgan Kaufmann Publishers, 1998.

22. See, for example, Paul Geoffrey Brown, *Object-Relational Database Development: A Plumber's Guide,* Upper Saddle River, NJ: Prentice Hall PTR, 2000.

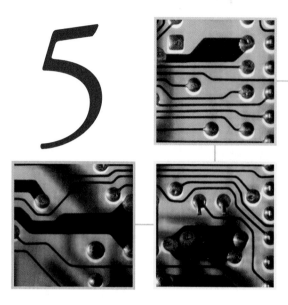

5

Telecommunication and Networks

LEARNING OBJECTIVES

After completing Chapter 5, you will be able to:

- Identify and define the elements of communication.
- Identify three dimensions of telecommunication that affect technological options.
- Describe the five steps in the telecommunication process.
- Identify a network's type based on the distance it covers and the organizational context of its use.
- Give examples of the business applications of telecommunication.
- Describe the communication industry in the United States and abroad.
- Discuss the role of the OSI model in creating telecommunication standards.
- List and compare the different types of media used for telecommunication.
- Identify four LAN protocols and four WAN services.
- Briefly describe the development of the Internet.
- Describe the functions of a network administrator and the tools that administrators use to manage telecommunication networks.
- Explain how the public key infrastructure assures message privacy, authentication, non-repudiation, and integrity.

Using Networks at the Miller-Dwan Medical Center

The Miller-Dwan Medical Center (MDMC), a 165-bed hospital located in Duluth, Minnesota, recently installed a wireless network to improve care for its patients and to increase the hospital's operational efficiency. Before the network was installed, doctors and nurses filled out paper forms and accessed patient information on terminals located near the nursing stations. Not only had these terminals become bottlenecks, but their distance from the patients also made service awkward. Patient information wasn't necessarily current or accurate because it had to be transferred from paper to computer when the terminals were available and the medical staff was free. Now, patient data can be input and accessed at the patient's bedside from laptops (and potentially handheld computers) that the medical staff members wheel with them on carts as they move from room to room. Doctors and nurses can perform tasks such as ordering a medical test, writing a prescription, or even ordering a special meal while consulting with the patient. In addition, patients are admitted in one-third the time needed before the network was installed, and nurses and doctors have the information that they need to treat patients faster and more accurately.

The hospital staff had considered several alternatives to the wireless network. A solution that required a terminal in each room was rejected because of its expense. Another solution, one that would put a network connection in each room, was rejected because plugging and unplugging the laptops would take time and the addition of wires to the jumble already in the rooms was thought to be hazardous.

The MDMC did not need to change its software systems to accommodate the new network. Most of the hospital's transactions are processed by the Meditech clinical information system that hospital employees used before the network was installed. However, now hospital employees are confident that the information that they obtain from the system is current and accurate. Furthermore, the network has considerably reduced the time spent doing useless paperwork.[1]

MDMC's management is convinced that it has chosen the right solution for the task at hand. But questions remain. Should doctors outside the hospital be connected to the network so that they can more closely monitor their patients? If so, how? Can the wireless signals be picked up outside the hospital? If so, how will the confidentiality of patients' medical records be maintained? And, how can the hospital best communicate with the regional community that it serves? The hospital's managers need to be able to answer questions such as these and provide the communication capability necessary to make the hospital the best it can be. This chapter addresses what managers, such as those at the MDMC, need to know about telecommunication and networks to manage effectively.

We start this chapter by presenting some basic principles and applications of telecommunication. We then address the public infrastructure that most long-distance communication requires. Next, we explore the technologies available for telecommunication, including those that the management of the MDMC might consider, especially the technologies associated with wireless networks and the Internet. Finally, we address the issues associated with the management of telecommunication and networks, especially the issue of security.

TELECOMMUNICATION PRINCIPLES AND APPLICATIONS

Communication is the exchange of information between two parties. **Telecommunication** is communication at a distance. In this section we address some basic principles of telecommunication and explore how telecommunication is applied to business.

Principles of Telecommunication and Networking

Communication is one of the most important of all human needs. It is how we understand the world around us, how we select our mates, and how we teach our children. We communicate primarily through sight and sound. Those who are born blind and deaf, such as Helen Keller, rely on other senses, such as touch, to communicate. It's hard to imagine life without communication, and hard to believe that the human species could exist if we could not communicate with one another.

A business is a complex organization that relies on communication among its employees to organize its internal activities and communicate with its customers and suppliers to generate and sell its products and services. Wal-Mart, for example, communicates constantly with its suppliers to keep them advised of their stock in its stores and to seek their input on what products to carry.[2] Not-for-profit organizations, governments, and other organizations also rely on communication among their members and the broader community to execute their missions. Nurses, doctors, pharmacists, and other employees at the MDMC communicate with one another to coordinate patient care.

Humans have evolved language to communicate complex ideas. We have also developed writing, which enhances our ability to communicate at a distance. We communicate not only to exchange information but also to establish and maintain relationships.

Elements of Communication

We consider the basic element of communication to be a message (see Figure 5-1). A **message** is one idea, or one unit of information, sent from one party to another. Although we can divide a message into pieces, such as sentences, phrases, words, letters, and even bits, these pieces by themselves have no meaning. Usually, the recipient of a message interprets its meaning within some context.

A *conversation* is an exchange of messages between two parties, usually but not always on a single topic or subject. The technical term for a conversation using telecommunica-

FIGURE 5-1

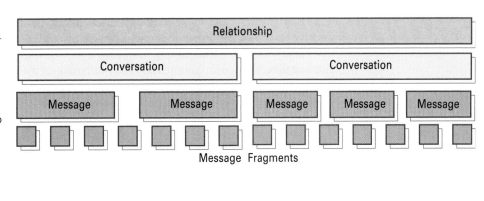

FIGURE 5-1

Elements of communication: A message is composed of message fragments; a conversation is composed of two or more messages; and a relationship is created over several conversations and establishes a context for interpreting new conversations.

tion equipment is a **session**, an extended series of messages having meaning and communicated over a period of time in some order.

A *relationship* defines the context of communication. Over an extended period of time, two parties establish a history of communication, adding richness to the context of any additional communication. The parties understand their roles relative to one another and establish expectations for how their messages are received and interpreted.

Dimensions of Telecommunication

We identify three dimensions that affect the technological options for telecommunication: distance, organizational context, and automation context (see Table 5-1). Distance significantly affects options for communication. In close proximity, face-to-face conversation is possible. At long distances, particularly internationally, communication generally requires the use of public equipment and facilities. In practice, options for telecommunication very greatly depending on whether we communicate within a building or campus (local area), within a city or metropolitan area, or over a longer distance (wide area). To make a telephone call, for example, employees in an office might simply dial a two-digit extension for someone in their building; they might need to dial a 9 to get to get a dial tone before dialing a seven-digit number to call someone within their metropolitan area; and they might need to use a special phone for long-distance calling.

The organizational context of communication is also important, as it establishes the nature of the relationships between the communicating parties. We distinguish among communication within an organization, communication between organizational partners, such as customers or suppliers, and communication with the public. Organizations typically share much more information among their employees than they are willing to share

TABLE 5-1

Dimensions of Telecommunication.

Dimension	Possible Values
Distance	Face-to-face Building or campus Metropolitan area Wide area
Organizational Context	Organizational members only Organizational members and partners Public
Automation Context	Human/Human Human/Computer (Input/Output) Computer/Computer

with their partners, and they provide even less information to the public. The need for security also becomes more important as communication becomes more public.

Finally, we distinguish among human/human, human/computer (input or output), and computer/computer communication. Where one of the parties to communication is human, the communication is relatively slow and typically involves language. When only computers are involved, the communication can be much faster, is typically digital, and may be highly encoded.

The Telecommunication Process

Telecommunication, at its simplest, usually requires the following five steps:

1. Sender initiates message communication.
2. Device puts sender's message onto a telecommunication medium.
3. *Telecommunication medium* transfers message to receiver's location.
4. Device takes message off the communication medium.
5. Recipient receives the message.

Figure 5-2 illustrates this process for the simple children's game that sends messages over a tightly stretched string between two tin cans. In this simple example, the tin cans represent the telecommunication devices and the string represents the telecommunication medium.

Telecommunication Capacity

The capacity for information flow over a telecommunication channel, called **bandwidth**, is usually measured in bits/second. This capacity is affected by many factors, especially the communication devices and the media used to transmit the information. Face-to-face bandwidth, however, is simply limited by how fast we can talk. Communication among computer devices usually occurs with much greater bandwidth. Managers need to forecast what bandwidth they will need when installing new systems so they can effectively guide their technical advisors in selecting the appropriate telecommunication equipment.

Telecommunication Networks

A **network** is simply a set of points and the connections between them. In a telecommunications network, the points represent message senders, recipients, and their associated

---

FIGURE 5-2

Children's game with tin cans and string illustrates the process of telecommunication.

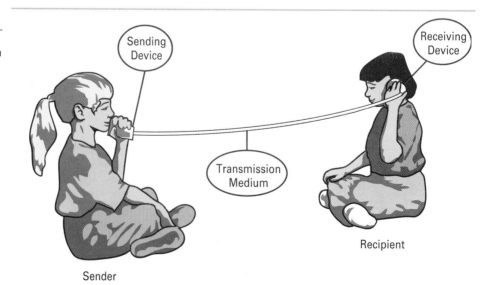

computer devices; the connections represent telecommunications media. Communication across a network is more complex than point-to-point communication because each message must be routed from its sender to its intended recipient.

We distinguish among different network types based on two of the dimensions of communication: distance and organizational context. On the distance dimension, networks are called **local area networks (LANs)** if they serve a building or campus, *metropolitan area networks (MANs)* if they serve a metropolitan region, or **wide area networks (WANs)** if they connect points over greater distances than a metropolitan region. On the organizational context dimension, networks are called **intranets** if they serve a company's employees, **extranets** if they serve employees and partner organizations, and public networks if they serve the general public. Public networks include telephone networks, cable networks, satellite networks, and the Internet.

Business Applications of Telecommunication

Organizations use telecommunication to coordinate business activities, facilitate group decision making, and transact electronic commerce.

Coordination of Business Activities

Managers at most companies use electronic mail, voice mail, videoconferencing, and corporate intranets to communicate with their coworkers, supervisors, subordinates, and others.

Companies with corporate networks have essentially replaced memos and other written correspondence with *electronic mail (e-mail)*, which uses computers to deliver messages. E-mail has reduced telephone traffic and time wasted by employees responding to telephone calls. Employees now send messages that are not time-critical by electronic mail, knowing that people can read them at their convenience. Electronic mail software allows users to share documents, both text and multimedia, by attaching them to a mail message. Employees can send electronic mail to and receive it from addresses outside the company if its internal network is connected to the Internet or other public networks.

Voice mail uses computers to deliver voice messages. The process works as follows. A caller dials the *voice mailbox* of the person to whom she wishes to speak. After receiving a signal to begin, the caller leaves a message. The recipient can access the message at his telephone or remotely by dialing into the voice mailbox. Communication technology records the voice data in the appropriate location and retrieves it for replay. Most voice mail systems today do not connect to the corporate data network. However, new products can now integrate voice mail with electronic mail and facsimile to produce a single listing of messages and allow users to route voice messages using their computer networks.[3] Some products even do voice to text translation, so that users can read a voice mail message before listening to it.[4] These developments provide good incentives for integrating voice mail systems with other organizational systems on a common network.

Videoconferencing allows people in different locations to hold a conference as if they were in one room. It overcomes the slow speed of typing versus talking and improves the context of communication by capturing body language. Videoconferencing can be an effective way to reduce the cost of travel. Figure 5-3 shows a typical setup for videoconferencing. Eliokem, a $150 million chemical manufacturer, uses videoconferencing to reduce travel between its operating companies in France and Ohio, saving both time and money. The Wendy's restaurant chain recouped the cost of its videoconferencing systems in just six months by reducing travel.[5]

A network helps managers and employees throughout their company to coordinate their functional activities. Manufacturing managers might collect and use information about costs, supplies, inventory, special product changes, and quality control tests. Corporate property managers might use records about real estate owned and managed by

FIGURE   5-3

Videoconferencing saves
the cost of travel and
permits users to see
each other and to work
on shared documents.

the company. Engineering departments might maintain the latest specifications of company products, updates on customer complaints, and design drawings online for access throughout the company. Marketing and sales departments might maintain a database of customer leads that employees at sites throughout the world can access. Human resource professionals might regularly update job descriptions, benefits, and other compensation information for the company's employees to access.

Hewlett-Packard (HP) uses an intranet for many human resource functions. The company's 88,000 employees in 150 countries can access HP's intranet to fill out forms about beneficiaries, address changes, tax withholding, and even bank information. Up to 150 different types of transactions are automated, with forms and instructions in eight languages available to employees 24 hours a day. Previously, human resource professionals had to enter these data manually taking time from their knowledge work to perform simple clerical functions.[6]

Computer networks also help employees communicate across functional areas. When a sales clerk in the order department takes an order, for example, people in warehousing, manufacturing, billing, and shipping have access to the order so that they can act on it. Communication becomes even more important in a global environment. A company might order its raw goods in one part of the world, assemble its product in another, and sell the product in still other locales.

The United States Department of State plans to use a secure intranet to share information with its embassies and foreign affairs offices using e-mail, databases, and other applications. The intranet could be used, for example, to do research on an applicant for a visa to visit the United States. Currently the information that employees need is scattered over many unlinked databases, and sharing that information is difficult at best.[7]

As these examples show, networks keep businesses running smoothly and efficiently. The exchange of information among employees in different locations is crucial for almost all operational and transactional systems. Information exchange is also critical for managerial decision making, particularly when teams or groups are involved. Chapter 7 addresses the coordination of business activities in more depth.

Group Decision Making

Managers may introduce groupware, computer hardware and software that support a group's interactions, to help teams perform their tasks and accomplish their goals more effectively. Groupware supports information sharing among group members and so improves task coordination, the conduct of meetings, and problem solving. Some futurists believe that improvements in communication and networking technologies will fundamentally change the way people work, deriving productivity not from the individual but from the group.[8] Members of the vestry of St. John's Episcopal Church in Brooklyn, New York use groupware from Groove Networks to communicate with one another and stay in synch, share and edit documents in real time or off-line, and even make minutes and bulletins available to parishioners.[9] Chapter 8 discusses groupware in more detail, focusing on the way it facilitates group decision making and group project activities.

Electronic Commerce

Companies increasingly use **electronic commerce (e-commerce),** electronic transactions related to the purchase and delivery of goods and services. Although some people define electronic commerce as including only transactions that involve the electronic transfer of money, we also include electronic transactions relating to a purchase by check, phone, or some other means. Electronic commerce includes retail trade between individuals and businesses as well as business-to-business trade. Companies use extranets and public networks for e-commerce.

In 1996, about 54 percent of all Internet users in the United States purchased products or services using the Web.[10] Many more shopped on the Web but purchased through traditional channels. As people gained confidence in the security of electronic commerce and more people obtained access to the Internet, sales grew dramatically. During the 2001 holiday season, for example, U.S. consumers spent $8.3 billion online. Of those who made online purchases, 41 percent bought half or more of their gifts online.[11]

The dollar volume of retail shopping, however, pales in comparison to online business purchasing. Worldwide, B2B e-commerce was estimated at more than $800 billion in 2001.[12] Furthermore, there is a great deal of business-to-business communication that would not be included in the dollar statistics given for e-commerce. Among these are electronic bill paying, electronic banking, product research, and bidding that does not result in the award of a contract.

Chapters 6 and 7 address electronic commerce in more depth.

TELECOMMUNICATION INFRASTRUCTURE

Although every organization is responsible for building its own infrastructure, all organizations depend, to some extent, on the public infrastructure that enables communication to take place broadly within and among organizations. Telecommunication **infrastructure** refers to the facilities available for carrying out telecommunication. Much of this infrastructure is owned or controlled by companies called communication carriers. In this section, we examine the nature of the communication carrier industry and the issues involved with telecommunication across country borders.

The Communication Carrier Industry

A **communication carrier** is a government agency or private company that provides communication services and facilities to the public. Private carriers are almost always regulated to some degree and are called **common carriers.** In many countries, a company called a *PTT* (Postal, Telephone, and Telegraph company), operated or owned by the government, provides communication services as a monopoly carrier. Cable television companies are not generally considered communication carriers, although cable TV lines are capable of providing some degree of two-way communication.

Telephone Carrier Structure in the United States

A local exchange carrier (LEC), such as Albany Mutual Telephone Association in Albany, Minnesota, provides telephone service within a region called a LATA (Local Access Transport Area), which covers approximately one metropolitan area or a large rural or semi-rural district. Long-distance carriers, such as AT&T and MCI, provide service between LATAs and internationally. LECs and long-distance carriers jointly handle long-distance calls and share the revenue according to federal regulations. As a result of the U.S. Telecommunications Deregulation and Reform Act of 1996, long-distance carriers, LECs, and cable television companies can now each provide long distance, local, and cable TV service. RCN is an example of a company that competes in all three markets.[13]

Cellular Services

Cellular technology enables message transmission without a cabled connection to a telephone company. Instead, cellular phones or mobile computers transmit users' calls over radio signals to the closest antenna of an array of antennas positioned strategically by the cellular carrier to cover an entire service region. As shown in Figure 5-4, the call is passed from antenna to antenna until it reaches the telephone office, which routes it by land or

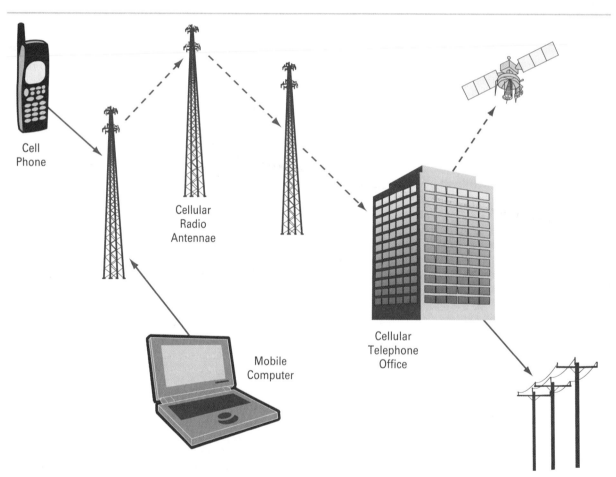

Cell Phone

Cellular Radio Antennae

Mobile Computer

Cellular Telephone Office

FIGURE 5-4 A mobile computer with a cellular modem or a cellular phone sends a message that is received by the nearest cellular radio antenna. The cellular system passes the message from antenna to antenna until it reaches a cellular switching office where it is routed by landlines or satellite to its ultimate destination.

satellite to other cities or countries. As a cellular phone moves out of the range of one antenna and into the range of another, computers track its movements so that they can route signals to it appropriately. Cellular phones operate in radio frequencies that are regulated by the Federal Communications Commission in the United States. The International Telecommunications Union, an agency of the United Nations, sets standards for the use of radio frequencies internationally.

Several incompatible standards exist for the signal that cellular phones transmit and receive. As a result, a cell phone that works in one country will not necessarily work in another country; even within a country or region, a single telephone device will not work everywhere, despite the existence of cellular coverage. Unfortunately, the number of standards is increasing, as cellular phone companies strive to provide better quality and increased bandwidth.

The first generation of cellular phones, available in the late 1970s and still in use today, communicated with an analog rather than a digital signal. The analog signal was prone to interference and had a very limited bandwidth, suitable only for voice transmission. The second generation of cellular phones, for which four major conflicting standards exist, became commercially available in 1992 and operate digitally at rates up to 9,600 bits/second (bps). This bandwidth is sufficient for e-mail, messaging, and other applications that require only the transmission and reception of text, very small computer programs, and very limited graphics. Technology for a third generation, operating at 384 Kbps, is now available, but implementation has been slow. Instead, most carriers are implementing an evolutionary upgrade of their equipment to standards known as "enhanced second-generation," or "2.5G." These standards, which again use different technologies, operate at between 57.6 and 171.2 Kbps.

Cable

The cable television industry has begun to leverage the capacity it has in its cable networks to deliver data communication services. After using most of its capacity for television transmission, cable still has plenty of capacity for simultaneous data transmission. Because cable companies mostly serve local areas, they work best for MANs and need to interact with long-distance carriers to provide WAN or Internet services.

Value Added Networks

Resellers of telephone and satellite capacity, commonly called **value added networks** (**VANs**), purchase communication services from common carriers in bulk and resell them for a profit. They bundle the messages of many companies and people and transmit them on lines leased from common carriers. Resellers achieve scale economies that let them offer lower prices. They may also offer extra services, such as electronic mail, access to electronic databases, and electronic banking.

DSI Toys, a $30 million manufacturer of high quality, value-priced toys and children's consumer electronics, uses CTI Communications, a Coeur d'Alene, Idaho-based VAN, for transacting business electronically with Wal-Mart. In addition to providing communication services, CTI Communications translates transactions from DSI Toys' computer systems into a form that Wal-Mart's systems can process automatically, and vice versa.[14]

International Issues

Foreign countries generally have a less well-developed communications infrastructure than the United States. Until recently, government monopolies regulated and controlled telecommunications in most companies outside the United States. However, increasing political pressures, especially within the World Trade Organization (WTO) and the European Union (EU), and the competitive pressure of mobile technologies have combined to increase privatization of telecommunication carriers and competition among them worldwide. For example, in October 2000, the EU Parliament adopted a regulation to open competition in telecom markets by the end of 2001. Although that regulation was superceded by a compromise that struck a balance between local regulation and EU rules, there is little doubt that competition is increasing in Europe both in law and in practice.[15] In 2000, China split its monopoly carrier, China Telecom, into two companies, one focusing on landlines and one on mobile telecommunication, to promote competition.[16] Still, in many parts of the world, particularly in developing countries, organizations requesting new service may have to wait several months or even years to obtain it.

Many countries have rules that restrict the flow of data across their boundaries or restrict or license the data that companies can collect. Some of these restrictions derive from local privacy laws that can't be enforced after the export of data. For example, the EU has more restrictive laws than the United States regarding the privacy of individuals. EU law prohibits the export of data to the United States unless the recipient of the information can protect the privacy of EU individuals to the extent guaranteed by EU law or unless the individual waives his right to privacy. Companies doing business in Europe must be aware of these laws and act accordingly, as they may be sued for failing to do so.[17] Some countries have even more restrictive rules. For example, Sweden prohibits, with very few exceptions, the processing of personal data that reveals membership in a trade union.[18]

TELECOMMUNICATION TECHNOLOGY

Telecommunication technology has been evolving so rapidly that it's unreasonable to expect business managers to keep current in the field. Fortunately, most IT departments employ telecommunication specialists who handle the design and development of communication systems. Also, despite the rapid advances in telecommunication technology, its components have remained remarkably constant over many years. So, although managers are wise to rely on technical experts for the design, installation, and maintenance of their telecommunication infrastructure, they should know enough to participate intelligently in its design to assure that their needs are adequately met. MDMC's network, for example, was designed and installed by Sisu Medical Systems, a consortium of Minnesota community hospitals formed to manage their IT needs. However, the participation of MDMC's managers, doctors, and nurses was critical to the proper design and acceptance of the network. This section summarizes what every manager and knowledge worker needs to know about telecommunication technology to communicate wisely with telecommunication specialists.

The technology to support telecommunication is built on a hierarchy of standards that assures its different parts will work properly together. We begin this section with a discussion of this hierarchy, known as the OSI model. We then address different components of the technology, starting with the devices that connect computers to transmission media, continuing with the transmission medium itself, and then addressing switching and routing technologies, which are critical for telecommunication in a network. Finally, we look at the existing and emerging standards that apply to local and wide area networks.

Industry Standards and the OSI Model

The computer and communications industries have developed *standards*—specific characteristics of telecommunications media, hardware, and software—that make it possible to mix computer and communications products from different vendors. The **OSI model (Open Systems Interconnection model)** provides a framework for thinking about communication standards. The International Standards Organization (ISO) created the OSI model to divide the communication process into layers, as shown in Table 5-2. This layered model simplifies the creation of standards and makes it easier to specify their scope.

A standard at any layer of the OSI model must either:

- Work with all standards at lower layers; or
- Specify which lower-layer standards it requires; or
- Specify its own standard at lower layers.

For example, **TCP/IP,** the standard that defines how messages are sent across the Internet, addresses layers 3 and 4 of the OSI model and works with any standard at layers 1 and 2. In other words, no matter what standard is selected for the medium of transmission (layer 1), wireless or wired, TCP/IP standards apply and messages sent according to

TABLE 5-2   The OSI Model divides the communication process into parts and identifies the responsibilities of standards within each part.

General Description	Specific Layer	At Origin	In Route	At Destination
Application Generates messages based on the user's applications (e.g. e-mail)	7 Application	Interface the communication with the application		Interface the communication with the application
	6 Presentation	Perform data compression Format messages for transmission		Decompress data Prepare data for receipt by application
Network Takes messages generated by the application level, breaks them into blocks, ensures their integrity, and reassembles them into messages; establishes and ensures the correct order of sessions.	5 Session	Establish session connection Associate message with session Terminate connection	Create end-to-end circuit if required	Establish session connection Associate message with session Terminate connection
	4 Transport	Divide message into blocks Determine end-to-end routing over subnetworks	Implement routing	Assemble blocks into messages Ensure integrity of message
	3 Network	Divide block into frames Determine routing on subnetwork	Implement routing Ensure integrity of block over each subnetwork	Assemble frames into block
Data link Controls the physical layer by determining how and when to send signals over it; breaks message into blocks and ensures their integrity	2 Data Link	Insert packet into frame	Ensure integrity of packet over each circuit	
Physical Deals with transmission media and hardware necessary to create circuits and send data as signals, and with the connections between the hardware and the media used	1 Physical	Type of connectors Timing of signal	Nature of cable	Type of connectors

these standards will be properly received. Higher-layer standards, such as HTTP, used for World Wide Web applications, might specify that it will work in any TCP/IP network. Many corporate networks, taking advantage of this fact, operate according to the TCP/IP standards so that users can browse their intranet just as they browse the Internet.

You will need to understand several communication concepts to understand the OSI model. Some standards divide a message into fragments called *blocks*. These blocks are sent sequentially: along its route from A to E, a message block might pass through devices at points B, C, and D. The path segments AB, BC, CD, and DE are called *data links*. Blocks might be divided into **packets** or *frames* for transmission over the data links. The packets might travel over different paths to reach their destination. At the receiving end, packets or frames are reassembled into blocks; blocks are held until a complete message is formed; and messages are sent to the terminal or application. At each layer of the OSI model, certain services assure the integrity of messages and improve security and/or performance.

Industry standards allow equipment and software manufacturers to develop products that work with other equipment and software. A company might also select internal standards from the industry standards to simplify the support of the interfaces between products and the management of a company's data communications. For this reason, MDMC's policies might have limited the hospital managers' choices in selecting the type of equipment for its wireless network.

The Computer/Medium Interface

Two types of devices connect a computer to the transmission medium—modems and adaptors.

A **modem** provides an interface between a computer or network on the one side and the phone line, cable line, or cellular connection of a communication carrier. Table 5-3 lists the types of modems. Standards define transmission speeds, compression technologies, and commands that direct the modem to perform such tasks as dialing a telephone number. The transmission speed and compression technology together determine how many bits can be transmitted in one second.

An **adaptor**, also called a **network interface card** (**NIC**), provides a direct wired or wireless connection between a computer and a network. The adaptor sends signals through connector ports to a network according to a selected standard. For example, an Ethernet adaptor provides a connector that conforms to Ethernet standards (see section on switching and routing technologies) and creates and interprets Ethernet signals and addresses.

TABLE 5-3

Numerous types of modems interface between the computer or terminal and the phone or cable lines.

Type	Characteristics
Internal	Located inside a computer; directly connects the computer's data bus and the telephone or cable line
External	Connects to the back of the computer through a serial or printer port and then to a telephone or cable line
Cable	Connects to coaxial cable
Wireless	Connects directly into the cellular telephone network without cables
Asynchronous	Has a data link protocol that makes them commonly used with PCs; operates at the speed of the lowest device it communicates with
Synchronous	Has a data link protocol that makes them commonly used with mainframes
Multi-port (or multiplexor)	Combines signals from several ports or computers (usually mid-range or mainframe) into a single phone line for long-distance transmission to another multiplexor that separates the signals at the receiving end

Transmission Media

Managers and computer professionals often select the medium of transmission for telecommunication. The most common media are **twisted-pair wire, coaxial cable,** and **fiber optic cable,** as well as electromagnetic signals in microwave, infrared, and radio frequencies. Table 5-4 highlights the most relevant characteristics of these media.

- **Twisted-pair wire** connects a telephone to its telephone jack in most homes. Because many buildings have excessive amounts of this wire that can be used for telecommunications purposes, it is inexpensive and readily available. Transmission speeds up to 10 megabits/second are possible. Higher grades of twisted-pair wire can support rates of up to a gigabit/second.
- **Coaxial cable,** used by cable television companies, brings television signals into the home. Although more bulky, more expensive, and less common in buildings than twisted-pair wire, it has a higher theoretical bandwidth than twisted-pair wire, and so it can transmit more data per second.
- **Fiber optic cable,** which has the greatest capacity of the telecommunications media, carries messages on a beam of light rather than using an electrical signal. Many long-distance telephone companies use it to carry telephone calls simultaneously between major switching stations. Private companies use it to carry data within their buildings and between closely spaced buildings. Fiber optic cable offers great security because of its low resistance to tapping and provides greater immunity to electrical interference than does electrical cable. It costs about 5 times more than the high-quality twisted-pair cable but exceeds its

TABLE 5-4		
Data communication media have different characteristics. Expense is calculated for the lowest capacity connection between two points and does not include the cost of signal boosting devices for long-distance connections.	Twisted-pair wire	Least expensive Widely available Moderate capacity Easy to install
	Coaxial cable	Moderately expensive Moderate to high capacity Cumbersome and thick wires Entry into homes through cable TV
	Fiber optic cable	Relatively expensive Very high capacity Very high security Difficult to bend or manipulate
	Microwave signals	Expensive Requires no cabling Can use satellite Best for high-volume, long-distance Limited to line-of-sight
	Infrared signals	Low to moderate capacity Inexpensive Short-distance limitation Requires no cabling Limited to line-of-sight Interference from hot objects
	Radio	Limited frequency range Potential interference Moderate to high capacity Limited distance Requires no cabling

capacity by more than one hundred. It also doesn't need *repeaters,* devices that twisted-pair and coaxial cable need to boost their signal, which weakens as it travels through the cable.

- *Microwaves* carry data. Relay towers, used for long-distance transmission, receive an incoming signal and retransmit it to another station within its view. Companies may buy capacity on an orbiting communications satellite that receives and retransmits their microwave signal. Microwaves effectively transmit data over long distances without using a telephone company.

- *Infrared signals* function only within line-of-sight. They carry data for short distances, such as within a building.

- *Radio signals* in special frequency bands reserved for short-distance communication and in unregulated frequency bands can carry data. Wireless LANs typically use radio signals to carry data between computers and a network interface. Although capacity varies, high-end systems can provide nearly the same capacity as most coaxial cable systems.

Switching and Routing Technologies

Telecommunication is relatively simple when only two people or computers are connected, as with a string-and-can play telephone. Real communication infrastructures involve networks, which allow message senders to choose who will receive their messages. In such an environment, equipment is needed to switch and route each message, and protocols are needed so that messages do not interfere with one another and so that the switches and routers can determine how each message should reach its destination.

Switching and Routing Devices

Four different types of devices determine the path of a message through a network: hubs, switches, routers, and gateways.

- A **hub** connects computers and sections of a network to one another. A hub forwards (without reading) every message it receives to everything connected to it. Network designers often use hubs to connect a group of computers to a network at a single point. All connections to a hub must have compatible standards for sending signals over the transmission media and hardware and creating and ensuring the correct order of sessions. Each computer station in a networked classroom will typically be wired to a hub connected to the campus's local area network.

- A **switch** connects two or more computers, hubs, sub-networks, or networks that have compatible standards for sending signals over transmission media and hardware and creating and ensuring the correct order of sessions. They examine the destination address of each incoming packet and forward the packet directly to the appropriate destination port without changing the packet. The Virginia Community College System uses switches at each of its 38 campuses to connect their local area networks to a college-wide wide area network.[19]

- A **router** connects two or more hubs, sub-networks, or networks that have the same network protocol and passes data between networks almost simultaneously. A router may modify the packet surrounding the data it transmits but doesn't change the data within the packet. A router examines the address of a packet's ultimate destination and determines the best path through the network to reach that destination. It then changes the packet so that it addresses the next router on the way to the ultimate address. A college might use a router to connect its campus network to the Internet.

- A **gateway** moves data between two networks that use different data link and network standards. It accepts data from one network, processes it into a format for another network, and then retransmits it. Some gateway products perform a specific conversion quickly; others combine software and hardware dedicated to the gateway and operate more slowly, possibly taking several hours before transferring messages between networks.

Network Protocols

A **network protocol** is a standard regarding how a message is packaged, secured, sent, routed, received, and acknowledged by the receiver within a network. Its purpose is to provide an environment in which the delivery of messages can be guaranteed. It may include any or all of layers 1 through 5 of the OSI model. We discuss LAN and WAN protocols separately, as they differ greatly.

LAN Protocols

The three most commonly used LAN protocols are Ethernet, Token Ring, and Wi-Fi. Bluetooth can also be considered a LAN protocol, although it is more commonly thought of as a protocol for a **personal area network (PAN).**

Ethernet

Ethernet is a group of standards that address media, connectors, and communication protocols. Every device on an Ethernet network has a unique address. To initiate communication, a device puts its data onto a bus cable (see Figure 5-5) along with the address of the intended recipient; the intended recipient reads the data. If two devices attempt to transmit at the same time, both notice that a collision has occurred and will each wait a random amount of time and then resend the data.

The Ethernet bus is located inside a single hub device as illustrated in Figure 5-6. Connections to the device appear to form a star shape. Ethernet standards limit the maximum distance between any two Ethernet devices, although these limits vary depending on

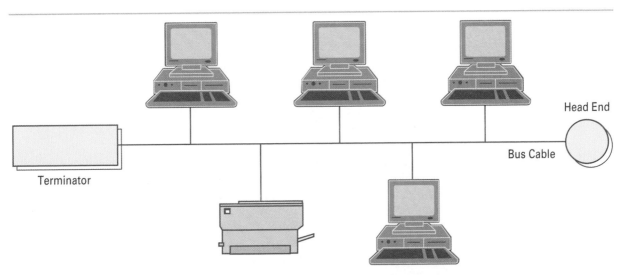

FIGURE   5-5   Computer adaptor cards, printer adaptor cards, and other devices put data on an Ethernet bus and take them off. All devices have access to every message but ignore all except those intended for them.

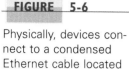

FIGURE   5-6

Physically, devices connect to a condensed Ethernet cable located inside an Ethernet hub.

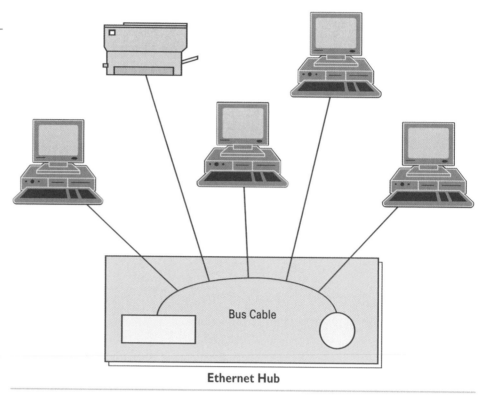

Ethernet Hub

the media and the bandwidth. Ethernet designers can overcome distance limits by linking several hubs to complete a LAN, as illustrated in Figure 5-7. Ethernet standards exist at several levels of price and performance, as shown in Table 5-5.

Tokyo DisneySea, a 300-acre theme park, uses a gigabit Ethernet network to connect its central control area with multiple rides, entertainment sites, and a 500-room hotel. In addition to controlling rides, the network transmits music in digital form from a central control room to amplifiers throughout the park without loss of sound quality. Using traditional analog cabling, Disney engineers estimate that they would have required cables up to two inches thick, and the quality would have been poorer due to signal interference.[20]

With optical fiber media, Ethernet limits can reach about six miles, making the protocol appropriate for metropolitan area networks. Cable Bahamas operates an Ethernet MAN that serves 50 businesses, 90 percent of the country's hotels, and residential customers on its four major islands at bandwidths ranging from 1 Mbps to 1 Gbps.[21]

Token Ring

The *token ring* protocol is designed to avoid message conflicts rather than detect and react to them. Devices in a Token Ring network are arranged in a unidirectional ring inside a hub, as shown in Figure 5-8. Unlike Ethernet, only one computer can directly read the output of another computer. When the network is turned on, the token monitor computer creates a message called an empty token. When a computer receives an empty token message, it will either resend the empty token or attach a message to the token and send it. Each computer in turn receives the message and passes it on until it reaches the intended recipient, which saves the message and attaches an acknowledgment to the token for the sender. Upon receiving the acknowledgment token, the sender either sends another message or creates a new empty token to pass to the next computer.

FIGURE 5-7

Ethernet hubs can be networked to provide Ethernet connections between devices that are too far apart to be connected by a single Ethernet hub.

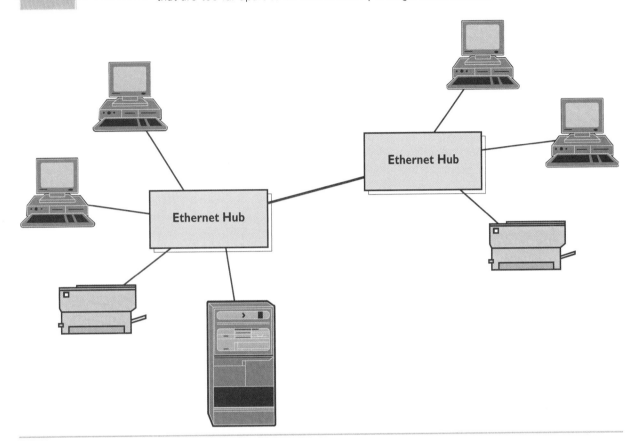

Collisions can't occur, but wasted capacity results. Computer failure also provides challenges for the operation of this type of network. Token ring standards vary from 4 to 16 megabits/second over regular or high-grade telephone wire. The popular FDDI standard permits data transmission rates of up to 100 Mbps on an optical fiber token ring network.

Wi-Fi

The **Wi-Fi** protocol is a standard for wireless LANs that operates like an Ethernet. Each device on the network has an address and communicates directly with a hub, in this case a hub that listens for and receives radio signals from the wireless adapters on the network. Initial Wi-Fi standards called for speeds of 11 Mbps and limited the range of the networks to a radius of 300 feet. Subsequent standards raise both limits.

TABLE 5-5

Ethernet standards vary in price and performance.

Standard	Speed	Requirements
10BaseT (Ethernet)	10 megabits/second	Standard twisted pair
Fast Ethernet	100 megabits/second	High-grade twisted pair or fiber optic cable
Gigabit Ethernet	1 gigabit/second	High-grade twisted pair (100 meters max) or fiberoptic cable
10G Ethernet	10 gigabits/second	Fiber optic cable

FIGURE   5-8

Circuits in a token ring connect each device to the next device. Messages are forwarded around the ring until they are received by the intended recipient.

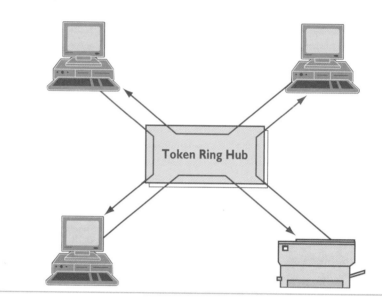

The city of Glendale, California is installing a Wi-Fi LAN to provide digital service to its police, fire, and public works departments. The city determined that the Wi-Fi solution would be cheaper than its cell phone service and would also provide additional bandwidth needed for such applications as transmitting mug shots to police cars in the field.[22]

Wi-Fi hubs can be connected to wired hubs or other wired devices, providing connection to the Internet or the phone system. McDonalds, the fast-food restaurant chain, plans to equip its 4,000 Japanese restaurants with Wi-Fi hubs so that its patrons can surf the Internet while they eat at a price of about $13 per month.[23] A number of Internet Service Providers have provided "hot spot" access points where their customers can link to their hubs for Internet service. Boingo has partnered with many of these firms, creating a large virtual network of Internet-accessible hot spots for its customers.[24]

Bluetooth

Bluetooth is a low-cost wireless (radio) protocol with a range of about 30 feet and a bandwidth of about 1 Mbps. Because of its short range, it is used primarily to connect devices of different types, such as a computer to a printer or a keyboard. Up to seven devices can be simultaneously connected into a small LAN or PAN called a *piconet.* Piconets can overlap, providing the capability of more complex networking. Devices on the piconet can include a hub, such as an Ethernet hub, providing connection to a wired LAN, the Internet, or the telephone system. DaimlerChrysler uses Bluetooth networking to connect its hands-free, voice-activated calling system, called U-Connect, to any Bluetooth enabled cell phone. The cell phone can be placed anywhere in a car, even in its driver's purse.[25]

Internetworking with LAN Backbones

What would you do if your company had a number of independent LANs that you wanted to integrate into one network? You might create a network of networks. You can implement this solution relatively easily using routers and switches if the networks are the same type. You can connect them using gateways if they are different types. In either case, the network that connects all the others is called a **backbone.** Figure 5-9 illustrates the use of a backbone to connect sub-networks into a complete LAN. Historically, *Fiber Distributed Data Interface (FDDI)*, a token-passing technology that uses two fiber optic rings operating in opposite directions at 100 megabits/second, was one of the most popular technologies for LAN backbones. Now, most companies prefer gigabit Ethernet or another technology called ATM.

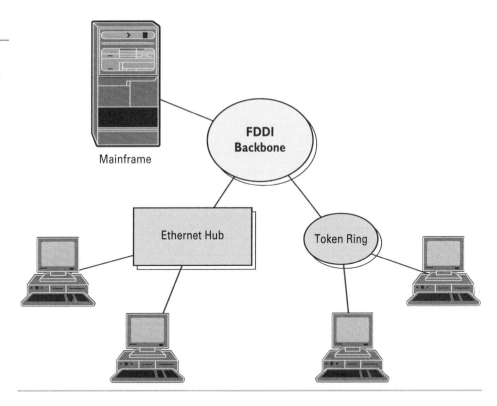

FIGURE 5-9

A backbone network connects subnetworks and devices with high messaging requirements.

Mainframe — FDDI Backbone — Ethernet Hub — Token Ring

Network designers typically plan the network backbone to have as much capacity as possible. This flexible planning approach allows them to expand the LAN by adding more LAN segments to the backbone. Most of the traffic will flow on the LAN segments, the original LANs, and any new ones. However, as the network grows, the backbone will experience increasing amounts of traffic.

WAN Services

Most organizations implement wide area networks using services purchased from cable or telephone companies. Table 5-6 compares various data services available.

TABLE 5-6

Organizations can choose from five types of wide-area networks.

Type	Examples	Comments
Leased line	T-1, Fractional T-1 (e.g. 1/4 and 1/2 T-1), T-4, SONET OC-48	A T-1 circuit works at 1544 Mbps and provides more than 24 times the capacity of a normal voice-grade telephone at less than 24 times the cost. Fractional T-1 lines are slightly more expensive. T-4 lines have much larger capacity (equal 168 T-1 lines) and cost somewhat more also. An OC-48 line provides 2.488 Gbps, the equivalent of more than 38,000 voice lines.
Switched circuit	ISDN BRI, ISDN PRI, SMDS, ADSL	The speed ranges from 128 Kbps to 1.544 Mbps for the ISDN lines. ADSL lines operate much faster: 8.192 Mbps from phone to subscriber and 1.088 from subscriber to phone company.
Packet switched	X.25, frame relay, ATM	Frame relay at 8 Kbps and ATM are replacing X.25 service.
Cellular	CDPD	This service operates at speeds of 19.2 Kbps.
Cable television		This service has delivery rates between 27 and 38 Mbps and return rates between 0.32 and 10 Mbps.

Leased Lines

A **leased line** creates a direct connection between two phone numbers rather than using a switch to provide a temporary connection to one or more circuits. When you sign a contract to lease a line, the telephone company hardwires the connection you requested. You pay for the capacity to send messages on that leased line whether or not you use it; nobody else can use it.

Leased line prices generally depend on the mileage between the points connected and the capacity of the line. A leased line costs less than paying for the same capacity on a pay-as-you-go basis. It establishes a better quality of connection between two points. In many areas of the world, telephone companies lease SONET (Synchronous Optical Network) circuits that use optical cable instead of telephone wire.

Switched Circuit Data Services

A normal telephone call uses a **switched circuit service**—a connection made between two points for the length of a session. Telephone charges may be fixed or based on usage.

- *ISDN (Integrated Services Digital Network)* describes a set of standards for integrating voice, computer data, and video transmission on the same telephone line. First introduced in the late 1970s, its acceptance varies dramatically by region. For example, in 2001, 31 percent of online Germans had an ISDN connection at home.[26] In the United States and Canada, less than 1 percent had ISDN at home and only about 7 percent had ISDN service from work.[27] European standards for ISDN differ from the U.S. standards, and no worldwide standards exist.

- *Digital Subscriber Line (DSL)* provides megabit/second speed over regular copper telephone lines. ADSL (Asymmetric Digital Subscribe Line) delivers data faster from the phone company to the subscriber and returns data at slower rates. Not all telephone circuits can handle DSL, and telephone companies have rolled out the service slowly. Nevertheless, estimates are that by 2006, 38 percent of U.S. households will use DSL for accessing the Internet.[28]

Packet Switched Services

Like switched circuit services, **packet switched services** provide a direct connection between any points on the telephone network but the packet switched services don't necessarily provide a fixed circuit for the entire session. Packet switched services break a message into packets, route these packets at the discretion of the phone company, and reassemble them at the destination, as illustrated in Figure 5-10. The telecom carrier can mix pieces of messages between different origins and destinations on the same long-distance line. Charges are based on the amount of data transmitted, not by the length of a session.

The most popular packet switched technologies are frame relay and ATM. A 20-year-old standard called "X.25" also has many installations worldwide, but has fallen out of favor with the availability of the newer technologies.

In the *frame relay* protocol, one computer opens a session by requesting a circuit of specified capacity to a destination computer. The network, if it accepts the request, creates a virtual circuit of the requested capacity using a series of circuits and switches. Frame relay breaks each message into variable length packets of up to 8 kilobytes and sends them sequentially through the virtual circuit. If the computer exceeds its requested transmission rate, excess packets are transmitted if capacity is available, but transmission is not guaranteed.

The Georgia Transmission Corporation (GTC) runs a frame relay system over leased lines to monitor and control its electrical transmission network. The frame relay system collects operational, maintenance, and revenue-metering data from the compa-

FIGURE   5-10

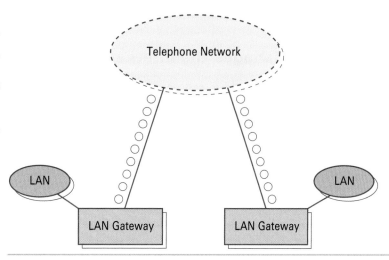

In a switched packet network, packets from different sources within the LAN are sent through the gateway to a public switched network. These packets will be mixed with other sources on their way to the destination where they will be reassembled with other packets from the same message.

ny's 700 power substations. The substation data is conveyed through frame relay to GTC's headquarters, its monitoring center, and the headquarters of each of GTC's 39 member companies. This system provides more capacity at lower cost and greater reliability than the network of leased lines that the company previously ran.[29]

ATM (Asynchronous Transfer Mode) resembles frame relay except that it has a fixed packet size of 53 bytes, and capacity responds to the demand. A fixed packet size results in faster, less costly equipment. The small packet size also assures that no packet has to wait for very long, enabling the carrier to provide better guarantees about the delay between transmission and receipt. Companies can also use ATM for their LAN backbone and so can eliminate the need for a gateway between their LAN and WAN. Kent State University uses an ATM wide-area network to support the voice, video, and data needs of more than 30,000 students on its eight campuses. The school plans to link its network to an ATM network that the State of Ohio is creating by putting ATM equipment into 3,800 K-12 schools around the state.[30]

Cellular Services

Cellular services allow data transmission across the cellular telephone network at about the same speed as voice landlines. *CDPD (Cellular Digital Packet Data)* uses a cellular carrier's spare capacity to transmit data packets. Because CDPD is packet-based rather than circuit-based, users do not have to dial to send and receive messages; they are always connected. Cellular providers charge for CDPD by the amount of data transmitted or by a flat monthly fee.

Andy Rodenhiser, owner of Rodenhiser Plumbing and Heating in Holliston, Massachusetts, uses a CDPD WAN to dispatch and manage his 27 plumbers. Rodenhiser's office computer is connected through the CDPD WAN to his plumbers' handheld computers no matter where the plumbers are working. The handheld computers attach to a Global Positioning System in the plumbers' trucks, so that the office knows the location of all trucks at all times. The cellular WAN has enabled Rondenhiser to greatly improve his customer service.[31]

General Packet Radio Service (GPRS) is an emerging packet-switched service that operates at up to 171.2 kilobits per second. Like CDPD, the GPRS service is always on, making it attractive as a protocol for operating a WAN over the Internet. Initially, however, GPRS has been used primarily to provide Internet service to mobile customers. For example, in 2002, 28 million people surfed the Web from their mobile phones using a GPRS service called i-mode provided by Japan's cellular carrier, ITT DoCoMo.[32]

INTERNET CONCEPTS

Who Manages the Internet?

Companies, individuals, and governments own pieces of the Internet, but the Internet as a whole has no owners or operators. Who, then, controls access to it? Who settles arguments when conflicts arise? Who makes sure that the pieces interconnect? Who sets standards for hardware and software? How does the Internet keep track of its composition? How does it know what users are on these networks? How can a person or company become part of the Internet?

The answers to these questions are complex because the Internet has no formal governance. Instead, individual technical volunteers and representatives of national governments and industry attempt to control the Internet through negotiation and the creation of non-binding agreements. In the past, this process has worked well. As the Internet has become larger and more commercial, the financial impact of decisions has increased, and stakeholders in the Internet have become more diverse. Therefore, it has become harder to reach consensus on critical issues. In 1998, a broad coalition of the Internet's business, technical, academic, and user communities created a private non-profit corporation called the Internet Corporation for Assigned Names and Numbers (ICANN) to provide technical coordination of the Internet. However, ICANN has power only to the extent that national governments cooperate.

The Internet began in 1969 as the ARPANET, a research network funded by the U.S. Defense Department that linked four computers in Massachusetts, Utah, and California. The ARPANET grew to 62 computers by 1974 and more than 100 research and university computers by 1976.

The military network, MILNET, split off from the ARPANET in 1984, although the Defense Department continued to fund the ARPANET. The National Science Foundation (NSF) began to pay for networks similar to and connected to ARPANET and intended for college and university collaboration. At about the same time, the British government created JANET, a network based on similar technology.

The NSF updated the backbone of its networks in 1991. At this time, more than half a million computers connected to the network and dues of its member organizations paid its operational costs. By 1994, World Wide Web (WWW) browsers became generally available, almost 4 million computers were connected, and growth skyrocketed to 15 percent per month (see Figure 5-11). An ATM backbone operating at 145 megabits/second was installed. In 1995, the NSF withdrew its funding for the Internet backbone, contracting it to a consortium of four companies authorized to sell access to other groups, organizations, and companies in the United States.

In early 1995, the U.S. government awarded a contract to MCI WorldCom to begin development of a *very high speed Backbone Network Service (vBNS)*. Currently WorldCom's vBNS backbone consists of two parallel networks operating at 622 Mbits/second and 2.5 Gbits/second, respectively. In 1999, the National Science Foundation funded the development of a third backbone operating at 2.5 Gbits/second and serving research universities only.

By the end of 2001, 498 million people worldwide boasted Internet connections from their home, 27 percent of them located in the United States.[33] The *Computer Industry Almanac* predicts that the number of Internet users will pass 1 billion by the year 2005.[34] By the end of 2001, about three quarters of U.S. small businesses were connected to the Internet with almost half of those featuring useful Web sites.[35]

FIGURE 5-11

Internet domains and hosts have grown exponentially between 1993 and 2002.

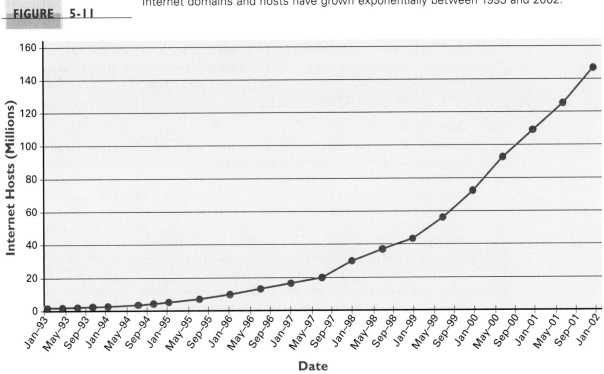

SOURCE: http://www.isc.org/ds/host-count-history.html. Used with permission.

Network Addressing

Every device attached to the Internet has a unique address called an **IP number.** This address consists of two parts—a network number and a device number. The Internet backbone routes a message between the network numbers. It then passes the message to a subnetwork that routes it to a specific device. The subnetwork is often an Internet Service Provider (see below in the section on Network Access), which further breaks the device address into a customer address and a device number on the customer network. The service provider routes the message to the customer, and the customer then routes the message to a device.

Organizations register their names with one of three registries—RIPENIC in Europe, APNIC in Asia and the Pacific, and ARIN in the United States (InterNIC before March 1998)—that maintain central routing tables for the network portion of Internet addresses. The current numbering scheme theoretically allows more than 4 billion addresses. However, current allocation schemes and the unavailability of addresses allocated in a prior addressing scheme eliminate many addresses. Oddly, the Internet is running out of addresses to assign. Most estimates are that new Internet addresses will become unavailable in some parts of Europe and Asia in 2005 unless something is done to correct deficiencies in the existing scheme.[36]

Potential solutions to the problem of insufficient addresses include changing the size of the address and modifying the scheme for allocating addresses. A new addressing standard known as IPv6 (Internet Protocol Version 6) has gained widespread acceptance in some parts of the world and has been mandated for Japan and Korea by 2005. The new scheme uses a 128-bit address compared to the 32-bit address of the current IP version. The number of addresses in this scheme is more than will ever be required (about 3 followed by 38 zeros), easily allowing each person and device in the world to have its own address. The major resistance to IPv6 is that many old routers and switches do not recognize the new standard, meaning that many companies will need to upgrade their equipment in order to access the new addresses.

Domain Names

Most managers know domain names for Internet addresses rather than their IP number. A **domain name,** such as mcdonalds.com, is a mnemonic for the network number portion of an Internet address. Users can more easily remember these names, type them without error, and associate them with their owner. You can always use a device's numeric address in place of its name. Name registries maintain the correspondence between domain names and their IP address and provide a look-up service for Internet users on **Domain Name Servers** (**DNSs**). When you specify a domain name, such as mcdonalds.com, your Internet server or service provider looks up the corresponding number in its copy of the domain name database. If it can't find the name, it requests a number lookup from a domain name server near it. It then uses the numeric address to communicate with the desired location.

Domain names come in two types—country domains and generic domains. Each country controls and assigns its own country domain names. An international registry assigns generic domain names on a first-come, first-served basis. Country domain names have a two-character suffix. For example, all names registered in the United Kingdom end with .uk and all those registered in France end in .fr. Each country may establish sub-domains. For example, in the United Kingdom, .co.uk represents a company sub-domain. In most cases, a company must have operations in a country to register a domain name with the country. The United States, in addition to its rarely used country registry, reserves .mil for the military, .gov for the government, and .edu for educational institutions.

Until recently, only three generic domains existed—.com for commercial organizations, .org for non-profit organizations, and .net for network providers. A single company, Network Solutions, Inc. (NSI), maintained the registry of all generic names. Some parties objected to the way that NSI handled the registry, the profits that NSI made as a monopoly, and the limits NSI established to the form of generic names. For example, if someone requested the domain name mcdonalds.com before the fast-food company McDonalds did, McDonalds would have to reach an agreement with the name owner or sue on trademark violations in order to obtain the name for its own use. If suffixes other than .com had been available, McDonalds could have used another suffix instead.

In November 2000, ICANN established seven new generic domains, including .biz for businesses, .name for individuals, and .pro for professional organizations. Different registries were selected to administer these domains, removing NSI's monopoly on domain name and IP number assignment.

Network Access

The Internet has no access restrictions. Any person or company that has an IP number, appropriate software, a dedicated telephone line, and meets a few additional criteria can request registration, thus obtaining access to the Internet. More commonly, people and companies connect to the Internet through an **Internet Service Provider** (**ISP**), a company such as America Online (AOL), MSN, or Road Runner (AOL-owned cable ISP), that already has an Internet connection, a large block of IP numbers for reassignment, and a high-capacity connection to the Internet backbone. Most ISPs sell additional services, such as software, trouble-shooting, and security.

ISPs provide dial-up service to the public through a *Point of Presence (POP)*. A POP is simply a location where the ISP has a bank of modems that connect to the ISP's Internet connection. When a user connects to an ISP through a POP, the ISP gives the user an IP number for temporary use, so that the user's computer becomes a device on the Internet.

NETWORK MANAGEMENT

When network traffic at the Deaconess Health System in St. Louis rocketed from 10 percent of capacity to almost 70 percent in one week, Chief Information Officer Bob Bowman used network management hardware and software to identify the problem. He found that a new application to track pagers worn by staffers caused the problem.[37]

Network Management Devices and Software

Most network devices, such as hubs, routers, switches, printers, and even servers collect information about the data they process and about their own performance. These devices can send data to a monitoring station when polled or when certain conditions arise. Network management software polls devices, logs responses, and helps network administrators identify problems and forecast capacity needs.

Network Devices

Most devices that operate on a network conform to a standard known as **SNMP** (**Simple Network Management Protocol**). SNMP defines how network devices maintain and communicate information about their own activity and performance. A Network Management Station uses the SNMP protocol to query network devices, get responses, and set SNMP parameters for each device on the network. These parameters determine how the devices operate and under what conditions, such as overload, they should send unsolicited messages to the Network Management Station. Network management software, discussed below, polls SNMP devices to create a picture of the network and graphs of network traffic.

A **network analyzer** plugs into a network and analyzes the traffic that passes by or through it. It displays this information in real time or produces reports for later review. Normally network managers use network analyzers when they have identified the location of a problem but don't know its cause. Network analyzers move among locations to solve different network performance problems rather than perform long-term monitoring.

Network Management Software

Many operating systems, such as Windows 2000/Server and Linux, provide a number of key network services, such as the following:

- *Device management* services recognize the devices, including computers and printers, that are connected to the network. Each has an address or label by which the client software can access it and network management can control it.
- *Security services* provide entry into the network and establish a relationship between a user and a client station. The network administrator determines who has access to specific services, devices, and data on the network. Figure 5-12 shows a screen that a network administrator can use from within Microsoft Windows 2000/Server to provide these functions.

FIGURE 5-12

Microsoft's Windows 2000/Server network operating system allows network managers to add or delete users and to specify their permission to access files, devices, and services.

- *File services* provide access to shared files. MDMC managers, for example, want pharmacy workers to be able to access patient files created by doctors and nurses.

- *Print services* provide central access to a common printer. Doctors and nurses at the MDMC should be able to output from a printer located at the nursing station on each floor.

- *Fax services* allow network users to send or receive a facsimile electronically, without having to create a hardcopy.

- *Directory services* provide an enterprise-wide telephone book that identifies and connects network users to each other and to software, such as electronic mail and groupware.

Network management software provides additional services, often related to the monitoring and routing of traffic. HP's OpenView, for example, (see Figure 5-13) monitors and reports on network protocols and devices; measures the performance and availability of specific network paths; enables problem detection with statistics, alarms, and maps on a single display; performs root-cause analysis of network problems and forecasts future bottlenecks.

Organizational Roles and Responsibilities

Networks serving more than 100 users typically require a full-time professional to manage network services. Network services include:

- Planning, upgrading, and maintaining the physical network.
- Monitoring network traffic and message delays.
- Adjusting the physical or logical network layout and number of servers to respond to transmission delays.
- Purchasing services for wide-area communication.
- Adding new workstations, printers, and other devices to the network.
- Adding and deleting users, user passwords, and modifying user authorizations.

FIGURE   5-13   Using HP's OpenView network management software, a network analyst can perform many network management functions.

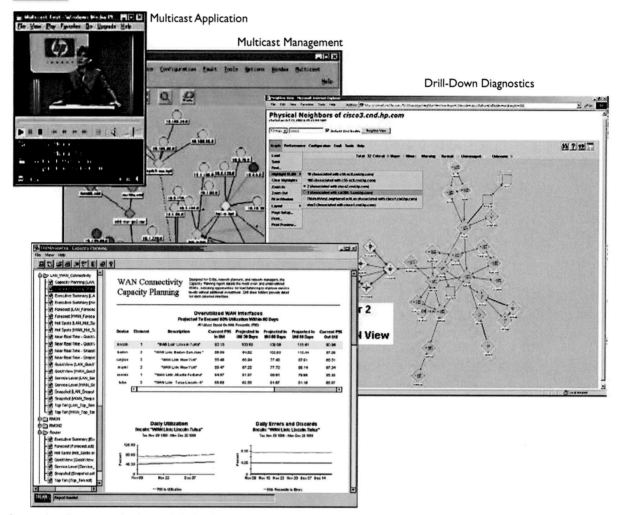

Multicast Application

Multicast Management

Drill-Down Diagnostics

SOURCE: http://www.openview.hp.com/solutions/categories/networkmgmt/index.asp. Used with permission from Hewlett-Packard Companies.

- Installing shared software; controlling the number of simultaneous users of shared software if limited by license.

- Providing appropriate backup of shared data and files.

In addition to a network administrator, many organizations hire specialists for specific network management roles. A network analyst, for example, typically troubleshoots switches and routers and deals with outages or other problems as they occur. A network engineer designs and configures networks, forecasts network capacity, and develops network plans. A LAN manager might be responsible for the performance of a single local area network. A network security manager analyzes known or expected network intrusions for prevention, damage assessment, and repair. A Web master or Web site director also may also have network responsibilities to assure the capacity for rapid service of Web pages and protection against intrusion.

ENSURING TELECOMMUNICATION SECURITY

Because data are vulnerable to theft, sabotage, and accidental corruption during transmission, managers of telecommunication networks care a lot about security. Information systems that permit access from physically remote facilities, such as wide-area networks, are particularly vulnerable to security breaches. The most important step to protecting data and limiting the implications of any breach in security is the development of a security plan, which Chapter 10 addresses in detail. Security plans rely, in large part, on a number of security technologies. This section discusses the technologies available for protecting data in a networked environment.

Cryptography and the Public Key Infrastructure (PKI)

Cryptography uses a secret code called a **key** to scramble a message or document so that it becomes unreadable. The key can also be used to unscramble the message. Anyone intercepting a scrambled message will be unable to read it unless they know the key. Assuming that only the sender and the intended recipient know the key and that the key cannot be deduced from the scrambled message, the message is secure.

But how can a message sender be sure that only he and intended recipient know the key? If the key is sent over the network, anyone intercepting communication on the network will observe the transmittal of the key and will be able to decode any additional messages sent using that key. The major problem with using cryptography for telecommunication is getting the key to the intended recipient securely.

The solution to the problem is a technology called **public key cryptography.** Public key cryptography uses a pair of keys. A message encoded with one of the keys in the pair can be decoded only with the other key. Assume that Arthur wants to communicate with Betty (see Figure 5-14). Arthur generates a pair of keys and sends one of them, called a *public key*, to Betty. Arthur does not reveal his *private key*, the other half of the pair. Betty generates a new key, called a *session key*, encodes it with Arthur's public key, and sends it

FIGURE   5-14

Public key cryptography is used to share a session key between two parties.

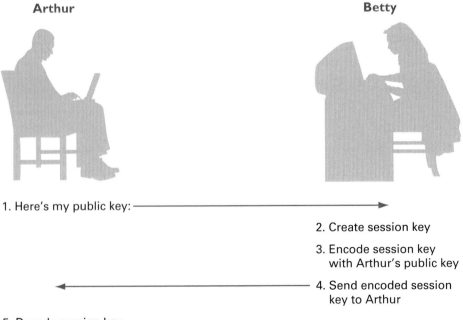

Arthur

Betty

1. Here's my public key: ⟶

2. Create session key

3. Encode session key with Arthur's public key

4. Send encoded session key to Arthur

5. Decode session key with my private key

back to Arthur. Anyone who might have intercepted the public key that Arthur sent to Betty would be unable to read Betty's message, as a public key cannot decode a message that it has encoded. Only Arthur can read the encoded message because he's the only one with the matching private key, the key paired to the one that Betty used to send the message. Once Arthur decodes the message, only he and Betty know the session key. Arthur and Betty can continue to converse privately using the session key.

An advantage of public key cryptography is that a session key is only valid for a session. New session keys are generated each time two parties want to converse. Because sessions are reasonably short, intruders usually don't have enough information to deduce the session key from the session itself. The difficulty of deducing a session key from encoded messages rises exponentially with the length of the session key. Mathematicians have calculated that it would take a hacker with a supercomputer two trillion years to break a session key having 128 bits.[38] If computers speed rises dramatically, it is only necessary to increase the length of the key to increase security. Adding just one bit to the length of the key doubles the time needed to break the code.

Public key cryptography can be used for three additional functions important to e-commerce: authentication, non-repudiation, and integrity. **Authentication** is the ability of a message receiver to ascertain the identity of a message sender. Before you send your credit card number to a vendor claiming to represent a company, you naturally want to verify that the message recipient is really who it claims to be. Authentication is achieved with the assistance of a trusted third party, known as a **certificate authority** (**CA**). The CA serves the same function that a notary public or bank would serve for a physical document. Here's a rough description of how it works: Arthur wants to make sure that nobody else can send a message pretending to be him. Arthur brings physical identification to the CA to prove that he's Arthur. The CA issues him a public and private key as well as a certificate (an electronic document) bearing the public key and encoded with the private key of the registry (see Figure 5-15). Now, when Arthur initiates a session, he sends his public key, a randomly generated number, and a copy of his certificate along with the same information encoded with his private key. The recipient knows that the message comes from

FIGURE   5-15

A decoded copy of Amazon's certificate as presented by the Netscape browser.

Source: courtesy of Amazon.com. Used with permission.

Arthur because when the copy is decoded with Arthur's public key, the random number matches the number in the first part of the message. The recipient can also verify that the public key is really Arthur's because the certificate says it is. The certificate is decoded with the CA's public key, meaning that nobody else could have created it. This process of exchanging a session key and verifying the identity of parties to a session is central to a standard protocol known as **Secure Socket Layer** (SSL).

Non-repudiation means that a message sender cannot deny having sent a message. With traditional commerce, a signature verifies that the sender, or signatory in this case, has authorized the message. A sender cannot deny having sent a message because his signature is attached to it. With e-commerce, non-repudiation is achieved with the help of a **digital signature.** To digitally sign a document, the sender applies a standard formula to the document that results in a large number called a digital hash of the document. Many documents could create the same digital hash, so it's not possible to reconstruct the document from its digital hash. The sender then encodes the digital hash using her private key, thereby creating the digital signature. The recipient verifies the signature by decoding the digital hash with the sender's public key and comparing it to the digital hash produced by the document. A match not only assures the recipient that the sender sent the message, but it also eliminates any possibility that the sender can deny having sent the message. Nobody else could have created a digital signature that matched the message.

Integrity means that nobody can alter a message after it's been sent. The integrity of any message signed with a digital signature is guaranteed. If anyone had attempted to change the message, the digital hash of the revised message would not correspond with the digital hash encoded in the message signature.

Firewalls

A **firewall** is hardware and/or software intended to separate an organization's intranet, and the data on it, from its extranet and the Internet. A firewall serves to:

- Hide information about the network by making it seem that all outgoing traffic originates from the firewall rather than the network.
- Block incoming data or programs that might compromise an organization's security.
- Screen outgoing traffic to limit Internet use and/or access to remote sites.

Firewalls provide a tremendous amount of flexibility to network administrators in the nature of the rules they can use to provide different levels of security. But, determining the appropriate level of security and associated rules can often be difficult. Major League Soccer (MLS) discovered this difficulty when it set up rules at its New York headquarters to prohibit users from surfing sites with objectionable content or downloading inappropriate data. Because software at the firewall identified *Sports Illustrated* swimsuit edition as too racy, the firewall blocked all access to the CNN/Sports Illustrated site. "Obviously, blocking the cnnsi.com site is not good for our organization," said Joseph Dalessio, network administrator for the MLS.[39]

Virtual Private Networks (VPNs)

A **Virtual Private Network** (VPN) is a *private* wide-area network that connects an organization's LANs and users to one another through a *public* network, usually the Internet. By creating a VPN, an organization can save the cost of leased lines, VAN charges, or the expense of other direct connections among its sites. A VPN provides long-distance connections virtually free of direct charges. Companies that have already paid for their connection to the Internet need only assure that they have sufficient capacity between themselves and their Internet Service Providers.

The Green Bay Packers of the National Football League experienced high communication costs because scouts, coaches, and administrators were dialing into their network via an 800 number whenever they were on the road. After installing a VPN, the team was able to cut its communication costs to one-third of its previous amount. No hardware changes were required, and users were able to use the same passwords they had used when accessing their network from the office.[40]

VPNs provide a high level of security by not only encrypting messages, but also by encrypting the header information that identifies the computers of the senders and recipients and other elements of each packet in a message, such as their sequence. A standard known as Internet Protocol Security Protocol (IPSec) provides this high level of encryption. Firewalls and routers that are IPSec compliant perform the encryption and decryption, ensuring that message information is invisible to potential theft or redirection once it has left the organization to travel on public pathways.

SUMMARY

Organizations use telecommunication, communication at a distance, to coordinate business activities, support group decision making, and conduct commerce electronically. The basic element of communication is a message, which has meaning in a context. Telecommunication is a five-step process that includes message initiation, placement upon a telecommunication medium, transfer through the medium to a destination, retrieval from the medium, and acceptance by the recipient. Telecommunication networks allow communication among any parties attached to the network. Networks are called LANs, MANs, or WANs, depending on the distance between their members. Networks are called intranets, extranets, or public networks, depending on how the network members are related to the organization.

Communication carriers, including PTTs, long-distance and local exchange carriers, cellular companies, and cable TV companies, operate public networks and provide communication services on them. Value added networks purchase these services in bulk and resell them, often providing additional services.

The OSI model divides the communication process into layers within which compatible standards can be set. Transmission media differ in their cost, capacity, and availability, and include twisted-pair wire, coaxial cable, fiber optic cable, microwaves, and infrared and radio signals. Communication hardware, such as a modems, hubs, switches, routers, and gateways, connects computers to networks and interconnects network segments. Network protocols define how a message is packaged, secured, sent, routed, received, and acknowledged. LAN protocols include Ethernet, Token Ring, Wi-Fi, and Bluetooth. WANs generally use the services of public carriers, which include leased lines, switched-circuit services, packet switched services, and cellular services.

The Internet is a network of networks, owned by nobody and managed by consensus. Every device attached to the Internet has a unique IP number as its address. Domain names identify servers on the Internet. Domain name registries maintain the relationship between domain names and IP numbers. Most people and companies connect to the Internet through an Internet Service Provider.

Smart devices, such as SNMP devices, and network analyzers ease network management. Network management functions include planning, upgrading, and maintaining the physical network; monitoring network performance; adjusting layout and hardware; purchasing wide-area services, managing network users; and providing security and backup.

Message privacy and security is achieved through cryptography using a key to encode and decode messages. Public key cryptography provides a means for securely sharing a session key between two parties. Certificate authorities issue digital certificates and private and public keys to allow message senders to authenticate themselves. Digital signatures provide for non-repudiation and message integrity. Firewalls separate and secure an organization's intranet from its extranet and public network connections. A virtual private network uses a public network to provide private WAN communication.

KEY TERMS

adaptor
authentication
backbone
bandwidth
certificate authority (CA)
coaxial cable
common carrier
communication
communication carrier
digital signature
domain name
domain name server (DNS)
electronic commerce (e-commerce)
extranet
Ethernet
fiber optic cable
firewall
gateway
hub

infrastructure
integrity
Internet Service Provider (ISP)
intranet
IP number
key
leased line
local area network (LAN)
message
modem
network
network analyzer
network interface card (NIC)
network protocol
non-repudiation
OSI Model (Open Systems Interconnection Model)
packet
packet switched service

personal area network (PAN)
public key cryptography
router
Secure Socket Layer (SSL)
session
SNMP (Simple Network Management Protocol)
switch
switched circuit service
TCP/IP (Transmission Control Protocol/Internet Protocol)
telecommunication
twisted-pair wire
Value Added Network (VAN)
Virtual Private Network (VPN)
wide area network (WAN)
Wi-Fi

REVIEW QUESTIONS

1. How does an intranet differ from an extranet?
2. What is the difference between a LAN and a WAN?
3. What five steps are required for telecommunication?
4. How is the telecommunications industry structured in the United States?
5. How does the telecommunications industry differ outside the United States?
6. How do cellular telephone services work?
7. What is the function of value added network (VAN) service providers?
8. What is the role of the OSI model in the creation of industry standards for data communication?
9. What are the characteristics of the six transmission media used for telecommunication?
10. What function do modems serve?
11. Compare and contrast the functions of a hub, switch, router, and gateway.
12. What are the most popular standards for local area networks?
13. How do leased line, switched-circuit, and packet-switched services differ?
14. How do SNMP devices simplify network management?

15. What are the major functions of a network administrator?

16. What is the Internet?

17. What is the role of an Internet Service Provider (ISP)?

18. How can two parties to a conversation agree secretly on a session key?

19. How does a digital signature guarantee non-repudiation of a message by its sender?

20. What is the role of a certificate authority (CA)?

FORD DEVELOPS AN INTRANET PORTAL

MINICASE

When Ford's former CIO Jim Yost took the first steps toward creating a new intranet, called MyFord.com, he had the full support and encouragement of former CEO Jacques Nasser. That support was crucial in shaping the Dearborn, Michigan-based company's internal Web site. Today, the site supports more than 175,000 employees who visit more than 500,000 times a day for anything from checking their benefits to getting the latest competitive information or signing up for company-run training classes. "The [intranet] would not have happened without senior management support," says Martin Davis, program manager for what Ford calls its ePortal project.

Ford's intranet began as a way to give employees a personalized online environment and grew into an enterprise-wide strategy to replace disparate desktop applications with standardized Web programs and access. The company has come a long way since it first provided an intranet to employees in 1996. "That was really just access to a search engine," Davis says.

The IT department started to revamp the site in 1999 when Nasser embarked on a business-to-employee initiative designed to bring every Ford staff member into the digital age. Nasser emphasized the importance of integrating Web capabilities into each of the company's business units in meetings and in *Let's Chat,* his weekly e-mail to every Ford employee. He also added e-commerce-related positions to all departments. Davis says Nasser wanted to create a corporate culture that embraced e-commerce.

"He didn't want to just spawn millions of Web sites, he wanted to have a rational approach to e-business," says Bipin Patel, director of management systems at Ford.

With Nasser's encouragement, Yost created the ePortal plan, which aimed to cut costs and increase efficiency by putting learning and collaboration tools online and by giving employees desktop access to human resources and job-related information. Considering the large scope of the project—the new intranet needed to reach almost 200,000 people at 950 locations worldwide—funding and resources to support a network of that scale were imperative. Nasser made sure Yost had all the funding he needed, a move that entailed a big leap of faith, Davis says, because any return on the cost of the project was extremely difficult to measure in terms of tangible dollar savings. "With a project like this, it's easy to demonstrate savings through an increase in efficiency, but it's very hard to translate that to ROI," he says. "They had the vision to see how the intranet would benefit the company."

The result was the May 2001 launch of MyFord.com. The site gives Ford staff access to personal information, links to benefits and human resources forms, demographics, salary history, and general company news. In addition, each business unit posts employee-specific job information. For example, a project manager in the engineering division can access engineering project information through his view of the intranet page. "We wanted to help people increase their business acumen by being able to read about company performance and what's new with the business, because that will help them make more informed decisions," Davis says.

Before the intranet launched, employees got information through time-consuming, paper-based manual processes, Davis says. Now, Ford employees can personalize their view of the intranet homepage by selecting what they want to see on the page and prioritizing the links they use most. Sensitive information can be shielded. Managers can view financial data on company performance, while other employees can access only general performance information.

The portal has saved Ford millions of dollars and thousands of man-hours by putting applications and documents at employee's fingertips, Davis says. Future plans call for deploying Microsoft Net-Meeting and eRoom applications. Under current CIO Marv Adams, Patel and Davis are looking at creating business unit-specific portals within the central infrastructure.

For Ford, the intranet is not just a tool for employees to manage their benefits efficiently; it's also a foundation for the company to become a digital business. In order for Ford to run a successful e-business with customers, suppliers and partners, its employees first had to be adept at using e-business technologies themselves, Davis says. "You're not properly doing e-business unless you're doing it inside the company as well," he says. "It starts on the inside."

Case Questions

Diagnosis

1. Generally, what are the information needs of Ford's employees?

Evaluation

2. What were the deficiencies of Ford's intranet in 1999?

3. What initiatives of Ford's former CEO, Jacques Nasser, made it necessary to improve Ford's intranet?

Design

4. What was the scope of the project in terms of the number of employees and locations that needed to be reached?

5. How did Davis justify the development of MyFord.com?

6. What security issues do you think needed to be addressed in the design of MyFord.com?

Implementation

7. What benefits has MyFord.com provided?

8. Why does Davis believe that the MyFord.com intranet is a tune-up for a future extranet?

9. What concerns should Davis have about opening the intranet to Ford's customers, suppliers, and partners? How might he address these concerns?

5-1 A LAN FOR CENTRAL AIRLINES

ACTIVITY

Step 1: Read the following scenario.

Ryan Daly is the operations manager for Central Airlines at O'Hare International Airport in Chicago. At O'Hare, Central leases 12 gates, handling roughly 150 flights/day and 15,000 passengers/day. In addition, Central has a significant cargo operation; it shares a cargo hanger/warehouse with a major international shipper.

Daly supervises a staff of 32 ticketing/baggage agents, 18 gate agents, 30 baggage handlers, a small maintenance crew, and a variety of lower-level managers, such as shift supervisors at the ticketing counters, a cargo manager, and a manager of customer service. He is responsible for the operation of all Central's passenger and flight services at the airport. Examples of his responsibilities include arranging overnight accommodations for flight crews, ensuring that the food that caterers load on the aircraft for in-flight meals meets Central's quality standards, and negotiating leases for space with the airport authorities. Daly reports to the vice president of operations at Central's headquarters in Kansas City.

For the most part, Daly relies on the information systems services provided by Central Airline's MIS group. This group has a staff of almost 200 people worldwide and an acquisition and operating budget that exceeds $3 million per year. Daly's office is equipped with a personal computer that is connected over a value added network to Central's mainframes in Kansas City. He obtains information about reservations, flight schedules, and other centrally collected or centrally produced data from the mainframe. Daly has also developed a few spreadsheets that he uses to keep track of his local operations and to help him evaluate decision alternatives.

Currently, Daly communicates with his employees and peers at other airports by phone and in person. Electronic mail systems were once available on the mainframe, but were discontinued for all employees except those at headquarters when a budget crunch forced cutbacks in communication expenses. He has proposed a local area network for O'Hare in order to improve communications among his managers and employees and to help them share data with one another. Daly has estimated the price to network his key employees to be $25,000. The twisted-pair wire needed for the network is already in place at O'Hare.

Step 2: Prepare the case for class discussion.

Step 3: Answer each of the following questions, individually or in small groups, as directed by your instructor.

Diagnosis

1. What do you think are Daly's information needs?
2. What are the information needs of Daly's employees?
3. What are the information needs of Daly's supervisor, the VP of operations.

Evaluation

4. How well are Daly's information needs currently being met?
5. How well are the information needs of Daly's employees and supervisor being met?
6. In what ways might a local area network improve Daly's effectiveness and the effectiveness of his employees?

Design

7. If you were Daly's supervisor, would you approve Daly's proposal? Why or why not?
8. Based on your current knowledge, would a 10 Mbps Ethernet network be appropriate?

Implementation

9. Will Daly need a full-time network manager for his operation?
10. What network issues will Daly or his network manager need to deal with after the network is installed?

Step 4: In small groups, with the entire class, or in written form, share your answers to the questions above. Then answer the following question:

1. What are the likely information needs of Daly, his employees, and his supervisor?

2. How well are those information needs currently being met?

3. Is a LAN the best choice for meeting these needs? Is 10 Mbps sufficient bandwidth?

4. What network management issues are likely to arise after the installation of the network?

5-2 CALCULATING TRANSMISSION TIME

ACTIVITY

The time it takes to transfer a file can be calculated with the following formula:

Transmission time (seconds) = Size of file in bytes ?
Number of bits per byte (8) /
Bits per second transmission speed.

Then add 10 percent to account for transmission errors and control characters.

Step 1: Calculate how long it would take to transmit a 95 megabyte file under each of the following network scenarios

1. Using a 28.8 kilobyte/second modem over dial-up lines.

2. Over a T1 leased line at 1.544 megabits/second.

3. Over a T3 leased line at 44.376 megabits/second.

4. Over a typical ISDN switched circuit at 128 kilobits/second.

5. Over a typical frame relay or ATM packet switched circuit at 10 megabits/second. For these services, use a 25 percent overhead for the packet rather than the 10 percent overhead you have used for parts a through d.

6. Over a 10 megabit/second Ethernet 10BaseT LAN.

7. Over a 100 megabit/second Fast Ethernet LAN

8. Over a Gigabit Ethernet LAN.

Step 2: Individually, in small groups, or with the entire class, as directed by your instructor, answer the following questions. For each of the network scenarios above, do you think would you be willing to wait that long if you needed the file to perform the following functions?

1. Start running a computer program.

2. As a doctor, obtain the image while consulting with a patient.

3. As a customer service representative, obtain information while talking to the customer on the telephone.

5-3 MONITORING NETWORK USERS

ACTIVITY

Step 1: Read the following scenario.

Alice Markin is the vice president of marketing for Almark Brands, a major snack-food manufacturer. She was hired to turn around the marketing department. The department's share of the company's budget had grown slowly over the last few years. Yet, the company's marketing programs and initiatives seemed to be failing badly. The consensus in the industry was the Almark was always just a step behind its competitors.

After a month on the job, Markin felt that she was beginning to understand the nature of the problem. The people who reported directly to her seemed to be knowledgeable and able employees. Under the previous VP of marketing, they were given a great deal of freedom, but had received no direction and no proper assessment of or accounting for performance. She felt that her staff could and would work harder and smarter if given appropriate goals and guidance.

As she thought about how to bring more discipline and direction to her department, the senior vice president of marketing, sales, and distribution, Jason Carter, knocked on her door. After a brief exchange of pleasantries, he came quickly to his point. "Alice," he said, "last week on the trip back from DC, I read about some software that can monitor any computer on a company's network. You can actually see exactly what's on the screen of another computer as if you were operating it yourself! I've ordered a few copies for us. I would like you to use the software to find out why we are not getting more productivity out of your department."

Markin was flabbergasted, but did not know what to say. She wondered whether or not her boss was spying on her. Finally she said, "Let's first see what happens in the next few weeks without the software." "It's your call," he said, "but I expect results quickly."

Step 2: Prepare the case for class discussion.

Step 3: Answer each of the following questions, individually or in small groups, as directed by your instructor.

1. Who benefits and who is harmed by the use of the monitoring software?

2. From the ethical principles of least harm, rights and duties, professional responsibilities, self-interest and utilitarianism, consistency, and respect, how would you evaluate the use of such software?

3. What course of action would you take if you were Alice Markin? Why?

5-4 NETWORKING AT DEBEVOISE & PLIMPTON

ACTIVITY

Step 1: Read the following scenario.

Debevoise & Plimpton (D&P), an international law firm with 500 lawyers worldwide, relies on its telecommunication network for document management, research, contact databases, and shared software. "If any of our networking systems go down, our practice is seriously affected," states Richard Hampson, director of information services for D&P. Therefore, when the company moved to a new building in New York City, it needed a reliable LAN to support transactions within its office complex and a reliable to WAN for worldwide communication.

D&P designed its LAN with a redundant fiber backbone, with each channel having a capacity of 1.2 gigabits/second. The design was intended to support the fastest ATM and Ethernet standards, support both voice and data, and to provide redundancy to withstand natural disasters, terrorist attacks, or accidental cable cuts. Redundant pathways had to be creatively designed, as the company occupies 15 floors dispersed throughout the 47-story building. The backbone cables rise through the 47 floors by way of an open airshaft, and terminate at a communication hub, which connects to the public telephone network for WAN services. Networks on each of the company's floors terminate in two hubs, which then tap into the backbone. In addition to the main data center and central communication hub, the network supports an elaborate conference facility with multiple conference/media rooms.

Step 2: Prepare the case for class discussion.

Step 3: Answer each of the following questions, individually or in small groups, as directed by your instructor.

Diagnosis

1. What are the information needs of Debevoise & Plimpton?

Evaluation

2. Why does D&P consider a reliable network to be of utmost importance?

Design

3. Why do you think that D&P's LAN backbone is based on fiber-optic cable?
4. Why did D&P use a redundant backbone?
5. What challenges did the company face in designing the network?

Implementation

6. What types of information are exchanged over D&P's network?
7. Did the network's design effectively meet the company's objectives?

Step 4: In small groups, with the entire class, or in written form, share your answers to the questions above. Then, answer the following questions:

1. What are the information needs of D&P's lawyers?
2. Why did D&P want a system with redundancy?
3. What were the challenges the company faced in designing its network?
4. How well does D&P's network solution meet its needs?

SOURCE: Extracted from Carol Everett Oliver and Arlene Franchini, "Redundant Cabling Practice Wins," *Communications News,* March 2002, 38. Used with permission.

5-5 WIRELESS NETWORKING AT HARKNESS HARDWARE

ACTIVITY

Step 1: Read the following scenario.

Harkness Hardware Company, a $60 million distributor of hardware, plumbing, and electrical supplies to steel companies, building contractors, and major retail outlets, stocks approximately 10,000 items in its 500,000-square-foot warehouse. The company publishes a catalog on the Web, where small customers can place orders. It regularly sends sales representatives to meet with larger customers to identify their needs. These customers place orders through their sales representatives, who enter the orders into their laptop and download them at the end of the day through the company's VPN via a call to the company's toll-free phone number. At the warehouse, orders are printed onto a form called a pick list. Employees pick the order items off the warehouse shelf and bring them to the packaging department where they are packaged and shipped.

The paper-based warehouse system at Harkness has been a problem for the company. The pick lists are often hard to read, and inaccuracies are common, especially in fulfilling multipage orders. Sometimes entire pages get lost. The company has called on you to evaluate the possibility of installing a wireless network in the warehouse. Handheld computers in the pickers' picking-carts would connect to the network and provide many benefits.

Step 2: Estimate the cost of the wireless network. Remember that each picker will need handheld computers that have wireless capability. Assume that the warehouse is approximately square and that about 15 pickers are active at any one time. Obtain cost estimates for the equipment you need by researching prices on the Web. Assume also that the order management software you currently use includes software to manage the warehouse processes, so you will not need to spend anything additional for software.

Step 3: Identify the potential benefits of the wireless LAN. Attach a dollar value to these benefits as best you can.

Step 4: In small groups or with the entire class, as directed by your instructor, answer the following questions:

1. What different solutions are possible for Harkness's wireless LAN? What are their relative pros and cons?
2. Which solution do you prefer?
3. What are the potential benefits of a wireless LAN for Harkness's warehouse operations?
4. What recommendations would you make to Harkness's management team regarding the installation of a wireless LAN?

IS ON THE WEB

IS ON THE WEB

Exercise 1: PGP (Pretty Good Privacy) is an encryption product for secure e-mail that is free for personal use. It incorporates public key encryption and hashing to create digital signatures. Research PGP on the Web. If your instructor allows it, download PGP, install it on your computer, and use it. If your instructor prefers, write a memo that addresses the following questions:

1. Which version of PGP is most compatible with your computer, operating system, and e-mail client?
2. What potential problems might arise from using PGP on your system?
3. How would you uninstall PGP if you had installed it and ran into problems?
4. What decisions (such as key size) would you need to make before using PGP?

Exercise 2: Check whether your university or company has an intranet. If it does, make a list of the information included in the intranet. What additional information would you like to be included? If it does not, make a list of the information that it should include for your organization.

RECOMMENDED READINGS

Bates, Regis J. *Broadband Telecommunications Handbook,* 2nd ed. New York: McGraw-Hill, 2002.

Gralla, Preston. *How the Internet Works,* 6th ed. Indianapolis, IN: Que Publishing, 2001.

Kaufman, Charles, Radia Perlman, and Mike Spiciner. *Network Security: Private Communication in a Public World,* 2nd ed. Upper Saddle River, NJ: Prentice Hall PTR, 2002.

Mikalsen, Arne and Per Borgesen. *Local Area Network Management, Design and Security—A Practical Approach.* New York: John Wiley & Sons, 2001.

Mueller, Milton L. *Ruling the Root: Internet Governance and the Taming of Cyberspace.* Cambridge, MA: MIT Press, 2002.

Rappaport, Theodore. *Wireless Communications: Principles and Practice,* 2nd ed. Upper Saddle River, NJ: Prentice Hall PTR, 2001.

Eifert, Rich. The Switch Book: *The Complete Guide to LAN Switching Technology.* New York: John Wiley & Sons, 2000.

Shepard, Steven. *Telecom Crash Course.* New York: McGraw-Hill Professional, 2001.

The following periodicals also provide regular features about telecommunication, data communication, and networks:

Business Communications Review, Network Computing, Network Magazine, Network World

NOTES

1. "Reaping the Benefits of Wireless," *Health Management Technology,* February 2002, 50–51. Nelson, Matthew G., "Doing Business without Wires: Bluetooth and 802.11b," *InformationWeek,* 15 January 2001, 22–24, 28. www.sisunet.org, accessed on 21 June 2002. http://www.miller-dwan.com, accessed on 21 June 2002.

2. Eric Sfiligoj, "Re-Examining 'Chain' Economics," *Croplife,* April 2002, 22.

3. Maggie Biggs, "Simplifying Communication," *Federal Computer Week,* 3 June 2002, 46, 47, 50.

4. Janet Kornblum, "Ameritech Service Gives E-Mail by Telephone E-Listen Targets Mobile Professionals' Need to Stay in Touch," *USA Today,* 17 May 1999, 6B.

5. Betty Lin-Fisher, "Companies Save Money, Avoid Corporate Travel with Videoconference Sessions," *Knight Ridder Tribune Business News,* 10 June 2002, 1.

6. Mike Moralis, "HR's Enterprise-Wide Portal: To Go Where No Intranet Has Gone Before," *Canadian HR Reporter,* 20 May 2002, G8.

7. Judi Hasson, "State Taps Accenture for Intranet Project," *Federal Computer Week,* 4 March 2002, 10.

8. Clark W. Gellings, Adam Serchuk, and Steve Hoffman, "Life in 2020: Imagine Yourself in the Future…," *Electric Perspectives,* May/June 2002, 40–52.

9. http://www.groove.net/solutions/testimonials/nonprofit/stjohns.html, accessed on 8 September 2002.

10. Scott Hamilton, "E-Commerce for the 21st Century," *Computer,* May 1997, 44–47.

11. Christopher M. Kelley, Retail & Media North America: *Consumer Technographics Data Overview.* Cambridge, MA: Forrester Research, 2002.

12. CyberAtlas staff, "B2B E-Commerce Headed for Trillions," accessed at http://cyberatlas.internet.com/markets/b2b/article/0,,10091_986661,00.html on 24 June 2002. Data is attributed to eMarketer, "E-Commerce Trade and B2B Exchanges," March 2002.

13. http://www.rcn.com, accessed on 24 June 2002.

14. Brett Pate, "CTI Communications Testimonial," 5 June 2002, accessed at http://www.cticomm.com/testimonials.htm on 11 July 2002.

15. "News from Europe," *Management Services,* March 2002, 22.

16. "China Telecom Monopoly Ends," *Reuters,* 20 April 2000, accessed at http://www.wired.com/news/business/0,1367,35797,00.html on 26 June 2002.

17. Demetri Tsanacas, "Transborder Data Flows in the Internet Era: Privacy or Control?," *American Business Review,* June 2001, 50–56. Francis Aldhouse, "The Transfer of Personal Data to Third Countries under EU Directive 95/46/ec," *International Review of Law, Computers & Technology,* March 1999, 75–79.

18. Sweden, *Personal Data Act* (1998:204), October 1998, accessed at http://www.datainspektionen.se/in_english/default.asp?content=/in_english/legislation/data.shtml on 26 June 2002.

19. http://www.cisco.com/warp/public/779/edu/build/profiles/vccs.html, accessed on 8 September 2002.

20. David Strom, "Disney Takes a Ride on Ethernet," *Network World,* 2 April 2001, 40–42.

21. Phil Hochmuth, "MANs in Paradise," *Network World,* 15 April 2002, 39–42.

22. Bob Brewin, "Calif. City Plans Wireless LAN for Critical Communications," *Computerworld,* 18 February 2002, 11.

23. Jim Wagner, "Want Broadband with Your Fries?," *Internetnews.com,* 7 May 2002, accessed at http://www.internetnews.com/isp-news/article.php/8_1038961 on 27 June 2002.

24. Janet Rae-Dupree, "Surf the Airwaves; You Can Tap into High-Speed Wireless Service Right Now at Thousands of Wi-Fi 'Hot Spots,'" *U.S. News & World Report,* 24 June 2002, 62–64.

25. Jeff Bennett, "Chrysler Embraces Hands-Free Calling," *Knight Ridder Tribune Business News,* 10 January 2002, 1.

26. Paul Jackson with Erwan de Montigny and Fraser Pearce, *Turning On Broadband Users: Consumer Technographics Europe.* Amsterdam: Forrester Research BV, 2001.

27. Jed Kolko with Tom Rhinelander, Gillian DeMoulin, and Resa Broadbent, *Devices & Access North America: Consumer Technographics Data Overview.* Cambridge, MA: Forrester Research, 2001.

28. Charles S. Golvin with David M. Cooperstein, Gregory J. Scaffidi, and Jennifer Schaeffer, *Sizing US Consumer Telecom.* (Cambridge: MA, Forrester Research, 2002): 11.

29. David Van Winkle, Keith Porterfield, and Charles Nash, "Utility Overhauls Its Communications Backbone," *Transmission & Distribution World,* October 2001, 40–46.

30. Paul Desmond, "Kent State's ATM Network," *ATM Newsletter,* December 2000, 1–4.

31. Bob Brewin, "Now, Even the Plumber May Be Using Wireless," *Computerworld Online,* 15 May 2002, accessed at http://www.computerworld.com/mobiletopics/mobile/story/0,10801,71189,00.html on 9 July 2002.

32. Scott Bradner, "Silly Question: Are the Carriers Smart Enough?," *Network World,* 18 March 2002, 24.

33. Michael Pastore, "At-Home Internet Users Approaching Half Billion," *CyberAtlas,* 6 March 2002, accessed at http://cyberatlas.internet.com/big_picture/geographics/article/0,,5911_986431,00.html on 9 July 2002. The original source for the total number is cited as the "Fourth Quarter 2001 Global Internet Trends Report" by Nielson/NetRatings. The original source for the U.S. percentage is cited as eMarketer.

34. "Internet Users Will Top 1 Billion in 2005. Wireless Internet Users Will Reach 48% in 2005," *Computer Industry Almanac,* Inc., 21 March 2002, accessed at http://www.c-i-a.com/pr032102.htm on 9 July 2002.

35. Michael Pastore, "Small Business Embraces Net, Shuns E-Commerce," *CyberAtlas,* 6 August 2001, accessed at http://cyberatlas.internet.com/markets/smallbiz/article/0,,10098_860861,00.html on 9 July 2002. Original sources are cited as eMarketer and International Data Corporation.

36. Peter Gwin, "Upgrading the Internet and the IPV6 debate," *Europe,* June 2002, 5. Ken Wieland, "Addressing the IPv6 Issue," *Telecommunications International,* May 2002, 27–30.

37. Richard Adhikari, "The Bandwidth Rainbow," *InformationWeek,* 10 April 1995, 45.

38. Steven Gardner, "Catching the Online Bus—Financial Institutions See Potential Profits from Internet Customers," *The Columbian,* 5 February 2002, E1. "Clash of Cryptography and Copyright," *The Hindu,* 13 September 2001.

39. Kelly Jackson Higgins, "Major League Soccer Fields a Deep Line of Defense," *Network Computing,* 16 April 2001, 79–81.

40. Marcia Savage, "Green Bay's Defensive VPN Line," *CRN,* 18 June 2001, 63.

Part III

Designing Systems for Business

Information systems use information technology to satisfy information needs. Part III investigates how information technology addresses these needs in the context of business systems. Chapter 6 explores e-commerce and e-business issues and practices, addressing the objectives and difficulties of doing business electronically and analyzing how information technology affects or enables various business models. Chapter 7 delves into the processes that businesses perform, showing how information technology adds value within a business and between business partners. It addresses customer relationship management, production, supplier relationships, logistics, human resources, accounting, and enterprise and cross-enterprise integration. Chapter 8 shows how information technology supports management decision making and coordination. It addresses business and competitive intelligence, decision support systems, group support systems, and executive information systems. ■

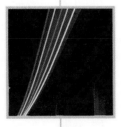

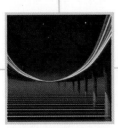

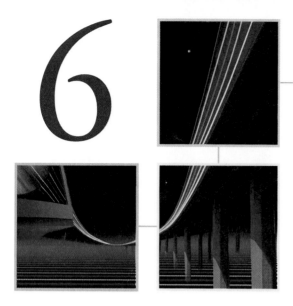

6

Introduction to E-Commerce and E-Business

LEARNING OBJECTIVES

After completing Chapter 6, you will be able to:

- Define the "value chain," identify its components, and explain how it differs from the extended value chain.
- Explain how e-business can help companies reduce the cost of executing transactions and increase the speed of business
- Explain how e-business helps reduce errors and improve quality.
- Describe three ways in which e-business helps companies collaborate with their suppliers.
- Identify the advantages and disadvantages of pure-play vs. click-and-mortar strategies.
- Define "business model" and describe six such models.
- Describe the effects of disintermediation on producers and distributors.
- Define "e-government" and give examples of its implementation.
- Identify and compare four technologies for exchanging information between organizations.
- Explain how companies can resolve channel conflict brought on by direct Web selling.
- Identify the decisions companies need to make when doing business internationally over the Web.
- Explain the implications of e-commerce for a company's security policy.

Enterprise Rent-A-Car
Connects with Insurers

Enterprise Rent-A-Car promises in its TV commercials, "We'll pick you up." Lately it's been providing a huge pick-me-up for perhaps its most important customers: insurance companies.

Occupying a unique niche in the rental industry, St. Louis-based Enterprise gets 95 percent of its business through local rentals—a significant chunk of which are replacement rentals paid for by auto insurers while the renter's car is in the repair shop. With its Automated Rental Management System (ARMS), Enterprise has brought the previously labor-intensive replacement rental process online, streamlining operations for insurers and protecting its niche in the process.

ARMS is a Web-based application that enables insurance companies, Enterprise branches, and auto-body shops to manage the entire rental cycle electronically. When someone gets in an accident and files a claim, the insurance adjuster can log on to the ARMS Web site and create a reservation for the client. Meanwhile, through the ARMS Automotive Web application, the auto-body shop can send daily electronic updates on the status of car repairs. If the repair takes longer than expected, the insurance company is automatically notified through ARMS. Once the body shop completes the repair and the customer returns the rental car, ARMS automatically generates an invoice and sends it to the insurer. Meanwhile, ARMS gives insurers access to a data warehouse where they can slice and dice information about their overall transactions, enabling them to better analyze and manage the rental process on a macro level.

This is a huge improvement over what used to be a cumbersome, paper-laden, manual process. In the past, an adjuster might have had to call an Enterprise branch three or four times before she hooked up with someone who could process a reservation. Enterprise has calculated that an average of 8.5 phone calls are cut from each rental transaction, as well as half a day from a typical rental cycle, saving the insurance industry between $36 million and $107 million annually. That means:

- Enterprise personnel are freed up to provide better personal service to the renter (who's typically disoriented and distressed over his accident and loss of car).
- Auto-body shops can concentrate on repairs instead of fielding annoying phone calls concerning the repair status.
- Insurance companies can cut, on average, a half-day out of the rental cycle.

Enterprise has reaped considerable rewards from ARMS. The company processes more than $1 billion worth of transactions annually through the system. And, according to COO and President Don Ross, Enterprise has been able, in large part because of ARMS, to forge several "preferred provider relationships" with insurers like MetLife and GMAC. Meanwhile, 22 of the nation's 25 biggest insurance companies and more than 150 companies in all use the system. And because ARMS makes it so much easier for insurance companies to do business with Enterprise, the company's business with major ARMS customers has grown dramatically faster than its overall insurance business, which includes insurers still conducting rental transactions manually. "We've seen our business more than double with certain companies since they've gone on ARMS," says Ross.[1]

Replacing paper and manual processes with electronic processes can save a company a great deal of time, effort, and money. When companies, such as Enterprise, do business electronically, not only do they stand to gain, but their partners also participate in the benefits. This helps cement the partnerships and build the business.

In this chapter, we begin by exploring e-commerce and e-business concepts: What are they and how do they relate to a company's business processes? We then explore the benefits of doing business electronically—as companies should to diagnose the need for e-commerce and evaluate alternatives. Next, we address various business models, analyzing how the business design affects the opportunity for and benefit of e-commerce. Finally, we explore the issues involved in implementing e-commerce and e-business.

E-COMMERCE AND E-BUSINESS CONCEPTS

What Are E-Commerce and E-Business?

Commerce is the exchange or buying and selling of goods and services.[2] We define **e-commerce** as the exchange or buying and selling of goods and services by electronic means. Examples of e-commerce include your roommate ordering a game over the Web, your college sending a purchase order by e-mail to its paper supplier, and the conclusion of a successful auction on eBay.

Business is a commercial or mercantile activity engaged in as a means of livelihood.[3] We define **e-business** as the use of information and communication technologies to perform business functions. E-business is, therefore, a broad term that includes e-commerce. For example, e-business includes such activities as entering information about a potential customer into a company's database, exchanging information about a new product design by e-mail, and scanning a part needed for manufacturing when drawing it from inventory. None of these examples would be considered e-commerce by our definition. Although we have defined e-commerce and e-business differently, you should be aware that many people use the terms interchangeably.

Value Chain Concepts

The **value chain** is the series of processes by which a company turns raw materials into finished goods and services. A proposition popularized by Michael Porter in 1980 is that each of the processes in the value chain should add value for the ultimate consumer and that a company can become more efficient by identifying and eliminating processes that do not add value.[4] Furthermore, a company can become more efficiently and strategically focused if it can identify and enhance the unique values that it adds. Each company, depending on its industry and niche, has its own value chain, but Figure 6-1 illustrates a generic value chain, adjusted somewhat from Porter's to align with this text. In Figure 6-1, arrows represent the direct value-adding processes in the value chain. The rectangle shown below the direct value chain illustrates additional processes necessary to support the value chain, either by tying its processes together or by providing analysis and information that improve process performance. E-business supports these processes and the flow of information among them.

Note that material flows *primarily* from supplier to customer. Sometimes, of course, as when products or materials are returned or reworked, material will flow in the opposite direction. Note also that information flows primarily in the opposite direction. This flow is dictated by the fact that customer purchases drive the operation of a company. When a customer purchases a product, information regarding that purchase is processed by outbound logistics, the processes associated with retrieving the product from inventory and shipping it to the customer.

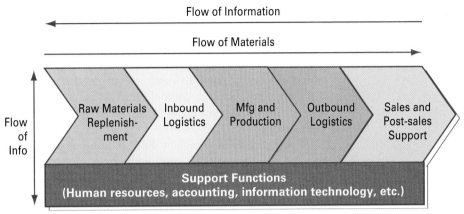

FIGURE 6-1

The value chain consists of processes that add value for the ultimate consumer. E-business supports the flow of information among these processes as well as among the functions that support the operation of the company.

That process, in turn, generates information that advises production whether to replenish inventory, which draws from supplies, which also need to be replenished.

The **extended value chain**, shown in Figure 6-2, is the sequence of value-adding activities that extend beyond the company boundaries. Every company should recognize that its suppliers are ultimately involved in the creation of its products' value. To the extent that your company, its suppliers, and its suppliers' suppliers act in concert to maximize value and drive out non-value-adding processes, your company can become more efficient and focused. The portion of the extended value chain on the supply side is called the **supply chain.**

Some of your customers might use your company's products as components of their own products; they might repackage your products for resale or simply provide distribution services that add value by reducing the distance or difficulty that consumers have in obtaining your products. To the extent that your customers or your customers' customers add value to your product, they are part of your extended value chain. To the extent that you and these customers act in a coordinated fashion to add value and drive out non-value-adding activities, you can reduce cost and add value for the ultimate consumer. The portion of the extended value chain on the customer side is called the **demand chain.**

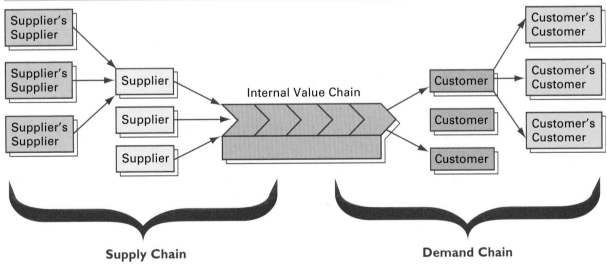

FIGURE 6-2

The extended value chain includes the value-added processes of your suppliers and their suppliers, your supply chain, and the value-added processes of your customers and their customers, your demand chain.

BENEFITS OF DOING BUSINESS ELECTRONICALLY

Organizations can analyze their value chain and their extended value chain on both the supply and demand sides to identify opportunities to improve business processes with information technology. To assess existing business operations, diagnose the need for change, and evaluate e-business alternatives, managers must understand the benefits and costs of doing business electronically. Only then can they design new systems and implement change.

Many good reasons exist for doing business electronically. E-business reduces the cost and increases the speed of executing business transactions; it allows business to be done seven days a week, 24 hours a day; it helps manage the flow of work, ensuring that tasks get handed off to the proper people and that people follow through with the tasks they are assigned; it helps monitor and improve product quality; and it improves coordination among businesses in handling the flow of raw goods and parts needed for production. In this section, we explore how these benefits of e-business improve the performance and efficiency of a business enterprise.

Reducing the Cost of Executing Transactions

E-business has the potential to reduce both the direct and indirect cost of executing transactions. Organizations can realize savings in the cost of mail, paper, handling, storage, logistics, labor, and other areas.

A typical business transaction involves several communications between the parties to the transaction. A purchase order initiates the purchase, a shipping notice and invoice are sent when the item is shipped; and payment is sent when the order is received. Some transactions will also require price quotations, authorizations, notification of receipt, and re-billings. When sent through the mail, these communications bear the cost of postage. When sent electronically, the cost can be much less. Also, electronic communication eliminates the cost of paper, especially forms, which can be expensive, and the cost of envelopes. It eliminates the handling required to stuff the envelopes. It also eliminates the labor required to cross-reference shipping notices against purchase orders to make sure that the items sent were the items ordered, invoices against shipping orders to make sure that the items billed were the items sent, and payments against invoices to make sure that the amount paid equaled the amount billed.

E-business reduces the cost of paper storage. It replaces files and filing cabinets with much cheaper electronic storage in much less space and, potentially, with much greater security. Saving space saves rent. Electronic records are also much cheaper to duplicate and to save off-site for backup purposes in case of fire, earthquake, or other natural or man-made disasters.

E-business reduces cost by improving logistics. Because electronic messages move faster than postal mail, much of the slack and guesswork can be taken out of the ordering process. Materials can be ordered shortly before they are needed with less fear of a stock-out. Therefore, the amount of inventory and the resulting inventory holding cost can be reduced. Also, electronic processing can help optimize shipping, combining less-than-truckload shipments into full truckload shipments and arranging for the carriage of goods on return trips, known as *backhaul.*

If the product being sold can be produced in electronic form, e-business produces even further cost savings. Books, magazines, newspapers, music, movies, television, catalogs, and many other products can be easily transmitted electronically, saving the cost of production on a hardcopy medium.

Increasing the Speed of Business

Increasing speed is as important as reducing costs. In competitive markets, the first company to produce a product has a tremendous marketing advantage. For example, in one industry, Hewlett Packard estimated the value of time-to-market, in terms of competitive advantage, at $1 million per day. The company was able to reduce time to market by as much as two weeks by posting on its intranet manufacturing specifications and code for reprogramming machines and assembly lines. Project team members around the world were thus able to work 24 hours/day on product design and rollout.[5]

Netgem, a leading provider of interactive TV technology, found that e-business tools allowed it to reduce the time to design a printed circuit board from six to two weeks. This allowed it to get complex products to market in a competitive timeframe.[6] Typically, reducing time to market requires not only the use of computers to aid in design (see Chapter 7), but also electronic tools for project management and for coordinating activities in design, engineering, marketing, manufacturing, and sales for a smooth product rollout.

The value of speed extends also to service and product delivery. Customers value quick turnaround. They will often pay extra for rapid service or go to a competitor if they can't get it. IP Communication (IPC), a broadband Internet access provider, used e-business to reduce the time it took to provision a new customer from 45 to 15 days. The process involves three external parties: the customer, a credit bureau, and SBC, which is the Local Exchange Carrier in IPC's region. When a customer signs a contract, credit has to be approved, a telephone line requested from SBC, and equipment installed at the customer's site. In addition, internal processes need to be set up for billing and trouble management. IPC used workflow software to streamline its internal processes and EDI and XML software, which are discussed later in this chapter, to streamline its external processes.[7]

Doing Business Any Time Anywhere

A great benefit of e-business is the ability to do business even when employees are not present. With the appropriate systems in place, a business can handle customer orders 24 hours a day, seven days a week. In addition, customers can shop, even if they don't place an order. They can also receive some level of customer support.

The ability to do business anywhere is a wonderful benefit for a small business that otherwise would have difficulty reaching distant locations. A store with a small number of physical outlets, or no physical outlet, can sell nationally or even internationally on the Web. Vosges Haut Chocolat, for example, a confectioner with two boutique locations in Chicago, attributes about 30 percent of its roughly $2 million in annual sales to its Web site.[8]

Improving Workflow

E-business improves workflow by replacing paper with electronic documents and notices. Electronic documents can be more readily accessed and the information on them more easily used. Duplication of paper, duplication of data entry, and loss of documentation are all eliminated. In addition, computer software can track the progress of processes, alerting managers when processes bog down, forecasting potential bottlenecks due to inadequate staffing, and providing audit trails and control.

Workflow software is built into most functional software, as well as the enterprise and cross-enterprise software that ties together processes in the internal and extended value chain (see Chapter 7). However, organizations can use workflow software independently to automate various processes. Workflow software operates in three phases: mapping, modeling, and implementation. In the mapping phase, the software helps record in a visual fashion, as illustrated in Figure 6-3, the manual and automatic steps involved in a business process. In the modeling phase, the software then helps identify inefficiencies in the process and potential areas for improvement, automation, and control. The software builds a model of the way the process should work, and automatically generates the code to enforce that process. In the implementation phase, the software uses the code, along with other tools such as e-mail, to provide the intended benefits.

Anova, a member of the Agis Group, one of the largest health care insurers in Holland, boasts 600,000 customers and annual revenues exceeding 1.3 billion guilders (about $600

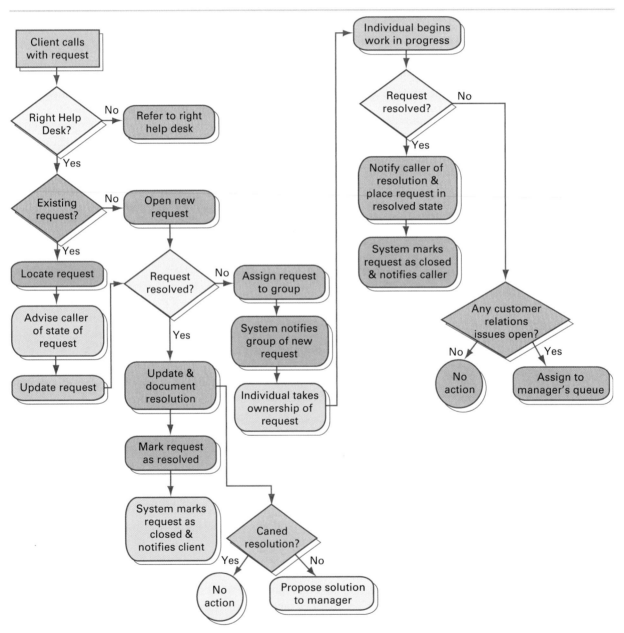

FIGURE 6-3 Mapping of the workflow of the computer service help desk at the University of Pennsylvania.

SOURCE: http://www.upenn.edu/computing/group/penntips/, accessed on 10 August 2002. Used with permission.

million). It processes approximately 1.2 million records each month, consisting of applications for reimbursement from patients, statements from specialists, doctors, and hospitals, and corrections and modifications of existing documents. To meet this enormous workload, it has computerized both its processes and its documents. Documents are scanned when they are received, stored in a database, and routed to those who need to enter missing information, get additional information from patients or doctors, or approve payment. The new system has had a fantastic impact on the efficiency of the organization. The number of outstanding work-in-progress jobs decreased 93 percent from 60,000 to 4,000, and the number of calls to the call center decreased from 18,000 to 10,000 per week. In addition, the average time to process an application or claim has decreased from 16 to 2 days, with 75 percent of the jobs now processed in a single day. Customer service agents are able to retrieve customers' applications or claims on their computer screen within seconds, so they can better respond to customer calls. They can make decisions and change documents while the caller is on the telephone. The system tracks and audits all changes made so that managers can review and control the process. In addition, Anova's managers should be able to improve their decision making because they have access to both transactional and statistical data and can perform analyses regarding their operations and strategy.[9]

Think about how ARMS has automated Enterprise Rent-A-Car's workflow. The benefits have included not only improving its relationships with insurers, but also speeding its processes and reducing errors.

Reducing Errors and Improving Quality

Doing business electronically provides many opportunities to reduce errors and improve quality. For example, when a customer uses a Web-based interface to enter data about her address or the details of her order for a pair of slacks, she can proof the information on the screen and make sure that it's correct. If instead she had given the information to an order taker over the telephone, the handoff between the order giver and the order taker would provide an additional chance for error. An electronic record also provides an opportunity for quality checks along almost every phase of every process. For example, when the order for slacks is filled, the picker can scan the item and the address on the box it's placed into. If the wrong item is placed into the box, computer systems can generate an error message. If a paper-based system were used, the only way to double check the process would be to have a second worker check the activities of the first worker.

E-business also reduces errors by providing an opportunity to automatically monitor all business processes. Q-Link Technologies, a Tampa, Florida-based provider of workflow software, cites the case of an anonymous Fortune 500 company that used its software to automate the process of resolving invoice discrepancies. When its process was manual, the company wrote off millions of dollars each year due to discrepancies that managers assumed were due to undocumented deals made by its sales force. The electronic process revealed, however, that as much as 80 percent of the problem was due to data entry errors. The e-business solution saved the company more than $2 million in the first year alone.[10]

Collaborating with Suppliers

Companies can benefit greatly by collaborating electronically with their suppliers. Collaboration can occur in several areas:

- *Joint product design.* A company can work with its suppliers to improve their designs and coordinate the designs of multiple suppliers for parts that are used in the same product. Suppliers can review a company's product design to advise how small changes in the design might produce large savings in the cost of its parts.

- *Synchronization.* A company can work with its suppliers to jointly forecast the need for supplies. Suppliers can then optimize their production schedules to reduce cost and share the cost savings with the company. Suppliers also save by not having to produce parts for products that are discontinued or out of demand.
- *Servicing.* Servicing is particular important in the service industries. Web-based interfaces, for example, greatly reduce the cost a company would incur in dealing with its insurance provider or 401K retirement plan provider.

A recent survey indicates that 62 percent of large firms already use the Internet to collaborate with their suppliers.[11] This percentage will surely increase as improvements in collaboration technology allow smaller companies to participate more easily and cheaply.

ELECTRONIC BUSINESS MODELS

E-business is not appropriate for every organization. Depending on the type of organization, the opportunities for doing business electronically may vary substantially. The Internet and Web-based technologies have also created the opportunities for businesses to earn revenue and to operate in ways that they couldn't have before. In this section, we explore how businesses differ from one another, what implications these differences have for the opportunities to do business electronically, and what threats exist to traditional businesses by new businesses operating with new models. We start by reviewing some basic concepts of business-to-consumer and business-to-business commerce. We then define what we mean by a "business model," and explore some of the more common business models to identify the impact of the Internet and e-business in general for companies following those models.

B2C and B2B Concepts

The popular press has paid a great deal of attention to the distinction between two types of e-commerce: **business-to-consumer (B2C)** and **business-to-business (B2B)**. As an individual and a consumer, you probably already know a great deal about B2C commerce. You've probably bought products on the Web, received promotions by e-mail and while Web surfing, and might even have downloaded commercial software or music products. The technology behind B2C commerce is quite simple, both for the business and the consumer. Once consumers began to trust the Web as a safe channel for buying, consumer purchasing exploded, as shown in Figure 6-4, with initial growth rates exceeding 150 percent a year. Although growth has slowed in percentage terms, online retail sales have grown consistently on a year-to-year basis and have outpaced the overall growth in retail sales since 1997. Today, nearly half of the U.S. adult population over the age of 17 and more than 80 percent of adults with Web access have purchased something online.[12]

Business-to-business e-commerce has existed at high volumes far longer than B2C e-commerce. As early as the 1960s, the transportation industry in the United States used an early version of a technology called Electronic Data Interchange (EDI), discussed in more depth later in this chapter, to transact business electronically. By 1991, about 20,000 companies worldwide were using EDI.[13] Currently, B2B e-commerce is roughly ten times the volume of B2C e-commerce as measured in dollar sales. It is expected to grow at a rate of about 68 percent annually through 2005 in the United States and at even faster rates elsewhere.[14]

Pure-Play vs. Multi-Channel

The initial wave of companies to popularize the Web for B2C e-commerce sold only through the Web channel, a strategy called "**pure-play.**" These companies were the first to

FIGURE   6-4

Growth of B2C sales in
the early years of
e-commerce.

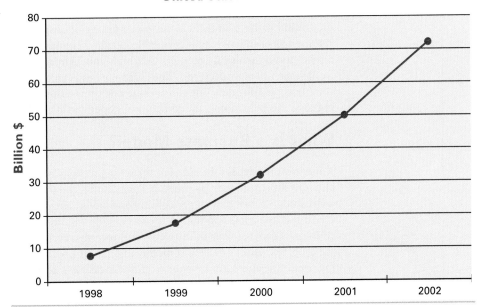

United States B2C Online Sales

recognize the power of the Web to take advantage of the opportunity to do business any time, anywhere and to reduce consumer prices and increase their own margin by bypassing distributors. A second wave of B2C e-commerce initiatives followed, with old-line companies reacting to the pressure of the pure-plays by initiating a **click-and-mortar,** or clicks and bricks, **strategy,** offering the same Web channel that the pure-plays provided (the "click") but also providing stores (the "mortar") where customers could return items more easily and where many felt more comfortable shopping.

Initially, many traditional companies hesitated to sell over the Web for fear of cannibalizing in-store retail sales and because they expected to incur huge costs to create a satisfactory Web presence. Companies, such as auto manufacturers, who sold through indirect channels, such as distributors or retail stores, often could not sell through Web channels without jeopardizing their retail relationships, a situation called **channel conflict.** Levis, for example, had to close down a successful Web site after complaints and threats from its retail partners.

Today, it is widely believed that a click and mortar strategy is more successful than a pure-play strategy. In fact, no large pure-play company other than eBay had been able to earn a profit through the year 2002. Many pure-play companies that had been darlings of Wall Street have gone bankrupt or ceased to exist. EToys, for example, opened its first day of trading at $20 per share, climbed to $85 per share before the day was out, and declared bankruptcy only two years later. MotherNature.com, which sold vitamins, supplements, minerals, and other natural products, as well as providing free information online opened trading in December 1999 at $13 per share, saw its share price rise to $14.56, and ceased operations less than one year later, in November 2000.

Nevertheless, the pure-play retail market continues to grow, with a year 2002 growth rate of about 33 percent, reaching nearly $23 billion in sales.[15] Evidence exists that many of the failures in the market were due to companies pursuing unreasonable growth rates to meet expectations of stockholders and the venture capital companies that funded their growth. These expectations were based largely on hype and sales potential, not profits. Companies that grew slowly, often using their own capital, and that paid attention to profits have continued to survive and thrive.

One example is FragranceNet.com Inc. Founded in 1997, the company bills itself as, "the world's largest pure Internet discount fragrance store, offering more than 3,500 genuine brand name fragrances at the lowest prices." It's listed on the Over The Counter market and has been marginally profitable despite being a public company. Bellacor.com, an online home furnishing retailer, sells high-end lighting and home decorating products from some 700 manufacturers. The company has been online since September 2000 and is completely self-funded. With an average sale transaction of about $400 and no warehousing costs except shipping, the company has operated at gross margins of 40 to 50 percent.[16]

What is a Business Model?

A **business model** is a broad plan for what products or services a company plans to sell and how it plans to earn its revenue. For example, the business model for most newspaper companies is to sell newspaper delivery and advertising. Television has two business models. In the free television model, a company distributes programming and advertising to consumers for free over the airwaves and receives revenue from its advertising clients. In the cable television model, a company distributes programming and sometimes advertising over cable and earns revenue from the local cable company, which collects revenue, in turn, from cable subscribers.

Business models apply to both standard business and e-business. The electronic channel offers different advantages for different business models. The electronic channel also offers different synergies with the standard channels in different business models. In this section, we focus on what advantages the electronic channel offers and also on how electronic and standard channels work together.

Thousands of different business models exist, but many share common features. We have identified several common models in this section. Nevertheless, many business models will not fall neatly into the categories we have created.

Producer Models

A **producer** is a business that earns revenue by selling the products that it builds, manufactures, grows, or creates, or the services it provides. A producer can sell through many channels, including directly to the end consumer, through a retailer, through a distributor, or through an *original equipment manufacturer (OEM)*, a company that incorporates the product into its own product. Examples of producers include farmers, automobile manufacturers, plumbers, consultants, and pay-per-view television. A business that makes circuit boards is a producer, but so is the computer company that includes the circuit boards in its own products. Logistics providers, such as UPS, can also be considered producers, as they sell a well-defined service.

The ability of a producer to do electronic commerce anywhere gives it the ability to bypass wholesalers and/or retailers in its demand chain, as illustrated in Figure 6-5. The process of bypassing intermediaries, such as these, in the distribution and sale of a product or service is called **disintermediation.** Often, the original producer of a product selling through the typical demand chain will receive only a small percentage of what the final consumer pays. For example, the author of a book typically receives royalties of less than 15 percent of the wholesale price, perhaps only 8 percent of the retail price. An apple grower in Ontario typically receives about 20 cents/pound at the farm, less than one third of the 90 cents/pound that the consumer pays for the apple. As shown in Figure 6-6, the storage company, the packing company, the wholesaler, and the retailer each earn revenue for the services they provide, raising the cost of the apple. Disintermediation occurs if the apple grower sells directly to the consumer, perhaps allowing her to pick her own apples at the orchard.

FIGURE 6-5

Electronic commerce gives rise to disintermediation, the ability of a business to bypass intermediaries in the distribution and sale of its product or service.

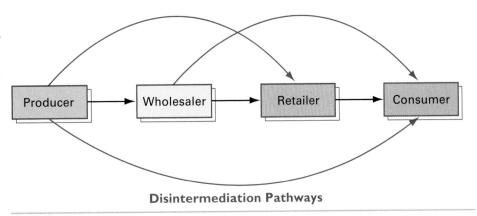

Disintermediation Pathways

FIGURE 6-6

Price of a pound of fresh apples when purchased from various companies in the value chain. The producer, in this case the grower, often receives only a small percentage of the eventual selling price.

SOURCE: Government of Ontario, Analysis and Review of the Apple Marketing Plan (Ontario, Canada: Queen's Printer for Ontario, 2002): Table 4-1, accessed at http://www.gov.on.ca/OMAFRA/english/farmproducts/apple/section_4.htm on 9 August 2002. Used with permission.

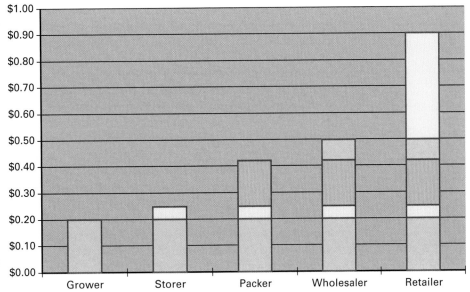

In bypassing intermediaries, producers not only receive a higher price for their goods but they also create a closer relationship with the final consumer. This relationship allows them to better sense the level of demand, which can help guide their production planning. In addition, direct contact with the consumer provides better feedback about their products or services, which can help improve design. The major disadvantage of disintermediation for the producer is the need to provide the services that intermediaries would otherwise provide. Selling in smaller quantities, a producer might need to increase its sales staff, support staff, and advertising, incurring additional costs. As the producer's primary competency is normally production rather than sales, it might even cost a producer more than it saves to bypass intermediaries in the demand chain.

Dell Computer is a well-known example of a company that has used electronic commerce to bypass intermediaries and sell directly to both businesses and consumers. It is highly efficient in both its production and distribution channels. Scholars debate how much of its success is due to a business model that bypasses retail stores and how much is due to its efficiency as a producer and its skills in marketing. Other computer makers attempting to emulate Dell's business model have not fared as well.

Distributor Models

A **distributor** is a business that buys in bulk and resells in smaller quantities. Examples of distributors include auto dealers, gas stations, and wine distributors. A distributor adds value by its marketing, sales, and post-sales support activities.

According to our definition, wholesalers and retailers also follow the distributor model, although many carry the products of different types of goods and even competing goods (see Aggregator Models later in this section). A **retailer** is a company, such as a grocery or department store, that sells products to consumers. A **wholesaler** is a company that buys from producers and sells to retailers. A retailer may buy directly from both producers and wholesalers.

Distributors are greatly affected by the threat of disintermediation. As e-commerce makes it easier for producers to sell directly to retailers and consumers, distributors must add clear value by the services they perform if they hope to survive. The air travel industry is a perfect example. Airlines had always sold some tickets directly to customers over the phone and at airports, but it wasn't until 1996 that Southwest began to sell tickets online. Other airlines followed suit, and within a few years, more customers were buying directly from airline sites than from ticket agencies. By 2001, only 6 percent of U.S. travelers booked their travel through a traditional agency.[17] At the same time as airlines began selling directly through the Web, the travel agency industry was hit by the entry of new online agencies pursuing a pure e-commerce strategy. Many traditional agencies went out of business, with one source claiming a loss of nearly 3,000 businesses between April 2001 and April 2002 alone.[18] Yet, many agencies continued to thrive. Their secret: rather than relying on commissions from airlines and hotels, they charged their customers for the services they performed, sold these services well, and performed them well. The successful agencies were those that had established long-term relationships with their clients. These clients understood that their agency could save them a great deal of search time, provide accommodations that best met their needs, and would run interference and solve problems when they ran into trouble. These agencies earned money less as a distributor and more as an agent (see Market Maker Models later in this section).

Reintermediation or **cybermediation** are terms applied to businesses that have replaced brick and mortar distributors with pure e-commerce distribution models. Travelocity or Expedia are examples from the travel industry.

Aggregator Models

An **aggregator** is a business that adds value by providing one-stop shopping. It buys products from many producers and distributors and resells them in the retail market. Examples of aggregators include grocery stores, department stores, hardware stores, and most catalog direct mail companies.

Although aggregators of physical goods can use e-commerce on their supply side to cut costs, improve supplier relationships, and optimize inventory, e-commerce has had very little impact on their demand chain. They are subject, however, to some degree to reintermediation by Web malls, which provide a small amount of competition, particularly in specialty markets. Amazon.com, for example, threatened Borders, Barnes & Noble, and other book aggregators. However, most aggregators found that they could compete satisfactorily by adopting a multi-channel model. The pure plays have some advantage in that they don't need to rent store space and don't need to pay sales clerks. These advantages, however, are offset by higher costs for shipping and technology. Also, click and mortar stores provide an advantage for customer service, providing a place to return items and to seek personal assistance in purchasing.

Aggregators of products that can exist in electronic form have faced reintermediation threats. Software and music are two such examples. Nevertheless, software and music stores continue to thrive.

Advertisement Revenue Models

Some companies, we will call them "advertisement runners," earn revenue primarily by selling advertising. Free television and many Web portals are examples of businesses that follow a pure advertisement revenue model. Many advertisement runners also earn revenue from other sources, following a mixed, rather than a pure, model. For example, newspapers are typically both producers and advertisement runners.

In many ways, the Internet is an ideal medium for advertising (see Table 6-1). One of the greatest benefits of Web advertising is that it can be easily targeted to the customer by the nature of the page on which it appears. This characteristic was the genesis of many business plans that sought to create communities of interest and earn revenue by advertising to those communities. The Motley Fool (www.fool.com) is a good example of success with this model. The company provides free advice and information to investors, and has built a community of loyal "customers" who return frequently to its Web site. It can guarantee, with near perfect certainty, that people viewing advertisements on its site are interested in investing. The company also sells research reports and has a few other sources of income, but it is primarily an advertisement runner.

The advertisement runner model based on a community of interest will not succeed, however, if its community doesn't use its Web site often. In 1999, former U.S. Surgeon General C. Everett Koop raised $450 million in the stock market on the strength of his business model to sell advertisements at drkoop.com, a Web-based community of people interested in health care.[19] The business was never able to earn a profit, filed for bankruptcy, and sold its assets to Vitacost Holdings Inc. in 2002 for just $300,000.[20]

A **click-through advertisement** is one that directs the viewer to the advertiser's Web site if the viewer clicks on the ad. Click-throughs are particularly potent because they:

- Identify customers who have an interest in the content of the advertisement.

- Provide an opportunity to provide more information to the customer in an interactive fashion. Customers become responsible for what they view.

- Provide an opportunity to obtain information about the customer through customer registration and other means.

Web portals, such as Yahoo and Google, take advantage of their search capability to position themselves as advertisement runners. **Web portals** are companies that draw a large volume of repeat visitor traffic because they provide free Web searching services.

TABLE 6-1	**Pros**	Advertising can be well targeted based on the nature of the Web page on which it appears.
Pros and cons of the Internet as an advertising medium.		Advertisements can be changed in real time to reflect market conditions.
		Advertising views can be easily measured.
		Click-through advertising can generate immediate sale or lead.
		Effectiveness of click-through advertising can be measured.
		Cost of advertising can be tied to its effectiveness.
		Compared to print, advertising can be dynamic.
	Cons	Overuse and clutter can lead to customer tune-out.
		Compared to TV, quality is poor.

Their ability to attract viewers makes them an ideal site for advertisers. In addition, a portal can customize its advertisements based on the user's search criteria, and it can charge sponsors (another form of advertising) for listing their Web sites at the top of the search list returned to the user. Recent research indicates that search listings are extremely effective advertising channels. Specifically:

- Consumers are three times more likely to recall the name of a company when it appears as a result of a search rather than in a banner ad.

- People are twice as likely to have a favorable opinion of companies in the top three search positions as compared to those featured in ads.

- Of all online purchases, 55 percent were made on Web sites found through search listings compared to only 9 percent found through banner ads.[21]

Total spending in online advertising is estimated at between 2 and 5 percent of total media spending.[22] Three quarters of forecasters in a recent eMarketer study are projecting that e-advertising in the United States will grow at annual rates of between 30 and 45 percent.[23]

Market Maker Models

A **market maker** is a business that earns revenue by bringing together buyers and sellers. The market maker generally never buys or sells a product. Market makers earn income by charging buyers or sellers to participate in the market or by charging a percentage or a fee for each transaction consummated. Examples of market makers include auction houses, real estate agents, B2B exchanges, and trade conventions. Market makers can be neutral, as most auction houses are, or they can be agents for buyers or sellers. An **agent** is a company or person that acts on behalf of another. A real estate agent, for example, usually acts on behalf of a seller to find a buyer for a property. Acting on behalf of one seller does not preclude the agent from acting on behalf of others.

Electronic Auctions

Electronic auctions are an ideal way of connecting buyers and sellers. By far the most successful pure e-commerce company has been the auctioneer eBay. Founded in 1995, eBay had 49.7 million registered users in 2002 with a market capitalization of more than $16 billion.[24] Some of its key features and services are listed in Table 6-2.

Many types of auctions exist, and almost all can be emulated on an electronic basis. In an *English auction,* most commonly used for B2C or consumer-to-consumer transactions, a seller declares a minimum price for an item to be auctioned. Buyers bid upwards until nobody is willing to bid any higher. The highest (last) bidder is then required to purchase the product or service at the price bid. In a *Dutch auction,* the auctioneer starts at a high price and slowly reduces the price until a bid is made. The last bidder is obligated to purchase the product or service at the price bid. In a *sealed bid auction,* all bidders secretly enter the highest price that they are willing to pay, and the high bidder wins the auction. Variants of these auctions occur when multiple identical items are sold.

A *reverse auction* occurs when a buyer declares the willingness to buy at the lowest price offered. In this case, the sellers bid against one another, lowering the price until nobody is willing to go any lower. At that point, the last (lowest) bidder is required to sell to the buyer at the price bid. A variant of this model is the name-your-price auction popularized by online auctioneer Priceline.com. In this case, the buyer commits to purchasing goods or services at a stated price. If any seller is willing to meet the price, the deal is consummated.

A problem with electronic auctions arises from the fact that, unlike brick and mortar auctions, the electronic auctioneer often does not take possession of the physical product. The bidders, in most cases do not see the physical product. Therefore, bidders must rely

TABLE 6-2

Features and services
available at electronic
auctioneer eBay.

Billpoint/PayPal	Handles credit card payments or transfers from customer's bank account.
Half.com	Seller sets fixed price for high-quality, previously owned, mass market goods.
eBay International	Users buy and sell into a global marketplace.
eBay Motors	Auction for automotive goods. Provides additional services, such as "financing, inspection, escrow, auto insurance, vehicle shipping, title & registration, and a lemon check."
eBay Stores	Sellers can create customized stores, such as wearables or collectable toys.
Buy It Now	Allows buyers to buy an item at a specified price without having to wait for the end of an auction.
eBay Professional Services	Serves professionals and freelancers for projects such as Web design, accounting, writing, technical support.
eBay Local Trading	Lets users find items located near them in 60 local markets.
eBay Premier	A specialty site where buyers can purchase high-value goods such as art, antiques, fine wines, and rare collectibles from leading auction houses.
eBay Live Auctions	Permits real-time online bidding on items being sold on the sales floor of the world's leading auction houses.

SOURCE: http://pages.ebay.com/community/aboutebay/overview/index.html, accessed on 9 August 2002.

extensively on the reputation and good will of the seller along with any guarantees that the auctioneer might offer. To satisfy this need, electronic auction houses offer buyers the opportunity to rate sellers, and their ratings are released in subsequent auctions to the bidders. An alternative means of guaranteeing the quality and delivery of products bought is to use an escrow service. For a fee, a third party will hold the bidder's payment in trust until the bidder receives and accepts the product or service. eBay, for example, uses escrow.com as its escrow agent.

B2B Exchanges

B2B exchanges, or marketplaces, serve buyers and sellers in specific industries or regions. For example, ChemConnect is a marketplace for buyers and sellers of chemicals and plastics. Paperspace is a marketplace for trading paper and pulp. CPGMarket serves the European consumer packaged goods industry.

Although some exchanges provide auctions, most operate on a many-to-many model similar to the stock exchange. Bid and ask prices are posted, and available for view. When a buyer or seller finds a bid or ask price that matches what he or she is willing to pay or receive, the exchange arranges the sale and takes a percentage of the price as its fee. Most exchanges also require membership, which also earns them a fee. To provide additional services to their members and additional sources of revenue, many exchanges offer market research, news, logistics support, and other enticements.

Infomediary Models

An **infomediary** is a company that collects and sells information. We could consider it to be a producer, as it creates a product or service, but we've put it into a separate category because its extended value chain is so different from that of most producers.

Information about consumers and their buying habits is particularly helpful to companies in designing and marketing their products and services and in setting strategy. Information about producers and suppliers is useful to consumers in making their product and service selections. Infomediaries serve either or both functions. Although they are not market makers, they are critical to the operation of an efficient market.

Market research firms follow an infomediary business model. Many operate on a contract basis, selling their research services to firms with specific questions about how to position or price a particular product or service. Other firms collect information from both public and proprietary sources and then sell that information in the form of reports. For example, Nielsen Media Research measures television and radio audience reach as well as print readership in 40 countries. The company sells its reports primarily to media providers in the markets it measures.

The Web provides many opportunities to collect data about consumer buying habits. Data are derived from a number of sources: Companies can analyze the logs of their Web servers to obtain such data as what sequence of pages their Web visitors followed, how long they looked at each page, how often they return, and what Web site sent them to the company's Web pages. Companies, such as DoubleClick, which feeds click-through banner ads to a network of sites, collect information regarding click-through activity and advertising impressions. Nielsen//NetRatings puts software on individuals' computers at home and at work to measure their click-by-click behavior in real time. The company collects and provides to its clients such data as the number of Internet visits to popular Web sites and overall, online advertising creatives, impressions, and expenditures, and information about Internet user lifestyle, demographics, and product purchases. The information is available through subscription to reports published periodically or access to the company's database. Figure 6-7 illustrates the types of information that a company such as Nielsen//NetRatings can provide.

E-Government

Electronic models are also applicable to the business of government. Government agencies, like all businesses, purchase goods and services from suppliers. Governments have employees. But do they have customers like other businesses? It's easy to think of the public, including citizens and business establishments, as governments' customers. Although the relationship between the government and the public is not identical to traditional business-customer relationships, the public funds the government with its taxes and fees and receives services and goods in return. **E-government** is the model of government in which information technology is used to the extent possible to facilitate interaction between the government and its suppliers, government and the public, government and its employees, and among government agencies and different governmental bodies.

Increasingly, governmental bodies are pursuing an e-government strategy to improve efficiency and provide better services to the public. Electronic tax filing is one type of activity that provides both benefits. The State of Minnesota, for example, estimates that it saved $1.5 million dollars in 2002 because 40 percent of individuals and 97 percent of businesses filed their returns electronically. The public benefited because the state issued refunds to electronic filers in five days, whereas it took about 90 days to process the refunds for paper filers.[25]

E-government can be implemented at many levels. At the lowest level, the government simply provides information electronically. Many governmental bodies provide more advanced features, including the ability to perform two-way transactions. Some, such as the U.S. Government at its www.firstgov.gov Web site, provide portals that simplify access to both informational and transactional Web sites for employees, other government agencies, and the public. At higher levels are the ability to personalize services and the implementation of a full enterprise model, involving the transformation of all business processes and their integration electronically using software similar to ERP business software.[26]

FIGURE 6-7

News releases from Nielsen//NetRatings during the month of July 2002 and sample data from the July 16 news release.

SOURCE: http://www.netratings .com/news_corporate.jsp ?thetype=date&theyear =2002&themonth=6, accessed on 11 August 2002. Used with permission.

Nielsen/Net Ratings Online Population by Race (U.S., Home)

Ethnicity	June 2001 Unique Audience	June 2002 Unique Audience	Year Over Year Growth
Hispanic Origin	6.7 million	7.6 million	
Percent Composition	6.60%	7.20%	13%
Asian or Pacific Islander	2.2 million	2.4 million	
Percent Composition	2.20%	2.30%	6%
White (Caucasian)	90.8 million	94.0 million	
Percent Composition	89.50%	89.60%	4%
African American	7.5 million	7.8 million	
Percent Composition	7.40%	7.40%	3%

07/31/2002	Home, Corporate and Government Web Sites More Than Double Audience Reach to Work Surfers in Germany
07/26/2002	Seasonal Sales Drive Shoppers Online
07/25/2002	NetRatings Announces Q2 2002 Financial Results
07/24/2002	UK House Buyers home in on the Web (United Kingdom)
07/19/2002	Traffic to Education and University Web Sites Soars as Fall Semester Nears
07/16/2002	Hispanics are the Fastest Growing Ethnic Group Online
07/16/2002	June Online: Holidays, Football and News (Italy)
07/12/2002	Fandango.com, Movietickets.com, and Moviefone.com Score with Fourth of July Weekend Moviegoers
07/12/2002	Résultats mensuels: Panel Univers Global - Juin 2002 (France)
07/11/2002	Nielsen//NetRatings Lanza la Primera Herramienta de Plantifiacion Online en España (Spain)
07/07/2002	Military Web Sites Spike in Traffic
07/05/2002	World Cup Scores Online in Hong Kong (Hong Kong)
07/02/2002	Nielsen//NetRatings veröffentlicht erste Internet Nutzerzahlen für Surfen am Arbeitsplatz (Germany)
07/01/2002	Google Gains Four Million Unique Audience Members in May

In the United States, the Office of Management and Budget (OMB) is promoting 24 broad cross-agency e-government initiatives for the years 2002 through 2004 (see Table 6-3). Also, OMB effectively has oversight for the entire $52 billion federal budget for information technology. It can withhold funding for an individual agency initiative if it finds that the initiative fails to provide a clear business case and an architecture consistent with the federal plan.

Europe is also making progress toward e-government. A recent survey of 15 EU countries plus Iceland, Norway, and Switzerland found that approximately 55 percent of 20 public services measured are now available online. Overall, 80 percent of public service providers have some online presence. The most developed services are income generating ones, such as tax filing, while the least developed services relate to documents and permits, such as drivers' licenses and passports.[27]

Other countries around the world, both developed and less-developed, are moving toward an e-government model. For example, China has had an active e-government initiative since 1999, focusing on e-service systems for customs, taxation, finance, public security, social security, agriculture, and water resources.[28] Brazil's government has saved 20 to 30 percent on purchases through its e-procurement portal Comprasnet.[29] Taiwan,

TABLE 6-3 Twenty-four e-government initiatives managed by the Office of Management and Budget.

Government to Business Initiatives

Federal Asset Sales: Customers will be able to find assets regardless of the agency that holds them, and will be able to bid and/or make purchases electronically for financial, real, and disposable assets.

Simplified Tax and Wage Reporting: Decrease the number of tax-related forms that an employer must file, provide timely and accurate tax information to employers, increase the availability of electronic tax filing, and simplify federal and state tax employment laws.

Business Compliance: Provide information on laws and regulations, and allow permits to be completed, submitted, and approved online.

Health Informatics: Provide a simplified and unified system for sharing and reusing medical record information among government agencies and their private health care providers and insurers.

International Trade Process: Create a single customer-focused site whereby exporters could be facilitated through the entire export process.

Online Rulemaking Management: Provide access to the rulemaking process for citizens anytime, anywhere through an expanded eDocket system.

Government to Government Initiatives

Disaster Assistance and Crisis Response: Create a one-stop portal containing information from applicable organizations involved in disaster preparedness, response and recovery.

E-grants: Create an electronic grants portal for grant recipients and grant-making agencies to streamline, simplify, and provide an electronic option for grants management across the government.

E-vital: Expand the vital records online data exchange efforts between federal agencies and state governments.

Geospatial Information One-Stop: Provide access to the federal government's spatial data assets in a single location.

Wireless Public Safety: Provide: Standards to enable interoperability among federal, state, and local officials during emergencies.

Government to Citizen Initiatives

EZ Tax Filing: Make it easier for businesses and the public to file taxes

Eligibility Assistance Online: Through a common Internet portal, citizens (with a focus on high need demographic groups) will have access to government programs and services coupled with a prescreening device.

Online Access for Loans: Allows citizens and business to find and apply for loan programs that meet their needs.

Recreation One-Stop: Provide a one-stop, searchable database of recreation areas nationwide, featuring online mapping and integrated transactions

USA Service: Use best practices in customer relationship management to enable citizens to quickly obtain service online, while improving the responsiveness and consistency across government agencies.

Internal Efficiency and Effectiveness

E-payroll: Consolidate systems at more than 14 processing centers across government.

E-records Management: Establish uniform procedures and standards for agencies in converting paper-based records to electronic files.

E-training: Provide a repository of government-owned courseware.

Enterprise Case Management: Centralize Justice litigation case information.

Integrated Acquisition: Agencies will begin sharing common data elements to enable other agencies to make better-informed procurement, logistical, payment, and performance assessment decisions.

Integrated Human Resources: Integrate personnel records across government.

Recruitment One-Stop: Automated federal government information re career opportunities, rèsumè submission, routing, and assessment. Streamline the federal hiring process and provide up-to-the-minute application status for job seekers.

Cross-Cutting Initiative

E-authentication: Establish a core federal public-key infrastructure with which federal employees and the federal community would interoperate and give the public a secure and consistent method of communication with government.

Source: U.S. Office of Management and Budget, E-Government Strategy: Simplified Delivery of Services to Citizens, February 27, 2002.

Australia, and Canada have been ranked second, third, and fourth, respectively, for the quality of their e-government services.[30]

E-COMMERCE IMPLEMENTATION ISSUES

So, you've decided to do business electronically. Now, what do you have to worry about? In this section, we look at four issues that companies face in implementing e-commerce: choosing the right technology, resolving potential channel conflicts, designing your Web site for international business, and keeping your systems and data secure.

E-Commerce Technologies

Picking the right technology for the job is to some extent a technical issue, but strategic differences exist among the most common technologies used to exchange data between business partners. In this section, we examine four commonly used technologies: EDI, Web forms, XML, and, recently, Web services.

EDI

Electronic data interchange (EDI) is the exchange of electronic documents between computers at different companies. A key feature of EDI is that it takes place directly between the computers without manual intervention. Companies routinely exchange purchase orders, invoices, shipping notices, and money using EDI. It eliminates the cost of data entry, printing, and mailing. For example, when sending an invoice to a customer using paper documentation, a company prints a copy of the invoice, stuffs it into an envelope with a window (or perhaps prints an envelope and matches it to the invoice), and mails it. The customer at the receiving end enters the invoice data into its accounts payable database. With EDI, software produces an electronic version of the document and delivers it over communication channels in a form immediately understood by the accounts payable program of the customer. EDI saves paper, mailing, and data entry work at the customer's end. The supplier receives a time-stamped electronic acknowledgment of the customer's receipt of the invoice.

EDI standards exist at two levels:

- *General EDI standards* specify formats for various types of documents and parameters within which industry standards must comply. The American National Standards Institute (ANSI) sets EDI standards, known as ANSI-X12, for the United States. Canada observes the same standards, but European companies and many Asian companies have embraced a standard called *EDIFACT*. Divergence in standards creates difficulties for companies that do business both domestically and internationally.

- *Industry standards* modify the general standards within the allowable parameters to reflect the unique ways that each industry does business. These standards not only add detail to the universal document types but also introduce additional documents that are common to the industry. For example, the insurance industry might create a common form for brokers to send claim requests to an insurance provider.

In addition, trading partners can establish their own EDI document forms for transactions unique to their partnership as long as these forms comply with the general and industry standards.

A company's application software packages must produce and accept EDI documents for EDI to work. Companies with systems that do not support EDI can use *mapping software* to translate their application's output into EDI documents and translate EDI documents received into input compatible with the company's software. Most VAN suppliers provide utilities that perform this translation at the time they transmit a document across their network.

Early resistance to EDI's growth derived in part from the fact that it takes two companies to transact business using EDI. In the late 1980s companies did not want to invest in EDI because few suppliers or customers transacted business using it. Now most large companies have adopted EDI. Some impose charges on non-EDI commerce to offset its increased cost. The retailer Nordstrom, for example, charges its vendors $25.00 for each non-EDI invoice it receives.[31] Other companies require their business partners to use EDI. For example, Mellon Bank, N.A., lost PPG Industries Inc. as a client when it could not process the EDI payments PPG received from General Motors, PPG's largest customer.[32]

Companies already using EDI can use the Internet to transact EDI business with companies that have not yet invested in EDI software. General Electric Lighting (GEL), for example, allows its non-EDI suppliers to submit bids using a Web interface. GEL's suppliers first download a browser plug-in that allows them to access GEL's EDI forms over the Web, request and receive product blueprints, and submit a bid directly into GEL's EDI system. Web-based EDI freed six to eight days a month for purchasing agents to perform strategic rather than administrative tasks, reduced material costs by 5 to 20 percent, reduced processing time from over seven days to just one day, and reduced overall cycle time by more than 50 percent. In addition, it reduced paper and mail costs significantly and allowed GEL to acquire more suppliers.[33]

Web Forms

If you've ever ordered something over the Web, you've probably filled out a form by entering your name, contact information, and credit card number. The form might have had pull down menus to allow you to select the state, for example, or the color of the product you ordered. When you press the SUBMIT button, the contents of the form are sent to the Web server that presented the form, and its contents are processed. Secure Socket Layer (SSL) technology (see Chapter 5) ensures the confidentiality of the information you've entered and allows you to be confident that your transaction is going to the company you thought you were dealing with. The combination of Web forms and SSL technology is the predominant method for transacting B2C commerce.

XML

Your Web browser understands several languages, such as HTML and javascript, which instruct it how to arrange the text and pictures on a Web page and respond to the click of your mouse. Most Web pages have meaning to you because you view them in a context and you're intelligent. Look, for example, at Figure 6-8, a Web page of online light bulb vendor Lite-House.com. You can easily distinguish the item number from the price even though both appear under the column "Item #." You probably also recognize that the word following "Mfgr:" is the name of the manufacturer, and that "120 V" refers to the voltage rating on the bulb. A computer program could also make sense of this data if it were programmed to recognize the fact that the beginning of every line alternates between an item number and price and that the manufacturer's name follows the letters, "Mfgr:". However, this program would not work properly if Lite-House.Com were to change the format of its Web page or if you wanted the software to work with the Web pages of other light bulb stores.

The solution to this problem is a language called **Extended Markup Language (XML)**. A Web page designed in XML includes tags that identify the meaning of the data. For example, the code for the Web page of Figure 6-8 might include the following notation:

<ItemNum>SL14623</ItemNum>. A matching pair of tags, in this case "ItemNum," appears inside the angle brackets, one without a slash starting the identification, and one with a slash ending it. Web browsers ignore these tags when displaying the Web page, but computer programs can interpret data between the two tags, in this example, as an item number. Of course, for this scheme to work, the light bulb selling industry would have to agree that every Web store would use the ItemNum tag to refer to item numbers.

XML has a few additional features that make it very powerful. For one, tags can be nested, as shown in Figure 6-9. Also, XML includes a data definition language, which defines what tags are valid, how they can be nested, and what additional properties they might have. The data definition language makes it relatively easy to create and use standards. The Organization for the Advancement of Structured Information Standards (OASIS) is a not-for-profit organization created to define general XML standards for business, such as standards for names and addresses, as well as standards for several industries. The organization boasts a large number of sponsors who are leaders in software development, such as Microsoft, IBM, Sun, Hewlett-Packard, and Netscape/AOL, as well as industrial leaders such as Boeing and Airbus.

Recently, Boston-based financial giant, Fidelity, converted its corporate data into XML format to ease the integration of its information systems. As a result, the company was able to eliminate many of the translations that took place between its Web site, mainframes, and application servers, allowing it to decommission 75 of the 85 servers that had been needed to coordinate the exchange of messages and data among them.[34]

Web Services

A Web service is software that accepts commands over the Web and optionally returns results over the Web. A command could be to run a process or to get some information. Two Web services, perhaps an order-taking service at one company and an order-placing service at another, could operate over the Web to conduct e-commerce without manual

FIGURE 6-9

Nested XML for a name
and address.

How the address appears:

Prof. John Knowitall
School of Business
Mustard Hall, Room 319
XML University
Xanadu, MA 10101

How the address might be represented in XML:

```
<Address>
        <NameDetails>
                <Title>Prof.</Title>
                <FirstName>John</FirstName>
                <LastName>Knowitall</LastName>
        </NameDetails>
        <AddressLines>
                <AddressLine>School of Business</AddressLine>
                <AddressLine>Mustard Hall, Room 319</AddressLine>
        </AddressLines>
        <CompanyName>XML University</CompanyName>
        <City>Xanadu</City>
        <State>MA</State>
        <PostalCode>10101</PostalCode>
</Address>
```

intervention, smoothly integrating processes across organizational boundaries. While EDI and XML allow companies to exchange data, Web services are more flexible in that they let companies open up their information systems to partners with far less programming and less structure in the format of exchanged information.

Nordstrom.com, the online arm of Nordstrom department stores, built a Web service to allow customers to buy gift cards online and by telephone. One approach would have been to link the company's Web site to a mainframe at its savings bank through middleware so that customers could query gift-card balances and the bank could process redemptions. Instead, Nordstrom.com built a Web services tool that allows the bank, the call center, and visitors to its Web site to query or update a gift-card balance. A shopper can, therefore, redeem a Nordstrom's gift card at a store or cash it in at Nordstrom.com.[35]

Resolving Channel Conflicts

Manufacturers operating through resellers and distributors often face a no-win situation in setting up their Web site. Consumers expect manufacturers to have a Web site where they can obtain information about the company's products. Once at the Web site, consumers often want to order products directly and are disappointed when they cannot. However, manufacturers have several good reasons to avoid selling directly to customers from the Web site, and few incentives to do so. They cannot undercut the prices of their distributors, resellers, and other channel partners without risking their loss and defection to another manufacturer. Most manufacturers don't want to ship in small volumes, as this practice runs counter to their distribution philosophy and requires them to operate in areas where they have no expertise or established business practices. Their core competencies are manufacturing, not distribution or logistics.

Two solutions exist to this problem. The first is to take orders directly at the manufacturer's Web site and then relay them to the distributor or other channel partner for handling. This strategy can operate in two ways. In one, the consumer is made aware of the fact that a channel partner will handle the order. The consumer is often not told who the partner will be. For example, FTD.com accepts orders for flower delivery over the Web, but does not identify the partner that buys the flowers, assembles the order, and delivers it. The Web site merely says, "Delivered by an FTD® Florist." One problem with funneling the order to a partner is that customers often don't like dealing with two parties to a transaction. If something should go wrong, they don't know whether to contact the manufacturer or the distributor, for example.

An alternative strategy is for the partner to handle the order as if it were the manufacturer. From the consumer's perspective, the partner becomes transparent, and the consumer often feels more confident dealing with a single source. A drawback of this strategy from the manufacturer's perspective is that the manufacturer needs to be able to service the customer, from the standpoint of following up on orders that don't arrive, handling returns, and handling questions about setup or use. The drawback from the partner's perspective is that it has no contact with the customer. It may make a small profit on its service, but it cannot easily follow up with the customer for service or future sales.

A second solution is to redirect the customer to a partner's site before taking an order. 3Com Corporation, the Santa Clara, California-based manufacturer of networking products, turned to this strategy after selling directly from its own Web site since November 1999. Although its direct order site eventually handled 5 percent of the company's total sales, 3Com preferred to sell through its distributors. Now, when you browse 3Com's catalog at its Web site, find a product you like, and click "buy online," a window pops up to with a list of online dealers for you to select. When you click on a dealer's name, the dealer's Web site appears with the product you selected, ready for you to add it to your shopping cart. Because 3Com partners with so many dealers and retail outlets, it has outsourced the redirection process to Channel Intelligence, whose software provides the linkage directly to product pages at reseller sites and whose services keep the links current. When it first experimented with this program, 3Com gave customers the option of buying directly or via an authorized reseller. However, within a month, more than 50 percent of customers buying online from the 3Com site selected a reseller to complete the sale. A month later, 3Com shut down the direct sale option. 3Com no longer has to support its own shopping cart application and has shut down the distribution center that delivered products directly to customers. Its partners are also happy, as they are getting more leads of high quality. One reseller reports having doubled its sales of 3Com products as a result of customers redirected from 3Com to its site.[36]

Doing Business Internationally

The ability to do business anywhere over the Web provides an opportunity for many companies to conduct business internationally, even without a physical international presence. Companies taking this route need to decide what markets to target, whether or not to provide foreign language interfaces, what currency to use in pricing products in foreign markets, and how to arrange the logistics for delivering and supporting their products.

The Sharper Image, a high-tech consumer products marketer based in San Francisco, used to sell its products internationally through licensees in Japan, Australia, and Switzerland. Now, although its only foreign licensee is in Switzerland, it does business throughout the world, avoiding the costs of a print catalog and overseas ground support, by selling on its international Web site. When a customer clicks "International" in The Sharper Image Web site banner, the site displays the flags of eleven countries (see Figure 6-10) and text explaining that customers in other countries can order from the domestic version of the Web site. The Sharper Image's e-commerce site provides three languages—English, Spanish, and German—and provides pricing in three currencies—euros for customers that use them in Europe, pounds sterling for customers in England, and dollars for all other customers. The Sharper Image made a conscious decision to offer a site in German because Germany's size and wealth made its market potential substantial. On the European and German Web sites, when the buyer clicks on a link to the product manual for any product, the manual is presented in four languages, English, German, French, and Spanish. On the European Web sites, a pull-down menu appears giving the user a choice of plug types to account for different European electrical outlet standards. To ship throughout Europe at a competitive time and price, The Sharper Image maintains a distribution center in the Netherlands. The company ships to Asia and Australia from the United States, but quotes prices in dollars to protect against loss due to currency devaluation. However, it does somewhat subsidize the shipping to remain competitive and continue to build its brand internationally.[37]

Security Management

E-commerce requires the transmittal of messages over networks, where they can be intercepted and modified. The costs of insecure message transmission are high. A thief can steal your customer's credit card number or can modify the ship-to address to receive the shipment of a product. A malicious competitor can change the prices on your Web site, causing you to lose money or face the anger of customers when you try to explain that the price on the Web site was incorrect. Competitors can determine the price you receive from your suppliers, allowing them to price their products strategically.

Fortunately, security technologies, such as public key encryption and SSL, if properly used, can protect confidential e-commerce information exchanges. Most companies

FIGURE 6-10

The opening page of the international Web site for The Sharper Image.

SOURCE: copyright © 2002 Sharper Image Corporation. Accessed at http://www.sharperimage.com/us/en/intlshopping.jhtml;$session-id$M4IPZNCRKTXT3QFIA2RSIIQ, on 7 August 2002. Used with permission.

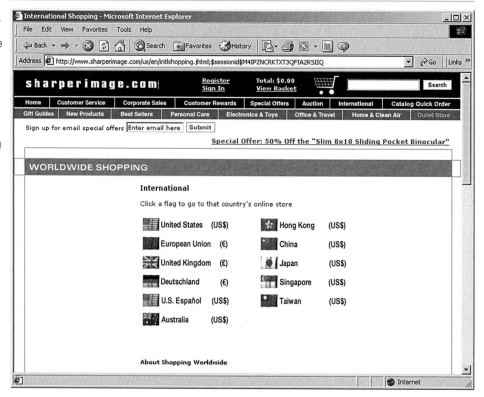

require the use of encryption for their e-commerce transactions. Staples, a Massachusetts-based retailer of office products, for example, requires its B2B partners to encrypt all Internet transmissions. However, the company doesn't require encryption for transmissions sent over private networks because it believes that security is what it's buying when it pays for private network transmission.[38]

An additional concern for companies doing B2B e-commerce is that their partners' security could be lax. To engage in B2B e-commerce, companies generally need to give authorized suppliers and customers access to selected information and applications. If an unauthorized person penetrates your supplier's computer systems, he would have access to your confidential information, just as if he had been an authorized employee of the supplier. Therefore, no company is secure unless its e-commerce partners are secure. Visa, for example, will not allow merchants and service providers to accept its credit cards unless they can demonstrate on an annual basis that they meet the company's standards for e-commerce security. Ma-and-Pa shops must undertake a through online self-assessment and merchants or service providers handling large volumes of cardholder information must undertake extensive third-party audits.[39]

SUMMARY

The value chain is the series of processes by which a company turns raw materials into finished goods and services. The extended value chain includes suppliers and their suppliers as well as customers and their customers. Firms that can coordinate planning and optimize operations in an extended value chain have a competitive advantage over those than cannot.

Doing business electronically has many benefits. Businesses reduce the cost of executing transactions through the elimination of paper, mail, handling, storage, logistics, and labor. They also increase the speed of business because electronic records are available at all times and can be more readily found than paper records. E-business decreases time to market for new products, streamlines internal and external processes, and leads to faster customer service and product delivery. E-business can be done any time anywhere, reducing the need for physical plant and employees and increasing market reach and customer satisfaction. E-business improves workflow, allowing companies to better control their processes and to collect information about process performance for managerial analysis. E-business reduces errors by reducing multiple data entry, eliminating paper loss, and controlling workflow. E-business helps companies collaborate with their suppliers for joint product design, synchronization of inventory replenishment, and servicing.

Companies using e-commerce to sell to consumers are said to follow a B2C strategy, those selling to businesses a B2B strategy. B2B e-commerce has been around longer than B2C e-commerce and exceeds its volume. A business model is a broad plan for what product or service a company plans to sell and how it plans to earn revenue. Producers sell the products or services they create and may elect to bypass distributors with a disintermediation strategy. Distributors, who add value by buying in bulk and selling in small units, face the threat of disintermediation. Aggregators earn money by providing one-stop shopping. They can use e-commerce to optimize their supply chain. Advertiser runners earn money through the sale of advertisements. The Internet is an ideal medium for this business model, but many companies have lost money doing it poorly. Electronic auctions and electronic marketplaces are market makers, companies that earn revenue by bringing together buyers and sellers. Infomediaries, companies that collect and sell information, have found that e-commerce has opened new markets for them. E-government uses information technology to improve governments' efficiency and service.

The implementation of e-commerce poses many challenges. Various technologies, such as EDI, Web forms, XML, and Web services, address the technical issues by helping companies exchange information electronically. Companies can resolve channel conflicts by handling orders on behalf of their channel partners or by steering orders to their partners. Doing business internationally requires making decisions about Web site languages, target markets, and currency choices. E-commerce requires a company to consider its partners' security as relevant to its own security policies.

KEY TERMS

agent	cybermediation	market maker
aggregator	demand chain	producer
business model	disintermediation	pure-play
business-to-business	distributor	reintermediation
(B2B) e-commerce	e-business	retailer
business-to-consumer	e-commerce	supply chain
(B2C) e-commerce	e-government	value chain
channel conflict	electronic data interchange (EDI)	Web portal
click-and-mortar strategy	extended value chain	wholesaler
click-through advertisement	infomediary	XML

REVIEW QUESTIONS

1. What is meant by a company's value chain?
2. How does a company's extended value chain differ from its internal value chain?
3. What are six benefits of doing business electronically?
4. How does e-business help companies reduce the cost of executing transactions?
5. How does e-business help increase the speed of business?
6. What are the three phases of workflow software?
7. How does e-business workflow improve the efficiency of an organization?
8. What is one advantage of a pure-play over a click-and-mortar strategy, and what is one disadvantage?
9. What is meant by a business model?
10. What are six business models?
11. What is meant by disintermediation?
12. How does the Internet make it easier for producers to bypass distributors?
13. What problems do producers have in bypassing distributors?
14. What is meant by reintermediation?
15. What does it take to be successful as a pure-play advertisement runner?
16. What are the pros and cons of advertising on the Web as opposed to other media, such as radio, print, and television?
17. How does a market maker earn revenue?
18. How does an infomediary earn revenue?
19. At what levels do EDI standards exist?
20. How does XML solve the problem of identifying the meaning of data on a Web page?
21. What are two ways to resolve channel conflicts?
22. What are the security concerns of companies doing B2B e-commerce?

CIRCUIT CITY'S MULTI-CHANNEL STRATEGY

MINICASE

In 1998, Circuit City, the $12.8 billion consumer electronics retailer, put Web-enabled kiosks in its stores to allow customers to build customized PCs. Surprisingly, 50 percent of the people who purchased PCs through these kiosks wanted to pick them up in the store rather than have them delivered to their home.

A year later, while the company was codifying its e-commerce strategy, it struggled with how to fund its vision of multi-channel retailing. Rather than appeal to venture capital, it decided to use its own assets to set up its e-commerce infrastructure. Had the company spun off its site as a separate entity (as so many other enterprises did in order to fund their Web initiatives), Circuit City (like others) would have wound up with a Web site that was not integrated with its other systems.

"We thought of the Web as just another store. We basically set it up as a virtual location," says e-commerce director Steve Duchelle. That notion that the Web store was no different from any other store led Circuit City to adapt its proprietary point-of-sale (POS) technology, which already let stores sell from one to another, to sell across channels and offer pickup services.

"We already had an existing capability, called 'alternate-location sales,' where you can sell the inventory of one store [to] another. It came to us that when you buy on the Web, you're basically doing an alternate-location sale," says CIO Bowman.

But, there were some differences that required complex systems interface changes and developing entirely new business processes. If, for example, a customer arranged to pick up a portable Sony CD player that was priced at $99.99 on the Web but was selling for $89.99 in her local store, the IT staff had to write some business logic on top of the merchandising system so that the POS system in the store would know to ring the CD player up at the lower price.

Once back-end kinks like that were ironed out, Circuit City was ready to roll. On July 21, 1999, shop online, pick up and return in store was inaugurated. The company soon found out, however, that it had some wrinkles on the front end to smooth over. For example, the process Circuit City used to ensure that online customers actually get the items they reserved for in-store pickup didn't always work. Ken Pacunas, technology manager at the Circuit City store in Natick, Massachusetts, said, "the biggest [problem] was that there was no time limit to how long an employee could take to pick a product." If an employee waited too long to get a pack of batteries off the shelf and put them in a back room with the customer's name on it, another customer might buy it before the first customer arrived. Result: one irate customer.

To prevent that scenario, Circuit City instituted a 15-minute rule. When an order for an in-store pickup comes in to the store from CircuitCity.com, the POS system prints a pick ticket with the product ID and the customer's name and starts a timer. Store associates have 15 minutes to pick the item, acknowledge that they've done so in the POS system, and put it on a shelf designated for in-store pickup. If the POS system doesn't recognize the completion of the task within 15 minutes of the pick ticket being generated, a beeping alarm will sound and a message will appear at the bottom of every POS terminal in the store reminding clerks that a pickup order needs to be taken off the shelf. If the POS system does not recognize the completion of the task within 30 minutes, an electronic alert is sent to the customer support center to call a manager and have him immediately set the product aside for the customer.

Pacunas says that people buy online and pick up items in his Natick store every day and that 5 percent of his store's business comes from individuals who shop online and arrange to pick up their merchandise in the store. "It's the convenience factor," he says. "Most people pick their items up the same day that they order them online. They want that instant satisfaction."

SOURCE: Adapted with permission from Meridith Levinson, "Your Place or Mine," *CIO,* 1 August 2002.

Case Questions

Diagnosis

1. Why do you think that Circuit City felt it needed to do business on the Web?

2. What were the information needs of Circuit City's online customers? What other needs did they have?

3. What are the information needs of Circuit City's in-store employees in dealing with multi-channel customers?

Evaluation

4. How well did Circuit City's initial design meet the needs of its multi-channel customers?

Design

5. Why did Circuit City decide to integrate the information systems for its online customers with its in-store systems? Do you think its decision was a wise one? Why?

6. What philosophy or way of thinking simplified Circuit City's design for its online customers?

7. How did Circuit City's online sales process differ from its alternate location sales process? How did that difference affect the design?

Implementation

8. What adjustments did Circuit City make in its process for handling multi-channel sales after it initially opened its Web site for business?

9. Do you think that Circuit City considers its multi-channel sales implementation a success? Why or why not?

10. Would you recommend that Circuit City continue to integrate its online and in-store channels, or should the company consider separating the two? Support your recommendation.

6-1 SELLING DIRECT

ACTIVITY

Step 1: Read the following scenario.

Your company, the BuiltRight Appliance Company, manufactures large appliances, such as stoves, refrigerators, dishwashers, washers, and dryers. The company is third in the market despite persistent attempts at boosting its market share. The president of the company, Bill Emalot, has promoted the director of sales, Eileen Ahnem, to assistant to the president and given her the task of evaluating possible e-commerce strategies. Among the strategies he would like to consider is the possibility of selling directly to consumers. In the past, BuiltRight and all other appliance manufacturers have sold to large retailers, such as Sears, and to small appliance service stores that have established reputations for quality sales and service in their communities. Bill has always felt that these resellers haven't given BuiltRight the proper attention, and he'd love to teach them a lesson by selling direct. Bill does not expect BuiltRight to install and service the appliances. Instead, the company will rely on Ma-and-Pa service companies that have been certified as "Authorized Parts and Repair" representatives for BuiltRight. In many areas, retailers use these companies to service the appliances they sell, and the consumers also find their names in the Yellow Pages when service is required.

Step 2: In groups of three to six, work out a strategy for selling directly to the consumer. Consider how you will deal with your traditional resellers, which you would like to keep in the fold. These resellers currently receive a 25 to 30 percent discount, depending on their sales volume. At the 30 percent discount, you retain only a 5 percent profit margin so it's unlikely that you can offer a larger discount. Of course, by selling direct, the entire profit would be yours, less what you pay to the installers if you need to subsidize the price you charge consumers for installation. Also, consider how you would set up your Web presence, what privileges you would give your resellers and installers regarding access to your information, what information you would expect to receive electronically from them, and what technologies you would use (EDI, Web forms, extranet, Web services, etc.) to implement cooperation between your partners and BuiltRight.

Step 3: Assign the following roles to people in your group: One person plays Eileen Ahnem. One person plays the role of president of a small, typical installation company. The remaining people in the group play members of a negotiating team created by the resellers to deal with BuiltRight. Your instructor will give you a set amount of time to try to reach agreement about the nature of the relationship between the parties and, if agreement can be reached, details about their electronic collaboration. Resellers should retain the option of not carrying BuiltRight products, but they do so at the risk of losing that source of profit and the possibility that some of their competitors will carry BuiltRight.

Step 4: With the entire class, share the outcome of the simulated negotiations. Then, individually, in small groups, or in the entire class, answer the following questions:

1. What are the pros and cons of the different strategies that BuiltRight might employ?

2. How susceptible are the resellers to disintermediation? How can they fight back?

3. Should BuiltRight pursue a direct-to-the-consumer strategy? What are the likely implications of doing so?

6-2 THE GATES RUBBER WEB SITE

ACTIVITY

Step 1: Read the following scenario.

Denver-based Gates Rubber Company, a wholly owned subsidiary of Tomkins PLC, is a global manufacturer of rubber and fiber parts and systems for automotive and industrial markets. The $2.5 billion company employs approximately 23,000 people in 70 factories, 20 distribution centers, and 18 countries. Gates sells its products through 150,000 distributors, jobbers, and dealers, as well as through direct sales to original equipment manufacturers—manufacturers who include Gates's products as components in their products.

Gates's e-commerce strategy is to combine marketing with transaction processing systems. Its Web site is designed to draw users to it and convert them into customers. The following features of the Web site illustrate this philosophy:

- The Gates Racing Game, where visitors learn about features of Gates belt drives while racing against each other.

- Easy Agent, software that recommends products to customers based on their needs.

- A calculator that compares the purchase and maintenance costs of polychain versus roller chain conveyor belts.

- An online catalog for Gates's vehicle parts.

- Software for engineers and distributors that helps automates the design of belt drives.

The Web site also includes an online procurement system called PowerPro where Gates's partners can order products and check on inventory levels, product availability, and order status. The implementation of PowerPro generated some channel conflict, as distributors worried that their sales would be cannibalized by direct sales through the system.

Step 2: Prepare the case for class discussion.

Step 3: Answer each of the following questions, individually or in small groups, as directed by your instructor:

Diagnosis

1. Why do you think Gates established its Web site?
2. How would you describe Gates's marketing needs prior to the implementation of its Web site? Be as specific as you can about how you would market Gates's product without creating a Web presence.

Evaluation

3. Why do you think Gates decided to use its e-commerce site as a marketing tool?

Design

4. How did Gates attract potential customers to its Web site?
5. What features of the Web site do you think existing customers used the most?
6. Do you think that customers would try the racing game while downloading catalog information? Do you think that it's beneficial to mix pleasure with business this way? Is it likely to make customers want to return or more likely to offend them?
7. Why did the introduction of the procurement tool for customers lead to channel conflict?

Implementation

8. If you were a Gates distributor, how would you respond to the implementation of Gates's PowerPro tool?
9. How should Gates minimize the impact of the channel conflict caused by PowerPro?

Step 4: In small groups, with the entire class, or in written form, share your answers to the questions above. Then answer the following questions:

1. Why did Gates embark on an e-commerce initiative?
2. What are the pros and cons of including the Racing Game on Gates's e-commerce Web site?
3. How should Gates minimize the impact of channel conflict caused by PowerPro?

Source: Kate Maddox, "Strange Webfellows," *B to B*, 15 October 2001, 1 and 19. http://www.gates.com accessed on October 27, 2002.

6-3 E-BUSINESS OPPORTUNITIES AND THREATS

ACTIVITY

Step 1: Read the following scenario.

Secretaries Inc. is a ten-person firm that provides secretarial and graphics design services to approximately 50 clients. A client calls Secretaries Inc., with job specifications, and the firm's office manager records the relevant information and then gives the client a price for the job. Assuming that the price is acceptable, the office manager then assigns the job to either the most qualified employee or a qualified employee with the lowest workload. Employees log in the job and then maintain a work log until it is finished. Currently, all record keeping is done manually.

Step 2: Individually or in groups of two to four students, answer the following questions:

1. How would you characterize Secretaries Inc.'s business model?

2. What threats, if any, does this business face from new firms that rely heavily on e-business?

3. Map the process of getting and completing a client's job. For e-business to help, does the process need to be redesigned? If so, how?

4. What other processes in the business are likely to benefit by becoming more electronic? Be sure to consider how the client is billed, how marketing is done, and how employees are scheduled?

5. What are the benefits of an e-business initiative at Secretaries Inc.?

Step 3: In small groups or with the entire class, review your answers to Step 2. Then answer the following questions:

1. How would you characterize Secretaries Inc.'s business model?

2. How can e-business help the process of getting and completing a client's job?

3. What are the potential benefits of an e-business initiative at Secretaries Inc.?

6-4 PRESSURE TACTICS

ACTIVITY

Step 1: Read the following scenario.

You are the purchasing manager for Officapplies, a chain of 30 office supply superstores headquartered near Chicago. Last week, you received a call from Wilbur Ibery, the sales manager at Paperdy Inc., one of your major paper suppliers. He invited you to attend a Cubs game as his guest. As the Cubs are your favorite baseball team, you accepted the invitation, not particularly upset at the likelihood of having to endure a sales pitch during the game.

But at game time, you didn't get the anticipated sales pitch. Instead, Wilbur asked you to be a reference account for an extranet linkage he intended to set up with an office supply store in another part of the country. In exchange, Paperdy would give Officapplies a 2 percent reduction in price for the next six months, and, although it was never specifically stated, Wilbur indicated that you could have his tickets to any Cubs game you wanted for the rest of the season.

After the game, you thought about what type of reference you would give Paperdy's customer. About two years ago, you had given Paperdy access to Officapplies' extranet on its promise to monitor its inventory and keep your shelves filled. In return, Paperdy gave you a 1 percent discount on its price. The system seems to be working well now, but Paperdy was the most difficult supplier you had ever had to work with before or since in setting up such an arrangement. Not only were its information systems poorly managed, but it took months to sign the nondisclosure agreement and, although your technology gurus could never prove it, they thought that Paperdy had attempted to bypass your security systems twice in the past year. Still, you probably could give them a good recommendation without lying, and the deal was favorable to the company—and probably favorable to you.

Step 2: Individually or in small groups, analyze the situation using the basic ethical criteria.

Step 3: Based on your analysis, decide how you will respond to Paperdy's customer's call. Share your plan with the rest of the class. What are the major ethical issues in this situation? How should they be handled?

6-5 BUYING A BICYCLE

ACTIVITY

Step 1: Make believe you are buying a bicycle and bicycle helmet. Visit the following Web sites with the view of eventually purchasing these products:

- Two bicycle manufacturers, such as Schwinn (www.schwinn.com) and Bianchi (www.bianchi.it).
- Two discounters, such as Wal-Mart (www.walmart.com) and Kmart (www.kmart.com).
- Two electronic department stores, such as Yahoo!Shopping (shopping.yahoo.com) and MSN eShop (eshop.msn.com).
- Two bicycle specialty shops, such as Harris Cyclery (www.sheldonbrown.com /harris) and Aaron's Bicycle Repair (www.rideyourbike.com).
- Two auction sites, such as eBay (www.ebay.com) and Yahoo!Auctions (auctions.yahoo.com).

Step 2: Individually, in small groups, or with the entire class, answer the following questions:

1. What features did each site provide?
2. At which site was it easiest to research the choices?
3. At which site was it easiest to make a purchase?
4. Where would you go to order a bike and helmet over the Web? Why?

IS ON THE WEB

IS ON THE WEB

Exercise 1: Follow the Chapter 6 Web links to three electronic auction sites. Then compare and contrast the sites regarding their features, the types of auctions they support, and the methods of payment they allow. In what ways are they similar? How do they differ? Which auction site would you most prefer as a consumer? Which auction site would you most prefer as a seller of consumer products? Which auction site would you most prefer as a seller of industrial products?

Exercise 2: Follow the Chapter 6 Web links to explore the options for bringing business to your Web site. In what different ways do advertisers charge for their services? How can you determine the best advertising strategy?

RECOMMENDED READINGS

Frances Cairncross. *The Company of the Future.* Boston, MA: Harvard Business School, 2002.

Coughlan, Anne T., Erin Anderson, Louis W. Stern, and Adele I. El-Ansary. *Marketing Channels,* 6th ed. Upper Saddle River, NJ: Prentice Hall, 2001.

Cunningham, Michael J. *B2B: How to Build a Profitable E-Commerce Strategy.* Cambridge, MA: Perseus Publishing, 2002.

Davis, William S., and John Benamati. *E-Commerce Basics: Technology Foundations and Business Applications.* Boston: Addison-Wesley, 2002.

Poirier, Charles C., and Michael J. Bauer. *E-Supply Chain: Using the Internet to Revolutionize Your Business.* Williston, VT: Berrett-Koehler Publishers, 2000.

Rosen, Anita. *The E-Commerce Question and Answer Book: A Survival Guide for Business Managers.* New York: AMACOM, 2002.

Wong, W.Y. *At the Dawn of E-Government.* New York: Deloitte Research, 2000.

NOTES

1. Extracted with permission from Eric Berkman, "How to Stay Ahead of the Curve," *CIO,* 1 February 2002, 72–74.

2. *Merriam Webster Collegiate Dictionary* defines commerce as "the exchange or buying and selling of commodities on a large scale involving transportation from place to place." Accessed online at http://www.m-w.com/cgi-bin/dictionary on 5 August 2002.

3. *Merriam Webster Collegiate Dictionary,* accessed online at http://www.m-w.com/cgi-bin/dictionary on 5 August 2002.

4. M. E. Porter, *Competitive Strategy: Techniques for Analyzing Industries and Competitors.* New York: Free Press,1980.

5. Wally Bock, "Study: Speed to Market," 2001, accessed at http://www.bockinfo.com/docs/speed.htm on 5 August 2002.

6. "Netgem is a Leading Provider of Interactive TV Technology," accessed at http://www.mentor.com/pcb/successes/netgem_success_story.pdf on 5 August 2002.

7. Nucleus Research, "ROI Profile: BEA WebLogic, IP Communications, Dallas, Texas," *Research Note #B32,* accessed at http://www.bea.com/customers/pdf/roi_ip_communications_120301.pdf on 5 August 2002.

8. Margaret Littman, "The State of Small Business/Internet: Stores Weaving Web Strategies," *Crain's Chicago Business,* 10 June 2002, SB9.

9. Staffware, "Anova," accessed at http://www.staffware.com/customers/163.htm on 10 August 2002.

10. Qlink Technologies, "CheMatch Using New Software to Quickly E-Enable Business Processes," *Chemical e-Business News & Networking* (www.eyeforchem.com), 23 May 2001, accessed at http://www.qlinktech.com/news_chematch.html on 10 August 2002.

11. Bruce D. Temkin, with Christopher Mines and Hillary Drohan, *Web Services Boots B2B Collaboration.* Cambridge, MA: Forrester Research, 2002.

12. Jennifer Fan and Maria Bumatay (NetRatings, Inc.) and Suzie Pileggi (BSMG Worldwide), "Nearly Half of All Americans Buy Online, According to Nielsen//Netratings and Harris Interactive," 24 April 2001, accessed at http://www.nielsen-netratings.com/pr/pr_010424.pdf on 6 August 2002.

13. Roger Clarke, "Electronic Data Interchange (EDI): An Introduction," December 1998, accessed at http://www.anu.edu.au/people/Roger.Clarke/EC/EDIIntro.html on 6 August 2002.

14. CyberAtlas staff, "B2B E-Commerce Headed for Trillions," 6 March 2002, accessed at http://cyberatlas.internet.com/markets/b2b/print/0,,10091_986661,00.html on 6 August 2002.

15. Calculated from data supplied in "Most 2001 Top 10 E-Retailers Are Multi-Channel," 1 August 2002, accessed at http://www.emarketer.com/news/article.php?1001447 on 6 August 2002.

16. Michael Mahoney, "Staying Pure in a Multichannel World," *www.EcommerceTimes.com,* 1 June 2001, accessed at http://www.newsfactor.com/perl/story/10000.html on 11 August 2002.

17. Henry H. Harteveldt, with James McQuivey and Gillian DeMoulin, *Travel North America: Consumer Technographics Data Overview.* Cambridge, MA: Forrester Research, 2002.

18. W. Scott Bailey, "Largest S.A. Travel Firm Buys Competitor," *San Antonio Business Journal,* 7 June 2002, accessed at http://www.bizjournals.com/sanantonio/stories/2002/06/10/story5.html on 9 August 2002.

19. Alan Abelson, "Up & Down Wall Street: Oh, Doctor!," *Barron's,* 14 June 1999, 3–4.

20. The Thomson Corporation, "Koop Clients' E-mail Addresses for Sale," *Technology in Practice,* 3 July 2002, accessed at http://www.technology-inpractice.com/html/news/NewsStory.cfm?DI=8776 on 9 August 2002. Fred Charatan, "Executives Fly the koop.com," *British Medical Journal,* 29 July 2000, 257.

21. Keith Boswell, "Digital Marketing vs. Online Advertising: Breaking Waves for Marketers to Catch," *The Marketleap Report,* 19 March 2002, accessed at http://www.marketleap.com/report/ml_report_24.htm on 9 August 2002.

22. http://www.emarketer.com/images/chart_gifs/037001-038000/037073.gif, accessed on 9 August 2002.

23. http://www.emarketer.com/images/chart_gifs/030001-031000/030594.gif, accessed on 9 August 2002.

24. Community size listed at http://pages.ebay.com/community/aboutebay/overview/index.html, accessed on 9 August 2002. Capitalization found at www.quicken.com on 9 August 2002.

25. "A Million Minnesotans Filed Taxes Electronically," *TwinCities.com,* 19 April 2002, accessed at http://www.twincities.com/mld/twincities/news/3097378.htm on 21 September 2002.

26. W. Y. Wong, *At the Dawn of E-Government.* New York: Deloitte Research, Deloitte & Touche, 2000.

27. "Europe Making Progress on Road to E-Government," *Europemedia,* 20 June 2002, 1.

28. "China Seeks to Promote 'E-Government' Services for Higher Efficiency," *BBC Monitoring Asia Pacific,* 20 September 2002, 4.

29. "Govt. Unveils Construction Portal," *Business News Americas,* 20 September 2002, 1.

30. Paul Gosling, "UK Is the Fifth Best at E-Government," *Public Finance,* 26 October 2001, 9.

31. The EDI Connection, "Retailer EDI Announcements," accessed at http://www.edi-connection.com/news05.htm on 9 August 1997.

32. Jim Brown, "Banks Increase Use of EDI," *Network World,* 25 January 1988, 1, 82. James Johnston, "EDI Implementation at PPG Industries," *Journal of Systems Management* 43 (February 1992): 32–34.

33. Julie Bort, "Big Money beyond EDI," *Client/Server Computing,* June 1997, 44–47.

34. Lucas Mearian, "Fidelity Makes Big XML Conversion," *Computerworld,* 1 October 2001, 12.

35. Susannah Patton, "Web Services in the Real World," *CIO,* 1 April 2002, 58–63.

36. Richard Karpinski, "3Com Opts for Channel over Own Online Store," *B to B,* 15 July 2002, 15.

37. Lisa A. Yorgey, "Test the E-Waters," *Target Marketing,* June 2002, 48, 50.

38. Eric Berkman, "How to Practice Safe B2B," *CIO,* 15 June 2002, 1.

39. Eric Berkman, "How to Practice Safe B2B," 1.

7

Functional and Enterprise Systems

LEARNING OBJECTIVES

After completing Chapter 7, you will be able to:

- Analyze a company's value chain and its support processes to identify the functional services that information technology can support.
- Explain why integrating a company's extended value chain can improve its operations and profitability.
- Explain how customer relationship management helps a company become more customer-centric.
- Describe the components of computer integrated manufacturing.
- Compare and contrast differing levels of customization.
- Describe the advantages and disadvantages of just-in-time inventory and vendor managed inventory from the perspectives of supplier and inventory user (manufacturer, distributor, or retailer).
- Describe two technologies for reducing inventory cost.
- Identify the major elements and functions of human resource information systems and accounting information systems.
- Explain why most companies need both ERP and middleware to integrate their information systems applications.
- Describe how supply chain management can help companies optimize their logistics and inventory.

Customer Service at Honeywell International

Pruitt Layton, vice president of sales and marketing for Honeywell International's Propulsion Systems Enterprise group, understands the value of customer service. Before the merger of AlliedSignal Aerospace with Honeywell Inc. in 1999, forming Honeywell International, Layton had been director of sales support for AlliedSignal. There, he recalls being told directly by several customers that his company, which made aircraft engines, engine parts, and other products, was hard to do business with. As a $13 billion company with a worldwide workforce of more than 85,000 employees and 40 independent product lines, the company had become too big to coordinate its various parts. Layton recalls customers complaining, for example, that several different sales people had solicited them on the same day, each apparently unaware of the others' calls.

Layton realized that AlliedSignal's sales processes needed to be more centralized. Part of the solution would have to be technological. AlliedSignal's first step was to provide a central system, called ATLAS, for managing customer relationships. The harder part of the solution was getting the different functional and product managers to use ATLAS rather than the systems they had used in the past. Layton created a Customer Relationship Management (CRM) program office, staffed it with business and technical people, and gave it the responsibility of helping sales and field service managers learn how they and the company could benefit by using ATLAS.

The merger with Honeywell made the need for ATLAS even more important, as the number of product lines and business units grew. But ATLAS paid off from the start, as it provided for a single sales process for all of Honeywell Aerospace and AlliedSignal. Currently 2,000 Honeywell International employees use ATLAS and 2,000 more are expected to use it as its functionality improves.

ATLAS now provides a single view of the customer through initial sales, account management, campaign management, field service, and post-sales support, with up to two years of customer history. For many accounts, a single employee provides the sole contact point, but everyone who works on the account works from the same information. The customer is never bothered with multiple calls and never has to repeat information previously told to another employee. Marketing and financial managers can evaluate trends for product sales and returns, and can analyze opportunities for new sales. And the system has provided financial returns as well. The first business unit to adopt ATLAS saw its sales immediately increase by $62 million, about a fifth of which was attributed to ATLAS.[1]

Keeping customers happy is one of Pruitt Layton's primary concerns as vice president of sales and marketing. But the information that his system, ATLAS, collects is of value to many parts of the business. Product sales, which ATLAS logs, affect shipping and billing. Sales also affect inventory, so they are a concern for inventory managers, as well as for manufacturers who have to replenish inventory. To manufacture new goods, supplies will have to be purchased, so procurement managers should also be interested in ATLAS's data. Engineering would love to see ATLAS's repair records so that they can focus on which products need to be redesigned and on how to minimize service calls. Even the human resources department would benefit by having access to the sales information so that it can appropriately reward the best performing employees. Layton would probably like to share his data with the other Honeywell Aerospace departments, and would like access to their data as well.

Recall the value chain concepts presented in Chapter 6 (see Figure 7-1). Layton would probably like to share information across his company' value chain. **Enterprise Resource Planning (ERP)** software does that and more; it not only shares information across functions but also feeds information from one application to another to support cross-functional processes in an integrated fashion. It also provides links for integrating the extended value chain (see Figure 7-2). In this chapter, we break ERP into its components and examine each in turn. We start with the customer, whose order directly or indirectly generates all other business activities. Temporarily ignoring logistics, we continue right-to-left in Figure 7-1 with production and then supply. We next address logistics, both inbound and outbound, in a single section called "warehousing and transportation." We continue with the support functions, such as accounting and human resource management. Finally, we examine the issues involved in making ERP work within an organization and between organizations.

CUSTOMER RELATIONSHIP MANAGEMENT (CRM)

Customer relationship management (CRM) is the philosophy that an organization should focus on the customer. CRM software is software designed to achieve this goal.

Table 7-1 lists some of the most frequently cited reasons why companies pursue a CRM strategy. Far and away the most common reason is to develop a single, consistent view of the customer.[2] But, each company has its own reason or reasons for acting. For example, the ultimate objective of Ohio-based Nationwide Insurance's CRM technology strategy is to maintain customers from age 16 until they are in their 80s.[3]

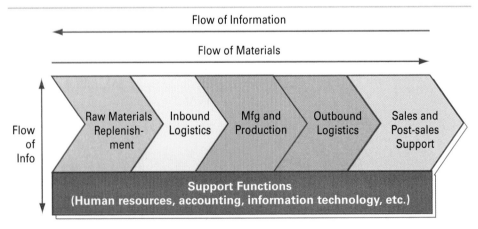

FIGURE 7-1

ERP software addresses the activities directly responsible for sales as well as the functions that support the operation of the company.

FIGURE 7-2 ──────── The extended value chain includes the value-added processes of your suppliers and their suppliers, your supply chain, and the value-added processes of your customers and their customers, your demand chain.

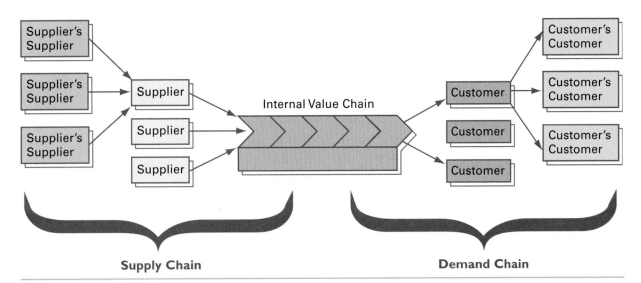

Reportedly, CRM initiatives have a high rate of failure, with estimates from knowledgeable sources generally falling between 30 and 70 percent. There are many reasons for such failure, as illustrated in Table 7-2, but the most common are that the reward system is misaligned or nonexistent and that various CRM initiatives lacked coordination.[4] Also, many researchers attribute the failure of CRM initiatives to confusion between CRM strategies and CRM technology implementations.[5] In fact, if you examine the reasons that companies implement CRM, you will find that most address organizational efficiencies rather than customer satisfaction.

In this section, we first look at what it means to be focused on the customer. Then we look at how information technology helps to improve a variety of customer-facing processes, such as selling, order handling, electronic billing, and post-sales support. Finally, we examine how information technology can help when the customer is a distributor rather than an end consumer.

Customer-Centric Management

The first step in implementing a CRM philosophy is not technological. Generally, organizational and cultural changes are needed before CRM software can be applied effectively.

TABLE 7-1

Reasons why companies implement a CRM strategy

- Develop one view of the customer for more successful sales, marketing, and service
- Improve customer satisfaction
- Improve retention by rewarding loyalty
- Increase up-selling and cross-selling of products and services
- Target markets more accurately
- Improve sales leads
- Increase sales closing rates
- Increase margin on goods and services
- Increase revenue and profits
- Respond to competitor's implementation of CRM

TABLE 7-2	• Lack of coordination among different projects
	• Emphasis on technology rather than business processes
Reasons why CRM initiatives fail	• Lack of executive support
	• CRM is implemented for the enterprise, not the customer
	• Inability to execute cultural change
	• Employees are inadequately trained or motivated to use CRM
	• Poorly defined business case
	• Inadequate assessment of the status quo
	• Poor technical architecture
	• Poor integration of people, processes, and technology
	• Poor or insufficient measurement of success
	• Insufficient resources allocated to initiative

Companies structured around product lines have a particularly difficult time viewing a customer holistically. Often, each product division has its own view of the customer, different customer numbers for the same customer, different incentive plans for its sales people, and an uncoordinated approach to selling to the customer, as illustrated by AlliedSignal in the opening vignette.

A common view of the customer is also difficult to obtain when the customer purchases through several channels. Salespeople at companies that have a Web presence, a direct (catalog) sales department, and a physical presence often are unable to view a customer's previous Web and catalog purchases when they encounter the customer physically in one of its stores. Having a sales history would allow salespeople to provide better in-store service and would allow catalog managers to better target their direct mail customers. A recent survey found that 43 percent of shoppers who shop online also purchase goods from the same company through catalog sales and 59 percent also purchase goods from traditional stores. In addition, shoppers who visit a retailer's Web site and then buy from the retail store spend 33 percent more annually than the retailer's other customers.[6]

Best Buy, a Minnesota-based electronic goods retailer, would like to treat its customers as if they had walked into a mom-and-pop shop. The company has tried hard to shift from a product-centered to a customer-centered focus. Although most of its customer contact is through a single channel, it deals with so many brands and has so many touch points, including phone, fax, e-mail, and point-of-sale interactions, that creating a holistic view of the customer has been difficult. It has managed to rationalize its 25 independent customer databases to 16 integrated ones, so that all employees, including in-store customer service representatives, in-home repair technicians, and tele-help phone operators, work from the same data, and can therefore provide the best service possible.[7]

But customer-centric management is more than simply having a common customer number and even good access to the customer's history and buying habits. A customer-centric philosophy aims to understand the customer, serve the customer well, and thereby build loyalty and trust. Attracting a new customer is a very expensive activity, requiring advertising and often discounts. Serving existing customers well so that you won't need to attract them again as a new customer is a cost-effective practice. Loyal customers spend more than new customers and return to your company more often. You can also serve them better and more cheaply, as you can know their preferences and tastes.

Sales Force Automation

Just as many office workers and managers still rely on paper to record, exchange, and store information, many salespeople use Post-it notes, index cards, and memo pads to track sales leads. Many district or regional managers still prepare typed summary reports for distribution to their salespeople. **Sales force automation** dramatically changes this way of doing business. It replaces manual systems of tracking leads, sales, service requests, and other sales-related information with computerized systems that use sophisticated database software and mobile computers. It supports sales people by taking care of routine activities and providing them with the information they need to close new sales and support current customers. The 800-person sales force at Yellow Freight System Inc., a Kansas trucking firm, uses automated sales software that allows it to retrieve customer information and complete administrative work on the road. In addition to using the system to solve more customer problems as they meet face-to-face with clients, the sales reps can use e-mail to easily obtain transportation plans designed for other reps' customers that might apply to their customers.[8]

Sales Support

Automating sales requires a set of software applications. At its core is a prospect database—the list of potential customers with key information to allow sorting by industry, company, company size, sales call history, purchasing history, product requirements, and other characteristics. Figure 7-3 shows a screen from such a database. Word processing, electronic mail, graphics, spreadsheets, and other applications work with the prospect database to provide instantaneous summary reports.

MCI invested $75 million in an automated system that included outfitting 5,600 field sales and technical employees with laptops and links to the corporate sales and customer service database. The salespeople submit orders and can access data about the customer and the product. They even have online remote access to other employees who can answer customer questions immediately. Six months after the rollout, sales representative productivity increased by 21 percent and sales branch revenue increased by 23 percent.[9]

FIGURE 7-3

This screen illustrates a prospect database, which includes key information about potential customers for use by salespeople.

SOURCE: accessed at http://www.salesforce.com/us/assets/tour/leads_ss.gif, on 2 August 2002. Used with permission.

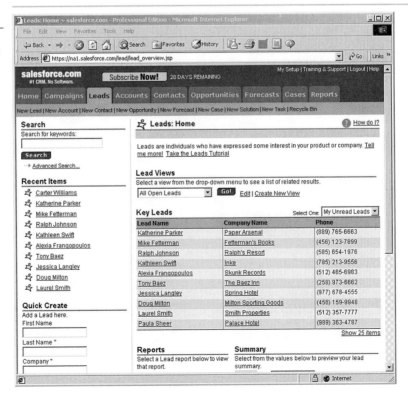

Pfizer Pharmaceutical's sales-automation system, Sherlock, pools the knowledge of the company's 2,700 sales representatives about physicians' prescribing patterns and requirements of their managed-care organizations with information about the company's promotional programs. Sales representatives use the system to access critical information faster to get the greatest payback from their short face-time with physicians. One year after implementation, sales rose 26 percent, in part due to Sherlock's impact.[10]

Order Handling

Point-of-Sale (POS) Systems

A **point-of-sale system (POS)** records the sale of a product or service and updates company records related to the sale. Figure 7-4 shows a typical POS transaction.

A customer brings an item to the sales counter or register. The sales clerk scans the product code with a bar-code reader, manually enters the code for the product into the POS terminal, or presses the appropriate button for that product on the POS terminal. The POS system retrieves the price for the item and uses it to create a receipt for the customer and the company. The system records the type of item, sale price, method of payment, and often the time and date of purchase into the corporate database.

If the customer pays by check, the POS system might check with its own or an external database to verify that the person doesn't routinely write bad checks. In addition, it will receipt the check for processing at the bank. If the customer pays by credit card, the POS system might access a similar database to verify the customer's credit. It will also process the request for payment by the credit-card company. If a customer uses a discount coupon, the system will also store information relating to the coupon. The POS system will store key elements of the payment, such as the credit card or check number along with the other transaction data.

FIGURE   7-4

A point-of-sale transaction starts with the customer bringing items to a cash register and ends with the system updating the company's inventory.

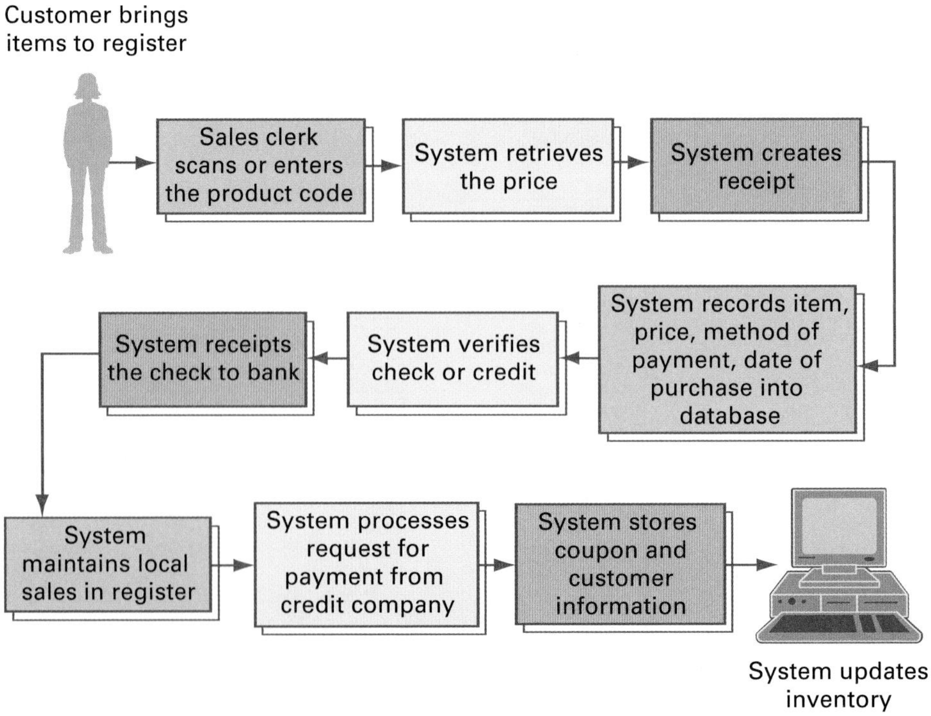

Customer brings items to register

Sales clerk scans or enters the product code → System retrieves the price → System creates receipt

System records item, price, method of payment, date of purchase into database

System receipts the check to bank ← System verifies check or credit ←

System maintains local sales in register → System processes request for payment from credit company → System stores coupon and customer information →

System updates inventory

The POS system might also store ancillary data, such as the zip code of the customer, entered by the sales clerk, and subsequently used for marketing research. It can track the amount of cash and checks in the register. Some systems also update inventory, either at the time of sale or in a batch process after the sales registers close. Point-of-sale systems can record service as well as sales transactions. For example, they might record service calls for appliance repairs or telephone installation. The State of Maine has designed a point-of-sale system for pharmacies to use in tracking Medicaid claims. Pharmacists, physicians, and Medicaid administrators can use an online database that stores all prescription information.[11]

Point-of-sale systems satisfy the business need to capture and supply information at the point of customer contact. They improve customer satisfaction by increasing the speed of the transaction, providing data to answer customers' questions, producing records and other receipts for the customer, and providing timely checks on transaction activities. They capture transactional and managerial information efficiently, accurately, and without delay.

Point-of-sale systems often use special input hardware to improve the speed, ease, and convenience of transacting a sale. They may include magnetic card readers to assist in processing credit card and bank cash-card transactions, and scanning devices to process bar codes attached to products and discount coupons. Wesleyan Assurance, for example, gives its agents laptops to use with its POS, named Faith (Financial Advice In The Home).[12]

POS terminals operate independently or are networked to a central computer. Independent terminals usually have more limited functionality because they have self-contained databases. For example, they don't contain pricing information or customer credit information. Diskettes can transfer transaction logs from independent POS stations located at a single site to a central computer for consolidation and batch processing to update sales and inventory databases. POS systems with stations located at several sites poll the POS terminals by telephone or over a WAN to collect the transaction records and provide an alternative to the real-time updating of inventory.[13] Diamond Shamrock, which operates 1,500 convenience stores, uses the Intelligent Retail Information System (Iris), which handles all in-store operations, including a point-of-sale system. The client/server system provides nightly feeders from the stores to the corporate databases by way of dial-up connections.[14]

Networked POS stations provide the benefit of centralized database management, greater storage, and increased computing power. If the central processor or the network fails, however, the failure affects all POS stations, which may significantly slow the selling process and reduce the number of sales. Installing a network may also be difficult and expensive and result in less flexibility for the organization. Wireless LANs can provide a solution to this problem.[15] Pepsi Cola Allied Bottlers use Fast Access, a wireless sales order entry system. Salespeople use hand-held computers to place orders and monitor deliveries at customers' sites. They enter the amount of beverage to be shipped for the next delivery. The warehouse receives the orders and places them on pallets for next-day delivery.[16]

Small companies often lack the expertise to select, purchase, install, and run a POS system. This problem has led to businesses that support the POS needs of small companies. For example, AT&T provides a service that links the POS terminals of a client company to computers at designated companies that perform the transaction processing for their clients.[17] Third party vendors also perform credit checking.

Companies that want to run their POS systems in-house can purchase *turnkey systems* from POS vendors. Such systems include hardware and software that have been sufficiently customized for the target industry that buyers can simply plug them in and turn them on. Buyers can also select from a broad range of customized input devices, monitors, and keyboards, all of which interface with standard PCs running any of a number of customized POS vertical packages.

Wave Riding Vehicles, a retail surf shop with stores in Virginia Beach, Virginia and Kitty Hawk, North Carolina, uses a POS that lets it track specific customer purchases, assists with receipt of merchandise, and supports inventory control. To perform their last physical inventory, for example, employees scanned the merchandise, downloaded the information, and ran the reports.[18]

Order Entry Systems

Order entry systems record and process the taking of an order. Businesses such as pizza stores, mail-order distributors, insurance companies, newspaper advertising departments, and steel manufacturers use these systems to support prompt and rapid customer service. Order entry systems can also capture information that helps obtain future orders from customers. Bell Atlantic, for example, introduced its Sale-Service Negotiation System to improve relationships between the customer and small-business telephone sales representatives and their customers. The system provides comprehensive information about customers, sales, and products. Bell Atlantic experienced a 30 percent increase in consumer product sales over three years, in part because of this order entry system.[19]

An order entry system typically functions as shown in Figure 7-5. When a customer calls to place an order, a clerk requests identifying information. For example, a customer number might appear on the merchandise catalog. Other companies use the customer's telephone number, birth date, corporate federal identification number, individual social security number, club membership number, or name. If the order entry system determines that the company database includes the customer, the system will display additional identifying information, such as the customer's telephone number and address, for verification. The order entry system may require the clerk to register an unregistered or incorrectly registered customer. This transaction updates the company's customer database. Occasionally order entry systems, such as in the restaurant industry, do not require or store specific customer information.

Private Spring Water Company found that its order entry system was too limited. It couldn't track the progress of orders after they were received. The company replaced the system with a more complete one that has since reduced order-processing time by 15 percent and saved thousands of dollars a month in rush shipping costs.[20]

An order entry system should include many features of a POS system, such as identifying and recording the price and quantity of specific items purchased as well as the method of payment. Unlike POS systems, however, order entry systems may also require a shipping

---

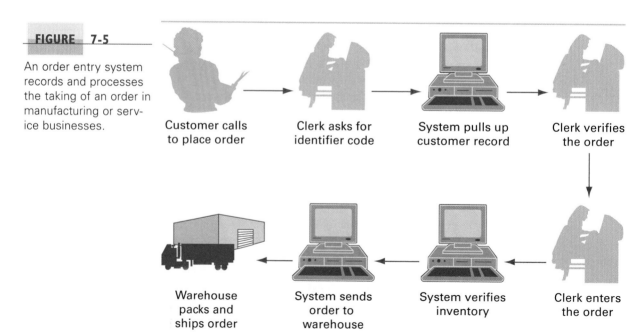

Customer calls
to place order

Clerk asks for
identifier code

System pulls up
customer record

Clerk verifies
the order

Warehouse
packs and
ships order

System sends
order to
warehouse

System verifies
inventory

Clerk enters
the order

address, a billing address, and the ability to deal with back-orders. Order entry systems must verify the inventory of ordered goods so that the sales clerk can inform the customer about shipping delays and the system can generate orders to replenish depleted stock.

Stanley Hardware, for example, uses a voice order entry system to provide service to smaller volume and stock order customers. First, customers contact customer service to obtain an account number and password. Then, they can dial into the system using a toll-free number. A recorded voice asks them to enter their customer number and password, which the system then verifies. Next, the voice order system prompts the customer to enter the item number and quantity desired. The system repeats the information entered as confirmation. The caller then accepts or changes the information. Upon completion of the order, the system says the customer's reference number and ship date. The system can also ask customers if they wish a hard copy of the order, which they then receive by fax. The system validates all inputs as well as information in Stanley's database.[21]

Order entry systems differ markedly by industry and often need customization for companies within an industry. How would the data needed by a mail order distributor, a fast food chain, or a newspaper's advertising department differ? A mail order distributor uses a product number, which displays a product description. A fast-food chain uses a food name and size. A newspaper's advertising department accepts advertising text, its size, and date of publication. The order entry systems need to be specially designed to include the precise information needed by the businesses. For example, Brigham and Women's Hospital in Boston, like many other hospitals, now has a medical order entry system that flags potentially dangerous prescription orders.[22]

Firearms dealers in California use a specially designed order entry system. Previously dealers sent a record of sale by mail to the state's Department of Justice for a criminal cross-check, a process that could take as long as 20 days. Now an automated transaction processing system sends the order electronically to the Justice Department for approval, significantly reducing the time between purchase and approval. The system automatically checks 60 items on the dealer's application to the Justice Department on behalf of the customer. MCI, the computer system vendor, will track purchases and bill dealers monthly for fees owed to the Justice Department.[23]

Electronic Bill Presentment and Payment (EBPP)

Electronic bill presentment and payment (EBPP) is the process of billing customers and receiving payments electronically over the Internet. The advantages of EBPP over paper processes are the reduction in paperwork and mailing costs. EMarketer estimates that between 84 percent and 98 percent of business-to-business invoicing involves paper processes, allowing for major opportunities to save costs by EBPP.[24] In addition, both parties to an EBPP transaction can capture the transaction more easily, increasing the amount and quality of data available for decision making.

In 2001, consumers viewed online only 2 percent of all bills from the nation's major billing companies and paid only 1 percent of all bills online. Nevertheless, that percentage is rising rapidly, and many consumers prefer the ability to pay online.[25]

Four major models exist for EBPP:

- Company bills its customers via its own Web site. Customers pay by presenting a credit card, authorizing the use of a credit file already on file, or authorizing a bank transfer. AT&T provides EBPP at its Web site as a way to build customer loyalty, provide better customer service, reduce customer service costs, and increase customers' use and visits to its Web site.[26]

- Company bills its customer through a third party's site. Many small companies accept payments through PayPal, for example, which presents the bill to the customer and collects either through credit card or bank payment.

- Consolidator aggregates bills from multiple companies, collects single payment, and distributes it among bill presenters. Benefits to the consumer include ease of payment, integrated reporting, categorization, and money management features. Banks have garnered the majority share of the consolidator market. Wells Fargo, for example, has three million active online users, of which nearly a third are using EBPP.[27]

- Company bills its customer at its customer's EBPP Web site or via EDI. This alternative is incidental to the billing company and is clearly not part of its CRM initiative. However, it does benefit the customer. General Electric provides incentives to its suppliers to use EBPP by offering them fast payment within 15 days of invoicing at a 1.5 percent discount as opposed to a 60-day wait to get paid.[28]

Business to business EBPP is becoming increasingly common. A recent study shows that the return on investment in EBPP is positive, with a payback within one or two years even if only 12 to 15 percent of customers adopt it. The benefits of EBPP that produce the rapid payback include reductions in customer service calls relating to bills, decreases in accounts receivable processing time, the opportunity to communicate consistently and personally with customers, and more rapid payments by customers, as it is easier for them to pay their bills and make partial payments on disputed items.[29]

Mercedes-Benz has developed an EBPP system to allow its car dealers in Spain to pay through the Internet. Depending upon whether the purchase is financed, the dealer can make payments online to Mercedes-Benz Espaa or Mercedes-Benz Credit, 24 hours a day. The transaction is a three-way transaction, between the dealer, the bank, and Mercedes. Upon completion of the transaction, the dealer receives an online confirmation from the bank.[30]

Post-Sales Support

Post-sales support is one of the primary determinants of customer loyalty. For many types of products, especially complex ones such as computers, customers pay for support. Whether or not the customer pays for support, the support function is a major way that companies can stay in touch with their customer. CRM software can provide benefits such as reducing the cost of customer support, providing 24 hour, 7 day per week service, and creating a database of interaction with the customer that can lead not only to improved service but also targeted selling.

CRM software for post-sales support includes systems to support a call center, a mobile field service, and Web services. In addition, CRM software collects data about the service transaction, which help diagnose and solve subsequent service issues and which also provide opportunities for cross selling.

Call centers are a major cost center for companies and can be a major annoyance for their customers. CRM software, such as Siebel System's "Call Center," shown in Figure 7-6, can help a company reduce the cost of its call center, provide better service, and help it cross sell its products. Call center software for banks, for example, uses information from the service call, customer account information, and demographic data to help agents make recommendations to customers, turning service calls into sales opportunities.[31] Call center software allowed Unilever Philippines to increase the number of calls handled by its call center from 3,000 to 6,000 monthly without any increase in staff.[32]

Honeywell's Automation & Control Solutions division, which services building systems, such as those for security, fire alarm, lighting, and energy control, provides an example of how CRM field service initiatives can be effective. As part of its Field Automation Service Technology (FAST) initiative, Honeywell provided its field service technicians with handheld computers that could connect with its WAN intranet. With their direct connection to dispatch, technicians could pick up service requests and keep dispatch advised of their status

FIGURE 7-6

Call center employees
may see an opening
screen such as this one
from Siebel Systems,
one of the leaders in
CRM software.

SOURCE: accessed at http:
//www.siebel.com/products
/service/call_center/con_demo
.shtm. Used with permission.

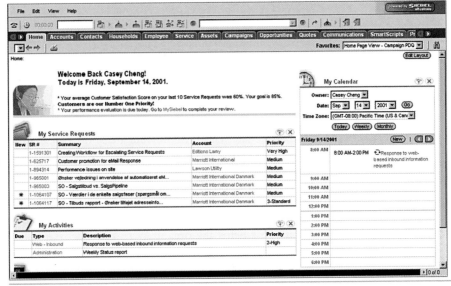

without ever having to call in. In addition, they automatically received on their computers all details regarding the purpose of the service call and the nature of the equipment to be serviced. Customers, too, could access their service records over the Web. In the near future, Honeywell plans to provide online detailed engineering and service drawings and instructions to replace the tremendous amount of equipment documentation that technicians now have to carry with them. Honeywell reports that in addition to improving customer service, the FAST system has allowed it to reduce the number of administrative steps between work completion and invoicing from 17 to 3 and cut the billing cycle from weeks to just a few days.[33]

Managing Distributors

Partner relationship management (PRM) is a philosophy of coordinating with distributors and other channel partners in the sale and distribution of a product or service. PRM software supports this philosophy by facilitating inter-organizational communication and sharing of data over an organizational extranet or the Internet. CRM software often includes PRM features.

PRM software helps companies evaluate potential channel partners, launch and track partnership programs, manage the funding of cooperative programs, such as joint advertising, and provide training information on new products. Lead management is one of the most desired features of PRM software. Lead management automates the matching and delivering of leads to distributors and other resellers based on their location, vertical expertise, and product specialization.[34] PRM software helps companies identify their best partners and customize the level of incentives, such as discounts, rewards, and leads, to keep the partnership strong.

Lion Apparel, headquartered in Dayton, Ohio, is a global manufacturer and distributor of occupational apparel, such as for firefighters and police. The company employs eight regional sales managers to oversee and track the activity of over 2,000 distributors throughout North America. The company introduced a Web-based PRM system that provided its sales managers with a comprehensive snapshot of day-to-day sales and gave its distributors access to product and sales information. In addition, partners can request proposals from Lion for jobs they intend to quote. Lion expects the PRM software to allow it to increase sales revenue by 40 percent in two years, in an industry that has been relatively static, without adding to its existing sales force.[35]

Marketing Systems

Marketing is often classified as a support function rather than a value-adding function. However we have included it in this section because it directly interacts with the customer and adds value by informing customers about product characteristics and by packaging information with the product. In its support role, marketing gathers information about the customer so that other functions, such as production and logistics, can add more value.

Table 7-3 lists some of the functions and objectives of marketing information systems. These can be broadly classified into four areas – market analysis, campaign and event management, channel management, and management of the marketing function. In supporting market analysis, information technology helps an organization to gather information about every interaction with the customer, including product or price inquiries, sales, calls on customers by salespeople, Web visits, contact at shows and conferences, service calls, and merchandise returns. Combined with demographic and sociographic information, market analysis helps the organization segment the market and customize responses, products, pricing, campaigns, and events to each segment or individual. Chapter 8 addresses in more depth the analysis tools available in such management software.

Campaign and event management software helps keep track of the details involved in executing a marketing campaign or event. It also helps marketers to funnel leads gathered through such campaigns and events to the salespeople or channels most appropriate for following up on them. The software helps campaign and event managers put together a budget, forward marketing materials for approval through required channels, and collaborate with employees within and outside the organization on promotion or event details. In addition, it can help managers to estimate the return on their marketing investments and optimize the allocation of their marketing dollars among alternative campaigns and events.

Channel management helps managers decide whether and how to use different channels to reach the end customer. Potential channels include the Web, direct mail, retail, and

TABLE 7-3 Functions and objectives of software to support the marketing function		
	Market analysis	Identify and retain the most valuable customers
		Optimize targeting and improve response rates by segmenting the market based on any data in the enterprise
	Campaign and event management	Execute permission-based multi-channel campaigns, including automated multi-stage, recurring, and event-triggered campaigns
		Engage customers in real time across any channel with the optimal offer to turn inbound interactions, such as service inquiries, into revenue opportunities
		Improve conversion rates through integrated response capture and automated lead assignment that enables rapid follow-up by direct and indirect sales teams
		Execute high-quality event-based marketing programs
	Channel management	Leverage lower cost Web channels to acquire new customers and build loyalty
		Increase revenues and grow customer lifetime value with more intelligent cross-selling and up-selling
	Management of marketing function	Improve marketing ROI using continuous test, real-time measurement, and analysis capabilities
		Apply best practices and automation to improve the effectiveness and velocity of marketing programs

SOURCE: Based on sales literature from Siebel Systems for its Siebel Marketing 7 product. Accessed at http://www.siebel.com/products/marketing/index.shtm on July 29, 2002. Used with permission.

distributors. Channel management also helps managers integrate information collected in different sales channels.

Finally, marketing software helps managers improve the marketing function by incorporating the best practices of marketers around the world and by monitoring the outcome of marketing decisions. It helps management develop an overall marketing plan for the organization and helps track how well the organization executes the plan.

MANAGING DESIGN, ENGINEERING, AND PRODUCTION

As director of sales at AlliedSignal, Pruitt Layton relied heavily upon his production and design departments. The sales department needed information about inventories and production rates to set prices and determine how fast they could promise product to their customers. But, information had to flow in the other direction as well. The design and engineering departments needed detailed information from the sales force about customer requirements to design the custom parts that AlliedSignal sold. These departments also had to learn about customer needs in designing mass-manufactured products. In this section, we look at how information technology assists in design, engineering, and manufacturing, and how it helps integrate these processes with one another and with other processes, such as sales. In addition, we review how the production function, along with distribution, provides different levels of customization for meeting market demand.

Computer-Aided Design (CAD)

Computers can help designers translate their mental images into physical drawings and specifications. Designers create and develop both products and processes:

- *Product design* refers to the creation of a concept and specifications for a finished good. For example, designers determine the specifications of a new video camera or television set.

- *Process design* describes the creation and specification of equipment and procedures for manufacturing the finished good. Designers develop the specifications for equipment to manufacture the video cameras or televisions.

Uses of Computer-Aided Design

Computer-aided design (CAD) automates both product and process design. Although computers recently have had some success in imitating human creativity,[36] they have contributed most to improving the design process by removing much of its drudgery. Today, for example, computers automatically transcribe the music that composers play on a piano-like keyboard input device. Computer-aided design has allowed carpet designers to create more daring designs, more easily custom-tailor orders, and manufacture them faster.[37]

Product and process designers can use computers to transcribe their ideas into engineering drawings, redraw designs from different angles, and evaluate the technical characteristics of alternative designs. Consider this. Designers use computers to make better basketballs, baseballs, and other sports equipment at Spalding Sports Worldwide. This company uses imaging software to improve its product development process. Developers create, share, discuss, and update product specifications online; they no longer send paper copies to offices around the world. The company now handles twice as many specifications and updates as before computerization of design and has reduced development time from one and one-half years to a few months.[38]

Engineers, architects, graphics designers, and others who compose their designs on a computer can view them from multiple perspectives, analyze them from an engineering perspective, edit them, document them, and output them in a format suitable for those doing the manufacturing. They also can save designs for subcomponents and insert them into other designs. Boeing used computers to design each part of the 777 aircraft and again used computers to fit each part into the three-dimensional puzzle of the finished aircraft before it reached the factory floor.[39]

Designers can also take their designs into the field. Members of the restaurant supplier Aramark's Design Group take laptops, projectors, and special software onsite to clients. They can change a drawing on the spot, show the client how the changes would appear, and then send the changes to the CAD department at their headquarters in Philadelphia.[40]

CAD software for networked computers allows several designers to work together on the design of complicated products. Web communication software can support global product design by letting designers send a 3-D product model to anyone with Internet access.[41] BAA PLC, owner of Heathrow Airport, is using CAD software to replace the design paper trail with electronic drawings of its $550 million fast track rail link to London. Contractors have instant access to the latest drawing revisions from remote design teams.[42]

CAD software allows technical service people to retrieve CAD models of products, such as the wire frame diagram shown in Figure 7-7. They can then use the CAD capabilities to see different views of the product as part of their repair instructions.[43] Consider how a CAD capability might help a technician service a Honeywell aircraft engine. The ability to obtain many views of the engine easily should ease troubleshooting and repair.

Computer-aided design can speed the design process by showing a true picture of the finished product. CAD can spot potential design mistakes before they occur in production. It also allows designers to focus more on the creative aspects and less on the mechanical aspects of product and process design.

Features of CAD Software

Computer-aided design (CAD) software automates many design processes and removes noncreative tasks associated with design. In selecting CAD software, users should consider how it handles composition, viewing, modeling, editing, documentation, output, and

FIGURE   7-7

CAD software can produce a wire-frame diagram to represent a model of a new product.

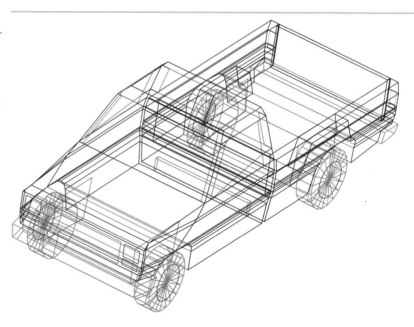

storage, as shown in Table 7-4. Think for a moment about designing part of an airplane engine. How might designers use the CAD software to make their jobs easier?

Rapid Prototyping

Rapid prototyping refers to the conversion of an electronic computer-aided design model into a solid physical model. Imagine designing a product, pressing a key, and having a plastic, wax, metal, or ceramic model of the product produced in your office. A variety of technologies now support rapid prototyping at relatively low cost.[44] For example, a product called Sculptor, by Visual Impact, creates a physical model of a design by building it in slices. It uses one material to correspond to solid parts of the design and another material to correspond to the void or empty areas. The process ends with heating the cube; the material corresponding to the void or empty areas melts and drains away, leaving a model of the design. Alternatively, the solid part can melt away, leaving a mold for casting the product. In many cases, rapid prototyping can reduce the design to market time by 75 percent or more.[45]

TABLE 7-4

High-quality CAD design systems aid designers in composition, viewing, modeling, editing, documenting, outputting, and storing designs.

- Composition. CAD products should allow the user to scan in a hand-drawn sketch; use a pen interface to draw directly on the screen; import sketches from business graphics packages; or compose directly using a mouse, trackball, or keyboard. The software should include numerous sketching tools that support the drawing of a three-dimensional design from either a single perspective, as two-dimensional slices at selected intervals, or as projections of the design from each of three dimensions.

- Viewing. Users should be able to rotate an object, view it from any angle, or zoom into or from a particular point on the object. CAD products should also show it in three-dimensions as it would appear with light coming from one or more lamps placed at the user's direction, render it as a wire-frame diagram display slices, or provide a physical model.

- Modeling. Modeling allows users to determine not only how a design looks, but also how well it likely will perform, e.g. how well it stands up to heat or pressure, creates drag or noise, conducts heat, or resists fluid flowing through or around it. Although modeling is a feature more often associated with computer-aided engineering, CAD packages increasingly supply CAE tools.

- Editing. Editing functions allow a CAD user to modify a design simply and easily by moving, rotating, sizing, coloring, shading, and applying new textures to previously-defined objects. CAD software also allows a user to simultaneously place several views of the design or parts of the design on the screen, thereby showing the complete implications of the editing.

- Documentation. Documentation consists of putting labels, measurements, and symbols on a design. Most CAD packages have standard tools that can rotate, size, and color text. CAD software can also attach non-printing attributes, such as a part number, vendor, price, or other descriptive information, to parts or subparts of the design.

- Output. CAD software generally supports a wide choice of printers and plotters that let the user zoom, position, and crop the picture during printing. Most software support standard graphic storage formats, such as GIF (Graphics Interchange Format) and TIFF (Tagged Image File Format) as well as the DXF (Drawing Exchange Format) and IGES (Initial Graphical Exchange Standard) formats used for exchanging designs between different CAD packages.

- Storage. Product information managers control large volumes of engineering information; they store such metadata about drawings and documents as part numbers, date of last revision, storage location, and acceptable viewers.

SOURCE: From Paul Dvorak, "FEA Software Shapes Manufacturing's Future," *Machine Design*, 28 May 1993, 102–114; and Seth B. Hunter, "PIM Systems Manage the Information Morass," *Machine Design*, 28 May 1993, 114–124. Used with permission.

Computer-Aided Engineering (CAE)

Engineering is the application of mathematics and science to the invention, design, and development of industrial and practical products. While CAD focuses on the aesthetics and manufacturability of products, **computer-aided engineering (CAE)** applies mathematical models and scientific theory to the designs to determine how well they work under varying conditions.

Increasingly, CAD manufacturers are including CAE capabilities directly into their products. However, the types of models that engineers use tend to be highly specific to the types of products that they deal with. For example, engineers designing an aircraft engine would probably be concerned with modeling the flow of fuel and air and perhaps the heat dissipation of the engine's materials, while a bridge engineer would be more concerned about the nature of stresses and strains on the structure caused by physical loading and wind vibration. As a result, many CAE products exist as stand-alone products or as products that can be imported into popular CAD software. For example, Pittsburgh-based ALGOR sells mechanical engineering software for use with the popular Autodesk line of CAD software.[46]

Computer-Aided Manufacturing (CAM)

Computer-aided manufacturing (CAM) is the use of computers to control equipment in the manufacturing process. CAM offers advantages in reliability, control, training, quality, speed, and flexibility, as described in Table 7-5.

Managers must decide to what extent automation can replace human judgment in machine monitoring and control. Ideally, companies should use computers and humans to each perform what they do best. For example, automated systems vary in their ability to determine when to shut production lines for maintenance, evaluate which machinery or parts may cause quality problems in a finished product, and schedule the order and length of production runs of multiple products sharing production equipment. Some activities, such as the repair of some equipment, remain too complex for automation; rapid technical advancements continue to address these limitations.

Managers need to assess the feasibility, cost, and appropriateness of automation for their own operations. Although a single computer may replace several people, it can cost more to buy, operate, and maintain than the labor it replaces. System failures can also have disastrous consequences. A computer malfunction may affect many machines and reduce

	Advantage	Description
TABLE 7-5	Reliability	Computers do not make as many mistakes, forget to act as expected, get sick as often, or tire.
Computer-aided manufacturing (CAM) systems automate production and assembly to provide advantages in reliability, control, training, quality, speed, and flexibility.	Control	A single computer can control more machines and monitor them more frequently and precisely.
	Training	Although automation requires training during start-up, workers can more easily transfer their knowledge to new computer systems.
	Quality	Through their consistency and predictability, automated systems increase the quality of products.
	Speed	Automated systems can produce goods more quickly by performing individual processes faster and reducing the time required for start-up
	Flexibility	Automated systems can more easily modify assembly lines and other parts of the manufacturing process to respond to changes in product and process.

production for days or weeks, while a pool of operators in a manual production environment can generally compensate for the loss of a single machine operator.

Flexible Manufacturing

Flexible manufacturing requires that machinery potentially have multiple uses. This approach contrasts with having factories designed to produce a single product, such as one car model or one type of steel. Computers have made flexible manufacturing possible. Streparava S.p.a., an Italian company, builds machine parts for the automotive industry. They use equipment that can produce an array of parts on demand to meet performance, service, and environmental requirements.[47]

Because changes in product design generally required significant changes in the manufacturing machinery and plant layout, in the past managers had trouble responding quickly to changing customer requirements. Now, flexible manufacturing can support a rapid response to changes in customer demands.

Robotics

A *robot* is a computer-controlled machine that has human-like characteristics, such as intelligence, movement, and limbs or appendages. General Motors purchased the first commercial robot, called Unimate, in 1961. The early robots of the 1960s and 1970s were expensive and unreliable. The second generation of robots evolved in the mid-1980s and benefited from technical advances in both mechanics and electronics. Today's robots, as shown in Figure 7-8, have gained from advances in computing technology that allow machines to perform tasks that were previously too complex for automation. The Scania Trucks plant in Oskarsham, Sweden uses a robotic system to cut interior panels for truck cabs. Operators can customize the cabs' size, color, and special equipment.[48] In the pharmaceutical industry, robots can sample drugs for quality control during the intermediate stages of production. They also reduce the risk of contamination when compared to workers.[49]

Small, precise motors allow robots to position items more accurately than people can. Video cameras and pressure-sensitive sensors give robots sight and a sense of touch, enabling them to align one item with another. The Meta Torch system gives welding robots

BMW, Audi, and DaimlerChrysler use Stäubli robots on their automobile assembly lines.

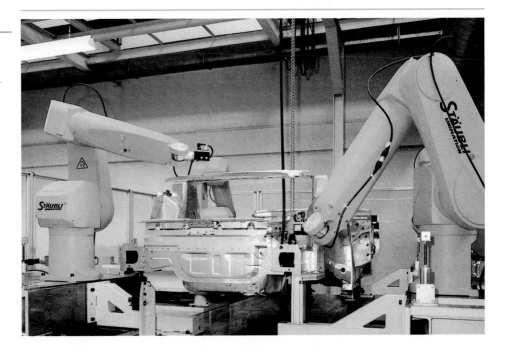

"sight" so they can avoid obstacles and deal with a changing welding environment.[50] Some experts believe that by the year 2025 robots will have replaced most machine operators, a job class that currently accounts for approximately eight percent of the work force.[51]

Software allows a computer to identify and classify different types of objects, select those required for a given task, and move obstacles to the tasks. Companies use robots to monitor and control almost every type of equipment. Sony Electronics' San Diego television manufacturing division, for example, routes finished TV sets to two robotic packaging stations. The use of these robots has increased production by more than 30 percent.[52]

CAD/CAM

Companies that design products that they can manufacture easily and efficiently have an advantage in the market place over companies whose products are hard to manufacture. CAD/CAM integrates CAD and CAM software so that engineering drawings are processed in such a way that their output can be downloaded directly to manufacturing equipment to produce a final product. CAD/CAM permits design engineers to anticipate and participate in the solution of manufacturing problems.

British manufacturer Amchem uses CAD/CAM software from VX Corporation to produce manufacturing systems that precisely position and drill rows of cooling holes into the blades of jet turbine engines.[53] Manufacturers of more mundane products also use CAD/CAM software. John Yair Designs Ltd. used the same VX software to design the ACME soccer whistle, and British lawnmower maker Hayter Ltd., uses the software to design its line of lawnmowers.[54]

Automated Guided Vehicles (AGVs)

Automated guided vehicles (AGVs), as illustrated in Figure 7-9, are computer-controlled vehicles that move along a guidance system built into a factory or warehouse floor. Primarily used for material handling, employees can program them to retrieve parts for constructing an assembled unit. Modern AGVs can even depart from the guidance system for short distances as long as no obstacles block their paths. Frymaster, a large manufacturer of fryers for restaurants, uses AGVs to deliver inventory to the plant floor.[55] The Aluminum Company of America (Alcoa) uses AGVs to transport 28,000-pound coils from hot rolling to cold mill, slitting, cut-to-width, and packing stations.[56]

FIGURE   7-9

A computer-controlled, battery-operated, unmanned transport AGV from Egemin Automation improves factory floor efficiency and lowers costs.

AGVs contribute to a flexible manufacturing environment. If a manufacturer mounts assembly line conveyors on AGVs, it can reconfigure its assembly lines simply by moving the AGVs. Workers and machines in such an environment then assemble the finished goods directly on the vehicles.[57]

Computer Integrated Manufacturing (CIM)

Computer Integrated Manufacturing (CIM) is the integration of product design, manufacturing planning, manufacturing execution, and shop floor control, as well as the integration of these production functions with the other functions of an organization (see Figure 7-10). CIM improves business processes by sharing information across departments, allowing companies to respond more quickly to changes and threats in the environment.

Many functional departments have a stake in product design. Marketing, for example, has a customer orientation and can provide substantial, valid input as to the value of a new product and the price it is likely to draw in the market. Production engineers can anticipate manufacturing difficulties and make recommendations that maintain the quality of the product while reducing production costs. Financial planners and controllers, with the assistance of marketing managers, can assess the cost of rolling out a new product and its implications for the financing of the company. Senior management can judge how well the designs reflect the company's strategic focus. CIM systems help bring these players together during the design process.

Production managers can better schedule their manufacturing equipment if they have access to product orders. Organizations can also integrate production schedules with inventory and purchasing systems to ensure the availability of materials for production. Because production requirements affect staffing, human resources information systems would benefit from integration with manufacturing systems.

FIGURE   7-10

Systems for computer-aided design, manufacturing planning, manufacturing execution, and shop floor control comprise CIM. CIM integrates with other functional and ERP systems through the corporate intranet.

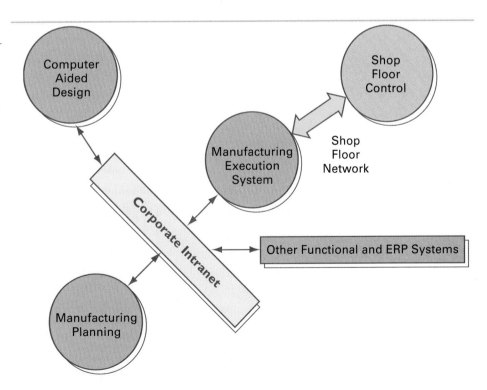

Manufacturing Execution Systems (MES)

A **manufacturing execution system (MES)** is software that monitors and controls processes on the shop floor, allowing managers and employees to observe activities at a specific work center or a specific machine. An MES is the central component of computer integrated manufacturing and generally interfaces with other enterprise software dealing with processes affected by or affecting manufacturing, such as accounting, warehousing, and purchasing.

Table 7-6 shows the key functions of an MES. The objective of the resource allocation and scheduling tasks aim to maximize productivity and throughput, minimize machine setup time, and reduce idle time and queuing. The scheduling component of an MES also allocates personnel, machinery, and devices, and sequences manufacturing orders through the required production steps. The objectives of the documentation tasks are to track personnel, machinery, and product. For personnel and machinery, the MES collects data such as machine usage, production rate, workers' performance, labor skill, hours between repairs, and condition of the equipment. On the product side, it collects data, such as who worked on it; specifics regarding components, such as supplier, lot number, and serial number; rework statistics; and lot and batch numbers.

Michigan-based Argent Automotive Systems manufactures custom adhesive-backed components for the automotive industry. It employs 86 line operators, who work in multiple shifts at 27 different stations. The company installed an MES initially to improve

TABLE 7-6		
Functions of a management execution system.	Operations/Detail Scheduling	Sequencing and timing activities for optimized plant performance based on finite capacities of the resources
	Resource Allocation and Status	Guiding what people, machines, tools, and materials should do, and tracking what they are currently doing or have just done
	Dispatching Production Units	Giving the command to send materials or orders to certain parts of the plant to begin a process or step
	Document Control	Managing and distributing information on products, processes, designs, or orders, as well as gathering certification statements of work and conditions
	Product Tracking and Genealogy	Monitoring the progress of units, batches, or lots of output to create a full history of the product
	Performance Analysis	Comparing measured results in the plant to goals and metrics set by the corporation, customers, or regulatory bodies
	Labor Management	Tracking and directing the use of operations personnel during a shift, based on qualifications, work patterns, and business needs
	Maintenance Management	Planning and executing appropriate activities to keep equipment and other capital assets in the plant performing to goal
	Process Management	Directing the flow of work in the plant based on planned and actual production activities
	Quality Management	Recording, tracking, and analyzing product and process characteristics against engineering ideals
	Data Collection/Acquisition	Monitoring, gathering, and organizing data about the processes, materials, and operations from people, machines, or controls

SOURCE: MESA International, "White Paper #6: MES Explained: A High Level Vision," September 1997. Accessed at http://www.mesa.org/whitepapers/pap6.pdf on 26 July 2002. Used with permission.

communication between shifts and departments and to improve workplace productivity. Every process is now tracked electronically in real time. A color touch screen at each employee station provides information that employees need to do their jobs and allows them to control and adjust the machinery. Production managers can now automatically adjust production schedules if a customer changes quantities or delivery dates. Among the most obvious benefit is the continuous stream of quality data that now flows from the factory floor.[58]

Mass Customization

Imagine the competitive advantage your company would have if it could produce the exact product that each customer wanted as cheaply and efficiently as if it were mass-produced. This concept, called **mass customization,** remains an ideal, but it has come closer and closer to reality with advances in information technology.

Researchers have identified several levels of potential customization, as illustrated in Figure 7-11. Segmented standardization allows no customization, but segments the market and presents customers choices depending on their preferences. Cosmetic manufacturers typically operate according to a segmented standardization policy. Customized standardization makes products from standard components. The basic design is standard and the components are all mass-produced, but each customer can configure the product as constrained only by the range of available components. Still, a great deal of customization can be achieved in this manner. Dell Computer has used this strategy, along with effective information technology, to create highly customized build-to-order products. Tailored customization changes the fabrication of the product to the customers' tastes. A tailored shirt and a decorated cake exemplify tailored customization. Pure customization involves the customer even in the design. A home renovation might exemplify such customization,

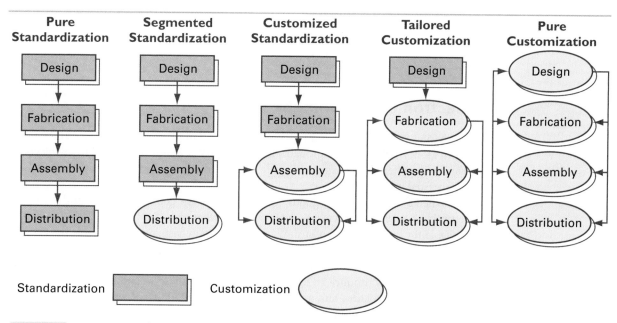

FIGURE   7-11   A continuum of customization strategies exists between standardization and pure customization.

SOURCE: Reprinted from "Customizing Customization," by Joseph Lampel and Henry Mintzberg, *Sloan Management Review,* Fall 1996, pp. 21-30, by permission of publisher.

because the homeowner works with the architect to create a design that is then fabricated to the architect's specifications.

Saleen Inc., located in Irvine, California, provides tailored, and sometimes pure customization, to transform standard Ford Mustangs into high-horsepower, great handling, fully-equipped, souped-up vehicles. Using a production line to disassemble vehicles and reassemble them with Saleen parts, the company has produced more than 8,000 customized vehicles at prices close to that of a mass producer, well below what one would expect to pay for a one-of-a-kind driving machine.[59]

Mass customization can also be applied to services. Mortgage underwriter Freddie Mac is planning to change the way it does business so that all its mortgages will be mass customized. It will provide a list of characteristics numbering in the hundreds that lenders can choose from in creating a mortgage for the borrower.[60]

MANAGING SUPPLIER RELATIONSHIPS

Honeywell International's Garrett Engine Boosting Systems Division, the world's leading supplier of turbochargers for automobiles, boats, and commercial vehicles, wanted to take charge of its supply process. It purchases supplies from a variety of companies, some with annual revenues as low as $35 million and others with revenues of as much as $1 billion. The company implemented a Web portal at which suppliers can access its internal enterprise-wide system. The system alerts suppliers if inventory levels for specific parts are out of line with consumption levels. It also allows Garrett's suppliers to plan for and commit capacity against projected production 12 months into the future. When Garrett posts requests for new part designs or volume contracts to the system, suppliers can view them and respond with designs, documentation, and price quotes.[61]

Garrett's portal is not ideal, as it is basically a one-way system. It provides Garrett's suppliers with views of Garrett's use of and plans for their products and allows them to plan better. However, it doesn't let Garrett see the state of its suppliers' inventory and production capability. Also, it fails to offer the capability of automating transactions between Garrett and its suppliers. Its benefit, on the other hand, is that it costs suppliers nothing to participate, which is particularly important for small suppliers who are often unwilling or unable to afford a more direct linkage.

Electronic Procurement

Purchasing and receiving systems document transactions between a company and its suppliers. Honeywell Aerospace probably uses such a system for ordering and receiving goods from its suppliers. Purchasing transactions have both internal and external implications, as suggested in Figure 7-12.

When a company orders goods, it either pays for the goods at the time of the order or commits to paying for them at a later date. In either case, the order reduces the budget available for further orders of a similar type. The purchasing system records the encumbrance on the budget so that other people who use the same budget can determine whether additional funds remain.

An order may produce an inventory notice to advise clerks and managers that inventory is being replenished. This notice reduces the likelihood that other employees will place or attempt to place duplicate orders. Also, the notice allows order entry clerks to advise customers that the items they need will shortly be in stock.

An order also produces and records a purchase order. A *purchase order* is a form sent to a supplier to document an order. The purchasing staff can reference the purchase order record when suppliers call with questions about the order. In some cases, the system may

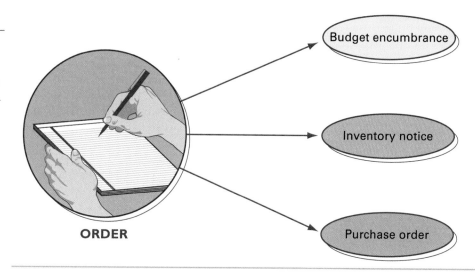

FIGURE 7-12

Ordering goods has numerous consequences for other parts of a purchasing system.

use EDI to transfer the order electronically to the supplier. An electronic copy of the EDI order sent to the supplier serves as the purchase order record.

When the supplier ships the items ordered, it may send an EDI or paper record of the shipment that usually arrives prior to the shipment itself. The system logs this record to alert receiving and inventory clerks and managers to the impending delivery. If the delivery does not arrive when expected, clerks can contact the shipping company to address the difficulty.

The arrival of the shipment generates additional transaction records. A record of the shipment's contents notes any discrepancy between the contents and the order. The customer can then accept or return the order. In addition, the customer may perform quality tests on the received goods. The system logs the results of these tests so that managers responsible for deciding what suppliers to use for future orders can base their decisions on concrete data. The system then updates the inventory with goods passing the quality tests. It may also generate an order return record, packing slips, and quality documentation for items not passing quality inspection. Finally, if the customer has not prepaid the order, the system makes a record of the amount owed to the supplier and enters it as an account payable. Companies that generate an accounts payable record at the time of order may need to modify that record to reflect differences between the goods accepted and received and those ordered.

Companies have also moved to the use of Web-based technology for their purchasing systems. General Electric, for example, launched a Web site that lets users give requests for bids to thousands of suppliers who can respond over the Internet. In 14 months, the site logged $350 million worth of industrial products purchased electronically by GE divisions. Now it sells the purchasing technology to other companies that want to handle purchasing using the Internet.[62]

Just-in-Time (JIT) Inventory

Just-in-time (JIT) inventory is the practice of receiving supplies just as a company requires it, neither too early nor too late. The early receipt of inventory increases costs by tying up capital and increasing the demand for warehouse space. It also adds to the costs of maintaining, searching for, and retrieving inventory. Inventory received too early might become out of date and need to be replaced, further increasing costs. Inventory received too late can be even worse, forcing a company to shut down or reschedule its production and generating costly rush orders and back orders.

JIT requires a tight relationship and real-time exchange of information between a company, its supplier, and often its suppliers' shippers. Imagine that you're the supplier of spokes to a bicycle manufacturer that practices JIT. If you fail to deliver the spokes on time, your customer, the bicycle manufacturer, will need to shut its plant when it runs out of parts. On the other hand, the manufacturer doesn't want to receive your spokes before it needs them. Because it takes you time to manufacture spokes, you need very detailed information about how fast the manufacturer is using your spokes and good forecasts regarding future use. Your customer would not be happy if the holiday season caught you without enough spokes to deliver. Your production schedule, then, needs to be tightly tied to your customer's schedule.

Good information systems and supplier relationships aren't always enough to keep JIT running well. Many companies find that it's important for suppliers to be located nearby, to reduce the variability in shipping time. Also, suppliers may be forced to keep a larger supply than they normally would so that they can respond to unanticipated changes in demand. For example, National Packaging Company (NPC), which manufactures boxes, found that to serve its JIT customers it needed to purchase warehouse space to hold extra inventory in the types of packaging that it could not manufacture quickly.[63] Although NPC's customers might think that their JIT policy has driven down inventory cost, more likely they've simply pushed those costs to NPC and their other suppliers, who eventually will have to charge them accordingly.

Vendor Managed Inventory (VMI)

Vendor managed inventory (VMI) is the process by which a supplier manages the inventory in its customer's facilities. Wal-Mart and Proctor & Gambel (P&G) pioneered this concept in the early 1990s. Wal-Mart gave P&G access to its information systems so that P&G could track the sales of its products, such as disposable diapers and toothpaste. Under this arrangement, P&G was responsible for noticing when inventory was low and for shipping and restocking the shelves allocated to their products. One advantage for P&G is that it had sufficient information about product sales to more accurately schedule its own production and to ship its goods in bulk. Another advantage was that it could maximize sales by making sure that its products were never out of stock. The advantage to Wal-Mart was that it didn't pay for any product until it was sold. As a result, Wal-Mart kept its cash longer (earning interest) and never had to worry about overstocking. P&G's interest was to move its product, and so it would try never to overstock a slow moving product, preferring instead to use the space for a faster moving product. Both companies reduced costs by eliminating invoicing and billing. The two companies acted in concert to provide the greatest value for the customer. Wal-Mart provided the distribution points, sales facilities, and information, and P&G provided the product.

Since the Wal-Mart/P&G experiment, vendor managed inventory has become a common practice in many industries. Although the nature of the practice varies by industry, the philosophy is always to optimize the extended value chain. In manufacturing industries, companies make their orders and manufacturing schedules available to suppliers, so suppliers can be sure to have supplies available before they are needed in the manufacturing process.

The initiative for VMI can come from customers or suppliers. Dallas-based Allied Fasteners, a distributor of bolts, nuts, rivets, and other fasteners, first implemented VMI in response to the demands of one of its customers. The experience was so positive that Allied now seeks customers who would benefit from and would like VMI.[64]

Vendor managed inventory relies heavily on information technology, particularly network technologies and functional systems. For the concept to have value, suppliers must have accurate and timely information about sales or orders and all factors affecting the use of their products. Some companies use Web-based software over their extranets to give their suppliers access to the same information that their internal employees receive. The drawback to this approach is that it's very hard for the supplier to extract the information from the Web-based view without manual intervention. Until recently, EDI was used more frequently because it provided direct computer-to-computer contact. Slowly, however, XML is replacing EDI because it allows a company to provide its suppliers with the same interface whether they are accessing the extranet using a Web browser or a computer. XML allows a supplier's computer to process the data on a Web page no matter what its format.

MANAGING WAREHOUSING AND TRANSPORTATION

Warehousing and transportation provide the major logistics functions of an organization. Inbound logistics includes shipping materials from suppliers, receiving the materials, and storing them in an appropriate way. Outbound logistics includes packaging the finished goods, loading them onto outbound transportation, and moving them to the customer. In this section, we examine some of the major components of warehousing and transportation systems.

Warehouse Management Systems

Warehouse management systems support activities inside the warehouse and at its shipping and receiving docks. Some of the features of warehouse management systems follow:

- *Receiving.* Systems help schedule pickup and deliveries to the warehouse. They identify incoming materials and corroborate them with purchase orders and advance shipping notices. They assign docks and schedule the arrival and departure of vehicles at these docks. They also support testing incoming materials for quality assurance.

- *Shipping.* Systems schedule outbound vehicles at docks. They optimize the picking process, so that products that need to be shipped together can be picked without moving back and forth at the warehouse. They coordinate picking with outbound shipping. They also support palletizing and pallet labeling for large shipments.

- *Picking.* Warehouse management systems support automated picking (see AGV's earlier in this chapter) and conveyor systems. They support the verification of items picked against pick lists by bar code or other means.

- *Storage.* Warehouse management systems help lay out the storage so that size and weight restrictions are observed and frequently used items are accessed most easily.

- *Reporting.* Warehouse management systems identify the number and value of items in stock. Product information, such as barcode, trademark, cost, and price, are also available.

- *Planning and monitoring.* Warehouse management systems schedule staff and capacity. They warn managers of processes that have not been completed on time.

Porsche uses a warehouse management system from SAP to manage its central spare parts warehouse in Ludwigsburg. The software also handles spare parts at other locations as if they were located as a virtual warehouse. Employees and distributors can query the system to find out which parts are in stock and where they are located. The system has smoothed and accelerated the retrieval of spare parts, allowing distributors to reduce their safety stock and thereby lower their costs.[65]

Cross-Docking Systems

Cross-docking is the process by which goods received at a distribution point are immediately loaded onto outgoing trucks without entering into inventory. To understand the advantages of cross-docking, you must first understand the traditional operation of a distribution warehouse. Distribution warehouses are used by companies, such as grocery chains, that have many stores in a region. If a grocery chain orders canned soup from one its suppliers, it saves a great deal of money if it can order it in bulk and have the supplier ship it in bulk. The grocery chain would have the soup shipped to its warehouse where it would be stored until it was needed at one of the chain's local markets. Then, the chain would combine the soup with any other products that the local market needed into a single load for delivery. The warehouse acts as a collection point, allowing the company to achieve economies of scale in receiving goods and in distributing them.

Many markets commonly receive at least one shipment per day. Many incoming goods, such as produce, fish, and meat, are received at least once per day. If the incoming goods could be routed directly to the outgoing trucks, the grocery chain could reduce the size of its warehouse, reduce the cost of storage, and increase the freshness of the product. Cross-docking systems track the schedule of incoming and outgoing vehicles, and manage the flow of product from dock to dock so as to minimize the need for storage.

National Retail Systems (NRS) has built a new warehouse and cross-docking facility in North Bergen, New Jersey, which serves its major mass retailing clients, such as Kmart and Marshalls department stores. NRS receives goods from a nearby Kmart distribution center and distributes them to 135 stores in the New York/Baltimore corridor. Marshalls ships products from distribution centers around the country for delivery to New York and New Jersey stores. Five miles of conveyors and computerized, barcode-reading sorters take only a few minutes to move each of some 45,000 cartons per shift from its receiving dock to the proper destination trailer, guaranteeing the rapid delivery of product to about 500 different retail stores with near perfect accuracy.[66]

Auto-ID Systems

Auto-ID is technology for tagging merchandise, boxes, pallets, containers, and moving vehicles in such a way that their location can be tracked. Current technologies use tags that either respond to a radio signal emitted at close range or produce a radio signal of their own that can be read at a longer distances.

Auto-ID tags eliminate the manual processes involved in scanning bar codes. Another advantage is that they're more reliable. If a receiving clerk fails to scan a box at a receiving dock, the inventory might appear to be lost. With auto-ID, the box can immediately be found.

Although the primary use of auto-ID technologies is in warehousing and logistics, other applications are also possible. One possibility is real-time promotions. For example, as a shopper passes the chips section of a grocery store, the grocer can automatically scan the items in the shopper's cart to see if it's likely that the shopper is planning a party. If so, it can flash a special price to entice the shopper to buy a certain brand of chips. Another possible application is for a smart refrigerator that can sense when a product is used and automatically add it to a shopping list, a process that might be considered personal inventory replenishment.

Currently, the major barriers to more widespread use of auto-ID systems are the lack of standards and the high price of auto-ID tags. However, the opportunity is so great that companies such as Wal-Mart, Procter & Gamble, Gillette, Philip Morris, Johnson & Johnson, Coca-Cola, and Target have sponsored research at the Auto-ID Center of the Massachusetts Institute of Technology that promises to create a standard and reduce the price of an auto-ID tag from its current $1 to nearly the price of a barcode label.

Managing E-Fulfillment

Shipping of goods comprises a significant part of logistics and distribution systems. Information systems support the logistics of shipment delivery particularly well. VF Corporation, which distributes women's apparel, such as blue jeans and lingerie, uses a computerized market-response system to help it restock the shelves. In contrast to the month it can take to replenish stock of Levis jeans, VF can stock Lee and Wranglers within three days of an order. For example, Wal-Mart sends sales data about Wrangler jeans collected on its register scanners directly to VF. If VF has the jeans in stock, it sends replacements the next day. Otherwise VF's computers automatically order them and ship them within a week. Of course, VF isn't the only company with such a system. J.C. Penney already has its own, so that it can restock as fast as VF can. [67]

Managers see reducing the costs of shipping as having a major potential for cost savings. Computerized systems can help them identify the fastest and lowest cost shipping routes. They also can identify the best sizes and combinations of goods for shipments. For example, Trane, manufacturer of residential heating and air conditioning systems, use software that produces a loading diagram designed to optimize the use of space for its shipment.[68] Tracking shipments also improves with these logistics systems.

When FMC Resource Management received complaints from customers that its shipments were too large, it made the decision to keep a larger inventory and ship goods to customers more often. But going from 25 outbound shipments daily to 500 or 1,000 created major logistical problems. It solved these problems by introducing an automated system that routes and tracks packages almost instantly and chooses from several overnight carriers to get the best price. Sales went from $600,000 to $16 million in about eight years.[69]

Companies can also use logistics systems to improve their own fleet management. Winston Flowers, a $12 million Boston-area florist, uses an order entry and tracking system that comes with electronic maps and bar-code scanners. When a person orders flowers, the operator enters his name and address. The computer looks through a database of maps to verify the address and assign the delivery to one of 15 delivery zones. The system prints the order and a bar-code tag in the flower design area. The designer arranges and tags the flowers. A warehouse worker then checks the zone on the tag and carries the flowers to the correct loading bay. The driver scans the tag before loading the flowers, recording the time the flowers left the building. The driver then radios the dispatcher or returns to the warehouse after the delivery and updates the record. The system keeps a running record of drivers' commissions, which is about 40 percent of the delivery fee, and can total them with a single keystroke. The system can also provide routes and maps for inexperienced drivers. The company believes that the new system has paid off, particularly in improved customer service.[70]

SUPPORT SYSTEMS

Support functions are those that do not directly add value to a company's products and services. They include human resources, information technology, accounting, facilities management, legal, and general management functions. Support systems are information systems that support these functions. In this section, we review human resource management systems and accounting systems as representative of organizational support systems.

Human Resource Management Systems

Human resource management (HRM) systems streamline the processes relating to employee recruitment, development, retention, assessment, and compensation. Table 7-7 shows the major functions of an HRM system and many of the subsidiary functions that

TABLE 7-7	Assessment	Initiate performance reviews and route workflow
		Maintain and archive review documents
A sample of the functions provided by human resources management systems.		Track performance against pay
	Benefits Administration	Define providers, rates, and beneficiaries
		Calculate coverage and premiums for employees
		Determine and track employee eligibility
		Calculate payroll deductions
		Calculate and track benefit/expense ratios and other benefits statistics
		Enable employees to update beneficiaries and coverage
		Administer health insurance and retirement benefits plans, including reports to employees and relevant agencies
	Compensation	Provide compensation history for employees and managers
		Manage the pay structure; evaluate impact of changes
		Collect and track external market pay data
		Interface with sales management to compute sales-based compensation and awards
	Development	Review required skills against education opportunities
		Retain information about certification and courses taken
		Allow employees to request training
		Manage the workflow around training requests, authorization, and payment
		Maintain education performance data, such as grades
	Payroll	Track time by employee and project
		Estimate scheduled time and overtime requirements
		Maintain information on vacation and sick leave accruals and use
		Produce paychecks or send needed information to third party to produce paychecks
		Produce pay documentation for employees and relevant agencies
	Recruitment	Forecast employment needs
		Automatically screen resumes
		Support interview and hiring workflow
	Workforce Analysis	Track employee productivity
		Analyze retention and employee turnover

an HRM system supports. Keeping track of employees and employee programs is relatively easy for small companies, and most outsource their payroll and reporting functions to payroll specialists. Larger companies, especially companies doing business in more than one state or country, can benefit greatly from HRM systems.

Auto manufacturer DaimlerChrysler has an international workforce of 370,000 employees with manufacturing facilities in 37 countries. Recruiting for DaimlerChrysler is big business. The company used the eRecruit module of PeopleSoft's HRM product to eliminate much of the paperwork and streamline its recruiting process. The software enables job applicants to fill out application forms and post and update their resumes online. Human resource professionals and managers hiring for specific positions can view and evaluate interview results, and keep themselves appraised of the state of the hiring process. Not only has the recruitment process become more efficient, but the company has also saved money and freed human resource professionals to do analytical work rather than paperwork.[71]

One of the major challenges of human resources management in global organizations is that labor rules and reporting requirements vary dramatically by country. HRM systems address this issue by having different products for each country or a core product with extensions for each country. Figure 7-13 shows an example of a data entry screen for the popular PeopleSoft HRM product, showing an area for common or core information and an area that opens up for country-specific information.

Accounting Systems

Every financial transaction affects the income statement and the balance sheet of the company. Fleet Capital, for example, has a general ledger system that automates key financial processes. Its integrated financial database provides the company information that supports decision making.[72] Accounting systems generally include the following subsystems:

- *Accounts receivable* tracks money owed to the company as payment for goods and services provided; the system may generate reports used for checking credit, monitoring bad debts, pursuing overdue accounts, and reducing payment lags.

- *Accounts payable* generates purchase orders and produces checks for paying the organization's bills. The accounts payable system may automatically review the discounts received by the company for early payment of bills, select the optimal time for paying the bills, and automatically generate the check.

- *General ledger* records all financial transactions and classifies them into specific accounts. Periodically, the system summarizes and consolidates these accounts so that managers and investors can assess the financial health of the company.

Table 7-8 identifies some additional modules that accounting systems often include. In addition, almost every functional information system processes transactions that affect the general ledger. As a result, most companies implement an accounting system as their first functional system.

Barrie Pace, a direct mail seller of women's clothing, replaced its accounting system with an internal, PC-based system that gives it instant access to data and produces reports in a timely fashion. For example, managers can view the general ledger account history and then easily show supporting documents.[73]

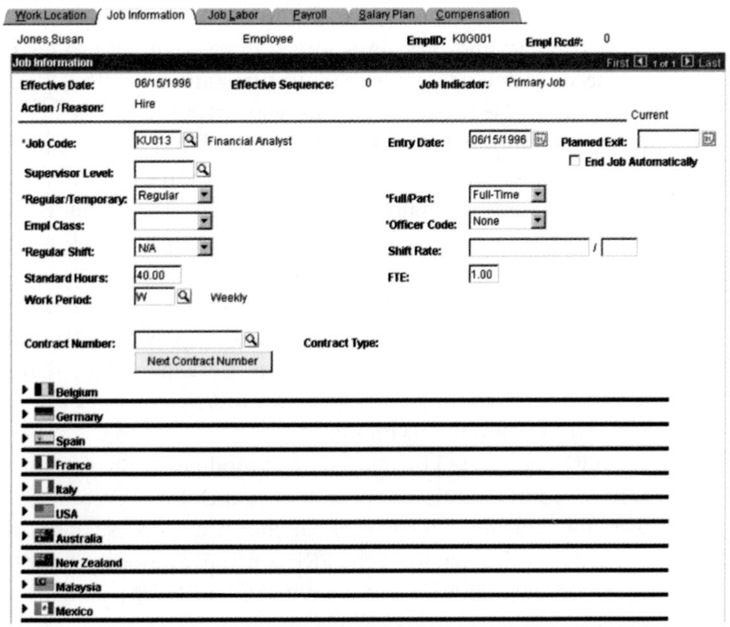

FIGURE   7-13

PeopleSoft HRM systems provide a screen area for common information and an area that opens up for country-specific information.

SOURCE: accessed at http://www.peoplesoft.com/media/en/pdf/hrms_global_strategy.pdf, on 30 July 2002. Used with permission.

	Software Module Outcome on Project	Function
TABLE 7-8 Accounting systems often include modules, such as those shown here, to process many types of transactions that can affect the general ledger.	Bank reconciliation	Reconciles bank statements with internal accounting
	Billing	Generates account statements and bills to customers
	Budgeting	Set limits or expectations of values of selected accounts, analyzes variances from these expectations, and sends notices or aborts transactions when limitations are exceeded.
	Cash management	Maintains information about the receipt and distribution of cash
	Credit-card authorization	Interfaces with order processing and accounts receivable
	Fixed asset accounting	Depreciates and amortizes fixed assets
	Investment tracking	Records investment transactions
	Work in Process	Adjusts the value of inventory for partially completed production

ENTERPRISE AND CROSS-ENTERPRISE SYSTEMS

You've already seen how information technology contributes to the operation and efficiency of an enterprise's value-chain and support processes. Now it's time to see how IT integrates these processes across the enterprise and across enterprise boundaries.

Enterprise Resource Planning (ERP)

ERP software is software that seeks to provide all the functional needs of an enterprise. It integrates the information across functions and even, at times, between corporate partners.

ERP software is vertical software. An ERP system for a retail company obviously needs to be much different than one designed for a manufacturing company. Even among manufacturing companies, information needs vary tremendously. For example, Honeywell Aerospace needs to track thousands of parts, but only produces a few different products for a few customers. Because it makes aircraft engines, quality assurance and component tracking are extremely important. A shoe manufacturer, on the other hand, uses relatively few parts and may have hundreds or thousands of customers. Its manufacturing areas are more compact and probably more automated. A gas producing company has even different needs. It doesn't exactly manufacture natural gas. But, it does have supplies for drilling, and it may also need to integrate with its refineries. It needs to manage the flow in its pipelines, a problem that neither Honeywell nor the shoe manufacturer must address.

Because no two companies, even in the same industry, use exactly the same processes, ERP software is normally customized upon installation. ERP vendors have written their software so that such customization is relatively easy. Still, an ERP implementation is complicated, involving most if not all of a company's processes. Most companies use consultants to help them customize and install their ERP software. The cost of an implementation varies greatly depending on the industry, the size of the company, and the number of features implemented. The average cost is more than $10 million and the average time nearly two years, according a recent survey of 63 companies with annual revenues that ranged from $12 million to $63 billion.[74]

ERP vendors sell their software in modules, so that customers don't have to implement software for the entire enterprise at once and also so customers can substitute their own software for some modules. Customers may decide to use their own software or software provided by another vendor if the ERP software cannot be made to match their own processes or if their own software is so good that the ERP vendor's software is unnecessary. For example, it's possible to license an ERP vendor's CRM module without necessarily licensing any of the other modules in the vendor's offering. Even within the CRM module, the vendor might provide submodules, such as field service, call center, and catalog management, which a customer might choose to license or not to license. Figure 7-14 illustrates, for example, the ERP modules of Waldarf, Germany-based SAP, one of the premier ERP vendors.

Supply Chain Management (SCM)

The term "supply chain management" means different things to different people. To some, supply chain management is synonymous with ERP. To others, supply chain management operates across the entire extended value chain, focusing on planning issues in parallel with ERP's focus on automation and transaction processing. Many ERP vendors object to this definition, as they believe that their software incorporates many planning functions. We define **supply chain management** (**SCM**) as the manner by which a company and its supply chain partners analyze, optimize, and control the acquisition and delivery of raw materials necessary for the creation of the goods and services that an organization produces.

Supply chain management software provides many functions to automate and simplify SCM. At the strategic level, SCM software allows companies to simulate the placement of warehouses and manufacturing facilities in relation to suppliers, and to determine the impact of such placement on transportation costs, safety stock, and material availability. Companies can use SCM software to simulate the operation of an individual plant to determine the best production levels and inventory requirements.

SCM software typically supports demand forecasting, which is needed to coordinate with suppliers so as to reduce inventory. Barnes & Noble (B&N), for example, improved its forecasting accuracy by more than 85 percent using software from i2 Technologies, one of the leading suppliers of SCM software. Because the typical B&N store carries 160,000 books, manual forecasting is impossible. B&N estimates that the improved forecasts reduced its inventory by 30 to 40 percent, saving the company $4 million annually in interest and making room for other books, which would increase revenue.[75]

SCM software also includes tools that allow supply chain partners to share forecasts and information about material use. Dell Computer, a leader in the use of SCM, uses SCM software to aggregate its orders every 20 seconds, compute the parts and other materials needed to complete these orders, compare these requirements to its inventory, and then transmit orders for any additional supplies that it needs. Dell has arranged with its suppliers to deliver orders placed in this fashion to its assembly plants within 90 minutes of the order's receipt. Then, again using SCM software, Dell unloads the delivery, placing it on

FIGURE 7-14

ERP vendor, SAP, offers a wide choice of modules in five different areas for a consumer products company thinking of implementing an ERP system.

SOURCE: accessed at http://www.sap.com/global/scripts/jump_frame.asp?content=/businessmaps/69F0899f40f311D397980000E83B54CE.htm&CloseLabel=, on 28 July 2002. Used with permission.

Enterprise Management	Strategic Enterprise Management	Business Analytics	Business Intelligence & Decision Support	Accounting	Workforce Planning & Alignment
Customer Relationship Management	Sales Force Management	Sales Cycle Management	Customer Service	Key Account Management	Trade Promotions	Category Management
Marketing & Innovation	Market Research & Analysis	Product Development	Brand Management	Marketing Program Management	Advertising & Consumer Promotion
Supply Chain Management	Strategic Planning & Coordination	Demand & Supply Planning	Procurement	Manufacturing	Distribution
Business Support	Human Resources Operations Sourcing & Deployment	Procurement	Financial Supply Chain Management	Treasury/ Corporate Finance Management	Fixed Asset Management

the assembly line in the exact order in which it will be used, all within 30 minutes of the time that the delivery arrives. For Dell, SCM software has reduced inventory from 13 hours to 7 hours and reduced paperwork by 90 percent.[76]

Supply chain management can be more difficult for smaller companies that cannot command the respect and response from their suppliers that Dell can. To implement supply chain management, most companies must secure the cooperation of many different suppliers, who use many different software products for their own internal operation. In these circumstances, standard interfaces such as EDI, XML, and Web services are necessary to achieve the degree of integration required.

Enterprise Application Integration (EAI)

Companies have many reasons for not implementing all the modules of a single vendor's ERP or SCM systems. Some companies, for example, follow a "best of breed" strategy, selecting the best software for their particular way of doing business to support each of the functional areas. Others find that they don't have the resources to implement all the modules they need or that their own systems are far superior to what they can find in the market for the way that they do business. The process of getting different software packages to work together as an integrated whole is called **Enterprise Application Integration (EAI).** By one estimate, EAI consumes 24 percent of the average corporate information technology budget.[77]

Two major strategies exist for integrating software products that weren't meant to work with one another. When a small number of products need to be integrated, IT professionals can build interfaces among them. At the simplest level, data can be extracted from one source and fed to another. Still, some programming is usually required because the extracted data need to be formatted properly for input into the receiving software package. Procedures also need to be established to make sure that the data get transferred sufficiently frequently between the packages and, potentially, to automate the transfer. Data exchange can be made more sophisticated by programming each package to automatically send data to the other packages whenever an interaction should occur. For example, when logistics software records the shipment of goods to a customer, it can send a message to the accounting software advising it to make whatever accounting entries are necessary and to the billing software so it can invoice the customer. However, programming real-time data transfers, such as this, can be extremely costly, and the programming might need to be repeated each time any of the software packages goes through an upgrade.

As the number of cooperating software packages increases, building interfaces among them quickly becomes infeasible. With six packages, there are 15 different combinations or package pairs, and with ten packages, the number of pairs grows to 45. Even more combinations exist if three-way cooperation is needed. The solution is to use software called **middleware** that interfaces with each of the cooperating packages (see Figure 7-15). When any package needs to communicate with others, it simply sends a message with data to the middleware, which determines what other packages need the data, formats the data appropriately, and sends it on. Commercial middleware packages have pre-built connections to packages of the major ERP vendors, so these interfaces do not have to be programmed. Some work is required to identify what data gets sent where, but the cost of achieving integration with middleware is much less than if a company were to try to build these interfaces on its own. Also, companies need to build interfaces to connect their proprietary software with their middleware solution.

FIGURE   7-15

Interfaces between
applications can be
replaced with fewer and
more standardized inter-
faces with a middleware
application.

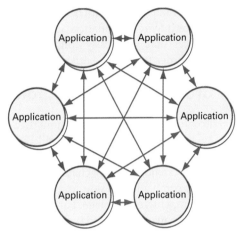

Without middleware, many application-to-application interfaces exist.

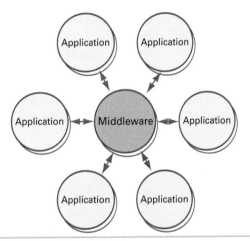

Steelcase, a Fortune 500 furniture company headquartered in Grand Rapids, Michigan, relies upon Hedberg Data Systems software to service its 800 global furniture dealers and automate many of its own business processes. But, it uses software from the German ERP vendor, SAP to set its prices. To connect these applications so that dealers can get accurate, real-time pricing for their customers over the Web, Steelcase uses Hewlett-Packard (HP) middleware. The HP middleware is also used to connect other applications because Steelcase operates in a complex environment with many different systems used internally and by its dealers.[78]

Companies are increasingly employing Web services as an EAI technology. Although Web services were originally envisioned as a tool to simplify cooperation among organizations (see Chapter 6), they can also be used as middleware.

IMP is a high-technology manufacturer based in San Jose, California. It uses Camstar's MESA product for its MES and Microsoft's Great Plains product for its financial systems. The problem is that the two products are not integrated. For example, orders have to be simultaneously entered into the financial and MES systems and, once produced and released from manufacturing, have to be manually entered into the financial system. Also, Great Plains does not account for work-in-process, the transformation of raw materials into intermediate products. To solve these problems, IMP and its contractor InSync Information Services used Cape Clear's CapeStudio product to build Web services that seamlessly connect the two products, providing automated integration from order taking through the receipt of payment.[79]

Cross-Enterprise Integration

According to a recent study, more than 85 percent of executives say that their firm considers the performance of its extended value chain to be one of its top priorities, yet fewer than 7 percent collect the information they need to track that performance.[80] Integration of the extended supply chain has proved to be difficult for a variety of reasons. For one, many companies are slow to recognize that their extended value chain is a potential source of competitive advantage. For example, only 5 percent of companies extend partner relationship management to their suppliers, viewing purchasing as a cost center rather than as a potential competitive weapon.[81] Also, integration across company boundaries is technically complex. Companies operate on different computing platforms and have incompatible ERP software. Adding to the complexity is the fact small suppliers and customers may have limited ability and funds to integrate, while very large suppliers and customers may try to drive the integration toward their own systems.

Nevertheless, cross-enterprise integration can pay off handsomely. For example, a recent study found that the best-in-class companies (top 20 percent) compared to the median companies turned over their inventory in 35 days versus 74 days, had a cash cycle of 36 days versus 84 days, and were able to respond to a 20 percent rise in demand in 9 days versus 20 days.[82]

SUMMARY

Enterprise resource planning software coordinates processes across the value chain. It includes modules for customer relationship management, production, procurement, logistics, human resources management, accounting, and other support functions.

Customer relationship management is the philosophy that an organization should focus on the customer. Sales force automation helps a company's sales force to interact with customers in an efficient and effective manner. Order entry and electronic bill presentment and payment systems smooth the customer-facing processes in the sales order cycle, leading to happier customers and quicker cash receipts. Excellent post-sales support, one of the primary determinants of customer loyalty, can be achieved with technologies that support call centers, mobile field services, and Web services. Partner relationship management systems help support and integrate with distributors. Marketing systems help managers segment the market, set prices, carry out promotional campaigns, and develop a better sense of market needs.

Computer-aided design helps designers translate their mental images into physical drawings and specifications. Computer-aided engineering applies mathematical models and scientific theory to designs to determine how well they work under varying conditions. Manufacturing execution systems monitor and control processes on the shop floor. Computer integrated manufacturing integrates product design, manufacturing planning, manufacturing execution, and shop floor control with other business processes, allowing companies to operate more efficiently and respond more rapidly to changes in the environment. Mass customization produces exactly what each customer wants nearly as cheaply as if it were mass-produced.

Electronic procurement, just-in-time inventory, and vendor managed inventory allow a company to reduce the cost of purchasing and inventorying supplies. Companies can achieve efficiencies in the supply chain by cooperating with suppliers, viewing them as partners rather than vendors, with the help of partnership management software.

Logistics support systems, including warehouse management, cross-docking, auto-ID, and electronic fulfillment systems, help track raw materials from the supplier and finished goods to the customer. These systems also help reduce time in inventory and shipping, getting product faster to manufacturing and ultimately to the customer.

Human resource management systems provide support for employee assessment, benefits administration, compensation, development, payroll, recruitment, and workforce analysis. Accounting systems interact with almost every functional system to trace the financial impact of transactions, assess the profitability of products and services, and set budgets.

Enterprise application integration is the process of integrating homegrown systems and non-ERP packages from different suppliers, often using middleware, so that they coordinate with one another. Coordination across enterprise boundaries is more difficult, but can provide substantial benefits.

KEY TERMS

auto-ID
automated guided vehicles (AGVs)
computer-aided design (CAD)
computer-aided engineering (CAE)
computer-aided manufacturing (CAM)
computer integrated manufacturing (CIM)
cross-docking
customer relationship management (CRM)

electronic bill presentment and payment (EBPP)
enterprise application integration (EAI)
enterprise resource planning (ERP)
flexible manufacturing
human resource management (HRM) system
just-in-time (JIT) inventory
manufacturing execution system (MES)
mass customization

middleware
order entry system
partner relationship management (PRM)
point-of-sale system (POS)
rapid prototyping
sales force automation
supply chain management (SCM)
vendor managed inventory (VMI)
warehouse management system

REVIEW QUESTIONS

1. What is enterprise resource planning?
2. What is customer relationship management?
3. Why do such a large percentage of CRM software implementations fail?
4. What is sales force automation?
5. How do point-of-sale systems differ from order entry systems?
6. What are the advantages of EBPP over paper systems to a company and its customers?
7. What functions does a CRM system need to provide to enable post-sales support?
8. What are the advantages to a company and its distributors of PRM software?
9. What are the functions and objectives of marketing information systems?
10. What are the major uses of computer-aided design?
11. How does rapid prototyping improve the design and development process?

12. How does computer-aided engineering differ from computer-aided design?

13. What are the components of computer integrated manufacturing?

14. What are four differing levels of customization?

15. What are the advantages and disadvantages of just-in-time inventory and vendor managed inventory from the perspectives of supplier and inventory user (manufacturer, distributor, or retailer).

16. How does cross-docking work?

17. What are the advantages of auto-ID systems as compared to bar code systems?

18. What are the major functions of human resource information systems?

19. How does supply chain management (SCM) differ from enterprise resource planning (ERP)?

20. What options exist for integrating an organization's functional information systems?

DRILLING FOR EVERY DROP OF VALUE

MINICASE

The Love Lane Chevron station on 145 Love Lane in Danville, California is the very model of a modern filling station, with all the amenities the residents of this wealthy San Francisco suburb expect: eight pay-at-the-pump lanes, a 24-hour convenience store, even a car wash. Underground, it's just as modern. The 14,250-gallon tank for super unleaded and the 19,000-gallon tank for regular (the midgrade fuel is a mixture of the two) are larger than the 10,000-gallon norm. Each tank is equipped with an electronic level monitor that conveys real-time information about its status through a cable to the station's management system and then via satellite to the main inventory management system for ChevronTexaco. Since it opened in August 2001, the Love Lane Chevron has never run out of gas.

During the last 10 years, ChevronTexaco, the nation's eighth largest company, with revenue of $104 billion, has used detailed consumer demand data to all but eliminate runouts and retains (the industry term for a delivery aborted because the tank is too full). That data, and the integration work that allowed it to be shared across the company, improved decision making at every point in what the industry calls the downstream, or customer-facing supply chain that begins once the oil is earmarked for the refinery (as opposed to the upstream chain, which includes hunting, drilling for, and pumping oil). In 1997, Chevron's confidence in the reliability of its demand data had reached the point where the company for the first time used demand-forecasting to determine how much oil it would refine on a monthly basis, with weekly and daily checks, thereby transitioning the company from a supply-driven to a demand-driven enterprise. That first year, Chevron's downstream profits jumped from $290 million to $662 million on the same refining capacity and number of retail stations.

Louie Ehrlich, ChevronTexaco's CIO for global downstream, says that while it's difficult to isolate the exact percentage of that jump and attribute it to the business model change—as opposed to a booming economy and the increasing ability to replace human workers with technology—the move has revolutionized the business. "It was a fundamental shift to take the customer view," he says. "[Before the shift] we acted like a manufacturing company, just trying to make products, when really the market was customer-driven."

But in 1997, the year Chevron decided to let demand, and demand only, drive production, the company's systems—station management, terminal management, transportation coordination, refinery scheduling and so on—were still isolated from one another.

Planners at the various points across the supply chain had to share data manually or flip between applications, introducing deadly costs. Since then, the company annually invests about $15 million in supply chain technology in the United States alone—a figure that doesn't include a $200 million SAP project, proprietary systems that capture real-time data, and even more advanced planning systems.

The downstream supply chain begins on an office floor in San Ramon and on another in Houston, where oil and gasoline traders are looking at an integrated marketing and refining sales and production plan to decide how much crude and how much gasoline to buy on the open, or spot, market. Traders used to be thought of as cowboys who relied just as much on instinct as they did on information. Now, they use up-to-date customer demand data.

Regional coordinating teams consisting of representatives from refining, marketing, and logistics use the same data—the information collected by all the integrated ChevronTexaco filling stations, plus other points of sale, such as airlines and trucking companies—to plan a refinery's load: for example, 50 percent gasoline, 30 percent diesel, and 20 percent jet fuel. ChevronTexaco, however, sells more than the company's seven domestic refineries can produce. Most of the difference is made up through long-term agreements with other oil companies. But those agreements don't take into account the changes in demand from month to month, says Doug Gleason, ChevronTexaco's regional manager of product supply east.

To respond to those changes, ChevronTexaco must buy gasoline on the spot market. In any given month, the company could buy up to 30 percent of its gasoline that way. The shift to a demand-driven model and the continued refinement of the demand-forecasting technology has allowed spot buyers to dramatically cut cost. Before, buyers would react to supply shortfalls, buying the gasoline they needed when they needed it, regardless of price. As with any market, when demand spikes, so does price. An accurate forecast at the beginning of the month means that buyers know exactly how much they need to buy and can spend the month looking for bargains. During the course of a month, says Gleason, buyers can average savings between a quarter to a third of a cent per gallon. That can add up to as much as $400,000 a month. "Good demand information causes a person to time their acquisitions much more intelligently," he says.

Tonight, the Love Lane Chevron is scheduled to receive 3,150 gallons of super and 5,950 gallons of regular (gasoline truck tanks have three compartments and hold a total of 10,000 gallons). Information from Love Lane's monitors is sent via satellite to ChevronTexaco's Customer Order Entry and Dispatch Center in Concord, California, where load planning software minimizes the number of deliveries needed to keep a station running while avoiding run-outs or retains. The demand forecasting and scheduling system has tentatively planned the next five deliveries as well, although they will be updated with new information. Shortly after 11 p.m., a truck picks up the gas destined for Love Lane at the Chevron terminal in Avon, about a half hour away. The Avon terminal has eight tanks, two truck-filling lanes, and a one-story tin-roofed office building on about 10 acres of land. Tank 108, one of the terminal's largest, holds 2.5 million gallons of unleaded gasoline. It is 70 percent full right now. Trucks enter and leave, taking 9,100 gallons at a time. Like at the filling station, terminal inventory is tracked in real-time. The terminal's inventory, combined with the demand data from the stations that it serves, helps ChevronTexaco determine how often Tank 108 needs to be filled.

Avoiding terminal run-outs isn't simply a matter of waiting until a tank is two-thirds empty and then filling it back up. Tank 108 alone takes two and a half days to fill. If the tank is low when a sudden spike in demand is caused by unusually warm weather, a sudden drop in prices, or a special event like the Olympics, it could run out of gas and force delivery trucks to be rerouted from terminals farther away, adding costs up and down the supply chain. A bigger problem is the demanding pipeline schedule. There are only a limited number of pipelines from each refinery, which are reconfigured based on the target terminal. And they are constantly in use. When Tank 108 isn't receiving gas, another tank—or another terminal—is. Schedulers use the demand data and the terminal inventory to create a tank-refilling plan that optimizes the use of the pipeline for all the terminals a refinery serves.

SOURCE: Extracted with permission from Ben Worthen, "Drilling for Every Drop of Value," CIO, 1 June 2002, 68–73.

Case Questions

Diagnosis

1. What problems existed before 1997, when ChevronTexaco decided to let demand drive production and the company's systems?
2. How do you think these problems affected ChevronTexaco's performance?

Evaluation

3. What information do ChevronTexaco's managers need to properly schedule and dispatch gasoline trucks?
4. What information do ChevronTexaco's managers need to allocate pipeline capacity?
5. Why do ChevronTexaco's gasoline buyers and refinery managers need to be able to react quickly to changes in demand for their products?

Design

6. What functional systems has ChevronTexaco built to acquire and process the information that its managers need?
7. How are the systems integrated?

Implementation

8. In what ways has ChevronTexaco's focus on demand and its new information system helped it to increase its profits?
9. Do you see any reason to extend ChevronTexaco's systems to its extended supply chain or demand chain? Why?

ACTIVITY

7-1 MASS CUSTOMIZATION AT FABULOUS CANDY

Step 1: Read the following scenario.

Fabulous Candy has just hired you as a consultant to advise it on a problem that it has with some of its customers. Fabulous Candy Company began in the owner's kitchen in 1980. The company soon opened a larger plant with ten employees who guided the manufacturing process. All candy was made by hand until the late 1980s, when the owner installed some assembly-line equipment to speed up the processing. In the 1990s, the company introduced a number of new products that sent sales skyrocketing. The company had difficulty keeping up with demand for chocolates at the original plant and soon opened several additional plants that produced more standard chocolate bars and other novelties. Company performance remained strong through most of the 1990s. Recently, some major accounts have threatened to defect to competitors, as Fabulous Candy was unable to provide the capabilities they wanted to customize their candies and wraps without negotiating each time with the company's sales department.

Step 2: Individually or in small groups, decide how to respond to the customers' requests.

Step 3: Share your plans with the entire class.

Step 4: In small groups or with the entire class, answer the following questions:
1. What level of customization, if any, should be offered?
2. What information will customers need to provide, and in what form, to allow the customization to proceed?
3. What hardware and software will be necessary to implement the recommended changes?

7-2 FUNCTIONAL SYSTEMS AT TACO CITY

ACTIVITY

Step 1: Read the following scenario.

Taco City is a national chain of fast-food franchises that sells Mexican-style food in the United States. Taco City recently made a public offering of stock and plans to expand from 150 outlets to 400 outlets in the next two years. Currently, Taco City provides franchisees with a point-of-sale system that records sales and sends them to company headquarters once a day. Franchisees are required to use this system. They are also required to purchase at least 80 percent of their food through Taco City.

Step 2: Individually or in small groups, diagnose the information needs of the franchisees and Taco City's executive managers. Decide what functional systems are necessary to support those needs.

Step 3: Share your conclusions with the rest of the class.

Step 4: In small groups or with the entire class, answer the following questions:
1. What are the information needs of Taco City's franchisees?
2. What are the information needs of Taco City's executive managers?
3. What functional systems should Taco City implement?

7-3 A MATTER OF TRUST

ACTIVITY

Step 1: Read the following scenario.

Six months ago, as vice president of sales and marketing at Fun Board Games, you negotiated a deal with Aaron Tyu Trusting at eNormous Toy Stores to obtain access to its extranet. According to the agreement, your company would charge eNormous Toy two percent less than any other toy store for each of your products. In exchange, eNormous Toy would provide access to its information systems, which show the number of your games in stock and on its shelves. You've calculated that this information will enable you to better schedule your production and improve your forecasts, reducing unsold goods and saving far more money than two percent of sales. It took only a few weeks to set up your computer systems to process the new information.

Yesterday you learned that Dee V. Us, one of the most capable employees of the information systems department, had figured out how to get access to the inventory and stock information of all eNormous Toy's products, including information about your competitors. Tracking the inventory information would allow you to quickly determine the rate of sales of your competitors' products. Obviously, eNormous Toy did not intend for you to see this information. Not only are you concerned with the ethical issues involved, but you are also concerned that your competitors might have figured out how to see information about your products. Your previous dealings with the head of the information systems department, Lee Vus Alone, have been cordial, but Mr. Alone has never been open to suggestion or criticism.

Step 2: Identify your alternatives for dealing with this situation.

Step 3: Answer each of the following questions, individually or in small groups, as directed by your instructor.

1. For each alternative, who benefits and who is harmed?
2. From the ethical principles of least harm, rights and duties, professional responsibilities, self-interest and utilitarianism, consistency, and respect, how would you evaluate each alternative?
3. What course of action would you take? Why?

7-4 ERP OR MIDDLEWARE?

ACTIVITY

Step 1: Read the following scenario:

Your company, a leading manufacturer of breakfast cereal foods, has just merged with the second largest manufacturer of breads and cookies. The logic behind the merger is that the combined company would have more power in buying wheat, rye, and other grains and that it would also have more power over grocers in negotiating prices and shelf space. There is no intent at the current time to merge the brands, so each will continue to operate under its own name. However, savings in overhead and logistics are expected. You have been put in charge of merging the two information technology departments.

Unfortunately, nobody ever looked at the difficulty of merging the information systems before the corporate merger took place. Your company runs an ERP system from SAP, but the baked goods company's ERP system is licensed from Oracle. You have a number of proprietary systems that are linked to your ERP system using middleware. So does the baked goods company. Very soon you will need to make the decision about whether to run the combined companies under a single ERP system or whether to link the two systems, where required, using middleware.

Step 2: Make a list of information that needs to be shared between the two companies.

Step 3: Your instructor will assign you to a team that will argue either to combine the operations of the companies under a single ERP system or to merge the two systems using middleware. Each team will have ten minutes to prepare its case, five minutes to present its case, and three minutes to rebut the other team's case.

Step 4: In small groups or with the entire class, answer the following questions:

1. What problems are likely to arise in converting to a single ERP system?
2. What problems are likely to arise if middleware is used to integrate the two ERP systems?
3. What are the advantages of merging the two companies under a single ERP system?
4. What are the advantages of using middleware instead?

ACTIVITY

7-5 AUTOMATING THE SALES FORCE AT RIGHT-TIME INSURANCE

Step 1: Read the following scenario.

You have just been hired as the regional sales manager for Right-Time Insurance. This medium-size family company sells all types of insurance to customers in a Midwestern city. The company has begun to computerize some of the office procedures, but all salespeople use manual systems for recording leads, obtaining and providing information about products to customers, keeping track of customers' insurance needs and policies, and generally conducting and completing the sale.

You believe that it is time for the company to computerize its sales and marketing activities. You know that software exists to handle most of the functions of the company, but you need to spend some time with the salespeople identifying their specific information needs.

Step 2: Individually or in small groups, diagnose the information needs of the sales staff and offer a plan for providing the sales force at Right-Time Insurance with information systems support.

Step 3: Share your plans with the rest of the class.

Step 4: In small groups or with the entire class, answer the following:

1. What types of processes should information systems support at Right-Time Insurance?
2. What functional systems are required to support these processes?
3. At this time, what hardware, network equipment, and software would you recommend for Right-Time Insurance?

IS ON THE WEB

IS ON THE WEB

Exercise 1: Follow the Chapter 7 Web links to vendors of CRM software. Visit the Web sites of three such vendors and examine the features of their software. Then, compare and contrast their software products. In what ways are they similar? How do they differ?

Exercise 2: The Chapter 7 Web links will direct you to Autodesk's AutoCAD product information page. According to your instructor's direction, either run the Interactive Overview or download and try out the trial version of AutoCAD.

RECOMMENDED READINGS

Anderegg, Travis. *ERP: A-Z Implementer's Guide for Success,* vol. 1. San Jose, CA: Resource Publishing, 2000.

Bergeron, Bryan P. *Essentials of CRM: A Guide to Customer Relationship Management.* New York: John Wiley & Sons, 2002.

Coyle, John Joseph, Edward J. Bardi, and C. John Langley. *Management of Business Logistics: A Supply Chain Perspective,* 7th ed. Mason, Ohio: South-Western/Thomson Learning, 2002.

Petty, D. J. *Systems for Planning and Control in Manufacturing.* Oxford, UK: Butterworth-Heinemann, 2002.

Pine, B. Joseph, II, and James H. Gilmore. *Markets of One: Creating Customer-Unique Value through Mass Customization.* Cambridge, MA: Harvard Business School, 2000.

NOTES

1. Meridith Levinson, "Cleared for Takeoff," *CIO*, 1 April 2002, 64–68. Jeff Morris, "Doing it Right," Customer Support Management, August 2001, accessed at http://www.quiq.com/docs/lo/176/SUPP/187790.pdf on 23 July 2002. Honeywell, "AlliedSignal: A Strong Local Commitment from a Global Player," accessed at http://www.asplastics.com/news/earchive/ aspr035e.html on 23 July 2002. Honeywell, "Aerospace Solutions," accessed at http://www.honeywell.com/about/page6_1.html on 23 July 2002.

2. Sharon L. Botwinik, with Bobby Cameron, Emily Jastrzembski, and Elizabeth Schneider, *Organizing to Get CRM Right.* Cambridge, MA: Forrester Research, May 2001. Of the 50 companies responding to the survey, 58 percent listed a single view as the driving reason to implement a CRM initiative. The next highest reason garnered only 28 percent.

3. Katherine Burger, "Strategies for Putting the Customer First," *Insurance & Technology Online*, 31 May 2002, accessed at http://www.insurancetech.com/story/specialReport/IST200 20531S0006 on 24 July 2002.

4. Botwinik, *Organizing to Get CRM Right.*

5. See, for example, Mitch Betts, "How to Run a CRM Project during a Recession," *Computerworld Online*, 18 February 2002, accessed at http://www.computerworld.com/softwaretopics/crm/story/0,10801,68262,00.html on 24 July 2002. Linda Hershey, "Why CRM Implementations Fail: A Business Survival Memo to the CEO/President," 7 August 2001, accessed at http://www.realmarket.com/required/lghcons1.pdf on 24 July 2002. Don Peppers, "Why CRM Initiatives Fail and What You Can Do about It," Inc.com, 1 November 2001, accessed at http://www.inc.com/articles/marketing/market_research/market_research_basics/23649.html on 24 July 2002.

6. J.C. Williams Group, "Joint National Retail Federation/J.C. Williams Group/BizRate.com Channel Surfing Study Validates Cross-Channel Influence," Press release on 25 September 2000, accessed at http://www.jcwg.com/channel-surfing-news.htm on 28 October 2002.

7. Meg Mitchell Moore, "Special Report: The Customer Agenda. Thinking Small," *Darwin*, May 2001, accessed at http://www.darwinmag.com/read/050101/thinking.html on 1 August 2002.

8. Julia King, "Trucking Firm Nets Automation Payback," *Computerworld*, 17 July 1995, 43.

9. Steve Alexander, "Sales Force Automation," *Computerworld Client/Server Journal*, October 1995, 41–50. Mindy Blodgett, Virtual Office Prototype Puts Field Service Reps to Work at 'Hearth' of MCI," *Computerworld*, 26 February 1996, 73–76.

10. Jill Gambon, "Sales Sleuths Find Solutions," *IW*, 22 July 1996, 51–52.

11. Thomas Hoffman, "Maine Drives Medicaid Reform with Decision-Support System," *Computerworld*, 20 January 1997, 67–68.

12. "How Laptops Helped Transform the Wesleyan," *Insurance Systems Bulletin*, July 1996, 3–4.

13. For example, Mrs. Fields Cookies operates in this fashion; see Jack Schember, "Mrs. Fields' Secret Weapon," *Personnel Journal* 70, no. 9 (1991): 56–58.

14. Rosemary Cafasso, "Diamond Shamrock, Inc.," *Computerworld Client/Server Journal Supplement*, August 1996, 26.

15 Judy Murrah, "Service Maximized in the Wireless Store," Chain Store Age Executive 69 (April, 1993): 76.

16. "Wireless Unclogs Pepsi's Distribution Bottleneck, Improves Merchandising," *Systems Management*, March 1996, 22–23.

17. Bob Wallace, "AT&T Rolls Out New Transaction Service," *Network World*, 29 March 1993, 25–26.

18. "Spotlight—Wave Riding Vehicles," http://www.retailpro.com/spotlights/wrvspot.html, accessed on 8 July 1997.

19. Tom Field, "A Good Connection," *CIO*, 1 February 1997, 70–74.

20. Wayne Seel, "Integrated Order Processing Helps Supplier Save Money and Keep Better Track of Jobs," *Marketing News*, 6 January 1997, 10.

21. "Application review: Order Entry at Stanley Hardware," http://www.midrangecomputing.com/tradeshow/link/hardware.htm, accessed on 10 July 1997.

22. Peter Fabris, "A Speedy Recovery," *CIO*, 1 February 1996, 34–36.

23. Kim Girard, "Gun Dealers Get a Shot in the Arm," *Computerworld*, 20 January 1997, 49, 51.

24. Julie Bort, "Build Tomorrow's Great Site Today," *Network World*, 18 February 2002, 62–68.

25. Paul Gores, "Wisconsin Data Services Firm Metavante Tries to Coax Customers to Pay Online," *Knight Ridder Tribune Business News*, 14 February 2002, 1.

26. IBM, *AT&T EBPP—Meeting Small Business Needs Via E-Business: A Hurwitz Group E-Business Case Study*, accessed at http://www-3.ibm.com/software/success/cssdb.nsf/CS/AWOD-4TR65W?OpenDocument&Site =default on 24 July 2002.

27. Paul Doocey, "Wells Fargo Inks Online Banking and EBPP Pact with CheckFree," *Bank Systems & Technology Online*, 27 June 2002, accessed at http://www.banktech.com/story/ebpp/BNK20020627S0006 on 24 July 2002.

28. A. Litan, "Management Update: GE Brings B2B Internet Invoicing and Payments to Life," *InSide Gartner Group*, 20 June 2001.

29. "Giga's Total Economic Impact Research Shows Electronic Invoice Presentment and Payment Improves Profitability Even with Only 12% Customer Adoption," Business Wire, 23 July 2002, accessed at http://www.manufacturing

.net/index.asp?layout=articlePrint&articleID=LN46BV-WCP0-010G-02G7-00000-00 on 26 July 2002.

30. "Mercedes-Benz Sets Up Online Dealer Payments," *Europemedia*, 19 February 2002.

31. "Cross-Selling Drives CRM Growth in Banking," *Call Center Magazine*, June 2002, 10.

32. Tao Ai Lei, "Unilever Gets Productivity Boost with mySAP CRM," *Asia Computer Weekly*, 15 July 2002, 1.

33. Erika Morphy, "Honeywell Embraces Field Service Automation," *CRMDaily.com*, 7 December 2001.

34. Eric Hills, "A Case for Gambling on PRM," *Online Magazine*, January 2001, accessed at http://www.saleslobby.com/Mag/0101/CMEH.asp on 25 July 2002. Hills cites August 2000 online survey conducted by Frontline Solutions as the original source for the most desired feature of PRM.

35. Partnerware, "Lion Apparel—Manufacturing Success Story," accessed at http://www.partnerware.com/customers/success.html on 25 July 2002. Jennifer Maselli, "Tools Track Customers, Boost Sales," *InformationWeek.com*, 26 November 2001, accessed at http://www.informationweek.com/story/IWK20011120S0017 on 25 July 2002.

36. See, for example, Kyle Heger, "Whiz...Bang...Eureka! The Automation of Creativity," Communication World, November 1991, 18–21. Patricia D. Prince, "A Showcase for Computer Art," *Personal Computing* 13 (October 1989): 132–134.

37. "With CAD, Carpet Goes High Tech," *Facilities Design and Management* 15 (October 1996): 50–52.

38. Tim Ouellette, "Spalding Sports' Imaging, Workflow System on Tap," *Computerworld*, 23 October 1995, 57, 62.

39. Rochelle Garner, "Flight Crew," *Computerworld*, 5 February 1996, 66–67.

40. "Road warriors: Aramark Brings Design Company to Its Clients," *Nation's Restaurant News*, 18 November 1996, 19.

41. Brian Kuttner and Dan Deitz, "Reviewing Designs in Cyberspace," *Mechanical Engineering* 118 (December 1996): 56–58. Uri Klement, "A Global Network for Plant Design," *Mechanical Engineering* 118 (December 1996): 52–54.

42. "CAD Network Helps Rail Link," *ENR*, 23 December 1996, 13.

43. Sidney Hill, "CAD Vendors Saying 'Ole!,'" *Manufacturing Systems* 13 (July 1995): 8.

44. See Dan Rasmus, "Conceptually Speaking," *Manufacturing Systems*, March 1993, 14–18, for examples of concept modeling.

45. Philip Balsmeier and Wendell J. Voisin, "Rapid Prototyping: State-of-the-Art Manufacturing," *Industrial Management* 39 (January/February 1997): 1–4.

46. http://www.feaincad.com/products/InCADD1505/default.asp, accessed on 25 July 2002.

47. "Italina Machine Builders Target Lean Production," *Manufacturing Engineering* 118 (January 1997): 22–24.

48. "Robots on the Cutting Edge," *Robotics Today* 9 (fourth quarter 1996): 6–7.

49. Dennis Melamed, "Robots on Drugs," *Robotics World* 14 (spring 1996): 21–23.

50. "Sensing a Better Robotic Weld," *Robotics Today* 9 (fourth quarter 1996): 6.

51. Robert K. Robinson, Ross L. Fink, and William B. Rose, Jr., "Attitude Survey on Robot Workers," *Robotics Today* 5 (third quarter, 1992): 5–6.

52. "Robots Tune in to Sony TVs Packing," *Packaging Digest* 34 (January 1997): 76.

53. http://www.vx.com/content/us/customer_spotlight/amchem.pdf, accessed on 25 July 2002.

54. http://www.vx.com/customer_spotlight/index.cfm?LangID=US, accessed on 25 July 2002.

55. "When It's Hot, It Sizzles," *Automatic ID News* 12 (September 1996): 18, 41.

56. John Schriefer, "Automated Coil Handling to Improve Efficiency and Quality," *Iron Age New Steel* 11 (August 1995): 60–62.

57. Guy Castleberry, "AGVs Critical to Development of Factories of the Future," *Robotics World* 10 (September, 1992): 10, 12.

58. "Paperless ERP System Overcomes Language Barriers and Enhances Data Collection and Communication," *Modern Machine Shop*, June 2002, 138–141.

59. Kermit Whitfield, "Saleen's Mass Customization Approach," *Automotive Design & Production*, January 2002, 52–54.

60. "Freddie Aims to Allow 'Mass Customization' of Home Loan Products," *National Mortgage News*, 15 April 2002, 7.

61. Peter A. Buxbaum, "Honeywell Unit Looks to Transform Itself through Partner Relations," *searchEBusiness.com*, 29 October 2001, accessed at http://searchebusiness.techtarget.com/originalContent/0,289142,sid19_gci778356,00.html on 23 July 2002. "Garrett Engine Boosting Systems," http://www.egarrett.com/index.jsp, accessed on 23 July 2002.

62. Scott Woolley, "Double Click for Resin," *Forbes*, 10 March 1997, 132–134.

63. "NPC Expands Warehouse," *Official Board Markets*, 20 April 2002, 33.

64. Bridget Mccrea, "Partners Going Forward," *Industrial Distribution*, March 2002, F7–F10.

65. SAP, "SAP Enables Porsche Dealers to Reduce Inventory and Meet Real-Time Demand for Parts," accessed at http://www.sap.com/solutions/industry/automotive/news/index.asp?pressid=981 on 2 August 2002.

66. David Maloney, "Crossdoc-King," *Modern Materials Handling*, January 2002, 23–27.

67. Joseph Weber, "Just Get It to the Stores on Time," *Business Week*, 6 March 1995, 66–67.

68. Tom Andel, "Load Plans Make Room for Profit," *Transportation and Distribution*, March 1996, 58–62.

69. Joshua Macht, "Delivering the Goods," *Inc. Technology*, No. 4 (1996): 34–41.

70. Ibid.

71. http://www.peoplesoft.com/corp/en/ent_strat/articles/daimlerchrysler.asp, accessed on 1 August 2002.

72. Holly Sraeel, "Fleet Capital Tackles Complex General Ledger Reporting Requirements," *Bank Systems and Technology*, September 1996, 61.

73. Linda Perri, "Barrie Pace Instant Accounting," *Apparel Industry Magazine*, September 1996, 124–128.

74. Elisabeth J. Umble and M. Michael Umble, "Avoiding ERP Implementation Failure," *Industrial Management*, January/February 2002, 4, 5, 26–33.

75. http://www.i2.com/web505/media/3A53A0D0-BA98-4F80-B0F76E4F0123F6B3.pdf, accessed on 22 September 2002.

76. http://www.i2.com/web505/media/D8610BF3-D7F1-432D-B9AA6EFBC8727186.pdf, accessed on 22 September 2002.

77. Tom Yeager, "The Future of Application Integration," *InfoWorld Online*, 25 February 2002, 1, 42–43.

78. HP, "Steelcase Embraces Web Services with Solutions from HP," accessed at http://www.hp.com/large/success_stories/pdfs/SteelcaseE.pdf on 31 July 2002.

79. Cape Clear and Insync Information Services, "Application Integration with Web Services: 'Partner-in-Action' Case Study," accessed at http://www.capeclear.com/customers/Case-IMP_Inc.pdf on 1 August 2002.

80. Miles Cook, *Why Companies Flunk Supply Chain 101*. Boston, MA: Bain & Company, accessed at http://www.bain.com/bainweb/pdf/hottopics/82-1.pdf on 1 August 2002.

81. Queenie Ng, "Supplier Collaboration: Still a Long Way to Go," *Asia Computer Weekly*, 29 July 2002, 1.

82. Ben Worthen, "Drilling for Every Drop of Value," *CIO*, 1 June 2002, 68–73.

8

Management Support and Coordination Systems

LEARNING OBJECTIVES

After completing Chapter 8, you will be able to:

- Describe the processes that organizations use to build business intelligence.
- Identify and describe three component practices of knowledge management.
- Explain the importance of institutional memory and describe the tools that support its development.
- List three types of management reports and describe the information they provide.
- Describe alternative schedules for producing reports.
- Discuss the components and uses of a decision support system.
- Identify and describe seven analytical tools often found in decision support systems.
- Compare and contrast OLAP and spreadsheet software.
- Explain how decision support systems can support group decision making.
- Identify the elements and major uses of groupware.
- Describe the typical features and uses of an executive information system.

Business Intelligence at Ace Hardware

Mike Cripe used to set prices at his three Ace Hardware stores near Chicago by drawing on his considerable experience and intuition. He sold wheelbarrows, for instance, at $80 apiece, more than a 100 percent markup over their $39 wholesale cost. Recently, Ace's corporate headquarters started issuing pricing recommendations to store owners. Among these recommendations was a suggestion to drop the price of wheelbarrows to $50. In the four months after the launch of the new pricing plan, Cripe sold eight wheelbarrows, compared with two in the preceding 12 months. "I made as much in four months on them as I did in a year before," Cripe marvels.

What was the key to this insight? Ace Hardware uses computer systems to analyze price and sales data from its own stores and from competitors. The goal: Calculate prices that will keep customers coming into Ace outlets and buying everything from hammers to light bulbs, while maximizing profits for the owners of local stores. For Cripe, the result has been better margins—up to 39 percent, from 32 percent. "With the data we're collecting, we can go back to the stores and say: 'Here's the money you're leaving on the table,'" says Mark Cothron, information technology manager at Ace headquarters in Oak Brook, Illinois.[1]

Managers, such as Mike Cripe, use information to make decisions. Managers who function in a global economy face complex, unpredictable events and problems that call for an effective managerial response. They must first diagnose and then process the information required to deal with these situations. Computer information systems can help them make smart decisions.

The functional and cross-functional transaction processing systems you learned about in Chapter 7 generate and gather a tremendous amount of data about the functioning of a company. In this chapter, we explore how managers use this information, along with information about competitors and the environment affecting their businesses, to form plans and strategies about future operations and solve short-term problems. We start with business and competitive intelligence, which focuses on deciding what information is important and how to obtain and retain it. We then examine decision support systems, which allow managers to analyze their data. Recognizing that decision making is not a solitary activity, that it often require consensus, and that it requires cooperation to be carried out properly, we next review coordination and group support systems. Finally, we look at executive information systems, systems that support the roles of executives at the highest level of an organization.

CREATING AND USING BUSINESS INTELLIGENCE

Business Intelligence (BI) is a combination of processes and tools for increasing a business's competitive advantage by using data intelligently to make better, faster decisions. In this section, we focus on the creation and use of business intelligence. We first examine the processes that managers need to establish for business intelligence to succeed. We then focus on two of the key processes—knowledge management and competitive intelligence. Finally, we explore how managers typically use business intelligence.

Processes for Building Business Intelligence

In order to use information intelligently, business managers first need to create a BI plan (see Figure 8-1). This plan establishes BI as a goal, identifies the components that need to be in place, creates a budget for software, hardware, and training that might be needed, and identifies metrics for measuring the success of the program. Implementing the plan will require several processes. Many of these fall under the concept of knowledge management. They include identifying what information is important for decision making, promoting a culture of information and knowledge sharing, designing and implementing systems to automate the retention of important information, and designing and implementing systems to simplify access to information by those who need it. In addition to knowledge management practices, BI requires the identification and collection of important competitive information.

Knowledge Management

Many executives would argue that their organizations' most important assets are their people. Of course, they don't literally mean their bodies—the bodies can be easily replaced. It's the knowledge and know-how that these employees and other organizational members possess that's so valuable. What if that knowledge could be bottled, stored away, and retrieved whenever needed or useful? Such an ability, which is the objective of the practice known as **knowledge management (KM)**, would be invaluable to any organization.

Knowledge management consists of practices for knowledge acquisition and creation, institutional memory, and knowledge retrieval and transfer. As illustrated in Figure 8-2, it

FIGURE   8-1

Processes for building
business intelligence.

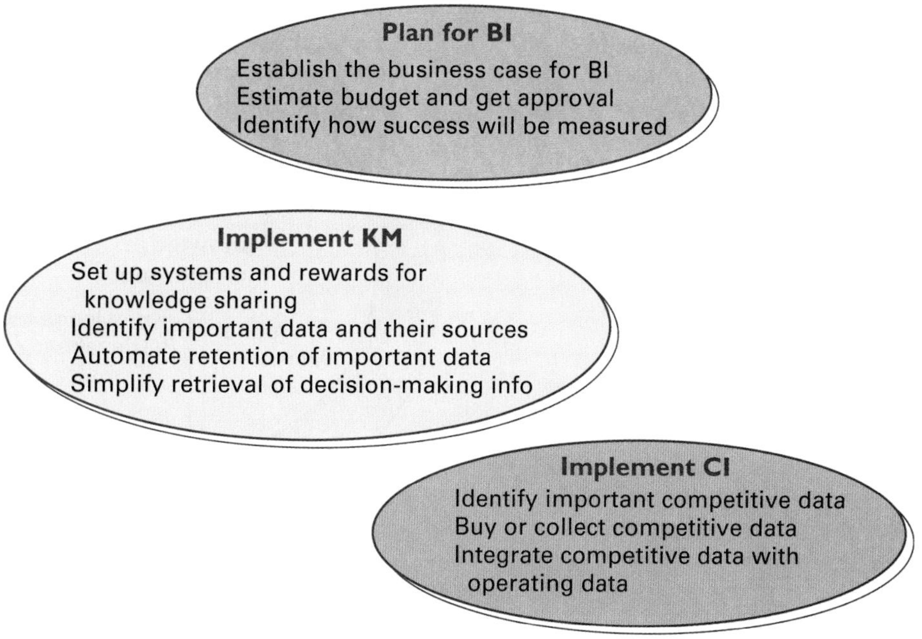

Plan for BI
Establish the business case for BI
Estimate budget and get approval
Identify how success will be measured

Implement KM
Set up systems and rewards for
   knowledge sharing
Identify important data and their sources
Automate retention of important data
Simplify retrieval of decision-making info

Implement CI
Identify important competitive data
Buy or collect competitive data
Integrate competitive data with
   operating data

requires a culture, environment, and reward structure that promotes knowledge sharing. The outcomes of knowledge management are improved decision making and organizational learning.

You may recall from Chapter 1 that knowledge is an understanding, or model, about people, objects, or events, derived from information about them. Organizations acquire data and turn that data into information rather easily. But how can an organization acquire knowledge? What does it mean for an organization to have knowledge? It doesn't seem possible for an organization to understand anything. But, of course, an organization may behave as if it understands. What we mean by an organization having knowledge is that it can provide its members whatever resources they need to understand the data that the organization collects and the information it provides so as to act knowledgeably on them.

Knowledge Acquisition and Creation

How does an organization acquire or create knowledge? It must first make sure that it acquires the appropriate data upon which the knowledge is based. Normally information systems are good at collecting transactional data. Other data, such as someone's intention or promise to buy a product or what type of products someone likes, reside in employees' heads and are harder to collect. A great deal of data lies hidden inside documents, not readily convertible into information for general use. Form-based documents can be scanned to extract important information. Chase Manhattan Mortgage, one of the largest mortgage originators and servicers in the United States, scans more than 2.5 million documents per month to extract data from standard mortgage documents into a more useful form.[2]

Organizations can use products called text mining or document mining software to extract information from other documents, such as letters, e-mail, reports, and news stories. At its simplest level, text-mining tools index documents for words or phrases that are relevant to the organization or its work. At a higher level, these tools can extract meaning from documents using artificial intelligence (see Chapter 3). In particular, sentences and paragraphs containing certain words or phrases, such as "purchased," can be analyzed for related information, such as what was purchased, from whom, by whom, when, and for how much. In addition, themes based on the repeated use of particular sets of words are

FIGURE   8-2

Knowledge manage-
ment consists of prac-
tices for knowledge
acquisition and creation,
institutional memory,
and knowledge retrieval
and transfer in an envi-
ronment that promotes
knowledge sharing. Its
outcomes are better
decision making and
organizational learning.

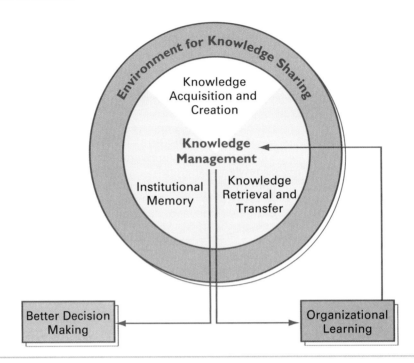

relatively easy to identify. For example, if a document contained words such as "brake,"
"steering wheel," and "bumper," the software might assume that it's about an automobile.
This makes text mining particularly useful if the knowledge acquisition is well focused.
The Centers for Disease Control and Prevention (CDC), located in Atlanta, used text mining effectively to gather data about the implementation of HIV-related biomedical intervention trials and vaccine efficacy trials.[3]

Extracting unwritten information from employees is much harder. Imagine that an auto
mechanic has just solved a particularly difficult problem regarding an intermittent failure in
the electrical system of a car. What process did he use to diagnose the cause of the failure
when others had been unsuccessful? If others are to learn from his success, he will need to
document his thinking process, the steps he took, and the decisions he made along the way.
For knowledge management to succeed in this environment, the employee will need to be
trained how to enter this information into a computer system and will need to be rewarded
for doing so. The repair shop will have to decide that the employee's time used to update the
repair process database is worth more than his time on the floor repairing cars.

Customer service is one function for which it is often easy to make the business case
for knowledge management. Boeing Commercial Airplanes in Seattle provides service
information regarding all aircraft that the company has manufactured, even its 50-year old
DC3s. The company's service engineers found that about half the questions they were
asked had already been answered for another customer, sometimes several times.
Unfortunately, because they answer so many questions about so many different aircraft,
the service engineers usually couldn't remember the answers or, even if they did, could not
be sure that their previous answers had not been outdated by an engineering change or
service memo. As a result, they would have to launch a new search. Boeing calculated that
if it could reduce the number of queries the engineers received by just 2 percent, a knowledge management system would pay for itself in 18 months. Boeing's knowledge acquisition system tracks the searches, screens, and engineering drawings pulled up by service
engineers as they are working, so that very little additional time is required for data entry.

The knowledge management system is made available directly to the company's field service staff, dramatically reducing the load on the service engineers.[4]

Institutional Memory

Institutional memory is the collective shared memory of an organization. Imagine how easy it would be for you to learn if you could just supplement your memory with the memories of all of the students in your class and all students who have taken this course before you. Imagine how productive employees would be if they could augment their memory with the memories of their coworkers, past and present. One of the primary goals of knowledge management is to build such institutional memory. Institutional memory improves employee effectiveness and productivity and creates a climate for organizational learning.

The absence of institutional memory can be a major problem when key employees leave. All of a sudden, people have to reinvent processes and remake contacts that had been second nature to the departed employee. A recent study of 105 company acquisitions found that companies that retained executives with long organizational tenures were four times as likely to be financially successful as those that dismissed such employees in favor of younger managers in the acquired company.[5] College clubs, unions, and other student organizations find the lack of institutional memory particularly troubling, because students have little time to develop expertise before they graduate and little incentive to organize their knowledge for those who follow.[6]

Institutional memory involves more than just collecting and filing information. The information has to be organized in a way that makes it easily retrievable. In addition, the context of the information needs to be addressed. For example, the memories of a prior student might be more harmful than helpful if the course has changed dramatically in the past year. So, to be most effective, institutional memory needs to be dynamic, with recent memories modifying older ones.

Database management systems, especially those designed for text and document management, are popular tools for organizing institutional memory. The Pan American Health Organization (PAHO), which acts as the regional office for the Americas of the United Nation's World Health Organization, uses such a tool to provide what it calls, "The PAHO Institutional Memory Database." The database, accessible to employees and the public over the Web, contains over 30,000 bibliographic items, 4,000 in full text, which document and present the organization's intellectual production since its inception in 1902.[7]

Many companies use content management software (see Chapter 4) to organize institutional memory. Sandia National Labs, which designs all non-nuclear components for United States' nuclear weapons, is using content management software to index, organize, and make available on its intranet videotaped conversations with many of its retired and soon-to-be-retired engineers. Sandia has been creating these video clips for several years knowing that many of the weapons systems that the designers created will need to be serviced long after the designers have retired.[8]

Knowledge Retrieval and Transfer

Knowledge transfer occurs informally through social interaction.[9] Employees learn from others by watching them work. Mentoring, a common practice in many organizations, is aimed at transferring knowledge in this way. However, the informal transfer of knowledge is less useful when employees with information needs are physically far from or out of normal contact with employees who might have solutions. Informal knowledge transfer is also less useful in cases where specialized knowledge is required, because it is often hard to find the people who have the specific knowledge needed. In these cases knowledge management can help.

Many organizations use intranet Web portals, Web sites that offer a broad array of content and services to its visitors, to disseminate information and knowledge to their members. Typically, a company will include on its portal material such as human resource information, commonly used forms, calendars of events, phone directories, and any other material that employees are likely to find useful. The idea is to have one place where employees can find any information that they need. Once employees get used to using the portal, it's likely that they will return frequently. Portals designed for knowledge dissemination are organized so that employees are able to navigate to the information they need quickly. In addition, they have search engines that allow employees to find information even if they don't know how the information is organized. IBM uses an intranet portal called w3, which the company believes offers a tremendous potential for increasing productivity. The portal allows IBM employees to access everything from one site.[10] Procter & Gamble's intranet site, available to about 18,000 employees, is designed to encourage greater collaboration and innovation.[11]

Competitive Intelligence

Competitive intelligence (CI) is the collection, management, and use of information about competitive organizations. It is particularly important for advertising, pricing, product design, and other marketing activities. However, it can be used in all areas of business to secure a competitive advantage and to keep others from obtaining such an advantage. Direct advantages can be achieved in areas of purchasing, logistics, and customer service. Even internal processes, such as manufacturing, materials handling, and warehousing, can be improved by looking at the best practices of other companies.

Sources of competitive intelligence include:

- Competitors' Web sites
- Legal documents
- Newswire, magazine, and journal articles
- Patent and trademark filings
- Trade organizations
- Benchmarking companies

A great deal of competitive intelligence can be purchased from market research companies. Approximately 15,000 supermarkets, 14,000 drugstores, and 3,000 mass merchandise stores in the United States provide weekly data from their checkout scans to Chicago-based Information Resources Inc. (IRI). The company processes these data and other data it collects from shoppers to provide reports on over 1.3 million consumer package good items, providing details on such characteristics as dollar sales, distribution channels, promotion, and pricing.[12] Customers of IRI can query these data and obtain reports by product, locale, and store chain, for example.

Using Organizational Knowledge

Organizations' transaction processing systems generate a great deal of data that managers can use in various ways. To address complex, unstructured, or unusual problems, managers may call upon a decision support system (see next section). More typically, managers use information extracted from transactional data for typical day-to-day decisions: What supplier should I order from? What happened to the order of the customer who just called? Should the bank loan money to the customer sitting at my desk? **Management reporting systems (MRSs)** provide the information that managers need to answer questions such as these.

TABLE 8-1		
	Report Types	Detail reports
Characteristics of		Summary reports
management report-		Exception reports
ing system outputs.	**Report Schedules**	Periodic
		Event-initiated
		On-demand

Management reporting systems provide outputs of different types and schedules, as shown in Table 8-1. In most cases, managers access the output of management reporting systems directly on their computer screens; in other cases, reports are centrally prepared and distributed in hard copy to managers according to a distribution list.

Types of Reports

Managers generally use detail reports, summary reports, and exception reports to monitor organizational performance and identify problems. Managers generally access summary reports on a regular basis, detail reports when they need to follow up on particular problems, and exception reports to identify problems.

Detail reports provide managers information useful in overseeing the day-to-day operations of a department or working group. For example, a front-desk manager at a hotel might use a detail report of reservations to resolve conflicts between what the desk clerk sees on his computer screen and the reservation confirmation form brought by a guest. Marketing analysts at Ace Hardware might want detailed information about product sales, as shown in Figure 8-3, so that they can adjust prices, promotions, or the products they carry.

Used primarily by low-level managers, detail reports provide data about individual transactions, such as payments made by customers, parts manufactured, and debits and credits to the general ledger. Detail reports can also offer managers competitive intelligence gathered from outside the organization, such as consumer purchasing power by zip code. Management systems should provide detail reports often enough for managers to readily use the information they contain.

Different detail reports contain information from the same transaction data arranged in different orders or containing different parts of the transaction. For example, one report of customer payment data might show only the customer name and amount of payment, sorted by customer. Another report referencing the same transactions might show the prior balance, the customer code, the amount of payment, the check number (or a cash indicator), and the final balance, sorted by open invoice number.

Summary, or statistical, **reports** show totals, averages, maximums, minimums, or other statistical data aggregated over time, personnel, products, or some other quantity. Each line of a statistical report summarizes large amounts of transaction data that a manager can examine in a detail report. Figure 8-4 illustrates a summary report that Mike Cripe might receive from Ace Hardware. Because data can be aggregated at many levels, each detail report may give rise to several statistical reports. As managers move up the organizational ladder, they deal with reports that have data aggregated to increasing degrees.

FIGURE 8-3		
	Product #	**Description**	**Quantity**

Product #	Description	Quantity
533	6′ fiberglass stepladder	13
625	Stanley box saw	12
699	Stanley tape rule	25
821	Marathon 7.25″ saw blade	8
822	CLC tool holder	5
827	ACE drum liners	34
902	ACE lawn and leaf bags	21
903	Circular mister fan	2

A detail report such as this can show the items sold at Ace Hardware throughout the week.

Summary Operating Statistics
Store #6
Week of 3/15/02

	Your Store	Average, All Stores
Customers	135	165
Customers/Day	27	33
store sales ($)	67,445	83,442
sales/customer	499.59	505.70
sales of specials	10,435	9,015
defective merchandise returns	–	–
incorrect order returns	–	–

Higher level managers may refer to detail reports when summary data fail to help them solve a particular problem. For example, a manager responsible for quality control in a manufacturing process might notice that product defects arise more frequently after replacing a certain part. She may review the detail reports for the previous several months to test that observation. Then, the manager can recommend appropriate corrective actions. Or, a national sales manager noticing an overall sales decline in a particular region may refer to the detail reports of sales of particular items in that region to try to identify more specific causes of the decline.

Exception reports alert managers to potential problems by showing only data that fall outside an accepted or expected range. For example, an accounts receivable exception report at Ace Hardware might show only seriously overdue accounts or accounts with outstanding payments later than usual based on an account history. A manufacturing exception report might cite all parts whose rate of defects exceeds company standards or the historical rate of defects for those parts.

Exception reports show data at either a transaction or summary level. Unlike transaction and summary reports, they don't show all data. As a result, they allow managers to quickly target problems without wading through a morass of data. Figure 8-5 shows an excerpt from a sales exception report like one that Mike Cripe might receive; it highlights items whose recent sales were less than predicted. Cripe can use this information to refocus the salespeople's efforts in selling the products, alter their prices, or remove them from stock. Ace Hardware's purchasing manager might receive a report that lists suppliers who do not offer discounts for early payment so Ace can attempt to renegotiate contracts with them or replace them with different suppliers.

Sales Exception Report
Month Ending 3/31/02
Store #5

Product #	Description	Code
533	6' fiberglass stepladder	A, M
821	Marathon 7.25" saw	M

Codes:

A: Sales of this item are at least 10% below that of the average store's sales as adjusted for total sales volume.

M: Sales of this product are at least 5% below that of last month as adjusted for total sales volume.

Notification systems, which occur as the result of a specific event, can replace exception reports in some situations. For example, a notification system might automatically notify Cripe when certain items reach a pre-specified level so he can order more. It might automatically notify sales managers when selling a different but equally good product would better meet specific sales targets. Notifications use alerts instead of reports to highlight exceptions. They reduce the number of reports managers need to review. They also can increase the value of a single report by honing in on particular information, rather than requiring the manager to scan the entire report.[13]

Report Schedules

Most organizations produce a large proportion of their reports on a scheduled basis and distribute them to a predetermined list of recipients. Management reporting systems may also produce reports on demand or generate them in response to specified events. Table 8-2 compares periodic, event-initiated, and on-demand reports.

Management reporting systems produce most **periodic reports** on an occasional basis and deliver them to a specified list of employees. For example, one company produces a report of sales by region every weekend so that all senior managers receive the report on Monday morning prior to their weekly planning meeting. Each day an airline produces a report of reservations by rate class for each flight so that managers can adjust the number of seats open for special fares. Most companies produce financial statements every month or every quarter. What types of reports might Ace generate daily? Weekly? Monthly? Periodic reports should provide information essential for managerial decision making and action without overloading the manager with too much detail.

MRSs may also generate **event-initiated reports** on the occurrence of a specified event, typically either a milestone or an expected problem. For example, a government contractor produces a contract status report each time the contractor completes part of its contract and each time a deadline passes without completion of the contracted work. A catalog company produces a backorder report when a customer orders a product that is out of stock and again when it replenishes the stock. A pre-specified list of recipients generally receives such event-initiated reports.

Management reporting systems provide **on-demand reports** for authorized managers when they request specific information. In most cases, the system already includes programs to generate the reports, and managers can activate them when they want. In some cases, technically skilled managers use a high-level report-generating language to prepare reports in a variety of formats. Mike Cripe might want a one-time report of recent advertising expenditures, employee hires, or customer complaints.

DECISION SUPPORT SYSTEMS (DSS)

Should a newer, more powerful machine replace two older pieces of equipment? Should your company sell directly to the retail market, continue to sell through distributors, or both? Should your company order parts more frequently and in smaller lots? Will lower

TABLE 8-2	Report	Frequency	Delivery	Example
Managers can prepare or request reports on a periodic, event-initiated, or on-demand schedule.	Periodic	Periodically—daily, weekly, monthly	To specified list of people	Financial report
	Event-initiated	After occurrence of specified event	To specified list of people	Contract progress report
	On-demand	Upon manager's request	To requested list of people	New customer report

marketing and sales expenses offset the revenue loss of a price decrease? **Decision support systems (DSS)** help managers make more effective decisions by answering complex questions such as these. For example, South African Petroleum Refineries Ltd., a joint venture of Royal Dutch/Shell and BP located in Durban, South Africa, uses a decision support system to identify the best time for shutting down its process units and to evaluate alternative trading and business opportunities. Such computer systems provide information required for effective planning and organizing.

Middle and upper level managers use DSSs to reach decisions in ambiguous and complex environments. Unlike management reporting systems, which provide managers primarily with current data to use in problem analysis, DSSs offer forecasts of future conditions. They also give managers the ability to analyze alternative decision choices quantitatively. Essentially, they model a complex set of circumstances. The decision maker can manipulate various parameters of the model to assess the impact of diverse conditions.

Decision support systems help managers better use their knowledge and help create new knowledge. They are essential components of a knowledge management system.

The benefits of DSSs include:

- Improved decision making through better understanding of the business
- An increased number of decision alternatives examined
- The ability to implement ad hoc analysis
- Faster response to expected situations
- Improved communication
- More effective teamwork
- Better control
- Time and cost savings

The extent to which DSSs help managers make more effective decisions depends to a large degree on the user's familiarity and expertise with the decision support tool, the user's knowledge about the problem to be solved, and the interaction of the cognitive style of the user with the DSS.[14]

Decision Support Systems Architecture

A full-featured decision support system consists of four major components, as shown in Figure 8-6: (1) a database, (2) a knowledge base, (3) a model base, and (4) a user interface.

A database provides access to internal or external data relevant to the decisions. Data from a database form a baseline that mathematical models use in extrapolating from past to future conditions. The data can help calibrate and validate parameters of models used for forecasting. For example, in evaluating a proposed price cut, the DSS should have the capability of analyzing how past price changes have affected sales

The **knowledge base** provides information about highly complex relationships among data that a database has problems representing. It consists of rules-of-thumb, known as *heuristics,* which define acceptable solutions and methods for evaluating them. For example, in analyzing the impact of a price reduction, the DSS should signal if the forecasted volume of activity exceeds the volume that the projected staff can service. Such signaling would require the DSS to incorporate some rules-of-thumb about an appropriate ratio of staff to sales volume.

A **model base** includes an array of analytical tools for building models of a business's processes and activities. It should also include previously developed models that managers may reuse. For example, a DSS that helps managers of mutual funds decide which stocks

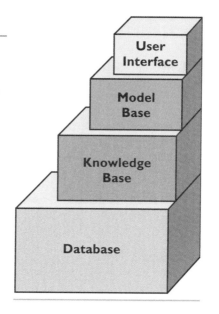

FIGURE   8-6

Decision support systems include a database, knowledge base, model base, and user interface.

to buy would include a variety of mathematical models that analyze various aspects of the potential purchase.

Finally, the DSS must include a sophisticated *user interface,* which allows users to control which data, models, and tools to include in their analyses. The design of user interfaces is an area of expertise that combines information and technology concepts with the rich realms of human factors and psychology.[15] A DSS must be designed to support the greater freedom users experience in manipulating data and processing information. The flexibility of the DSS user interface contrasts with that of transaction processing systems and management reporting systems, where the user is more passive, receiving the data in limited formats or entering data into carefully crafted screens or forms.

A state-of-the-art DSS should ease the assembling of data and knowledge from a variety of sources. It should support their use as inputs to previously developed models or models currently under development. Because DSSs support complex decision making and users typically analyze many alternatives and extensive data about each alternative, a quality DSS should compare, contrast, and aggregate data in a wide range of graphical and tabular formats.

A decision support system should give managers the opportunity to evaluate the impact of alternative decisions, such as whether to locate a new restaurant in a city or suburban location of a large metropolitan area. Because a decision's impact will not be felt for a period of time, a DSS must include an ability to forecast the effect. In addition, the impact of decisions often depends on numerous factors outside the manager's control, such as the general economic conditions, introduction of new technology, or changing customer requirements. A DSS must provide opportunities for managers to vary the assumptions inherent in the forecasting process to account for such factors. For example, buyers at Deere & Co., the Illinois-based manufacturer of farm machinery, when forecasting the prices of Deere's supplies, can enter the impact of expected design changes and can vary materials cost projections and exchange rate fluctuations.[16] Such a DSS can support the manager in comparing, contrasting, summarizing, and evaluating the alternative scenarios that arise from the forecasting effort. Ace Hardware can use a DSS to help it decide whether to offer a new line of gas grills and whether to open another store.

The analytical elements of a DSS vary dramatically among organizations, depending on the industry, the sophistication of the DSS users, and the computing resources available in the organization. A manager should evaluate whether the product meets his specific needs. Table 8-3 lists an array of elements that DSS may incorporate. In this section we discuss the most common tools available in a state-of-the-art DSS: data mining, online analytical processing (OLAP), simulation languages, optimization (goal-seeking) software, statistical packages, geographic systems, and expert systems.

Data Mining

Data mining is the use of software to extract previously unknown, unsuspected, and potentially useful information from data. Imagine entering a large store that stocks all kinds of products, but everything is so disorganized that you aren't able to find what you need quickly enough. Companies that have large amounts of data can suffer from the same problem.

TABLE 8-3 A DSS can incorporate numerous tools, some specific to an industry or job function.	• Simulation languages	• Forecasting models	• Risk assessment and evaluation models
	• Optimization model	• Data mining tools	• Stochastic modeling support
	• Statistical software	• Graphical analysis tools	• Multicriteria decision models
	• Geographic systems	• Word-processing integration	• Capital finance models
	• Expert system shells	• Markov process models	• Pert/CPM and other project management models
	• Accounting modeling support	• Decision tree models	• Conjoint analysis

Data mining helps organize information by analyzing huge quantities of data and looking for patterns, trends, associations, irregularities, exceptions, and changes in data that are too complicated for normal human detection. Data mining uses a variety of tools, such as artificial intelligence and statistical and visualization tools, to analyze the data in a database or a data warehouse. The discovery that Mike Cripe was charging too much for his wheelbarrows was probably made by data mining software combing through the millions of transactions and thousands of prices for each of Ace Hardware's products and stores.

The First Bank of Puerto Rico uses data mining software to identify cross-selling opportunities and potential problems with its customers. For example, the bank's data mining software identified a group of doctors whose bank balances were steadily declining, indicating that, although they had been customers for 20 years, they were likely to defect to another bank. A call to the group indicated that a change in the bank's policy in accepting certain types of checks caused the problem. The bank quickly changed the policy. The bank's vice president of customer relationship and quality, Maria Christina Oruna, estimates that use of data mining software along with timely customer service follow-up will increase the bank's profit by about $1.4 million annually.[17]

Knowledge workers in the health-care industry also use data mining effectively. Florida Hospital in Orlando uses data mining to identify the best practices for the treatment of different diseases. Workers there learned, for example, that the amount of time that elapses between when a pneumonia patient is admitted and when medication is administered affects the speed of recovery. They also found that patients in a certain areas of the city were admitted with the same strain of pneumonia and that other areas of the city generated specific gastrointestinal diagnoses.[18]

Online Analytical Processing (OLAP)

Online analytical processing (OLAP) software allows users to analyze multi-dimensional data easily and quickly. Imagine that a marketing analyst is given an hour to analyze the impact of a recent price increase that applied to 40 of her company's 150 products. She decides to compare this year's sales with last year's sales for products whose prices have increased and for products whose prices have remained the same. On the fly, she creates a grouping for products whose prices have changed and one for those whose prices have remained constant; she then simply calculates the ratio of this year's to last year's total sales for each group. Using OLAP, creating each group is simple, because the groups can be defined by the value of an attribute of a data element—the date of last price change. Once the group is created, data, such as sales dollars, are automatically aggregated. So, calculating the ratio of this year's to last year's sales for the group is as simple as calculating it for any individual product. Other elements of the database, such as returns or unit sales, can be analyzed just as easily. It is also easy to break down the results by sales channel, region of the country, sales person, or any other dimension on which the data has been aggregated.

OLAP software, like spreadsheets, presents data in row-column or graphical format. It differs from spreadsheets in that it excels at grouping and ungrouping data. Any type of analysis that can be applied to a single data item can be applied to a group. Characteristics of the data on which groups can be created, such as sales channel or geographic region, are called *dimensions.* A spreadsheet has only two dimensions: rows and columns. An OLAP "data cube," as it is called, has multiple dimensions, often hundreds. Usually an OLAP analyst views the data in only two dimensions, selecting which appear as rows and which appear as columns. The other dimensions are aggregated, or collapsed. The user can also easily sample from among the collapsed dimensions. The analyst who examined the impact of the price increases probably started with two columns, one for each year, and two rows, one for each group of products. She probably displayed sales dollars in each cell. These sales dollars represent the total for the group over the year. However, she could have restricted the amount shown to sales in the Northeast region at department stores only. Or, she could have restricted the products analyzed to a particular type of product, for more comparable results. The process of slicing and dicing the data in this manner is typical in an OLAP analysis.

Figure 8-7 shows an example of a screen from an OLAP application. The data cube for this example was built on data from the National Center on Health Statistics regarding the demographics of new mothers. The data shows a graphical display of average birthrate along the dimensions "years of education" and "age of mother at birth." But it's easy to change the display to show the data by race rather than years of education, or to slice the data currently shown so that it appears for a selected race, as you can see by examining the choices above the display.

OLAP products differ in their target audience and their structure. They were originally targeted at users of specific application products. In particular, vendors of financial and marketing applications offered OLAP as an optional feature for users who wanted to perform analyses on the data collected by the application rather than simply rely on the fixed reports that the software generated. While such products remain popular, other companies have targeted an audience that would like to analyze data from any source or database. These vendors offer stand-alone OLAP products.

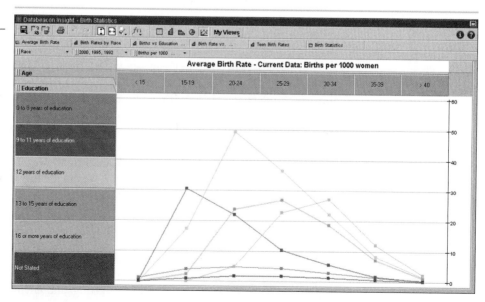

FIGURE 8-7

Databeacon's OLAP product displays demographics of mothers based on data from the National Center on Health Statistics.

SOURCE: accessed at http://www.storydata.com /rele/user53/storydata/index .html?cube=mothersday.html, on 30 October, 2002. Used with permission.

The major structural difference among OLAP products is how they interface with the sources of data. Relational OLAP (ROLAP) processes data directly from a relational database. Other OLAP products extract data from relational or other databases into a form that is more suitable for aggregation and analytical processing. The major advantage of the ROLAP design is that data are available to be used immediately, without the need to first construct a data cube. This one-step processing is attractive to managers, who can use any or all of the data in a data warehouse, for example, to feed their analyses. The disadvantage of ROLAP is that processing, particularly of large data sets, can be very slow. For this reason, ROLAP products have never captured a large share of the OLAP market. To make it easier for managers to deal with non-ROLAP products, most organizations automate the creation of an OLAP data cube and populate the cube overnight with data drawn from their databases or data warehouses. This approach generally limits the types of analyses that can be done because it's impossible to anticipate all the dimensions and breakpoints in these dimensions that are most appropriate for every type of analysis. For example, in Figure 8-7, if an analyst wanted different groupings of the mothers' birth rates or years of education, it would not be possible with a predefined cube.

The major applications of OLAP remain in marketing and finance. Businesses collect a tremendous amount of information from their point of sales systems about the types of products purchased as well as customer information, particularly when credit cards or loyalty cards are used. In some industries, particularly pharmaceutical and grocery, market and competitive data can easily be purchased and merged with internal data. OLAP products help managers sift through these large databases to answer questions such as whether new products are achieving their desired penetration, whether or not advertising and discounts are effective, and what stores and sales people are underachieving or overachieving. OLAP tools can also be used to analyze clickstream logs to determine the effectiveness of an organization's Web site design. OLAP is particularly good for financial consolidation and financial analysis. The ability to aggregate accounts, time periods, and business units or to drill down to provide detail at any level to examine the cause of unexpected results helps analysts make financial decisions and impose financial control.

The Oregon Department of Education uses OLAP tools to analyze financial data for its 16 K-12 school districts. Its 220 MB OLAP cube draws from a 900 MB database, updated with more than 5 million rows of new data each year. Since implementing the database and OLAP product, the state has been able to re-deploy much of its staff to more productive activities. "Instead of tabulating data, our staff can better analyze it," says associate superintendent Nancy Heiligman. The department is now better able to analyze financial data and quality metrics to drive school improvement and accountability. It is also able to close its books six months earlier than it could previously.[19]

Philadelphia-based Pep Boys, an automobile parts and service chain with 6,500 service bays and 629 stores, uses OLAP extensively to analyze products, budgets, store performance, employee productivity and retention, inventory, sales trends, and many other business processes. Roughly 1,000 users query one or more of the company's 20 data cubes at the rate of about 10,000 queries per day. Greg Russ, the company's director of service operations, says that "rather than spending time trying to figure out which store we need to focus on, we can identify strong and weak areas right away. If a store that typically performs 50 alignments in a week has sold only 7, we can identify the issue behind the decline and address it immediately."[20]

Geographic Information Systems (GIS)

Certain decisions require the ability to examine and manipulate geographical information, such as that represented by maps, telephone directories, and other locators. Industries such as public utilities, transportation, retail marketing, and environmental management are driving a dramatic increase in the use of geographic information systems, which can improve customer service and cut costs.

A **geographic information system (GIS)** is software that simplifies the analysis and visualization of information about entities whose physical location is important. GIS combines digital mapping with databases to allow graphical representations, sophisticated access and storage of geographical data, and analytical tools that address location and distance. Most high-quality GISs can manage geographic information, do geographic analyses, and provide geographic and mapping capabilities for custom applications.

Western Exterminator, a pest control company based in Irvine, California, uses a GIS to help manage its 650 employees and 33 service centers. Before the company acquired its GIS tool, managers spent a great deal of energy updating maps and related documents whenever they needed to open a new service area. Now, the company's customers and service areas can be managed with the help of its GIS (see Figure 8-8). According to Mike Lawton, vice president of sales and marketing, it takes 80 percent less time to create a new service center, the work can be done by one person instead of several, and mistakes have been virtually eliminated, saving the company thousands of dollars. The company also uses the GIS to identify new service opportunities and to segment its market based on demographics.[21]

In addition to managers, knowledge workers, particularly in scientific areas, use GIS extensively. Research Systems International, a subsidiary of Kodak, for example, has created the RiverTools GIS to visualize and analyze watersheds and river networks. The software helps scientists and engineers measure channel lengths and elevation drops, delineate catchment boundaries, and calculate basin and subbasin parameters.[22] Such tools are important for such tasks as evaluating the environmental impact of new development or tracing the source of pollution.

Many organizations, particularly government agencies, use GIS to communicate better with their customers. Figure 8-9 shows an example of a map showing traffic volume created with a GIS by the Washington State Department of Transportation. The map, updated once every minute, 24 hours a day, 365 days a year, is available to commuters over the Web to help them plan their commutes in the Puget Sound area.[23]

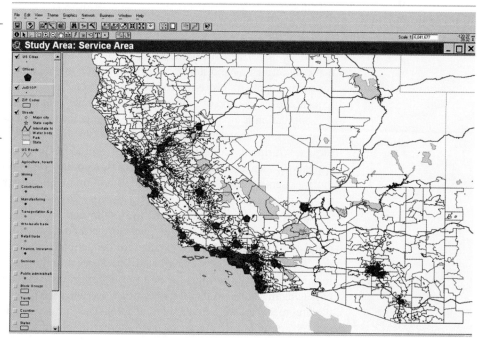

FIGURE   8-8

This screen shot from Western Exterminator's GIS plots out its pest control customers. Large blue dots show Western Exterminator's service center locations.

Source: accessed at http://www.esri.com/news /arcnews/winter0102articles /winter0102gifs/p27p2-lg.gif, on 15 July 2002. Used with permission.

FIGURE   8-9

Washington State's Web-based GIS provides a traffic map for commuters in the Puget Sound area.

SOURCE: accessed at http://www.wsdot.wa.gov /PugetSoundTraffic/, on 15 July 2002. Used with permission.

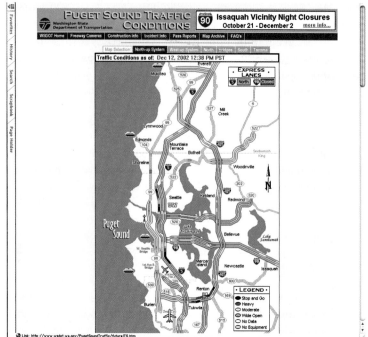

Simulation

Simulation refers to representing real processes with analytic models. Organizations can save money and time, reduce injury, and increase quality by simulating changes to their processes and product designs before trying them in the real world.

Most DSSs provide several computer languages and environments to assist in the development of simulations. Spreadsheet software, the most common tool for simulation, provides a simple one-, two-, or occasionally multi-dimensional way of interrelating data using formulas. Most simulation languages, including spreadsheets, offer a way to represent random occurrences in nature or business, such as unexpected changes in the Gross National Product, the rate of inflation, or unemployment rate. Some simulation languages, such as SIMSCRIPT and GPSS, are particularly well suited to performing random processes many times and automatically calculating and storing statistical information about the outcomes. Such languages effectively represent processes that perform operations in sequence or in a variety of sequences over a period of time, such as occur on the floor of a manufacturing shop.

Simulation is a particularly useful technique for product design, making it easier for engineers to estimate the cost and quality of alternative plans and manufacturing techniques. Whirlpool, for example, uses simulation to design the molds for parts used in its appliances, such as refrigerators.[24] Nissan uses simulation to position robots on its automotive assembly line.[25] ABC-NACO, a $97 million manufacturer of advanced products for the rail industry, uses simulation for the design of casts for its steel parts.[26]

Many companies use simulation to simplify and improve their logistics. Elkes Biscuits, a Uttoxeter, England-based subsidiary of Northern Foods employing over 1,400 people, used simulation to design a conveyer system for its manufacturing facility. The conveyors transport tote boxes with partially completed packages through eight manufacturing lines. The simulation helped determine the best throughput rate for the conveyors, load systems, and packaging machines, so that the totes never overfilled the packing machine buffers and the packing machines were never short of totes. This simulation, like many others, produced graphic output to help managers judge alternative solutions visually (see Figure 8-10).[27]

FIGURE 8-10

Simulation output helps managers visualize alternative designs. Here, different color tote boxes go to different manufacturing lines.

SOURCE: Logistics Simulation, accessed at http://www.logsim .co.uk/cs_elkp2.htm, on 16 July 2002. Used with permission.

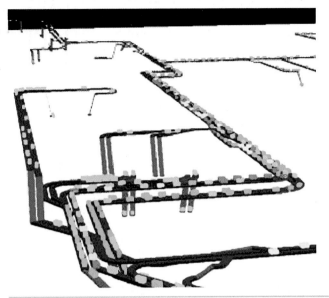

Simulation is heavily used for training. Airline pilots, for example, train in simulators to expose themselves in a risk-free environment to all types of situations that they might encounter in flight. Managers use simulation for similar reasons. Lufthansa, a German airline, uses its General Airline Management Simulation to train its managers by exposing them to different business processes and alternative scenarios.[28] Although simulation is not directly used for decision support in training applications, it ultimately helps managers make decisions by honing their decision-making capability in a risk-free environment.

Optimization

Simulation models excel in analyzing the impact of a few decision choices. When the number of choices becomes large or infinite, **optimization** (goal-seeking) **software** can quickly narrow the best choices to one or a few. Optimization software requires that the user specify in advance criteria (e.g., cost, speed, or revenue) for evaluating the outcomes of different decisions. The major drawback of optimization as an analysis tool is that it's often difficult or impossible to represent the goal or goals of a decision by a formula.

Because different types of problems require different optimization techniques, most optimization software supports a variety of techniques, including linear programming, integer programming, goal programming, quadratic programming, and unconstrained optimization. Model builders trained in optimization, and some managers, know which tools to use for which types of problems. After the models are built, untrained managers can use the tools repetitively to solve problems and make decisions. For example, airline schedulers use optimization techniques to allocate aircraft and crews to published schedules at the lowest cost, taking account of the capacity required, flight rules for pilots and cabin crews, and aircraft maintenance requirements.

Fairchild Semiconductor, a $1.5 billion manufacturer of high technology electronic components, uses optimization software to help fine-tune its pricing. Fairchild's model calculates the price for each product so as to maximize profit. The model reflects how consumers respond to changes in price given such factors as the price and substitutability of competitive products and external market conditions. The ability to include such factors in calculating the optimal price can increase profit margins from 3 to 5 percent, resulting in profit increases of 25 to 100 percent in tight-margin industries.[29]

Virginia-based Columbia Gas Transmission Company operates 12,750 miles of pipeline, 130 compressor stations, and 3,500 natural gas storage wells to deliver 1.3 trillion cubic feet of gas per year to 72 local distribution companies and several hundred end-users of gas in 11 Northeastern, Midwestern and Mid-Atlantic states.[30] The company uses optimization software to minimize the amount of fuel used in its pumping and compressor stations. The software accounts for compressor status and performance limits, maximum and minimum pressure and flow limits, and gas delivery demands. The company estimates that the optimization software saves it about $6 million per year in fuel costs.[31]

Statistical Inference

Statistical packages assist managers in drawing inferences about the relationships among data elements. Building effective models calls for developing such relationships and having confidence that they reflect underlying processes rather than random occurrences. For example, suppose that an 8 percent increase in sales historically accompanied every 10 percent decrease in price. But, this relationship was not perfect. Sometimes sales increased by a larger amount and sometimes by a smaller amount given the same price change, reflecting differences in economic conditions, type of product, or time of year. Statistical packages would determine the degree of confidence a manager can have in the 10/8 formula and its likelihood of applying to future price cuts or increases.

Statistical inference along with data mining allows analysts to construct sophisticated models of human behavior that are frequently important in pricing and other marketing activities. For example, the Bank of Montreal analyzed its 8 terabyte database to build a predictive scoring model that ranks customers based on profitability, identifies their likely preference for certain financial products, and estimates their likelihood of switching banks. The bank's marketing department can use this information to address its customers' needs before the competition can woo them away, and can also identify good potential customers based on demographics.[32]

Expert Systems (ES)

Expert systems (ES), a type of artificial intelligence (see Chapter 3), capture and apply the collective wisdom of experts in a particular field to help make decisions. Ace Hardware might use an expert system, for example, to assist with pricing, staffing, advertising, or expansion decisions. Escobois, one of France's largest lumber producers, uses an expert system to get the greatest yield of high-quality lumber and the lowest waste from crooked, fast-growing trees that grow in the Aquitaine region of France.[33] Expert systems add power to DSSs by improving analyses when data are unreliable, contradictory, or of limited validity.[34]

An expert system often takes many years to develop and fine tune. As a result and also because it tends to address a single problem rather than being a multi-purpose tool, an expert system is more likely to be a stand-alone system rather than a component of a DSS. Many companies, however, include both tools for ES development and ES models in their DSS architectures.

An ES consists of four components, as shown in Figure 8-11: (1) a knowledge base, (2) an inference engine, (3) an explanation module, and (4) a user interface. Each expert system has a unique knowledge base; the other parts of the ES function in any expert system and are sold off-the-shelf as **expert systems shell** software.

A *knowledge base* consists of specific facts, rules-of-thumb, examples, and relationships that an expert knows and might use to solve problems in a particular area or domain. Expert systems software can treat facts and rules as the same or as different types of information. When they are treated alike, the software simply views rules and/or relationships as one of sev-

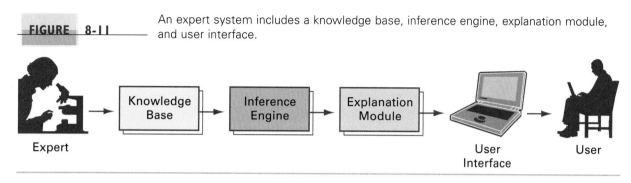

FIGURE 8-11 — An expert system includes a knowledge base, inference engine, explanation module, and user interface.

eral types of facts and makes no distinction between the fact and rule parts of the knowledge base. Expert systems that treat facts and rules differently draw their facts from databases whose information may change continuously. The rules they use, however, are placed in a special **rule base** by the expert systems developer, who changes them rarely. An expert system commissioned by the Mekong Secretariat (Southeast Asia) for assessing the environmental impact of various projects on the Lower Mekong River Basin used a rule base of over 1,000 rules.[35]

The **inference engine** applies the knowledge base to a particular problem. For example, suppose the knowledge base states the following: A and B are brothers; C is A's daughter; and a niece is defined as the daughter of one's brother or sister. If a user asks the ES to identify B's nieces, the inference engine applies the rules and data to determine that C is B's niece. The **explanation module** then tells the user how the inference engine applied the rules and facts to reach its conclusion. In this case it would say that C is B's niece because C is the daughter of B's brother A.

Inference engines work not only upon known facts but also upon suspected facts, or facts that are probably true. Most inference engines can understand and process facts expressed in terms of likelihood—in terms of probability or in ordinal terms—just as human experts would. For example, if a medical ES knows that John is 70 years old and that older people are likely to suffer from heart disease, its inference engine will conclude that John likely suffers from heart disease as it performs its other diagnoses.

The user interface acquires and modifies the rules and knowledge in the knowledge base, accepts a description of the user's problem, asks the user for additional information if necessary or desirable to address the problem, and presents its conclusions, recommendations, and explanations in an understandable fashion. Expert systems software user interfaces can be textual or graphic, depending on the nature of the problems to be solved. Figure 8-12 illustrates the presentation of the explanation module for the Lower Mekong River Basin environmental impact ES mentioned above.

GROUPWARE

Groupware, also known as **computer-supported cooperative work (CSCW)** and **group support systems (GSS)** is software that provides an electronic mechanism for enhancing communication among group members and hence for improving group coordination, discussions, problem solving, and meetings. Groupware supports the group activities of managers and other workers. Because managers participate in groups both as supervisors and as members working on common tasks, groupware assists them in exchanging information, coordinating activities, and managing workflow. Table 8-4 illustrates how groupware reduces the impact of separation among group members in time and space.

Nabisco, an $8.27 billion manufacturer of biscuits, snacks, and other premium foods, uses Microsoft Exchange Server, a groupware product, to enable the collaboration of its prod-

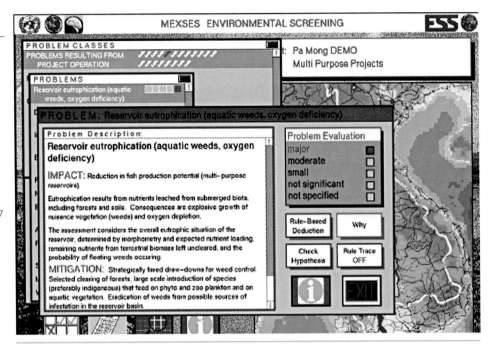

FIGURE   8-12

The expert systems user interface provides access to the explanation module, as shown here, and can also be used to add rules or obtain facts about the problem to be solved.
SOURCE: Accessed at Environmental Software and Services, GmbH, http://www.ess.co.at/EIA/mx7.html, on 16 July 2002. Used with permission.

uct design and launch teams. Project managers can track issues, assemble virtual teams, and manage project timetables. They can create group calendars for their work teams and use a feature called "public folders" to maintain shared contact and task lists. The team members, crossing multiple departments and located in different offices, can work together efficiently, and can access all group information on the Web when they are away from their offices.[36]

In global organizations, groupware can reduce the costs of assembling team members from around the world into a single meeting room by simulating such a meeting electronically. Advertising agency Grey Worldwide uses videoconferencing to assemble creative teams in the company's Hong Kong, Beijing, and Shanghai offices. The teams review advertising storyboards in real time. Videoconferencing makes it easier for the participants to share ideas visually and assess the reactions of other team members.[37] Groupware also helps managers and other group members resolve problems and answer questions as they occur, rather than waiting to convene a meeting.

Elements of Groupware

Groupware technologies include message systems, multi-user editors, computer conferencing, coordination systems, and group decision support systems. Many companies choose to run their groupware applications over their corporate intranet.

TABLE 8-4

Groupware helps eliminate the barriers of time and space among group members, establishing means of communication and coordination.

		Time	
		Same Time	Different Time
Place	Same Place	Electronic meeting rooms GDSS	Data management Message systems
	Different Place	Message systems Computer conferencing	Message systems Workflow systems

Message Systems

Electronic mail and lists, bulletin boards, instant messaging, and polling systems enhance group work through improved communication. **Electronic mail** allows members of an organization to send messages to people inside and outside the organization. Electronic messages are sent to recipients' e-mail addresses, where they are held until the recipient decides to read them. Managers and employees may send text or multimedia information to specific users whose electronic addresses they know. Electronic mail systems allow users to keep an address book and to group addresses into a mailing list, so that a message can be sent to all members of the list.

Electronic lists allow people interested in a particular topic to share electronic mail. When people subscribe to a list, they receive any mail sent to the list. Depending on the nature of the list server, they may set parameters, such as whether to make their e-mail address available to other list members or whether to receive messages as they are sent to the list or to receive one message per day that includes all the messages received that day. Electronic lists may be unmonitored or monitored, in which case a censor must approve messages before they are acknowledged by the list.

Electronic bulletin boards resemble electronic lists except messages they receive are simply stored, never mailed. People interested in the bulletin board's topics may read the messages once they subscribe. Messages are organized in what's known as a **threaded discussion.** A threaded discussion organizes messages by topic, subtopic, sub-subtopic, etc. Often, a message will be considered a topic, and all responses to that message will be organized within it as subtopics. Responses to responses will be sub-subtopics.

Instant messaging (IM) allows you to create and maintain a list of friends or contacts known as "buddies." When you use IM, you are notified if any of your buddies is connected to the Internet or an organizational intranet. You can then send messages to them and they can send messages to you. When either party sends a message, a small window opens up on yours and your buddy's systems, where you can type in messages that both of you can see. If you'd like, you can create a chat room, which allows several buddies to join in an IM conversation.

Electronic polling assists groups in making decisions. It encourages groups to express their preferences frequently by creating a "vote early, vote often" mentality. One company that was experiencing a major budget shortfall used electronic voting to decide whether to make cuts across divisions or to eliminate a single, ineffective division. Electronic voting allowed the decision makers to make the best choice—to eliminate the division, a choice they had been unable to make because they feared offending the division's head.[38]

Multi-User Editors

Groupware technology includes software that allows multiple users to access and modify a common document. Each user can view a copy of a master document on the screen. As each user edits this copy, the computer program alters the master copy to reflect the changes made by group members. Users can either see others' changes as they work on their own changes or after they've saved their copy. **Multi-user editors** generally allow asynchronous editing, providing access controls to limit who can change which parts of a document and allowing updates to be combined and synchronized at a later time. Groups whose members maintain different portions of documentation can benefit greatly from multi-user editing.

Computer Conferencing

Telecommunication technology has created four ways to hold conferences: real-time conferencing, teleconferencing, desktop conferencing, and Webcasting.

Real-time conferencing allows people at the same or different locations to hold meetings electronically. Using networked computers, the participants type their contributions into their computers. The text of their speech appears simultaneously on all of the conferenced computers. Protocols exist to allow participants to interrupt and take the floor as with normal meetings.

Teleconferencing, which includes audio and video conferencing, allows people in different locations to hold a conference as if they were in one room. It overcomes the slow speed of typing versus talking and the absence of video to capture body language, which limit the effectiveness of real-time computer conferencing. It requires special rooms to hold the hardware necessary to capture and forward the video and voice, as well as technical operators to work the equipment effectively.

Desktop conferencing offers a compromise between real-time computer conferencing and teleconferencing. Sophisticated workstations that include a video camera connected over a network or high-capacity conference line can transmit text, graphics, voice, and video. Participants see others in windows of their computer and hear them in voice output played through the computer. However, it works best for fewer than four people. As the quality of video and voice improve, the benefits of desktop conferencing match those of teleconferencing. It costs more than real-time computer conferencing, but less than teleconferencing.

Deutsche Bank has rolled out desktop conferencing equipment and software to 2,000 of its employees. The system has cut the bank's travel expenses in half. Senior managers, in particular, like the system because it helps them manage direct reports in different locations around the world. For example, Paul Spillane, managing director and global head of relationship management, notes, "it's much easier to use this (video technology) to talk to one of my people than to pick up the phone, because I can look him in the eye, and they can know whether I'm in a good mood or a bad mood, and I can get a sense of who they are and what they're thinking about."[39]

Webcasting is a cost-effective way to reach a large number of people if two-way interaction is not needed. A Webcast transmits live or recorded audio or video so that recipients can receive it using a Web browser. Companies can use Webcasting to make a slide presentation, a class discussion, or a videotape of a meeting available to members of the company who were not able to attend in person.

Coordination Systems

Coordination systems improve project management by providing managers with information required to coordinate the scheduling of project activities and team member participation. Coordination systems assist with all phases of project management.

In the planning stage, project management software can determine the order of tasks, estimate their time to completion, and identify the most time-constrained tasks. It can schedule employees efficiently so that they work on the most appropriate tasks and have a reasonable workload. Coordination systems can also evaluate trade-offs in labor overtime and cost. The group features of project management software particularly aid planning when the project spans diverse departments. Although functional managers can plan independently, the groupware features of project management software help them to identify and resolve potential conflicts in interdepartmental interactions, such as the timing of tasks or the use of labor resources. During project performance, project management software can compare actual to planned performance.

Coordination systems also support the creation and manipulation of joint calendars and schedules. For example, Allegheny College administrators and department managers use calendaring groupware called WebEvent to schedule classrooms, laboratories, and even equipment, such as laptops and digital cameras. The Inter-Lakes public school district, serving Meredith, Center Harbor, and Sandwich, New Hampshire, uses the software to avoid conflicts in scheduling events and activities at its three schools. In addition to providing internal coordination, the district's use of this software allows parents and the community to easily find scheduled events online.[40]

Using DSS for Group Decision Making

The increasing use of teams in the workplace has prompted the need for decision support systems to support cooperative decision making. **Group decision support systems (GDSS)** address any or all of the following aspects of joint decision making: idea generation, alternative analysis, alternative evaluation, and consensus building.[41] Companies use GDSSs for tasks such as long-term planning, setting standards, redesigning processes, and setting budget priorities.

In addition to the elements found in a standard DSS, GDSSs include analytical and operational tools to improve group decision-making processes. For example, polling software allows group members to vote on alternatives, with or without anonymity. Other software implements a variety of brainstorming techniques, guiding group members to react in various ways to the ideas of other group members. GDSSs often include software to help group members identify areas of agreement and areas of disagreement. They may include software to help elicit and explain the underlying reasoning and preferences of group members as they search for common ground when making difficult decisions.

Many GDSSs require **electronic meeting rooms.** Participants work at their own computers on a U-shaped table facing a common computer at the front of the room, which can be seen by all participants, as shown in Figure 8-13. Any participant can control the common computer. Alternatively, the computer can merely assimilate the entries of the participants onto a single, large screen. This approach allows participants to contribute anonymously to the problem-solving effort. Such anonymity allows GDSSs to improve conflict management and foster group cohesiveness.[42] Groups focusing on a public screen tend to perceive all ideas as "our" ideas rather than "my" idea or "your" idea. This perspective tends to reduce the emotional ownership of ideas and allows decisions to be made with less conflict.

FIGURE 8-13

Computer conferencing rooms can be set up in a variety of ways, one of which is shown here.
SOURCE: Courtesy of Andrullis Corporation.

Problems in Managing Groupware

Groupware does not solve all group performance problems.

- *Inappropriate information sharing.* Some people will not share information despite the technological capability. The corporate culture may also not support the sharing of information electronically. Alternatively, they can easily share irrelevant or unnecessary information, making it difficult to stay focused. Groupware also encourages socializing, which may interfere with job performance.

- *Information overload.* When faced with a flood of information, managers often cannot differentiate important from unimportant information. Workgroup editors that screen, edit, and consolidate messages, especially with electronic lists, offer one solution to the overload problem.

- *Too many or inappropriate meetings.* Groupware may increase the number of meetings because it reduces the time needed to arrange them. Online meetings do not work for all types of communication. Managers need to diagnose when face-to-face contact benefits team members. They need to diagnose both the information required and the best context for delivery.

EXECUTIVE INFORMATION SYSTEMS (EIS)

Executives require somewhat different information from middle and lower-level managers. Generally, they need information at a more summary level. They also tend to focus more on external factors, such as the financial markets, the satisfaction of customers, the public's perception of their company, and the competitive environment. Executives also use information differently. They are constantly interrupted and on the run. Therefore, they need to be able to access information quickly. Their focus is usually broader. They need to rapidly switch attention among different geographical regions, operating functions, and even different business units. They must have access to information across the entire enterprise, yet the information they need to address any type of issue must be easy to find. Finally, executives generally prefer to spend less time at their desks and more in personal conversation. Therefore, when they do settle down to do any type of analysis, it must be quick and easy.

Executive information systems (EISs), also called **executive support systems (ESS)**, resemble decision support systems, but respond to the particular requirements of top-level managers. Unlike DSSs, which deal with specific problems, EISs are characterized by enterprise-wide and external data. They focus less on modeling and more on assembling and displaying data, recognizing trends, determining underlying causes, and communicating knowledge.

Executives use an EIS to answer specific questions or monitor performance, which requires greater efficiency in looking at information. Some executives scan information in an EIS without specific questions in mind. For them, an EIS helps broaden their outlook, challenge their assumptions, and provide greater insight into their businesses.[43]

Most EISs include mainly hard information, such as financial data, sales, shipments, and other historical information. Increasingly, they include soft data, such as predictions, opinions, explanations, and forecasts. Table 8-5 compares these two types of information.

External pressures, such as the increasingly competitive and dynamic environment, and internal pressures, such as a need for timely information, improved communication, and access to data, lead to the development of an EIS. Usually an organization's chief executive officer or president sponsors development of an EIS, but over time its use spreads to

	Information Characteristics	Hard Information	Soft Information
Usefulness	Perceived accuracy	High	Questionable
	Perceived value	Low	High
	Interpretation	Generally accepted	Individually assessed
	Richness	Low	High
	Application	Operational	Strategic
Source	Org. context	Generally internal	Often external
	Ownership	Generally available	Often tightly held
	Communication channel	Formal	Informal
Time frame	Timeliness	Historical	Current/Future
	Lifetime	Long	Short
Accessibility	Frequency	Regular	Ad hoc
	Existence known	Generally so	Generally not
Format	Computerized	Often yes	Generally no
	Standardization	High	Low

TABLE 8-5

Executive information systems can include both hard and soft information.

lower-level employees as subordinates become aware that they can access unique information available to the organizational leaders.[44]

Typical Features of an Executive Information System

Because most executives use executive information systems without the benefit of technical intermediaries, EISs must have a friendly user interface. In addition, an EIS must provide access to company data, electronic mail, external databases and news, work processing, spreadsheets, and automated filing.

User Interface

Many executives cannot type well and so dislike using a keyboard to request information. An EIS generally includes a graphical user interface to limit keyboard use. Most systems present numeric data in a variety of tabular and graphical formats. The user can select among the formats with a mouse or touch screen. The systems use color and graphics consistently to cue the user to the information. For example, red might highlight any number outside an expected range, and blinking red might highlight an item that requires immediate attention. Often the screen shows the name and telephone numbers of those individuals responsible for acting on the data presented on the screen.

Most EISs also provide a drill down capability. They first present data at their most aggregated levels. The executive can then select a line and request the detail behind it. The executive can drill down through greater and greater levels of detail or return to higher levels of aggregation as desired. Recent studies, however, show that executives tend not to use the drill down features of their EIS. Instead, they use the EIS to identify issues and then directly contact the people most involved or affected to discuss alternatives or solutions.[45]

Communication with Employees

Most EISs contain a variety of groupware features, including calendaring systems, electronic mail, and electronic bulletin boards. Well-designed EISs directly link many of these features into the information displays. When an executive identifies a problem or issue that needs to be further explored, clicking on the display should provide an opportunity to send mail to the managers responsible for the data, check their calendars to identify potential times to meet on the issue, and access any electronic discussions on the relevant topic.

News Updates

Although executives read newspapers and magazines widely to learn about events that might have an impact on their organization's operations, searching through news sources for relevant articles is time consuming and relatively unproductive. Many organizations now purchase news services that scan the media for relevant items. In their EISs, executives specify the types of articles and subjects that they find relevant. The EIS links to the news service and provides abstracts of articles meeting the executive's criteria. An executive can obtain the full article by clicking on the abstract. Many systems allow the executive to rate each article as to its relevance. The EIS uses this feedback to be more accurate in selecting future articles.

Query Features

EIS systems can pass through to OLAP and database products to give the computer-savvy executive the option of performing more detailed analyses. Most EISs also provide common canned queries from the EIS menu system.

Functional Support

Increasingly EISs support functional applications. For example, they may provide software that addresses corporate functions, such as sales, budgeting, and marketing. They may also include software that supports the needs of vertical industries, such as financial services, insurance, or retailing.[46]

Development and Implementation of Executive Information Systems

The development of executive information systems was popular in the early 1990s, but has fallen somewhat out of favor as Web-based corporate intranets became increasingly available. Executives are used to searching the Web in their personal lives and seem increasingly able to use corporate intranet portals to get the information they need. In addition, executive information systems have been expensive to develop because they need to be designed to reflect the interests and preferences of a particular executive. When changes occur in executive ranks, the systems serving the old executive usually become worthless. The high cost and short life of executive information systems has made their development difficult to justify.

An alternative to developing executive information systems from scratch is to use a commercial package designed to interface with a corporate intranet and OLAP cube. Figure 8-14 illustrates the ExecDash product from iDashes. Developers can customize the product's dashboards to display any measure accessible from the company's intranet. Upon clicking on any of the graphics, the executive may select from options such as drill down, show trends, and identify data owner and date updated. Many commercial products, such as this one, are configured so that their output is available on the Web to authorized users, enabling their data to be accessed any time anywhere.

The business case for executive information systems depends on the executive's information needs and operating style. As executives rarely understand the value of an EIS, information systems professionals must usually diagnose the need and analyze alternatives. Then, specific designs can be prototyped so that the executive can make an informed decision about whether or not to approve implementation.

SUMMARY

Business intelligence increases a business's competitive advantage by using data intelligently to make better and faster decisions. To build business intelligence, companies must create a

Commercial products, such as this one from iDashes.net, ease the development of an EIS. The dashboards of this product can be easily modified to show any company metric, and trends and drilldowns are available by clicking on any of the graphics.

SOURCE: iDashes demonstration of Exec Dash™ at http://www.idashes.net. Copyright © 2002 iDashes, Inc. Used with permission.

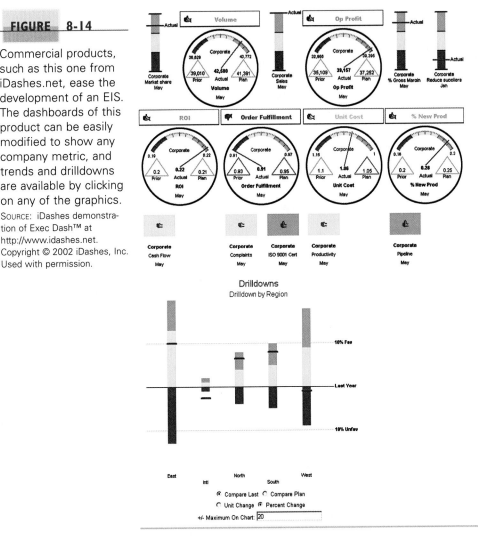

BI plan and implement knowledge management and competitive intelligence. Knowledge management requires the acquisition of knowledge, institutional memory, and knowledge retrieval and transfer. It results in better decision making and organizational learning.

Management reporting systems (MRS) make use of business intelligence to address day-to-day operational problems. They provide detail, summary, and exception reports that are produced periodically, are initiated by a particular event, or are published on demand. MRSs in many organizations comprise the reporting components of a transaction processing system.

Decision support systems (DSS) help create knowledge using a database, knowledge base, model base, and user interface. DSSs can answer unforeseen questions by supporting ad hoc queries and providing analytical abilities. A DSS usually obtains its database from an organization's transaction processing system. The analytical elements of a DSS can include data mining, OLAP, geographic information systems, software for simulation, optimization, and statistical inference as well as expert systems.

Groupware, computer-supported cooperative work, or group support systems support a group's interaction in performing a task or reaching a goal. Groupware can include group decision support systems, message systems, multi-user editors, computer conferencing, and coordination systems. Organizations can face challenges with appropriate information sharing and with scheduling of meetings in managing groupware.

Executive information systems (EISs) address the unique information needs of executives and the different ways that they work. The typical EIS includes a user-friendly interface, facilities for communicating with employees, and options for scanning news updates. EISs have fallen out of favor because of their high costs and the increasing ease of executives with the Web; however, new commercial products have decreased the cost of developing an EIS.

KEY TERMS

business intelligence (BI)
competitive intelligence (CI)
computer-supported cooperative work (CSCW)
data mining
decision support system (DSS)
desktop conferencing
detail report
electronic bulletin board
electronic list
electronic mail
electronic meeting room
event-initiated report
exception report
executive information system (EIS)

executive support system (ESS)
expert systems
expert systems shell
explanation module
geographic information system (GIS)
group decision support system (GDSS)
group support system (GSS)
groupware
inference engine
instant messaging (IM)
institutional memory
knowledge base
knowledge management (KM)
management reporting system (MRS)
model base

multi-user editor
on-demand report
online analytical processing (OLAP)
optimization software
periodic report
real-time conferencing
rule base
simulation
summary report
teleconferencing
threaded discussion
videoconferencing
Webcasting

REVIEW QUESTIONS

1. What is business intelligence?
2. How does knowledge management contribute to business intelligence?
3. What is competitive intelligence, and how do companies use it?
4. What is a management reporting system?
5. How do detail, summary, and exception reports differ?
6. How do periodic, event-initiated, and on-demand reports differ?
7. What is the relationship between an MRS and a transaction processing system?
8. What are the benefits of a decision support system?
9. What are the components of a DSS?
10. How does a DSS answer unforeseen and ad hoc questions?
11. What types of analytical capabilities do DSSs provide?
12. What is the purpose of data mining?
13. How does OLAP software differ from spreadsheet software?
14. Why do companies use geographic information systems?
15. What are some applications of simulation? Why might simulation tools be included in a DSS?
16. How does an expert system work?
17. What are the major elements of groupware?

18. What are the advantages and disadvantages of group decision support systems?
19. What three ways can managers hold conferences electronically?
20. How do executive information systems differ from decision support systems?
21. What are the typical features of an EIS?

MINICASE

EIS AND OLAP AT WEGMANS

Danny Wegman has rearranged his office furniture and installed a big screen TV. The president of Wegmans, which operates 59 Wegmans Food Markets and 17 Chase Pitkin Home Centers in New York, Pennsylvania, and New Jersey, isn't getting ready for a Buffalo Bills season still four months away. No, his concerns are more businesslike. Wegman wants to view his company's month-end numbers with his management team assembled, and leafing through printed reports just won't cut it anymore.

"They all pivot their chairs to the screen, pass a mouse around a table and query the 'Essbase [OLAP] cube' online," Wegmans financial systems business manager Paul Wawrzyniak said, referring to the data mart that now holds a copy of all the information in the company's general ledger. "'How is produce doing compared to last month?' They call it up and mull it over. And there's not a piece of paper on that desk."

Analyzing Wegmans month-end results is a very different process from what it was just seven months ago. "We cut a full week out of the time it takes to get month-end numbers into the hands of executives," Wawrzyniak said. "Last year, they'd get paper reports a week after the fact. We had over 2,000 spreadsheets for financial reporting. Now, everyone who can benefit from that information is viewing it via the Web. We don't want people poring over paper reports. We want them to look at quick screens and make informed decisions."

Wegmans decision makers are not accessing canned electronic reports online, either. Rather, they are actively querying the data mart. "The screens are generated dynamically from the data as users query the Essbase cube. The screen layouts are intuitive, so people don't have a terribly difficult time getting the hang of this."

The reliability of the information on which executives base their decisions is just as important as the speed with which they access it. "Our people can have faith in the information they're working with because it comes from the general ledger, not from different transactional systems," Wawrzyniak said. "They're on the same page."

The information, however, does begin with Wegmans' transactional systems. Wegmans runs numerous Lawson financial applications in addition to the general ledger, as well as homegrown applications and systems from other vendors. Data makes its way from those systems to the general ledger and then on to the Hyperion Essbase data mart.

Power to the people: Just six months after the data mart went live, as may as 360 individuals accessed it on a daily basis. Unlike retail companies that give number-crunching financial analysts the first crack at querying a new data warehouse, Wegmans followed a much more democratic strategy. Executives, such as Danny Wegman and his father, company chairman Robert Wegman, are accessing the data mart, as are a raft of store managers, merchandising directors, and store operations personnel.

"Eventually, 1,800 people will access the database on a daily basis," Wawrzyniak said, adding that Wegmans soon hopes to flow general ledger information into the data mart weekly—a move that would give decision makers the power to be much more proactive.

Financial analysts, though not the primary user base of the data mart, are making much better use of their time now that the Essbase cube is up and running. The system, according to Wawrzyniak, has significantly altered the way Wegmans' 15 financial analysts interact with store managers. "Say produce sales are down 3 percent for a store in a given month," he said. "Store managers used to rack their brains trying to figure out why that happened. Now, a store manager can compare the performance of his produce department to the produce departments of all Wegmans stores. The power of the Essbase cube is that the information from all the stores is rolled up into the database."

Before Wegmans began pumping all its monthly figures into the data mart, store managers would call on 15 financial analysts at corporate to make sense of troublesome results. "You want to know what the financial analysts used to do?" Wawrzyniak said. "Basically, they crunched the numbers and sent out a lot of paper reports. Then, they'd wait for the phones to ring. Store managers and regional managers would call in saying, 'What does this mean?' or 'How can we get back on track?'

"Now that all the figures are available online, the analysts can spend their time out in the stores going over results with store managers in person," he continued. "We want the financial analysts in the field where they can do the most good."

There are many questions, however, that the store managers can answer on their own, thanks to some behind-the-scenes work on the part of Wawrzyniak and his staff. "We took a look at all the Daner reports we used to send out to store managers and turned them into graphic on-screen presentations," he said. "Store managers can look at figures on year-to-year variations on actuals and budgets via a PC and a browser. And the drill-around capabilities of the system have reduced the time spent asking questions and getting answers."

Source: Excerpted with permission from Matt Nannery, "Wegmans Informed Decisions," *Chain Store Age*, May 2000, 258–260.

Case Questions

Diagnosis

1. What are the information needs of Danny Wegman's executive team?
2. What are the information needs of his financial analysts?
3. What are the information needs of his store managers?

Evaluation

4. Before the use of executive information systems and OLAP at Wegmans, what problems existed in meeting the needs of Wegmans' managers and analysts?

Design

5. How does OLAP address the deficiencies of the previous information systems?
6. What features of executive information systems are embedded in the software that Wegmans' managers and analysts use?
7. How do the systems assure that all managers are working from the same data? Why is this important?

Implementation

8. What do you think accounts for the widespread use at Wegmans of the systems described in this case?
9. How do the systems described in this case promote business intelligence at Wegmans?
10. Currently, Wegmans' data mart and OLAP tool seem to be loaded only with financial data. What do you think are the problems and benefits of adding operational and competitive data? Do you think it would be wise for Wegmans add these data in the future?

8-1 FINE JEWELRY AT HAMPSTEAD DEPARTMENT STORES

Step 1: Read the following scenario.

Carl Elkins manages the fine jewelry division of Hampstead Department Stores, a major retail chain of 19 stores in the southwestern United States. Unlike managers in other departments at Hampstead, Carl manages all employees who work in the fine jewelry departments in all of the chain's stores, a total of 3 buyers, 5 assistant buyers, and 70 salespeople across the country. Carl has bottom-line responsibility for the fine jewelry division. He needs to have a good understanding of the sales in his departments so that he can stock and staff them appropriately.

Step 2: Individually or in small groups, as directed by your instructor, design a set of reports that provide the information Carl needs to run the fine jewelry division. Your design should indicate what information each column of the report includes, what totals (if any) should appear, and on what schedule the report should be produced.

Step 3: Exchange your report designs with another student or group. Compare the designs you received with your own designs. Then answer the following questions:

1. How many reports are necessary to give Carl the information he needs?
2. Are detail, summary, or exception reports most useful for providing this information?
3. What reporting schedule is best for providing this information?
4. Would a decision support system be more appropriate than a management reporting system for providing the required information?

8-2 L&A SCALE COMPANY

L&A Scale Company manufactures digital industrial scales. The company has expanded greatly in its 20 years, going from a job shop of 5 employees with sales of $500,000 to a bona fide manufacturer with 100 employees and $30 million in annual sales.

Donald Jenner, the president, has installed an array of computer systems over the years. They mainly support the processing of transactions around ordering, shipping, and payroll. The system provides numerous management reports, but Jenner's managers find that they can't easily get answers to questions such as the following: How have customers' buying patterns changed over time? Does offering discounts for early payments successfully reduce accounts receivable? Do piece-rate incentive systems lead to better productivity than paying workers straight salary?

Step 1: Individually or in small groups, as directed by your instructor, write five questions that Jenner probably would want answered.

Step 2: List the characteristics of a decision support system that would answer these questions. Be as specific as possible in identifying the type of information the system should include, the queries it should address, and the screens it should produce.

Step 3: Share your lists with the rest of the class. What types of information can a DSS provide? What costs and benefits would be associated with developing a DSS for Jenner's managers? What issues must Jenner address in integrating a DSS with the rest of the information systems in the company?

ACTIVITY

8-3 THE OFFENSIVE SCREEN

Step 1: Read the following scenario.

Iris Blair is the applications manager at Tolliver Investments, a three-year old broker-age firm. Two nights ago, after most people had left, Iris was in the office of Arthur Amanita and Ronald Conway, two of the most highly respected brokers at Tolliver. Her job was to install a new virus-protection program. She noticed that Art and Ron's 88-meg system cartridges were in their protective cases, properly shelved away from the hardware. Art and Ron were gone for the day. She inserted Art's cartridge and booted the system. The screen lit and, instead of the usual smiling-face start-up screen, the display showed a bikini-clad woman in a provocative pose. After about 15 seconds the screen blinked, then showed the usual desktop. Iris installed the virus-protection software, shut down Art's computer, and repeated the process on one of Ron's computers. The start-up screen was exactly the same as Art's.

SOURCE: Excerpted and adapted with permission from "The New Job," in Ernest A. Kallman and John P. Grillo, *Ethical Decision Making and Information Technology: An Introduction with Cases* (New York: McGraw-Hill, 1993).

Step 2: Individually or in small groups, analyze the situation using the basic ethical criteria.

Step 3: Based on your analysis, develop an action plan for Iris. Share the action plan with the rest of the class. What are the major ethical issues in this situation? How should they be handled?

8-4 DESIGNING AN EXECUTIVE INFORMATION SYSTEM

ACTIVITY

Step 1: Read the following scenario.

John Campbell Brewing has grown from a small microbrewery to a company that produces 15 types of beer and distributes it worldwide. The company has information systems to support its financial management, human resources management, production, and marketing. Most of these systems, however, provide operational information at a fine level of detail. Thomas Patton, its current president, wants to use information systems to help him get the "big picture." He has been reading about executive information systems and believes that an EIS could help him keep better tabs on the business.

Step 2: Individually or in small groups, as directed by your instructor, identify Patton's information needs.

Step 3: List the screens that an executive information system should include to address these needs.

Step 4: Choose one screen and design it, specifying the information it includes, the graphical presentation, and its links to other screens.

Step 5: Share your designs with the entire class. Then discuss the advantages and disadvantages of an executive information system for John Campbell Brewing.

8-5 DECISION MAKING USING GROUPWARE

ACTIVITY

Step 1: Your instructor will organize you into small groups and provide you with a decision problem to solve.

Step 2: Now your instructor will arrange for you to use groupware to solve a similar decision problem.

Step 3: Individually, in small groups, or with the entire class, compare and contrast your experiences. Then answer the following questions:

1. What are the advantages of using groupware for making decisions?

2. What are the drawbacks of using groupware for making decisions?

3. What types of decision making would groupware help?

4. What types of decision making would groupware hinder?

5. How does the groupware product you are using affect your ability to make your views known?

6. How does the groupware product affect your opinion of the views of the other members of the group?

IS ON
THE WEB

IS ON THE WEB

Exercise 1: Locate and visit the Web sites of a company that provides a Web interface to an OLAP tool. At the time of publication, www.storydata.com was one such site. Learn to use the tool and apply it to one or more of the sample data sets provided on the Web site. Then write a one-page analysis comparing the OLAP tool to Microsoft Excel or any other spreadsheet software with which you are familiar. Address differences in both ease of use and functionality.

Exercise 2: Locate and visit the sites of two companies that produce videoconferencing systems. How are their systems similar? How do they differ?

RECOMMENDED READINGS

Conway, Susan, and Char Sligar. *Unlocking Knowledge Assets.* Seattle, WA: Microsoft Press, 2002.

Fayyad, Usama, Georges G. Grinstein, and Andreas Wierse. *Information Visualization in Data Mining and Knowledge Discovery.* San Francisco: Morgan Kaufmann Publishers, 2001.

Kluge, Jurgen, Wolfram Stein, and Thomas Licht. *Knowledge Unplugged: The McKinsey and Company Global Survey on Knowledge Management.* New York: Palgrave Global Publishing, 2001.

Kostner, Jaclyn. *BIONIC eTeamwork.* Chicago: Dearborn Trade, 2001.

Rumizen, Melissie Clemmons. *The Complete Idiot's Guide to Knowledge Management.* Indianapolis: Alpha Books, 2001.

Sterman, John D. *Business Dynamics: Systems Thinking and Modeling for a Complex World with CD-ROM.* Burr Hill, IL: Irwin/McGraw-Hill, 2000.

Thomsen, Erik. *OLAP Solutions: Building Multidimensional Information Systems.* New York: John Wiley & Sons, 2002.

The following periodicals also provide regular features about topics covered in this chapter:

Data Mining and Knowledge Discovery

KMWorld Magazine

NOTES

1. Jim Kerstetter, "Information Is Power," *Business Week,* 24 June 2002, 94–96.

2. Kim Ann Zimmerman, "KM Helps Ease Home Mortgage Marathon," *KMWorld Magazine,* July/August 2002, accessed at http://www.kmworld.com/publications/magazine/index .cfm?action=readarticle&Article_ID=1317 &Publication_ID=74 on 17 July 2002.

3. Megaputer, "TextAnalyst Simplifies Data Analysis at CDC," http://www.megaputer.com /company/cases/cdcp.php3, accessed on 17 July 2002.

4. Pimm Fox, "Making Support Pay," *Computerworld,* 11 March 2002, 28.

5. Donald D. Bergh, "Executive Retention and Acquisition Outcomes: A Test of Opposing Views on the Influence of Organizational Tenure," *Journal of Management* 27, no. 5 (2001): 603–622.

6. Aaron Kass, "Lack of Institutional Memory Dooms Clubs to Repeating Past," *The Hoya*, 13 November 2001, accessed at http://www.thehoya.com/viewpoint/111301/view4.cfm on 18 July 2002. Alan Kalish, "Institutional Memory and Changing Membership: How Can We Learn from What We Don't Recall," *Workplace*, February 1998, accessed at http://www.workplacegsc.com/features1/kalish2.html on 18 July 2002.

7. http://www.paho.org/English/DBI/DBL/IMdatabase.htm, accessed on 18 July 2002.

8. Beth Cox, "Case Study: Bringing Nuclear Science into the Digital Age," *Datamation*, 13 August 2001, accessed at http://itmanagement.earthweb.com/entdev/article/0,,11979_865071,00.html on 18 July 2002.

9. W. Tsai, "Social Capital, Strategic Relatedness and the Formation of Intraorganizational Linkages," *Strategic Management Journal*, 2000, 925–939.

10. "One Access, Many Functions," *Computer Times*, 10 July 2002.

11 Igor Kotylar and Alan M. Saks, "Using Technology for Knowledge and Skill Transfer," *Canadian HR Reporter*, 22 October 2001, G9.

12. http://www.knowledgegroup.com/index.html and http://www.knowledgegroup.com/resources/resources.pli?pageid=methodology, accessed on 18 July 2002.

13. Stewart McKie, "Notification Systems," *DBMS*, February 1997, 55–56, 71.

14. Jane Mackay, Steve Barr, and Marilyn Kletke, "An Empirical Investigation of the Effects of Decision Aids on Problem-Solving Processes," *Decision Sciences* 23 (1992): 648–672.

15. Ben Schneiderman, *Designing the User Interface*, 2d ed. Reading, MA: Addison-Wesley, 1992.

16. Doug Smock, "Deere's New Web System Tracks and Forecasts Product Costs," *Purchasing*, 7 February 2002, 12–13.

17. Peter Fuller and Kenneth Hein, "A Two-Way Conversation," *Brandweek*, 25 February 2002, 20–22, 24–26, 28.

18. Harry R. Kolar, "Caring for Healthcare," *Health Management Technology*, April 2001, 46–47.

19. Microsoft, "Web-Based Solution Enables Better Decision-Making Productivity for the Oregon Department of Education," http://www.microsoft.com/business/casestudies/bi/kpmg_ode.asp, accessed on 15 July 2002.

20. IBM, "Pep Boys Tunes into Its Data, Driving Sharper Decision-Making with DB2," http://www-3.ibm.com/software/success/cssdb.nsf/CS/NAVO-4YM2L9?OpenDocument, accessed on 15 July 2002.

21. ESRI, "Western Exterminator Boosts Business with ArcView Business Analyst: Leading Pest Control Company Redefines Marketing and Sales Efforts with GIS," *ArcNews Online*, winter 2001/2002, accessed at http://www.esri.com/news/arcnews/winter0102articles/leading-pest.html on 15 July 2002.

22. Research Systems International, http://www.rsinc.com/rivertools/, accessed on 15 July 2002.

23. Washington State Department of Transportation, "Puget Sound Traffic Webpage Questions," accessed at http://www.wsdot.wa.gov/PugetSoundTraffic/faq/ on 15 July 2002.

24. Charmaine Jones, "From Simulation to Solution," *Appliance Manufacturer*, June 2001, 46–50.

25. Tristan Honeywill, "Car Sparks," *Professional Engineering*, 13 February 2002, 43–44.

26. "Conference Showcases: Steel Casting Technology," *Foundry Management & Technology*, February 2002, 20–23.

27. Logistics Simulation, http://www.logsim.co.uk/cs_elkes.htm, accessed on 16 July 2002.

28. Lufthansa Consulting, http://www.lhgams.com/, accessed on 16 July 2002.

29. Malcolm Wheatley, "Programmed for Profit," *MSI*, March 2002, 58–66.

30. Columbia Gas Transmission Corp., http://www.columbiagastrans.com/tco_overview.html, accessed on 16 July 2002.

31. Richard Carter, Mary Goodreau, and Henry Rachford, "Optimizing Pipeline Operations through Mathematical Advances," *Pipeline & Gas Journal*, October 2001, 51–53.

32. Jim Middlemiss, "Bank of Montreal Aims to Score with Clients with Data Mining Product," *Bank Systems & Technology*, December 2001, 37, 42.

33. Ted Blackman, "The Mission: Saw Crooked Logs into High-Quality Lumber," *Wood Technology*, March 1999, 34–36, 38.

34. Alfs T. Berztiss, "Software Methodologies for Decision Support," *Information & Management* 18, no. 5 (May, 1990): 221–229.

35. Environmental Software and Services Gmbh, "EIAxpert: Rule-Based Screening-Level EIA,"

http://www.ess.co.at/eia/, accessed on 16 July 2002.

36. Microsoft, "Nabisco Expects 72% IRR from Enhanced Product Development and Sales Collaboration Using Microsoft Exchange 2000 Server," March 23, 2001, accessed at http://www.microsoft.com/business/casestudies/nabisco-exc.asp on 21 July 2002.

37. Yasmin Ghahremani, "Techsavvy E-Business: Not Being There," *Asiaweek*, 23 November 2001, 1.

38. Jay F. Nunamaker, Jr., Robert O. Briggs, Daniel D. Mittleman, Douglas R. Vogel, and Pierre A. Balthazard, "Lessons from a Dozen Years of Group Support Systems Research: A Discussion of Lab and Field Findings," *Journal of Management Information Systems* 13 (winter 1996/1997): 163–207.

39. Robert Sales, "Deutsche Bank Sees Future in Desktop-Video Software," *Wall Street & Technology*, May 2002, 23.

40. http://www.webevent.com/about/quotes.html, accessed on 9 September 2002.

41. Kenneth R. MacCrimmon and Christian Wagner, "The Architecture of an Information System for the Support of Alternative Generation," *Journal of Management Information Systems* 8, no. 3 (1991/1992): 49–67.

42. Laku Chidambaram, Robert P. Bostrom, and Bayard E. Wynne, "A Longitudinal Study of the Impact of Group Decision Support Systems on Group Development," *Journal of Management Information Systems* 7, no. 3 (1991): 7–25.

43. Betty Vandenbosch and Sid L. Huff, "Searching and Scanning: How Executives Obtain Information from Executive Information Systems," *MIS Quarterly* 21, no. 1 (1997): 81–105.

44. Hugh Watson, R. K. Rainer, Jr., and Chang Koh, "Executive Information Systems: A Framework for Development and a Survey of Current Practices," *MIS Quarterly* 15, no. 1 (1991): 13–30. C. Barrow, "Implementing an Executive Information System: Seven Steps for Success," *Journal of Information Systems Management* 7, no. 2 (1990): 41–46.

45. Choton Basu, Sandra Poindexter, Janes Drosen, and Theo Addo, "Diffusion of Executive Information Systems in Organizations and the Shift to Web Technologies," *Industrial Management & Data Systems* 100, no. 6 (2000): 271–276.

46. Eckerson, "Drilling for Data."

Part IV

Managing the Information Resources

Organizations face the ongoing challenge of designing, implementing, and maintaining information systems and delivering IS services effectively. Part IV concludes this text by examining issues associated with systems planning, development, implementation, and delivery. Chapter 9 investigates key system development concepts, including the stages of the systems development life cycle, the development and management of Web sites, and why development projects succeed or fail. Chapter 10 explores ways of structuring and managing the information systems function, as well as managing change in information systems and technology. ■

9

Systems Planning, Development, and Implementation

LEARNING OBJECTIVES

After completing Chapter 9, you will be able to:

- Identify and describe the stages of the systems development life cycle.
- Describe four pathways for the development of new systems, and identify the pros and cons of each.
- Discuss the role of data, process, and object models in the design and development of new systems.
- Explain how CASE tools simplify and support SDLC activities.
- Specify six ways of collecting information for a needs assessment.
- Describe the key elements of interface design, data design, process design, object design, physical design, and test design.
- Specify the key decisions and activities in the development stage of the systems development life cycle.
- Cite the advantages and disadvantages of four implementation strategies.
- Describe how nonWeb applications and Web sites differ in their development and management.
- Describe why systems projects succeed and fail.

Developing a CRM Solution at Royal Bank

As senior manager in client relationship marketing at Royal Bank, one of Canada's largest financial institutions, Cathy Burrows needed to understand the bank's customers, anticipate their needs, and measure their value. The bank had already implemented a large data warehouse that captured millions of daily transaction, maintained a historical record of customer activity, and segmented the bank's clients by profitability. However, the bank had no way to use the collected information to analyze alternative products, services, or processes that the bank might establish to be more responsive to its clients.

Senior managers at the bank understood that they needed to be more responsive to their customers. As Burrows said, "Our clients have told us very clearly that an integrated client relationship strategy is differentiating." So, Burrows set out to implement such a strategy.

Her first step was to identify what systems and data were in place and what additional development was needed. She determined that the bank's systems needed to be focused on customer behavior and perceived needs, able to provide actionable information to support decision making, scalable as the bank evolved and its environment changed, and flexible enough to serve each of the bank's five business units. These business units ranged from personal and commercial banking, to insurance, to wealth management.

The next step was to develop a clear set of specifications and select a vendor to implement them. It was important that the solution would integrate easily with the bank's data warehouse, that it aligned with the bank's overall strategy, and that Burrows have a high degree of confidence in the vendor and the proposed solution.[1]

It appears likely that Cathy Burrows will assume a major role in the design and development of the new systems for Royal Bank. Her situation is not unusual. If you think that you won't need to understand the systems development process because you can always delegate it to your technical staff, you will probably be surprised. Most companies will not undertake a major systems project without the active participation of the business units funding the project. Many companies require a business manager to be the leader or one of the leaders of the project. Functional and general managers should expect to participate in at least one major information systems project every year or two.

KEY SYSTEMS DEVELOPMENT CONCEPTS

Managers involved in developing or updating information systems should understand the systems development life cycle, development pathways, and the importance of systems models and computer-aided design tools. They should also learn to treat systems development as a business process rather than as a series of independent projects.

The Systems Development Life Cycle

The **systems development life cycle (SDLC),** also known as the "software life cycle" or the "application life cycle," refers to stages in the conception, design, creation, and implementation of an information system, as shown in Figure 9-1. Our model of the SDLC consists of the following six stages: **needs assessment, alternative analysis, design, development, implementation,** and **maintenance.**

- *Needs assessment* describes a formal, integrated, and usually time-limited process of gathering data about the needs and opportunities of end users and their managers; evaluating and ranking the importance of these needs; and addressing the possibility that they can't be satisfied by incremental improvement of existing systems.

FIGURE 9-1

The systems development life cycle describes the stages in the conception, development, and maturity of an information system.

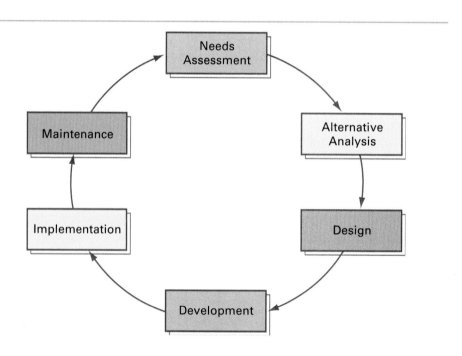

- *Alternative analysis* considers one or more alternate designs and analyzes their advantages and disadvantages. Alternative analysis ends when developers select a preliminary design for further analysis.

- *Design* refers to the creation of detailed specifications for the proposed system. Just as a contractor would not begin to build a house without knowing the size and placement of its rooms and the location of plumbing and electrical fixtures, systems developers need to work to detailed specifications to produce desired results. If the organization plans to contract the development of the system, detailed specifications enable contractors to estimate costs and submit bids.

- *Development* refers to the creation or purchase of the hardware and software necessary to implement the design. It also includes the testing required to ensure that the system meets the design specifications.

- *Implementation* refers to deactivating the old system and activating the new one. Implementation includes converting data from the old to new system, training employees to use the new system, and pilot testing or phasing in the new system.

- *Maintenance* refers to fixing errors, or **bugs,** in the way that the system operates. It also refers to modifying the system to provide new features or improved performance beyond that included in the design and possibly even beyond what was envisioned during needs assessment.

No uniformly accepted model of the SDLC exists. Some models combine development and implementation into a single stage. Others combine needs assessment and analysis into a single stage. Still others offer more detail, dividing each of the stages into several parts. One model, for example, divides design into logical and physical design stages.

The concept of a life cycle implies that companies replace or renew systems as they age. Business managers, such as those at Royal Bank, examine new opportunities, assess information needs, and address weaknesses in existing systems on a regular basis. As maintenance demands become more frequent and difficult to implement, the organization will probably want to undertake a formal needs assessment, starting the cycle anew. Needs assessment and alternative analysis might occur several times before an organization actually decides to move beyond these stages and replace the existing system.

Large systems usually require several years before they reach stability and maturity. During that time the organization may grow or shrink, move into new markets, or acquire new businesses. Technology will also change. Hardware that met initial needs may remain adequate, but failing to incorporate more recent, advanced technology into its systems may leave an organization at a competitive disadvantage. For example, a company that developed its inventory systems before bar-code scanners became widely available would have less information than companies that use more recent technologies. Similarly, systems that incorporate voice-input and multimedia devices will surpass the capabilities of earlier systems that lack these technologies. Software technology also improves and becomes more efficient with time. Systems developers who maintain existing applications must use older, less efficient technology, and cannot modify their applications to meet new demands as rapidly as competitors who use newer technology. These old, hard-to-maintain systems are called **legacy systems.**

The decision to replace rather than modify an old system is difficult. Legacy systems often represent an investment of many years and thousands or millions of dollars. Managers, users, and the information systems staff feel comfortable and secure in using them; they know that despite their limitations, they work. A new system poses potential risks. It should work better than the legacy system it replaces but may fail in unexpected ways. The organization must retrain its systems development staff in the new technologies and train end users in the new system.

Management typically has no reliable way to quantify the benefits of a new system and faces some uncertainty in estimating the system's development costs and time. The typical manager who faces these concerns will often try to keep current systems operating. As maintenance costs mount and competitors' new products display more advanced, sleeker features, managers consider replacing older systems. Sometimes technology changes that make it difficult or impossible to maintain a legacy system will force managers to scrap it before they are ready to do so. More commonly, however, the initiative to replace an old system will originate with business leaders who become frustrated with the inability of existing systems to support their needs.

Systems Development as a Process

Many organizations view each systems development initiative as a project. More sophisticated organizations, however, treat systems development as a process. They recognize that although systems may differ substantially from one another, their development follows a somewhat predictable, well-defined, and manageable path. Such organizations learn from their successes and mistakes. They create workbooks of materials that help managers and developers repeat successful activities and avoid unsuccessful or wasteful ones. They gradually accumulate a set of tools that help institutionalize, automate, and audit the activities associated with systems development. They may measure the success of their systems development initiatives using metrics, such as time to completion, manpower required, and flaws in the finished product, all relative to the number of features in the new system.

Organizations can use commercial process management software to help them standardize and improve their systems development processes. Most process management software products emphasize a particular development methodology. A **methodology** is a prescribed and documented set of practices, tools, documents, reports, and, often, notations. Commercial process management packages provide support for dozens of popular methodologies, such as the Dynamic System Development Method[2] and the Rational Unified Process.[3] Such software typically includes templates to guide developers in the creation of intermediate products, such as designs, specifications, and other end-of-stage outputs associated with the methodology it supports. It might include tutorials to help users apply various software tools associated with their tasks, metrics that managers can use to measure and evaluate performance, and task lists that can be exported into a project management package, such as Microsoft Project.

Southwest Airlines realized many benefits when it abandoned the practice of treating software development efforts as independent projects, each with its own methodology, and standardized on the Rational Unified Process methodology, supported by Rational Software's set of process and software development tools. In comparing projects before, after, and during the transition, Southwest found that projects using the methodology were calmer, the development staff was more focused and knew better what it needed to do, and schedules were more frequently met with not as much slippage. In addition, the best practices of experienced development teams were easy to share and convey to new developers.[4]

Some commercial packages support an organization's development of its own best practices. These products come with customizable process libraries, which often include several of the widely accepted methodologies as starting points.[5] Developers may select a methodology based on factors such as the size of the project, how risky it is, how strategic it is, how soon it needs to be completed, and the extent to which development is likely to be internal or outsourced.

Organizations sometimes assign a **process manager** or **process librarian** to customize templates and tutorials to the organization's standards and collect metrics and best practices for customizing the process library. The process manager may also have training responsibilities and a mandate to educate managers, such as Cathy Burrows, who are newly involved in projects and may not be familiar with the company's systems development methodologies.

Organizations that treat systems development as a process often strive to apply principles of total quality management and process improvement to their methods. The Software Engineering Institute (SEI) has developed and popularized a model called the Capability Maturity Model (see Figure 9-2), which helps these organizations measure how well they achieve these goals and guides them in improving their systems development processes. Many companies use third-party assessors to attest to the quality of their development processes. Generally, firms are pleased to be certified at level 2 out of a possible five; for example, RCG Information Technology, a national leader in IT professional services with 45 of the top 100 Fortune 500 companies among its clients, issued a press release when it received its level 2 certification.[6] According to recent figures, only 42 firms worldwide have achieved the highest rating.[7] New Jersey-based Telecordia Technologies, a worldwide leader in telecommunication, achieved a level 5 certification after a complex review of the software development practices of its 3,500 software engineers in eight company divisions.[8]

Project management software complements process management software with tools that project leaders can use to help manage a complex software development project. Microsoft Project and other such packages help managers assign responsibilities to individuals or groups, identify tasks on the critical path, estimate time to completion, and track the percent completed. When a project falls behind schedule, project management software can notify appropriate managers and help them adjust resources and priorities to get it back on schedule.

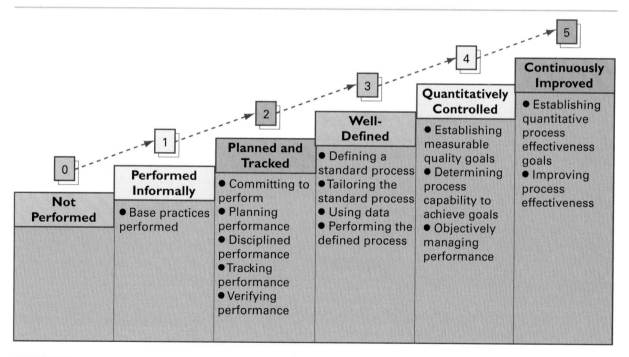

FIGURE 9-2 The Software Engineering Institute's Capability Maturity Model describes an organization's sophistication in regard to the establishment and development of best practices for systems development.

Source: Software Engineering Institute, *A Systems Engineering Capability Maturity Model, Version 1.1, SECMM-95-01, CMU/SEI-95-MM-003* (Pittsburgh, PA: Software Engineering Institute, 1995): 2–28.

Development Pathways

The SDLC might seem to suggest that new systems always progress smoothly and sequentially from one stage to the next. In practice, systems do not always follow this progression. Managers and computer professionals can move through the SDLC by using the waterfall model, the spiral approach, prototyping, or agile programming.

The Waterfall Model

The **waterfall model** follows the SDLC in sequence (see Figure 9-3). Like water flowing over a waterfall, the development moves in only one direction, so stages cannot be repeated. Needs assessment, for example, occurs only once. After completing each stage, the project team creates products and reports that document the results of that stage. Project sponsors approve these outputs, which become input to the next stage of the process. The waterfall approach's linear structure and absence of rework make it relatively easy to manage. The project manager can set deadlines and monitor progress toward those deadlines.

At the same time, the waterfall model is highly inflexible. If, for example, user needs change during the course of the project, no formal mechanism exists for adjusting the development process. If the project manager follows the waterfall model strictly, he saves all proposed changes in a database and examines them at the conclusion of the project to see if another project should be started to meet these needs.

Using the waterfall model also means that no component of the system is delivered until near the end of the project. Often, this delay in delivery leads to tension between users and developers, especially if deadlines slip. Sponsors wonder why they spend millions of dollars yet see no results. The final product may also surprise the sponsors. Despite the mass of documentation accompanying the waterfall model, sponsors rarely understand exactly what they have bought until the product is delivered. At that point, they cannot make changes without major costs and delays.

Despite these disadvantages, Royal Bank will probably use the waterfall model for its CRM system. The system has an enterprise-wide scope with implications for many existing software applications in the company. Royal Bank will want to ensure that the new system meets all users' needs and that the scope of the project doesn't change as development proceeds.

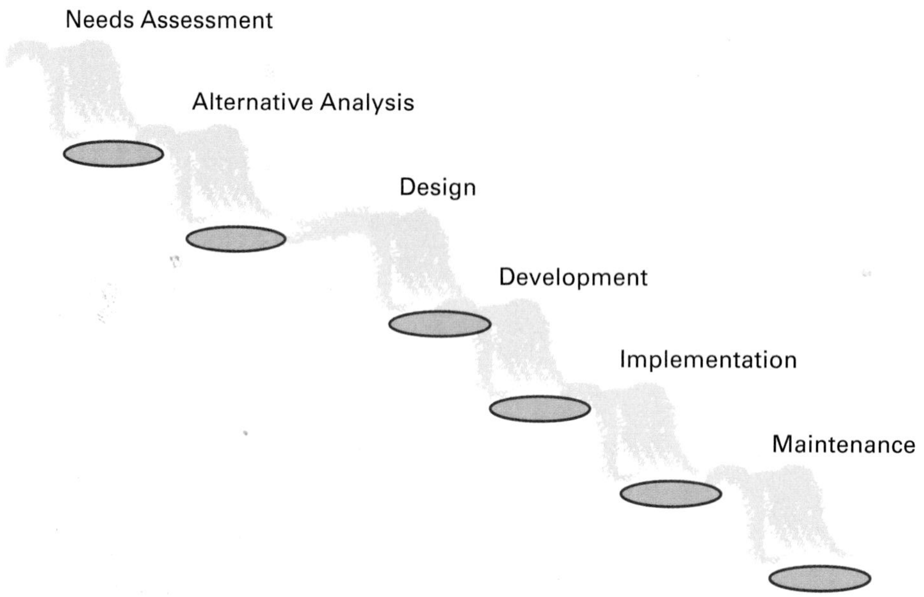

FIGURE 9-3

The waterfall model of systems development demands that stages in the SDLC be performed in sequence, with no possibility of repetition or return to steps already performed. Water does not flow uphill.

Needs Assessment

Alternative Analysis

Design

Development

Implementation

Maintenance

The Spiral Approach

The **spiral approach** implements systems based on the concept of greatest need. As illustrated in Figure 9-4, the spiral approach delivers a system in versions. Each version goes through all the steps of the SDLC except implementation, which may apply to some versions, and maintenance, which applies only to the last version.[9]

The "80/20 rule" drives the spiral approach: 80 percent of users' needs can be met with only 20 percent of the functions they want. Producing a basic system to satisfy 80 percent of needs then becomes simple, if you can believe this rule. The first version attempts to achieve a basic system that will meet most user needs. Adding the "bells and whistles" takes the most time.

Advocates of the spiral approach often use a time-box concept to pace development. A **time box** is a set period, usually three months, within which developers must complete each version. No product specifications exist because meeting such specifications may be impossible within the time allowed. Instead, developers add features in order of priority until time runs out. Then, they release the new version. Caterpillar Financial Services and its contractor ThoughtWorks used a time box approach to develop a financial and credit approval system for dealers of Caterpillar's products, such as tractors and earth moving vehicles. Every three or four months, the contractor delivered parts of the system, such as credit approval, pricing, and documentation. The entire system took three years to develop and cost several million dollars, but users appreciated having whatever features were available as soon as they were available.[10]

An alternative to time boxing involves planning each version as much as possible at the beginning of the project. In effect, this divides the project into smaller subprojects, each more easily managed than the main project and each providing a working product as a deliverable. At the end of each project, the remaining subprojects are redefined considering user feedback.

The spiral approach delivers the product rapidly. No laborious documentation of specifications occurs because users can revise the product with later versions. Users can see

FIGURE   9-4

The spiral model of systems development creates new systems in versions, with the most important needs being addressed first. Each subsequent version goes through many of the SDLC stages.

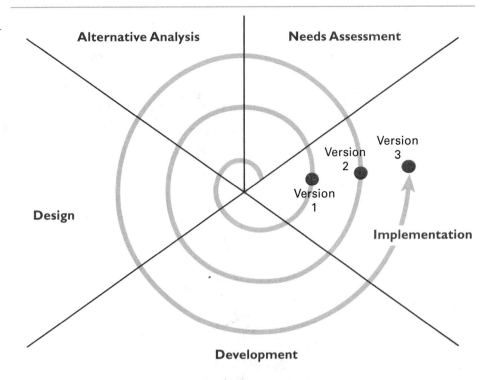

progress and judge how long it will take before the development system meets enough of their needs to replace the existing system.

The spiral approach also means constant rework of existing versions. Although companies can reuse some parts of old versions, they must discard and rewrite others. This rewriting generally increases the cost of the project. The product might not be usable until later versions are complete.

Prototyping

Prototyping describes an approach that tries to satisfy user needs by focusing on the user interface. The design and development stages, as they apply to the user interface, repeat until the user is satisfied, as illustrated in Figure 9-5. Occasionally, developers discover new user needs in the process and may need to do additional analysis.

A variation of prototyping called **joint application development (JAD)** works essentially as follows. Users meet with systems developers periodically, often every day at the start of the project. The users describe their needs during the initial meetings. Software developers use prototyping software to create a prototype of a system that appears to meet these needs before the next joint meeting. The prototype that they create might include data entry screens, reports, query screens, and other parts of the user interface, but rarely performs much processing. Developers sometimes create dummy data to present an illusion of a working system. At the next meeting, the developers present their prototype to the users for their review.

Discussion meetings alternate with development time for the systems developers. These ongoing discussions between users and developers allow the users to communicate their needs more accurately to the developer than would occur by building a formal specification statement during the design phase of the SDLC. As the system develops and unmet needs diminish, the frequency of meetings between users and developers decreases. Developers then spend their time more on implementation issues, optimizing the use of system resources, such as storage and computing, and completing the code for processing.

FIGURE   9-5

Prototyping calls for the iteration of the design, development, and occasionally analysis stages. Software tools are used to develop the user interface rapidly and to keep data and process models current.

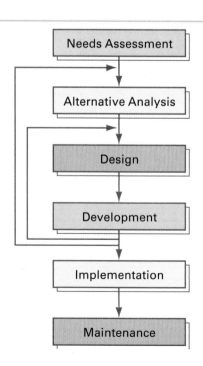

Prototyping offers several advantages over the waterfall approach:

- Decreases the amount of time that elapses between analysis and implementation.
- Ensures that the new system addresses user needs.
- Shows the benefits of a new system before the effort and costs become excessive.
- Exploits the skills that users have in articulating what they don't like about a system more easily than what they like about it.

Prototyping also has disadvantages relative to the waterfall model:

- It tends to raise the expectations of users to levels that developers can't achieve within their budget. When users see how rapidly developers can produce a prototype, they believe that the entire systems development effort will be equally fast and easy. Users continually ask for more features as they experiment with each prototype. Rapid prototyping hides the cost and risk of increasing the scope because no full analysis occurs after each prototyping cycle.

- The software programs that enable software developers to quickly develop the shell of a new system and rapidly customize it to user demands currently command high prices. Although the code that many of them produce may reduce the final cost of development by more than the cost of the tool, such savings are not guaranteed.

- It delays the demonstration of system functionality. As much as one-half of the functionality may not appear until the final 10 percent of the development schedule.[11]

- The benefits of prototyping decrease if the company buys existing software rather than develops its own. Because Royal Bank, for example, planned to purchase and adapt a CRM vendor's software, it probably would not follow a prototyping approach.

Agile Programming

Agile programming is a name given to several methodologies that focus on being reactive to changing user demands and that target small development groups and projects requiring minimal documentation. One example of agile programming that has recently become popular is extreme programming (XP), a methodology that pairs two programmers with one of the customers for whom the software is being written. Despite contradicting many long-held beliefs about software development, experience shows that XP can reduce development time and software defects while increasing satisfaction among developers and users. Automobile manufacturer, DaimlerChrysler AG, uses XP for some of its systems development projects in both the United States and Germany.[12] Extreme programming, despite being agile with regard to customer needs and development speed, has been criticized as being very prescriptive in its methodology.

Other agile methodologies, such as Crystal, allow the development team to script and refine its own process.[13] Crystal is probably closer to a philosophy and menu of methodologies than a methodology itself. For example, it embraces the principle that every project needs a slightly different methodology, depending on factors such as size and the experience and personalities of the project team. When Crystal advocate Jens Coldewey was called in to rescue a failing project to develop a complex enterprise-wide system at a bank, he took the development team off-site to help its members remove themselves, however briefly, from the day-to-day pressures of getting the work done and to focus instead on how they were doing the work. He asked the developers to write down what processes and activities improved development speed on one set of index cards and what processes slowed development on another set. After the team members analyzed the data and refined their development methodology, they were able to finish the first phase of job within a few weeks, meeting a deadline that had seemed impossible just days before.[14]

Selecting a Pathway

Table 9-1 summarizes the differences between the four pathways. The best approach for a given project depends greatly on the nature of the project and the nature of the organization. The waterfall approach works best with large, complex projects that have numerous stakeholders, affect the entire enterprise, and cannot easily be divided into subprojects. It also works well with organizations that have a formal culture and a hierarchical structure.

Spiral and agile programming approaches work well in dynamic organizations that can tolerate ambiguity and need results quickly. The spiral pathway is best adopted for projects that easily divide into subprojects and for more simple projects, especially the development of single-user systems or systems that affect a small department. Agile programming succeeds in environments where user needs are difficult to specify or rapidly changing.

Prototyping works best for small- to medium-size projects. It works well where the culture supports cross-functional teams. Prototyping can be combined with the spiral approach and be used for one or more of the subprojects in a spiral development.

Systems Modeling

Systems developers use data, process, and object models to understand existing systems and design new ones. These models provide a language that analysts, designers, and devel-

TABLE 9-1   Systems developers can choose from four pathways.

Model	Description	Uses	Advantages	Disadvantages
Waterfall	Follows the stages of the SDLC in order	Large, complex projects with many stakeholders	No rework Easy to manage	Highly inflexible No interim deliveries
Spiral	Delivers a system in versions according to the 80/20 rule of greatest need	Dynamic organizations that can tolerate ambiguity and need results fast	Rapid product delivery Progress easy to see	Constant rework High costs
Prototyping	Focuses on the user interface through repetition of design and development stages	Small-to-medium projects where the requirements are vague or unclear	Short time between analysis and implementation System better meets needs Avoids unnecessary costs Increased communication and interaction between users and developers	Raises user expectations Cost savings not guaranteed Delays system functionality
Agile Programming	Assesses needs and develops specifications during development	Small projects with experienced, competent developers and users willing to take part in the development process	Rapid product delivery Responsiveness to user needs	Harder to apply quality concepts such as process measurement and improvement Can fail dramatically with weak developers

opers can use to communicate efficiently. Managers on systems development teams will benefit from understanding these models so they can better communicate their needs.

Products that generate computer programs directly from systems models can dramatically speed software development. Products that generate system models from existing programs can help developers understand and maintain these programs. Many products also support translation among models of the same type, for example, from one data model to another.

Data Models

Data models describe the relationships among the elements of data that an organization uses. The entity-relationship model (see Chapter 4) is one of the most widely used data models (see Figure 9-6 for an example). The American National Standards Institute supports a different standard, the IDEF1X data model. This model resembles the entity relationship model, but translates more directly to a relational database implementation. Products, such as Visible Analyst from Visible Systems and System Architect from Popkin Software, support both models as well as several others.

Process Models

Process models divide a process into its parts, show how these parts relate to one another, and indicate which outputs of one process are input to other processes. The most popular process models include **structure charts, function boxes,** and **data-flow diagrams (DFDs).**

- *Structure charts* show the relationship among the programs and subprograms that will comprise the finished system. Figure 9-7, a structure chart for a payroll system, emphasizes the modular design of the system. Performing a given task, such as calculating net pay, requires completing all tasks below (e.g., calculating taxes and calculating deductions).

- *Function boxes,* illustrated in Figure 9-8, implement the American National Standards Institute's IDEF0 model. Each function box corresponds to a box in a structure chart. The lines between boxes show the relationships between the

FIGURE 9-6

This E-R diagram shows the relationship between sales representatives and their customers.

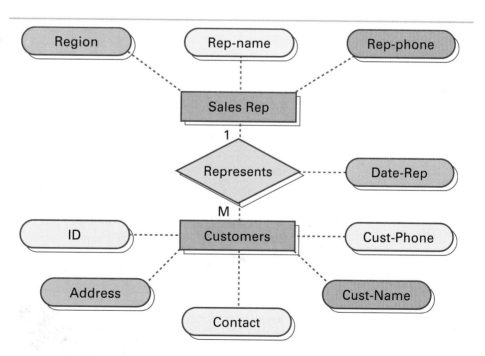

A structure chart of a payroll system divides the payroll process into three subprocesses. Subprocesses are further divided.

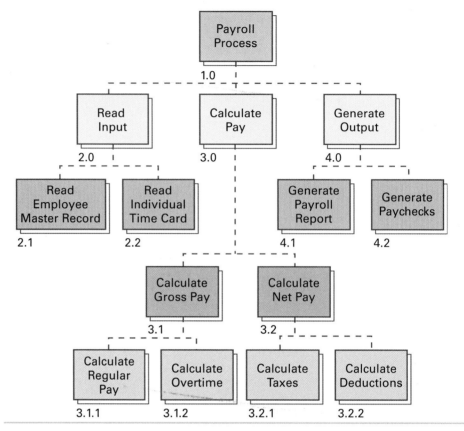

An IDEF0 function box shows how a process connects to other processes. Function boxes are labeled by levels, corresponding to a level of a structure chart hierarchy.

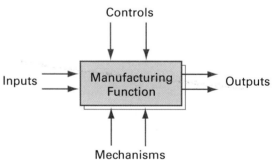

inputs and outputs of the procedures. Documents that support the IDEF0 methodology show a single function box along with the division of that box into its subtasks on each page, as illustrated in Figure 9-9.

- **Data-flow diagrams (DFDs)** model the flow of data between processes. They don't model the breakdown of processes into subprocesses or the order in which tasks are performed to accomplish a process. Figure 9-10 illustrates a data-flow diagram for a simplified payroll system. Arrows indicate data flows; open-sided rectangles represent stored data; round-edged rectangles indicate processes; and squares represent sources of input or users of output. This example shows the employee as both a source of input (time card) and a user of output (paycheck). An employee file maintains stored data about the employee's pay class, pay rate, and deductions; processes to determine gross pay and calculate net pay use these stored data.

FIGURE   9-9

The bottom page shows an IDEF0 model with function boxes. The upper page provides the IDEF0 model of the parent process, allowing the modeler to view the current process in its proper context.

SOURCE: *Federal Information Processing Standards Publication 183: Integration Definition for Function Modeling (IDEF0)* (Knowledge Based Systems, Inc. and U.S. Department of Commerce National Technical Information Service, 1993): 55, accessed at http://www.idef.com/idef0 .html on April 2, 2002.

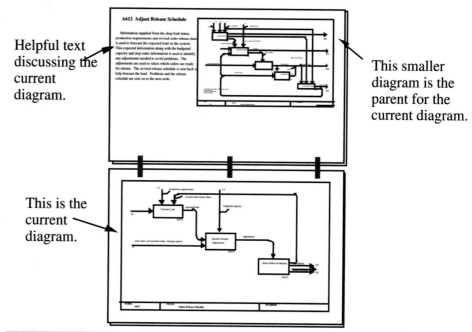

Helpful text discussing the current diagram.

This smaller diagram is the parent for the current diagram.

This is the current diagram.

FIGURE   9-10

A data-flow diagram of a payroll system shows the inputs and outputs of each procedure, and the sources and uses of data that are outside the system boundary. The data-flow diagram also shows intermediate files and outputs.

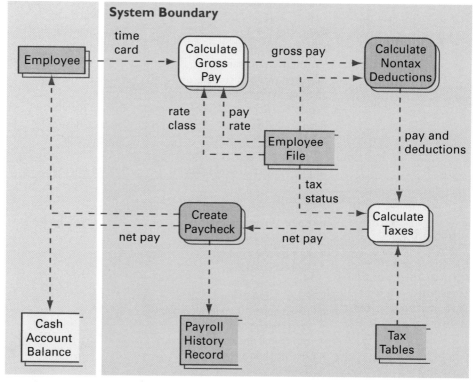

Object Models

Object models describe the properties of objects, their relationship to one another, and the functions they perform (see Chapters 3 and 4). Object models typically include inheritance diagrams that show how objects derive their properties from other objects. Object models may also include state diagrams to show how object characteristics change as external events affect an object and how the object responds differently to messages depending on its state.

You may recall that objects incorporate both data and the operations that can be performed on the data. The relationships among objects, data, and processes have motivated the development of models that incorporate all three elements. Among the most popular is the Unified Modeling Language known as UML.[15]

Computer-Aided Software Engineering (CASE)

Computer-aided software engineering (CASE) describes the use of software to automate activities performed in needs assessment, systems analysis, design, development, and maintenance. **CASE tools,** as shown in Table 9-2, refer to the software products themselves. Managers and developers might use CASE tools for a single activity or element of the SDLC, such as developing an ER diagram, or for almost all activities during the cycle. Table 9-3 shows a list of typical CASE features.

	Company	Product	Application
TABLE 9-2 Managers can choose from a variety of CASE tools.	+1 Software Engineering (www.plus-one.com)	+1 suite	Metrics, testing, reuse, and reengineering
	Aonix (www.aonix.com)	Select	Full suite Business Solutions
	Computer Associates (www.ca.com)	AllFusion Modeling Suite	Full suite
	IBM	WebSphere Studio	Application development
	KBSI (www.kbsi.com)	AI0 Win 6.0	Process modeling
	Merant (www.merant.com)	PVCS	Change management
	Microsoft (www.microsoft.com) application development	Visual Studio .Net	Data and object modeling,
	Popkin Software (www.popkin.com)	System Architect	Full suite
	Rational Software (www.rational.com)	Rational Rose	Full suite
	TogetherSoft	TogetherSoft	Object modeling, application development
	Visible Systems (www.esti.com)	Visible Analyst	Full suite

TABLE 9-3

CASE products have features, including those listed in this table, that support software development.

- Common debugger
- Data modeling
- GUI builder
- Problem tracking
- Process management
- Project scheduling
- Rapid application development
- Reverse engineering
- Structured analysis and design
- Technical documentation
- Testing

A suite of CASE tools that support and integrate the activities performed throughout the life cycle is called a **CASE toolset** or **CASE workbench.** CASE workbenches provide a consistent interface between the various CASE tools in the suite, a smooth transition for moving between tools as they follow one or more methodologies, and a common database of information about the project under development. In addition, they provide consistent and cross-referenced documentation of user needs, application processes, data flow and structure, and software design. System methodologies and CASE tools ease the development of systems that respond to users' needs in a cost-effective, timely, and technologically current fashion.

STAGES OF THE LIFE CYCLE

The role of managers in the development of new systems varies depending on the stage of the life cycle. In order to participate properly in development activities, managers need to understand what occurs at each stage. This section provides an overview of the activities associated with each stage of the SDLC.

Needs Assessment

Needs assessment, also called **requirements analysis,** identifies the information needs of an organization. As part of this effort, analysts compare the identified needs to the specifications and performance of the current information system to determine what needs remain unmet. In later stages of the SDLC, managers evaluate the costs and benefits of developing new systems to satisfy these unmet needs.

Business managers analyze current systems and needs periodically. Some organizations have no formal review process. They have users who rarely complain or who constantly demand changes that force IS managers to conduct ad hoc reviews. Other organizations have formal systems for examining current systems and prioritizing and scheduling changes.

Documenting all the information needs of an organization presents a major challenge because these needs constantly change. Research shows that when systems developers identify needs early in the development cycle, the likelihood of development success increases and the costs of corrections in later stages of the cycle decline.[16]

Collecting Information for Needs Assessment

Analysts determining organizations' or users' information needs typically focus on three types of needs: outputs, inputs, and processing.

Output analysis describes the systematic identification of ways people in an organization use information: What type of reports do people receive? How frequently do they obtain the reports? What information do they retrieve from manual files? What information do they gain from online queries? What information would they like to obtain, and in what form?

Analysts can easily identify the formal uses of information by looking at reports and query screens that existing information systems generate and by asking employees how they use hard-copy files stored in file cabinets. Analysts can also help users compose wishlists of information that would help them perform their jobs better. Without analysts' help, end users often include on these wish lists only information they believe they can obtain. They often don't know the breadth of information that the organization can secure.

Business managers, along with IS professionals, can expand a traditional output analysis by benchmarking similar applications developed at other companies and in other industries. For example, in assessing Royal Bank's needs, Cathy Burrows can benefit from studying the screens and reports produced by customer relationship management programs run by real estate companies, accounting firms, or even manufacturing firms, such as computer companies and chemical manufacturers.

Input analysis refers to a formal cataloguing and review of the information an organization collects, stores, and uses. It also includes an analysis of the data collection process. Typically, input analysis follows output analysis so that analysts can identify missing or duplicate sources of information needed to produce the desired output. Input analysis also addresses the potential input of information that an organization collects but currently doesn't input into its information systems. Most organizations informally collect large amounts of data, such as word-of-mouth opinions, that don't reside on formal information systems. For example, sales agents rarely enter more than a small percentage of the data they obtain when conversing with prospective or existing customers into manual or computerized information systems. Because informal data can provide useful information, product designers, executive strategists, and marketing managers would highly value a system that captures them. Educating users to identify what information they collect can be difficult because most users lack an awareness of how they and others use and collect information.

Procedure analysis attempts to determine whether the organization collects the information it needs, uses the information it collects effectively, and has efficient processes to address the organization's information needs. Procedure analysis should examine all computerized and manual systems. Data-flow diagrams and structure charts might document existing processes and compare them with desired practices. Designers might simply compile a cross-reference between processes and data, showing what data each process creates, reads, updates, or deletes (see Figure 9-11).

The Role of the Systems Analysis

Users of information systems often can't understand the jargon that computer professionals use, and computer professionals often don't know enough about specific business processes to understand the needs and language of its users. This communication gap may reduce the quality of a company's requirements analysis. A **systems analyst**, a person who provides an interface between information systems users and information systems developers, can bridge this gap. A successful systems analyst understands the technical aspects of a system and can assess their implications for users.[17]

Data		Process			
		Maintain employee file	Calculate employee pay	Prepare pay by job class report	Maintain tax tables
Employee	Name	CRUD	R		
	Wage rate	CRUD	R		
	Job class	CRUD	R		
	YTD pay		U		
Tax Rates	State		R		
	Rate		R		U
Time Cards	Employee		R		
	Hours		R		
Summary Data	Hours		U	R	
	Pay		U	R	

FIGURE 9-11 — This portion of a CRUD diagram shows which processes Create, Read, Update, and Delete specified data in a payroll system.

Systems analysts should have strong interpersonal skills: they should listen well and ask probing questions in an unthreatening manner. The complexity of business processes often motivates systems analysts to work in a single applications area for several years to maximize their knowledge of the business specialty and its requirements. Line managers rely on such specialists to interface with IS managers. In many large organizations, systems analysts report directly to a line manager rather than an IS manager.

Methodologies and Tools for Needs Assessment

Systems analysts use varied techniques and data sources to perform needs assessment. These include interviews, onsite observation, questionnaires, structured analysis, data dictionary, and reverse engineering.[18]

Systems analysts typically obtain information about existing systems and needs by interviewing users and their managers. Users and managers know the most about the systems they use, although they perform many activities almost subconsciously. Because users often report only standard operating practices, forgetting the exceptions that occur infrequently, analysts must ferret out these exceptions for the new system to operate effectively and efficiently. Users might resist reporting how they bypass the formal or standard systems to perform their work more efficiently. They might fear being fired or demoted if they tell what they actually do rather than what they should do. An analyst may require several interviews with the same people to verify their understanding of the processes performed, provide feedback on the use of the collected information, and build the trust necessary to reveal exceptional and nonstandard processes.

Systems analysts can watch users doing their jobs or work alongside them.[19] This approach, called **contextual inquiry,** lacks efficiency because it can require several days or weeks to obtain information that an analyst could obtain in an hour's interview. But it can reveal exceptional and nonstandard processes more often and more completely.

Systems analysts, such as those at Royal Bank, may use questionnaires to collect information when many people or geographically disbursed workers should provide information about the processes affected by the new system. Analysts may also use confidential questionnaires to obtain information about hidden processes. Questionnaires may not yield quality data because employees often fail to complete them, and those that do often offer incomplete answers. Small companies have too few employees in each area to merit the use of questionnaires for data collection. Analysts prefer techniques that involve users and build a sense of ownership in the proposed system; questionnaires may fail to develop such a stake in users.

Structured analysis uses process modeling tools to diagram existing and proposed systems so that users can understand and critique an analyst's perception of information relationships. Royal Bank's analysts will probably use structured analysis to share their understanding of customer relationship management processes with Cathy Burrows. Burrows will need to understand these models to ensure that the proposed system meets her needs and those of her staff.

A **data dictionary** refers to a database that contains descriptions of all of the computerized data items maintained by the organization (see Chapter 4). Users can access the data dictionary to validate their perceptions of the data an organization collects and uses and identify gaps in the data they require for their business functions. Analysts use a data dictionary to specify and clarify terms used by end users to describe their business activities. For example, when a user refers to *revenue from sales,* the analyst working with that user can refer to the data dictionary to learn whether the term means the undiscounted price of items sold, the money that changes hands at the time of the sale, or the revenue adjusted by any returns after the sale.

Reverse engineering describes the process of analyzing existing software to understand how it works. Legacy systems typically consist of thousands of programs written and modified over ten to twenty years. Often, these programs and the processes they implement have such complex interrelationships that no one in the organization knows exactly how they work. For example, programmers no longer employed by the organization might have made significant changes in the programming code ten years ago. Even if these programmers documented the changes that they had made, they may not have documented why they made the changes. The size of legacy systems compounds the problem of identifying what they do. Unless legacy systems used structured techniques and tools and had good documentation, analyzing them manually is an expensive and time-consuming task. Reverse engineering software automates much of this process by performing at least the following functions:

- Identifying and organizing the names of variables used by the code to represent data.
- Identifying where the code performs input and output.
- Identifying, organizing, and diagramming the sequence of operations performed.
- Determining under what circumstances the operations are performed.
- Monitoring the frequency of use of various parts of the software.
- Translating the software into languages that provide clearer or terser code or conform to current software standards.

Figure 9-12 illustrates two screens from a reverse engineering tool showing the structure of an application written in C++.

FIGURE   9-12

The Imagix 4D reverse engineering product reveals the structure of a legacy application written in C++.

SOURCE: accessed at http://www.imagix.com/, on 1 April 2002. Used with permission.

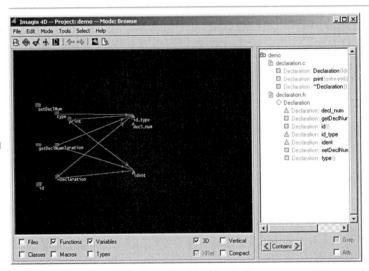

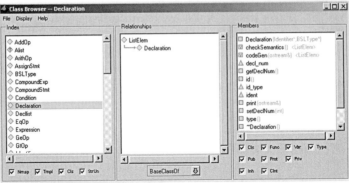

Reverse engineering often requires specialists to interpret the output of the programs and make decisions about the way the current system operates when the software can't specify the system's functioning. Although improvements in artificial intelligence allow reverse engineering software to make many decisions about the code, it remains more an art than a science.

Alternative Analysis

The second stage of the SDLC includes the identification and evaluation of alternative systems, ultimately focusing on a single design more extensively. Often the chief IS manager or senior executives will establish a committee consisting of managers from the user departments and IS specialists to make the decisions required at this stage. Burrows might form a committee primarily composed of top management, with a few representatives from the rest of the professional and nonprofessional staff. Decisions about the nature of the system made at this stage often encumber sufficient funds to warrant review by senior executives. Afterwards, they can't abandon a project without a substantial loss of effort and money.

The selection of an alternative for further design involves making trade-offs between designs that meet few user needs but have low costs and designs that meet many needs but have high costs. In addition, some designs are more likely than others to be successfully completed, installed, and used. Executives analyze return on investment (ROI) and risk to help them assess the relative costs, benefits, and risks of alternative solutions. A key decision focuses on whether to renovate an old system or build a new one. Renovating a system requires that significant energy be spent on assessing and improving the quality of the code, checking and augmenting the documentation, and making other functional and technical improvements.

ROI Analyses

Return on investment (ROI) is a ratio of the benefits (return) of an investment to the amount of the investment. The higher the ratio, the greater the benefit per dollar invested. All else being equal, organizations seek to use their assets in projects or investments that provide the greatest return. Organizations that use ROI analysis regard investing in information systems as one of many ways in which they can invest their assets. They will rank all projects they are considering, not just those for new information systems, and approve only those with the highest returns. Tellabs Inc., a Fortune 500 telecommunications equipment and service provider, ties the bonuses of its managers to the ROI of the investments for which they are responsible.[20] Such a practice ensures that managers will do as good a job as possible predicting the return of investments that they approve. Nevertheless, a recent survey revealed that more than two-thirds of companies rarely, if ever, examine their actual ROI six months after a project is completed.[21]

Alternative designs meet different needs and require different investments. Consider, for example, a shipper who wishes to trace the location of a package in route without waiting for the daily transport report. One solution might locate the package within an hour, another within five minutes, and a third within seconds. Each solution meets the need with a different relative benefit and required investment. An ROI analysis weighs the benefits of meeting the needs against the projected investment in a formal, documented way.

Estimating the cost of a project, and the associated investment required, may be difficult at this early design stage. Various techniques exist to estimate software development costs based on the number of application functions the software will provide.[22] However, knowing the number of functions is difficult even for a fully specified design. Estimates at this stage may err by 50 percent or more. It is also necessary to consider ongoing costs. At Delta Airlines, for example, ROI calculations for information system investments include the costs of hardware, software, maintenance, and support for four years after the project is complete.[23]

Estimating a system's benefits may be even more problematic. For example, how can a manager assess the value of responding to customers more rapidly? Although a rapid response should lead to greater sales, calculations of the impact on sales and profits may contain significant errors. Intangible benefits, such as improving morale by changing the nature of an employee's work, may be almost impossible to quantify accurately.

ROI analysis techniques address the differences in the timing of investments and benefits. Most costs for new systems occur during their development and when procuring hardware. Benefits accrue over time and may decline as competitors develop similar systems. ROI analyses may use economic and portfolio analysis techniques, such as discounted cash flow, internal rate of return, and payback period, to compare investments and benefits on a current basis.

Risk Analysis

Every IS project involves risks as well as benefits. One proposed system might provide more benefit than another with the same or lower investment, but it might require the use of unproven technology or the mastery of new technology by the IS staff. Risks exist both with technology and people. Some designs might automate a job previously done manually, causing the company to lay off some staff. While benefits accrue from reduced labor costs, risks arise from possible labor unrest or loss of morale. **Risk analysis** requires managers to identify where risks might arise and trade risk against costs and benefits.[24] Generally, companies require more risky projects to produce a greater ROI than less risky projects. Some companies take a portfolio approach to the information systems investments. They might balance a few risky investments having high projected ROIs with several less risky investments having lower ROIs so as to manage their overall risk and return.[25]

The McFarlan Risk Questionnaire (see Figure 9-13), one of the most widely accepted instruments for measuring risk assessment, estimates risk as a function of project size, the intended technology, and the structure of the relationship between the project, its users, and other projects. For example, breaking a project into smaller components can reduce he risk associated with a large project size. Other risk avoidance techniques include using small teams of highly skilled and experienced professionals, minimizing the dependencies among projects, and reducing the amount of time between deliverables and review points.

Design

The third stage of the SDLC focuses on providing detailed specifications for the selected design. These specifications include designs of the user interface, the database, processes and procedures, and objects. In the design stage of the SDLC, designers will also determine the physical characteristics of the system, such as the number, types, and locations of workstations, processing hardware, and network cabling and devices. They should also specify the procedures for testing the completed system before installation. During design, no programming occurs. Designers must provide enough information to developers to let them turn the design into software code during the development stage of the SDLC.

Some practitioners overlap the design and alternative selection stages. For example, they may select two or three alternatives for additional design, partially proceed through the design stage, and then return to the alternative selection stage to make a final decision. Rapid prototyping overlaps design and development of the user interface. Design and development can also be iterative because unacceptable system performance might not be observable until development is nearly complete.

Design elements include the interface design, data design process design, physical design, and test design. The design stage results in a set of specifications that can direct

FIGURE 9-13	The McFarlan Risk Questionnaire is popular for assessing the risk of a systems development project. Here are selected questions from that questionnaire.

CATEGORY/QUESTION	RISK SCORE	WEIGHT
Size		
Total systems and programming man-days for system:		5
( ) 12 to 375	Low=1	
( ) 376 to 1875	Med=2	
( ) 1876 to 3750	Med=3	
( ) Over 3750	High=4	
What is the estimate for the elapsed time to complete the project?		4
( ) 12 months or less	Low=1	
( ) 13 to 24 months	Med=2	
( ) Over 24 months	High=3	
To how many existing systems must the new one interface?		3
( ) None or one	Low=1	
( ) Two	Med=2	
( ) Three or more	High=3	
Structure		
The system is best described as:		1
( ) Totally new	High=3	
( ) Replacement of existing manual system	Med=2	
( ) Replacement of automated system	Low=1	
Has a joint IT/user team been established?		5
( ) No	High=3	
( ) Part-time user involvement	Med=2	
( ) Yes, full-time user involvement	Low=1	
Technology		
Is additional hardware required?		1
( ) None	Low=0	
( ) Central processor type change	Low=1	
( ) Peripheral/storage changes	Low=1	
( ) Terminals	Med=2	
( ) Platform change	High=3	
How knowledgeable is the IS team in the proposed application area?		5
( ) Limited	High=3	
( ) Understands concepts but no experience	Med=2	
( ) Has implemented similar systems before	Low=1	

SOURCE: Extracted from Graham McLeod and Derek Smith, *Managing Information Technology Projects* (Danvers: Boyd & Fraser Publishintg Company, 1996): 143–148. Used with permission.

developers if a new system will be built or compare the fit with alternative products if the new system will be purchased.

Interface Design

Interface design refers to the specification of the media, content, and form of input and output. Output media might include a computer screen, paper report, microfiche, or microfilm. Designers might also consider transferring some output elements directly into a spreadsheet or database on a user's personal computer. Input media might include keyboarding, scanning, or bar code entry.

Interface design also specifies content, the elements of data that appear on an output report or screen. Designers must separate important from unnecessary information. Extraneous information clutters a screen or report making the required information more difficult to find. The designer might also provide options to obtain related information, such as clicking a button on a screen to select a more detailed report about certain aspects of the output.

On the input side, designers must determine whether users will enter data in batch or online modes, the characteristics of input screens, the nature of error checking during data entry, and the standards that apply among data entry screens. For example, they might decide that the F1 function key on the keyboard should always request help about the function that the data entry clerk performs and the F2 key or a mouse click on a scroll button will display a list of options.

During interface design, designers determine the form of output—the way information is presented. They determine whether data should appear in tabular form or graphically. Designing the display of tabular data includes determining the layout, the amount of white space, page margins, page length, the frequency of breaks, and the location of subtotals in the data, among other features. Designing graphical displays involves deciding these issues as well as the graphical form to use (pie, bar, or line chart) and options for switching among forms. Interface design also considers the choice of color. Some systems give every color a different meaning: for example, red may always show data outside the usual range or identify items that demand user attention.

Data Design

Data design refers to creating the model of data supporting the system. Data models that analysts used to describe the existing system now model the planned system. Database specialists help data users and managers formalize relationships among data elements to create a logical design. Ultimately, the data users and managers, such as Burrows at Royal Bank, are responsible for the design's accuracy.

Database specialists generate a physical design to structure the data for ease and speed of retrieval and to keep storage requirements as low as possible and promote data integrity (see Chapter 4). They will also specify the database model (relational, for example) to use. The database model constrains the physical data design and forms the basis for the way the designers view and process the data. Designers may also select the DBMS vendor at this time, although this selection more typically occurs in the development stage. Data designers work with the organization's data administrator to coordinate the storage and use of data that independently designed information systems might share.

Process Design

Process design refers to the design of both the computational and logical processes underlying the system. The calculation of pay for hourly employees illustrates a computational process. Process designers for a payroll system will identify the procedure for calculating the payroll of the employees who receive overtime pay. Users and business managers most familiar with the business processes form the core part of the process design team.

The removal of an item from inventory illustrates a logical process. The system should check whether an item has fallen below a prespecified level. When the stock of certain types of items reaches the prespecified level, the system should alert affected managers by producing a report, sending an electronic mail message, or initiating an EDI transaction to automatically reorder the item. This example demonstrates the computer taking one or more procedural steps in response to a transaction. Process designers must specify the precise steps the system should take in response to any transaction that might occur. They must also specify what steps the computer must take to process inputs and outputs.

Although IS specialists may generate the computer code, business managers, such as Burrows, will be heavily involved in writing the process specifications.

Object Design

Object design refers to the generation of an object model. Object-oriented programming techniques will translate the object model almost directly into software code. The object design identifies and isolates the characteristics and behavior of objects for programming, testing, and then assembly into a working system.

Object-oriented development requires that a software object represent a business object. The object can be used and reused, not only in the project for which it was designed, but in all future projects. If this objective is to be achieved, the software object must model the characteristics and behaviors of the business model as completely as possible.

Physical Design

Physical design refers to decisions about the hardware used to deliver the system. Physical design usually follows data and process designs because they determine the required amount of data storage, the volume of transaction processing, the amount of data communication activity, and the complexity of processing. Designers use such information to determine whether existing hardware will accommodate the new system or whether the organization must procure new hardware. For example, designers who recommend new hardware purchases should determine whether centralized or decentralized development and delivery of the system should occur. Although analysts might address these issues during the alternative selection phase of the SDLC, they can't develop accurate estimates of cost and response time until they have complete data and process designs. Costs and response time that fall outside the ranges forecast during alternative analysis might call for revisiting the second stage of the SDLC.

Test Design

Test design refers to the creation of tests that ensure the proper operation of developed systems. Test design includes the generation of a sample data set and a series of processes, transactions, or activities that simulate the eventual use of the system. The test design also specifies acceptable performance criteria. Test design becomes particularly important for purchased systems because it affects whether to pay the supplier.

Design Specification

Design specification refers to means for communicating the design to the programmers who will implement it. Prototyping most readily communicates the interface design. The tools available to design input and output screens, sample reports, and GUI interfaces ease the prototyping of these interfaces and consequently their design. Common interface standards can be specified in hard copy as an interface standard guide. A data dictionary or an entity-relationship diagram can also communicate the data design. In addition, a variety of software can perform data design as well as store and print the result.

Development

The development stage includes development or purchase of software, potentially the procurement of hardware, and testing of the new system. IS professionals assemble a working system that meets the specifications formulated in the design stage. Users test the new system during the development phase, but will not use it until the implementation stage of the SDLC. Unless development is by prototype, IS professionals work more independently of end users and their managers than at any other stage of the SDLC.

The Develop-or-Purchase Decision

The choice to develop or purchase a new system is one of the most difficult decisions that senior information systems managers and other top executives must make. Medium to large organizations usually find that packaged vertical application software will not entirely satisfy their complex information needs. The requirement of organizations such as Royal Bank to interface the new system to other systems, such as the bank's data warehouse, may preclude their buying packaged software unless they can customize it to provide the interfaces they need.

A company's ability to modify purchased software depends on the vendor's licensing agreements. Some prohibit any modification of the software except by the vendor itself. Some authorize value added resellers (VARs) to modify their software. Some provide all or portions of their computer code to the purchasing company so that its staff can modify the software.

An alternative to modifying purchased software is to modify existing software to interface with the purchased product. Most vendors who restrict modification of their own code provide an application program interface (API) that facilitates the exchange of data with external programs and allows external programs to execute selected processes in the purchased software.

Companies that do not have the resources and skills to develop their own software but need functionality not provided by packaged products may hire another company to develop software for them.

Development Tools

A variety of products, including **screen, report,** and **code generators**, exist to simplify and speed the development of information systems. **Rapid application development (RAD)** describes the use of such tools, in conjunction with rapid prototyping, to speed the ultimate development of new systems.

- *Screen generators* create and edit a screen and generate programs for screen-based data entry or queries (see Figure 9-14). For example, the designer lays out the text and data portion using standard text and drawing tools and specifies where the data will appear or be entered.

- *Report generators* help examine design options, lay out reports using standard text and drawing tools, test the report, and generate a computer program to create it. For example, they identify the placement of headings and determine what triggers breaks or subtotals. They identify the sources of data for columns, specify the order for sorting rows, and identify what criteria will determine the display of rows.

FIGURE   9-14

A user designs a data entry screen using Microsoft Access's screen generator.

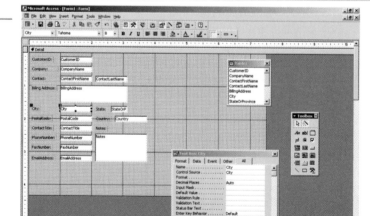

- *Code generators* create complete and working programs based on designer specifications. This code derives directly from data, process, or object models that the developers have created. It uses the outputs of screen and report generators as input.

Selecting and Procuring Hardware

The design stage of the SDLC requires many hardware decisions, particularly those related to selecting processing, peripheral, and telecommunication equipment. For example, when Carlson Hospitality, the owner, manager, and franchiser of some 750 hotels, designed an application that would allow its 2,000 users to access a central database on reservations and occupancy, the company determined that it would be best to present this information on handheld computers synchronized over wireless local area networks at many of the hotel properties. The company then had to select vendors for the wireless LAN equipment and for the handheld computers.[26] To make decisions such as these, designers analyze product reviews in the trade press, request quotations from vendors, talk to industry groups about their experience, and contact reference sites supplied by the vendors. Depending on the nature of the procurement, the choice of vendors may be limited by those the company has already approved for similar purchases. On large purchases, the purchasing company can often bargain with potential vendors to achieve the best long-term deal.

If a company chooses to buy rather than develop its software, it may deal with software manufacturers who sell **turn-key solutions.** Organizations that purchase a turn-key system can plug it in and turn it on (historically with a key), and it will run. The software will already be loaded onto the computer, and the system optimizes the hardware/software combination for the buyer's needs. ABN AMRO Mortgage, the fifth largest loan originator in the United States, purchased a turn-key solution from NetByTel to automate its telephone processing of new loan applications. NetByTel, a leader in speech recognition systems, had a prepackaged solution that needed very little modification to produce the solution that company managers sought. Garth Graham, the company's vice president of customer acquisition and relationship management, claims that the system allowed the company to generate an additional $2.5 million in revenue in its first six months of operation.[27]

Selecting an Appropriate Language

The choice of languages for systems development depends on several factors. The company may have standards that limit the choice of programming language. At small companies, even without formal standards, staff expertise is often limited to, at most, one or two languages. The DBMS selected may restrict the languages to a small number that it supports. Customization of third-party software may require a language that interfaces with that used by the third-party vendor.

Chapter 3 discusses some common issues in language selection, including the choice of interpretive versus compiled, procedural versus nonprocedural, and command/data oriented versus object oriented language. Although selecting computer languages for software development is a technical decision in most organizations, business managers should address the impact that language choice has on their functions, including their ability, for example, to make changes or to have IS professionals make changes in a timely fashion.

Testing

Testing describes the process of ensuring that the system works as designed. A testing plan, typically created in the design stage of the SDLC, states precisely how users will recognize whether a delivered system meets their needs and expectations.

The development phase of the SDLC includes the following four levels of testing to ensure quality: **unit, component, integration,** and **system testing.**

- *Unit testing* refers to testing each small component of the system to guarantee its proper operations.

- *Component testing* examines the interaction of a series of programs within the system that likely will be used in concert, such as those that process a transaction.

- *Integration testing* addresses the interaction between large, independently developed components of the new system that were internally checked at the unit and component testing levels.

- *System testing,* also known as **alpha testing**, refers to testing the entire system under realistic conditions.

In the first stage of system testing, **performance testing,** developers identify and correct problems that might cause a system to slow down or fail when stressed with too many users or too much data. To simulate a realistic level of activity in a laboratory, developers use software load-testing products. These products can generate transactions from a transaction profile, provide statistical data about the speed with which the system responds, and compare outputs and final values of data elements to expected outcomes.

The second stage of systems testing, **usability testing,** compares the developed system to users' expectations and needs. Users ideally test the system in a **usability lab,** a place where developers can observe and record their reactions to the system for later analysis. A typical usability lab includes two rooms connected by a one-way mirror, as shown in Figure 9-15. Video cameras record and store users' reactions to the system. Computer equipment, including software to log the user's keystrokes, tests the application. An audio system allows users to communicate with application developers and usability professionals. Professionals look for the time required to complete specific tasks, the types of errors made, the ways errors are corrected, whether errors are repeated, the speed of learning, the frustrations users experience, and so on. Organizations too small to have their own usability labs can hire the services of a usability consultant and use the consultant's labs to test its software.[28] Other usability testing techniques include conducting focus groups and polling users. Staples.com, for example, used such techniques to determine that the "Favorite Aisles" feature of its initial Web-site release confused and distracted people rather than helping them. Without usability testing, they would never have been able to determine that this feature, requested by their designers, didn't work as expected.[29]

FIGURE   9-15

Developer monitors and observes users testing a new system in a usability lab.

SOURCE: accessed at http: //www.theuegroup.com /usability.htm, on 1 April 2002.

When Visa completed a major overhaul of its credit-card clearing system, it needed to be sure that the system operated properly before moving it into production. Because of the importance and complexity of the product, Visa allocated almost 40 percent of the project budget and nearly a full year to the testing process. One group of testers selected and tested 60,000 transactions from prior production data, making sure that each of the fifty types of services was represented in sufficient quantity. Another group ran 350,000 transactions, representing five full days' worth of data, through the system, comparing the results to the actual runs on those days. Member banks were also called upon to test complex, multi-part transactions, both for accuracy and usability. As a result, product was rolled out without any significant downtime in the processing of credit-card transactions.[30]

Implementation

Once a new system satisfactorily passes its acceptance tests, it can be moved into the production environment. IS professionals or other organization members must manage the transition from the old system to the new system. Burrows probably will manage such a transition at Royal Bank; alternatively, she can hire a consultant or assign an employee to oversee the transition and implementation.

Companies generally use some combination of the four implementation strategies summarized in Table 9-4. The proper strategy or combination of strategies for a given organization depends on the project, the amount of risk the organization can tolerate, the budget, characteristics of the target users, and the culture of the organization.

Direct Cut-over

The **direct cut-over strategy** describes the replacement of the old with the new system overnight, over a weekend, or over some other period of time when the company does not operate. Theoretically, a direct cut-over from one system to another can occur almost instantaneously. A direct cut-over requires that the new system have the data that it needs to run. Transferring data from the old to the new system poses one of the major challenges of the direct cut-over approach. Programmers should write utility programs during the development stage to transfer data from the old system to the new. They should test these programs well in advance of implementation to ensure that they work properly. The cut-over period, when neither system is in use, involves the automatic transfer of data from the old to the new

TABLE 9-4   The four implementation strategies differ in their risk and cost.

Strategy	Description	Time Required	Cost	Risk
Direct cut-over	Replaces old system with new system overnight	Minimal	Low	High
Pilot implementation	Uses the new system in one or more parts of the organization and later in entire company	Moderate	Moderate	Moderate
Phased implementation	Introduces components of the new system one at a time	High	Moderate to High	Low
Parallel implementation	Uses both the old and new systems simultaneously for a period of time	High	High	Low

system. Performing such a data transfer on a large system and confirming that the data transfer usually take many hours, but can generally be completed over a weekend.

Companies that must operate continuously experience difficulties in using the cut-over approach. One or two days before implementation data transfer from a backup copy of the old system to the new system occurs. Then transaction logs from the old system are fed into the new system. The new system should process these transaction logs as fast as or faster than the old system originally processed the transaction. When the new system has processed these logs, the almost instantaneous switch of processing from the old to the new system can occur. An alternative approach keeps old files online and accesses them as needed. This approach requires development of extra code that will not be used after the cut-over is complete.

The direct cut-over approach has the lowest cost but the highest risks of the implementation strategies. Organizations might use this approach if they willingly trade reduced cost for high risk. Having the new system maintain a transaction log that can update the old system and return it to action if necessary can reduce this risk. Using such a backup doesn't eliminate the risk completely because improper processing might not appear until it has affected business transactions in a way that harms the business. For example, if the new system fails to generate invoices for specific products or services, the company might not notice this defect until its cash flow deteriorates.

The direct cut-over strategy might also result in employees lacking sufficient training to use the new system properly. Although employees receive training in the new system before the cut-over date, no employee will have used the system for an extended period and no one can act as an expert to assist users who have trouble with the new system. In addition, their dissatisfaction may not surface immediately. Experiencing difficulty in retrieving information for customers may affect the business only after longer term use of the system. Returning to the old system then may be difficult or impossible.

Pilot Implementation

A **pilot implementation strategy,** often called **beta testing,** requires one or more segments of a company, or perhaps even just a few employees, to use a new system before the entire company uses it. Concentra Health Services, a billion-dollar private occupational health provider based in Addison, Texas, employed a pilot implementation strategy for the roll-out of a custom physical therapy application designed for wireless handheld computers. The company found that its physical therapists and physicians were annoyed by the three- to four-second delay between the application's screens. It rectified the problem by removing much of the software from the handheld devices, running it instead on the company's servers. After another pilot, they successfully rolled out the software to 1,000 physicians and physical and occupational therapists at 250 clinics across the country.[31]

Pilot implementation reduces risk by limiting exposure to a small fraction of the business. This limited implementation doesn't eliminate risk because even a few costly mistakes in a small branch of an organization can harm its performance. Even if a new system works properly in one part of the organization, it may not function properly when the entire organization uses it. The increased load on the system, for example, can slow response time to an unacceptable level.

Implementing a pilot system increases the cost of a changeover. Particular difficulties arise in dealing with transactions that cross the boundary between old and new systems. Consider the problems of a company piloting a new order entry system in its Los Angeles office while running an existing system in its New York office? What happens if the Los Angeles office wants to serve one of its customers by pulling from New York's inventory? Systems developers must address questions such as these before implementation by building often expensive programs that allow the new system to access the old system's data and vice versa.

Phased Implementation

A **phased implementation strategy** introduces components of the new system one at a time. For example, the organization implements the accounts payable portion of an accounting system before the rest of the system. It reduces risk by limiting exposure to the new system. Users can slowly become accustomed to the new system. The cost of building interfaces to deal with transactions that cross the boundary between the new and old systems becomes a problem, particularly as the number of phases increases. Practitioners can reduce the cost of the phased strategy by combining it with parallel implementation.

Parallel Implementation

A **parallel implementation strategy** refers to the use of both the new and the old system for a period of time. The parallel implementation essentially eliminates the risk of failure because ongoing comparisons of the results of the two systems identify inaccuracies. Parallel implementation remains infeasible where employees lack the time to use both systems or when the cost in employee time of using two systems becomes excessive.

Managing Risk in Introducing Systems

Employing quality measures throughout previous stages of the SDLC and paying particular attention to training can reduce the major risks of implementation. To achieve quality, users and their managers must involve themselves in system design from the outset, demand that designs meet their needs, and ensure that they have a forum to communicate their expertise regarding the processes they perform. Quality also requires a rigorous testing program that detects errors of design or development early, thereby preventing a defective system from reaching the implementation stage.

Training ensures that employees have the proper skills to make the new system work. Even the best system can fail if employees cannot use it properly and efficiently. Training should occur both before and after implementation. Pre-implementation training prepares employees to use the features they need and deal with exceptional conditions. Post-implementation training focuses on using the system efficiently.

Maintenance

Maintenance refers to all activities related to a system after it is implemented and before a full-fledged needs assessment. It should include such activities as fixing software that doesn't operate properly, adding features to systems in response to new user demands, and performing periodic **post-implementation reviews.** Post-implementation reviews evaluate how well the system meets user needs, set priorities for new development, and determine when to begin a new needs assessment. A recent survey of Fortune 1000 companies found that 97 percent of all programmers are involved in maintenance activities rather than new systems development.[32]

During the maintenance stage, systems undergo continuous improvement, initially to fix bugs in the system and ensure that it continues to operate as implemented. Bugs almost always exist and may even appear after a system has operated for several years because testers can't foresee all possible contingencies that might arise in using the system.

Users also tend to discover new needs after they have used a system for several months. These needs may arise from changes in the nature of the business or environment. For example, the company may develop a new product having sales data or post-sales data needs that differ from those for other products. Or, a competitor may launch a new program, such as a frequent-buyer discount program or extended warranty program, that the company must emulate but which requires data not captured by the existing system, reports not currently generated, or even new operating procedures. Ensuring that the information system responds to such needs generally doesn't require a complete redesign or rebuilding of the system.

Once users assimilate the process improvements supported by the new system, they begin to realize that they expressed too few wishes in the needs analysis phase. They now propose changes to make the system more usable; allow managers to make better, faster, and more informed decisions; or improve the workflow of employees using the system. These users, together with IS professionals, must evaluate each change on the basis of its costs and benefits. Those judged worthwhile will require redesign and reprogramming as part of maintaining the system.

What distinguishes the activities that take place in the maintenance phase of the SDLC from those in the needs assessment phase? The activities in the maintenance phase resemble those of the needs assessment phase, but maintenance is less rigorous, more informal, less comprehensive, and more reactive. While needs assessment addresses the possibility of completely redesigning and rebuilding existing information systems, maintenance implies continuous improvement to these systems.

Modifying a system without introducing new bugs poses a significant challenge. Any changes in complex systems very likely have side effects. Following the SDLC should minimize and document the interactions among different parts of the system, thereby reducing the likelihood and scope of side effects. Maintenance remains problematic because some interactions are unavoidable and documentation may not always be complete. As more maintenance is done on a system, the likelihood of new bugs increases and the accuracy of the system's documentation decreases.

Business managers should understand the political pressures that face the IS staff during the maintenance phase. Because IS managers view end users as their customers, they often find refusing their requests difficult. Limits on IS resources mean that accepting too many projects puts too few resources on each, resulting in delivery delays, an overworked and demoralized staff, and poor product quality. Forming steering committees composed of end user managers and IS professionals who rank projects and allocate additional resources to the IS staff can help overcome the dilemmas of choosing among projects. In the absence of such committees, managers should internally justify their maintenance requests before acting on them.

Life Time Fitness, a Minnesota-based operator of operator of 27 Sports and Fitness Resorts boasting 400,000 members, uses a steering committee consisting of the company's CEO, CFO, CIO, and five corporate executive vice presidents to align IT projects with corporate goals. Before the committee was established, the executive vice presidents of each division fought hard to get their individual needs addressed, putting a great deal of pressure on an IT group with limited resources. Now, in once-a-week meetings, these executives are taking an enterprise view, making decisions that are in the best long-term interests of the company as a whole, and communicating them clearly to the IT staff.[33]

Post-Implementation Review

The first post-implementation review should occur several months after the release of a new system. This first review should audit the SDLC product and process. The IS staff and the users involved in the needs assessment and design stages should reconvene to examine any flaws in the final product, determine their causes, and modify the systems development process to prevent these mistakes in the future. This committee should also identify any remaining changes necessary to rectify the most major problems.

Subsequent system reviews should focus on establishing priorities for maintenance and determining whether the cycle should be restarted with a full needs assessment. An effective redesign strategy is proactive and attempts to implement changes before the system reaches capacity or experiences other major problems. Post-implementation review, like system maintenance, involves both IS professionals and end users in an ongoing process.

DEVELOPING AND MANAGING WEB SITES

The development and management of Web sites is fundamentally no different from that of any other type of business application. The major distinction between Web applications and most other applications is that the end user of a Web application is much more likely to be a customer of the company than an employee. The development of Web applications for employees and other internal customers follows the approximately the same life cycle, pathways, methodologies, and stages as most other systems. This section focuses, therefore, on Web sites intended for the general public or other external customers. It addresses the key issues of brand management, security, and content management.

An organization's Web site presents a public view of the organization that, like any other piece of marketing or public relations material and unlike most application systems, needs to be controlled carefully to ensure that it conforms to and supports the image that the organization hopes to convey. The content, structure, design, and performance of an organization's Web site all contribute to this image. Organizations should view their Web site as an extension of their brand. Indeed, responsibility for Web-site management at many organizations falls to the marketing or public relations department, even for applications, such as customer support or mortgage approval, that are not traditionally assumed by the marketing function. If the marketing or public relations function does not control the Web site, they could set Web-site policies to ensure the protection of the company image. Table 9-5 lists some of the policies that organizations might apply to their Web sites.

Because an organization's Web site is available to the public, security of its Web applications is a prime concern of Web-site developers. In particular, the following protections need to be established:

TABLE 9-5	Policy Category	Category Elements
	Design	Layout
Policies organizations might apply to their Web site development and management.		Stylesheets
		Typography
		Color palette
		Logos
		Background color or picture
		Metadata
		Navigation (e.g., max depth)
	Performance	Response time (to serve page)
		Page size (in bytes, determines transmission response)
		Browser compatibility (browser type, version)
		Platform compatibility (computer, phone, PDA)
	Process	Development language(s)
		Approval process for site updates
		Appeal processes
		Frequency of review
	Content	Frequency of update
		Ownership
		Content sources
	Privacy	Use of cookies
		Use of collected data
		Disclosure

- ***Protection of customers' data.*** To secure the trust of its customers and often to fulfill its legal obligations, organizations must protect data provided by customers. For example, if an organization collects customers' credit card numbers, addresses, medical data, or other confidential data, these data should not only be secured from the view of outsiders, but they should also be encrypted so that if the intended protection fails, those stealing the information cannot make sense of it.

- ***Protection of operational data.*** Unprincipled competitors can put a company out of business if they have the ability to change or delete orders, alter shipping information, or otherwise interfere with a company's operational data.

- ***Protection of trade secrets.*** Company trade secrets should not be vulnerable to theft over Web connections.

- ***Protection of access.*** Hackers can cause irreparable harm by tying up a Web site so that it is unavailable to others with legitimate needs, such as placing orders.

Chapter 5 addresses the technologies available for managing the security of Web services and Chapter 10 addresses the organizational issues surrounding the management of security.

Most non-Web applications are designed for stability. These applications are expected to change infrequently; developers properly place an emphasis on getting the design right to minimize the need for maintenance. In contrast, Web site developers expect their Web sites to change frequently. Such change keeps customers interested and promotes their return to the Web site. Because developers anticipate the need for continual maintenance, they focus less on the initial design and more on assuring that maintenance will be easy and inexpensive. To the extent possible, organizations automate the maintenance of their sites, using powerful products called **content management software** (see Chapter 4). These products catalog information on a Web site so that it can be easily tracked, modified, and used in differing contexts. They allow employees who have little or no Web development experience to create material for an organization's Web site. All they need to do is enter the material into a form that indicates its type and relevance. Based on the information the employee provides, the content management software massages and fits it into the style and structure of the Web site and makes it available where and when appropriate. Content management software also helps frequent Web-site visitors customize what they see each time they return to an organization's Web page.

WHY SYSTEMS DEVELOPMENT PROJECTS SUCCEED OR FAIL

Burrows and managers like her can learn a great deal by studying systems development successes and failures. Large-scale systems development poses major challenges to organizations, even those with extensive IS experience. Statistics indicate that only about 26 percent of all IT projects are completed on time, within budget, and with the functionality originally proposed. About 28 percent of IT projects are cancelled before they are even delivered.[34] Another study claims that faulty software costs businesses $78 billion per year.[35]

Much research has addressed the question of why systems projects succeed or fail. The reasons vary from project to project, but most fall into the following five categories: riskiness of the project, definition of project scope, quality of project management, quality of process design, and adequacy of resources.

Risk

Every project involves some element of risk. We have already addressed how companies can assess and manage risk. We've also seen that if the potential return is great enough, most companies will undertake even a highly risky project and expose themselves to a high likelihood of failure.

Scope

Successful projects have a clearly defined scope. Unfortunately, a variety of forces tend to put pressure on a project's scope. Often, new products or services from competitors create the need for an immediate reaction that had not been anticipated when the project began. Even without such competitive pressures, users needs will change, and they will find additional features that they feel they absolutely must have. Technology advances will also provide the opportunity for additional capabilities that are very hard to forego. Changing requirements, known as scope creep, can keep a project from ever being finished and is one of the leading causes of project failure.[36]

Management

Projects more often succeed when experienced and effective managers run them. Project managers need to know how to plan, organize teams, assign responsibilities, set milestones and deadlines, seek and obtain resources, and resolve crises. Business managers, even those not on a project team, can affect a project's success. Managers who do not support a project can undermine or sabotage it. Top management support can help employees affected by the project to accept change. Lack of top management involvement and support can result in the development of systems that fail to anticipate the long-term needs of the organization and conflict with strategic organizational goals.[37]

Process

As we have seen, systems development is a complicated process with many alternative paths. Those familiar and experienced with the process can more readily guide development through the obstacles it might face. The process of systems development has been widely researched. Several academic and trade journals and many books and studies are devoted to it. In addition, a variety of software tools exist to guide project managers through the tasks they need to perform to maximize their chance of success. Managers, such as Burrows, should familiarize themselves with these tools and with current thinking about the process before actively participating in it. Those unfamiliar with the process will make many mistakes unless they follow clear guidelines.

Resources

Systems development requires time, money, and people. We have studied ways to estimate the resources needed. Organizations that commit the required resources more often succeed. Those organizations that can't or won't commit the resources necessary for success will likely encounter failure.

SUMMARY

The systems development life cycle (SDLC) refers to a sequence of stages in the conception, design, creation, and implementation of information systems. It includes needs assessment, alternative analysis, design, development, implementation, and maintenance. Sophisticated organizations view systems development not as a series of independent projects but rather as a process, subject to incremental improvement and following specified methodologies. Pathways through the SDLC include the waterfall model, the spiral approach, rapid prototyping, and agile programming.

Systems developers use data models, process models, and object models to understand existing systems and design new ones. Process management tools help standardize and assure quality throughout the SDLC. CASE tools can help automate the activities in the SDLC.

Needs assessment begins the SDLC. End users, their managers, and IS professionals analyze current systems and document users' needs as completely and accurately as possible. Systems analysts often serve as liaisons between the IS department and the users to facilitate the complete identification of needs. They use interviews, onsite observation, questionnaires, structured analysis, data dictionaries, and reverse engineering to collect information about inputs, outputs, and procedures.

The alternative analysis stage of the SDLC focuses on specifying and evaluating various options for the system and tentatively selecting a single system. Such selection involves both cost/benefit analyses and risk analyses. The design stage of the SDLC provides detailed specification for the selected system. Elements of design include the interface, data, process, objects, the physical design, and a design for testing.

Development, the fourth stage of the SDLC, focuses on procuring hardware, procuring or developing software, and testing the system. IS professionals and system users must determine whether to purchase or develop the new system. Development tools include screen generators, report writers, and code generators. Developers test systems for performance and usability.

Organizations then implement the new system using one of four strategies. Direct cut-over involves the overnight replacement of one system by another. Pilot implementation means replacing the system for a targeted population in the organization and increasing that target over time. Phased implementation means introducing each component of the system individually and sequentially. Parallel implementation refers to the introduction of the new system without disabling the old system.

Maintenance and post-implementation review conclude the SDLC. These activities involve finding and fixing bugs in the system and introducing required process improvements.

Web site development differs from other systems development in that site content changes frequently and security is paramount. Developers use content management software to control Web content while assuring consistency with format and brand.

Systems development projects succeed or fail because of their risk, definition of scope, management, process design, and resources. Managers who understand and observe the processes and tools for developing new systems can reduce the likelihood of failure.

KEY TERMS

agile programming
alpha testing
alternative analysis
beta testing
bug
CASE tool
CASE toolset
CASE workbench
code generator
component testing
computer-aided software engineering
    (CASE)
content management software
contextual inquiry
data design
data dictionary
data-flow diagram (DFD)
design
design specification
development
direct cut-over strategy

function box
implementation
input analysis
integration testing
interface design
joint application development (JAD)
legacy system
maintenance
methodology
needs assessment
object design
output analysis
parallel implementation strategy
performance testing
phased implementation strategy
physical design
pilot implementation strategy
post-implementation review
process design
process librarian
process manager

prototyping
rapid application development (RAD)
report generator
requirements analysis
return on investment (ROI)
reverse engineering
risk analysis
screen generator
spiral approach
structure chart
structured analysis
system testing
systems analyst
systems development life cycle (SDLC)
test design
time box
turn-key solutions
unit testing
usability lab
usability testing
waterfall model

REVIEW QUESTIONS

1. What are the six stages of the systems development life cycle?
2. How does maintenance differ from needs assessment?
3. Compare and contrast the waterfall and spiral approaches to the implementation of the SDLC.
4. What are the advantages of rapid prototyping relative to the waterfall approach?
5. Why do managers and systems developers use models to describe an organization's data, processes, and objects?
6. What are two types of data models?
7. What are three types of process models?
8. How might managers use the Capability Maturity Model to improve systems development in their company?
9. What three types of needs do analysts focus on during the needs assessment stage of the SDLC?
10. How can managers assess and reduce the risk of new systems development?
11. What are the key elements of interface design, data design, process design, object design, physical design, and test design?
12. How do content and form design complement each other in interface design?
13. What choices do managers have in the develop-or-purchase decision?
14. What are four types of testing, and how do they differ?
15. How is usability testing done?
16. What are the advantages and disadvantages of the four implementation strategies?
17. Why do bugs often exist even after testing?
18. Why should managers perform a post-implementation review?
19. Why do systems projects sometimes fail?
20. How does the development and maintenance of Web applications differ from that of other business applications?

MINICASE

HOW HYGEIA TRAVEL HEALTH SELECTS WHICH PROJECTS TO FUND

Toronto-based Hygeia Travel Health provides health insurance for foreign tourists to the United States and Canada. Say a sightseeing Spaniard falls and needs hip replacement surgery. Hygeia works with the traveler's home country health insurance provider, finding a local doctor and handling the paperwork.

Hygeia is basically a middleman between a foreign HMO and a network of American doctors and hospitals. Any HMO has a network of doctors who, in return for a guaranteed customer base, give the HMO discounted rates. Hygeia basically does the same thing. It has a network of American doctors to whom it guarantees a customer base of sick travelers—a profitable clientele because most require only minor treatment and never come back for follow-up visits. Hygeia then passes the savings along to the foreign HMO, which would otherwise be forced to pay full price to a doctor not on its plan.

The travel health market has grown radically during the past few years, and Hygeia has grown along with it. In 2000, Hygeia had a relatively easy time hand-processing the 20,000-plus claims submitted. But in 2001, that number will grow by 300 percent, and within five years, says CIO Rod Hamilton, it should reach millions.

With the company growing so quickly, each business project has to be successful either in raising revenue, cutting costs, or substantially increasing Hygeia's standing with its customers, says Hygeia CEO Virgil Bretz. Last summer Hygeia developed a process through which every project—whether it's a new e-commerce system or simply a change to the Web site—is evaluated.

The process itself is relatively straightforward. The project evaluation committee, consisting of six senior executives, splits into two groups. One group includes CIO Hamilton and the heads of operations and research and development; it analyzes the costs of every project. The other group consists of the two chief marketing officers (for insurance providers and payers) and the head of business development; it analyzes the expected benefits, including the impact on revenues, the impact on profitability in the first year, and client retention. The groups are permanent, and to stay objective, they don't discuss a project until both sides have evaluated it. The results are then shared, both on a spreadsheet and in conversation. Projects are then approved, passed over, or tabled for future consideration.

Bretz says the process works for two reasons. First, it considers only objective measures, such as revenue possibilities and costs. That way, Hygeia avoids favoring pet projects and other potential hazards. "The process is very deductive," says Bretz. "We see all the options and then find the winners."

The process also fosters communication among departments. The committee meets every Monday to discuss and evaluate new proposals. It is a large time commitment, but Bretz feels it builds understanding and consensus within the organization.

The following example shows how the process was used in a typical application.

The Small Claim Automation Project Proposal

In early 2001, the payer marketing team proposed a project to automate the system for processing doctors' smaller claims by integrating the processing with Hygeia's Web site.

The proposal came out of an important observation: Most of the company's revenue comes from claims for in-patient hospital stays, clinical tests, and the like, which can run more than $100,000. These claims represent about 20 percent of Hygeia's business and 80 percent of its revenues. The remaining 80 percent of business consists of physician claims, most of which are less than $1,000 and often less than $100. In many cases, the cost of paying someone to process these claims, and thus get the discount promised to customers' health plans, is actually greater than Hygeia's processing fee. Sometimes, Hamilton says, Hygeia processes these claims for larger clients and absorbs the financial hits. Many times, Hygeia simply pays the bills in full. The project proponents reasoned that if the physicians' claims forms could be moved online, allowing doctors to fill out the forms themselves, then it would eliminate staff processing costs for these small claims.

The benefits team estimated that the project would help the company recover $840,000 in revenue. Based on assessments of past business and projections for future growth, the team also estimated that the project would provide for a 5 percent profit increase and a 10 percent rise in customer retention.

The costs team, meanwhile, determined that building a fully automated application that could handle the claims would cost $266,000 (about 104 weeks' worth of an application developer's time, at $1,600 a week, plus contingencies for consultants and two full-time data managers).

In this case, the assessment teams felt the costs did not outweigh the benefits. However, the project depended on two applications: the automated processing and the online claims entry. Each one would have to be built, then the two would have to be integrated. So, when the two teams returned to the table, they reached a compromise: To speed development and limit the cost, the applications would be built, but not integrated.

Collecting the data online but processing it after the data had been checked by the data managers was a substantial improvement over the current system and still allowed Hygeia to guarantee processing within 24 hours. It's not real-time, but it's still fast. And, Hygeia could have the system in place sooner.

After the Green Light

Once a project has been approved, it gets added to one of two lists, depending on its size. Typically, the line dividing large and small ones is a cost of $100,000. Hygeia generally pursues three large projects at a time, says Hamilton, provided that the primary workload falls in different business areas. Small projects are spread out in similar fashion, although, says Hamilton, "usually eight out of every 10 are IT projects."

Hygeia weighs two factors when determining the order in which to undertake the projects. The first is the bottom line: How much money will a project return? In this case, Hygeia relies on the committee's estimates and proceeds based on which promised the largest financial return. For many of the smaller projects, such as redesigning the company Web site, the dollar benefit is hard to calculate. In these cases, the committee looks at the benefit to customers, the unquantified product of the benefit team deliberations. Hamilton acknowledges that this is less objective than the financial estimates used to evaluate large projects. But since these are small projects, they tend to take less time and Hygeia can pursue a number of them at once.

Of the 27 projects that have gone through the process so far, 14 have been approved. "I have a high degree of faith [in the process]," Bretz says. "I am betting the future of the company on it."

SOURCE: Adapted from Ben Worthen, "Two Teams are Better than One," *CIO Magazine*, 15 July 2001, 74–77. Reprinted through the courtesy of CIO. ©2002, CXO Media Inc. All rights reserved.

Case Questions

Diagnosis

1. What were Hygeia's information needs with regard to processing small claims?

Evaluation

2. How well were those needs being met?

Design

3. How did Hygeia evaluate the proposal to automate small claims processing?

4. Why did Hygeia modify the proposal?

Implementation

5. How did Hygeia determine whether the proposed claims processing automation was more or less worthy of being funded than other projects?

6. How did Hygeia reduce the risks associated with the project?

7. How will Hygeia measure the success of the project?

8. What are the benefits and costs of the process that Hygeia has put into place to evaluate project proposals?

9. Do you think that Hygeia's process could be improved? How?

9-1 TEDDY BEAR COMPANY TRIES AGAIN

ACTIVITY

Step 1: Read the following case.

After a three-year saga that included a $10.3 million financial hit from the failed installation of packaged applications, teddy bear maker Russ Berrie and Co. is taking another crack at retiring its legacy systems.

The Oakland, New Jersey-based distributor of toys and gifts last week finalized plans to roll out J. D. Edwards & Company's suite of enterprise resource planning (ERP), customer relationship management, and financial applications. The company has scheduled the multimillion-dollar project to be implemented in phases over an 18-month period.

Russ Berrie CIO Michael Saunders said that the company, which had sales of $225 million during the first nine months of last year, hopes the ERP system will help it reach $1 billion in annual revenue in the coming years.

Within the next 12 months, he said, Russ Berrie plans to begin installing the applications one department at a time, starting with a stand-alone implementation in purchasing. "We're not going big bang," Saunders said. "We're mitigating implementation risks by taking a phased-in approach."

The company has reason to be cautious. Three years ago, it attempted to migrate its homegrown distribution, financial, and customer service systems to a packaged ERP application because the old systems, programmed for two-digit dates, could not properly handle calculation for years 2000 and beyond and because these systems could not store four-digit dates. In 1999, the migration to the ERP package hit a brick wall. Saunders said the problems were severe enough for Russ Berrie to take many of the new applications off-line. That forced the company to resurrect and modify its aging Digital Equipment Corp. VAX systems so that they could handle the four-digit dates. "It was not a fun process," Saunders said, adding that it strained both the IT department and business units.

Saunders wouldn't identify the software vendors that were involved in the failed implementation, but sources said that SAP AG's applications were part of the 1999 project. A spokesman at SAP confirmed that Russ Berrie was one of its customers, but he declined to offer further details because of pending litigation between the two companies.

Joshua Greenbaum, an analyst at Enterprise Applications Consulting in Daly City, California, said it appears that Russ Berrie "bit off more than they could chew" on the 1999 project. Company-wide rollouts are especially risky for midsize businesses, Greenbaum said.

In an attempt to protect itself the second time around, Saunders said, Russ Berrie hired a law firm with experience in the IT market. Washington-based Shaw Pittman LLP assisted the company during the software selection process. Saunders declined to disclose the exact cost of the J. D. Edwards project. Some limited software customization work will be required, he said.

SOURCE Extracted and adapted from Marc L Songini, "Teddy Bear Maker Prepares for Second Attempt at ERP Rollout," *Computerworld*, 4 February 2002, 16.

Step 2: Prepare the case for class discussion.

Step 3: Answer each of the following questions, individually or in small groups, as directed by your instructor.

Diagnosis

1. What information needs did Russ Berrie have in 1999?

Evaluation

2. How well did the old system meet these needs?

Design

3. What advantages was the new system supposed to offer?

4. What alternative was selected for the new system? Was this alternative appropriate?

5. What elements of the SDLC were not performed in 1999?

6. How has Russ Berrie modified it approach to the SDLC for the current ERP project?

Implementation

7. Why do you think Russ Berrie has decided on a phased implementation approach for the current project?

8. What does Russ Berrie need to do to ensure the success of the current project?

Step 4: In small groups, with the entire class, or in written form, share your answers to the questions above. Then answer the following questions:

1. What information needs did Russ Berrie and Company have?

2. How well did the old system meet those needs?

3. Why did the first implementation fail?

4. What should Russ Berrie do to ensure the success of the current project?

9-2 MORAL MINORITY

Step 1: Read the following scenario.

"What changed?" Janice Devin asked. "Is it just me, or does anybody else feel like this?" Devin reflected back on her decision four months ago to join the development team for Liberty Hospital's new imaging and workflow system.

Her manager Robert Harding did not know how to respond to her question. He began to realize that Devin had underestimated the impact the project would have on the people in the accounts payable department and, by extension, on her own feelings about her work at the hospital.

In the past 12 months, the hospital's financial situation had improved significantly. Much of the credit had gone to the administration and finance team, which, two years before, had begun an aggressive effort to examine every critical business process at the teaching hospital.

A year ago the administration team began to translate the results of its analysis into an action plan. However, while their effort had improved the hospital's bottom line, it had also caused stress among staff in different departments. There had been rumors that the union representing the maintenance staff was considering a strike over proposed changes in work rules, and several of the hospital's senior medical staff had filed a protest over what they described as "interference" from nonmedical personnel.

Until she joined the new project team, Devin's interaction with staff outside her own department had been limited. As a result of another of the process changes proposed by the new administration, most members of the IS department had, for the most part, operated in isolation from the groups they served.

Harding had been an internal advocate of the new approach to working with the IS department's internal "customers" and had encouraged Devin to participate on the project team. Harding had painted an attractive picture of the opportunity. In addition to letting Devin work with exciting new technology, it would give her visibility outside her own group. After some friendly encouragement, she volunteered for the team.

But once she had joined the team, things began to look different from the picture Harding had painted. Devin found Robin Groaci, the administration and finance member of the project team, difficult to work with. Robin had joined Liberty straight out of a health care management program three months after the senior management team turned over. This was her first job. Mary Trayte, the head of the accounts payable department, was pleasant enough, but seemed intimidated by Groaci. Devin liked the two other IS members of the team, but they were more focused on the technical architecture for the application, whereas she had to worry about how the application's functions matched up with the system spec.

Things got worse when Devin discovered—relatively late in the project life cycle—that once the application was completed and phased in, more than 20 members of the accounts payable department stood to lose their jobs. When she inquired further, Groaci told Devin that it was not any of her concern and that she should concentrate on getting the application completed on time.

Realizing that she had to talk with someone about how she felt, Devin approached Harding and requested a private meeting. During the meeting, she stated her discomfort with the work she was doing and asked for Harding's advice on what to do.

SOURCE: Damian Rinaldi, "Moral Minority," *Client/Server Computing*, April 1994, 33. Used with permission.

Step 2: Prepare the case for class discussion.

Step 3: Answer each of the following questions, individually or in small groups, as directed by your instructor.

1. How might Harding respond to Devin?
2. For each alternative, who benefits and who is harmed?
3. From the ethical principles of least harm, rights and duties, professional responsibilities, self-interest and utilitarianism, consistency, and respect, how would you evaluate each alternative?
4. How should Harding respond to Devin? Why?

9-3 USING A CASE TOOL

ACTIVITY

Step 1: Read the following scenario.

Benson College is a business school with a student body of about 2,000 undergraduates, 300 full-time MBA students, and 1,500 part-time MBA students. The part-time MBAs take courses in the evenings, and full-time MBAs take most of their elective courses in the evenings as well. Ninety percent of the undergraduates live on campus.

Currently, the college sends out registration material to students listing the available courses and the times that they are offered. Students register for courses by filling out and returning registration forms. The forms are processed by the registrar's office and posted to the registration system in the evening. Students may check the status of their registration by touch-tone phone. Although the registrar updates the availability of courses daily, students still need to check to make sure that they were not closed out of courses for which they had registered.

The college registrar has sponsored a project to reengineer the student registration process so that student registration will be paper-free and require no human assistance. The impetus for this project includes a need to reduce the cost of running the registrar's office and to respond to competitive pressure in the evening MBA market by making registration easier and more pleasant for part-time students.

A start-up team consisting of the registrar, an assistant registrar, the graduate dean, the undergraduate dean, the chief information officer (CIO), and a member of Benson's quality office have met a few times and have established the following parameters for the project prior to setting up a project team.

Students will be able to register by telephone or World Wide Web. If they have paid in advance, this registration will be effective immediately. Otherwise, the registration will be provisional pending receipt of payment (by check) and will remain in effect for one week. A project team will be formed shortly consisting of the current start-up team, a software developer, and possibly volunteer members of the faculty and undergraduate and graduate student body.

The current registration system, which is built on proprietary software using a proprietary database, will be replaced rather than modified. Although functional, it is considered too inflexible to change and too costly to maintain. Benson does not have the staff or resources to develop this system from scratch. It will have to be purchased. The system will have to interface with the existing accounting system, which maintains student account information. It will also have to interface with the room and faculty scheduling system. The project team may identify other required interfaces. The system will have to check for prerequisites and time conflicts. The project team will likely identify other system requirements and information needs. A budget of $50,000 has been allocated for the preliminary analysis and design.

The college has standardized on a TCP/IP network infrastructure running Windows NT servers, Windows 95 desktop systems, Microsoft Outlook for e-mail, Microsoft SQL-Server for enterprise database management, and Visual Basic for GUI development. It is using both Lotus Workflow and Microsoft Exchange for workflow management.

Step 2: Your instructor will show you how to use a CASE tool available within your college environment. If no such tool is available, your instructor will direct you to download a demonstration copy of such a tool from the World Wide Web.

Step 3: Using the CASE tool, develop a ER diagram, a DFD, a structure chart, an IDEF1X model, a function box model, or a UML model, as directed by your instructor, of the data, processes, or objects suggested by this case.

9-4 THE HINDENBERG GAS COMPANY

ACTIVITY

Step 1: Read the following scenario.

You are Pete Bogg, the IS manager of the Hindenberg Gas Company, a regional utility providing service to more than 10 million locations. As with many large monopolies, your company suffers from a reputation for poor customer service and weak community relations. An ancient billing system, in which customer bills are usually late, wrong, or missing, contributes to its poor reputation. There is little information available to customer-service representatives about current bills, and no history information whatsoever.

The good news is that your department is funded to replace the system for the billing department, and everyone is very excited. The bad news is that everyone wants something very different from the project. Capp deFumes, your systems and programming manager, sees the opportunity to expand his department with many of the group technicians taking the long-awaited step into supervisory roles. The users have a long list of traditional detailed requirements and, having waited for years, are not prepared to accept any compromises. The very influential vice president of public relations, Shirley U. Jest, and the president, Dick Tator, want something very soon to put the ground swell of customer complaints and attendant nonpayment into remission. They feel that it could even be temporary, as long as it is quick, and it does not have to be perfect. The vice president of finance, Amanda B. Reconwith (the likely next president, but not directly in charge of billing) on the other hand, believes that a high tech, sophisticated, state-of-the-art system is the way to go. Not only would it generate positive customer relations and favorable press, but it would last for a long time. Everyone knows, based on experience, that this system will have to last for a long time.

You must decide which development pathway to use. You know that a decision on direction needs to be made and the project started.

SOURCE: Excerpted from Robert K. Wysocki and James Young, "Situation 10-1: The Hindenberg Gas Company," *Information Systems: Management Practices in Action* (John Wiley & Sons, 1990): 70–71. Used with permission.

Step 2: Individually or in small groups, outline three plans for developing the new system, one using each of the following approaches: waterfall, spiral, and prototyping.

Step 3: Share your plans. Then assess the risks associated with each of the development approaches? How prepared is the company to assume these risks? Overall, which approach do you favor? Why?

9-5 SYSTEM ANALYST HIRING AT VAILTON COLLEGE

ACTIVITY

Step 1: Your instructor will divide you into five groups. One group will represent the Registration Redesign Committee (RRC) at Vailton College, and the other competing systems analyst candidates.

Step 2: Read the following scenario.

Vailton College is a small but well-respected business school located in the southeastern United States. Six years ago, the college computerized its class registration process. Nevertheless, much of the process remains manual and cumbersome. Students have complained, year after year, about waiting in line to register, having to re-register after being closed out of their selected classes, and having to make frequent trips to the registrar's office during the drop-add period. Faculty members have complained about the length of time it takes before they receive final class rosters.

The computer system also allows students to register for classes for which they do not have the necessary prerequisites. Although students are supposed to have their registration plans approved by their faculty advisor in advance of registration and faculty are supposed to check prerequisites, this process has not eliminated this problem and others associated with students not completing their requirements.

The president of the college has commissioned a committee of faculty members, staff from the registrars office, and staff from the information systems division (the technical group that runs the college's computer systems) to redesign the registration process and the information systems that support it. The committee has developed a broad outline of a new telephone-based registration system and must now design the information systems to support it. Its current task is to hire a systems analyst to coordinate the project. After an initial screening, the committee has narrowed the search to the following four candidates:

- *Gene/Jean Smith:* A 54-year-old systems manager who has recently been laid off from Digital Equipment Corporation (DEC) when the division he/she worked for was closed. Smith's background includes more than 30 years of systems development work at DEC, exclusively in the DEC environment. Smith has dealt with many different DEC products, customers, and their needs. Although Smith has never previously been at Vailton, he/she is thoroughly familiar with Vailton's current DEC computer equipment.

- *Bobbie/Bobby Jones:* A 23-year-old Vailton graduate with a recent MBA, an undergraduate major in MIS at Vailton, and limited work experience. Jones is currently self-employed as an IS consultant, but is looking for more permanent employment in a small company. Having gone through the registration process at Vailton, Jones is familiar with it and agrees strongly with the need to revise it.

- *Pat McDonald:* A 32-year-old former employee of Pacific Bell who has relocated near Vailton. At Pacific Bell, McDonald worked in the customer relations department and has experience dealing with customers and using computer systems. He/she enrolled in the part time MBA program at Vailton upon returning to the area and was one of the people affected by problems with the current registration system. He/she has some wonderful ideas for improving the system.

- *Terry Wilson:* A 38-year-old programmer for the Shawton Bank, the largest bank in the state. He/she learned how to program at Georgia Tech in the late 1980s and has been a very reliable, well-liked, easy-to-get-along-with employee of Shawton ever since. The bank has recently undergone some restructuring and appears headed for further restructuring if the recession runs its course; Wilson is looking for a more stable environment. His/her programming skills are excellent in four languages: FORTRAN, COBOL, BASIC, and C. He/she feels that a college community would permit further enhancement of his/her skills and valuable opportunity for additional education.

Step 3: If your group is assigned the role of one of the candidates, select one of your group members to represent your candidate in an interview. Prepare a short presentation to explain why he/she is the best person for the job. Also anticipate the questions that the committee will ask and prepare your candidate to answer them in the most favorable light. If your group is assigned the role of the RRC, prepare a job description for the systems analyst and a set of questions to ask each candidate.

Step 4: The instructor will call each team's representative to present its case. Members of the RRC will sit at the front of the class and ask the prepared questions and any additional questions they may have after each candidate has presented his/her case. Please be advised that it is illegal to ask candidates about their personal lives and families.

Step 5: The RRC will discuss the merits of the candidates in open executive session. It will then vote on the four candidates.

Step 6: With the entire class, answer the following questions:
1. What are the most desirable attributes of a candidate for the job of systems analyst?
2. In selecting an analyst for a project, which is more important: familiarity with the business process or familiarity with the role of systems analyst. What are the pros and cons of each?
3. Did the RRC use appropriate criteria in selecting the candidate?

IS ON THE WEB

IS ON THE WEB

Exercise 1: The Web page for Chapter 9 will direct you to a story about a company's successful or unsuccessful implementation of a new information system. Using principles from this chapter, identify the characteristics of the project, the way it was managed, and the company's development process that contributed most to the success or failure of the new system.

Exercise 2: Go to the Web site of two consulting firms that provide systems development assistance. What types of services do they offer? In a short report, compare and contrast the two firms.

Exercise 3: Download and demonstrate a CASE tool from the Web. Learn how to use it. Briefly present an application of it.

RECOMMENDED READINGS

Ambler, Scott W. *Agile Modeling: Effective Practices for Extreme Programming and the Unified Process.* New York: John Wiley & Sons, 2002.

Kaner, Cem, James Bach, and Bret Pettichord. *Lessons Learned in Software Testing.* New York: John Wiley & Sons, 2001.

Murch, Richard. *Project Management: Best Practices for IT Professionals.* Upper Saddle River, NJ: Prentice Hall, 2000.

Niederst, Jennifer. *Web Design in a Nutshell,* 2nd ed. Sebastopol, CA: O'Reilly & Associates, 2001.

Vredenburg, Karel, Scott Isensee, and Carol Righi. *User-Centered Design: An Integrated Approach.* Upper Saddle River, NJ: Prentice Hall, 2001.

Whitten, Jeffrey L., Lonnie D. Bentley, and Kevin C. Dittman. *Systems Analysis and Design Methods,* 5th ed. Boston: Richard D. Irwin/McGraw Hill, 2000.

NOTES

1. Extracted and adapted from Len Ptak, "Measuring Client Value," *CMA Management* 75 (June 2001): 38–40.

2. http://www.dsdm.org, accessed on 18 March 2002.

3. Philippe Kruchten, *The Rational Unified Process: An Introduction,* 2nd ed. Boston: Addison Wesley Longman, 2000.

4. http://programs.rational.com/success/Success_ VideoDetail.cfm?ID=225, accessed on 13 September 2002.

5. http://ca.com/products/alm/process_continuum/processware.htm.http://catarina.usc.edu/danzig/cs402/prog3/doc/internal/section3_3.html. http://www.mitre.org/resources/centers/sepo/docs_guidance.html, accessed on 18 March 2002.

6. http://www.rcgit.com/news/Current/seilevel2.cfm, accessed on 13 September 2002.

7. Gary H. Anthes and Jaikumar Vijayan, "Lessons from India Inc.," *Computerworld,* 2 April 2001, 40–42.

8. http://www.telcordia.com/aboutus/background.html, accessed on 13 September 2002.

9. Barry Boehm, "A Spiral Model of Software Development and Enhancement," *IEEE Computer* 21 (May 1988): 61–72.

10. Lee Copeland, "Caterpillar Digs into Agile Development," *Computerworld,* 7 January 2002, 14.

11. John G. Voltmer, "Selling Management on the Prototyping Approach," *Journal of Systems Management* 40 (July 1989): 24–25.

12. Lee Copeland, "Developers Approach Extreme Programming with Caution," *Computerworld,* 22 October 2001, 7.

13. Alistair Cockburn, *Agile Software Development through People* (Boston: Addison Wesley Longman, 2001).

14. Alan Radding, "Extremely Agile Programming," *Computerworld,* 4 February 2002, 42, 44.

15. Object Management Group, "OMG Unified Modeling Language Specification, Version 1.4." Needham, MA: Object Management Group, 2001.

16. Hubert F. Hofmann and Franz Lehner, "Requirements Engineering as a Success Factor in Software Projects," *IEEE Software,* July/August 2001, 58–66.

17. "Firm Size & Experience Drive Pay for Business Systems Analysts," *Ioma's Report on Salary Survey 1* (November 2001): 4, 5.

18. For a more complete list and description, see Terry A. Byrd, Kathy L. Cossick, and Robert W. Zmud, "A Synthesis of Research on Requirements Analysis and Knowledge Acquisition Techniques," *MIS Quarterly,* March 1992, 117–138. See also Suzanne Robertson and James Robertson, *Mastering the Requirements Process.* Boston: Addison-Wesley, 2000.

19. See H. Beyer and K. Holtzblatt, *Contextual Design: Defining Customer-Centered Systems.* San Francisco: Morgan Kaufmann, 1998.

20. Thomas Hoffman, "ROI on IT Projects Difficult to Measure," *Computerworld,* 11 March 2002, 6.

21. Ibid.

22. See, for example, Capers Jones, *Software Assessments, Benchmarks, and Best Practices.* Boston: Addison-Wesley, 2000.

23. Melissa Solomon, "ROI: It's About People, Not Numbers," *Computerworld,* 14 January 2002, 26.

24. ohn R. Schuyler, *Risk and Decision Analysis in Projects.* Newtown Square, PA: Project Management Institute, 2001.

25. Robert L. Scheier, "Stabilizing Your Risk," *Computerworld ROI,* May/June 2001, 16.

26. Danielle Dunne, "Wireless That Works," *CIO,* 15 February 2002, 60–66.

27. Caitlin Mollison, "ABN AMRO Mortgage Turns to Speech-Recognition Technology," *Internet World,* February 2002, 40–41.

28. Kim Halskov Madsen, "The Diversity of Usability Practices," *Communications of the ACM* 42 (May 1999): 60–62.

29. Mark Leon, "How to Make Sure the Customer Comes First," *InfoWorld,* 29 October 2001, S26–S27.

30. Gary H. Anthes, "When Five 9s Aren't Enough," *Computerworld,* 8 October 2001, 48- 49.

31. Kelly Jackson Higgins, "Concentra Health Finds a Cure for Wireless Growth," *Network Computing,* 22 July 2002, 51–53.

32. Nina Lytton, "Maintenance Dollars at Work," *Computerworld,* 16 July 2001, 14.

33. David Joachim, "Where the Gloves Come Off," *Network Computing,* 8 July 2002, 54–58. http://www.xtime.com/press/archives/aug142001.html, accessed on 13 September 2002. http://www.averisoft.com/press_020708_1.php, accessed on 13 September 2002.

34. H. Jeff Smith, Mark Keil, and Gordon Depledge, "Keeping Mum as the Project Goes Under: Toward an Explanatory Model," *Journal of Management Information Systems* 18 (fall 2001): 189–227. Original source: Standish Group International Inc., CHAOS: A Recipe for Success, 1999.

35. Meridith Levinson, "Let's Stop Wasting $78 Billion a Year," *CIO,* 15 October 2001, 78–83.

36. "India: Making IT Projects Tick: Five Simple Rules Can Make All the Difference to an IT Project's Success, Says Brian Katzen," *Businessline,* 24 September 2001, 1. David Raths, "Managing Your Three-Ring Circus," *InfoWorld,* 13 March 2000, 93–94.

37. W. J. Doll, "Avenues for Top Management Involvement in Successful MIS Development," *MIS Quarterly,* spring 1985, 17–35. M. L. Markus, "Power, Politics, and MIS Implementation," *Communications of the ACM* 26 (June, 1983): 430–444. K. B. White and R. Leifer, "Information Systems Development Success: Perspectives from Project Team Participants," *MIS Quarterly* (1986): 214–223. Robert A. Rademacher, "Critical Factors for Systems Success," *Journal of Systems Management* 40 (June, 1989): 15–17.

10

Managing the Delivery of Information Services

LEARNING OBJECTIVES

After completing Chapter 10, you will be able to:

- Describe three ways of organizing the information systems function.
- Discuss the advantages and disadvantages of outsourcing.
- Compare and contrast the concepts of unallocated cost center, allocated cost center, and profit center.
- Discuss the roles and positions of employees who provide information services.
- Describe the purpose of a service level agreement and list its typical components.
- Discuss the advantages and disadvantages of setting standards for investments in information technology and systems.
- Explain why disaster planning is desirable, and describe the elements of a disaster plan.
- Explain why organizations draft security policies, and describe common business practices that compromise security in the absence of such a policy.
- Explain why organizations draft acceptable use policies, and describe how they enforce them.
- Describe two ways that IS managers can align IS and business priorities.
- Discuss why companies develop an information technology architecture.
- Offer two strategies for keeping technical staff current.

Delivering Information Technology at Nestlé

Nestlé is the world's largest food and beverage company. A global giant with a workforce of about 225,000, Nestlé operates almost 500 factories and has offices in more than 75 countries. The company's line of 8,000 products includes chocolate bars, Nescafe instant coffee, Perrier bottled water, and Cheerios breakfast cereal.

Delivering information technology at the scale of Nestlé's operations is a daunting task. The task is complicated by Nestlé's organizational structure. While its water and pharmaceutical businesses are managed globally, its food businesses are managed through three geographic zones, with many national companies. The national companies have a great deal of autonomy, including the responsibility for providing their own infrastructure and support services. A wholly owned subsidiary, Nestec, is available to support corporate services, including information and communication technology, but national companies have a great deal of liberty to arrange their own technology services to meet their local needs.

Over the last decade, the company has worked hard to rationalize and standardize technology to make operations more efficient and promote information sharing. For example, in the late 1980s, Nestlé's companies operated many different e-mail systems. In the early 1990s, they integrated these systems using an X400 switch and gateway. However, the lack of a global directory continued to hinder communication. Eventually, the company standardized on Microsoft Exchange. Still, it took two to three years for all the users to agree to be integrated into the network, for the transition to take place, and for the full benefit of the integrated e-mail system to be realized. Ten years ago, the company operated multiple spreadsheet and word processing systems. Today, the common use of Microsoft Office makes information exchange much easier.

In 1991, Nestlé began to standardize its enterprise operation and planning systems on SAP. Yet, as of June 2001, only two-thirds of the company runs on that platform. Some subsidiaries continue to operate on stand-alone PC systems or AS/400-based systems. In Syria, for example, where laws require invoices to be printed in Arabic, the company uses a different ERP product because SAP does not support the Arabic character set.[1]

Organizations, such as Nestlé, whether they operate in a decentralized or centralized mode, periodically evaluate their information technology **infrastructure**—their investment in hardware, software, systems, and people—to ensure that it takes advantage of new technological developments and responds efficiently to the organization's information needs and changing competitive position. They might develop an **architecture**—a plan or framework to shape the future of their technical infrastructure. They might also revisit the **organizational structure** of their information delivery system. This structure defines reporting responsibilities and identifies who manages and controls key resources.

In this chapter, we focus on managing the delivery of information systems services. We start by examining decisions that shape and constrain systems management at the enterprise level, such as those related to organization and control. We then investigate issues associated with the day-to-day operations of information systems delivery. Finally, we explore how to plan for and manage change.

STRUCTURING THE INFORMATION SYSTEMS FUNCTION

Nestlé uses a combination of centralized and decentralized control to manage the delivery of its information systems effectively despite the company's decentralized organizational structure. In addition to the locus and control of resources, the type and extent of outsourcing and the method of accounting for information technology costs also affect the delivery of information systems at companies such as Nestlé.

Locating Control and Resources

Organizing the IS function involves deciding how much control to centralize in a corporate IS staff and how much to distribute throughout the organization. Some organizations have structures in which a corporate IS department performs all IS activities, as shown in Figure 10-1. Advantages of centralization include ease of creating and implementing a consistent vision, economies of scale in purchasing, reduction in costs associated with the duplication of systems procurement and development, and ease of standardization for sharing information.

Dow Jones & Co., the publisher of the *Wall Street Journal,* recently recentralized its information systems group when it found that various parts of the company had developed their own standards and practices and that the company was unable to share data among its business units. Although the redesign cost the company almost $40 million, chief technology officer Bill Godfrey felt that it was necessary to meet the company's business needs, including aggregating its market data, providing a consistent customer relationship management system, and becoming more efficient globally.[2]

Many organizations place most IS activity under the control of separate business units and have only a few employees in a corporate IS department, as shown in Figure 10-2. Internet technologies and the widespread use of corporate intranets have eased the movement of information systems functions into the business units. The advantages of decentralization include moving decision making closer to those affected by the decisions, improving the speed of response to external or local changes, and being more flexible to the needs and demands of each business unit. The attack on the World Trade Center (WTC) in New York City on September 11, 2001 also alerted many companies to the importance of decentralizing operations and data storage and increasing redundancy so that a single disaster can't disable their operations. For example, the law firm of Harris Beach & Wilcox lost all of its paper files, e-mail, and computer hardware when the WTC towers collapsed. Now, the company scans key paper documents and maintains electronic copies of these documents and other important files at other offices in New York City and Rochester.[3]

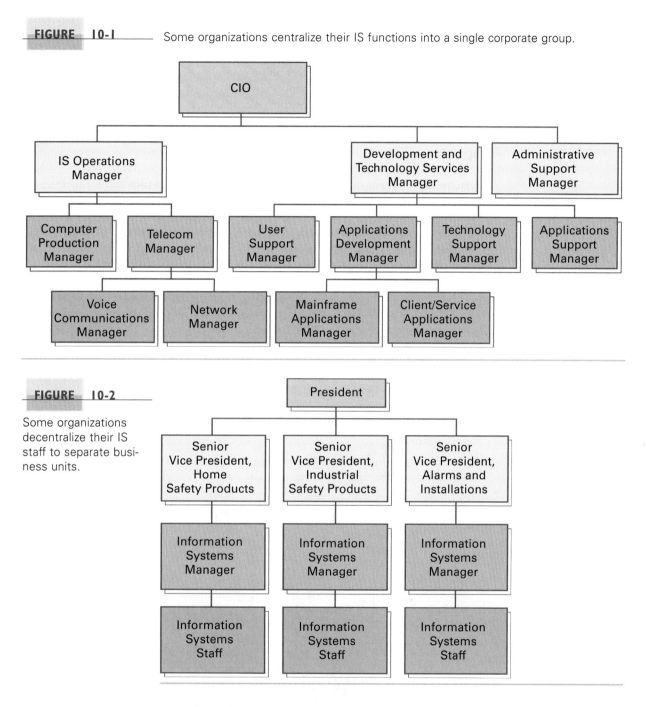

FIGURE   10-1 — Some organizations centralize their IS functions into a single corporate group.

FIGURE   10-2

Some organizations decentralize their IS staff to separate business units.

Mitre Corporation, a government contractor headquartered in Bedford, Massachusetts, is an example of a company that has adopted a decentralized structure. Its CIO, Dolly Greenwood, has a budget of nearly $1 million but no full-time IT staff. The information technology staff reports to each business unit and may draw from the IT budget. On projects that affect all units, Greenwood must draw from the technical staff in each business unit.[4]

Many companies adopt a mixed structure. One strategy, for example, might decentralize application development and centralize operations, as shown in Figure 10-3. Another strategy might centralize all functions for some business units and not for others. Federal

Express, for example, after acquiring a number of companies such as RPS Ground Services, found that its IT services were highly decentralized into its various business units. To improve cooperation among its units and to operate more efficiently, it reorganized most of its information technology services into a centralized IT department. However, some groups, such as its Asia systems, were not easily assimilated. Because of the need to support languages other than English and the difference in customs and regulations, FedEx found it better to keep the Asia systems independent.[5]

Outsourcing

Outsourcing, hiring an outside organization to perform services such as information processing and applications development, can reduce or eliminate a company's information infrastructure. Nestlé, for example, recently signed a $500 million contract with IBM to operate its server hardware, software, and information technology services. The contract allows Nestlé to replace more than 100 of its IT operation centers with five regional data centers, which not only saves money, but also increases operational efficiency.[6]

Outsourcing moves both capital and human investments to a company that specializes in the outsourced service. The outsourcing company hopes to obtain better service at the same price or similar service at a lower price. The service provider leverages its expertise and investments over many companies to provide economies of scale that an individual company could not obtain.

Before 1989, few large companies considered it viable to outsource significant portions of their information services. They viewed information systems and technology as strategic resources and their information as too important and confidential to entrust to

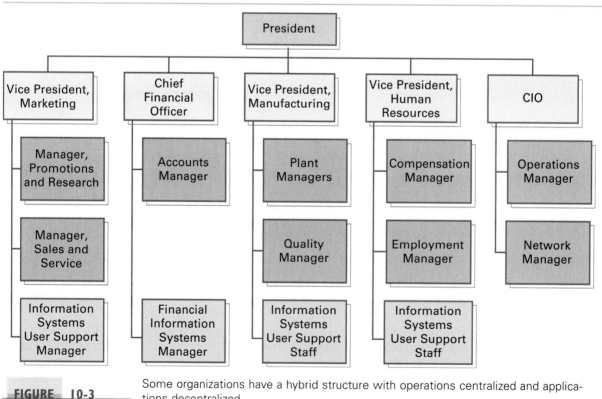

FIGURE 10-3 Some organizations have a hybrid structure with operations centralized and applications decentralized.

others. In 1989, Eastman Kodak stunned the business world by selling its mainframes to IBM and hiring IBM to process its data for the next ten years.[7] Although experts disagree on whether Kodak made a wise decision or a terrible mistake, its deal with IBM legitimized the outsourcing of information services. Outsourcing has since become a popular alternative to the internalization of the information infrastructure. Experts predict the outsourcing market will reach $160 billion by the year 2005.[8]

Table 10-1 displays a sample of recent outsourcing contracts to indicate their size and scope. The large, $4 billion deal between American Express (Amex) and IBM covers the operation of Amex's major data centers, which process about 1 billion transactions per day, and other parts of Amex's operations infrastructure. As part of the deal, IBM acquired about 2,000 of Amex's technology employees. Amex retained responsibility for its technology strategy, its voice and data networks, application development, and databases.[9] The smallest deal shown is for EDS to manage the operation and administration of the State of Kansas's Medicaid program.[10]

Outsourcing of the operation and maintenance, and often customization, of specific software applications is becoming increasingly common. Companies that provide such services are known as **Application Service Providers (ASPs)**. For example, Robinson Nugent Inc., an $80 million designer and manufacturer of high-technology electronic connectors, sockets and custom cable assemblies, uses a suite of financial, distribution, and manufacturing software developed and sold by the ERP vendor PeopleSoft. However, the company does not use any of its own computers to run the software. It pays a monthly fee to Surebridge, an ASP headquartered in Lexington, Massachusetts, to access the software over the Internet. Surebridge also helped Robinson Nugent configure the software for the way it does business and converted the company's data from its previous system.[11]

Table 10-2 lists some of the advantages and disadvantages of outsourcing information services and technology. Questions exist about whether or not outsourcing reduces costs. Outsourcing at least makes costs more explicit, leading to better decisions about where to spend company money. In addition, service providers, such as IBM and EDS, can realize economies of scale that they can share with their customers.

Outsourcing can also ease staffing and other resource problems encountered in software development efforts. Consider a company that needs to develop a large application rapidly. Such an organization often can't add staff simply for that effort because it would have excess staff at the end of the project. Instead, the company can contract out a fixed quantity of software development concentrated into chunks or spread over a long period. The service provider can more easily move its staff from one company's project to another's. This flexibility applies to all IS resources, not just staffing.

	Outsourcer	Contractor	Start Year	Years	Amount ($)
TABLE 10-1	American Express	IBM	2002	7	4 billion
	PacifiCare Health Systems	IBM and Keane	2002	10	1.2 billion
These outsourcing	National Bank of Canada	IBM Canada	2001	10	700 million
contracts range from	Scotiabank	IBM Canada	2001	7	578 million
five to ten years and	Gulfstream Aerospace	CSC	2002	10	510 million
$160 million to $4 bil-	Nestlé	IBM	2002	5	500 million
lion. Experts forecast	Fireman's Fund Insurance	CGI Group	2001	10	380 million
the total market to	Nextel Communications	EDS	2002	5	234 million
exceed $160 billion by	7-Eleven	EDS	2002	7	175 million
the year 2005.	State of Kansas	EDS	2002	6	160 million

TABLE 10-2

Outsourcing provides advantages and disadvantages. Some attributes of outsourcing, such as its cost, fall into both categories because of the variability of technology costs over time.

Advantages	Disadvantages
Could reduce cost	Could increase cost
Reduces cost of fluctuations in size of systems development staff	Locks company into a provider
Takes advantage of scale economies in hardware where they exist	Fails to guarantee responsiveness
	Reduces control
Makes cost/service tradeoffs explicit; improves decisions	Removes knowledge of processes from the company
Allows more rapid or timely development	Decreases ability to use information technology strategically
Consolidates operations	
Frees management to focus on business	
Offers improved reliability and stability	
Provides opportunity to learn from the contractor	

Outsourcing creates a major disadvantage by locking the outsourcing company into a long-term contract. A company may have difficulty firing a provider that misses deadlines, develops poor quality programs, delivers insufficient processing capacity, or generally acts unresponsively. Although the contract may specify performance penalties and divorce clauses, an unsatisfied outsourcer may have to sue its service provider to terminate the contract. Long-term contracts also don't necessarily reflect rapid changes in the cost of technology, which may penalize either party. A recent survey found the majority of respondents were frustrated with their outsource provider;[12] however, only about 15 percent of companies are likely to switch their outsource provider when their contract is due to be renewed.[13]

Outsourcing also requires organizations to relinquish control in an area of potential strategic advantage. Although a company directs its contractor, it loses expertise in IT and may experience difficulty reclaiming the outsourced functions. For this reason organizations generally outsource only selected functions. Figure 10-4 shows the distribution of spending on outsourcing.

Even within a particular function, outsourcing need not be exhaustive. For example, a contract for PC maintenance may cover only Intel compatible computers and exclude Macintosh computers. Similarly, organizations may limit outsourcing of systems development to major projects and handle minor projects in-house.

Successful outsourcing occurs when companies can divide their IS activities into meaningful segments for outsourcing, identify appropriate segments to outsource based on sound business analysis, and treat the outsource provider as a partner. A company should consider outsourcing if information systems have little ability to provide it a competitive advantage, its technological capabilities are limited, or it does not have the financial resources to acquire the technological capability that it needs.

Accounting for Information Technology Costs

How an organization accounts for its information systems has implications for both the acquisition and application of information technology and information systems resources and the structure of the IS function. A company such as Nestlé must determine whether its corporate information systems department should exist as (1) an unallocated cost center, (2) an allocated cost center, or (3) a profit center. Table 10-3 summarizes the advantages and disadvantages of these options.

SOURCE: Christine Spivey Overby with John C. McCarthy and Emily H. Boynton, *US Outsourcing Decelerates,* (Cambridge, MA: Forrester Research, 2002). Used with permission.

FIGURE 10-4

The data center dominates the spending on information technology outsourcing; however, outsourcing for network management and application development is growing most rapidly.

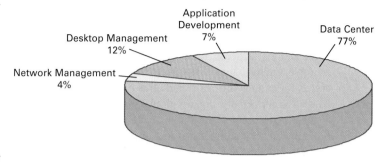

Spending on Outsourcing, 2001

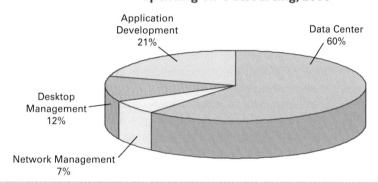

Spending on Outsourcing, 2006

TABLE 10-3

Companies can account for IT costs in three ways. Each has advantages and disadvantages.

Allocation Method	Description	Advantages	Disadvantages
Unallocated cost center	All IS costs are considered an organizational expense.	Experiments with technology can occur. Users can request the development of new systems. IS can develop systems regardless of economic benefit.	Costs can get out of control. IS professionals can't easily allocate their budget among conflicting requests.
Allocated cost center	IS department allocates costs to departments that use its services.	Users request only beneficial services. It works well in organization where charges are regularly made to all internal customers.	IS can have problems determining allocation of costs. Friction among user departments and between them and IS can occur. IS has no reason to operate efficiently.
Profit center	IS charges internal and external users the same and attempts to get both kinds of business.	Users can choose who will perform their IT services. IS department has incentives to operate efficiently.	Outsourcing may become more common. Fees may be higher than with other methods.

Unallocated Cost Center

End users and their managers who view information services and technology as a free resource from an information systems department establish an **unallocated cost center.** This setup considers all costs of operating the IS department and related IS services as an organizational expense, rather than attributing costs to departmental budgets. Nestlé, for example, might charge all IS costs to the central IS department rather than charge them separately to manufacturing or marketing budgets. Viewing the IS department as an unallocated cost center benefits organizations just developing their information architecture because it encourages users to experiment with and learn about the technology and subsequently build the infrastructure. It also encourages users to request the development of new systems.

The unallocated cost center approach allows the development of systems without regard to their economic return. As a result, the costs of information technology can quickly rise out of control. Companies then tighten their budgets for systems development and resource acquisition to control costs. Because no economic basis exists for choosing any particular budget level, financial officers usually determine the budget for information systems and technology as a percentage of sales according to the experience of similar companies in similar markets. This approach fails to consider the company's current status, whether it needs to build its infrastructure to catch its competition, or whether it can coast and wait for its competition to catch it. Also, setting the budget using an industry benchmark probably squelches any opportunity to achieve a competitive advantage by spending extra on innovative information technology initiatives.

The unallocated cost center approach fails to give information systems professionals a way of allocating a fixed budget among conflicting requests for resources. When the IS staff or other executives decide not to fund or to delay certain projects, the user community may become angry at the lack of response and long lead times for their projects. The information systems department then becomes an antagonist rather than a partner in systems development. Having IS staff determine the cost of requested services and the user department identify and quantify the expected benefits of its request can alleviate some problems with an unallocated cost center. This approach helps the IS department determine which projects are most likely to have the greatest net benefit and allows it to justify its decisions to end users.

Allocated Cost Center

As an **allocated cost center,** the IS department allocates and charges its costs to the departments that use its services. Nestlé, for example, could allocate the costs of IS usage to its individual business units, and within them to product development, manufacturing, and marketing departments. Unlike the unallocated cost center approach, the allocated cost center approach avoids the use of and request for services that do not provide an ample benefit. Managers become intelligent consumers when their business units have to pay for the services used.[14] This approach works particularly well in environments where departments charge other services to their internal customers.

Allocating the costs of an allocated cost center can pose problems. Ideally, a cost center should charge user departments for resources in proportion to their usage and the costs of those resources. The charges levied should fully reimburse the cost center for its expenses. Calculating costs in this way uses information about technical factors, such as units of computer use, internal memory use, input-output use, and data storage requirements, which users may find unintelligible and which probably change between periods. For example, the per-unit charge for computer time is low in a period of high usage, whereas the per-unit charge must be higher in a period of low usage to recover the fixed costs of owning and running the computer system. This variation in charges motivates additional usage during the peak periods of the year.

The average cost in the allocated cost center approach doesn't reflect the marginal cost—the economic way of allocating resources. For example, a company that upgrades its equipment for a new application distributes the cost of the new equipment among all applications. The purchasers of the application see their own unit costs. They don't experience changes in unit costs for other applications which, although likely to be small, when added together might have made the application uneconomical. In addition, other users see fluctuations in their costs without any changes in their activity. This strange costing behavior can lead to friction among user departments and between user departments and IS.

Finally, an allocated cost center has no reason to operate efficiently. Since it receives reimbursement for all costs, it has no incentive to keep these costs low. If some users attempt to bypass high charges by outsourcing, the cost center simply charges each of the remaining users more. This leads to over-investment in IS and IT resources and results in dissatisfied users.

Profit Center

An IS department that operates as a **profit center** becomes an internal option to the outsourcing of IS services. It bids for the work of internal users, charges internal users what it would charge external users, and often actively seeks external users. For example, Fairmont Hotels and Resorts Inc., operates as its own ISP, operating and maintaining the broadband links necessary to connect its guest rooms to the Internet. The hotel chain has also brought its applications in-house and now operates as its own ASP. It plans to earn a profit through the Internet charges and voice over IP phone services that it offers to its guests.[15] Maimonides Hospital in Brooklyn, New York, used its technology expertise to create an ASP, which it calls 4 Healthcare LLC. The business unit will provide, among other services, patient scheduling, picture archiving and communication services, and electronic patient record services not only to Maimonides, but also to other hospitals in New York, New Jersey, and Connecticut. It hopes to generate revenues of as much as $80 million over four years.[16]

Typically, internal users of IT services in companies following the profit center model aren't required to use the services of their IS department, although they are strongly encouraged to do so. IT is part of an operating unit's budget, and its managers purchase the services they need. The company may limit the fees the profit center can charge internal users to make purchasing services internally more attractive. This type of pricing avoids monopoly prices for those projects that share data with other applications and for which the users have no other choice of IS supplier.

The profit center approach provides the IS department incentives to operate efficiently. It motivates users to request only economically viable services. But it may encourage outsourcing because internal prices and service probably resemble those of outsource providers. Also, because the profit center attempts to earn a return on its investments, it generally charges users more than it would as an unallocated cost center or allocated cost center (assuming that such centers operated with equal efficiency). These higher costs tend to discourage the use of information systems and technology for solving business problems.

MANAGING THE INFORMATION SYSTEMS FUNCTION

Many activities contribute to delivering information services efficiently and effectively. In this section we focus on the people who do the IS work, their interactions with the service recipients, and the tasks involved in measuring and improving the process of service delivery. We also examine three behind-the-scenes management functions normally delegated to information systems groups—standard setting, disaster planning, and security management. Finally, we examine the legal and social issues that information systems managers typically face.

Staffing the Technical Functions

Having good people in well-defined positions is critical for providing an effective information systems organization. The human infrastructure supporting information services includes a broad array of jobs.

Most IS positions require good communication and problem-solving skills. Some also require strong management skills. Technical skills, although usually necessary, generally have a lower priority. Applicants for an entry-level IS position should be computer literate and should know how to program in at least one computer language or have experience with GUI or Web software development tools. Although some companies look for experience with certain equipment, computer languages, or software development tools when hiring, others will train applicants on their equipment and the software that they use on the job.

The positions described here, and shown relative to their usual skill and pay in Figure 10-5, present a sample of the positions found in many organizations.

Chief Information Officer (CIO)

An organization's **chief information officer (CIO)** manages its information-related resources and activities. The CIO might also be called manager, director, or vice president of data processing, information services, or management information systems. The CIO usually reports to the chief financial officer, the chief operating officer, or the president of the company. Organizations that don't have a full-time CIO generally delegate the CIO functions and responsibilities to the chief financial officer. Companies with multiple business units often employ CIOs within each unit to direct the technology services of that unit. The CIO should:

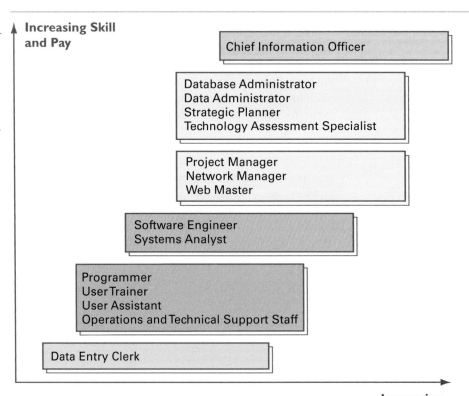

FIGURE 10-5

Information systems range from clerical to technical to managerial. The figure shows a sample of job titles and their associated responsibility and pay within each job class.

- Be a leader.
- Have a vision for the IS architecture.
- Possess the managerial savvy and political clout to implement that vision.
- Act as the technology adviser for major organizational restructuring and reengineering.
- Educate upper management about the application and value of information technology for securing a strategic advantage.
- Secure the financial resources to appropriately shape the infrastructure.

Most chief information officers have significant technical experience. As information technology becomes more strategic, however, management and business experience become increasingly important. For example, Greg Volan, the CIO of Bloomington is a lawyer by training. He not only practiced law, but was also the CEO of BlueMarble Telecom, where he acquired some of his technical know-how before taking the CIO position.[17]

Strategic Planner and Technology Assessment Specialist

Most large companies have at least one full-time employee who monitors advances in information technology, educates the key managers about these advances, and plans how the company can take advantage of them. Often such specialists, frequently called **chief technology officers (CTOs)**, have a staff and budget to pilot new technologies on real or hypothetical applications. Large organizations might have separate jobs in specific areas of technical specialty, such as communications, expert systems, and object-oriented technology. Such specialists tend to be highly technical, although those who supervise a staff and have long-term planning responsibilities should have both a technical and managerial education.

Data Administrator and Database Administrator

The **data administrator** and **database administrator** organize, manage, and guarantee the integrity of an organization's data. Most organizations combine the data and database administrator position into a single job. Otherwise, the data administrator:

- Maintains the data dictionary.
- Assists project managers in defining and coordinating data needs associated with their projects.
- Develops an enterprise-wide data model.
- Sets and implements company policies regarding data security and data access.
- Specifies data integrity rules.

The database administrator has more technical responsibilities:

- Sets and fine-tunes database parameters that affect performance.
- Performs database backups.
- Manages database recovery upon system crashes.
- Installs DBMS updates and software tools.

Network Administrator

The **network administrator** oversees the corporate network, including both LANs and WANs. This responsibility includes not only operations and maintenance, but also planning and the supervision of a network support staff. Because of the dire consequences of network failure, network administrators with proven track records command salaries well above those of most other technical managers. Some organizations expand the role of network manager to communication manager, giving that person the responsibility for voice and data networks.

Web Master

A **Web master** is responsible for the management, evolution, and sometimes development of an organization's Web site. Originally a technical position, it has become much more managerial as Web services have increased in importance and scope. In many organizations, the Web master maintains and troubleshoots the Web servers, determines the look and feel of the Web site, sets policy for Web site updates, and selects the technologies that support the interfaces between organizational systems and the Web.

Project Manager

A **project manager** directs a software development project and ensures that the project meets user requirements within a specified budget and time frame. He has significant supervisory responsibilities for technical and personnel decisions and, therefore, typically has both technical expertise and strong management skills. Project managers may have prior experience as analysts or programmers. Alternatively, project managers act as business specialists who report to line managers rather than or in addition to IS managers. The project manager position may be temporary, lasting only for the duration of a project. In some organizations, however, project managers have permanent positions, moving from project to project or supervising several projects at once.

Applications Development Manager

Some companies have a person who monitors and coordinates the development of all software applications. This jobholder helps enforce software standards. She may advise managers and computer professionals about the outsourcing of development projects, the selection of software, and the sharing of applications throughout the company. This position is particularly useful when decentralized development occurs.

Systems Analysis and Software Engineering

Systems analyst refers to a technical position associated with all aspects of the systems development life cycle (see Chapter 9) except programming and focused most directly on needs analysis. Companies often recruit systems analysts from the graduating class of four-year colleges, especially those offering degrees in business or information systems. They sometimes require analysts to show proficiency in one or more programming languages. Many combine the analyst and programmer positions into a single job. Others focus more on the links with business and call the jobholder a *business analyst*. As the power of CASE increases, more companies train their systems analysts to use CASE tools. They often call analysts with CASE skills **software engineers.** Some systems analysts and software engineers who work on one application or in one application area for several years acquire expertise in that application through the process of designing and implementing software. Because of their expertise, they may join the line function where they may assume project management responsibilities.

Programmer

Programmer describes a highly technical position associated with the production of custom software. Companies expect applicants for this positions to have a two-year or four-year college degree with a computer-related major or a certificate from a technical training school and working knowledge of at least one programming language. Programmers need not have a business education or background.

User Trainer and User Assistant

Employees who train users of computer hardware and software and help users diagnose and solve problems with their equipment and software require both technical and interpersonal skills. Some companies hire full-time trainers, although many organizations prefer to use consultants as trainers or send their employees to intensive off-site training courses. Almost all medium to large companies employ people who only assist end users of information technology. These employees often work from a help desk, discussed later in this chapter.

Operations and Technical Support Staff

Operations and technical support personnel install, maintain, and operate the computers and communications equipment. In a typical organization, the operations and technical support staff performs such tasks as monitoring and maintaining the organizations servers, performing system backup and recovery, refilling paper and toner in laser printers, installing software upgrades, and repairing users' computer equipment. The staff may also perform some hardware upgrades, such as installing new network cards in users' computers, increasing the amount of RAM or disk in users' workstations, and configuring or reconfiguring communication equipment, such as routers.

Although operations and technical support employees must have a general technical background, typically they still require in-house or outside training shortly after hiring because they lack extensive experience with the specific hardware or communications equipment their employer uses. In addition, they must receive additional training as the IT infrastructure changes.

Data Entry

Data entry clerks hold a relatively low-skilled, low-paid position in the IS hierarchy and work for companies that process large numbers of paper transactions. An insurance company, for example, often employs data entry clerks to process its customers' paper claims. Organizations that use online data input generally don't have data entry positions. Department stores or fast food companies may use employees trained for another function, such as sales, to perform data entry as part of their job.

Interacting with Information Technology Users

End user describes a consumer of IS services. She uses a computer for tasks such as word processing, electronic mail, statistical analysis, and report generation. End users at Nestlé include warehouse workers, plant managers, marketing managers, package designers, purchasing agents, and sales people, among others.

As end users become more computer-literate, they increasingly perform their own systems development. While not officially part of the human IS infrastructure, they contribute to building the technical infrastructure through the development of systems and the creation and storage of data. Increasingly, such users play a more formal role in systems development by serving on development task forces, participating in rapid prototyping efforts, or engaging in sophisticated needs assessments. IS staff can support end users informally or by using a help desk.

The Help Desk

The **help desk** refers to the IS staff and associated systems that help end users solve immediate problems with their equipment or software. The staff of the help desk addresses problems as diverse as how to turn on the computer, replace the cartridge in a laser printer, handle an exception in an otherwise routine data-entry application, and produce a customized report from the corporate database. In some organizations, the user training staff also reports to the help desk. In small organizations, typically one or two individuals recognized for their technical expertise informally perform the function of the help desk.

The organization of the help desk varies. Many large companies maintain several specialized help desks scattered geographically or organized by expertise. A centralized help desk can reduce costs by achieving economies of scale and improve service by creating a single point of contact.

Help desks operate in different ways. Some companies use help desk operators with extensive expertise in the company's hardware and software who, with the help of expert systems, can handle most problems independently. Other companies ask help desk operators only to identify the problem and route it to an appropriate technical person or function in the company. This approach distributes the help desk function throughout the organization. Still other companies outsource help desk services. For example, IBM supplies the IT help-desk services for the 29,000 desktop users in 400 locations of Invensys, a London-based global manufacturer of automation and control systems.[18]

A help desk can identify system flaws or user training needs by monitoring problems and tabulating the speed of their solution. Recently, many help desks have focused extensively on their role as problem-logger rather than problem-solver. This change in role typically results in end-user dissatisfaction because it motivates end users to solve their own problems rather than using the help desk. The type and quality of services provided, users' expectations about the information center, the technological environment in which the information center functions, and the organization's commitment to the information center influence its success.[19] In addition, the information center must have a competent staff and deliver effective end-user training.[20]

Measuring and Improving Performance

Managers can track the performance of information services over time and benchmark them against other companies. They can hire an outside consultant to perform the benchmarking study or they can conduct it themselves. For example, Prudential Financial, the $27 billion insurance giant, annually employs one of the big consulting firms to assist in its benchmarking. The consulting firms can compare Prudential's spending on various technology initiatives with the spending of other firms in the industry on similar initiatives. Prudential's IT managers use these comparative data to adjust their technology budgets.[21]

Table 10-4 identifies various statistics and measures that managers can use to evaluate the quality of their information services. These statistics measure not only the efficiency and response of the organization's information systems, but also customer satisfaction with systems and services and their cost and quality. Tracking such measures can help information systems managers identify and repair weaknesses in their operations and processes.

Service level agreements (SLAs) help business managers trade off cost against the level of service they want from their technology support staff. An SLA specifies in detail a guaranteed level of performance on a variety of dimensions. These include the following:

- *Service objectives.* A statement of the objectives of the agreement.
- *Parties.* The department, customers, vendors involved.
- *Points of contact.* The people who serve as the liaisons to the parties involved.
- *Responsibilities.* The specific responsibilities of each jobholder involved in providing service.

TABLE 10-4

A variety of measures can assess information service quality.

Customer Satisfaction

Overall satisfaction of users/managers with information services

User satisfaction with contacts with IS organization

User satisfaction with response to problems

Manager satisfaction with cost and speed of development

Operations

Availability (% of time)

Mean time between failures

CPU Usage (% of capacity)

Disk Usage (% of capacity)

Average MIPS

Number of jobs handled

Quality Assurance

Defects found per 1000 lines of code

Percentage of erroneous keystrokes on data entry

Financial

IT expense as a percent of revenue

IT investment as a percent of assets

Total system cost

Average cost per job

Average cost per input screen

Average cost per report produced

Staffing

Percentage of professional staff with college degree

Payroll as percent of IS budget

Percentage of staff with advanced degrees

System Development

Projects completed in period

Average function points per employee per period

Lines of code per employee per period

Fraction of projects done on time and on budget

Technology

Percent of IS expense in R&D

Percent of employees having a workstation

Training

Courses taken per IS employee per year

Average courses taken per IS employee

Average IS courses taken per non-IS employee

Communications

Percentage of cost for telecommunication

LAN contention in peak periods

WAN cost per packet, per byte, and per message

Help Desk

Percentage of problems solved by 1st contact

Average time to problem solution

Number of problems handled per FTE

Number of problems handled

SOURCE: Steven R. Gordon, Working Paper Series 94-08: *Benchmarking the Information Systems Function* (Boston: Babson College, Center for Information Management Studies, 1994).

- *Performance measures.* The metrics that reflect whether the objectives have been accomplished, including ongoing milestones or performance expectations and responses.
- *Escalation guidelines.* The procedures for changing the contract or expediting various processes.
- *Renegotiation.* The provisions for renegotiating the service level agreement.[22]

Within a particular category, an SLA can also specify different service levels depending on how critical the task is. For example, it might require a 15-minute response to some conditions and a 24-hour response to others. It also specifies penalties if information services can't provide the guaranteed level of service. Figure 10-6 shows an excerpt from a service level agreement between Network Appliance Inc., a supplier of enterprise storage systems, and its customers.

SLAs work particularly well when information services operate as a profit center. Information service managers then have the greatest incentive to provide good service and business manager have the option of obtaining similar service from outsource contractors. Many organizations also use SLAs to guarantee adequate service levels from their outsourcers.

FIGURE 10-6

This service level agreement shows the response a customer can expect from Network Appliance, Inc.'s Global Support Center.

SOURCE: https://now.netapp .com/public/gscsla.shtml, accessed on 25 April 2002. Used with permission.

Priority Definitions & Response Targets

Problems where a customer cannot access their data are always given priority over other types of issue. They will immediately be worked by a certified engineer who will focus on rapid restoration of data access. We ask customers to always contact us by telephone for this type of problem to ensure the issue can immediately be worked by an experienced, certified engineer who will focus on restoring data access as quickly as possible. Other problems whether received by phone, NOW, or Autosupport will be assigned and initial assessment targeted to be provided as follows.

Priority Level	Description	Initial Assessment Target
1	Appliance not serving data	Immediate
2	Serious or repetitive disruption or very poor performance	Within 1 hour
3	Occasional disruption or problem	Within 1 hour
4	Other questions or issues	Within 1 hour

Data Access Restoration Guidelines (P1 Cases)

The purpose of this process is to restore access to data as quickly as possible as the highest priority activity. Root cause analysis of the underlying problem and its resolution may take longer. Escalation can occur sooner if it is recognized that additional resource or expertise is needed sooner. Escalation may be deferred when an agreed action plan is in place, e.g. when waiting for parts or collecting diagnostic information.

Elapsed Time with No Agreed Action Plan	Function
0–1 hour	Worked by Technical Support
1–3 hours	Escalate to Product Support Team
3+ hours	Escalate to Product Engineering

Management Notification (P1 Cases)

All open P1 cases are subject to internal management notification within Network Appliance to ensure awareness of critical customer issues and to ensure appropriate resources are being applied to resolution of the problem. Customers who are not comfortable with the progress of any problem may call the Duty Manager at anytime.

Selecting and Enforcing Standards

A **standard** refers to rules governing the types of investments an organization may make in information technology and systems. Standards strive to impose organization-wide control over IT decisions without directing those decisions. Standards can be set broadly or strictly and can apply to some or all types of products and services.

Table 10-5 identifies some types of products for which a company might set standards. Many companies, for example, standardize on Windows-compatible equipment for personal computers. An employee who wants to use an Apple Macintosh may have difficulty obtaining one in such an environment. Depending upon how rigorously the standard is enforced, the company may do one of the following: prohibit the employee from using a Macintosh at work, allow the employee to use one if he pays for it, purchase one for the employee with the understanding that he will receive no support in dealing with hardware or software problems, or refuse to connect the Macintosh to the office computer network. Hardware and software manufacturers often standardize on ISO 9000, a set of five related quality management standards that ensure complete documentation and rigorous business practices in manufacturing.

Computers
    Specific configurations
        (e.g., Compaq with 40 GB disk,
        256 MB memory, etc.)
    Specific vendors (e.g., Compaq)
    Level of compatibility
        (e.g., WinTel compatible)
Communications Equipment
    Network interface cards
    Network protocol compatibility
    LAN media
    Router and hub models
Office Automation Software
    Office suites
    Word processors
    Spreadsheets
    Personal DBMS
    Presentation graphics

Software Development Tools
    Languages
    CASE products
    Methodologies
Database Management Software
    Specific vendors (e.g., Oracle)
    Compatibility (e.g., SQL, Corba)
    Type (e.g., relational, object)
Systems Software
    Operating systems
    Network operating systems
    Virus checkers
Other
    Browsers
    ERP software (e.g., SAP)
    Electronic mail

Table 10-6 identifies some benefits and drawbacks of standardization policies. Many of the benefits illustrate how standards can help reduce costs, sometimes substantially. For example, standardization can reduce costs by minimizing the duplication of software development. If each division of a company develops its own inventory system, the company will probably spend much more money in development than if the company standardized on a single inventory system that could handle the needs of all divisions. Other examples of cost saving include economies of scale in purchasing and improving the company's negotiating position for better pricing. A company that buys 1,000 PCs can expect to pay less if it orders them from a single supplier than if it buys 100 of ten different kinds of computers from ten or more suppliers.

Many of the benefits shown in Table 10-6 relate to efficiency rather than cost. For example, standards improve managerial and operating efficiency by increasing the integration of systems and easing the interchange of information among systems. A work team that writes a proposal under tight time constraints will fare better if each staff member prepares her component of the proposal with the same word processor. Standardizing on a word processor guarantees that the company's staff can easily integrate the parts of the proposal into one document. The absence of such integration would prevent cross-referencing, and changes to one part of the document, such as deleting a figure, would require reworking other parts of the document to achieve a coherent product.

Standards can increase efficiency by increasing flexibility in the use of IS personnel. If a company standardizes on a single DBMS, its managers can assign programmers to different projects as needed. Managers in a less standardized environment could only assign programmers who are proficient with the DBMS that the project uses. Most organizations also find that they must provide some control over the variety of computers that their employees purchase. Otherwise they can't effectively achieve a critical mass of experience to provide the know-how and support that users need.

Standardization also increases managerial effectiveness. Managers who can easily obtain data related to their decisions will probably refer to the data and make more informed choices than managers who find access to the data difficult. Standards, particularly in the user interface, database management systems, and data dictionary systems, increase the likelihood that managers can find the data they want quickly and easily.

	Benefits	Drawbacks
TABLE 10-6 Companies should consider the benefits and drawbacks of standardization in deciding the nature and degree of their policy on standards.	Increases the quality of developed software	Reduces flexibility in applications
	Reduces number of specially built interfaces	Stifles innovation and creativity
	Minimizes duplication of software development	Interferes with other requirements of applications
	Increases integration of systems for improved efficiency	Reduces ability to go with lowest cost solution in each case
	Increases ability to exchange data among systems	Requires more review and consensus for software/hardware selection
	Achieves economies of scale in purchasing and maintenance	Increases frequency of revision and upgrade installation
	Improves negotiating position for better pricing	Decreases users' comfort about opportunities to meet their direct needs
	Promotes and facilitates coherent mission and strategy	Increases cost of purchasing due to reduced supplier options
	Reduces training costs and time	Increases impact of any major changes
	Reduces outside projects with runaway costs	Decreases ability to make major changes
	Increases flexibility in use of IS personnel	Consumes political good will
	Reduces the cost and increases the quality of support	Increases impact of poor decisions
	Reduces application development time and cost	Impedes the acquisition of new technology
	Lifts burden of product research from the user	

SOURCE: Steven R. Gordon, "Standardization of Information Systems and Technology at Multinational Companies," *Journal of Global Information Management*, Summer 1996, 6.

Standards don't automatically increase the ease of systems integration and data exchange. For example, in the 1970s and 1980s exchanging information among a variety of personal computers and minicomputers was easier than exchanging information among different types of IBM computers. Companies that standardized on IBM had difficulty exchanging data among their mainframes, minicomputers, and PCs because these products used incompatible operating systems and supported different database managers. These companies might instead have standardized on a DBMS such as Oracle that ran on mainframes, minicomputers, and personal computers, and easily exchanged information among its databases on different systems.

Standardization may conflict with the objective of letting business needs determine systems development and acquisition priorities. In particular, standards reduce a company's flexibility in selecting its application software and decrease users' comfort about whether new systems can meet their needs. For example, one type of computer might work best for accounting applications whereas a different type might work best for laboratory applications. One inventory system might function better for discrete items, such as chairs, which exist in whole quantities, whereas another might function better for continuous items, such as chemicals, which can be stored in any volume. Most organizations respond to the inflexibility of standards by specifying a standard that allows for different alternatives. For example, a company may specify one type of computer for its personal computer needs, a second for business applications, a third for network servers, a fourth for scientific or laboratory work, and a fifth for computers on its manufacturing floor. A company should review its standards frequently so that it can respond to its changing needs in a dynamic business environment.

Standardization can also require a significant organizational effort to support its implementation. IS executives and other top managers must acknowledge that employees resent having limited choices. An employee who uses a Macintosh at home, for example, might resent having to learn to use a new system at work, especially one he does not like as well. The political significance of standardization increases when it affects a division or business unit. Managers of a subsidiary may object to changing its inventory system for the sake of standardization when its employees have the training to use the existing system and it works perfectly well. In particular, managers are likely to object if the standard system does not provide features of the old system they used and valued.

The organizational cost of standards includes the time and effort required to establish and review them. Setting a standard that affects the entire organization involves gathering input from many people to assess the impact of the standard properly. High-level managers with a stake in the outcome should and usually will lobby extensively for their choice. Standard setting thus uses time that they might better spend on more pressing business issues.

Ironically, standards may increase costs if poor decisions result. For example, many companies that standardized on Digital Equipment Corporation's DEC-Mate personal computer in the early 1980s discarded their entire investment in PCs when the IBM PC and compatibles became the industry standard. While software vendors produced numerous products for the compatibles, users of the DEC-Mate had little or no choice of word-processing, spreadsheets, and other productivity software. Eventually, even Digital abandoned its PC product. Similar stories abound for terminal equipment, network products, and software.

Standards may also increase costs by requiring more frequent updates of hardware and software. Companies that require a common configuration for their personal computers for easier maintenance and exchange must upgrade all computers when one user needs more capability. Similarly, many organizations require that all workstations use the same version of word processing software. When one or two people need the features of a new release, the organization must purchase the new release for everyone. If the company lacked or didn't enforce standards, it would pay to upgrade only for those demanding the new release. These users, however, can't easily share their documents with others using the older software.

Disaster Planning

A **disaster plan,** sometimes called a **business continuity plan,** refers to the process of anticipating disasters and providing for appropriate responses to keep a business operating after a disaster. A disaster is any event that disrupts operations in a major way. Some disasters are natural, such as hurricanes, earthquakes, or floods, and others are man-made, such as the terrorist attacks on New York's World Trade Center and the Pentagon on September 11, 2001.

One of the most effective ways for a company to address the possibility of disaster at a single site is to build site redundancy into its systems. With site redundancy, when a company's computers fail to operate at one location, its systems, data, and processes are available from computers at another location. These computers automatically assume the functions of those at the failed site. Site redundancy is particularly costly to achieve for transaction processing systems, as every transaction would presumably change data at multiple sites. Also, site redundancy requires having at least twice as much computing power as a company would otherwise need, as well as high-capacity networks to assure the rapid exchange of information between sites. Additional personnel would also be required.

Most companies adopt the less stringent approach of periodically backing up their data. The backup copy is stored somewhere far from where the original is kept. If a disaster should occur, the backup data can be reloaded into computers at another location so that the company can continue to operate. Because backups are not done in real time, some data may be lost. The backup strategy requires that the company have spare computing power, storage, bandwidth, and personnel at designated disaster recovery sites. Companies that do not have multiple sites or spare capacity may contract with companies that provide recovery services. The New York Board of Trade, for example, paid $300,000 per year to Comdisco Inc., for space and computer systems in Queens, New York. When its systems were destroyed in the September 11, 2001 attack on the World Trade Center in Manhattan, they were back up and running within a day at the Comdisco site.[23]

An important component of disaster planning is practice. If you have a disaster plan, it's important to periodically run a disaster drill. The purpose of such a drill is to make sure that the plan is current, that employees are aware of it, and that they are able to execute it.

Managing Security

In Chapters 4, 5, and 7, you learned about the technologies available to secure information, communication, and information systems. Unfortunately, no technology will compensate for poor security management practice. No technology will prevent an employee from maliciously deleting company records if that employee has the authority to delete those records in the normal course of business. No technology will prevent unauthorized access to records accessible by your suppliers if your suppliers permit their systems to be hacked. No technology will prevent your employees from giving acquaintances, and even strangers, their passwords to your system. And no technology will force your technology administrators to plug security holes when they are discovered.

Effective security begins with organizational control systems that treat information as a valuable asset, similar to cash. Effective security also demands a **security policy** that addresses proper security practices and methods of enforcing those practices. The pervasiveness of security policies is unclear. One recent survey reports that 97 percent of companies recognize the importance of security management and have a security policy in place,[24] while another survey, taken at about the same time, reports that only 54 percent of companies have such a policy and only 32 percent regularly assess and track their security measures.[25]

Table 10-7 identifies common organizational practices that compromise security in the normal course of business. A security policy addresses the activities that need to be undertaken to correct those practices identified in the table and other practices that could affect security. The security policy begins with the identification of what information assets are most important to the organization. It proceeds with an assessment of the vulnerability of each of these assets and the development of a plan, or set of practices, that sets an appropriate level of security in relation to the value and vulnerability of the assets.

Cardinal Health Inc., a $20 billion health-care manufacturing and distribution company, employs an Information Protection Team of 15 security specialists to protect its data. The director of the team, John Hartmann, a former FBI special agent, advocates a holistic approach to security because in a decentralized networked organization, such as Cardinal's, lax security in one business unit that has low-risk assets can adversely affect the security of assets in a different business unit needing a greater degree of protection. Hartmann's holistic approach also recognizes the relationship between the security of physical and digital assets. In 2000, Cardinal combined the physical and digital security functions into one unit. This security group acts as a consultant to the other Cardinal business units, but the implementation of security measures rests with each business unit.[26]

Legal and Social Issues

Managers of information systems and technology need to be keenly aware of the legal and social implications of their decisions regarding the uses of information technology in their organizations and the possible uses of systems developed under their supervision.

TABLE 10-7	**Policy Faults**	Failing to create a security policy
Ways in which organizations easily compromise their security.		Maintaining email and login accounts of terminated employees
		Failing to assess importance of information assets and cost of their compromise
		Failing to require encryption of data and messages
		Failing to educate employees about proper security practices
		Failing to install and use firewall hardware and software
		Failing to periodically test the ability of outsiders to crack your security
		Ignoring or downplaying the existence and importance of security threats
	Faulty Operational Practices	Failing to enforce security practices
		Failing to back up data regularly
		Failing to secure servers and networks physically
		Failing to update virus software regularly
		Failing to install software patches regularly
		Using easy-to-guess passwords and leaving passwords in easily found locations
		Leaving the default passwords on newly installed systems
		Leaving workstations logged in while unattended

Use of Workplace Technology

Many organizations rely on their information systems department to control computer-based activities that violate the law or have negative social consequences. Examples of such activities include employees producing documents containing copyrighted text or pictures downloaded from the Web, sending lewd or objectionable e-mail to other employees or to people outside the organization, running pirated software on company computers, and using corporate computers or networks to launch a virus or a denial of service attack.

To minimize the likelihood of employees inadvertently misusing company computers, many companies create an **acceptable use policy** or a **computer code of ethics.** Such a policy or code clarifies and makes explicit for employees what uses of corporate computer and network facilities are acceptable. Table 10-8 provides examples of the types of topics found in a typical acceptable use policy. At many companies, acceptable use policies are so extensive that they are bound and issued to employees as a book. Employees may be required to sign a statement saying that they have read the policy, are familiar with its contents, and agree to abide by it. Good practice keeps acceptable use policies online so employees can access them whenever in doubt. Some organizations display portions of their acceptable use policy whenever a user logs on to their network.

In most cases, the only way to enforce acceptable use policies is to monitor the content of employee e-mail, the content and source of Internet traffic, and even the content of files kept on employees' computers. Recent studies have concluded that U.S. companies continuously monitor the Internet activity and e-mail use of more than one-third of their Internet-connected connected employees[27], and that more than three-quarters of U.S. companies record their employees activities and communications and subject them to spot

TABLE 10-8 Topics of a Typical Acceptable Use Policy	• Physical Security • Electronic Security • Personal Use of the Internet/Online Services • Personal Use of the Computer for Word Processing, etc. • Loading of Non-Organization Software • Downloading from the Internet/Online Services • Pornography • Information Usage • Levels of Access • Allowable Uses of Access • Ownership of Software, Data, etc. • Data and Information Security • Trade Secrets • Confidentiality of Organizations Records • Logon Banners • Use of E-mail • Organization's Right to Inspect Computers • Organization's Right to Access E-mail • Document Retention Schedules • Voicemail • Telecommuting

SOURCE: Rehman Technology Services, Inc., "A Guide for Drafting Comprehensive and Effective Computer Policies," at http://www.computerpolicy.com/, accessed on 24 April 2002. Used with permission.

checks.[28] Clearly, such monitoring invades the privacy of an organization's employees. Nevertheless, it has almost always been found legal when challenged in court as long as employees are notified about the nature of the monitoring and told that the organization has a legal obligation to enforce acceptable use policies. Organizations may run afoul of the law if they collect information about employees that is not needed to enforce reasonable policies, if they fail to safeguard the information they collect, or if they use the information for purposes other than its intended use. Also, organizations may not collect information about employees' finances or health.[29]

Responsibility for Faulty Systems

Who is responsible when faulty software causes an airplane's autopilot to malfunction resulting in a crash and loss of life? Who is responsible when faulty systems cause medical imaging systems to malfunction resulting in a deadly dose of radiation to a patient? Fortunately, disasters of this magnitude rarely occur. However, as we have seen, software development is prone to error. Who is responsible when decisions based on faulty data result in a company losing money? Who is responsible when a bank denies credit to a credit-worthy applicant because a computer determined that the applicant didn't meet the specified criteria?

A computer glitch at Barclays Bank PLC left 20,000 business customers without access to funds, such as paychecks, electronically deposited to their accounts over the 2002 Easter weekend. If a customer needed that money to pay bills, Barclays would have been liable.[30] United Airlines sold 142 tickets between San Francisco and Paris at an unintentionally low price of $24.98 when a software problem caused the price to appear in error on its Web site. The airline decided to honor the tickets, although it believed it could have cancelled them legally.[31]

Generally, the developer of systems can be held liable for their flaws, whether the systems are used in-house or sold to another party. Increasingly, companies are suing not just for recovery of the price of the software that they purchased, but also for consequential damages. In a recent case, FoxMeyer sued SAP and Accenture for $1 billion on claims that SAP's software and Accenture's implementation were so badly flawed that the company was forced into bankruptcy. In August 2000, a jury awarded the State of Mississippi $475 million for failure of an automated tax collection system bought from American Management Systems. Although most cases are settled out of court, the financial impact of lawsuits on software developers can be significant.[32]

MANAGING CHANGE

Business change and technology change constantly affect information systems. Managing such change is one of the CIO's chief responsibilities. In this section, we start by exploring how technology managers assess changing business priorities and align their plans with these priorities. We then examine the role of the information technology architecture, the blueprint for changing the infrastructure to reflect new technology and new business needs. Finally, we address the need to develop the staff, the human infrastructure, which must also change in order to implement change.

Aligning with the Business

Surveys of IS managers show that aligning IS and corporate goals is always a top priority.[33] Companies can achieve such alignment by giving each business unit control over its IS function. Each unit would have a CIO and an information systems staff, an alternative we examined in the context of the structure of the IS function. Even with this structure, architectural and other needs cross business unit boundaries, so IS managers need a way to coordinate IS and enterprise-wide plans and strategies. Steering committees of top business managers help to attain this goal.

Steering Committees

An IS **steering committee** includes top business managers, selected users, IS managers, and technical specialists who provide direction and vision about the use and development of the IS infrastructure. Such a steering committee increases the likelihood that IS investments and activities align with organizational goals and increases the participation and buy-in of key managers in the development of the IS architecture. A steering committee, however, may have limitations:

- It may take too long to make decisions.
- Meetings may take valuable time of high-level managers.
- Arguments in committee may divide rather than unify the approach toward IS.
- Committee participants may lack the expertise to help make good decisions.

Steering committees work best when IS helps accomplish organizational goals and the organizational culture supports a participative management style.[34] IS managers in less participative cultures may resent committees that infringe on their managerial prerogatives.

The organization and composition of a steering committee influences its effectiveness. The committee should include current and potential user managers with some exposure to information technology. Many practitioners believe that having a user manager chair the committee improves alignment by reducing the likelihood of IS people dictating the agenda. Companies in which IS has strategic value should include top-level managers, such as the executive vice president, president, or CEO, on the committee. Companies for which IS plays a less strategic role might include only middle-level managers if top-level managers feel that the committee requires too much time.

Developing an Information Technology Architecture

Information technology architecture describes an enterprise-wide, long-term structural plan for investing in and organizing information technology. The architecture for an advertising firm with 30 employees, for example, might involve networked PCs, each loaded with word processing, presentation, and electronic mail software, with the long-term addition of groupware and some CAD software. Although each of Nestlé's country companies has its own architecture, Nestlé's corporate IT group also has a vision for how the company can best operate. This architecture addresses the network that ties the companies together, e-mail systems, word processing packages, and ERP platforms.

An organization's architecture determines the types of equipment it should acquire, the types of software it should use, and the telecommunications technology it should buy. Decisions about the architecture also involve decisions about standardization and global performance. The architecture may specify both the current and future state for the infrastructure, as well as a transition plan for reaching the desired state.

Not all organizations develop an information technology architecture. Many companies instead make their investment decisions on a project-by-project basis. Although an architecture increases the likelihood that an organization will make coordinated decisions that reflect its long-term strategy, developing an architecture takes time, effort, and money. Because an architecture has diffuse and long-term benefits, organizations often can't find anyone to sponsor its development. Unless top management acts as a sponsor, a company probably will remain without an architecture.

An architecture may reduce an organization's flexibility to respond to technological change. Once an organization implements architectural plans and purchases the technology that the architecture prescribes, technology managers and others resist investing in nonconforming technology. Such resistance may be counterproductive in periods of rapid technological change. Some companies with an architecture retain flexibility by seeking less rigid technologies and formalizing a structured approach for trying, evaluating, and eventually adopting appropriate technological advances.

Application Architecture

An organization's application architecture addresses its portfolio of software. The application architecture identifies existing systems, their strengths, weaknesses, and interdependencies. It specifies corporate policy about whether application development should be centralized, decentralized, or outsourced. It may specify methodologies to be used in the development of new applications. It should also address how decisions are made regarding which software to run in-house and which to outsource to ASPs. The application architecture should identify priorities for new application development. It might specify a preference or requirement to limit new software products to those compatible with a particular DBMS or middleware product or to particular user interfaces, such as GUI or Web-based interfaces.

Home Depot, the $40 billion home building goods chain, has an application architecture that tightly controls the development of its new systems. The company uses commercial packages whenever possible. For systems developed in-house, programmers must conform their code to an architecture based on reusability of code. CIO and chief architect, Ron Griffin, says, "functions like error checking, error handling, date comparisons and suspend/resume are written once." This has allowed the company to keep its systems compact, to change existing software quickly and inexpensively, and to develop new systems rapidly by linking together existing pieces of code.[35]

Network Architecture

An organization's network architecture addresses both its wide area and local area strategies. It may address only data networks or voice and data networks, and it should address the decision of whether or not data and voice should be combined over a digital network. Network architecture might also include a plan for assuring security of digital communication. It will usually include a personnel plan, designating roles and responsibilities for network operation, management, and oversight, especially in a distributed environment. It usually includes pictorial representations of the desired network, sometimes specific as to layout and sometimes more conceptual, as illustrated in Figure 10-7.

Network architecture might also address the servers that support a data communication strategy. In particular, the use and capacity of Web servers, the nature of proxy servers, and

FIGURE   10-7

Examples of layout and conceptual representations of network architecture.

Source: Cisco Systems referencing its customer NuSkin Enterprises, Inc., a direct marketing company. Accessed at http://www.cisco.com/warp /public/cc/pd/rt/3600/profiles /nuskn_ss.htm on 26 April 2002. MTG Consulting accessed at http://www .mtgconsulting.com /consulting/reference_models /network_architecture.shtml on 26 April 2002. Used with permission.

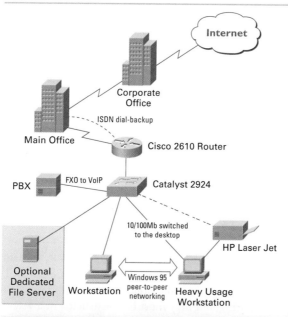

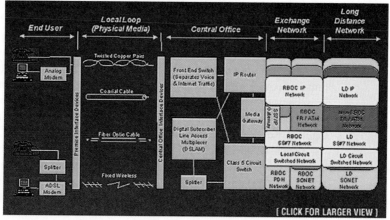

the types and configurations of firewalls, both hardware and software, are often included. Many organizations consider server load balancing to be a network architecture issue.

An organization's wide area network architecture should address not only intranet connectivity among its own sites, but also its extranet strategy for connecting to suppliers and customers. The architecture may specify whether the organization uses dial-up networking, broadband connections, such as DSL or cable through an ISP, or direct connections to the Internet. Large organizations might run their own microwave or satellite networks. Wide area architecture should also address current bandwidth use and forecasted needs, as well as the need for backup or redundant connectivity.

Local area network architecture addresses network topology, the type and capacity of switches and routers used, the nature of the LAN backbone, extent of redundancy, physical security of network hardware and cabling, network maintenance strategy, the protocols that the organization supports, and which protocols are used on each network and subnetwork. Many organizations are now considering how to incorporate wireless technologies into their existing infrastructure. Multisite organizations may centralize their local area network architecture, specify standards to apply to locally defined architectures, or leave the specification of local LAN architectures to the local sites.

Hardware and Platform Architecture

The hardware and platform architecture refers to planning for computer systems and operating systems software. It addresses both personal and enterprise systems. For example, it might address who in the organization should have a computer, whether they should have desktop, laptop, or handheld computers, how often their computers should be upgraded, how much RAM and disk they should have, who should have CD-ROM or DVD drives, what size monitors should be used, and whether maintenance is provided in-house or by a third party. Most medium and large organizations accept a multi-platform architecture with the understanding that deviations from the primary platform must be supported by a strong documentation of need.

At the enterprise level, hardware and platform architecture addresses the types and sizes of systems needed to serve large-scale applications, such as ERP. The architecture addresses what operating systems are supported and what DBMS products are used.

Global Issues

Companies that operate internationally, such as Nestlé, have unique problems in the architecture and building of a coordinated infrastructure. Standardization and networking have eased global differences in some organizations. Standards provide a common infrastructure for data sharing, but they must be constructed in a way that allows for local autonomy to respond to differences in culture, regulations, and constituencies.[36]

Language poses the most obvious barrier to coordinating the software infrastructure. Software tools exist to help developers simultaneously create software to be run in multiple languages. These tools work by separating textual screen prompts and textual report headings from the rest of the software, allowing for easier customization. Difficulties still remain because some languages are much more compact than others. Programmers often lay screens differently, adjust report columns, and change the display of dates and currency for each country. Displaying and printing characters for languages such as Japanese, Chinese, Korean, and Arabic may require special hardware.

Global architecture must consider the international support hardware and software vendors provide. Companies may have difficulty standardizing on either hardware or software if vendors don't support the product selected in all countries in which the company does business. Some companies provide multiple standards to deal with this problem so that each foreign office can find local support for at least one standard. Other companies select standards only from products that receive support worldwide. Accepting multiple standards increases the cost of support and integration. Limiting selection of products reduces a company's flexibility in meeting its needs and generally increases the cost of its investments.

The laws and regulations of foreign countries may also confound a company's attempt to implement a consistent architecture. Countries differ in their laws regarding accounting practices, documentation of business transactions, and reporting requirements. Although some vendors provide packaged software that deals with the laws in many countries, such software is expensive and requires frequent updates. Most companies either customize their systems for the countries in which they do business or allow the organization in each country to make its own IS decisions. Some countries even insist that companies purchase all or a percentage of IT investments from local companies.

The organization of a global company affects whether it can implement a global architecture. Centrally organized companies, typically domestic companies doing international business, usually have the easiest job of designing and controlling the infrastructure. Such organizations have a central IS department that can make and implement plans. Most companies organized along geographical lines, even if not centrally controlled, rely on a central IS staff to coordinate their infrastructure. Individual geographical divisions rarely have the critical mass for developing their own IS planning expertise. Global companies organized along product lines are more likely to establish their own IS planning capabilities.[37] This capability typically exists because different product divisions have very different business needs. Also, such organizations often evolve from mergers between companies that had already developed their own IS capability. Coordinating the infrastructure in such an environment poses political challenges unless strong business needs can overcome the parochial perspectives of local managers.

Developing Staff

To deal with changing technology, IS managers need a concrete human resources strategy for hiring, developing, and compensating staff. Replacing staff involves hiring new employees while moving existing employees to other positions or laying them off. Most companies prefer to maintain their investment in human capital and ensure morale by keeping staff current. This strategy requires effective training programs and a culture that values and rewards development.

Nestlé develops and nurtures its IT staff members by moving them among its operating companies and headquarters. In this way, Nestlé gives high potential individuals both a global perspective and an understanding of the diverse needs of local operating units. Jeri Dunn, for example, the CIO of Nestlé USA, worked for several years in the United States, first as associate director of development for Nestlé's Stouffer's business unit, and then on a project to implement worldwide an SDLC methodology and CASE toolset. Then, she spent three years at company headquarters in Vevey, Switzerland as assistant vice president for global technology and standards decisions, before returning to the United States in her CIO position.[38]

Technical training is an important component of staff development and satisfaction. Certification programs assure that professional are trained to a standard level of competency. A recent survey of 18,000 IT managers found that 34 percent of IT employees who received certification were rewarded through pay increases, promotions, and new responsibilities.[39] Many vendors of hardware and software, such as Microsoft and Cisco, offer certificates for professionals who have taken their training courses and demonstrated competency with their products. Many companies run their own training programs so that they can customize them to their immediate needs and reduce the cost of their training programs. Market research company IDC estimates that corporations in North America spent $12.9 billion for IT training in 2002.[40]

To maximize the effectiveness of technical training, experts suggest the following:[41]

- *Do just-in-time training.* Plan training sessions so that trainees can immediately use their new skills in an assigned project. For example, at United Stationers, a distributor of business, computer, and facilities management products headquartered in Des Moines, Illinois, 75 percent of the time after completing a class, IT professionals are assigned projects that relate to what they just learned.[42]

- *Use computer-based training to teach technical subjects or provide refresher courses.* Use teacher-lead classes mainly for concept training and developing soft skills, such as project management. Computer-based training can be significantly less expensive than teacher-led training, more flexible in its timing, and more directly responsive to individual needs. IDC expects the electronic learning market to reach $15 billion by 2005.[43]

- *Include training in procurement contracts.* Vendor training is often the most effective for "train-the-trainer" education.

- *Train on company time.* Training on company time sends the message that the company cares for its employees and expects them to keep current, not as an option but as a responsibility of the job.

- *Use help desk trainers.* Train your help desk staff to provide just-in-time training as they solve users' problems.

SUMMARY

Organizing the IS function involves deciding how much control to centralize in a corporate IS staff and how much to distribute throughout the organization. Some organizations create structures in which a corporate IS department provides all IS activities to simplify control and security and to reduce cost. Others place most IS activity under the control of separate business units to increase responsiveness to business needs. Outsourcing gives responsibility for operations and development to a contractor. The IS function can operate as an unallocated cost center, an allocated cost center, or a profit center.

The human infrastructure includes the IS jobs individuals hold. These include the positions of CIO, CTO, strategic planner, data and database administrator, network administrator, Web master, project manager, systems analyst, software engineer, programmer, user trainer, user assistant, operations and technical support staff, and data entry clerk. These positions require a combination of technical, managerial, and interpersonal skills for successful job performance. End-user computing focuses on the consumers of the IS services. Increasingly, end users contribute to systems development. Most organizations establish a help desk to help end users solve their information systems problems.

Information systems managers can track the performance of information services over time and benchmark them against other companies. Business managers can use service level agreements to guarantee adequate levels of information services. Managers may set standards that improve the efficiency of and flexibility of IS personnel, create opportunities to exercise power in purchasing, and improve coordination among applications. Standards may constrain an organization's ability to meet the needs of its end users and may stifle creativity and innovation.

Organizations should develop a plan to prepare for operating through and recovering after a disaster. They should also create an acceptable use policy. Enforcement of acceptable use policies must balance a company's need to avoid lawsuits with employees need for privacy.

IS managers manage change by aligning their priorities with business needs, developing an architecture, and training staff. Steering committees can help assure the alignment of IS and business priorities. An architecture lays out the plans for changing the information technology and systems infrastructure. Global organizations need to consider differences among national laws, accounting practices, and communication infrastructure in developing an architecture. Training staff ensures that an organization's employees can accommodate change.

KEY TERMS

acceptable use policy
allocated cost center
Application Service Provider (ASP)
architecture
business continuity plan
chief information officer (CIO)
chief technology officer (CTO)
computer code of ethics
data administrator
data entry clerk

database administrator
disaster plan
end user
help desk
infrastructure
network administrator
organizational structure
outsourcing
profit center
programmer

project manager
security policy
service level agreement (SLA)
software engineers
standard
steering committee
systems analyst
unallocated cost center
Web master

REVIEW QUESTIONS

1. What are the advantages of a distributed structure where each business unit controls its own information services?
2. How might a manager use outsourcing to ease problems encountered in staffing software development?
3. Why might managers outsource only selected information services?
4. What is the advantage of an unallocated cost center for companies with primitive information systems?
5. What problems are associated with unallocated cost centers?
6. What problems arise in distributing the costs of an allocated cost center?
7. What is the primary advantage of operating information services as a profit center?
8. How do a data administrator and a database administrator differ?
9. How do a programmer and a software engineer differ?
10. Why might a company centralize its help desk?
11. Why might business managers seek service level agreements from their information service providers?
12. Why do information service managers impose technology standards on the organization?
13. What are some disadvantages of standard setting?
14. On what technologies might information service managers apply standards?
15. Why is site redundancy so expensive for companies using transaction processing systems?
16. Why should companies develop a security policy?

17. How can companies keep their employees from using corporate computers and networks in inappropriate ways?

18. How do IS managers align IS and business priorities?

19. Why do companies develop information technology architectures?

20. What issues must managers consider in developing an IS architecture for a global company that they do not need to consider for domestic companies?

21. What rules should companies follow to train technical staff efficiently and effectively?

MINICASE

MANAGING INFORMATION TECHNOLOGY SERVICES AT DOMINION

To expedite its merger with Consolidated Natural Gas (CNG) of Pittsburgh, Dominion, a $10 billion energy company based in Richmond, Virginia, centralized IT. Lyn McDermid, CIO and senior vice president of IT, placed a director-level IT account manager in each of the company's five major business units to keep track of IT needs. Then, she grouped employees by expertise, such as mainframe, applications development, and servers.

A year later, that arrangement has improved the quality of IT services, McDermid says. "We're just getting to really capitalize on this, but we have the advantage of cross-pollination and cross-communication, and we aren't reinventing the wheel for every project or issue," she says. "We have tremendous checks and balances where people who [have solved specific IT problems] will give advice or be part of quality processes in other areas."

McDermid has struggled with cultural issues, particularly among non-IT people in various business units. "Centralization makes the business units nervous because they think they're losing control over their IT resources," she says, because the IT decision-making process is no longer localized. "So we've had to always make sure customers are aware of what we're doing and what the business case is." That's why the IT account managers meet with the stakeholders in each unit. "[These IT liaisons] help create common goals and expectations, and they help build the alignment between business and IT that's critical to delivering an acceptable product," says McDermid.

For example, Dominion is an SAP shop for enterprise resource planning, and CNG was an Oracle/PeopleSoft shop. After the merger, McDermid wanted to convert CNG to SAP in six months. She was successful, she believes, largely because the IT account managers from Dominion who were placed in CNG trained former Oracle/PeopleSoft users on SAP and made sure SAP was configured to meet the new users' needs. As a result, Dominion now has consistent HR policies, a single supply chain process, and more strategic sourcing because there's one source of information about all purchase orders and vendors. McDermid says achieving the same result in a decentralized organization would have taken months longer because she'd have been dealing with a separate IS staff in the new business unit with no way to bridge the divide between it and the rest of the enterprise.

McDermid's new organization follows a model called "Centers of Excellence" which has its roots in consultancies that organized themselves that way to create nimble teams quickly, drawing from various pools of IT workers grouped by specialty. The approach first spread into IT organizations in the late 1980s and early 1990s, but soon fell out of favor, says V. Sambamurthy, an associate professor at the Robert H. Smith School of Business at the University of Maryland. Centers of Excellence failed largely because they were rolled out for the whole IT organization rather than just for application development and solutions delivery, which Sambamurthy says they're best suited for.

Resentment from the business side as it loses a measure of control over IT is a natural risk of rolling out skill-based Centers of Excellence for the whole IT organization because it's traditionally used to owning its project team. "It's a departure from the past model of decentralization, because with the centers you are recentralizing technical people by putting them into a corporate group," Sambamurthy says. That's a danger, he adds, because IT can become an island that invents solutions that are irrelevant to the business unit.

Another potential problem with that model is downtime. Employees sit in the bullpen with other specialists and leave the pen to join a project. When the project ends, they go back to the bench and wait for the next one. "The danger here is human anxiety, especially in a bad economic environment," Sambamurthy says. "The concern is 'I'm visible because I don't have a project to work on. Will I be the first target of a cutback?'"

Appointing career managers to focus exclusively on IS employees can help, assuring them that bench time is no cause for concern. McDermid also uses that time for training as well as for development of new technologies and applications. It keeps the group sharp and takes away the pressure of predicting necessary staffing levels by discrete skill.

McDermid stresses that just as in decades past, centralization will fail if your company's culture does not already emphasize business–IT alignment. "When the business units first took back IT, it happened because we weren't responding to their needs," she says. "We were doing a terrible job, victims of the old glass-house syndrome. Outsourcing and the threats of new technology have shown us that the only way to survive is to understand where the business is going."

SOURCE: Adapted from Eric Berkman, "Next Stop: Centralization," *CIO Magazine,* 15 September 2001, accessed at http://www.cio.com/archive/091501/centralization.html on 26 April 2002. Reprinted through the courtesy of CIO. ©2002, CXO Media Inc. All rights reserved.

Case Questions

Diagnosis

    1. What are the information needs at Dominion?

Evaluation

    2. How well did the old organizational structure support those needs?

Design

    3. What characteristics of the organizational structure and the technical infrastructure did McDermid change?

    4. What improvements did McDermid see after the change?

Implementation

    5. What potential problems did McDermid face in implementing the organizational change at Dominion?

    6. How did she address these problems?

    7. Will it be easier or more difficult for McDermid to retain an alignment between IT and business units now that IT has been centralized?

    8. What are the pros and cons of the Centers of Excellence model for the company? What are the pros and cons for the employees?

    9. How has McDermid addressed the personnel issues raised by the Centers of Excellence model?

    10. Will McDermid's solution work for Dominion in the long term?

ACTIVITY

10-1 MISSING AN ARCHITECTURE AT THE DLA

Step 1: Read the following scenario.

The Defense Logistics Agency (DLA) is a U.S. Department of Defense agency that provides worldwide logistics support for the missions of the U.S. military. In 1988, the DLA, which employs 28,000 civilian and military workers at 500 sites in U.S. and abroad, determined that it needed to replace its 1960s, mainframe-based, legacy systems so that it could use the Web to handle transactions. Initial trials of some off-the-shelf products in 1999 worked well, and the DLA staff became excited about the possibility of replacing the old systems. In 2000, the agency awarded a contract to Accenture to implement SAP enterprise software and Manugistics supply chain software beginning in 2003. The new systems promised to greatly improve both the workflow and the management of the procurement and logistics processes.

The problem: The U.S. General Accounting Office (GAO), the investigative arm of Congress regarding the use of public funds, criticized the agency for beginning the modernization program without first creating an enterprise architecture. Not only did the DLA's approach violate Defense Department policy, according to the GAO, but without an architecture the DLA would run the risk of improving some systems but not improving, or even worsening, the way that its systems worked together.

The DLA, however, does not believe that its approach is risky. Its program manager, David Falvey, has argued that the agency has followed the lead of private-sector business. He argues that the agency can implement an ERP system at the same time as it builds a new architecture and that building the architecture first will slow down the agency's modernization efforts.

SOURCE: Dawn S. Onley, "FAA's DLA Takes an Industry Approach to Modernize, Handle Business on Web," *Government Computer News, GCN.com,* 20 August 2001, accessed on 27 April 2002 at http://www.gcn.com/20_24/news/16878-1.html. Bill Murray, "DLA Modernization Plan Called Flawed," *Federal Computer Week, FCW.com,* 16 July 2001, accessed on 27 April 2002 at http://www.fcw.com/fcw/articles/2001/0716/pol-dla-07-16-01.asp. Nick Wakeman, "GAO Urges DLA Modernization," *Washington Technology,* 16 July 2001, accessed on 27 April 2002 at http://www.washingtontechnology.com/news/16_8/federal/16843-3.html.

Step 2: Prepare the case for class discussion.

Step 3: Answer each of the following questions, individually or in small groups, as directed by your instructor:

Diagnosis

    1. Why does the DLA believe that its current systems are operating inefficiently?

Evaluation

    2. Is it likely that the new systems will meet the DLA's needs?

    3. Why has the GAO criticized the DLA's processes?

Design:

    4. How would an architecture satisfy the needs of the teams managing the modernization?

Implementation

    5. Why is developing a formal architecture difficult for the DLA?

    6. What should the head of the DLA do now?

Step 4: In small groups or with the entire class, share your answers to the questions in Step 3. Then answer the following questions:

1. Why does the DLA believe that its current systems are operating inefficiently?
2. Is it likely that the new systems will meet the DLA's needs?
3. How would an architecture satisfy the needs of the teams managing the modernization?
4. What should the head of the DLA do now?

10-2 IS JOB INTERVIEW

Step 1: Interview three information systems job holders about the job responsibilities, past and anticipated career paths, and interactions with other IS professionals and non-IS job holders in the organization. (Your instructor may direct you to conduct your interviews outside class or may convene a panel of IS jobholders for you to interview).

Step 2: Prepare a job description for each position.

Step 3: In small groups or with the entire class, share the job descriptions.

Step 4: In small groups or with the entire class, answer the following questions:

1. What types of jobs exist in information systems?
2. What types of career paths exist in information systems?
3. How do IS jobholders relate to other organizational members?

10-3 END-USER QUIZ

Step 1: Complete the following quiz. Interpret each statement as a stand-alone situation; there is no relationship among the various scenarios. Answer each question according to this scale: I sympathize ...

1. with the user.
2. with IS.
3. with both.
4. with neither.

Then indicate the major problem that exists in each situation.

Scenario 1:

User manager: The marketing department paid an exorbitant amount for technology services last quarter, and each quarter your rates increase. You've given us a breakdown of our use and charges, but I don't see anything we can do to lower them in the future. We have no choice but to pay what you ask—it's like blackmail.

IS manager: We're really trying hard to keep our costs down, but you have no idea how expensive technology is. We have to upgrade our systems constantly to meet the needs of your department and others, and the salaries of technical people have been rising much faster than the rate of inflation.

Scenario 2:

User manager: The laptops that we've standardized use a trackpoint to move the cursor. Personally, I just can't stand them. I've polled my department and found that the large majority prefer touchpads to trackpoints. I've also checked pricing, and I've found a computer with the same capabilities as ours, a touchpad, and a lower price. I'm almost always a team player, but I'm going to fight the team on this and buy our own computers despite the standard.

IS manager: The reason that we have a standard is to make sure that we can support the equipment and to provide a high level of uniformity. We also get a better price and better support from our vendor. Your department had input into the standard. You can get your own systems, but don't come running to us when they break down, the software fails to work, or you need assistance of any kind.

Scenario 3:

User manager: When we designed the new procurement system, you told us that it would be ready at the end of last month. Now you're saying it will be another three months. What going on? Why can't you stick to your estimates?

IS manager: Don't blame us. Every time we show you a prototype, you change the requirements. The changes you've asked for may seem small to you, but they put a monkey wrench into our development schedule. If you were more careful specifying your needs at the start, we would have been finished on schedule.

Scenario 4:

User manager: One of our major customers is complaining that they can't send us e-mail. They say that they can't seem to get through our firewall.

IS manager: I'm aware of the problem. We've identified a lot of viruses and Trojan horse attachments coming from their site. We've asked them to tighten their security, but they seem unable or unwilling to do so. Our security plan requires that we quarantine sites that attack us at greater that a certain frequency, and they've passed that limit. My hands are tied.

Step 2: Your instructor will provide directions for scoring your responses.

Step 3: In small groups or with the class as a whole, answer the following questions:

1. What issue does each scenario describe?
2. Which party presents a better analysis and perspective on the situation?
3. What actions would improve the situation described?

SOURCE: The idea of an end-user quiz pitting the user manager against the IS manager is drawn from Dennis Vanvick, "Getting to Know U(sers)," *Computerworld*, 27 January 1992, 103–104,107.

10-4 ACCEPTABLE USE POLICY

ACTIVITY

Step 1: Read the acceptable use policy at your school and at one other organization. (Your instructor may direct you to the other organization or to its Web site).

Step 2: Individually or in small groups, compare and contrast the two policies.

Step 3: In small groups or with the entire class, share your analysis. Identify the common elements in each plan. Then answer the following questions:

1. What elements are common to each plan?
2. How do the plans differ?
3. In which organization would you prefer to work?

4. What security and legal risks do the plans address?

5. What security and legal risks remain for each organization?

6. How do differences in their plans reflect differences in the organizations' missions and exposures to risk?

10-5 PUBLIC SECTOR OUTSOURCING

ACTIVITY

Step 1: Read the following scenario.

Halverton County Executive Andrew McLumis recently awarded a seven-year contract to JBM to outsource all of its information technology services. Most, but not all, of the county's 112 IS employees were offered jobs with JBM. Some who were offered jobs with JBM chose to fight the move. The employees' union filed a legal complaint with the state court, but the outcome has not yet been decided.

Step 2: Prepare the case for class discussion. Consider the viewpoints of JBM, the county, employees who welcomed the move, and employees who brought the suit.

Step 3: From the perspective of the each of the parties in the dispute, answer each of the following questions, individually or in small groups, as directed by your instructor.

1. What alternatives now exist? What compromises might you propose?

2. For each alternative, who benefits and who is harmed?

3. From the ethical principles of least harm, rights and duties, professional responsibilities, self-interest and utilitarianism, consistency, and respect, how would you evaluate each alternative?

4. If you were McLumis, what course of action would you take? Why?

IS ON
THE WEB

IS ON THE WEB

Exercise 1: Do a Web search on the term "privacy and security policy." Examine the security policy of two organizations, one governmental and one private, identified in the Web search. Compare and contrast these security policies.

Exercise 2: Visit the Web site of an outsourcer shown in Table 10-1. Prepare a brief summary of the types of projects it undertakes.

RECOMMENDED READINGS

Aalders, Rob. *The IT Outsourcing Guide.* New York: John Wiley & Sons, 2001.

Applegate, Lynda M., F. Warren McFarlan, and James L. McKenney. *Corporate Information Systems Management: Text and Cases,* 5th ed. Chicago: Richard D. Irwin, 1999.

Boar, Bernard H. *The Art of Strategic Planning for Information Technology,* 2nd ed. New York: John Wiley & Sons, 2000.

Clarkson, Mary. *Developing IT Staff: A Practical Approach.* New York: Springer-Verlag, 2001.

Hiatt, Charlotte J. *A Primer for Disaster Recovery Planning in an IT Environment.* Hershey, PA: Idea Group Publishing, 2000.

Martin, Wainright/ed., Carol V. Brown, Daniel W. Dehayes, Jeffrey A. Hoffer, and William C. Perkins. *Managing Information Technology: What Managers Need to Know,* 4th ed. Upper Saddle River, NJ: Prentice Hall, 2002.

Tipton, Harold F. and Micki Krause. *Information Security Management Handbook,* 4th ed. Boca Raton, FL: CRC Press, 2001.

NOTES

1. www.nestle.com, accessed on 18 April 2002. Malcolm Wheatley, "Nestlé's Worldwide Squeeze," CIO, 1 June 2001, 52–56. Stephen McClelland, "Nestlé: Global Customers," *Telecommunications,* April 2000, S2–S3.

2. Tony Kontzer, "Centralization Redux for IT," *Informationweek,* 17 September 2001, 179–182.

3. Jaikumar Vijayan, "Sept. 11 Attacks Prompt Decentralization Moves," *Computerworld,* 17 December 2001, 10.

4. Diane Rezendes Khirallah, "The Changing Face of IT," *Informationweek,* 31 July 2000, 42–54.

5. Ibid.

6. Todd R. Weiss, "Nestlé shifts from HP to IBM in Data Center Pact," *Computerworld,* 11 March 2002, 5.

7. David Kirkpatrick, "Why Not Farm Out Your Computing?," *Fortune,* 23 September 1991, 103–112.

8. Jaikumar Vijayan, "The Outsourcing Boom," *Computerworld,* 18 March 2002, 42–43.

9. Todd R. Weiss, "American Express Signs $4B IT Services Deal with IBM," *Computerworld,* 4 March 2002, 20.

10. Steven Burke and Marie Lingblom, "EDS Bullish on Outsourcing," *CRN,* 18 February 2002, 74.

11. http://www.surebridge.com/customers /cus_case2/0,1147,,00.html, accessed on 17 April 2002.

12. Christine Spivey Overby with John C. McCarthy and Emily H. Boynton, US *Outsourcing Decelerates.* Cambridge, MA: Forrester Research, 2002.

13. Geoffrey Downey, "Outsourcers Facing Uneasy Clients," *Computing Canada,* 24 November 2000, 1–2.

14. Barb Gomolski, "Get Rid of IT Burnout," *InfoWorld,* 11 June 2001, 72.

15. Bob Brewin, "Hotel Chain Becomes Its Own Service Provider," *Computerworld,* 15 October 2001, 10.

16. Julekha Dash, "Hospital Moves into ASP Niche," *Computerworld,* 23 April 2001, 1, 16.

17. Tom Field, "Former CEO Takes CIO Post in Bloomington," *CIO,* 1 February 2002, 32.

18. Jaikumar Vijayan, "Invensys Outsources IT to IBM in $1B Deal," *Computerworld,* 1 April 2002, 14.

19. Simha R. Magal and Dennis D. Strouble, "A Users' Perspective of the Critical Success Factors Applicable to Information Centers," *Information Resources Management Journal,* Spring 1991, 22–34.

20. Robert L. Leitheiser and James C. Wetherbe, "A Comparison of Perceptions about Information Center Success," *Information & Management* 21 (August 1991): 7–17.

21. Lucas Mearian, "IT Benchmarking Is Aid in Measuring Investments," *Computerworld,* 18 March 2002, 10.

22. These are drawn from the CES Service Level Agreement, Draft 10/23/96, accessed at www.his.ucsf.edu/~gif/stddsktp.html, on 12 December 1997.

23. Carol Sliwa, "New York Board of Trade Gets Back to Business," *Computerworld,* 24 September 2001, 8.

24. Mandy Andress, "Effective Security Starts with Policies," *InfoWorld,* 19 November 2001, 56–57.

25. Matt Hicks, "Survey: Even after Sept. 11, Security Lags," *Eweek,* 3 December 2001, 49.

26. Tracy Mayor, "Someone to Watch Over You," *CIO,* 1 March 2001, 82–88.

27. Andrew Schulman, *The Extent of Systematic Monitoring of Employee E-Mail and Internet Use.* Denver, CO: The Privacy Foundation, 2001.

28. American Management Association, *2001 AMA Survey: Workplace Monitoring and Surveillance, Summary of Key Findings,* http://www.amanet .org/research/pdfs/ems_short2001.pdf, accessed on 25 April 2002.

29. Dan Verton, "IT Shops Balance Security, Privacy," *Computerworld,* 25 February 2002, 1, 16.

30. Brian Sullivan, "Computer Glitch Disrupts Deposits at Barclays," *Computerworld Online,* 28 March 2002, http://www.computerworld.com /storyba/0,4125,NAV47_STO69645,00.html, accessed on 25 April 2002.

31. Linda Rosencrance, "United to Honor Dirt-Cheap Online Ticket Fares," *Computerworld Online,* 20 February 2001, http://www .computerworld.com/cwi/story /0,1199,NAV47_STO57853,00.html, accessed on 25 April 2002.

32. Ann Bednarz, "IT Malpractice," *Network World,* 8 April 2002, 54.

33. Eric Berkman, "Why We're Still Talking about Alignment," *CIO,* 15 December 2000, 68–76.

34. Harish C. Bahl and Mohammad Dadashzadeh, "A Framework for Improving Effectiveness of MIS Steering Committees," *Information Resources Management Journal,* Summer 1992, 33–44.

35. Matt Nannery, "Home Improvement," *Chain Store Age,* June 2000, 78–84.

36. Lori Chordas, "Solving the Global Disconnect," *Best's Review,* January 2002, 75–79.

37. Steven R. Gordon, "Standardization of Information Systems and Technology at Multinational Companies," *Journal of Global Information Management,* Summer 1993, 5–14.

38. Elizabeth Heichler, "A Head for the Business," *CIO,* 15 June 2000, 172–184.

39. Joel Schettler, "To the Certified Go the Spoils," *Training,* March 2002, 14.

40. Lisa Vaas, "Companies Cut Spending on IT Training," *eWeek,* 18 April 2002, accessed at http://www.eweek.com/article /0,3658,s=25210&a=25696,00.asp on 26 April 2002.

41. Based on Joseph Maglitta, "Train in Vain: Training Tips," *Computerworld,* 25 August 1997, 81.

42. Julekha Dash, "The ROI of Training," *Computerworld,* 18 March 2002, 58.

43. Kathleen Melymuka, "Executive Education on a Shoestring," *Computerworld,* 11 March 2002, 24–25.

GLOSSARY

A

acceptable use policy An organizational policy or code that clarifies and makes explicit for employees what uses of corporate computer and network facilities are proper.

adaptor Also known as a controller, it resides inside the computer and converts commands and data from the data bus into signals that peripheral devices can use

agent A company or person that acts on behalf of another.

aggregator A business that adds value by providing one-stop shopping through buying products from many producers and distributors and reselling them in the retail market.

agile programming Any of several systems development methodologies that focus on being reactive to changing user demands and that target small development groups and projects that require minimal documentation.

alliance An official working partnership with another organization.

allocated cost center An accounting scheme in which the IS department allocates and charges its costs to the departments that use its services.

alpha testing See system testing.

alternative analysis Considers one or more alternate designs and analyzes their advantages and disadvantages.

application programming interface (API) Software interface built into a program allows other programs to communicate with it.

application Service Provider (ASP) A company that provides outsourcing services for the operation, maintenance, and often customization, of specific software applications.

architecture The long-term structural plan for investing in and organizing information technology; it acts as the blueprint for the technology portion of an organization's information systems infrastructure.

artificial intelligence (AI) The branch of computer science that emulates human behavior and thought in computer hardware and software.

atomicity The property of a transaction that prevents its division into parts.

attribute A characteristic of an entity, such as a phone number, hair color, height, or weight of the entity "person"; a column of a relation in the relational model.

authentication The ability of a message receiver to ascertain the identity of the message sender.

auto-ID Technology for tagging merchandise, boxes, pallets, containers, and moving vehicles in such a way that their location can be tracked.

automated guided vehicle (AGV) Computer-controlled vehicle that moves along a guidance system built into a factory or warehouse floor.

automation system System that uses information technology to perform tasks or to make them easier or less labor intensive.

B

backbone A network that connects other networks.

bandwidth Theoretical capacity of a telecommunication channel

beta testing See pilot implementation strategy.

bit The smallest amount of data that can be stored; holds a zero or a one.

bug An error in the way that a system operates.

business-level strategy Strategy that matches the strengths and weaknesses of each business unit or product line to the external environment to determine how each unit can best compete for customers.

business-to-business (B2B) Electronic commerce between two or more businesses.

business-to-consumer (B2C) Electronic commerce between a business and consumers.

business continuity plan See disaster plan.

business intelligence (BI) A combination of processes and tools for increasing a business's competitive advantage by using data intelligently to make better, faster decisions.

business model A broad plan for what products or services a company plans to sell and how it plans to earn its revenue.

byte One byte equals eight bits Most manufacturers measure storage capacity in bytes

C

cache memory A small amount of primary storage that is faster than the rest of the primary storage in a computer.

CASE tool Software that helps automate the software development process.

CASE toolset Also called a CASE workbench, it is a suite of CASE tools that support and integrate the activities performed throughout the software development life cycle.

CASE workbench See CASE toolset.

Certificate authority (CA) A trusted authority that provides an authentication function for electronic documents similar to that provided by a notary public or bank for a physical document.

channel conflict Conflict caused by a company selling through indirect channels, such as distributors or retail stores, at the same time as selling directly to consumers through Web channels.

chief information officer (CIO) Person who manages the information-related resources and activities of an organization.

chief technology officer (CTO) Specialist who frequently has a staff and budget to pilot new technologies on real or hypothetical applications.

click-and-mortar strategy A business strategy that calls for a company to sell its products and services both over the Internet and at a physical location; a company that follows a click-and-mortar strategy.

click-through advertisement An advertisement that directs the viewer to the advertiser's Web site if the viewer clicks on its ad in a Web page.

client/server architecture Design that divides processing between clients and servers; design that divides DBMS processing among networked computers while centralizing permanent storage on a database server.

client/server model Software design that divides processing between two programs, one called the client that provides a user interface and requests information from another, called the server.

coaxial cable Transmission medium used by cable television companies to bring television signals into the home.

code generator Software that creates complete and working programs based on designer specifications.

command/data oriented programming language A computer language, such as FORTRAN, COBOL, and Pascal, that separates data storage from procedural parts of a program.

commercial off-the-shelf (COTS) software Uncustomized vertical software.

common carrier Private carrier that sells communication services to the public.

communication The exchange of information between two parties.

communication carrier A government agency or private company that provides communication services and facilities to the public.

competitive intelligence (CI) The collection, management, and use of information about competitive organizations.

compiler Software that translates a program's source code into object modules.

component testing Testing that examines the interaction of a series of programs within the system that likely will be used in concert, such as those that process a transaction

computer-aided design (CAD) System that allows engineers, architects, graphics designers, and others to compose their product and process designs on a computer rather than paper.

computer-aided engineering (CAE) The application of mathematical models and scientific theory to design to determine how the designed product will work under varying conditions.

computer-aided manufacturing (CAM) System that automates machine monitoring and control through the use of flexible manufacturing, robotics, and automated guided vehicles.

computer-aided software engineering (CASE) The use of software to automate activities performed in needs assessment, systems analysis, design, development, and maintenance.

computer-supported cooperative work (CSCW) See groupware.

computer code of ethics See acceptable use policy.

computer hardware Equipment used in electronic information processing.

computer integrated manufacturing (CIM) The coordination of CAD and CAM automation systems with each other and with information systems that relate to design and manufacturing.

computer software Instructions, in the form of computer code and its accompanying documentation, for processing data electronically.

concurrency control The proper management of simultaneous data updates when multiple users or multiple tasking occurs.

content management software Software that facilitates the creation of dynamic Web pages by pulling selected information from a database into a Web page template.

contextual inquiry A way of collecting information about how users perform their work by watching them working or working alongside them.

corporate-level strategy Strategy that addresses which lines of business a company should pursue.

cost leadership A strategy that seeks to achieve competitive advantage by allowing a business unit, by keeping its costs low, to make more profit than its competitors at the same price.

cross-docking The process by which goods received at a distribution point are immediately loaded onto outgoing trucks without entering into inventory.

cross-functional team Also known as an interdisciplinary team, team that includes employees from several functional areas in the company

customer relationship management (CRM) The philosophy, generally supported with the appropriate practices and software, that an organization should focus on the customer.

cybermediation See reintermediation.

D

data Raw facts whose uses and application are undefined.

data administrator A person whose responsibility is to ensure the integrity of the data resource The data administrator must know what data the organization collects, where it stores the data, and how it names data items.

data bus The electrical connection between various parts of the computer that manages the flow of data between the processing hardware and the rest of the computer.

data communication technology Company networks, the Internet, and other technology for the transmittal of digitized data.

data design The process of identifying and formalizing the relationships among the elements of data in a database.

data dictionary The part of a database that holds its metadata and acts as a CASE tool for automating programming.

data entry clerk A relatively low-skill, low-paying job position with the responsibility of entering data into a computerized system.

data-flow diagram (DFD) A diagram that graphically illustrates the creation and use of data by system processes and provides a complete picture of the relationship between inputs and outputs.

data mart Provides summary and historical data for management decision making for a single department or division.

data mining The process of identifying patterns in large masses of data.

data warehouse An enterprise-wide database designed solely to support management decision making.

database An organized collection of related data.

database administrator (DBA) A person with responsibilities to focus on the overall performance and integrity of a single DBMS on one or more databases.

database management system (DBMS) Software comprising programs to store, retrieve, and otherwise manage a computerized database and provide interfaces to application programs and to non-programming users, as well as provide a host of other data creation, manipulation, and security features.

database model The underlying methods that a database uses for associating, storing, and retrieving related data.

database server In a client/server architecture, a computer that stores data and runs the software to access its data in response to requests from client computers.

decision support system (DSS) System that assists managers in evaluating the impact of alternative decisions and making the best possible choice.

demand chain The portion of the extended value chain on the customer side.

density The number of dots an output device produces per inch horizontally and vertically.

departmental information system Information system that addresses the needs of individual functions or departments.

design The creation of detailed specifications for a proposed system.

design specification The means for communicating a system's design to the programmers who will implement it.

desktop conferencing A method of conferencing featuring the use of sophisticated workstations incorporating a video camera connected over a network or high-capacity conference line that transmits text, graphics, voice, and video.

detail report Provides managers information useful in overseeing the day-to-day operations of a department or working group.

development The creation or purchase of the hardware and software necessary to implement a system's design It also includes the testing required to ensure that the system meets the design specifications.

differentiation Strategy that seeks to distinguish the products and services of a business unit from those of its competitors through unique design, features, quality, or other factors.

digital signal processor (DSP) Processor that converts an electronic wave signal, such one arising from sound or other sensory inputs, to a stream of digital bits and vice versa.

digital signature Encrypted code attached to a message that verifies the identity of the sender.

direct cut-over strategy The replacement of an old with a new system overnight, over a weekend, or over some other period of time when the company does not operate.

disaster plan The process of anticipating disasters and providing for appropriate responses to keep a business operating after a disaster.

disintermediation The process of bypassing intermediaries, such as wholesalers and retailers, in the distribution and sale of a product or service

distribution architecture Plan that specifies how data and database processing are physically distributed among the computers in an organization.

distributor A business that buys in bulk and resells in smaller quantities.

docking station Special port on desktop computers that can transfer data between mobile and desktop units.

domain name A name that uniquely identifies a server on the Internet.

Domain Name Server (DNS) Server that looks up the IP address of a domain name for Internet users

E

e-business The use of information and communication technologies to perform business functions. E-business includes e-commerce.

e-commerce See electronic commerce.

e-government A model of government in which information technology is used to the extent possible to facilitate interaction between the government and its suppliers, government and the public, government and its employees, and among government agencies and different governmental bodies.

electronic bill presentment and payment (EBPP) The process of billing customers and receiving payments electronically over the Internet

electronic bulletin board A system for electronic conversation and messaging controlled by a central manager that uses a central repository to store messages.

electronic commerce (e-commerce) Electronic transactions related to the purchase and delivery of goods and services.

Electronic Data Interchange (EDI) The exchange of data (usually transactions) between two business organizations using a standard electronic format.

electronic list A feature of some electronic mail systems that allows people interested in a particular topic to share electronic mail.

electronic mail A message sent electronically between two users on a computer system or on networked computers; also the software that supports the sending of electronic mail.

electronic meeting room Room in which participants work at their own computers on a U-shaped table facing a common computer at the front of the room, which can be seen by all participants.

encryption Use of a code to change (encode or encrypt) a message, making it unreadable.

end user A consumer of information systems and services.

Enterprise Application Integration (EAI) The process of getting different software packages to work together as an integrated whole.

enterprise information system Fully integrates the functions of a company or enterprise and provides a single, comprehensive repository for its information.

enterprise resource planning (ERP) software Software that provides seamless support for the supply-chain, value-chain, and administrative processes of a company

ethernet A widely-used group of standards that address media, connectors, and communication protocols on a local area network.

ethics The study of how to apply a given set of moral standards to particular situations.

event-initiated report A report generated by a management reporting system that is designed to alert managers to potential problems by showing only data that fall outside an accepted or expected range.

exception report Report that alerts managers to potential problems by showing only data that fall outside an accepted or expected range.

executable module A program created by a linker combining object modules that perform related tasks with already-compiled object code from a library of commonly-used functions Also called a load module.

executive information system (EIS) System that allows executives easy access to their favorite reports, lets them focus on interesting items in more detail, and scans news-wire and other information services for items of greatest interest to the executive.

executive support system (ESS) See executive information system.

expert system (ES) Computer software that automates the role of an expert in a given field.

expert systems shell Off-the-shelf expert systems software that provides all the components of an expert system except the knowledge base.

explanation module The part of an expert system that tells the user how the inference engine applied the rules and facts to reach its conclusion.

Extended Markup Language See XML.

extended value chain The sequence of value-adding activities extending beyond a company's boundaries starting from those required to develop a product from the basic raw materials that comprise its components to its delivery to the end consumer.

extranet An internal network that a company opens to selected suppliers and customers to reduce the cost of transactions and create inter-organizational linkages that can become strategically advantageous.

F

fiber optic cable Transmission medium that carries messages on a beam of light rather than using an electrical signal.

field Data about one of the characteristics or attributes of a record; it is the lowest element of data that has meaning.

file A group or collection of data about similar things.

firewall Hardware or software that acts as a blockade between an internal network and an external network such as the Internet.

five forces model A model popularized by Michael Porter in which the bargaining power of suppliers and buyers, the threat of new entrants, the possibility of product or service substitutes, and the rivalry of competitors, all affect the success of an organization's strategy.

flash memory An electro-magnetic storage device that stores data onto computer chips in a non-volatile fashion.

flexible manufacturing Philosophy of manufacturing that requires that machinery to potentially have multiple uses.

focus Strategy that achieves competitive advantage by concentrating the organization's resources on a single market segment, allowing it to become a big player in a small market rather than a small player in a big market.

function box System design tool that shows how one process connects to other processes.

functional information system Information system that addresses the needs of individual functions or departments.

functional strategy Direction for individual departments to perform their tasks so as to accomplish organizational objectives.

fuzzy logic The reasoning of an expert system that includes rules to deal with ambiguities, rather than only "either/or" choices.

G

gateway System that moves data between two networks that use different data link and network standards.

geographic information system (GIS) Software with the ability to examine and manipulate geographical information, along with associated databases containing geographical information.

group decision support system (GDSS) Software that supports group decision making.

group support system (GSS) See groupware.

groupware Also known as computer-supported cooperative work (CSCW) and group support system (GSS), information technology that facilitates the sharing or communication of information among members of a group and helps the group to perform common tasks and to accomplish its goals, including such products as electronic mail, electronic notes, bulletin board systems, and electronic meeting systems.

H

hard disk The most common type of a fixed media storage device It consists of magnetic-coated metal platters arranged on a spindle, encased in a vacuum chamber, and packaged with a motor, electronics, and magnetic sensors.

hardcopy Output on a medium such as paper that can be removed from the computer.

hardware See computer hardware.

help desk The IS staff and associated systems that help end users solve immediate problems with their equipment or software.

hierarchial model See hierarchical model.

hierarchical model Also called hierarchial, views data as organized in a logical hierarchy.

horizontal software Software that performs generic tasks common to many types of problems and applications within and across industries.

hub Device that connects computers and sections of a network to one another.

human resource management (HRM) systems Information systems that streamline the processes relating to employee recruitment, development, retention, assessment, and compensation.

I

implementation Deactivating an old information system and activating a new one.

individual information system Information system designed to be used by a single person.

inference engine The component of an expert systems shell that processes the knowledge base supplied by users to reach conclusions, answer questions, and give advice.

infomediary A company that collects and sells information.

information Processed data — data that have been organized and interpreted, and possibly formatted, filtered, analyzed, and summarized.

information glut An overload of information.

information leadership The strategy of increasing the value of a product or service by infusing it with expertise and information.

information system The combination of information technology, data, procedures for processing data, and people who collect and use the data Information systems also include automation systems, which perform tasks that had been done manually; transaction processing systems, which process and record business activities; management systems, which supply information to managers; and strategic systems, which support the implementation of organizational theory.

information technology (IT) Computer hardware, software, database management systems, and data communication systems.

infrastructure An organization's investment in hardware, software, systems, and people.

input analysis A formal cataloguing and review of the information an organization collects, stores, and uses.

instant messaging (IM) A protocol for real-time communication via the instant exchange of messages over the Internet.

institutional memory The collective shared memory of an organization.

integration testing Testing that addresses the interaction between large, independently developed components of the new system that were internally checked at the unit and component testing levels

integrator Company that packages hardware and software to meet a customer's specification.

integrity Property of a secure messaging protocol that ensures the fact that a message can not be altered after it's been sent.

inter-organizational system (IOS) An automated information system that two or more companies share.

interface design The specification of the media, content, and form of input and output.

internet A worldwide network of computer networks.

Internet Service Provider (ISP) A company that sells access to the Internet; it owns a large block of IP numbers for reassignment and has a high-capacity telephone connection to the Internet backbone.

interpreter Software that translates language commands into computer code one instruction at a time and then executes each instruction before translating the next instruction.

intranet Internal network that relies on hypermedia to make information available and browsers to access the media.

IP number Unique address for every device attached to the Internet; this address consists of two parts - a network number and a device number.

J

joint application development (JAD) A variation of prototyping.

joint venture Agreement among two or more companies to jointly develop or market specific products or services.

just-in-time (JIT) inventory The practice of obtaining inventory precisely as needed, neither too early nor too late.

K

kernel See operating system kernel.

key A secret code used to scramble a message or document so that it becomes unreadable.

knowledge An understanding or model about people, objects, or events, derived from information about them.

knowledge base A database of facts and rules that an expert system uses in its reasoning.

knowledge management (KM) The identification, capture, systemization, and dissemination of knowledge so that it can be used it improve the operation and efficiency of an organization.

knowledge worker Employee, such as an engineer, accountant, lawyer, or technical specialists, who has specialized skills and knowledge.

L

leased line A direct communication connection between two points that bypasses the telephone switch.

legacy systems Large, entrenched systems, consisting of thousands of programs written and modified over ten to twenty years that cannot be changed because of their complexity or lack of documentation.

link loader Software that links object modules into one complete program.

linkage The strategy of obtaining a competitive advantage by establishing special, exclusive relationships with customers, suppliers, and competitors.

load module See executable module.

local area network (LAN) A network that connects devices in a single building or a campus of nearby buildings.

logical view A view of data based on a data model that is independent of the way in which the data are physically stored.

M

machine language The language of zeros and ones that instruct a computer's processor.

mainframe A computer designed and marketed to handle the largest processing tasks of an organization, typically costing at least several hundred thousand dollars and usually requiring a separate, air-conditioned room and a staff of trained professionals to support its use.

maintenance Fixing software that does not operate properly and adding features to systems in response to new user demands.

management The process of achieving organizational goals by planning, organizing, leading, and controlling organizational resources.

management reporting system (MRS) A system that helps managers monitor the operations and resources of an organization and the environment in which the organization operates.

management support system (MSS) An information system that supplies information that managers need to make decisions and coordinate their activities.

manufacturing execution system (MES) Software that monitors and controls processes on the shop floor, allowing managers and employees to observe activities at a specific work center or a specific machine.

market maker A business, such as an auction house, that earns revenue by bringing together buyers and sellers.

mass customization The concept of producing the exact product that each customer wants as cheaply and efficiently as if it were mass-produced.

message A basic element of communication that conveys one idea, or one unit of information, from one party to another.

metadata Data about data.

methodology A prescribed and documented set of practices, tools, documents, reports, and, often, notations for systems design and development.

MICR (Magnetic Ink Character Recognition) Input technology that senses the shape of characters written with magnetic ink.

middleware Software that coordinates software applications so that the output of any application can be fed automatically into other applications as input.

model base The analytic part of a decision support system that includes tools such as spreadsheets, simulation packages, forecasting tools, and statistical packages.

modem Device that provides an interface between a computer or terminal and the phone or cable lines of a communication carrier.

modular structure An organizational structure that breaks an organization into key processes and lets individual sub-contractors perform these key processes.

Moore's Law An observation that the amount of information storable in a square inch of silicon doubles about every 18 months

morality Refers to what is good or bad, right or wrong Philosophers differ as to whether or not morality is relative or absolute.

multi-user editor Software that allows multiple users to access and modify a common document.

N

nanotechnology Technology for building structures on a scale of one-billionth of a meter.

needs assessment A formal, integrated, and usually time-limited process of gathering data about the needs and opportunities of end users and their managers; evaluating and ranking the importance of these needs; and addressing the possibility that they cannot be satisfied by continuous improvement of existing systems.

network A set of points and the telecommunication connections between them.

network administrator Person responsible for the oversight of the corporate network, including both LANs and WANs.

network analyzer Device that plugs into a network and analyzes the traffic that passes by or through it.

network interface card (NIC) Also called an adaptor, provides a direct connection between a computer or terminal and a network.

network model A DBMS model that builds a tight linkage, called a set, between elements of data.

network protocol A standard regarding how a message is packaged, secured, sent, routed, received, and acknowledged by the receiver within a network

neural network Approach to artificial intelligence that operates by mimicking the human brain.

non-procedural language Computer language such as SQL and many expert system shells that can operate without step-by-step instructions.

non-repudiation A property of a secure message protocol that confirms that a particular sender sent a given message, and which refutes any attempt by the sender to deny having sent the message.

non-volatile storage Computer storage that retains its data even in the absence of electrical power.

normalization The process of grouping data elements into tables in a way that simplifies retrieval, reduces data entry and storage, and minimizes the likelihood of data inconsistencies.

O

object design The generation of an object model

object model A data model derived from object-oriented programming that encapsulates data and methods and organizes objects into object classes, among which there can be a hierarchical relationship.

object module Computer code to perform a particular task after it has been translated by a compiler; these may be linked together into an executable module.

object oriented language Merges procedures and data into a structure called an object Examples of object oriented languages include C++, Java, and Smalltalk.

ODBC (Open Database Connectivity) A standard that allows programs to access their databases in a uniform way and makes moving databases from one DBMS to another easy.

on-demand report Any report that a management reporting system provides for authorized users upon request.

online analytical processing (OLAP) Tools that aggregate, display, and analyze data to draw inferences and make decisions.

operating system Programs that perform the most basic housekeeping, resource allocation, and resource monitoring functions for a computer with a minimum of input or control by the user.

operating system kernel Operating system software that performs the most basic housekeeping, resource allocation, and resource monitoring functions for a computer.

opportunity An external or environmental factor that might help an organization to meet its strategic goals.

optical character recognition (OCR) Software that converts images received from image capture devices into data that word processing and spreadsheet programs can use.

optimization software Analytical software that identifies the best feasible choice or choices to meet a given objective.

order entry system Records and processes the taking of an order.

organizational structure A structure that defines reporting responsibilities in an organization and identifies who manages and controls key resources

OSI model (Open Systems Interconnection Model) Divides the communication process into layers within which compatible standards can be set.

output analysis The systematic identification of ways people in an organization use information.

outsourcing Hiring an outside organization to perform services such as information processing and applications development.

P

packet A division of data used by communication software; for example, many data communication software packages send data in a packet having a fixed number bytes.

packet switched service Provides a direct connection between any points on the telephone network but does not necessarily provide a fixed circuit for the entire session.

parallel implementation strategy The use of both a new and old system for a period of time.

parallel processing The use of two or more cooperating processors in a single computer.

partner relationship management (PRM) The philosophy and practice of coordinating with distributors and other channel partners in the sale and distribution of a product or service.

performance testing The first stage of system testing in which developers identify and correct problems that might cause a system to slow down or fail when stressed with too many users or too much data.

periodic report A report that a management reporting system produces on a periodic basis for delivery to a pre-specified list of employees.

permanent team A team that works together for long periods of time, generally at least one year, on a repetitive set of tasks.

personal area network (PAN) A network connecting the devices of a single person or computer.

personal computer (PC) A computer designed and marketed to be used by an individual or a small number of people and to be owned and managed by an individual.

phased implementation strategy An approach to the implementation of new systems that introduces the components of a new system one at a time.

physical design Decisions about the hardware used to deliver a system.

physical view View of data that includes how they are compressed and formatted, which data are stored near each other, and which indexes exist to simplify and speed finding data on its storage medium.

pilot implementation strategy Often called beta testing, requires one or more segments of the company to use a new system before the entire company uses it.

pixel A dot on the computer screen.

plotter An output device that operates by moving a pen or pens over paper, much the way a person writes.

point-of-sale system (POS) System that records the sale of a product or service and updates company records related to the sale.

port A socket usually located at the back of a computer through which the monitor, keyboard, and other input and output devices are connected via cables to interface cards inside the computer.

post-implementation review Process that evaluates how well a new system meets user needs, sets priorities for new development, and determines when to redo a needs assessment.

primary key The attribute or attributes of a table that uniquely identify a row in that table.

primary storage Electrical device or devices that store data, resides on the bus, and is directly accessible to the processor.

procedural language A computer language, such as C, COBOL, and FORTRAN, that requires the software developer to give step by step instructions to the computer

process design The design of both the computational and logical processes underlying a system.

process librarian See process manager.

process manager Also called a process librarian, a person assigned by an organization to customize templates and tutorials to the organization's standards and collect metrics and best practices for customizing the process library.

processing hardware Computer chips and other devices that manipulate information according to instructions encoded into software.

producer A business that earns revenue by selling the products that it builds, manufactures, grows, or creates or the services it provides.

profit center An organization of an IS department in which the department bids for the work of internal users, charges internal users what it would charge external users, and often actively seeks external users.

programmer A person who writes computer programs.

project manager A person responsible for one or more systems development projects Project managers typically supervise teams of workers who together must accomplish a specific goal.

prototyping A systems development approach that tries to satisfy user needs by focusing on the user interface.

public key cryptography Technique for providing telecommunication security that requires two codes - one secret code called a private key and another that is not secret called a public key Messages encrypted with one key can only be decrypted with the other.

pure play A business strategy that calls for a company to sell its products or services only on the Internet; a business that follows a pure play strategy.

R

RAID (Redundant arrays of inexpensive disks) Device that uses a large number of relatively small hard disks in a single unit.

random access memory (RAM) Volatile primary storage.

rapid application development (RAD) The use of tools, in conjunction with rapid prototyping, to speed the ultimate development of new systems.

rapid prototyping The conversion of an electronic computer-aided design model into a solid physical model. Also the development of software prototypes using rapid application development, for the purpose of verifying system specifications.

read-only memory (ROM) Nonvolatile primary storage; ROM holds the instructions that a computer uses when it is first turned on.

real-time conferencing Meeting in which information is exchanged electronically Participants do not have to be at the same location.

record Entry in a file containing one example of instance of the type of data the file contains Each record generally holds data about a person, place, or thing, concrete or abstract.

reintermediation The act or process of replacing brick and mortar distributors with a pure e-commerce distribution model.

relational model A database model that provides for logical connections among files (known as tables) by including identifying data from one table in another table

replication A feature of distributed DBMS in which the DBMS changes the data at all locations if a user or application changes the redundant data at one location.

report generator Software that automates the creation of programs that produce reports.

Request for Proposal (RFP) A document that identifies the information processing requirements and information needs of an organization and requests software developers to submit bids for software development responding to these needs.

requirements analysis Also called needs assessment, identifies the information needs of an organization.

resolution The quality of computer output.

resource An input to the production of outputs.

retailer A company, such as a grocery or department store, that sells products directly to consumers.

return on investment (ROI) The ratio of the benefit (return) of an investment to the amount of the investment.

reverse engineering The process of analyzing the software that comprises a legacy system.

risk analysis The process of identifying where risks might arise and analyzing the tradeoff of risk against costs and benefits.

robotic Output devices that physically move in response to signals from a computer.

router A device that connects two or more hubs, sub-networks, or networks that have the same network protocol and passes data between networks almost simultaneously.

rule base The component of an expert system that expresses rules that are rarely changed.

rule-based system Artificial intelligence software which directs the computer to make decisions based on logical rules.

S

sales force automation System that provides computerized systems for tracking sales leads, sales, service requests, and other sales-related information.

schema An integrated, enterprise-wide view of how an organization's data relate to one another.

screen generator Software that creates and edits a screen and generates programs for screen-based data entry or queries.

secondary storage Data storage, usually magnetic or optical, from which data must first be transferred into primary storage before they can be accessed by the processor.

Secure Socket Layer (SSL) A process used by most Web browsers to securely exchange a session key and verify the identity of parties to a session.

security management Policies and procedures that reduce the likelihood of a security breach and increase the likelihood of detecting security breaches that occur.

security policy A policy that addresses proper security practices and methods of enforcing those practices.

self-managed team A team having members who share responsibility for managing the work group without an officially appointed leader.

sensor Input device, such as a microphone, electromagnetic receiver, pressure detector, chemical detector, and temperature detector, that respond to the environment with a signal that a computer can interpret.

server In a client/server architecture, a computer dedicated to performing special services for client computers on the network.

service level agreement (SLA) An agreement between information technology providers and users that specifies in detail a guaranteed level of performance on a variety of dimensions.

session An extended series of messages having meaning and communicated over a period of time in some order.

set In the network model, the combinations of owners and members in a one-to many relationship.

simulation The process of representing real processes with analytic models.

situational analysis The process of collecting and analyzing information about a company's strengths, weaknesses, opportunities, and threats.

SNMP (Simple Network Management Protocol) A protocol that defines how management devices operate and the data they keep.

softcopy Output on an unmovable medium, such as a computer screen.

software See computer software.

software engineer Analyst with CASE skills.

source code A program written in the developer's computer language.

spiral approach A software development approach that delivers a new system in versions Each version goes through all the steps of the SDLC except implementation, which may apply to some versions, and maintenance, which applies only to the last version.

SQL An easy-to-use nonprocedural language that has been adopted as a standard for the relational model.

standard Rules governing the types of investments an organization may make in information technology and systems Also industry-wide agreements about characteristics of specific hardware, software, or telecommunications devices and protocols.

storage area network (SAN) A virtual storage device created by connecting different types of storage devices, such as tape libraries, RAID disks, and optical jukeboxes, over a high-speed network.

strategy The long-term direction or intended set of activities for an organization to attain its goals.

strength An internal characteristic of an organization that enhances its ability to compete.

structure chart A diagram that shows the relationship among the programs and subprograms that will comprise the finished system.

structured analysis An analysis technique that uses process modeling tools to diagram existing and proposed systems so that users can understand and critique an analyst's perception of information relationships.

subschema A logical view of how data in a database or portion of a database relates to other data in the database.

summary report Also known as a statistical report, a report that shows totals, averages, maximums, minimums, or other statistical data aggregated over time, personnel, products, or some other quantity.

supply chain The portion of a company's extended value chain on the supply side.

supply-chain management (SCM) The manner, generally accompanied by enabling software, by which a company and its supply chain partners analyze, optimize, and control the acquisition and delivery of raw materials necessary for the creation of the goods and services that an organization produces.

switch Device that connects two or more computers, hubs, sub-networks, or networks that have compatible standards for sending signals over transmission media and hardware and creating and ensuring the correct order of sessions.

switched circuit service A connection made between two points for the length of a session.

system call An application software request to the operating system kernel to obtain computer resources such as memory, storage, the network, or the display unit

system testing Also known as alpha testing, testing an entire system under realistic conditions.

systems analyst A person who provides the interface between the information systems user and the information systems developer.

systems development life cycle (SDLC) A sequence of stages in the conception, design, creation and implementation of information systems.

T

table The relational model's representation of a file with rows called tuples and columns called attributes.

TCP/IP (Transmission Control Protocol/Internet Protocol) Protocol for data communication that originated for transmission across the Internet but is now widely used by local and wide area networks.

telecommunication Communication at a distance.

telecommuter Mobile employee who rarely, if ever, visits his or her employer's office.

teleconferencing Technology that allows people in different locations to hold a conference as if they were in one room Teleconferencing includes both audio and video conferencing,

temporary team A team formed for short, pre-specified amounts of time to complete a unique set of tasks or projects

test design The creation of tests that ensure the proper operation of developed systems.

threaded discussion A series of messages that respond to an original message or to a response to that message.

threat An external or environmental factor that might hinder an organization from meeting its strategic goals

time box A fixed period, usually three months, within which developers must complete each version of software developed under the spiral approach.

total quality management (TQM) A management philosophy that attempts to achieve zero defects, emphasizes responding to customers' needs, gives workers more responsibility for making decisions, fosters continuous improvement in both an organization's product and the processes for creating it, and uses statistical control techniques to improve its products and processes.

traditionally-managed team A team having an individual designated as the official leader or manager.

transaction A unit of business activity, such as purchasing a product, making a banking deposit, or reserving an airline seat.

transaction processing monitor (TP monitor) Software that enforces transaction atomicity and provides other generic transaction processing services.

transaction processing system (TPS) An information system that records and processes an organization's routine business activities.

tuple In the relational DBMS model, a row in a table.

turn-key solution Hardware and software bundled for sale as a single product.

twisted-pair wire Connects a telephone to its telephone jack in most homes.

U

unallocated cost center A way of accounting for information services that considers all costs of operating the IS department and related IS services as an organizational expense, rather than attributing costs to particular budgets.

unit testing Testing each small component of a system to guarantee its proper operations

universal server Common name for hybrid object-relational DBMSs

usability lab A place where developers can observe and record users reactions to a new system.

usability testing The second stage of systems testing in which the developed system is compared to users' expectations and needs.

V

value-added network (VAN) A reseller of telephone and/or satellite transmission capacity.

value-added reseller (VAR) A software manufacturer's representative authorized to customize its software.

value chain The series of processes by which a company turns raw materials into finished goods and services.

vendor managed inventory (VMI) The process by which a supplier manages the inventory in its customer's facilities.

vertical software Software that performs tasks common to a specific industry and often has some or extensive options for customization.

videoconferencing Holding a meeting in which information is exchanged electronically.

virtual organization A modular structure tied together by computer technology.

Virtual Private Network (VPN) A private wide-area network that connects an organization's LANs and users to one another through a public network, usually the Internet.

volatile storage Computer storage that requires electrical power to retain its data

volumetric display Device that produces a three-dimensional image that the viewer can walk around.

W

warehouse management system An information system that supports activities inside a company's warehouses and at its shipping and receiving docks.

waterfall model An approach to systems development that follows the SDLC in sequence.

weakness An internal characteristic of an organization that impedes its ability to compete Having costs above the industry average typifies a weakness.

web master The person responsible for the management, evolution, and sometimes development of an organization's Web site.

web portal A company that draws a large volume of repeat visitor traffic because it provides free services such as Web searching.

webcasting The process of transmitting llive or recorded audio or video so that recipients can receive it using a Web browser.

wholesaler A company that buys from producers and sells to retailers.

Wi-Fi A protocol, which operates like an Ethernet, for wireless LANs.

wide area network (WAN) A network that covers a larger area than a LAN

wisdom The ability to use knowledge for a purpose.

X

XML A computer language that identifies the meaning of data by surrounding it with special tags The language can be extended by the user, who can create new tags using language-definition rules and features that XML provides.

XML model A database model that has as its fundamental entity an XML document.

BUSINESS INDEX

SUBJECT INDEX

W

X

PHOTO CREDITS

Figure 3-2: Data-processing keyboard, PhotoDisc, Inc. Point-of-sale keyboard, Courtesy of International Business Machines. Unauthorized use not permitted.

Figure 3-3: Joystick, Courtesy of International Business Machines. Unauthorized use not permitted. Lightpen, Courtesy of Fastpoint Technologies, Inc.; Mouse, PhotoDisc Inc.; Touchscreen, Corbis Digital Stock; Touchpad, PhotoDisc, Inc. Trackball, PhotoDisc Inc.; Trackpoint, PhotoDisc Inc.

Figure 3-4: Matrix barcode, Courtesy of National Barcode Inc.

Figure 3-7: 256 megabit chip, Courtesy of International Business Machines. Unauthorized use not permitted.

Figure 3-8: Cartridge disk, Copyright © 2002 Iomega Corporation. All Rights Reserved. Iomega, the stylized "i" logo and product images are property of Iomega Corporation in the United States and/or other countries. Cdrom, © Corbis; Diskette, PhotoDisc, Inc. DVD, © Corbis; Flash memory card, Courtesy of Kingston Technology Company, Inc. Cartridge tape, Courtesy of Verbatim Corporation.

Figure 3-10: Volumetric display of the HIV virus, Courtesy of ComputerWorld.com.

Figure 3-11: Plotter, Photo Researchers.

Figure 3-21: Xenon atoms on a nickel surface, Courtesy of International Business Machines. Unauthorized use not permitted.

Figure 5-3: Videoconferencing, Andreas Pollok, Stone;

Figure 5-12: WIN 2000 screenshot, Screenshot reprinted by permission from Microsoft Corporation.

Figure 7-7: CAD wireframe diagram, Courtesy of Imaginit Technologies.

Figure 7-8: Automobile factory, Courtesy of Stäubli Corporation.

Figure 7-9: Unmanned transport AGV, Courtesy of Egemin Automation.

Figure 8-13: Computer conference room, Courtesy of Andrulis Corporation.

Figure 8-14: Dashboards, Copyright 2002 iDashes, Inc., Patent pending. From ExecDash demo found at http://www.idashes.net.

Figure 9-15: Usability labs, Courtesy of theUEgroup.com.